THE HERO IN AMERICA

A Chronicle of Hero-Worship

BY DIXON WECTER

with headings by Woodi Ishmael

Ann Arbor Paperbacks
The University of Michigan Press

TO EUGENIA AND ELIZABETH

Second printing 1966
First edition as an Ann Arbor Paperback 1963
Copyright © by Charles Scribner's Sons 1941
All rights reserved
Reprinted by special permission
Published in the United States of America by
The University of Michigan Press and simultaneously
in Rexdale, Canada, by Ambassador Books Limited
Manufactured in the United States of America

Contents

CHAPTER ONE

HEROES IN WAR AND PEACE

Some got their medals and the plums,
Some got their fingers burnt,
But every one's a native son,
Except for those who weren't.
—Rosemary and Stephen Vincent Benét,
A Book of Americans.

I

HERO-WORSHIP answers an urgent American need. The fan and the autograph hunter, now imitated elsewhere, are as native to the United States as the catbird and the Catawba grape. To fix our relation with greatness by means of a signature in an album, a lock of hair, a photograph, or a baseball that has scored a home run; to haunt stage doors and entries to locker-rooms; to pursue our favorites with candid cameras and sound recorders, invading their meditations and their honeymoons—this passion has made us the premier nation of hero-worshippers. Others, of course, have like impulses. The phlegmatic Cockney collects Famous Cricketers from the coupons in cigarette packets; the Spaniard helps to carry off a great matador on his shoulder. But only in the United States has the greeter become a profession and the ovation a fine art.

Homage to heroes is a vital part of our patriotism. Patriotism springs traditionally from love of place; it is a filial relation toward mother country or fatherland. The earth upon which our feet are planted, from which we draw our livelihood, becomes an over-soul, the greatest hero of our national loyalties. The "patria" of the ancient Romans, "this precious stone set in the silver sea" of Shakespeare's England, and "la belle France" of many generations, sprang from this piety of place. Even the "blood and soil" of current Nazi mythology and the "magnetic mountain" of Communist mysticism are attempts to build on the old foundation; while these new masters of Europe, on the negative side, seek to destroy the folk integrity of those whom they have conquered by uprooting whole populations. But with us, in the New World, there are certain differences. We love the broad span of America, and sing of our affection for its rocks and rills, its woods and templed hills. But we are a restless people, moving from New York to San Francisco as our job demands, and in old age deserting the windswept homestead for a sunny bungalow in Florida. We have lost something of that warm devotion to the soil which stirred the embattled farmers of 1776, or even the agrarian days of Andrew Jackson and young Lincoln.

In 1820 about 93 per cent of all Americans lived in the country, 60 per cent as late as 1900, but only 43 per cent a generation later. Even in 1838 Francis Grund, a visitor from overseas, remarked that an American does not love his birthplace with the ardor of a Frenchman or an Englishman: "an American's country is his understanding; he carries it with him wherever he goes, whether he emigrates to the shores of the Pacific or the Gulf of Mexico; his home is wherever he finds minds congenial to his own." His patriotism is apt to be curiously abstract. Save for old-fashioned groups in New England and in the South, American loyalty in the pure geographical sense is a trifle cold and bloodless. Even the majority of our forty-eight states, as a Frenchman lately observed, are bounded by rectangles that suggest plane geometry more than esprit de corps. However much we love and would fight for America, as a concept and a way of life, our feeling for place is hardly more than a booster's slogan—such a one as used to hang, in electric lights, over the main street of a Texas town known to the writer: "Greenville—The Blackest Land, The Whitest People." With the passing of time, the floods of immigration and migration, the rise of cities and railroads and highways, our ancient roots into the earth of America have had an anchorage less firm. To many, the United

States as geography means many interchangeable places where one may hang his hat. It is a continent and civilization too vast for the warm immediate embrace possible to the patriot of Patrick Henry's day, when one's farm stood well enough for America, and its defense brought to mind the squirrel rifle that lived beside the chimney.

Because of these things, our collective symbols—the Flag, the Declaration of Independence, the Constitution, and the touchstone of our heroes—are more precious than such institutions are in the Old World. They nourish our sense of national continuity. Not even Englishmen appeal to their Magna Charta with the fervor that we—conservatives, liberals, radicals alike—appeal to the Constitution. With a faith not untouched by pathos, we accept its framers, as Thomas Jefferson described them, as "demigods," and their work as without flaw. Its guarantees, in a sense, mean America to us. In an earlier day, when political oratory flourished in the barbecue era, and the defiance of tyranny seemed more glorious than the unity symbolized by the Constitution, our most prized document was the Declaration of Independence. That was before the Civil War fused us into a nation. Likewise, the Supreme Court, standing for a "fundamental law" conceded to be more stable than the fickle will of the people, is another sacred symbol of government—as Theodore Roosevelt in 1912, after advocating a popular referendum on judicial decisions, and the second Roosevelt in 1937, by proposing to pack the Court, discovered to their surprise. Recent scholars, ranging from the playfully cynical Thurman Arnold to the soberly sympathetic Ralph Gabriel, have written about these symbols. Emblems even more homely, like Uncle Sam, have had a great influence upon our national character. Lincoln's Secretary of State, Seward, told of a man just after the Revolution who had put up a Liberty pole in his village. Neighbors asked him why, wasn't he free enough now? And he answered, "What is liberty without a pole?"

But after reviewing these symbols of government, one must not forget an equally vital force in building our concept of what is "American." It comes from the voices of our heroes, who, we like to think, are our counsellors from beyond the grave—Washington, Franklin, Jefferson, Lincoln—directing us with a wisdom hallowed by time. Europeans do not invoke the spirit of Charlemagne, of Pitt, of Danton, of Garibaldi, as we appeal to our national heroes. In a sense they have ceased to be persons, and have become institutions. Like Alma Mater, or the True Church, or America the Beautiful, they have grown into talismans with a strong emotional tone. Their words are like holy writ.

In the presidential campaign of 1940, by orators and candidates of both parties, Abraham Lincoln was quoted more than any other man—his words, that "we shall nobly save or meanly lose the last best hope of earth," running as a motif of debate between the rival camps. The hero also serves as the model of personal conduct for great and small—as the mighty Washington became to young Lee at West Point and to young Lincoln on the Illinois prairie, as both Lee and Lincoln have since become to untold thousands, even millions, of ordinary Americans.

A white-haired daughter of Alabama, known to the writer, has a son who in his senior year at Harvard married a Boston girl and brought her home for family inspection. Before the arrival of a daughter-in-law of whom she soon grew very fond, the old lady hung a portrait of Lee over the double bed in the guest-room, with the firm remark, "She must learn to appreciate Southern gentlemen, and she may as well begin with General Lee."

These are the great gods of the tribe, the sentinels of our earth and skies. Mark Van Doren has written, in "America's Mythology":

> America's tall gods are veterans here:
> Too close for view, like eagles in the eye;
> Like day itself, impalpable and clear;
> Like absolute noon's air, unflowing by.

The student of this homage to great Americans must write—as impartially as he can—of myths and men. Here and there he will come upon ironic circumstance, but mockery is no part of his purpose. For hero-worship, satisfying a hunger of the human heart, is always an inspiration to good if its objects are good. Scarcely any man is so poor in spirit that he has no heroes, that he finds nothing to stir his blood in the memories of his race and nation, or the acts of his fellows.

II

If it were not for books, newspapers, and cameras, which now put men and their acts upon immediate record, heroes might draw still richer substance from legend. When the world was young and there were men like gods, no reporters were present, but only poets. Achilles and Ulysses, Siegfried and Roland, Beowulf and Richard the Lion-Hearted were the supermen of those days. Surpassing all others in bravery, loyalty, and strength, they were the idols of a culture moving from the Old Stone Age to the gentler codes of chivalry. They were taller by a head than any of their tribesmen, could cut iron with their swords, throw the bar farther or wind the horn louder than their fellows. Their sinews held up the sky beneath which a whole nation lived and fought—for they generally appeared in times of racial struggle for survival, holy wars, and crusades, when ardor burned bright. Their very names, chanted by minstrels in battle, were a charm of victory. These men had the virtues prized most highly in the green youth of a race, when—as in the adolescence of the individual—hero-worship flowers most freely. The old, the wise, the tired, and the disenchanted always offer more sterile soil.

How are heroes born? Some believe in "the great man theory of history": at certain times—often in response to crisis—nature or God seems to bring forth a superman who can bend a people to his purpose. Plutarch, who was the father of hero-worship in biography and notably admired Spartan kings and the ideals of military stoicism, appears to have had a conviction of this sort. Many centuries later, under the dazzling phenomenon of Napoleon, this theory found clear expression. Carlyle held that the history of the world is the history of its great men—Moses, Mohammed, Cromwell, Frederick the Great. Between them are the unimportant valleys, the stagnant pools of time. Emerson thought that an institution is the lengthened shadow of a man. He also was fascinated by Bonaparte, and saw leadership in terms of an iron will sweeping multitudes before it and remaking civilizations as it pleased. Observing his own generation in America, and the nomination of four battered soldiers for the Presidency, he concluded that "the sword runs away with all the fame from the spade and the wheel." Meanwhile the age of science had begun to deflate the great man theory. Spencer, Galton, and the environmentalists asked whether the superman might not be the product of his age, a puppet gesturing on the ventriloquist's knee and speaking with the voice of multitudes. To the frank hero-worshippers this was a disturbing thought. Was the hero ruled by free will, or by racial predestination? William James tried sensibly to reconcile the two points of view. He held that the social environment selects the "great man," even as the biological environment breeds sports to advance the species. Such a man may vary from the norm just as a moth with brighter colors or longer proboscis differs from his species, but this apparently small difference will have a powerful effect upon future generations. If his variation is not useful to the times, he will be rejected or destroyed. Otherwise he will be honored above all men. Of course his influence is not a pure genetic one, as with the moth, but comes instead from establishing an effective and admired pattern of leadership. Clive in India, Bolivar in South America did more than all their fellows to mould the political destiny of millions. But, born out of their time, these men would have been broken by mass forces working not for them but against them. William James saw that Washington was the man of the hour, that without a chain of circumstance, and the aid of Everyman, he would have been helpless; yet James endorsed the popular judgment, that glorifies Washington above all fellow patriots. Washington had the exact variation, the magic formula, for success. The great leader (who becomes almost inevitably a hero) is thus both master and servant of his era. He is selected because he seems to fit the mould desired by the masses—and, once his work is done, he is idealized to fill that mould even better.

The question may be asked in current terms. Is Adolf Hitler the creator or the creature of Nazi Germany? Foreign idealists, eager to discriminate between the ruler and his docile millions with whom they have no quarrel, see Hitler as a superman of evil. Others—political observers with a fund of slightly cynical knowledge and artists with a gift of intuition—lately have inclined to a different conclusion. Peter Fleming in a recent fantasy about Hitler's parachute landing in England, Charlie Chaplin in his movie about dictators, suggest that Hitler is merely a chip bobbing in the whirlpool, a man of almost pathetic unimportance in comparison with the forces that sustain him. William James might have said that the truth lies somewhere between these extremes. Hitler is a "sport" whose variation from the norm made his leadership inevitable, effective: none could have succeded as he has done. On the other hand, only in Germany since 1925, among the times and nations of the earth, could he have succeeded.

Hitler, Stalin, and Mussolini vividly illustrate the vices of modern hero-worship. Whatever the complex of forces behind them, it is clear that leadership still focuses sharply upon single personalities. To the perverted ends of nationalism—which has been defined as "the snobbery of patriotism"—with its mass egotisms and mass hatreds, a hero is essential. The common man's bewilderment in a changing world, and his quest for security, have bred a lack of that faith in himself which democracies once tried to encourage; instead, he turns with superstitious trust to the magic of a hero. It is no longer necessary to think, but only to adore and obey.

The Fascist-Communist hero differs, in a way, from the kings and would-be kings of the past. He represents the third stage in a cycle which the world has travelled since the Middle Ages, in seeking its pattern of prestige. First came the king and aristocrat, moulded from the primitive strong man but transmitting his powers by heredity. Epic, romance, music, painting, and in fact all art glorified him or the scions of his ideal, like the warrior, knight, and gentleman. Then, under the industrial revolution, the French revolution, and the Napoleonic legend, arose the cult of the middle class and the romanticism of the self-made. The brownstone house supplanted the castle, the inspirational novel the lyric of chivalry. Much American hero-worship, as will be seen, falls into this span of the cycle. Lastly came the idealization of the little man, with a broad drift toward the doctrines of socialism. The collective ideal of the little man, whether sincerely or falsely, is personalized in the Fascist-Communist hero. He appeals not to the divine right of kings but to the dictatorship of the proletariat. Long ago Plato, in the eighth book of *The Republic*, showed how hero-worship might enable the so-called "protector of the people" to become a tyrant. Today the new hero claims to be both the Superman and the Little Man. Of humblest origins himself, he does not take the purple as did Cæsar and Napoleon. He clothes himself in blouse or simple military uniform, and has his picture taken blessing peasant children or stripping to the waist to get the crops in. He professes to speak for the masses, to save them from privilege groups and greedy internationalists—playing skillfully upon their folk emotions and prejudices. He is the triumphant sublimation of a million inferiority complexes, springing from the soil of economic discontent, and from such national humiliations as Brest-Litovsk, Caporetto, and Versailles. Although he is only a Little Man, the lamps of publicity project him upon the map of the world as a great shadowy giant. The poorest citizen of Soviet Russia or the Reich rejoices to think that this magnified image of himself is awesome and terrifying to other nations. Such a citizen is even willing to give up his individuality, and often life itself, so that the glory of this over-person may be greater. Demagogues thus become demigods. And thus, with something to die for, a heroic temper is bred which democracies in their years of fatness had forgotten. Whether it is not yet too late for democracies to recall their strenuous age, the exhilaration of their own ideals and traditions of leadership, remains to be seen. A nation that cannot evoke the spirit of its dead heroes and the birth of new ones, in a time of crisis, is doomed. France bitterly proved this fact.

III

Hero-worship is a secular religion. In so far as it looks backward, it is a form of ancestor worship. The child's first heroes are his parents. Similarly, in the childhood of the race, primitive man believed that his forefathers, vaguely remembered, had strength and wisdom greater than his. These forefathers, like the Catholic saints of later times, offered a sort of "treasury of merit" upon which one might draw by prayer and sacrifices. The ancient Greeks and Romans, and the Orientals, shared that feeling. Pericles, in his oration over the Athenian war dead, kindled patriotism by appealing to the founding fathers, with their ancient sagacity, and to the heroic dead, who live forever. These men watched over the destiny of the tribe, like King Arthur over the Britons. In a traditional sense they were immortal. It might be noted that the first use of the term "hero-worship" was in 1757, by that famous skeptic David Hume, who after making an analysis of polytheism wrote that "the same principles naturally deify mortals, superior in power, courage, or understanding, and produce *hero-worship.*"[2] *The Golden Bough,* which tells how the King of the Wood had to die, ere he grew feeble and discredited by old age, in order that he might become a god, is a primer of the hero-making process.

To some people, sainthood or godhead may seem terms too strong for a description of American hero-worship. We like to think we are a hard-headed nation of realists. But our folk attitude toward our greatest heroes approaches the religious. We insist upon stainless perfection for our greatest idols—like Washington, Lincoln, Lee—and many of our biographers, seeking to make them into Christlike characters, have succeeded only in converting them into Sunday school prigs. This mould of perfection is set, and any attempt to break it (whether through malice, love of sensation, or a passion for truth) is hotly resented by the majority. This the age of "debunkery," in the 1920's, discovered. More recently, as a milder instance, Grant Wood in 1940 was swamped with angry letters about his painting, "Parson Weems's Fable," which showed Weems pointing proudly to his handi-work—a youthful Washington, with the Gilbert Stuart face, confessing to his havoc beside the cherry tree. It was not unlike the popular indignation caused some years ago by Epstein's Christ. That Christ's nobility has no need of beauty, any more than Washington's integrity needs the cherry-tree story, does not occur to the sentimentalist, who loves the pictures that he carries about in his head. There are other religious traits in American hero-worship. One of them is fetishism. To us souvenirs are what holy relics were to the Middle Ages. The beds our heroes slept in, the clothes they wore, the houses they dwelt in, draw hundreds of thousands of pilgrims each year. Autographs, bits of wood, leaves from trees, are sought eagerly—but probably not preserved with much purposeful care. The impulse is not a new one: on the side of comedy one recalls that Thaddeus Stevens, pestered for a lock of hair by a female admirer who did not know that he was quite bald, pulled off his whole wig and offered it to her; on the side of tragedy, one reads of that little boy whom newspapermen saw on the morning after Lincoln's assassination, rubbing bits of white paper on the steps of the house across from Ford's Theatre, who said in answer to questions, "That's the President's blood, and I want to save it." In 1915 when the Liberty Bell journeyed from Philadelphia to San Francisco, in the tension of that pre-war atmosphere, throngs of ladies met it at stations by the way and kissed it with reverent lips. The birthdays of heroes are saints' days, and the scenes of their deeds are shrines. During and after the Great War, a ritual called "the worship of the Flag"— with psalms and responses by the congregation, and actors impersonating Washington, Jefferson, Jackson, Lincoln, Cleveland, Theodore Roosevelt, and Wilson as symbols of the seven red stripes—was performed in the Episcopal Diocese of New York.[3] We have only to gaze up at the central canopy inside our National Capitol to see an immense painting of angels and shadowy hierarchies called "The Apotheosis of Washington." And guards at the Lincoln Memorial say that on quiet evenings people often come alone and kneel, with moving lips, before that softly lighted figure in stone who from his Greek temple broods over the great republic.

Others, too, from rival camps try to steal our tribal gods—as men did of old. At the last great rally of the German-American Bund, at Madison Square Garden on February 20, 1939, a picture thirty feet tall of George Washington served as a back-drop. His image, often shown leaning upon the fasces as in Houdon's statue, was used repeatedly in Bund posters and symbolism. Washington was a soldier, a man of stern discipline, therefore presumptively a Fascist *in petto*. (An attempt from the same camp to make Franklin into an anti-Semite, by the simple process of forgery, will be examined later.) Lincoln's effigy, on the other hand, appeared as the back-drop at a large Communist rally in Chicago the following September. And the Abraham Lincoln Brigade, from the days of the Spanish Civil War, was perpetuated into a kind of Leftist American Legion. Earl Browder, trying again and again to convince the nation that Communism is twentieth-century Americanism, has urged his party to carry on "that democratic work begun by Washington, Jefferson, and Paine, and continued by Lincoln."[4] Lincoln is not only an earthier symbol of democracy, and the emancipator of the black man, but was also the recipient of an admiring letter from Karl Marx! Heroes, as will be seen, become all things to all men. Traditionalists see in Washington, Jefferson, and Lincoln the stays of an unbending Americanism—a gospel of orthodoxy that is safely beyond the reach of cross-question or denial. Liberals see in them an honest aspiration toward the golden future we have not yet reached. But radicals, as Professor Merle Curti has suggested, are prone to debunk our symbols of government in their seasons of gloom and bitter combativeness, and to adopt them eagerly when the "cause" is moving upgrade toward a united front.[5] When they are down and out, Washington is a dour Federalist, Jefferson a time-server, and the Constitution is "a covenant with death and an agreement with Hell," as William Lloyd Garrison, one of the angriest radicals of 1843, called it. Now that the United Front of 1935 has crumbled, with the Marxists in retreat, it is probable that their old spirit of scorn for our national emblems will reappear.

Conversely, upon the right wing, there are groups who claim the exclusive right of defending our heroes, and of interpreting the true American faith. The most vigorous, politically, is the American Legion, inheriting the place held a generation ago by the Grand Army of the Republic. But the Daughters of the American Revolution are the most watchful vestals of our patriotic fires. They place markers over historic spots, pass condemnations against subversive books and cinemas, and on occasion have gone so far as to demand that school-patrols stop using red flags as traffic signals.[6] Perhaps the most sentimental are the United Daughters of the Confederacy. Not long ago the president of one of those chapters lamented privately that most boys, these days, seemed to prefer the Boy Scouts to the junior affiliate of their organization. "Yes," she said wistfully, "and if this goes on, what will become of *feeling?*"

IV

Among the military powers of Europe one has seen how hero-worship can be forged into a weapon for dictatorship and conquest. Worship of the State, as personated by its head, becomes religion of a far more fanatic sort than that just described in America. Certain safe-guards, whose moorings are still holding fast, protect America from the worst excesses of hero frenzy. Today, under the gathering storm-clouds, they are worth counting.

First of all, in a democracy the hero must be the people's choice. This is not to deny that skilled publicity while he is alive, and friendly biography and oratory long after he is dead, may do much for him. George Rogers Clark, a great but little-known American, illustrates the plight of a hero in search of an author. William Henry Harrison, on the other hand, thanks to the Log Cabin Campaign, probably re-ceived better than his deserts. Nor is it denied that the hero of today may be scrapped tomorrow—of which the most spectacular instance, in recent times, is Lindbergh. But over a long stretch of time, the pre-vailing American favorites—national leaders like Washington, Jeffer-son, Jackson, Lincoln, Theodore Roosevelt, as well as others not na-tional leaders, such as Nathan Hale, Daniel Boone, David Crockett, Robert E. Lee, Thomas A. Edison—are men whom the American democracy picked, of its own free will, because it admired what they did or stood for. The purely synthetic hero, like Horst Wessel in Ger-many, has never been rammed down our throats.

In the second place, the major idols of America have been men of good will. The strong man without scruple—from Barbarossa to Lenin —does not belong in our halls of fame. The man who would be king, like the legendary Aaron Burr, becomes a villain rather than a hero. Personal arrogance is disliked by average Americans; hence Burr's adversary Hamilton, who called the People "a Great Beast," has never been a national favorite. The braggart may be an amusing folk char-acter—like Paul Bunyan, Mike Fink, Old Stormalong—but he is sharply set apart from even our most self-confident leaders like Wash-ington and Andrew Jackson. The boast of a Napoleon, echoed by Mussolini, "I am not a man, but an event," does not chime with the spirit of a democracy. No hero must announce that he is infallible. He must be greater than the average, but in ways agreeable to the average. He may know their collective will better than they know it themselves, and he may wield even the dictatorial power of Lincoln or Wilson: but he must keep his personal modesty, his courtesy toward the People who gave him that power. The hero is an instrument. Among Anglo-Saxons, the doer of brave deeds is expected to belittle himself—to credit luck, or his soldiers, or his mother, or God. It is another way of saying he is the servant of his age.

Moreover the strong man *par excellence,* the professional soldier, the military victor, has never been a very durable idol in the United States. He will always find staunch partisans, to be sure, among his own men; they have marched and grumbled and fought with him, through rain, sun and snow, and after the war is over, in the long twilight of peace, they muse upon the past and the grandeur of their cause and leader, until their lives are transfigured by the association. Anybody who has gone to a reunion of the G. A. R. or the U. C. V., or sat on the sunny veranda of an old soldiers' home, appreciates the spell under which great generals sometimes became President. Zachary Taylor was a professional soldier, pure and simple, who had done a good job in Mexico; but he was a mediocre President, died in office, and is largely forgotten. William Henry Harrison, long retired from campaigning, was presented to the country as the old farmer of North Bend, more vividly than as the victor of Tippecanoe; he was also a mediocrity rescued by death. Other famous soldiers hoped to be President but failed—Winfield Scott and Frémont and McClellan were rejected; Admiral Dewey became a laughing-stock; while Leonard Wood and Pershing (after the first war in our history which yielded no military President) were passed by in the search for "normalcy." Even Grant's fame tarnished badly, while Mr. Dooley poked fun at a history of the Rough Riders written by the then reigning President as "Th' Biography of a Hero by One Who Knows, or Th' Account of th' Destruction of Spanish Power in th' Ant Hills." To regard our greatest soldier-Presidents, Washington and Jackson, as sheer military men is a grave error. Their popular affection and enduring fame rise from a much broader context. Jackson was a pungent personality, a great democrat, whose battle with the banks seems more important than his battle with the redcoats. As for the noblest of all, it is not Washington the victor at Yorktown who stirs the deepest appeal, but the legendary Washington on his knees in the snow at Valley Forge, the Washington who was hardly a brilliant soldier by anybody's standards but who held grimly to his duty and faith. Like his friends Putnam the farmer and Greene the iron-worker, he was an "American Cincinnatus"—the antithesis of professional soldierhood, who longed to lay down the sword for the plow. Americans have a special affection for the man of peace—like Sergeant York in the World War—who leaves his trade only long enough to beat the military at their own game.

Of the hero our first requirement is likely to be unselfish service, rather than either the splendor or the efficiency that intoxicates the average European. Parades are not enough. Democracies are not grounded upon personal glory and magnificence. A disgruntled Federalist of Jefferson's day, Fisher Ames of Massachusetts, put the case humorously: "A monarchy is like a merchantman: you go on board and ride with wind and tide in safety and elation, but by and by you strike a reef and go down. But democracy is like a raft. You never sink, but, damn it, your feet are always in the water." This muddling through of democracies, so irritating to some citizens, is our best check upon the rise of imperial personalities.

As a further protection against the superman, we refuse to take too seriously our living heroes. No man is really a hero until he is dead, and, as in the making of a saint, all the evidence is in. Posterity then decides that he is wholly good—worthy the company of Washington and Lincoln—or else wholly bad—as with Benedict Arnold and Tom Paine. But Americans are prone to be critical of living men. Ancestral voices of the Puritans, perhaps, whisper that no mortal creature is worthy of worship; American knees are not supple. So long as the hero is still alive, the Bronx cheer will never fail to reach his ears. Our freedom of speech and press makes sure of that. The more formidable a public man, the more tempting he becomes as a target. Benjamin Harrison and Calvin Coolidge missed most of the vilification that was heaped on Washington and Lincoln. Less reverent of the office than our English cousins, we impersonate our Presidents on the stage and in vaudeville. In the campaign of 1940, both the President and Mr. Willkie were in peril from ripe fruit and eggs—though sportsmanship at large approves verbal but not physical attack. A President's dignity and privacy have often been violated, for it is felt that he is the people's man. Old Hickory, going by steamboat to his inaugural, was queried brutally by an unknown laborer about the recent death of Mrs. Jackson ("Well, I knew one of ye was dead"). General Grant, visiting Central City, Colorado, in 1873, and—in the grandiose style of that era—walking on silver bricks from stage-coach to hotel door, had to duck when snowballs from small boys threatened his tall silk hat. In any guidebook to political favor in the United States, any manual on how to win public friends and influence the People, the answers will be very different from those found in Machiavelli's *The Prince*.

Nicknames show the informality of our hero-worship. We like to be on comradely terms with even the great dead. A recent Hollywood "short" about the Declaration of Independence showed Franklin ad-

dressed by his fellow-patriots, often and jovially, as "Ben." (Yet the
evidence shows that his associates, from Washington down, invariably
called him "Doctor Franklin.") Nicknames like "Andy," "Abe," and
"Teddy" were heard much oftener outside the White House than
within—and the last of these names, at least, always made its victim
wince, though he learned to bear it with a politician's fortitude. "T.
R.," like the later "F. D.," was the dignified equivalent of a nickname.
"Old Hickory," "Old Rough and Ready," "Father Abraham," and
"Marse Robert" suggest various degrees of patriarchal affection. We
like names, too, that suggest homely origins: "the Mill Boy of the
Slashes," "the Railsplitter," "the Boy Orator of the Platte." Both Jef-
ferson and Lincoln were called "the Man of the People"; Clay and
Bryan alike were known as "the Great Commoner." Nicknames can
also damn to oblivion, suggesting self-importance and other unfavorable traits: Millard Fillmore, whom his friends tried to name "the
Wool-carder President," came instead to be known as "the American
Louis Philippe," while James Buchanan was dubbed "the Old Public
Functionary," Rutherford B. Hayes "Granny," and Chester A. Arthur
(at a day when Ward McAllister was gaining notoriety for the male
butterfly) "the Dude President." It was perhaps unlucky that so many
people knew that Wilson had changed his name, in young manhood,
from Thomas to Woodrow, as if to keep the public at arm's length.

And we have a final safeguard against the dominion of the superman. It might be described variously as our sympathy for the underdog, our respect for minorities, our sentimental weakness for lost
causes, even our admiration of failure. We have heard so much about
the success motif, in American life, that this statement looks at first
like a paradox. Always, the crowd loves victory, but it also likes the
salty sacrificial taste of disappointment and tragedy, which from its
own life it knows so well. There is a subconscious wish that the hero
should not in every way appear to be strong, resourceful, lucky, and
invincible. The crowd is thus able to achieve closer kinship between
him and themselves.

It is a feeling not peculiar to democracies. The beloved soldiers of
legend tend to become saints, exchanging physical for moral magic,
in defeat or death. Roland dies in the pass at Roncesvalles with his
captains slain; Joan of Arc is greatest in her imprisonment and martyrdom. The idol of Spain, fictitious but real, is Don Quixote, the mad
and foolish knight who dies with the sunset glory of a saint. King
Arthur, mocked and cuckolded, the Round Table broken and his best

men killed in battle, is grandest in his passing. Even to modern England, Nelson, struck down in the heat of Trafalgar, is a greater hero
than Wellington, who lived prosperously till his eighty-fourth year
and heard himself hooted by the mob on the anniversary of Waterloo.
In folklore, this trend runs to the extremes of comedy. King Alfred
sleeps while the cakes burn, and is soundly scolded by the housewife.
Whenever Robin Hood dares to fight a stranger single-handed, Robin
is rolled in the dirt and sometimes given an emetic as a final prank
of insult: then up come his merry men in green to win for him, or
to discover that the stranger is only one of the boys in disguise.

In a democracy, where the strong man is always secretly suspect,
this sympathy for handicap, struggle, and failure has much to do
with the popularity of heroes. Emerson, who declared that "heroism
feels and never reasons, and therefore is always right,"[7] had much to
say of that grandeur whose essence is sacrifice of self. Walt Whitman
called for

Vivas to those who have failed!
And to those whose war-vessels sank in the sea!
And to those themselves who sank in the sea!
And to all generals who lost engagements, and all overcome heroes!
And to the numberless unknown heroes equal to the greatest heroes known!

He too felt, with Emerson, that "a hero's, a man's success is made up
of failures . . . defeated all the time and yet to victory born." Many
times, during the Revolution, George Washington seemed to answer
that description. Lincoln, who tasted the dregs of poverty and heartbreak, and always bore the marks of his climb up the hill of difficulty,
Lincoln with his battered hat and shawl about his bony shoulders,
trudging down the lonely road to a martyr's grave—this is he whom
the artists, from James Russell Lowell to Robert E. Sherwood, have
chosen to honor. It is not the successful politician or victorious war
President. Certainly, Father Abraham, and not the generals in Blue
like Sherman and Grant, emerges as the supreme hero-symbol of
the North. While the rest of our tender homage has gone to the
defeated South, with her Stonewall Jackson killed in the dusk of
Chancellorsville by his own men, and her Robert Lee, the best of
those good losers whom Americans always love. Garfield and Mc-
Kinley became better heroes than they deserved to be, by virtue of
tragic death. William Jennings Bryan, with all his faults, stirred the
sympathy of millions because of his first gallant defeat for the Presidency. It is not yet decided whether Woodrow Wilson—a figure of

far deeper tragedy by reason of his greater powers—will become a major god. But at least, after his heartbreaking repudiation and his years of paralysis, men and women with tear-stained faces knelt on the pavement outside his window, for three winter days and nights, while he lay dying. The uniform success and good luck of a man like Coolidge hold no heroic attraction. Franklin D. Roosevelt's long battle against infantile paralysis has won widespread sympathy for a life which otherwise might seem too easy.

Our feeling for handicap and failure springs from the same root as our popular distrust of the man with hereditary place and fortune: we ask that our few aristocrats, like Jefferson and the two Roosevelts, balance things by a dash of "radicalism." In fact, neither Bourbons nor Cromwells fit into our scheme of democratic favor. No great American idol, in review, has lacked a touch lent by the struggle against odds, or by discouragement and passing failure. He must be a man who fights uphill. Unlike the dictator, or the superman as hero, he cannot display the arrogance of victory; but rather must be attuned to the still sad music of humanity. In the fabric of our success cult, this, as Henry James might say, is the figure in the carpet—on the under side.

CHAPTER TWO

CAPTAIN JOHN SMITH AND THE INDIANS

In kenning of the shore,
Thanks to God first given,
  O you the happiest men,
  Be frolic then;
Let cannons roar,
Frighting the wide heaven.

And in regions far
Such heroes bring you forth,
  As those from whom we came;
  And plant our name
Under that star
Not known unto our north.

—MICHAEL DRAYTON, "To the Virginian Voyage."

I

THE wine of the Elizabethans went to the head of Captain John Smith. His life was hardy and brave enough, but when he came to tell about it he drew a still longer bow. His tales of youth—how he left a humdrum apprenticeship to go soldiering; how at the "siege of Regall" he slew three Turkish champions in succession "to delight the ladies," but was finally captured by the paynims; how the beauteous Lady Traga-bigzanda, to whom he was sent as a present, fell in love with him; how he journeyed to Tartaria, overcame the bashaw, and was succored by the merciful Lady Callamata; how he escaped from pirates in a small boat, landing upon the coast of France and into the charitable arms of Lady Madam Chanoyes—reveal him as a sturdy wayfarer and perennial bachelor, who always contrived to be rescued by a beautiful lady of the highest social rank. His heroines' very names show that Captain Smith was steeped in Amadis of Gaul, Palmerin of Constantinople, and other courtly romances which Anthony Munday was rendering into English the decade before Smith's alleged adventures. When in 1607 he set foot in North America, on the first Virginian voyage, it was a foregone conclusion that the *leitmotif* of his life would somehow be repeated.

His first book from the New World, written the next year, said nothing about the saving of his head by Pocahontas. But in 1616, long after his return to England, the dusky princess herself, now "Lady Rebecca" and the Christian wife of John Rolfe, arrived at the Court of James I and Anne and became a seven days' wonder. Captain Smith could not resist basking in her glory. At this time, according to his later account, he sent the Queen a little book about Pocahontas, telling how "after some six weeks of fatting amongst those Salvage Courtiers, at the minute of my execution, she hazarded the beating out of her owne braines to save mine." But Smith's first recorded account of the rescue was not given until 1622, after Pocahontas had died of smallpox on the eve of her return home. His vague remark at this time, that "God made Pocahontas the Kings Daughter the meanes to deliver me," was much expanded in 1624 in his *Generall Historie of Virginia*, where she appears as "the blessed Pokahontas" who ran to the block and clasped him in her arms, to keep the braves from crushing his skull with their clubs.

Pocahontas thus became a great legend, as the white man's saviour. A fine ship's figurehead of her, which sailed the seas of Colonial trade, is now preserved in the Ludwell-Paradise house at Williamsburg. A settlement near Petersburg was called "Pocahontas." Her name appears as a favorite even upon Virginia family trees which claim no kinship with the Rolfe strain; while Randolphs and other First Families have been exceedingly proud of their descent. In Jefferson's day the best hotel in the new capital of Washington, on Pennsylvania Avenue, was named "The Indian Queen," and displayed a large swinging sign with the gaily painted image of Pocahontas. Numerous crossroads taverns through the West and Southwest took as their patron "The Indian Queen" or "Indian Princess." Over the west door of the rotunda in the National Capitol is carved in marble Antonio Capellano's "Pocahontas saving the life of Captain John Smith," while a painting inside that structure shows her baptism at Jamestown, as conceived by J. G. Chapman in 1836.

She and the Captain have gone hand in hand to immortality. The latter, as the self-attested hero of a dozen hairbreadth escapes, was held up to admiration of youth in Noah Webster's *The Little Readers Assistant* (Hartford, 1791), which, beneath a woodcut of Smith tied to a tree with Indians advancing murderously upon him, exclaimed: "What a *hero* was Capt. Smith! How many Turks and Indians did he slay! How often was he upon the brink of death, and how bravely did he encounter every danger! Such a man affords a noble example for all to follow, when they resolve to be *good* and *brave*." To his credit, Smith never implied that Pocahontas was in love with him. In fact, according to his *True Relation,* she was "a child of ten years old" in 1608, when as reported by his later memoirs the rescue took place. The embellishment of romance seems first to have been added with notable effect by John Davis, an Englishman who came to the United States in 1798 looking for literary employment. In 1805 he published his tale of *Captain John Smith and Princess Pocahontas,* in which Pocahontas, "all heavenly woman," becomes a willowy figure of distraught love. John Smith—with "the graceful manliness of the Belvidere Apollo," as Davis elsewhere describes him—suspects from her peculiar behavior that she loves him: "Yet, like a true soldier, unwilling to put his unhoused free condition into circumspection and confine, though he behaved to her with marked attention, he never dropped the slightest hint about marriage." Smith's embarrassment, however, causes him to drop his colonizing schemes in the New World, and after giving out the report that he is dead to sail secretly for England. Young Rolfe wins her hand, after moonlight walks and honeyed sonnets which bear little resemblance to Rolfe's authentic confession that he was desperately "in love with one whose education hath bin rude, her manners barbarous, her generation accursed." In Davis's tale the princess goes to London and is only momentarily piqued to learn of Smith's ruse. But she becomes such a social success that "carriages bearing coronets were often drawn up before her door . . . and Pocahontas, whose penetration was intuition, soon learnt to receive her visitants with appropriate variations of deference." One is reminded of Mrs. John Adams at the Court of George III.

But the first play about the princess and her captain, staged at the Chestnut Street Theatre, Philadelphia, in 1808, shows Pocahontas regarding him merely as a big brother. This "operatic melo-drame," *The Indian Princess; or La belle sauvage,* was written by the first Comptroller of the Treasury, J. N. Barker, and in accord with a financier's ideas about the increment of romance, contains no less than five pairs of lovers. Pocahontas, an "angel of purity," grieves over a flamingo she has shot and puts aside her bow and arrows forever; in the same mood she saves Smith from her tribesmen's tomahawks. Here, and elsewhere in popular writing, she comes to be Jamestown's patron saint. Thus in 1817 James Kirke Paulding writes fondly of the Virginia argonauts: "Fortitude, valor, perseverance, industry, and little Pocahontas were their tutelary deities; and their golden fleece the fields of corn and plantations of tobacco."[1]

But by the sterner moralists of New England, Captain Smith was not always accepted in his entirety as a safe model for youth. "Peter Parley," that favorite mentor of the Jacksonian era, was one of them. Parley is pictured as a benevolent old gentleman beckoning sedately to a group of wide-eyed youngsters, while he rests a bandaged foot on a stool beside a basket of kittens, and cajoles: "Come, come, boys and girls, no laughing, no tittering, while I tell you my stories about America—and mind you take care of my great toe!" His creator was a Connecticut clergyman's son named Samuel Griswold Goodrich. According to Goodrich's own statement, his books for American children sold upwards of seven million copies, and the effect of Peter Parley's priggish viewpoint upon the youthful reading of history is undoubted. Parley's *Stories about Captain John Smith* in 1829, written at a time when New England boys yearned to run off to sea, announces that John Smith "in his younger days was no great credit either to himself or his friends. . . . When only thirteen years of age, he laid a plan to run away from school, for he did not love to study. . . . This was a wicked step." Scorning his mother's advice he roves over Europe, but returns at last, to the gratification of "his mother and friends. It is always pleasant to see friends return, even if they have acted improperly." Now an incurable vagabond, he ships for Italy and falls in with a company of pilgrims. (The stout Protestant narrator explains that "Pilgrims are persons who pretend to be very religious.") After exploits in Egypt and Turkey, Smith lands by an abrupt jump in America, where Pocahontas saves his life: "What a worthy girl this was! She was a savage, but her deed was noble!" Powhatan lets Smith return to Jamestown "provided he would send him two cannon, and a grindstone. What he wanted of a grindstone I could never discover; but I suppose it was to sharpen tomahawks on." Although Smith's barter of two pounds of blue beads for 300 bushels of corn is a little too shrewd for Peter Parley's business ethics ("We should not take advantage of the ignorance of others"), his bravery is constantly praised. "Our fathers were distinguished for their courage; and hence they succeeded much better than if they had been timid." These tales about Captain Smith close with suitable reflections: "that persons, at an early age, have very *wicked hearts*. . . . How much more useful, and honorable, and happy would he have been, had he stayed at home —had he been sober and industrious; and, especially, had he assisted his mother! How much evil would he have escaped!" But also it may be learned "that it is never too late to amend a bad life, and lead a useful life. I am happy to say that Captain Smith did this. From the time he sailed for America, he was a useful man." It is a little breathtaking, even under the tutelage of a pious Congregationalist, to find Captain Smith emerge as a witness to conversion—transformed by God's grace from a prodigal son into a worthy citizen and canny trader.

Peter Parley's, however, is not a universal portrait of the great Captain. Two books of anecdotes written at the same time, one published in 1828 and the other in 1830, describe him in identical language as "the pure abstraction of chivalry—a very knight errant, as ever perilled his life for a lady's smile; brave to a fault, and high-minded to a miracle."[2] The same spirit of romance shines through a long play written by the son of Washington's stepson, George Washington Parke Custis, a florid little man who gloried in his sentimental title of "the child of Mount Vernon." In the cavalier rather than the Calvinist tradition was his drama *Pocahontas*, produced in Philadelphia in 1830 and later in the provinces. Smith is rescued at the end of the play by his princess, who long before has accepted the hand of Rolfe, rather than that of a redskin warrior who "lacks the best attribute of courage —mercy."

Seven years later another play about Pocahontas and Smith was written by Robert Dale Owen, member of the Indiana Legislature and son of the socialist mill-owner Robert Owen. Young Owen was a great friend of the first doughty feminist Frances Wright, pioneer of birth control and companionate marriage, and we discover in this play that the dusky princess is an advocate of women's rights. When her sister Nomony, a humdrum squaw, asks her in wonderment—

> Thinkest thou
> Woman was made to be the friend of man,
> To share man's confidence—win his respect—
> To be—to be—his equal?

Pocahontas sturdily answers

> I am born
> To aid, but not to slave.

With quickening interest in America's past, curiosity about John Smith grew apace. In 1846 William Gilmore Simms, the South Carolina romancer who was quarrying the epics of the Old South, of the Yemassee War and of Marion the Swamp-Fox, wrote a hero-worshipping life of Smith, "the founder of Virginia," to satisfy popular interest. Four years later Frank Lister Hawks, in gathering his *American Historical Tales for Youth,* held up for admiration Smith's boyhood integrity, "of too much principle to steal"; unlike Peter Parley's wastrel, he embarks upon adventure with his mother's blessing. Pocahontas saves Smith's life, but there is no love story—just clean action for boy readers.

As the frontier retreated deeper and deeper into the West, and redskins ceased to be a serious threat to manifest destiny, the noble savage grew increasingly a hero—whether as Pocahontas, a symbol of mercy, or as the stalwart chief, often the last of his clan, fighting against overwhelming odds, like Pontiac, Logan, or Tecumseh.[3] James Fenimore Cooper, who passed over the Pocahontas story as outside the scheme of his chronology, devoted himself to praise of the stern-souled brave, Chingachgook, Uncas, Conanchet, set off against the snivelling Puritan pastor Meek Wolfe. Time had brought many changes since the day when Deerfield, Wyoming, and Cherry Valley lingered in folk memory, and the legendary Indian was endowed with cruelty, treachery, and greed. In those times the applauded hero had been the sanguine Indian fighter like Ranger Rogers—whom Kenneth Roberts has lately rediscovered—or the iron-willed overlord like Sir William Johnson; while the classic villain had been Simon Girty the white renegade, who was said to have watched with glee the burning alive of Washington's friend Colonel Crawford. But when the Indian became the vanishing American, all this was altered. He was exalted into herohood by that *amende honorable* which the popular imagination often makes. During the earlier years of the nineteenth century the warrior and the Indian princess were hailed by a dozen poets in the urban East, and bodied forth into drama of highfalutin' sentiment like the record-breaking *Metamora.*

In time, by another swing of the pendulum, comedy overtook sentiment. The American itch to lay hands upon a too solemn idol prepared the way for John Brougham's celebrated farce of 1855, "An Original Aboriginal Erratic Operatic Semi-Civilized and Demi-Savage Extravaganza, being a Per-Version of Ye Trewe and Wonderfulle Hystorie of a Renowned Princesse Pocahontas: or The Gentle Savage." The prologue sings the praise of

> Jonsmith the valiant soldier,
> Sailor, buccaneer, explorer,
> Hero, trader, colonizer,
> Gent, adventurer, commander,
> Lawyer, orator, and author,
> Statesman, pioneer, and bagman.

With frankness Smith informs Powhatan, "a Semi-Brave," that "we came out here your lands to ravage." The chief consoles himself, at this melancholy intelligence, by ordering "some whiskey neat" and bursting into an Irish song to the tune of "Mother Machree." Smith is captured and sentenced to die. But Pocahontas, leading a "vociferous irruption of Juvenile Squaw-lers," grows so rowdy on behalf of rights for women that her father quickly agrees—among other concessions for the sake of peace—to let Smith's fate be determined by drawing a hand of poker. Smith of course wins, and pops the question to Pocahontas. The play ends on a note of cynicism, suiting the generation which saw the rise of Boss Tweed and of Tammany Hall, named after a great sachem. A procession bearing glass ballot boxes marches across the stage, chanting:

> Grab away
> While you may.
> In this game, luck is all,
> And the prize
> Tempting lies
> In the rich City Hall.

It was a decade of debunkery for the legend of Captain Smith and his princess. In 1860, for the first time since the ink had dried upon Smith's *Generall Historie,* his tale of the rescue was challenged by sober history. The skeptic was Charles Deane, Boston merchant and scholar, who pointed out that Smith wrote of his hairbreadth escape after the lapse of many years, that he was a notorious liar, and that none of his fellow-colonists seems to have known about the episode. In January, 1867, when the wounds of war-torn Virginia were still smarting, Henry Adams—scion of America's most tactless family of worthies—took it upon himself to attack her earliest hero. In an article in *The North American Review* Adams derided the myth of the rescue, also taxing Smith with being colossally vain and wholly incompetent as an official. It is said that Adams was egged on by some Northern friends, who observed that a stone thrown at the Virginia captain would "break as much glass as a missile heaved in any other direction."[4] Southern historians quickly rose to the bait, and were joined in Smith's defense by a redoubtable amateur scholar, William Wirt Henry, grandson of Patrick Henry. It was evident that a sensitive nerve had been touched. Curiously enough, in Smith's role as founder and patron of Jamestown, his equally important services to New England, whither he went in 1614, in charting a course which proved so helpful to the Pilgrims, have been ignored by friend and foe alike. But during post-bellum years his colors were worn upon the sleeve of various patriotic Virginians. John Esten Cooke paused in his saga enshrining Lee and his "paladins" in heroic fiction, to write in 1885 a novel called *My Lady Pokahontas*. Here Smith falls tenderly in love with his princess, woos her to Christianity and teaches her to say "God" as they walk hand in hand beside the sparkling James and the russet woods. To relieve the Victorian mind, Pocahontas appears "decently clad in her robe of birds' feathers"—hardly recognizable as the damsel whom the first secretary of the Virginia colony, William Strachey, had seen as a "wanton yong girle . . . [who would] get the boyes forth with her into the markett place, and make them wheele, falling on their hands, turning their heeles upwards, whom she would followe and wheele so her selfe, naked as she was, all the fort over."[5] In the pages of John Esten Cooke, Pocahontas and her captain decide their careers lie far apart, and take leave with tears and "a long kiss." Wooed and won by Rolfe, she goes to England—and attending a first night at the Globe Theatre, sees *The Tempest,* by Captain Smith's good friend Master Shakespeare, and recognizes herself as the heroine Miranda!

Margaret Junkin Preston, sister-in-law of Stonewall Jackson, made a fervently sentimental poem out of "The Last Meeting of Pocahontas and the Great Captain," at Court in 1616, in which Smith cajoles her as "My Sparkling-Water." Another minor poet of that era, George Pope Morris, wrote some often-quoted verses about the rescue—

> 'Tis ever thus, when in life's storm
> Hope's star to man grows dim,

An angel kneels, in woman's form,
And breathes a prayer for him.

There are many variations on this simple story and meager theme. John Smith, as "the last professional knight-errant that the world saw,"[6] is a figure whose appeal is easily understood; but the "heart interest" which has been attached to his story springs from pure folk and literary fancy, largely because he remained the lonely, world-wandering bachelor. His own explanation of his single blessedness—that the New World colonies "have been my wife, my hawks, hounds, my cards, my dice, and in total my best content"—has the right Elizabethan ring, but it failed to satisfy Victorian romance.

The Jamestown Tercentenary of 1907 stirred new interest in Pocahontas and Smith. A statue of the princess, "her hands outstretched to the starving colonists," by William Ordway Partridge, was then erected on the right-hand side of the old church by the Pocahontas Memorial Association; a bronze of Captain Smith flanked it on the left. Although neither has become the symbol of idealism into which the Pilgrim Fathers have grown, both will long live side by side in American folklore. Time and again we see how the pictorial quality of a story, doubtful or true—Washington and the cherry tree, Franklin and the loaf of bread or the kite, Paul Revere swinging into his saddle in view of the beacon lantern, Daniel Boone "shining" the eyes of his future bride while hunting for panther—has preserved it in imperishable amber. The truth or falsity of Pocahontas's rescue probably will never be proved to everybody's satisfaction; after several generations of scholarly doubt, the foremost Colonial historian of our day, Charles M. Andrews, has lately set down his belief in its likelihood.[7] At any rate, to the average American, Captain John Smith conjures up a figure in an Elizabethan ruff kneeling before a painted savage with an axe, while a dark maiden with feathers in her hair—blending the lineaments of Minnehaha and Ramona with a thousand chromo calendars—rushes protectively to his side.

II

The American temper has a marked sympathy for rebels, nonconformists, and cross-grained dissenters. It can be seen clearly in respect to Puritan and regicide. It appears in Hawthorne's *Grandfather's Chair*, and in the legend of the Charter Oak. Among the worthies of colonial New York many a name of civic obedience has been passed over in favor of Jacob Leisler—a firebrand of crude and selfish motives fondly imagined by some to have been "the people's friend"—who has his fine statue by Solon Borglum at New Rochelle. Leisler, along with Claiborne—who kindled much religious prejudice in his insurrection against the Proprietary in Maryland—inspired popular tales of the pre-dime-novel stripe about 1845.[8] No Virginian of the Colonial period stirred fiercer loyalties than Nathaniel Bacon "the Rebel," although he soon fell into oblivion until Thomas Jefferson led the antiquaries and novelists back to rediscover him as an evangel of the Spirit of '76. And of course his adversary Berkeley, who had thanked God there were no public schools or printing-presses in Virginia, readily became a symbol of British tyranny.

Just a century before the Revolution, in 1676, Bacon, a young English gentleman lately arrived in Virginia, dared to beard a Royal Governor. It was a season of discontent—with tobacco prices falling, navigation acts crippling Virginia commerce, and huge land grants from the Crown hamstringing the small farmer, whose acres were quickly going sterile—and the last straw was Berkeley's refusal to bestir himself in protecting the colonists from Indian marauders. At this juncture they began to rally round this bold young man, who was dubbed "General Bacon, by consent of the people."[9] He seems to have had a natural genius for leadership. His wife Elizabeth wrote proudly to her sister in England: "The country does so really love him that they would not leave him alone anywhere."[10] He quickly routed the Pamunkey Indians, and then turned his attention to the overbearing Governor. After Berkeley had given and betrayed promises, Bacon led an assault upon Jamestown and burnt it. He is described as a man of few words, but to the people his voice was like the sound of a trumpet. Leading the attack on Jamestown he called out, "Come on, my hearts of gold! He that dies in the field, lies in the bed of honor!"[11] He had not only the magnetism but the magnanimity of a hero. Even his foes witnessed that he "was not bloodily inclined in the whole progress of this rebellion," and that he had only one man—a spy and deserter—put to death, yet offered to spare his life if any soldier in the ranks would speak a word to save him. Once in power, Bacon began, it appears, to strip the Church of England of some of its clerical privileges, and to set up a more democratic government in Virginia, with pardon for all.[12] But in October, 1676, he died suddenly of a fever, or possibly poison, and his body was buried deep in a river-bed in Gloucester County. His rebellion soon collapsed, and Berkeley, coming out of hiding, reasserted himself with great cruelty.

The episode stirred excitement at home and abroad. A pamphlet, far from hostile to Bacon, was soon hawked on the streets of London, and Mrs. Aphra Behn wrote a play, *The Widow Ranter; or, The history of Bacon in Virginia*. Its fiction of Bacon's love for an Indian queen, Semernia, is absurd enough, but the speeches in which Bacon urges his men to revolt are so ringing that a Virginia historian born in Jefferson's day has asserted "one or two expressions in the Declaration of Independence occur in this old play."[13] Yet for all his meteoric deeds Bacon did not become a noteworthy hero, even to Virginia, in the century that followed his death. He seems to have been remembered chiefly as a trouble-maker. The author of a well-known satire, *The Sot-Weed Factor*, in 1731 published an account of Bacon's rebellion, "done into Hudibrastick verse, from an old manuscript." By this tale, Berkeley governed well enough

> Till little Nat, presumptuous Hector,
> (Aspiring, like the Lord Protector)
> O'er the Atlantick ocean came,
> And put the People in a flame.

The hanging of Bacon's followers is told with relish.

Bacon's memory, in fact, did not begin to attract hero-worship until well after the Revolution. A manuscript called "The Beginning, Progress, and Conclusion of Bacon's Rebellion," written for Secretary Harley in London in 1705 by an impartial merchant-planter of the Northern Neck, one Thomas Mathew, remained for many years in the famous Harleian Library—but in an unknown way it fell into the hands of a London bookseller, who sold it to Rufus King, the United States Minister, in 1801. King in turn presented it to President Thomas Jefferson, whose interest appears to have been keen. Jefferson sent a manuscript of it, "carefully copied, and with his own hand," to *The Richmond Enquirer*. That newspaper printed it in three installments in September, 1804. Jefferson, who believed that the tree of liberty should be watered at intervals with the blood of tyrants and was not loath to think the worst of royal governors, was warmly attracted to Bacon. The letter to the Richmond editor, which accompanied this manuscript, ends thus:

If this little book speaks the truth, Nathaniel Bacon will no longer be regarded as a rebel, but as a patriot. His name will be rescued from the infamy which has adhered to it for more than a century; the stigma of corruption, cruelty, and treachery, will be fixed on the administration by which he was condemned; and one more case will be added to those which prove, that insurrections proceed oftener from the misconduct of those in power, than from the factions and turbulent temper of the People.[14]

With such resounding Jeffersonian blessings, the long-forgotten author was allowed to tell his story. The narrator, although he shows Bacon as a well-liked champion and dismisses the charge that for selfish reasons he fished "in the troubled waters of popular discontents," describes the rebel more critically than Jefferson's preface leads us to expect. Bacon appears as a hotspur, swearing and raging in a "paroxism of phrenetick fury," and in some respects is the tool of a more clear-headed conspirator named Lawrence. Nevertheless, the rehabilitation of Bacon's fame had begun. In the next year, 1805, John Burk's *History of Virginia* praises his classical education, personal charm, handsome face, and the dignity of his "guarded silence and reserve." His uprising is now termed a civil war, and his motives are of the noblest:

We must not then regard him as the desperate adventurer, a bankrupt in fortune and reputation: But as a youth amiable and popular, of bright hopes and shining talents, and already advanced to the first offices in the government. . . .

Had this man's position on the globe been more favorable, or his means more ample, it is not easy to say how exalted had been his rank in history. He might have been the Brutus or the Cromwell of his country: but as it is, he is fated to pass off without fame and almost without notice.[15]

Another forgotten manuscript written soon after Bacon's rebellion was found about this time by Congressman William Burwell, among his family papers. He lent it in 1812 to Josiah Quincy of Massachusetts, who arranged for its publication two years later by the Massachusetts Historical Society. The original was kept in the archives in Boston, and the refusal of that Society after Burwell's death to return the manuscript to Virginia caused one of the minor antiquarian feuds which added to ante-bellum bitterness. Finally in 1866 when the War was over, and a letter had come to light from Burwell to Quincy saying that his manuscript was a loan, Massachusetts restored it at last to the Old Dominion. This account of the rebellion shows Bacon as more cunning than honorable, a man whose schemes, "having (like the hoggs the devill sheared) produced more noise than wooll," collapsed with little good accomplished. His needless burning of Jamestown church is branded as "barbarous," by one who evidently sensed the anti-clericalism which wrought some of Bacon's deeds. Yet the narrator gives what is probably the first hero-worshipping poem to come out of Virginia, "Bacons Epitaph," said to have been made "by the Man that waited upon his person"—

> Soules repleate
> With dull chilled cold, he'd animate with heate
> Drawn forth of reasons Lymbick. . . .
> [But] none shall dare his obsequies to sing
> In deserv'd measures, untill time shall bring
> Truth crown'd with freedom, and from danger free,
> To sound his praises to posterity.[16]

This man, it appears, was a hero to his own valet.

Bacon soon came to be a favorite in romance, especially as written by Virginians. William A. Caruthers, a doctor of the Old Dominion, published his novel *The Cavaliers of Virginia* in 1834, describing "Natty Bacon" as a bold and graceful Robin Hood in "a green hunting jerken, buttoned close up to his throat so as to show off to the best advantage a broad and manly chest." He is brave, but talks with bookish swagger, fearing often that the heroine is "irreconcilably offended" with him. To our surprise, the novel ends happily when Bacon—famous, successful, and in the best of health—"leads to the altar" the fair Miss Virginia Fairfax. That Bacon had married a devoted wife before emigrating to America, the daughter of Sir Edward Duke, is conveniently forgotten. Another Virginian, St. George Tucker, wrote in 1857 a romance of the rebellion called *Hansford*, after one of Bacon's aides, who had the "honor to be the first Virginian that was ever hanged." Here Bacon's "proud and imperial bearing" is joined to the most exquisite chivalry and dashing valor. From the first paragraph, praising the Cavalier at the Puritan's expense, to the last sentence of the novel (in which the bereaved heroine moves "through the world, like the wind of the sweet South, receiving and bestowing blessings"), one perceives the touch which lent aptness to a novel, written in 1857, about a great Virginia rebel. A host of later novels made him into a Byronic hero, dark, fiery, solitary, irresistible to women, "the wandering outlaw of his own dark mind."[17] To Maude Wilder Goodwin, who describes him rather curiously as having "an aspect ominous, pensive, melancholy, such as marks the portrait of every great man that has come down to us," Bacon is the forerunner of George Washington. His only full-dress biographer, Mary Newton Stanard, whose book came out in the year of the Jamestown Tercentenary, wrote: "If he had lived a hundred years later the number of heroes of the American Revolution would doubtless have been increased by one—and his name would have been at the top of the list, or near it."[18] The same celebration saw a four-act play written about him, hailing Bacon as America's first great patriot, who died in the prospect of a new liberty which "shall spread and ripen to the golden harvest—America! A brother-land to be!"[19] And that author of some three hundred dime novels, Edward S. Ellis, wrote of him "as a knight of the olden times," who laid the foundation for Virginia's defiant motto "Sic semper tyrannis!"[20] Most recently, in 1940, Thomas Jefferson Wertenbaker, a Princeton scholar and Virginian, published a book about Bacon named *Torchbearer of the Revolution,* calling him "as truly a martyr to American freedom as Nathan Hale or Hugh Mercer."

Nathaniel Bacon, after long neglect, was thus brought forth under Jeffersonian auspices as the symbol of righteous rebellion, democracy, and religious liberty. Scholars and romance-writers looked upon him with favor, and in Virginia—where "Bacon's Castle" in Surry County is something of a shrine to tourists in the motor age—his name is well known to school children today. But he has never become a national hero.

CHAPTER THREE

THE PILGRIM FATHERS AND THE AMERICAN WAY

> Let us thank God for having given us such an-
> cestors; and let each successive generation thank
> him not less fervently for being one step further
> from them in the march of ages.—NATHANIEL
> HAWTHORNE, *Twice-Told Tales*.

I

THE thirteen colonies had no lack of brave men, who dared
perils by sea and land, and went through a thousand adventures as picturesque as anything later times can show.
Yet they bred no individuals whose names keep the magic,
for average Americans today, of Paul Revere and Daniel
Boone, not to mention Lincoln or Lee. A colony has no heroes. Not
until the umbilical cord is cut which binds a colony to the Mother
Country, does a people begin to draw its own breath and have its great
folk legends. In the shade of dependence a racial hero cannot grow;
his essence is superlativeness and free will. He cannot be a subaltern,
a vice president, a second fiddle. The prime weakness of colonies, in
fact, is their dearth of rich traditions. Canada has no great national
idol, whose words she quotes and whose birthday she keeps (along
with the King's) as a holiday. Yet Canada has borne statesmen like

Sir John Macdonald and Sir Wilfrid Laurier, orators like Thomas
D'Arcy McGee, romantic types like the Royal Northwest Mounted,
and has contributed fine soldiers and aviators to European wars. A
popular candy in the Dominion is named for Laura Secord, who in
the War of 1812—in an episode unknown to United States schoolbooks
—slipped past the American sentries near Queenston, with a milk-pail
on her arm, and trudged through twenty miles of flood to carry the
news that enabled FitzGibbon to rout Colonel Boerstler and the 14th
U. S. Infantry. Similarly, Australia has a few locally famous bush-
rangers like "Starlight" celebrated in Ralph Boulderwood's *Robbery
under Arms,* and, collectively, the Anzacs of two European wars. But
neither country has giants like Washington and Andrew Jackson,
Wellington or Nelson. They have never been swept by the acclaim of
millions for a man.

Colonial America was in the same plight. A climate of dependence—
which called its wars by such revealing names as King William's War,
Queen Anne's War, King George's War, the French and Indian Wars
—was joined to the handicap of poor communication, in spreading the
fame of heroes. Newspapers were few, roads bad, postal systems costly,
and provincial isolations severe. Tidewater and frontier were not in sympathy. Jealous colonies bickered over boundaries and charter claims,
and spiritually Virginia was closer to London than to Massachusetts.
Such hero-worship as existed was apt to turn toward the Crown and
a few popular generals and governors from overseas. Benjamin Franklin's cartoon in 1754 of the snake cut into eight pieces, with the caption
"Join or die," was an emblem of cultural disagreement. To the Pilgrim
Fathers and John Winthrop the South felt no devotion; while Massachusetts knew little of Pocahontas or Nathaniel Bacon, but may have
remembered that Captain John Smith was an individual not wanted
aboard the *Mayflower.*[1] Lovewell's fight with the Indians at Pigwacket
in 1725 was extolled in the ballads of Maine, and in honor of his
chaplain, "good young Frye," who fell in that skirmish, a town was
named Fryeburg; but the Down East trader took small interest in
Roger Williams or William Penn. Even in the Revolution—when the
King had ceased to be a hero to the mass of Americans, and had
become a villain—this sectionalism still existed, and time and again
hampered effective action. New England, having chased the redcoats
from her borders, was loath to send soldiers to help the middle states,
while Southern militiamen had no enthusiasm for service in the North.
Eventually George Washington, a man upon whom New England and

Virginia managed fairly well to agree, became what the Freudians might call a "surrogate Father" in place of the King; at last his power-ful and noble leadership fused the colonies into a nation, and gave them a new pattern for hero-worship.

Yet traces of old regional jealousies survived a long time, even in respect to the earliest symbols of American patriotism. Although a poet like James Kirke Paulding might write, early in the nineteenth century—

> Jamestown, and Plymouth's hallowed rock,
> To me shall ever sacred be—

an historical feud between the Pilgrims and the Jamestown settlers simmered for many years. We have seen how Henry Adams and other Northern historians took impish delight in throwing stones at Captain John Smith. Yankees never tired of pointing out that the Virginia Company was an economic enterprise, whereas the first settlers of New England came to build an ideal commonwealth—pinning their brave hope not upon royal charter but upon royal sufferance.[2] Ergo, as dis-senters from English ways and the Established Church, these Pilgrims were the first true Americans. Southerners, on the other hand, have long distrusted the way in which the Pilgrims have been sold to the country at large as pure idealists, above and beyond the mercantile spirit, and as the founders of religious liberty and democracy. An extreme instance of the Southern point of view is a book called *Truths of History*, published in 1921 and unanimously recommended as a school text by the next convention of United Confederate Veterans. The author was Miss Mildred Rutherford, Georgia state historian of the U. D. C., and evidently a valkyrie of sectional patriotism. After scolding Yankee historians for describing the first settlers of Georgia as "filthy, ragged, dirty prisoners taken from the debtor's prison by Oglethorpe," Miss Rutherford remarked acidly that most textbooks "magnify and exalt the New England colonies and the *Mayflower* crew, with bare mention of the Jamestown colony, thirteen years older, and the crews of the *Susan Constant,* the *Discovery,* and the *Good-speed.*" She objected specially to the popular glorification of New England piety, to the neglect of praise for Sir Thomas Dale's code at Jamestown, "which enforced daily attendance at Divine worship, penalty for absence, penalty for blasphemy, penalty for speaking evil of the Church, and refusing to answer the Catechism, and for neg-lecting work." Miss Rutherford's eagerness to claim for Virginia the first fruits of bigotry, as well as the gospel of enterprise, is itself an unconscious comment on our long worship of Puritanism as true Americanism.

Touches of even closer sectional jealousy may be found. Cape Cod —where the Pilgrims first went ashore, on November 11, 162c, and tarried for such quaint acts as digging up Indian graves to examine the beads and pottery buried there, taking "sundry of the prettiest things away with us," as John Robinson related[3]—has long felt a grievance against Plymouth. On the Cape, at Provincetown, a stone tower has been built to hallow the real spot upon which the Fathers first landed. Compilers of the recent Federal Writers' Guidebook to Massachusetts report that old Cape Cod folk exclaimed, with a snort of pride: "Plymouth Rock? That's the name of a chicken. The spot where the *Mayflower* people first stepped on American soil is right here in Provincetown, and you ought to freeze on to that fact in your guide book, for it's been rising three hundred years now, and most off-Cape folks don't seem to know it yet!"[4] Yet Plymouth, the site of Daniel Webster's oration and Mrs. Hemans's poem and the National Monument to the Forefathers, continues to steal the show and the carriage trade. The Pilgrims' last port steadily draws more than 100,000 visitors each year, and holds its "Pilgrim's Progress"—a march of *Mayflower* descendants—every Friday in August.

II

It is plain that the founders of New England have had an immense effect upon our concept of Americanism—that collective symbol which means those things for which the Pilgrims settled this country, for which the Revolutionary fathers bled, for which the Civil War was fought and Abraham Lincoln suffered, and possibly for which our boys in France offered their lives. It is a vague but important concept, which always grows more dear to us in times of crisis. For all its vagueness, nobody will deny that Americanism has a rich kernel of truth and reality we all prize. But, on the other hand, all will agree that this emblem has been abused by generations of doctrinaires with axes to grind. Walter Lippmann some years ago compared collective symbols, like "Americanism," to strategic railroad centers, where many roads meet regardless of their point of origin or where they are going. A political strategist claiming these junction centers successfully enough to convince the public of his right to be there, controls the highroads of mass policy. He may attack or defend proposed legislation, call for more or less taxes, urge or decry government control of business, win support for war or peace, because his platform is "American." With such a fulcrum he can move a hundred million people. It is useful, therefore, to sift some of the myths and the truths concerning the Pilgrims and the Puritans as guides to the American way.

First, for the myths. One of the most innocent is the widespread belief that these pioneers lived in log cabins, the cradles of American enterprise. For generations now, poets, orators, and historians as eminent as James Truslow Adams and Charles M. Andrews have seen these early settlers—in their mind's eye—dwelling in log cabins. A typical illustration, in the Yale-sponsored *Pageant of America*, shows an all-log village of Plymouth, as well as a Jamestown being built in the same way—with Captain Smith flourishing a hatchet, while other adventurers lounge about in elegant attitudes, Sandys reading his Ovid. Yet a book published in 1939 by the late Harold R. Shurtleff, former head of the research department at Williamsburg, proves that the log cabin was brought to America late in the seventeenth century by Swedes and by Germans from the Black Forest—who had long lived in huts built of logs, a type of construction unknown to England then as now. English settlers were slow to adopt this outlandish way of making a house, and seldom did so until they began to settle the wilderness beyond the Alleghenies. The term "log cabin" apparently is not found in print or manuscript before 1770.[5] But with expansion of the frontier, log cabins grew to be emblems of American enterprise as classic as the long rifle, bowie knife, and buckskin hunting-shirt. In 1840 this symbol entered politics, when a Baltimore newspaper curtly remarked that William Henry Harrison, as candidate for President, might better be drinking hard cider and quietly sitting at home in a log cabin. Harrison's friends, the Whigs, jumped at the opportunity. By slogans, songs, tableaux, torchlight parades they glorified the log cabin—with latchstring hanging out and a barrel of cider at the door—as the essence of homespun Americanism. "Old Tippecanoe" was suddenly built up into the hero of the hour, the first synthetic one in American politics. That he really lived in a spacious mansion overlooking the Ohio River, and was an F. F. V., did not matter; on the strength of the Log Cabin Campaign he was swept into the White House in the heaviest voting known to that era. Soon, it appears, people with historical imaginations began to assume that the first Americans had lived in log cabins. Mr. Shurtleff found what he supposed was the first statement of this myth in a book published in 1841 by a Whig clergyman of Boston. But an earlier statement will be found in the files of a Whig newspaper, *The Newark Advertiser*, for May 18, 1840, in an editorial linking "the illustrious Harrison" and Daniel Boone with the first settlers:

Log Cabins were the dwelling places of the founders of our republic. It was a Log Cabin that received the daring pioneers of liberty who exchanged the dangers of the half-sinking *Mayflower* for the dangers and perils of an inhospitable clime. It was in view of the Rock of Plymouth that the Puritans of New England first erected their Log Cabins. . . . Honored, then, through all time, be these memorials of the trials, the sufferings, the triumphs of our forefathers.

Likewise, at the 250th anniversary of the Jamestown settlement, in 1857, Harrison's running mate and successor, Ex-President John Tyler, declared that the Virginia pioneers had built themselves cabins of logs. It is now clear that neither Captain John Smith nor Governor Bradford ever saw a log cabin—that not until the nineteenth century was a type of architecture, brought to these shores by immigrants from Continental forests, made into a symbol of self-help.

In other respects as well, the Pilgrims and Puritans have passed so far beyond the Lethe of legend that we have lost touch with their reality. Some moderns have charged them with greater dourness than they actually had—forgetting, for example, their abundant use of rum and wine even at the ordination of ministers, and their still shocking practice of "bundling"—while other moderns have praised them for liberal virtues which they heartily detested. Between the common picture of Pilgrims in sugar-loaf hats and kerchiefs, with angel faces, trudging to church through the snow, and the equally familiar caricature of the blue-nosed, lank-haired hypocrite labelled "Bigotry" or "Prohibition" by Rollin Kirby and other cartoonists a couple of decades ago, runs the whole span from white to black.

Various attempts have been made to solve this paradox. A century ago, growing hostility to the memory of the Puritans—in some circles a synonym for "demure rogues" or "formal hypocrites," as John Foster noted in 1826[6]—led to a feeling that the Puritan builders of the Bay Colony should be divorced from the Pilgrim Fathers who arrived ten years earlier. A piece of fiction like Harriet Cheney's *A peep at the Pilgrims* in 1824 shows the Plymouth settlers as kindly, hospitable, tender-hearted, while their neighbors to the north are stern bigots. But the distinction was not altogether common: another novel of the time, Lydia Maria Child's *The first settlers of New England,* in 1829, draws them all as cruel and bloodthirsty toward the Indians, on account of the Jewish strain in their religion! The label "Pilgrim Fathers," which suggests the spiritual patriarch and takes away the odor of priggishness attached to "Puritan," is one which the original settlers at Plymouth did not use about themselves. Surcharged with its present sentiments, it was first used by Cotton Mather and other divines three generations later in seeking to recall the good old days. These later Puritans were eager enough to identify themselves with the traditions of Plymouth. Of course there were some initial differences between Plymouth and Massachusetts Bay, in social rank, education, and ideas of church government. But soon they drew together, Boston swelling to a metropolis while Plymouth with its stony acres and poor trading-ground shrank to a village. "It was in Massachusetts Bay, not Plymouth," as Samuel Eliot Morison has written, "that were worked out those characteristic forms of state, church, and school, which have set off New England as a province apart."[7] The Puritan of the Bay is, therefore, the effective moulder of "the American way," while the Pilgrim fades into sentimental legend. Today the average American is prone to lump them together.

Both have been appealed to as founders of democracy in America. Timothy Dwight, president of Yale from 1795 to 1817, was one who (although a foe of Jeffersonian democracy, as befitted a kinsman of New England's first industrial families) extolled the Puritans for giving us a pattern of equality. Unlike the Virginians, said Dwight, the fathers of New England had banned primogeniture and entail, thus fostering

> The noblest institutions man has seen
> Since time his reign began. In little farms
> They measured all their realms, to every child
> In equal shares descending.[8]

Many Northern orators in Daniel Webster's generation said the same thing. This, however, is not the complete picture. Though the plantation covenant of Plymouth was more democratic than the charter of Massachusetts Bay, neither fits the modern American concept. The Pilgrim Fathers began as communists—laboring jointly upon the common land, and feeding from a communal store of supplies, to each according to his needs—but like the early communists of Jamestown they found that the experiment soon collapsed, thus proving, as William Bradford admits, "the vanitie of that conceite of Platos."[9] On the other hand, the Puritans of the Bay emphatically were not democrats. Birth, breeding, education, wealth, and religious orthodoxy gave prestige that was both social and political. Governor Winthrop in 1642, when litigation between rich Captain Robert Keayne and poor Mistress Sherman over the ownership of a sow roused some popular sympathy for the widow, rebuked such meddling as tending toward a democracy, and of course "there was no such Governm! in Israel." Likewise this haughty governor, in a famous letter to Thomas Hooker, expressed his conviction that "the best is always the least, & of that best part the wiser part is always the lesser."[10] Puritanism itself, beginning in England in the fiery furnace of minority loyalties, when dominant quickly cooled into the clinkers of authoritarianism. Pride, among all the seven deadly sins, was the one to which the Puritan was most susceptible—and this flaw left its mark upon the ruling caste. Many recent scholars have agreed with the late Frederick J. Turner, who said that American democracy as we now know it "was not carried in the *Susan Constant* to Virginia nor in the *Mayflower* to Plymouth. It came out of the American forest, and it gained strength each time it touched a new frontier."[11]

These early settlers are often praised, also, as pioneers of religious liberty. Freedom of thought and speech and worship we rightly regard as precious to Americanism. Do we owe them to the Puritans? Mrs. Felicia Hemans, who loved the sentimental heroic—now out of fashion with a younger generation which persists in linking the boy upon the burning deck with an invincible passion for peanuts—wrote a poem that used to be found in every school reader. The stern and rock-bound coast, a nobler frame for arduousness than the mild shores of the James River, she thus rhapsodized:

> Aye, call it holy ground,
> The soil where first they trod!
> They have left unstained what there they found—
> Freedom to worship God!

But it is plain that neither Plymouth nor Boston, but rather Rhode Island and Connecticut, were the nurseries of New England liberalism. Such a jolly dissenter from Calvinism as Morton of Merrymount was suppressed twice—first by the Pilgrim Fathers under Miles Standish, and later by the Puritans of the Bay under Endecott. Orthodoxy in Massachusetts, as is well known, agreed to whip Quakers and Baptists; to banish Anne Hutchinson, who in her friendless state was slain by the Indians; and to expel saintly Roger Williams, who wrote back to the elders: "Yourselves pretend liberty of conscience, but alas! it is but self, the great god self, only to yourselves."[12] The spirit of John Calvin —who had burned Servetus for disagreeing with him—did not foster much true charity. Too many of the first settlers came, not to set up an asylum of religious liberty for all men, but to establish their own brand of intolerance. Later, after Puritanism in evaporating left behind such crystals as Unitarian intellectualism, easy-going Congregationalism, and democratic evangelism, it became easier to read into the early spirit of Massachusetts the liberal virtues admired by modern times. But they were hardly there in the beginning. Of political and religious liberalism, as understood by the Republic of Jefferson and Madison, these Forefathers had few traces.

On the other hand, the Puritans have often been praised as the epitome of rugged individualism and free competition. Old guard Republicans frequently appeal to them in this way. Yet evidence shows that the Puritans favored government regulation of business, price-fixing for the common good, and curbing of excess profits made by an individual at the public expense. In some respects they were convinced New Dealers. This same Captain Keayne was fined £200 by the General Court for making a profit of sixpence or more in the shilling; while the Reverend John Cotton in 1639 condemned the thesis "that a man might sell as dear as he can, and buy as cheap as he can."[13] This aspect of the Puritan has been forgotten, probably because it ran against the grain of later mythologies in New England. Within a few generations after the first settlers, with the heroic age of Puritanism waning fast, more and more attention came to be paid to the gospel of business enterprise. Weber, Tawney, and others have suggested that Calvinist ethics was the seed-plot from which modern capitalist philosophy sprang. Unlike Luther, who taught that work in the sweat of one's brow was the orginal curse God laid upon Adam, Calvin held that work is man's holy duty. Idleness is shameful. "Work, for the night is coming," exhorted a later Protestant hymn. The first Puritans believed that good works—including thrift, soberness, and the making of money to be used wisely—were a badge of God's favor. Prosperity was important only because it showed that God was on one's side. John Cotton wrote of the "mystery" of Puritanism, namely "diligence in worldly business and yet deadnesse to the world." His grandson Cotton Mather described the two callings of man as his eternal salvation and his daily business: "If he mind but one of his callings, he pulls the oar but on one side of the boat, and it will make but a poor dispatch to the shoar of Eternal Blessedness."[14] In his book of hero-worshipping biographies called *Magnalia Christi Americana,* Mather wrote his longest and most enthusiastic life about a self-made man, Sir William Phips, who from poverty rose to riches and knighthood—"Behold one raised by God!" cried Mather, defying "pale Envy" to "fly-blow the Hero." That Phips had burnt his fingers at piracy did not seem to matter. The Puritan, in fact, was an idealist tinged with cynicism—cherishing dreams of utopia but knowing that on account of corrupt human nature they could never be realized on earth. The Yankee could skin a stranger at a horse-trade because he was convinced that his fellow-man was a bottomless well of original sin.

Soon, in the waning moon of Puritanism, Poor Richard after his Boston boyhood would help to secularize the gospel of wealth—preaching, in a hundred proverbs, diligence in business, thrift, and that self-improvement which was a Yankee passion. The sign of God's grace, prosperity, in time came to seem more important than the grace itself. When Irving came to write with the pen of Diedrich Knickerbocker, "the ingenious Yankee" was already a stock type, hard-fisted and God-fearing, sprung from "such a squatting, bundling, guessing, shingle-splitting, pumpkin-eating, molasses-daubing, cider-watering, horse-jock-eying, notion-peddling crew." His clipper ships rounded the Horn with argosies of the Indies; his outposts of the fur trade rose along the Columbia River; his tall chimneys at Lowell and Taunton belched forth the smoke of a new industrialism. Doctrines took shape concerning the holy stewardship of business, preached by President Porter of Yale and President McCosh of Princeton. "Acres of Diamonds," a lecture given six thousand times by the Reverend Russell H. Conwell, declared:

Money is power. Every good man and woman ought to strive for power, to do good with it when obtained. Tens of thousands of men and women get rich honestly. But they are often accused by an envious, lazy crowd of unsuccessful persons of being dishonest and oppressive. I say, Get rich! get rich! but get money honestly, or it will be a withering curse!

(Today the issue of "smearing success" still enters into Presidential campaigns.)

John D. Rockefeller said to the first graduating class at his new university, "The good Lord gave me my money, and how could I withhold it from the University of Chicago?"[15] while Bishop Lawrence of Massachusetts in 1900 asserted that "Godliness is in league with riches."[16] Indeed, the old Calvinist link between religion and business returns in many guises. In 1920, for example, post-war Puritanism began a spirited campaign against Sabbath movies and golf—appealing both to "the Christ spirit" and to the alleged fact that workmen "who had no sport on Sunday do their best day's work Monday."[17] During the Depression, on December 10, 1933, a *New York Times* editorial praised the economist Doctor Sprague for saying penitently of the bull-market days, "We were all miserable sinners," and Alfred E. Smith for stating that the causes of the stock-market crash were "as old as original sin." Thanks to the old Puritan heritage of American business, it sometimes shows a strange groping after the concepts of that faith.

In the making of American legends, therefore, the Puritan Fathers are often praised for contributions not very well deserved—such as religious liberalism and democracy in government—but slighted as pioneers both in State control of business and in the quite different cult of idealizing the merchant prince, a hero type to be discussed later. On the whole, the more personal qualities of the Puritan, like courage, stubborn will, and keen appreciation of the intellectual and spiritual life, have a place in legend better merited than that given to their group traits. The Puritan, in fact, seems to have been more attractive as an individual than *en masse*.

III

How then did the Puritan myth, somewhat at odds with the facts, arise? It was built by two forces working in contrary directions. One was the impulse of later times to exalt the first settlers as belonging to "the good old days." The other was an urge to read into Puritan life those qualities which moderns prize more than did worthies of the seventeenth century. The first was prone to measure the modern man by the Puritan yardstick; the second to give the Puritan credit for all the progressivism of a latter day. Both impulses ran to hero-worship.

Those early settlers themselves had had few individual heroes. They did not bow down before any man, choosing even in portraiture to show "the warts on Cromwell's face." Group egotism—of feeling themselves the anointed of God—they did have, but of persons they were fiercely critical. Miles Standish, nicknamed "the Hero of New England" on account of his valor against the Indians, might have stood forth as a great man in a society where the soldier was king.

But in a Puritan theocracy that looked first of all to its clergymen, Standish's fame, like his physique, never reached great height. To this day New England remembers him as a doughty little man, "Captaine Shrimpe," as he was called by the irrepressible Morton of Merrymount. He owes most of his present fame to Longfellow's poem, telling of his tongue-tied courtship of Priscilla—a story for which there is no basis in fact.[18] (To take off the dour edge of Puritan memory, the Massachusetts Development and Industrial Commission often proclaims the Old Bay State "the land of America's greatest lovers! Priscilla! John Alden! America's greatest love-match!") And there was John Winthrop, practically governor *in perpetuo* of Massachusetts, the most admired layman of his time. In funeral sermons and elegies—the Puritan equivalent of fan mail, offered when the admirer was no longer suspected of bootlicking, or the recipient of vanity—he was recalled as "the chiefest of our Peers," "New Englands Pelican," and "The Loadstone of America." Richard Greenough made a marble statue of him, Bible in hand, for the National Capitol in 1876, and another for Scollay Square in Boston, but to most Americans today he is neither an important symbol nor legend. There were eloquent divines, and the heroes of Indian captivity, and the Regicide Judges who took refuge from England in Connecticut and on account of their hiding inspired much popular folklore—but in general, colonial New England is pretty bare of individual idols.

The spirit of romance, therefore, has turned to a composite ideal called the Pilgrim Fathers or the Puritans. As early as 1676 a Boston schoolmaster named Benjamin Tompson—who seems to have been the first native-born American poet—dreamed about the first settlers and their "golden times, too fortunate to hold," when there was more praying for one's neighbors than gossiping about them, and when redskins were handled sternly—

> No sooner pagan malice peepèd forth
> But valor snubbed it. Then were men of worth,
> Who by their prayers slew thousands; angel-like,
> Their weapons are unseen, with which they strike.[19]

As Puritanism grew still colder, early in the next century, the great preachers like the Mathers and Stoddards from their pulpits loved to praise the good old times, in summoning their flock back to the strenuous temper. They extolled the Fathers, "who for an undefiled conscience and the love of a pure Christianity, first left their native and pleasant land, and encountered all the toils and hazards of the tumultuous ocean"—but were now prone to apologize (the difference is significant) for the brusque treatment these men had meted out to the Indians.[20] But this homage to the past had not yet grown sentimental: the first centenary of Plymouth, in 1720, for example, seems to have passed quite unnoticed.

The symbol of the Pilgrim Fathers did not become important, for the country at large, until storm clouds of the American Revolution began to gather. Then the flight of the Pilgrims, from English tyranny to the New World, was seen to have patriotic meaning. In 1768 a Marylander, John Dickinson, stirred by the recent events in Boston, wrote the most popular poem of that day, "The Liberty Song":

> Our worthy Forefathers—let's give them a cheer—
> To Climates unknown did courageously steer;
> Thro' Oceans to Desarts for Freedom they came,
> And dying bequeath'd us their Freedom and Fame.

"The Massachusetts Liberty Song" in the same year bade Americans take heart from the courage of their ancestors, who won "through deaths and through dangers," and a little later Peter St. John in his "Taxation of America" called on his countrymen to be worthy of their sires who for ideals had defied the British Crown. In January, 1769, twelve young men of Plymouth started a club to commemorate the traditions of their town; on the next December 22 they held the first dinner honoring the landing at Plymouth Rock. This spirit ran through the Revolution. The Pilgrims had now begun to be national heroes.

In Boston a scheme for annual celebration of the Pilgrims was first proposed in 1774, but was not adopted until December, 1798, when the "Sons of the Pilgrims" kept their first feast. Thereafter December 21 or 22 was observed widely in Massachusetts. The term "Pilgrim Fathers," fixed in the popular mind by this observance, soon became the usual designation for them throughout the nation.[21] Forefathers' Day grew into a great New England tradition, with the eating of turkey and pumpkin pie and the placing of five kernels beside each plate, in memory of the daily ration said to have been allotted during the "starving time" of April, 1622. In 1820, the Bicentenary of the landing, Forefathers' Day at Plymouth reached a new high. Daniel Webster spoke one of his greatest orations, and the banquet was eaten from huge blue dinner-plates specially made by Enoch Wood & Sons of Staffordshire—showing a boatload of Pilgrims landing before the eyes of the Indians, who were standing on the Rock itself, already carved with the names of Miles Standish, William Bradford, and others. Linking this historic event with the cause of Independence were scrolls at the top and bottom of this design, reading "America Independent, July 4, 1776" and "Washington, born 1732, died 1799."

Apart from Forefathers' Day but fostering the same cult was Thanksgiving, looking back to Governor Bradford's celebrated proclamation in 1621. It was a Puritan substitute for the "Popish" or High Church revels of Christmas—a holiday still frowned upon in Plymouth as late as 1840, when even the placing of wreaths in windows was regarded as a "'piscopal" custom.[22] Thanksgiving, in colonial times, was unknown outside New England. But in the tense days of the Revolution both thanksgivings and fasts were decreed by Congress, and came to be linked with the patriotic cause. In 1817 the Puritan harvest-home jumped its local borders when New York State adopted an annual Thanksgiving Day. Other states in the North followed suit, and the great tides of migration from New England to the West carried the sentiment of Thanksgiving with them—although the South looked upon the custom with suspicion, fearful lest a grain of Yankee propaganda be wrapped in the sheaves of patriotism. Not until the dark days of the Civil War—when all the states remaining in the Union were more or less friendly to New England traditions—did Thanksgiving become a national holiday, on the last Thursday of November, 1863. Lincoln's proclamation first bowed all loyal heads over the festal board, and since his time every President has set aside the feast of the Pilgrims. But, as will be recalled, President Franklin D. Roosevelt's departure from the customary date in 1939 and 1940 was disapproved, in conservative New England circles, as tampering with a hallowed rule "for a purely mercenary reason," as a Republican editorial sadly remarked.

Into the West, at an early date, Pilgrim and Puritan were carried as household gods—honored not only by feasts, but also by religious and ethical homage. They had become in fact the keepers of the Protestant conscience. When Benedict Arnold had joined the British and issued a handbill urging his fellow citizens to follow, he had the effrontery to appeal to the Pilgrim Fathers:

What security remains for you even for the enjoyment of the consolations of that religion for which your fathers braved the ocean, the heathen, and the wilderness? Do you know that the eye which guides this pen, lately saw your mean and profligate Congress at Mass for the soul of a Roman Catholic in purgatory, and participating in the rites of a church, against whose anti-christian corruptions your pious ancestors would have witnessed with their blood?

Arnold's handbill had little effect; many no doubt concluded that the devil could quote Calvinist scripture. But the call to prejudice is significant. With the southwest expansion that followed the Louisiana Purchase, Down East traders came into collision with an alien culture —that part Catholic, part radical naïveté of the frontier which tended to identify sin with sharp trading and the Yankee flair for commerce. On the other hand, the Puritan Northeast began to fear lest developments in the West—Romanism, freethinking, rampant democracy and lawlessness, the saloon, the gambling table—should strangle "true Americanism." The gaiety of New Orleans and St. Louis did not seem to those sharp blue eyes the American way. Nor were the Sunday games and folk dances of Continental immigrants, nor the passion of German peasants along the Wabash for music and flowers ("a strong symptom of simplicity and ignorance," as Hulme remarked on his travels). Hence, mingled as ever with economic considerations, sprang a certain missionary impulse to claim this new Canaan for the mores of Calvin and John Cotton. The unassimilated spirit of French and Irish Catholics, brought into the Union by immigration and annexation, clashed with the Puritan heritage—and the latter took political shape in the Know Nothing party. The sons of New England were aggressive and, in this generation at any rate, polyprogenitive. The tensions of this rivalry grew taut.

Meanwhile the American schoolhouse, under the growing secularization of life, took the old place held by the church as the builder of group attitudes. Whatever his parents' church, every Protestant child attended the village school, learning his ideas of history and social consciousness from it. New England had long bred schoolmasters for America at large: even in late colonial times the Virginia aristocrat, in search of a tutor for his children, went naturally to Harvard College and Princeton. The reasons were logical enough: New England had better libraries and academies, with its stern intellectual traditions and its passion for self-improvement (even its theology, as Perry Miller has lately remarked, being based upon Ramus's theory that truth needs only to be known in order to prevail). These schoolmasters carried with them a deep respect for the New England fathers and their ways, and a creed in which Puritanism stood for the true American faith. They taught textbooks written by Noah Webster, Jedidiah Morse,

William H. McGuffey—who re-enforced the young idea with tl̤e whalebone of Puritan ethics. Most of the historians and literary men in this generation sprang from New England, or were tinged by its thought. They nourished the attitude, later powerfully fostered in the North by the Civil War, that Puritan ways were synonymous with patriotism, simplicity of life, sterling worth, democracy, and all other desires of the young Republic. "For the progress and enjoyment of civil and religious liberty in modern times," wrote Noah Webster in his *History of the United States,* in 1832, "the world is more indebted to the Puritans in Great Britain and America, than to any other body of men, or to any other cause."

At length, therefore, the ark of the covenant brought overseas by the *Mayflower* was speeded on its way by the Conestoga wagon—to be set up in the little red schoolhouse of the prairies, and displayed on the platforms of political oratory. The center of Puritanism followed the center of population deeper and deeper into the interior, unaware that the old homestead was mellowing in the pale sunshine of Channing and Emerson and Frothingham, or feeding the vine of Latin art and liberalism whose shoots Yankees had lately brought home from France, Italy, and Spain. The Puritan had become an all-American hero. His mores filtered through to other regions. The Southerner who assailed John Quincy Adams for setting up a billiard table in the White House—hardly conscious of the past, when Increase Mather had first taught that games of chance are direct appeals to God, and hence "may not be used in trivial matters"—passed on the faith to Adin Ballou, from Roger Williams's Rhode Island, who in the 1850's crusaded against alcohol and tobacco, and a generation later to Carrie Nation of Kansas, editor of *The Smasher's Mail* and *The Hatchet* who asserted that McKinley should have recovered from the bullet "but his blood was bad from nicotine," and grieved over the poor Yale student who reported he had "brandy so strong on the food it made his head dizzy." The old New England point of view set the didactic tone of American life—decreeing that the best-loved books of the century, supplanting Fox and Bunyan, should be *Ten Nights in a Barroom, Uncle Tom's Cabin,* and *In His Steps.* This heritage, scattered abroad, came to supply the pruderies and reticences of America, its absurdities as well as its brave idealisms. Only among the gentle and wise was its spirit of meddling sublimated into the humanitarian urge.

Not until the 1920's under the effete morality of Prohibition—age of the bootlegger, the night club, jazz, nudism, companionate marriage, and *The American Mercury*—did "Puritanical" become an epithet worse than swearing. Henry L. Mencken and Stuart P. Sherman fought over whether the Puritans had themselves been Puritanical. New debunking biographies of the Mathers and Jonathan Edwards appeared. Boston, with its Watch and Ward Society, was—along with the mores of Iowa—good for a laugh at any cocktail party. Hitting below the Bible Belt became the chief pastime of metropolitan wit. William Jennings Bryan was widely mocked as the last Puritan. It seemed possible to blame all modern vices upon the old steeple-hatted Puritan —either as the result of, or the reaction from, his code—leaving us his grandchildren plainly helpless, in the grip of a more genial predestination to sin.

Yet even in this decade the hero-worship of the Puritan was not dead. Less sophisticated citizens, a sprinkling of fundamentalists and Klansmen, some New England brahmins of business, and the more excitable foes of Romanism still loved him, even in modern caricature. The high priest of his cult was probably that President of the United States whom William Allen White has described as "a Puritan in Babylon." In 1930 at Watertown, Massachusetts, Mr. Coolidge paid tribute to the Puritans in general: "They were a very wonderful people. . . . If they were narrow, it was not a blighting and destructive narrowness, but a vital and productive narrowness. The narrowness was like that of a mighty torrent which makes a smooth path, that after it the stream may flow on smoothly to its destination."[23] At the decade's beginning, Mr. Coolidge had been Governor of Massachusetts, and had assisted at the Tercentenary of the *Mayflower*. This episode, reflecting the rather confused hero-worship of that day, merits description.

In spite of the proverbial punctuality of New England, preparations were not ready in time for a real jubilee on December 21, 1920; nor, fittingly to grace the occasion, had a Republican President-elect succeeded to office. Hence a kind of rehearsal, which seems to have been informal enough, was held on the actual date. Governor Coolidge was met at the Plymouth railway station by a welcoming committee. But he did not give himself into their hands, as the official Tercentenary booklet sets forth: "Gov. [*sic*] Coolidge boarded a one-man trolley car and rode away, up in front, and some of the others took the trolley cars, but the majority walked, in no special order, along Court and Main Streets to the Old Colony theatre." There Mr. Coolidge briefly praised the Pilgrims who "sailed up out of the infinite . . . sailed hither seeking only for an avenue for the immortal soul." After Mrs. Hemans's poem had been sung by a male chorus, Senator Henry Cabot Lodge spoke the oration of the day. The Senator quoted Daniel Webster's anticipation back in 1820 of this Tercentenary, when, he prophesied, "the voice of acclamation and gratitude, commencing on the Rock of Plymouth, shall be transmitted through millions of the sons of the Pilgrims; till it lose itself in the murmurs of the Pacific seas." At this juncture, we are told,

a telephone bell on the stage tinkled and the speaker paused. Willard Parsons, local manager of the telephone company, advanced from the wings, picked up the transmitter of the desk set and queried "Is this the Governor of California? Just a moment. I introduce to you Governor Coolidge of Massachusetts." The instrument was passed to His Excellency, and the latter took up the conversation which was fulfilling the prophetic utterances of Webster a century previous, saying, "Governor Stephens, Yes. This is Governor Coolidge of Massachusetts. Yes, I am seated in the chair of Gov. Bradford at Plymouth. I wish to say that Massachusetts and Plymouth Rock greet California and the Golden Gate, and send the voice which is to be lost in the waves and roar of the Pacific. I'll do so. Goodbye."

As Senator Lodge resumed his discourse, he remarked: "It was the merest accident that I read that sentence." The incident had been planned as a surprise. . . . As a matter of fact, Gov. Stephens was away on a hunting trip and the conversation was with his official secretary, but the Webster prophecy had been fulfilled, nevertheless.[24]

In 1921 the real celebration took place, with a pageant for a cast of 1300 written by Professor.George Pierce Baker of Harvard. Called "The Pilgrim Spirit," it began with the Voice of the Rock—

Of me, the rock in the ooze, they have made a cornerstone of the Republic.

William Bradford is the chief actor; he reviews the noble temper of the Pilgrims. Gazing into the future of America he discovers its two greatest leaders, Washington and Lincoln, standing in a recess behind the Rock. At length a martial flourish of French and British flags that "wave and beckon," is answered by a bugle call from the *Mayflower;* the Spirit of the Rock summons America to join the Allies. Through deepening shadows the Rock speaks its benediction: "With malice toward none and charity for all. . . ."

The gala performance of the pageant was given on "Plymouth Day," when President and Mrs. Harding and some 100,000 visitors thronged the town. In his Address—delivered, to be sure, before he had seen Professor Baker's pageant—President Harding expressed America's "penitent realization" of "the wastes and the sorrows and the utter disarrangements of a cataclysmal war." Normalcy, rather than heroism, was on the march. The pageant that night, accompanied by a search-light drill of warships in the bay, drew a mammoth crowd. In fact, because of the out-of-town invasion, the booklet recalls, there was such a run on tickets that "parties who were within reach of later productions disposed of their tickets at considerable advances." Perhaps the Fathers themselves would have understood, and forgiven.

The Rock itself, carved with the numerals "1620," remains an American shrine. Although historians long ago attacked the tradition attached to this particular boulder—pointing also to the fact that most of the Pilgrims stayed aboard ship for about a month after the *Mayflower* anchored—the Rock serves a human need for the tangible symbol. Now housed in a Greek temple of granite, it has weathered the passing of time though not without casualties. A crack "which has existed in it from Revolutionary times and probably before that," caused the Rock to split on December 20, 1920, when it was being moved to accommodate its new setting, but the fissure has been mended several times with cement. One night a few years later Plymouth Rock was painted red by stealth; alarmed citizens first reported that Communists had done this outrage, but later it was discovered to be the work of Harvard jokesters.

In truth, as the dramatist said, Plymouth Rock has become a cornerstone of American patriot lore. Today, long after the Jazz Age and Repeal, unfair blame and equally partisan praise of the Puritans have both grown fainter. Now that the vortex of national discussion has shifted from private morals to economic and international issues, the Puritan has ceased to be the object of fierce debate that he was twenty years ago. Still a somewhat blurred symbol of religious freedom and of moral intolerance, to the popular eye, he wins more respect than affection. Today it is possible more calmly to weigh his defects against his virtues. With his narrow life, his lack of beauty and poetry, his pride and bigotry, he ran counter to some of the best impulses in the modern world. But as a hero he had stern self-discipline, courage physical and moral, a sense of reality that foreswore easy optimisms, and an acceptance of the need for sacrifice—a need that the Republic, in its less complacent moods, always discovers anew for itself. By reason of these traits, and because the men who had them stand at the door of American history, Pilgrim and Puritan will not soon be forgotten in our national legendary.

CHAPTER FOUR

POOR RICHARD: THE BOY WHO MADE GOOD

The sleeping fox catches no poultry. Up! Up!
—*Poor Richard's Almanack,* 1743.

I

PHILADELPHIA has two heroes. The second, Benjamin Franklin, held no very good opinion of the first. William Penn, he thought, had "the subtlety of the serpent with the innocence of the dove," and in pretending to be the man of God overbore popular self-government with the fist of a petty despot.[1] Franklin in fact detested all the Penns, and his judgment is somewhat harsh. Certainly others disagreed. In Penn's own day he received, and enjoyed, his meed of applause. The first martyr to the American passion for ovations was one B. Bevan of Chester, who in 1699 celebrated Penn's second landing by firing off a rusty cannon, relic of the Swedish regime, which burst and removed the arm of its firer. Penn's cash book shows that he paid the surgical fees, nursing costs, and finally the sum of three shillings fourpence to the gravedigger, for the melancholy expenses of his most enthusiastic greeter.[2] Pennsylvanians have long held their founder's memory in respect—while thinking of him as the stout burgher with a blue sash about his waist, concluding his pact

with the Indians under the Treaty Elm, as Benjamin West painted
the scene long afterward in 1772. The story of the sky-blue sash and
the elm—now a shrine at Kensington, which has its memorial park
and monument—is quite mythical, although Penn's fair treatment of
the Indians is true to fact.[3] Voltaire's remark, that this Treaty was the
only one made by Christians with the Indians which was never sworn
to, and never broken, helped to lend it worldwide fame, and West's
painting has done the rest. It is damaging to the heroic aspect of Penn
that he appears here, and in the familiar statue placed in front of the
Pennsylvania Hospital in 1804, as a fat pursy old man, following an
ivory medallion made from memory after the subject's death. From
the time of Weems, who described Penn at his mother's knee as "a
fine, plump, fleshy boy," to the modern effigy upon a million packages
of rolled oats, William Penn has been gifted with the corpulence
which really came upon him in old age. True zealots love the portrait
of the slim youthful Penn in armor, now in the Pennsylvania Historical
Society—whose patriarchs refuse to admit that its authenticity has been
impeached by recent research. Once the idol of abolitionists and
pacifists, William Penn remains essentially the scholar's hero—as
lauded from the days of Bancroft and Fiske to those of Albert Cook
Myers—rather than a great popular favorite. His cult, though minor,
is substantial. In 1881 the Pennsylvania Legislature tried to persuade
the sober Quakers who owned the burial-ground at Jordans, Bucks,
to surrender the body of Penn and at least one of his wives, for trans-
portation to a tomb "in the center of the city of Philadelphia . . . to
serve as an example of honesty and uprighteousness of character to
millions, among whom his name is a household word." But these
gentlemen in gray looked with no favor upon the son of an apostate
Quaker, who, unfortunately, had been sent as the emissary of Pennsylvania, and coldly vetoed the plan as a booster's scheme "to increase
the prestige, or promote the prosperity of a great city."[4] Also they
maintained that Penn, as an Englishman, should not rest in alien soil
where he had spent only four years of life. Yet in 1911, when the
Pennsylvania Society of New York City sought to place a tablet to
Penn in Westminster Abbey, they were told that "its limited space
was necessarily restricted to the greatest of England's sons, and could
not be extended to the great men of other countries."[5] Instead, the
Society consoled itself by dedicating a tablet in the London church
where Penn was baptized, Allhallows Barking-by-the-Tower, and the
City of Philadelphia was solaced by placing a bronze statue of him,

weighing 52,400 pounds, atop the City Hall in 1892. Because this statue towers above a church whose stained-glass window bears an effigy of Charles I, the rhyme of a local patriot once ran——

> Quoth Martyr Charles to William Penn,
> 'Tis best to let things be;
> They're used to looking up at you,
> And they can see through me.

But if Philadelphians look up to William Penn, they gaze with still greater homage upon Benjamin Franklin. He is the town's first citizen of all time. Doctor Oliver Wendell Holmes's quip that Franklin was a "citizen of Boston who dwelt for a little while in Philadelphia," is not relished in Market Street, where Franklin is accepted as the sturdy, rubicund essence of Philadelphian prosperity and enterprise. If it was in Boston that he paid too much for his whistle, and gained a fatherly rebuke for persuading his playmates to build a wharf out of stolen stones, it was in Philadelphia that he learned that a penny saved is a penny earned and also that honesty is the best policy. Philadelphia has the added advantage of being the setting for the two pictorial episodes—the munching of a loaf of bread which Franklin's future wife watched with merriment, and the flying of a kite in the thunderstorm—which everybody knows, and which have contributed so much to Franklin's reincarnation among the common folk. They are the pegs upon which most Americans hang their meager knowledge of Franklin. It is hard to feel on speaking terms with "the modern Prometheus" or even "the friend of mankind"—as the age of universal benevolence called him, translating the Latin tag *amicus humani generis*. It is even more difficult to take to one's bosom a syncretism of thrift, prudence, and serene wisdom. But the shabby, hungry boy and the inquisitive kite-flyer talk the Esperanto of common speech.

Almost everybody claims Franklin. He is "the father of all the Yankees," but in France he is known as a true Gallic spirit. He is invoked by printers, merchants, Masons, Sons of the Revolution, publicists, diplomats, postmen, efficiency experts, scientists, advertisers, newspapermen, purveyors of correspondence courses in success, inspirational preachers, Christians, deists, and atheists. The manufacturer of a popular safety razor once built an advertising campaign upon Franklin's observation in the *Autobiography* that "if you teach a poor young man to shave himself, and keep his razor in order, you may contribute more to the happiness of his life than in giving him a thousand guineas." And once more in 1939 peace-lovers began to quote his celebrated remark to Bishop Shipley, "There has never been or ever will be any such thing as a good war or a bad peace"—a bit of Quakerism which did not get in the way of Franklin's Revolutionary activities. In fact, Franklin comes close to being a universal oracle. He was versatile by nature, and complaisant by disposition. Thomas Jefferson noted that "it was one of the rules which, above all others, made Doctor Franklin the most amiable of men in society, never to contradict anybody." And since, like Jefferson, he uttered a good many ambiguities, it was possible for rival camps to appeal to Franklin even while he lived.

Since that day, the staking out of claims upon the testamentary body of Poor Richard has gone steadily forward. Mr. Coolidge, in a message read at the unveiling of the great printer's statue in the Hall of Fame in 1927, asserted that "Franklin is claimed by more groups than any other person in our history." Thus in 1840, when the first vapors of Civil War were visible in the sky, John Tyler, Jr., in an oration at William and Mary College called for another Franklin, the mild conciliator, to arise and tame the lightning of "civil strife and misrule" lowering from the North.[6] Yet when Greenough's statue of the sage was unveiled in Boston in 1856, while a crowd of 300,000 thronged the streets, a great banner across the entrance to Franklin Square proclaimed: "Benjamin Franklin—First President of the Pennsylvania Society for Promoting the Abolition of Slavery."[7] Similarly in 1864 James Parton in his two-volume life of Franklin pictured the hero's enemies the Lees as the spoiled aristocrats of the "plantation system," and suggested that Franklin had become "the secondary Providence of that portion of North America which lies between Mason and Dixon's Line and British America—where, certainly, the Spirit of Franklin is universally manifest."[8]

Prohibitionists loved to cite that passage in the *Autobiography* which tells how young Franklin in London excelled in muscular strength his fellow-printers who were "great guzzlers of beer," and how he won the name of "the Water-American." But the Wets, as long ago as the *Cozzens Wine Press* of 1855, delighted to quote a letter Franklin wrote to the Abbé Morellet. He there proved—by the argument from design so dear to Christian theologians—that God wants us to tipple, because He has made the joints of the arm just the right length to carry a glass to the mouth, without falling short of or overshooting the mark:

"Let us adore, then, glass in hand, this benevolent wisdom; let us adore and drink."[9]

Samuel Gompers in 1924 lauded the self-respect with which Franklin stood "before thrones, voicing the aspirations of democracy," while William Green more recently has called him "the Patron Saint of Labor."[10] Apropos of the vested interests, liberals have been pleased to quote Franklin's words written in 1789, about a plan to make the State Senate of Pennsylvania the representative of wealth: "And why is property to be represented at all? . . . Private property is . . . a creature of society. . . . I am sorry to see . . . a disposition among some of our people to commence an aristocracy by giving the rich a predominancy in government."[11] On the other hand, William Guggenheim, retired copper millionaire and honorary president of the International Benjamin Franklin Society, in his message to that Society on January 17, 1938, called for "a non-partisan league, to be founded on the common sense and wisdom of Benjamin Franklin," which should attack the New Deal and uphold an economic ideal which he daringly described as that of "big business."[12] Just four days later the New York *Times* observed, in a bland editorial:

Mr. Roosevelt's description of Dr. Franklin as "an inspiration to every American citizen," must be taken as gracious general approval of an illustrious and a varied career. It should not be thought approval of certain blemishes that enlightened citizens of today have to pass over or forgive. Poor Richard appeals now only to vulgar minds. Young Franklin was the Industrious Apprentice. His narrow principles of conduct are as outworn as apprenticeships. How can Industry and Frugality dare to show their heads in the midst of the more abundant life which is the portion of this happier era? Why count the pennies when millions of dollars are pouring out from the inexhaustible Federal Horn of Plenty? . . .

He ran the Postoffice so that it showed a profit. That proves too clearly the unworthiness of his motives as an administrator. . . . He wished that every member of the Convention of 1787 would, with him, "doubt a little of his own infallibility." How remote seems doubt, so paralyzing to executive and legislative vigor, in this Age of Devaluated Gold.

Poor Richard, like any great symbol, becomes Scripture for all the warring sects, and the connection between Franklinian enterprise and the now defensive philosophy of rugged individualism is easy to see. In 1939 John De Meyer's book, *Benjamin Franklin Calls on the President,* showed the philosopher rising from his long sleep—like a fly preserved in Madeira, after the lapse of ages "recalled to life by the solar warmth of my dear country," as Franklin himself once playfully dreamed. In the fantasy of Mr. De Meyer, Franklin visits Washington, where he is enchanted with the silent ingurgitation of modern plumbing but shocked by another American invention, namely purchase on the installment plan. Upon reaching the White House he reads a rebuke to the incumbent: "I would have you look well to your oath of office. When you took office, your people were in distress. Relieve this distress!" It is a lecture from America's first great comic spirit, so stern, so reminiscent of Mr. Hamilton Fish, that one concludes—apart from all political views—that the good Doctor's sense of humor is still asleep.

During the Depression it was popular to quote Franklin on "croakers," a passage in the *Autobiography* inspired by Samuel Mickle, who gloomily tried to dissuade the youth from opening a printing-shop in Philadelphia, "this decaying place." It serves to remind us that Franklin is the patron of optimists, good fellows, joiners, and those whose creed is distilled into the slogan "Don't knock—boost!" Young Franklin's club, the Junto, for self-improvement and service, "the promotion of our interests in business by more extensive recommendation," has been claimed as the first Rotary. During National Thrift Week, in January, 1922, a Philadelphia investment house published a widely circulated booklet called "What America Owes to Franklin"—the debt consisting of maxims concerning owning one's home, paying bills promptly, sharing with others, and making a will. The campaign by some ten thousand bankers, during and after the Great War, to promote savings and investments by the masses, relied heavily upon Franklin's picture—the effigy found upon the penny postage stamp, rather than the less familiar image upon the $100 Federal banknote. He has become such an emblem of solvency that the Associated Press, on January 9, 1940, carried as dramatic news the disclosure, from early records of the Bank of North America, that Franklin's account was frequently overdrawn.

Franklin the oracle has even been abused by forgery. A speech in which he is said to have assailed the Jews as a "vampire" race, and to have called for 100 per cent Nordic Americanism, seems to have appeared first in a newspaper of the Silver Shirts called *Liberation,* printed in Asheville, N. C., on February 3, 1934. Although a crude fabrication, it was copied and spread by oral rumor wherever the soil was fertile for its growth; by way of Germany and Switzerland, it travelled to New York.[13] Franklin's only known adverse experience with Jews occurred in early manhood; it was more amusing than bitter. While shifting from a canoe to a stageboat near Staten Island, Franklin was spilled into the water when the canoe capsized. But being a superb swimmer—who once thought of supporting himself by giving lessons in that art—he was in no danger. Nevertheless a passenger on the stageboat, a Jew named Haynes, claimed forever after that he had saved the philosopher's life—and wearied him with duns for money, which were sometimes met out of the easy-going generosity so typical of Franklin. But when forty years after the mishap Franklin received a begging letter from Haynes's relict, he could not help writing humorously to a friend that his self-styled preserver seems "to have left me to his widow as part of her dowry."[14] There is no proof that Franklin was anti-Semitic; in accord with his custom to contribute to all worthy schemes, he subscribed five pounds to build a Hebrew synagogue in Philadelphia. Doubtless he would appreciate the fact that the Benjamin Franklin High School in the Bronx has as many poor but ambitious Jewish youths as any school in the United States. An almost sentimental bond draws many American Jews to Franklin. He was a liberal, a freethinker, a successful man, a citizen of the world who earned and gave away money. Rabbi Krauskopf of Temple Keneseth Israel, Philadelphia, delivered an eloquent eulogy on the Bicentenary of Franklin's birth; Doctor Nathan G. Goodman of the same city has written many popular pamphlets on Franklin; Charles Blum is a former president of the Poor Richard Club there; Doctor A. S. W. Rosenbach collects Franklin medals, and the late Colonel Michael Friedsam collected Franklin portraits. The International Benjamin Franklin Society, essentially a New York organization, has William Guggenheim as honorary president, Mrs. Simon Guggenheim and Doctor Cyrus Adler as vice-presidents, and Louis F. Rothschild among its trustees. For Franklin to fall into the hands of the Nazis is therefore a circumstance of some irony. If he had symptoms of race prejudice they are found in an essay he wrote in 1751 on the populating of America; regarding the Germans in Pennsylvania he asked somewhat theatrically, "Why should the Palatine boors be suffered to swarm into our settlements, and by herding together establish their language and manners, to the exclusion of ours?"[15] But this passing mood of irritation is not of a piece with Franklin's prevailing tolerance.

II

How did the living Franklin first become a celebrity? He came to attract notice in Philadelphia about 1730, as the first successful newspaper editor of the town. He began as a "hustler," who not only did his work well, but contrived it should appear so, "to secure my credit and character as a tradesman." He burned a late candle, and had no time for the frivolities of hunting and fishing. His other great bourgeois roles came later—the homespun patriot at the bar of the House of Commons, the fur-capped philosopher at Versailles, the silent patriarch of the Constitutional Convention. Franklin's supreme originality consisted in becoming a great man without recourse to pomp and scarlet. In a century which had begun with Marlborough and the Sun King, Franklin walked on the stage of action with neither sword nor wig—and at length the applause grew deafening. If he had tried to ape Old World traditions he would have felt as foolish as he did in 1756, when, during his brief career as a soldier, his officers, in full dress and with drawn swords, insisted on escorting him to the border of Pennsylvania, while he bounced about uncomfortably in his saddle. Franklin the hero was not the man on horseback, and he wisely knew it.

Outside Philadelphia he first became famous because of *Poor Richard's Almanack*, begun in October, 1732, and continued for more than a quarter century. Soon it began to sell ten thousand copies every year, and to be quoted everywhere. Franklin cheerfully admitted that he wrote few of these maxims himself. They were encrusted with the mould of folk wisdom, old as the world of Æsop, and hence they stressed—even more than Franklin in his own right might have done—the common man's reliance upon prudence, hard work, close-mouthed counsel, and horse sense. Daring and prodigality, marks of the aristocrat, had no personal or professional value for the butcher, the baker, the candlestick-maker. And Franklin, son of a candlemaker, knew what the most diligent readers of almanacs wanted.

Sometimes, in borrowing the lore of the Old World, Franklin gave it a democratic twist which augured the Revolutionary patriot. The plain man's rebuke of royal extravagance, "The king's cheese goes half away in parings," becomes in *Poor Richard* "The king's cheese is half wasted in parings; but no matter, 'tis made of the people's milk" (1735). Some of his maxims ring profoundly true to American ways of thought, and suggest a Franklin who shared the tastes of his country as simply as when he dined in Craven Street on cranberries and Indian meal his wife had shipped overseas, and when he bestowed American apples upon Lady Bathurst and other favorites among the British peerage. The ancient saying "God helps those who help themselves" (1738) is the pith of New World self-reliance, the essence of Franklin's passion for improving himself and his fellow man. "Having been poor is no shame, but being ashamed of it is" (1749) serves as a democratic rebuke to success turned snobbish. "Write with the learned, pronounce with the vulgar" (1738) was later the practice of American statesmanship, when senators in the silver age of oratory quoted Tully and Shakespeare with a Yankee or a Southern drawl. The blend of the good neighbor with the sturdy yeoman, smacking of the frontier as well as of the hills north of Boston, gives savor to the advice, "Love your neighbor, yet don't pull down your hedge" (1754).

To deny the kinship between Poor Richard and the real Franklin would be foolish. The latter had many mercantile moments. As a young man he fell tepidly in love with his landlady's relative, inflamed by cosy suppers *à deux* which had been carefully prearranged by the family; but refused to marry the girl when he discovered that her parents were not willing to mortgage their house to raise a dowry, finally yoking himself to plodding and simple-minded Deborah Read. He thus followed Poor Richard's advice, "Keep your eyes wide open before marriage, and half shut afterwards." The old commercial strain in less selfish guise reappeared when, after a lifetime of international honors, returning from the glittering salons of Paris, Franklin devoted some of his best efforts to selling quantities of Crown soap, made according to the Franklin family recipe by the grandson of his sister Jane. Parton, Franklin's first great biographer, explains the sage's devotion to Crown soap somewhat sentimentally by quoting Wordsworth,

My heart leaps up when I behold
A rainbow in the sky,

suggesting that to a man of Franklin's temperament "a cake of soap becomes as poetical as a rainbow."[16] Franklin's essential materialism stands nowhere more pleasantly revealed than in his comment that "many people are fond of accounts of old buildings and monuments, but for one I confess that if I could find in any Italian travels a receipt for making Parmesan cheese, it would give me more satisfaction than a transcript of any inscription from any old stone whatever."[17] Franklin lacked the æsthetic and spiritual; his imagination had none of the tenderness of an artist's. Hostile critics have called him the father of American vulgarity.

Yet this is but one aspect of Franklin's nature, upon which the folk mind has seized. Even Poor Richard once said, in a reckless proverb which bankers never quote, "An egg today is better than a hen to-morrow." In respect to his own almanac lore, Franklin often behaved as did the listeners to Father Abraham's harangue on "The Way to Wealth," who "approved the doctrine, and immediately practised the contrary, just as if it had been a common sermon." Franklin was too generous to refuse loans even when the risk was great. He confessed that frugality was "a virtue I never could acquire myself," but that his wife's thrift balanced his imprudence.[18] At the age of forty-two he retired permanently from his printing shop in order to enjoy life, "uninterrupted by the little cares and fatigues of business."[19] In later years William Strahan was one among the sage's good friends who were often vexed by his "natural inactivity." In the days of his youth, as Poor Richard, Franklin had reminded himself that "time is money," and "there will be sleeping enough in the grave," but in his eighty-first year, from a sunny back garden in Philadelphia where he romped with grandchildren and played a little cribbage, he reached a different conclusion: "I have indeed now and then a little compunction in reflecting that I spend time so idly; but another reflection comes to relieve me, whispering, 'You know the soul is immortal; why then should you be such a niggard of a little time, when you have a whole eternity before you?' "[20]

But Franklin could not shake off the mantle of Poor Richard. Among people who knew nothing about his habits of free spending, he found himself saddled with a reputation for penny-pinching. As a single instance, the aged Franklin planned to give a welcoming dinner to members of the Constitutional Convention, who were supposed to meet in Philadelphia on May 2, 1788. They were very tardy in arriving, and when after waiting a fortnight Franklin at last gave his dinner, not many guests were present. Gossip promptly reported that Franklin had given his entertainment ahead of time, to save expense.[21] Franklin's emergence as Poor Richard, apostle of thrift, is characteristic of that false simplification often seen in folk hero-worship. His subtleties, his self-contradictions, were stripped away to leave a pattern of unity.

H. W. Schneider has well said that whereas Jonathan Edwards

"attempted to induce New England to lead a godly, not a sober, life, it was Franklin who succeeded in teaching Americans to lead a sober and not a godly life."[22] The mystic belonged to an outworn metaphysic; the sage to the dawning age of science and business. His cult helped vastly in transforming Puritanism into the gospel of getting on, as described in an earlier chapter. Franklin's was a God without thunder, whose fiery bolt had been tamed by the genial skepticism of "Old Fulmen Eripuit"—as Jeremy Belknap gaily termed Franklin —but the residue of Puritan morality was still there. Temperance, silence, order, resolution, frugality, industry, sincerity, justice, and a moderate degree of chastity were the aims of Franklin's quest for self-improvement. These virtues were now perceived to mark the road to health and wealth, even though the flinty path of Cotton Mather (to whose essays Franklin candidly admitted his debt) grew dimmer year by year. In Poor Richard we find the reason why Franklin has failed to reach the sublimity of Washington and Lincoln. The chink of silver and gold was not audible in the Farewell Address or at Gettysburg, whereas it was the dominant note of the Franklin legend. In the ranks of the Founding Fathers, then, Franklin appears as the Sancho Panza, rejoicing in the homely wisdom of proverb and precedent, thinking of belly and pocketbook, as he ambles by the side of a greater idealist, the godlike Washington.

Poor Richard was early approved as a mentor for youth. The collection of maxims called "The Way to Wealth" which Franklin had made in 1757 by skimming his earlier almanacs for sayings about hard work and thrift—ironically enough, to show the colonists how they might thrive and at the same time pay their mounting tax-bills to the British Crown—achieved a worldwide popularity. It became the gospel of the rising bourgeoisie in many lands. Thought eminently suitable for American children, it was issued by publishers of juvenile books in an age when such books were few. It was copiously illustrated as early as 1808, and sold with fine engravings for twenty-five cents. A broadside called "Bowles's Moral Pictures: or Poor Richard Illustrated. Being Lessons for the Young and Old, on Industry, Temperance, Frugality, &c.," first appeared about 1796. Grouped around a medallion of Franklin with a sharp-looking face, were twenty-four woodcuts illustrating such precepts as "The used key is always bright," "A rolling stone gathers no moss," "Keep thy shop, and thy shop will keep thee." Great seems to have been the demand for these pictures of gentlemen in broadcloth overseeing a field of busy reapers, shopkeepers weighing sugar behind counters, and in contrast a knot of elegant triflers lounging over a billiard table while the bum-bailiff waits without. As late as 1859 the firm of Allen & Holland was still publishing the same quaint broadside.

Franklin's *Autobiography*, first published in 1791, contributed to the same legend. It was as shrewdly gauged as *Robinson Crusoe* to interest young readers and gain the approval of their elders. This tale offers the pluck and luck, not of survival on a desert island, but of winning one's way as a friendless boy with scarcely enough silver to jingle in the pocket, shipwrecked upon the streets of Philadelphia and London —cheerful, persistent, resourceful as Dick Whittington, confident that a man who is diligent in his calling will stand before kings. (Five of them in Franklin's career, as he recalled, and one of them the King of Denmark, invited him to sit down.) That the *Autobiography* stops short of Franklin's richest and most cosmopolitan years has had much to do with moulding the apprentice fable, with its marks of arrested development. A century before the novels of Alger and Timothy Shay Arthur, Franklin lived the career of their heroes, and told the success story with a matter-of-fact charm and frankness which no one else has ever touched. He well knew what he was doing. After penning the last pages in October, 1788, he wrote to La Rochefoucauld that his dwelling upon the early years was "of more general use to young readers, as exemplifying strongly the effects of prudent and imprudent conduct in the commencement of a life of business."[23] Franklin's examples of imprudent conduct—"errata," as he called such episodes as his attempt to seduce the little milliner whom his friend Ralph had left him to support in London, tried under the Franklinian assumption that maintenance should carry its privileges—are generally left out of editions printed for the young. Thus the legendary Franklin, through no connivance of his own, has remained to stand for prudent conduct alone.

Scores of "Franklin Almanacs" published in the earlier nineteenth century by Cramer, John Armstrong, and others, invariably pointed to him as "a beautiful illustration of what may be effected by industry and application."[24] It was the fashion to show him as the cunning Yankee trader, to be admired or disliked according to one's point of view—the "philosophical Quaker full of mean and thrifty maxims," as the poet Keats saw him. Some rejoiced in the fact that Franklin alone, out of all the important framers of state and federal constitutions, was not college trained—or rather, that he was bred to what

Abraham Lincoln later called "the poor boy's college," the printer's shop. Hawthorne in 1842 imagines a Boston father telling his children the story of Franklin:

"But pray, dear father, tell us what made him so famous," said George. "I have seen his portrait a great many times. There is a wooden bust of him in one of our streets, and marble ones, I suppose, in some other places. And towns, and ships of war, and steamboats, and banks, and academies, and children, are often named after Franklin. Why should he have grown so famous?"

"Your question is a reasonable one, George," answered his father. "I doubt whether Franklin's philosophical discoveries, important as they were, or even his vast political services, would have given him all the fame he acquired. It appears to me that Poor Richard's Almanac did more than any thing else, towards making him familiarly known to the public. As the writer of those proverbs, which Poor Richard was supposed to utter, Franklin became the counsellor and household friend of almost every family in America. Thus, it was the humblest of his labors that has done the most for his fame."[25]

But the father is careful to tell his children that these maxims "teach men but a very small portion of their duties." Similarly in 1854 Herman Melville brings his character Israel Potter, in the novel of that name, into the ken of Doctor Franklin in Paris. The sage keeps French pastry and *eau de cologne* and the brandy bottle from his greenhorn guest, bestowing such reproof as "Never joke at funerals, or during business transactions," and leaving upon his bedside table, as improving reading matter, a copy of *Poor Richard*. "Oh, confound all this wisdom!" cries poor Israel Potter when left alone.

Poor Richard, whose life revolves about the axis of prudence—least heroic of the virtues—remains even today, to the average American, the real Franklin. The liberalizing effort of Jared Sparks, James Parton, Carl Van Doren to rescue him from "the dry, prim people" who have kidnapped him, touches only a minority. Benjamin Franklin has told his own story better than any one else can ever do. But for popular consumption he chose to tell only a part of it, and this part has come to stand for the whole.

III

Franklin's repute as the father of Yankee practicality owes much to his pioneer work in science. This proved to be his second great step toward worldwide fame. Such work flourished best between his retirement from business and his later immersion in diplomacy, although Franklin's curiosity about nature remained an ever keen appetite. Its empiric slant marks him as the forerunner of such geniuses as Edison, Burbank, Bell, Ford, and the Wright brothers. He invented the Franklin stove and the lightning rod and bifocal spectacles, tested the heat absorption of white and colored fabrics, introduced the cabbage turnip to America, speculated sensibly on ventilation and the common cold, studied the Gulf Stream on his voyages across the Atlantic, contrived a mechanical arm to fetch down books from his shelves, devised a musical instrument, and when at last the gout and stone laid him low played with the fancy of "a balloon sufficiently large to raise me from the ground . . . being led by a string held by a man walking on the ground."

His most celebrated experiment, that of the kite in an electrical storm, held such dangerous possibilities that it might have made him a martyr to science rather than allowed him to survive as the apostle of prudence. His son, the only witness of the discovery, by a curious quirk of folklore is shown in innumerable woodcuts and engravings as a small boy, although William was twenty-one at the time. On the other hand, Benjamin West's famous painting of "Franklin and the Lightning," made about 1805, portrays the kite-flyer of 1752 not as a vigorous man of forty-six but as a wrinkled, fat patriarch, his white locks streaming to the wind like Lear's, while cupids and aëry sprites flutter about his electrical apparatus. Franklin showed a casual modesty about his exploit which legend has chosen to ignore: he told no one about it until four months later, upon learning of similar experiments in France, and left no written account whatever. When his practical corollary of the lightning rod drew the applause of French scientists and praise from Louis XV, Franklin wrote in 1753 to a friend that he felt like the girl described in *The Tatler* "who was observed to grow suddenly proud, and none could guess the reason, till it came to be known that she had got on a new pair of garters." It is plain that Franklin enjoyed his part on the world's stage—of being a Yankee handy-andy about whose head the great of Europe had hung the halo of a Solomon or Merlin. He loved parlor tricks slightly tinged with sacrilege, such as stilling the waves by flourishing his bamboo cane filled with oil. His reputation as a wizard enhanced his career as a diplomat. Turgot's too familiar epigram, that "he snatched the lightning from the sky, and the sceptre from tyrants," was echoed even by Franklin's enemies. Doctor Samuel Johnson grumbled that he had taught his compatriots "how to put in motion the engine of political electricity," and it was said the credulous North Ministry believed "that Doctor Franklin had invented a machine of the size of a tooth-pick case and materials that would reduce Saint Paul's to a handful of ashes."[26] In France a multitude of prints showed him seated calmly in a great curule-chair while forked lightning played about his venerable shoulders. With American zest for tall stories, the *New Jersey Gazette* of December 31, 1777, announced that the Doctor was about to startle the world with a machine whose powerful shock could raise water-spouts or disunite kingdoms.

The poet Robert Treat Paine in "Adams and Liberty" boasted that "we're a world to ourselves" in being able to produce a man like Franklin, whom effete Europe could not match. America took great pride in Franklin among the magi. A typical woodcut of the sage and his kite, published in 1828, recounted his "grand experiment" and con-cluded: "This discovery astonished the philosophers of Europe. 'What!' said they. 'An American, being of an inferior order, make discoveries! Impossible!' "[27] A fellow printer of Boston, Mr. Gordon Forrest, cele-brated his hero in 1856 in a lyric called "Boston Boy":

> Some write in blood a name
> Which Fame is ever brightening;
> But Franklin had a heavenly aim,
> And wrote his name with lightning.[28]

In the person of Benjamin Franklin, acclaimed by the crowned heads and savants of Europe, America first thrilled to the native son who had made good.

IV

The further expansion of the Franklin legend came from his career as colonial emissary to England and later as American minister to France. The sunrise of his diplomatic fame cast a reflected glory in Western skies. To the average Philadelphian, Franklin abroad was a hero, the foremost citizen of Penn's "green country town," a man whose background of laundry soap and newsprint did him no dem-ocratic disservice. When in 1764 Philadelphia heard the news that he had arrived safe in London, "the bells rang on that account till near midnight."[29] Yet in the next year, learning that Franklin was lending his compliance to the Stamp Act ("We might as well have hindered the sun's setting"), the fickle public tolled the same bells to express "execration" of him, and there was talk of setting fire to his trim new house.[30] Stout-hearted Deborah, his wife, got together arms and provisions for a siege. But Franklin, hearing the news, like a good politician reversed his course and began to assail the Stamp Act. With his "examination" before the Commons in 1766 his favor at home returned. Philadelphia toasted Franklin as her champion, and named a forty-foot barge in his honor. When in 1774 Franklin was baited before the Privy Council—to the applause of peers who always saw the printer's ink upon his hands rather than the wisdom upon his face —his glory as America's defender reached its apogee. In Boston even the Adamses, who had distrusted the heresy of his religion and the moderation of his politics, began to favor him. At last to patriots at large he had become a political idol.

Pious Franklinians still refuse to admit that their hero, in England upon the eve of the Revolution, played a cleverly expedient part. Cooler critics see him torn between the desire to be popular at home and the desire to be an office-holder in London. He loved his sinecures as deputy postmaster-general and as agent for four colonies. When it was hinted that he might obtain an even juicier plum from the Crown, he assiduously danced attendance upon the Duke of Grafton, in the face of repeated rebuffs ignoring the adage of Poor Richard that "a ploughboy on his legs is higher than a gentleman on his knees." Even while tea was being dumped in Boston harbor and redcoats were shooting at the citizenry, he worked hard to get the British Government to favor his pet project in western lands, the Vandalia scheme— named in honor of Queen Charlotte, "as her Majesty is descended from the Vandals"—by which the Franklins would be enriched.[31] While most Americans were convinced that he was their Saint George fronting the royal dragon, Franklin was writing privately about "a people who are ungratefully abusing the best constitution and the best King . . . any nation was ever blessed with."[32] Indeed, the decisiveness of Franklin's break with all things British has been frequently exaggerated—typified by the fact that every one knows Franklin's famous letter to Strahan, the King's printer, at the beginning of the War, "You and I were long friends, but you are now my enemy, and I am—Yours, B. Franklin," but hardly anybody knows that their relations continued cordial, and that Strahan sent a Stilton cheese to his enemy in February, 1778.[33] Franklin's attitude toward the Revolution was more complex than Washington's or John Adams's. Though irritated by shabby treatment in England, and sensitive to American grievances, Franklin was sorry to make a clean break with the pleasant

life and friends he held dear. Upon peace and comfort he set a very
human value. At first glance his philosophic mind looked on war as
a childish way of settling disputes. Franklin, like other statesmen
with an honest mercantile background, saw all the arguments for appeasement. He kept his foot in the door of conciliation so long that
it nearly got pinched.[34] When at last aroused, he could hit hard and
tellingly; but by nature he was fonder of the easy-going way than was
Washington, most invulnerable of American heroes. And since there
could be one, and only one, supreme niche of glory in a struggle like
the Revolution, justly it has gone to one even more unselfish than
Franklin.

These indecisions, fortunately for the public confidence, were not
known in Philadelphia, which hailed his return on May 6, 1775 to

> fan the flame which Liberty inspires,
> Or fix the grand conductor, that shall guide
> The tempest back, and 'lectrify their pride.[35]

The next day he was chosen a member of the second Continental
Congress. He embarked upon much useful work, sketching a plan
of union, organizing the postoffice, seeking to draw Canada in upon
the American side. It has been said that Franklin was not asked to
draft the Declaration of Independence for fear he might put some joke
into the middle of it. He had indeed converted an earlier Declaration
of grievances into jest by inserting a passage reproaching England for
ingratitude "to Saxony, *her* mother country . . . an example we hope
no provocation will induce us to imitate."[36] At the signing of Jefferson's document Franklin was reminded of a good story, about the
hatter's sign, and (if tradition alone can be believed) made his
famous pun about hanging together in preference to hanging sepa-
rately. Years later, at the Constitutional Convention, he remained almost silent, save for his notable quip about the rising sun. To a solemn
and starchy generation, which looked for great men on the Plutarchan
scale—before the rise of frontier democracy, the crackerbox philosopher, and the phenomenon of Abe Lincoln, who might have said,
as Franklin did, "You know, everything puts me in mind of a story"
—this attitude smacked of frivolity. They laughed at his jokes, but
looked upon him as a little light-minded. Gaiety was hardly an attribute of the conventional great man. Washington's jokes were as dull
as they were rare, and this seemed just as it should be. Hence another
bar to Franklin's sublimity was his wit.

His journey to France in the autumn of 1776, on a mission of persuasion, began a new era in his life. At the age of seventy he became a great propagandist for revolution. The fur cap which kept his head warm on the November voyage in lieu of a wig, the mark of Old World caste, symbolized the new Franklin. Bernard Faÿ, like many earlier Frenchmen, has hailed it as the frontier badge, the oriflamme of democracy.[37] That Franklin in reality wore it on account of eczema of the scalp has long been forgotten. Henceforth the cap, the homely spectacles, and the crab-tree stick were inseparable from the Franklin fable. He discovered that the French, whom Rousseau had prepared for the advent of just such a sage from the primeval forests and Quaker meetings of the New World, were enchanted with his garb. That he was neither forester nor Quaker mattered little. With wise simplicity he lived up to his role as the strayed Utopian. His only fastidious note, which saved him from any reproach of slatternliness—even as it did Abe Lincoln in his rusty broadcloth—was the "very white linen" which went with his homespun, as the French police noted in their official files.[38]

It was soon reported with satisfaction back home that Franklin was "followed by a genteel mob" wherever he went, and that good views of him from Paris shop windows were sold to spectators.[39] Busts, engravings, medallions, likenesses in snuffbox lids soon made his face "as well known as that of the moon," Franklin wrote to his daughter Sarah. Louis XVI, growing a little bored with the enthusiasm of the Countess Diane de Polignac, presented her at New Year's with an elegant *vase de nuit* in Sèvres bearing Franklin's countenance and inscribed with Turgot's immortal epigram about the tamer of thunderbolts.[40] On one occasion the most beautiful of a throng of three hundred ladies placed a crown of laurel upon the sage's thinning white hair and kissed his cheeks. An unpublished letter, now among the Bache Papers, from a Madame Bachelier, December 9, 1777, informs Franklin that her husband has just swallowed a pin and that she fears for his life, but she cannot resist taking time to tell Franklin how she rejoices in the glorious victory at Saratoga of Franklin's cause and that of humanity.

Franklin's eight years in France are a splendid commentary on Gallic hero-worship. The snobbery which had hampered his every move in England, and the green provinciality which kept even his compatriots from taking the full measure of Franklin's stature, were here nullified. Of course he had the good luck to catch in his sails

the powerful winds of hate—the Anglophobia which even without
Franklin might have carried France to the side of America, and the
egalitarian stirrings which presaged a day not merely when a plain
man without wig and sword should stand before a king but when a
king should stand before a tribunal of plain men. But beyond all controversies, the triumph of Franklin was richly personal. He was *le
bonhomme Richard* to whom they gave a frigate as a namesake, and
even though it was not a very good ship the magic of its name and
the bravery of its captain sailed it to victory. Franklin was the friend
of liberty and justice, like M. Voltaire—whom, in response to popular
demand, he kissed before an applauding throng. The French have
long shown special homage to the heroes of humanity and of intellect
—artist, author, scientist, physician—which is denied the military hero
par excellence. The cult which made Germany adore Frederick the
Great is not so popular in France. A quality of moderation, balance,
and a sense of humor are apt to prick the inflated sufficiency of the
conquering hero. After all, Papa Joffre was a better French idol than
Napoleon.

It is good to think of Franklin, that aging philosophic Silenus, begotten in Boston and nurtured among the Quakers, who at last found
his Indian summer at Passy and in the most worldly Court in Europe.
He has been called "the only man in history who never bored anybody."[41] Certainly the French were enchanted with him, and whether
he was engaged in rebuking the arrogance of Gibbon or making love
to Madame Helvétius, the vein of Franklin's wit never ran more
limpid. With truth he may be called the father of the American wisecrack. Also, as the father of the American newspaper, he knew the
value of a good press for his cause and country. He wrote and circulated political catechisms, squibs about Hessian mercenaries, imaginary
accounts of Indians scalping and burning his countrymen at the in-
stigation of the British. From the viewpoint of strict truth the last
was not quite defensible, nor were the occasional lies which Franklin
told, without injury, to his friends to avoid unpleasantness.[42] Sometimes he winked at a little profiteering among his relatives, for whom
Franklin always had an amiable weakness.[43] But was it not Cotton
Mather himself who had given Franklin his first lesson in expediency,
"When you come to a low place, stoop"? In the main his faults were
not serious and his services were great—as he negotiated with France
but kept in touch with England through secret agents, speaking his
mind with partial candor to everybody but divulging all his thoughts

to no one, and going his untroubled way through an amazing net of spies set to trap him.

With victory achieved and peace concluded, he returned to Philadelphia in August, 1785, while cannon boomed and bells rang joyfully. Only a few crustacean families of the Quaker City, then as now, never approved of him. The masses thought otherwise. He was thrice elected President of the State of Pennsylvania. In councils of state, like Washington and Jefferson, he was a man of few words, but his prestige was immense. In suspicious Boston a newspaper in 1788 grumbled that the popular notion that "General Washington and Doctor Franklin" had made the new Constitution, was "too strong an argument in the minds of many to suffer them to examine, like freemen, for themselves."[44] Undoubtedly Franklin's most blissful admirer in the State of Massachusetts was his favorite sister Jane, who wrote to him that "it is not Profanity to compare you to our Blessed Saviour who Employed much of his time while on Earth in doing good to the body's as well as souls of men & I am shure I think the compareson just."[45]

Franklin's funeral on April 21, 1790, brought forth 20,000 mourners for the greatest demonstration of public grief Philadelphia ever made, up to the time of Abraham Lincoln's cortège. The death of the hero is often likened to the crashing of a mighty oak in the forest, which —as in Markham's phrase about Lincoln—"leaves a lonesome place against the sky." The first great American to be so remembered was Franklin, in Philip Freneau's elegy, which begins:

> Thus, like some tall tree that long hath stood
> The glory of its native wood,
> By storms destroyed, or length of years,
> Demands the tribute of our tears.

And then, as if aware of Franklin's twinkling mirth at all the funeral rhetoric sprinkled on his hearse, Freneau a month later published some "Verses from the Other World," in which the philosopher pokes fun at his panegyrists for saying that "Nature wept" at his death, and similar nonsense. Even in death Franklin looked homeward as the comic spirit.

The Federal House of Representatives voted unanimously to wear mourning for a month in Franklin's honor, but the Senate—a stage further removed from the hearts of the common people—refused. Thomas Jefferson wrote:

I proposed to General Washington that the executive department should

wear mourning: he declined it, because he said he would not know where
to draw the line if he once began that ceremony. . . . I told him that the
world had drawn so broad a line between him and Dr. Franklin, on the one
side, and the residue of mankind on the other, that we might wear mourning
for them, and the question still remain new and undecided as to all others.
He thought it best, however, to avoid it.[46]

It was inevitable that the public should measure Franklin's height
against Washington's. A few, who were strong for religious liberalism,
inclined to value the discoveries of science above the valor of war, and
who looked upon Washington as cold and austere, regarded Franklin
as the greater man. Tom Paine, whom Franklin had introduced to
America and had helped as pamphleteer and bridge-builder, while
Washington had snubbed him, belonged to this school. Probably Jefferson did too, in calling Franklin "the greatest man and ornament
of the age and country in which he lived . . . whose name will be
like a star of the first magnitude in the firmament of heaven, when
the memory of those who have surrounded & obscured him, will be
lost in the abyss of time."[47] But after the feuds of Washington's administration had cooled, and he too was gathered to the immortals, it
became plain that to the average American Franklin offered a more
practical symbol for imitation, but that Washington was the greater
hero.

V

Against the background of another age, the legendary Franklin
like the fabulous Lincoln might have taken on the tinge of a Rabelaisian story-teller, earthy, gusty, ironic. But the mythology of America
—which had to build upon the Puritan Fathers, and the idealistic pitch
of its great wars—had other uses for its heroes. Franklin had to become
the business ideal, and Lincoln the martyr president. Hence we hear
little of the Franklin who wrote "Advice to a young man on the choice
of a mistress"—counselling that before marriage one should quench
his lusts in a sensible way, choosing old women rather than young,
since the former run no risk of pregnancy, are more grateful for favors,
and because "regarding only what is below the girdle, it is impossible
of two women to know an old one from a young one." Or his burlesque letter "To the Royal Academy of Brussels" setting for their
consideration a prize question: "To discover some drug, wholesome
and not disagreeable, to be mixed with our common food, or sauces,

that shall render the natural discharges of wind from our bodies not only inoffensive, but agreeable as perfumes," scented with rose or bergamot. One of Poor Richard's least quoted maxims is an easy-going piece of morality in the Almanack for 1734:

> Be temperate in wine, in eating, girls, and sloth,
> Or the gout will seize you and plague you both.

In the *Autobiography* Franklin's twelfth precept of virtue is "Chastity: Rarely use venery but for health or offspring, never to dulness, weakness, or the injury of your own or another's peace or reputation." The editor Jared Sparks, in the early day of American Victorianism, reduced this passage to a simple but eloquent "Chastity. . . ." It is singular that the two best and most accessible books of advice to young men which the English-speaking world can claim—Franklin's *Autobiography* and Chesterfield's *Letters,* those sensible lessons in the gospel of getting on—should be frank and tolerant upon the one topic about which Anglo-Saxons are thought to be so reticent. But how could they well be otherwise? Each was addressed to the writer's natural son, and hypocrisy would have carried its own rebuttal.

Some people, distressed by this son of Franklin sprung out of wedlock, have tried to show that he was borne by the printer's future common-law wife Deborah Read, and so was later legitimized. Others, rushing to the opposite extreme, have asserted that Franklin had an illegitimate daughter also, and that in France as a septuagenarian he was a great lecher. All these statements appear to be moonshine. That in youth Franklin's morals were lax he himself has said, although the inconvenience and fear of disease caused his chief self-reproaches. And, as some have suggested, his failure to make acquaintance in those days with women of cultivation (the one flaw in his program of self-improvement) probably fostered a certain grossness in his attitude toward sex. The nineteenth century worried over this aspect of Franklin far more than did his own times, which took both his behavior and his candor for granted. But the mature Franklin was neither rake nor blackguard. He was a man with singular charm for the ladies, and believed with the French that there is no such thing as an ugly woman. None save prudes need to blush very deeply for him.

A second stumbling-block to the nineteenth century hero-worship of Franklin had been his religion. Was he an unbeliever? Assuredly he was not indifferent to religion. But from an emancipated Calvinism in early youth to a mellow old age, he showed the same pliant temperament which on the practical plane made him a successful entrepreneur and experimental scientist, and on the moral plane something of an opportunist. Borrowing the pun from Bishop Warburton, Franklin once remarked, concerning the relativity of dogma, "Orthodoxy is my doxy, and heterodoxy is your doxy." (Many a modern clergyman has repeated this saying from his pulpit, innocently unaware that in Franklin's day "doxy" was a real word, meaning a whore.) Tinged by deism in youth, he began each day's routine by praying to a decorous First Principle: "Rise, wash, and address Powerful Goodness!" He was a good money-raiser for Christ Church, Philadelphia, and the faithful subscriber to a pew in which he seldom sat.[48] Even to the chapel door he brought his abiding practicality. In the French and Indian campaign of 1755, when Mr. Beatty the Presbyterian chaplain complained of poor attendance at prayers, Franklin gave him a suggestion he followed with excellent results—namely that after prayers each day the clergyman ladle out the gill of rum to which every soldier was entitled.

Franklin once proposed to found a church for men like himself to be called "the Society of the Free and Easy"; a lately discovered manuscript shows that Franklin in London once began to draft a "philosophical liturgy" whose chief article of belief was in "the God of Newton."[49] He had faith in some kind of immortality, possibly the Pythagorean idea about transmigration of souls. In his own day the New England clergy were somewhat disturbed about him. Even on his death-bed Franklin received a point-blank inquiry from the Reverend Ezra Stiles, president of Yale. (Doctor Stiles's only theological vagary was "the hope that in the future life he would be permitted to visit the planets, and to examine the rings of Saturn and the belts and satellites of Jupiter."[50]) Franklin answered Doctor Stiles's letter with some frankness, trusting "that you will not expose me to criticism and censure by publishing any part of this communication." He wrote modestly of his beliefs and doubts, chiefly concerning Jesus of Nazareth, whom Franklin accepted as the noblest of men but not Divine. But he placidly declined to dogmatize about the future life, "when I expect soon an opportunity of knowing the truth with less trouble."[51] But in Philadelphia, where his generosities to many churches were known, and his eminence as first citizen towered above any metaphysical crotchets, "all the Clergy of the City" walked before his corpse to its last resting-place.

In France many of the sage's admirers liked to think of him as a forthright skeptic, an *esprit fort*, but in America most people kept assuring themselves that at heart he had been a conventional believer. In delivering his funeral eulogy before the savants of Philadelphia, the Reverend William Smith—an individual, by the way, of whom Franklin had no very high opinion—displayed a letter written in Franklin's hand asserting belief in the soul's immortality, but left the rest of his creed to be taken for granted.[52] Weems was the first biographer to tell how Franklin had died with his eyes fixed upon a picture of the crucified Savior. Parton repeated the unsupported story, and it has found favor with clergymen even to the present day.[53] Peter Parley told his young readers how Franklin had "roused himself from the stupor of approaching dissolution" to counsel a young man to believe the Holy Scriptures.[54] In the 1890's in clerical circles Franklin was hailed as "a devout Christian believer."[55] Yet a popular agnostic lecturer of Colonel Ingersoll's day, John Remsburg, glorified Franklin and Jefferson as the patron saints of freethinking in America. And in 1907 a Chicago pamphleteer named Mangasar Mugwiditch Mangasarian retorted to a Chicago preacher—who had said that no unbeliever could be, in effect, an American hero—by pointing to Franklin as one who rejected "the Christian superstition, imported to this country from Asia," and adding also the names of Jefferson and Washington.[56] That there was a link between deism and political revolution —a revolt against authority temporal and spiritual, in France and America in the eighteenth century—can hardly be denied. The bond between the two ideas is however as much exaggerated by the crusading "infidel" as it is ignored by the average D. A. R. Nobody knows what the close-lipped Washington believed. Like Shakespeare, he abides our question. But six important patriots—Thomas Paine, Ethan Allen, Thomas Jefferson, Gouverneur Morris, John Adams, and Benjamin Franklin—left indubitable traces of freethinking. Posterity, which likes to bolster its established institutions by the example of its heroes, has dealt with these heretics in different ways. It has chosen to execrate Paine's infidelity, which was most notorious, and to forget Allen's little-known *Reason the only oracle of man* (most copies burned miraculously in a printing-house fire) for the sake of his brave deeds and his invocation of the "great Jehovah and the Continental Congress." Arrogant Gouverneur Morris never was a hero, while John Adams kept most of his doubts dark. Jefferson is forgiven, save by the stricter clergy, because he is a major idol of the democracy. And Franklin, who caused no more scandal than he could help, and taught by precept and example so many useful lessons in the school of Puritan self-help, has been perhaps easiest of all to assimilate. The honey of his doctrine catches more flies than the gall of Tom Paine.

VI

The Reverend Mason·Locke Weems, who stands as the first hierophant in the temple of hero-worship for American youth, as early as 1796 had picked Franklin "the great economist of America" as a symbol of monetary success, in a book grandly called *The Immortal Mentor; or, Man's unerring guide to a healthy, wealthy, and happy life*. Later, after his best-selling lives of Washington and Marion, Weems decided to exploit Franklin more fully. On July 31, 1813, he wrote Jefferson asking for material for his collection of Franklin "Bons Mots, Anecdotes, Stories, etc., etc., all which, if only tolerably *cooked up* wou'd make a savoury dish for Juvenile palates." Soon he set to work in earnest. But Franklin, whose life was an antithesis of the sugared preachment and rhetoric upon which Weems throve, proved to be stubborn material for the hand which had turned Washington into the patriot prig. The first edition of Weems's Franklin appeared in Baltimore in 1815. Weems started out well by inventing a great-great-grandmother, "old Mrs. Franklin," who in the days of bloody Mary had played a shrewd trick on "a most violent priest," by removing from his saddle-bags a commission to burn heretics and substituting for it "a pack of cards with the knave of clubs uppermost." But the book's total effect was pretty flat. Weems was not inspired to lie gorgeously about Franklin himself. The biography went through eleven editions by 1845, but in comparison with Weems's other efforts it was a sad disappointment. For a long time he did not give up hope that Franklin might be made to sell, and on November 27, 1820, wrote to Carey, his printer: "When we think of what we have done with his illustrious compat. Washington we must keep up our hopes." That a life of the apostle of success should have been a commercial failure was, to Weems, intolerable.

Better justice was done Franklin by Jared Sparks, who from 1836 to 1840 published his works in ten stout volumes, and added to the *Autobiography* an account of Franklin's later years in which the sage appears as wise, honorable, and generous. He did his best to deflect the Franklin legend from the hands of prigs and misers. Sparks as a Connecticut boy of eleven, reading eagerly while he fed logs into a sawmill to earn his bread, had first come upon the *Autobiography;*

the book helped fire his ambition to attend Harvard, whose president he eventually became. But it was natural that Sparks, having been born out of wedlock, desperately poor in boyhood, nourished in a climate of hard toil and snobbish respectability, should have understood Franklin the successful American better than Franklin the child of a lustier age. While rebelling against Franklin the dumpy little figure who had been used as a kind of spiritual savings-bank to hold pennies, he still failed to reckon with the whole man.

America's growing industrialism and the rise of the success cult shortly before the Civil War brought forth a new appreciation of Franklin. Theodore Parker called him "the most popular man in America. . . . No man now has so strong a hold on the habits and manners of the people."[57] Robert C. Winthrop in Boston in 1853 gave a famous lecture on "Archimedes and Franklin," in which the latter came off with higher honors. Although, as Winthrop remarked, every lightning-rod and every penny stamp is Franklin's memorial, Boston should honor her greatest son with a statue, showing

that bland and benevolent countenance, which seems to say even to the humblest and least hopeful of God's creatures: "I was once as you are now, houseless and penniless, without fortune and without friends. But never despair: be just and fear not, be sober, be diligent, be frugal, be faithful, love man and love God, and do your whole duty to yourself, to your neighbor, and to your country, in whatever circumstances you are placed—and you, also, may do good in your day and generation, and you too may haply leave a name that shall be remembered and honored in all ages and throughout all climes.[58]

In reply to this plea a statue of the sage by R. S. Greenough was unveiled in 1856, with the biggest parade Boston had ever seen, the ships in the harbor decked with flags, and every spot associated with Franklin festooned with bunting. Every shop had its banners with Poor Richard's sayings. Printers, stove-makers, mechanics, fire brigades, Masons, the Boston Corn Exchange—with a tableau illustrating "It is hard for an empty bag to stand upright"—united in acclaim. All minds were fixed reverently upon the glory of Franklin and his statue, except (as the official brochure reports) for some "gallant students of Harvard College" who were distracted by a group of ladies waving handkerchiefs from an upstairs drug-store in Clinton Street.[59] The sage himself would have appreciated their distraction.

It is fitting that Franklin's tutelary genius appears to evoke some comic relief from the most solemn occasions of his apotheosis. Thus in 1872 when Albert de Groot, steamboat captain and crony of Commodore Vanderbilt, gave New York City a monument of Franklin for Printing-House Square—"viewed from the north, it is rather lacking in dignity," reported the *Tribune*—the mood of anticipation before the unveiling was broken in an unforeseen way. "A person, supposed to be crazy, rushed down Chatham Street with a huge knife in his hand, and climbing upon the large pedestal on which the statue of Franklin is placed, proceeded to tear the flag off and to hack the Statue with his knife. . . . The police seized him but he fought terribly . . . taken to the station house, he gave his name as Diedrich Barr, 37 years of age, of German birth and a sailor by occupation. He stated that he was passing by, and desired to know what was concealed under the covering of the flag, and that he meant no harm. He laughed heartily over the matter, being rather slightly intoxicated and full of mischief."[60]

On the threshold of the business era, the appreciation of Franklin was steadily mounting. Horace Greeley's well-known lecture, "Self-Made Men," first given in 1862, traced a career which owed nothing to inherited wealth, family, or formal education, yet carried Franklin from a tallow-chandler's shop "crammed full of hungry brothers and sisters, to the gilded saloons of Versailles." The philosopher's legend gave promise of outstripping Washington's. One cannot help suspecting that war between an industrial North and an agrarian South had something to do with the printer's tardy ascendancy over the Virginia planter. In Greeley's eyes Franklin is the 100 per cent American:

I think I adequately appreciate the greatness of Washington; yet I must place Franklin above him as the consummate type and flowering of human nature under the skies of colonial America. . . . [Washington] began responsible life on the vantage-ground that Franklin toiled twenty arduous, precious years to reach. . . . I realize that there are elements of dignity, of grandeur, in the character of Washington for which that of Franklin affords no parallel. But when I contemplate the immense variety and versatility of Franklin's services to his country and to mankind . . . I cannot place Franklin second to any other American. . . . And, great as Washington was, he was not great enough to write and print, after he had achieved power and world-wide fame, a frank, ingenuous confession of his youthful follies and sins for the instruction and admiration of others.[61]

What youthful follies and sins the publicist believed Washington had committed is unknown, but to Greeley's New Hampshire mind it was no doubt a highly suspicious circumstance if a man did not have some sins to confess. A generation later it is significant that Franklin is sometimes bracketed with Lincoln rather than with Washington. At the unveiling of Philadelphia's statue to Franklin, given by Justus C. Strawbridge in 1899, the Honorable James M. Beck described the sage as coming like Lincoln from the heart of the masses, inheriting the physique of generations of blacksmiths from Ecton forge, and in his will writing himself down as "Benjamin Franklin, printer." With Lincoln he shared a vein of optimism and good humor, genial fellowship, simplicity, inventiveness, industry, and love of freedom—"the peculiar characteristics of our people."[62] However, it was unlikely that an orator dedicating a statue of Lincoln would have drawn so lengthy a parallel with Franklin, who lacked Lincoln's idealism and pathos and remained essentially subordinate to him in the American mind. For a hundred years Franklin had been the most popular subject in American biography; but near the beginning of the twentieth century the flood of Lincoln literature swept past him.[63] As an inspiration to biographers he remains still second to Lincoln, although superior to Washington and Jefferson in the number of recent books he can claim.

Throughout the years Franklin's most loyal fans probably have been the Masons and the printers. Both have been ready to accept him without hairsplitting or apology. Since the day in 1731 when the Freemasons took Franklin into their fellowship—after he had drawn their notice by a provocative piece announcing that "their Great Secret is THAT THEY HAVE NO SECRET"—Franklin gained much from their personal friendship, power, and international connections. They, in turn, seeking to spread their "new light" of liberty and equality, with a tinge of anti-clericalism, found in him their perfect exemplar. They have never failed to keep his memory green, by writing and speech-making and entering into public celebrations of him.[64] Likewise he has been the patron saint of a guild, the printers. Starting early in the nineteenth century the typographical societies of New York, Boston, and Philadelphia, joined later by Chicago, kept his birthday as an annual feast. At a typical banquet at Niblo's on January 17, 1850, by the New York Typographical Society, birthday toasts were offered by James Fenimore Cooper, Horace Greeley, and Samuel F. B. Morse. In view of the gold fever then attacking many an idle apprentice, one toast of the evening proclaimed: "The Best Route to the Gold Fields—Through the Pages of 'Poor Richard.'"[65] Richard S. Greenough the sculptor—in studying his subject while making the Franklin statue for Boston City Hall—concluded that Franklin's fondness for portraits of himself in fur could be traced to the fact that early printers used fur as a professional badge.[66] The loyalty between Franklin and his craft is unquestioned. Among out-of-the-way modern tributes is a pamphlet written and printed to the number of one hundred copies in 1929 by a fellow guildsman named Earl H. Emmons, called *Odeography of B. Franklin*. The author's foreword declares, "I think he is by far the greatest white man this country ever produced." In hearty if rough-hewn grammar this printer celebrates his hero as versatile, robust, and amatory—adding that, like Franklin, the writer himself has often been looked at down the noses of respectable people, for much the same reasons:

> And though he trod the festive paths
> And played with ladies in their baths,
> He gave the world his gifts in boundless measures;
> And damned be weasel-minded men
> Who dare reproach the glorious Ben
> For lightening his toil with human pleasures.

And in Philadelphia America's most popular five-cent magazine claims him as its founder and editorial genius, despite the fact that his *Pennsylvania Gazette,* always a newspaper and never a story magazine, closed its files in 1815, and *The Saturday Evening Post* did not begin till 1821.

The first United States postage stamps, issued in 1847, bore the likeness of Washington (ten cents) and of Franklin (five cents). The sage has had many namesakes. Massachusetts named a town for him in 1775; in accepting the honor, Franklin passed over the citizens' request for a bell and gave them a library instead, "sense being preferable to sound." From 1784 to 1787 the territory that later became Tennessee called itself the State of Franklin. Elsewhere squares, streets, early steamships, fire-engines, colleges, lyceums, hotels, and banks were labelled Franklin. In 1864 Parton found that every state in the Union had at least one town called Franklin, and Ohio (no doubt to the confusion of postmasters) boasted nineteen of them. On the map of the United States the name then occurred 136 times, exceeded only by the Washingtons and Jacksons. As for personal namesakes, today in Chicago there is the Club of Benjamin Franklins, with some sixty members whose parents christened them after the sage.

In the flush times of 1928 Franklin narrowly escaped one of the most grandiose tributes ever planned in New York City—a $25,000,000 memorial and office building to be called "The Benjamin Franklin Temple of Peace," seventy-five stories high, with vast panels showing scenes from the philosopher's life. "The shaft of the building would portray *genius* in the vertical elements and *science* in the parallel elements. . . . The tower would bear a gilded dome, supported by thirteen huge columns typifying the thirteen original colonies. The crowning motif would be 'Lightning,' so planned that by a series of lights an effect would be produced of lightning bolts thrown from the sky." Although conceived as a shrine to Franklin, "the majority of the space would be devoted to offices which would render the structure self-supporting." Its sponsor was the International Benjamin Franklin Society, and its architect Mr. Franklin Bache Huntington, great-great-great-grandson of the sage—who incidentally is the greatest living impersonator of his ancestor, having appeared at numerous dinners and ceremonies in "authentic Benjamin Franklin costume," sometimes remarking, "When I speak, the blood of Franklin prompts and inspires my tongue."[67]

In Philadelphia the philosopher's finest monument is the huge building of the Franklin Institute, dedicated in May, 1938, to house a project founded in 1824 for the promotion of mechanical arts and popular scientific knowledge. Its stress is upon "science for youth," with exhibits of the graphic arts, engineering through the ages, and a fine planetarium. There is a very early Wright plane made for Grover Cleveland Bergdoll, himself no hero. Visitors may work many of the devices for themselves, as Franklin surely would have approved; there one may see first-generation Americans eagerly manipulating a manual printing-press, or a group of pickaninnies exploring the wonders of a telegraph key. The vast circular memorial chamber holds a heroic-size statue of Franklin by James Earle Frazer—a seated figure in white marble who gazes into the future with benign faith. The director, Henry Butler Allen, describes the reverence with which schoolchildren enter that sanctum, and predicts it will become "one of the most famous shrines in the world." In the building of this memorial, five million dollars were raised in ten days by the Poor Richard Club of Philadelphia, which does much to foster the Franklin cult. It is a group of those "who make, buy, or sell advertising," whose former leader was Cyrus H. K. Curtis. Over the doorway of this Club is a bust of the sage illuminated by an "Eternal Light" kindled in 1930 by Admiral Byrd from Little America. Each year on Poor Richard's birthday the Club, assisted by several thousand people and a half-dozen bands, makes a pilgrimage to Franklin's grave in Christ Church burial-ground. Early visitors to that spot complained of its inaccessibility, because one had to climb a high wall or tip the sexton. But, during the great upsurge of Franklin's popularity on the eve of the Civil War, an aperture was made in the wall and set off with an open grill fence. Since, in 1850, Fredrika Bremer visited the grave of her "hero of peace" and bound "clover and other field-flowers" into a garland, uncounted millions have passed beside the spot, in the heart of a great commercial city, where "Benjamin Franklin, printer" lies forever in state.

CHAPTER FIVE

THE EMBATTLED FARMERS

Life for my country and the cause of freedom
Is but a cheap price for a worm to part with:
And if preservèd in so great a contest,
  Life is redoubled.
  —NATHANIEL NILES, "The American Hero" (1775).

I

AMERICA is the only country in the world which pretends to listen to the teaching of its founders as if they were still alive," a French journalist has lately observed.[1] The fathers of American Independence, who declared it in 1776, the minute-men who fired the shot heard round the world to herald it, and the Founding Fathers of the Constitution who laid the keel for our ship of state—these are powerful symbols.

To the law office of Lincoln and Herndon came the widow of a Revolutionary soldier, "crippled and bent with age," to report that a pension agent named Wright had charged half her pension of $400 for getting her claim allowed. Lincoln instantly undertook her case, and his famous notes for the suit against Wright read thus:

No contract. Not professional services. Unreasonable charge. Money retained by Def't not given by Pl'ff. Revolutionary War. Describe Valley Forge pri-

vations. Ice—Soldier's bleeding feet. Pl'ff's husband. Soldier leaving home
for army. *Skin Def't.* Close.

Herndon, who says of his partner that "I never, either on the stump
or on other occasions in court, saw him so wrought up," describes
Lincoln's speech more fully. He pictured the young soldier leaving his
cabin home, bidding farewell to his weeping wife and kissing the babe
in its cradle.

Time rolls by; the heroes of '76 have passed away and are encamped on the
other shore. The soldier has gone to rest, and now, crippled, blinded, and
broken, his widow comes to you and to me, gentlemen of the jury, to right
her wrongs. . . . Out here on the prairies of Illinois . . . she appeals to us,
who enjoy the privileges achieved for us by the patriots of the Revolution,
for our sympathetic aid and manly protection. All I ask is, shall we befriend
her?

By this time, Herndon reports, half the jury were "in tears" and
Wright was "writhing." After the inevitable verdict in favor of his
client, Lincoln paid her hotel bill and fare home, charging no fee for
his services.² Such is the homage of sentiment paid to the soldiers of '76.

Poets sing repeatedly of those Emerson later called "the embattled farmers"—in homespun, with rifle and powder-horn, simple,
clear-eyed and brave—the pride of an agrarian civilization. After Concord, it was easy enough to teach successive generations of American
schoolchildren that "the old squirrel rifle from the mantelpiece will
repulse any foe," as a military officer drily observed some years ago,
in deprecating this attitude of effortless victory as a stumbling-block
to true preparedness.³ Poems about the Revolution found most often
in school readers—Emerson's "Concord Hymn," Longfellow's "Paul
Revere's Ride," Bryant's "Song of Marion's Men," Lowell's "Under
the Old Elm"—stress the freelance aspect of that great venture. Thus
Lowell described George Washington taking command over

> An army all of captains, used to pray
> And stiff to fight, but serious drill's despair,
> Skilled to debate their orders, not obey.

Washington—who quickly sensed that native sons fought well in local
skirmishes or bushwhacking larks under a popular captain like John
Stark or Francis Marion, but deserted from the regulars, and refused
to go far afield—took a less indulgent view of things than did the later
poets. Trying to get New Englanders to re-enlist in the fall of 1775,
he wrote: "Such a dearth of public spirit, and want of virtue, and

stock-jobbing, a fertility in all the low arts to obtain advantages of one kind or another, I never saw before and pray God I may never be witness to again."[4] Washington was far from sharing the present assumption of the D. A. R., that any Revolutionary soldier was a Revolutionary hero. Washington's magnificent control of his temper was often exercised to its full. Eventually, however, he was able to carve this knotty and cross-grained material into an army of sorts, with the help of such an iron taskmaster as the Prussian Von Steuben, during the bitter winter at Valley Forge.

General Washington probably would have been surprised by a description of his rank-and-file soldiers, given in a speech in Congress on August 15, 1916, in the ferment of that pre-War summer. The speaker was New York Congressman Walter M. Chandler, ex-cowboy, schoolteacher, and Wall Street lawyer:

No ignorant, vulgar rebels they! The Revolutionary ranks were filled with accomplished scholars, with men who read the tragedies of Æschylus in Greek as easily as the tragedies of Shakespeare in English. Government, philosophy, and religion were themes of daily and familiar converse around colonial camp fires. The soldiers of the Revolution knew the richness of their blood. They traced their lineage along a noble line to Crécy, Poitiers, Malplaquet, and Ramillies. They read the military achievements of their race in the recovery of the holy sepulchre, in the battle at Hohenlinden, in the capture of Quebec. They felt no inability to multiply these brilliant deeds.

The rank-and-file of that army was a mixed lot. About the anonymous hero, the unknown soldier of the Revolution, little has been written. Probably he was neither the "stock-jobber" of whom Washington complained in moods of fatigue nor the patriot highbrow whom the poets and Congressman Chandler have imagined. The almost-forgotten diaries that survive, by humble patriots, give us a picture that has no traces of Æschylus and Shakespeare, but does not lack simple quiet courage. Joseph Joslin, aged eighteen, a Connecticut teamster in the Continental Army, kept a placid journal that tells of "hard carting, Sir," through snow and mud, of unruly oxen and broken wheels, of eating sour bread and "stinking beef" and weathering the homely miseries of chicken pox and poison ivy.[5] He mentions his wages, to be sure, but for him cash probably did not outweigh loyalty any more than it did with the three irregulars who captured André and refused his bribe of "any sum of money"—those "poor Men Heroes of the Revolution," as Lippard called them. And there was Sergeant John

Smith, a Yankee with a dry humor, in Washington's army during the winter of 1776, who wrote a diary that abounds in the problems of forage rather than logistics: about the lack of salt and of bivouacs on wet ground in windy nights, of bare feet wrapped in the hides of newly killed cattle, of raids on orchards and barnyards ("my brother soldiers seamed hearty in the Cause of Liberty of taking what came in the way"), of cheerful endurance and final joy over the rout of the Hessians at Trenton, "to meak Genll. Washingtons heart glad once more."[6] And there are a few mutely eloquent prison diaries. One of the least known is that of a young American sailor, Charles Herbert, confined for two and a half years in Mill Prison at Portsmouth, England—enduring the itch and smallpox, expecting to be hanged if the Revolution failed, but celebrating Independence Day with his compatriots by cutting out paper cockades with thirteen stars and the motto "Liberty or Death" and hoisting a flag in the prison yard.[7] The daily acts of such men have little in common with the heroics of poetry and oratory. But their patience and bravery are not less convincing.

The composite patriot of '76 has been treated in a somewhat unreal way. Like the poets, most novelists write of fife and drum rather than lice, of glory more than shaking knees. The "proletarian" point of view—of Stephen Crane in the Civil War and Kenneth Roberts in the eighteenth century—is still rare. The Revolutionary soldier, in art and in books for the young, has commonly been disembodied, idealized, made uniform and perfect. The flag for which he fought has been unfurled to various winds of doctrine. Thus, in generations of textbooks he was used to teach hatred of the English. Then, about the time of the Great War, the Revolution was rewritten as a struggle between the Hessians and English-speaking freemen, in revolt against a German king. After the war, Mayor Thompson of Chicago and others angling for the Irish and German vote demanded that the accent on British tyranny be restored. There must be "no disparagement of the achievements of American heroes."[8] In California,[9] as well as in New York, bills were drawn up to safeguard the rightful teaching of Revolutionary history in public schools.[10] Then, in the vogues of education, came a time of debunkery and pacifism. Our patriotism—which burns brighter on the eve of wars until it bursts into the flame of self-sacrifice during the crisis—is apt to gutter, once the crisis is safely past, into a fume of "patrioteering" and intolerance, until apathy and cynicism serve as a pair of snuffers. At length the process starts anew, and the nation once more thrills to its great traditions. The schoolbook treatment of the Revolution, from the World War up to present days, follows this cycle.

In 1921 an investigator for Mr. Hearst, Charles G. Miller of *The Chicago Herald and Examiner,* severely took to task Albert Bushnell Hart of Harvard, for daring to say of the embattled farmers, "Many served from the purest motives of patriotism, but others were drawn into the army by money, bounties, and promises of land."[11] Other mention of bounties,[12] or mild rebuke of the patriots' childishness in burning the king's picture,[13] and other trivial details in textbooks have drawn the fire of excitable groups.[14] In 1931 the school board of Franklin, Pennsylvania, threw out, as "wet propaganda," a text by Vannest and Smith because it showed that Revolutionary heroes drank liquor and even trafficked in West Indian rum.[15] A "learn American" movement in New Hampshire, in 1933, called for the expulsion of *Silas Marner* from English classes and the substitution of stories about John Stark and Ethan Allen.[16] Among American generals, Benedict Arnold alone is freely thrown to the lions.

There must be no economic motivation behind the Revolution, but solely a passion for "liberty." Agitators against the Stamp Act in Boston must never be called "mobs" by any inadvertence, nor the leaders of 1776 "radicals." No residue of Marxism can be tolerated in the phenomena of this Revolution. So that there can be no mistake, the *D. A. R. Manual for Citizenship* explains to aliens seeking naturalization:

A revolution usually means an attempt to tear down or overturn a government or wreck the existing institutions of a country. The American Revolution did none of these things; on the contrary, it was a war fought to PRESERVE the principles of the colonial governments; it was fought to MAINTAIN the liberties of the colonists which George the Third had tried to take away. Americans abhor the kind of revolution which destroys and overturns, which murders, loots, and burns.

The compiler goes on to prove that the Revolutionists were fighting really upon the side of tradition, "to save and build up the free governments the American colonists already had," and hence that the British were actually the rebels in this War.[17] Most writers of history and civics texts have been willing to cut their cloth to suit the times— knowing how powerful certain groups are in promoting or blocking the adoption of schoolbooks. A survey made in 1930 of civic attitudes in textbooks found that the majority describe the Revolutionists *en masse* as "noble," "brilliant," full of "dogged persistence," but winning against overwhelming odds, when they wish, by an almost effortless miracle, while the redcoats are described as "haughty" and "cruel" and "tyrannical." A text by Willis M. West was denounced for saying that "the Tories, on the whole, represented respectability and refinement."[18] The brief attempt made during the first World War, and thus marred by special pleading, to do better justice to our then allies apparently was quickly revoked. That one can be truthful and fair to Britain, and still make out an excellent case for George Washington, seldom occurs to our zealots.

II

The first poem celebrating Paul Revere is quite forgotten. It is found in a manuscript now in the Massachusetts Historical Society, signed "Eb. Stiles" and dated "March 15, 1795." Called "Story of the Battle of Concord and Lexington and Revear's [sic] ride Twenty years ago," it begins:

> He speard neither Horse nor whip nor spur
> As he galloped through mud and mire
> He thought of nought but "Liberty"
> And the lanterns that hung from the Spire
> He raced his Steed through feild and wood
> Nor turned to ford the river
> But faced his horse to the foaming flood
> They swam across together
>
> He madly dashed o'er mountain and moor
> Never slackened spur nor rein
> Untill with shout he stood by the door
> Of the Church by Concord green
> "They come They come" he loudly cried
> "They are marching their Legions this way
> Prepar to meet them ye true and tried
> They'l be hear by Break of day."

Boston remembered the son of Apollos De Revoire, who upon setting up in business as a silversmith had simplified his name "merely on account that the Bumpkins should pronounce it easier."[19] It was a name which had the ring of heroism. Helen F. More's poem "What's in a Name?" tells the story of his fellow courier, William Dawes, who, while Revere was captured by the British, safely brought the news to Concord. He rode as valiantly but rode into oblivion—

> Why, should I ask? The reason is clear—
> My name was Dawes and his Revere.

The Dawes family seems foredoomed to produce runners-up and vice-presidents. Yet Paul Revere's exploit, when "the fate of a nation was riding that night," has received all the poetic tribute—despite the fact that he was a man of forty mounted on a stout work-horse, and that this night's work was but one of his many valuable services as a Revolutionary courier, before he fell into disgrace and was charged unfairly with cowardice.[20] His later and nationwide fame he owes solely to Longfellow. Prior to Longfellow's poem Revere's name was not included in a single dictionary of American biography—such as Hardie's which went into three editions between 1802 and 1808, John Eliot's in 1809, or William Allen's which enjoyed three editions between 1809 and 1857 and came latterly to embrace accounts of 7000 worthies. Next to April 18, 1775, the most important date in the Revere legend was April 5, 1860, when Longfellow, accompanied by a guide, climbed the tower of the old North Church, "now the home of innumerable pigeons," as he noted in his Journal. "From this tower were hung the lanterns as a signal that the British troops had left Boston for Concord." The next day he began to write "Paul Revere's Ride," and finished it apparently within a fortnight.[21] In 1863 it was published in *Tales of a Wayside Inn,* and, helped by the renascence of patriotism during the Civil War, quickly became a favorite. Revere's name appeared for the first time in a biographical reference book in 1872, Francis S. Drake's *Dictionary of American Biography.* Thenceforth he was a great American hero, by the same might of the pen which made Santa Claus the idol of generations of American children after Clement C. Moore's " 'Twas the Night Before Christmas" in 1823—lending a vivid physical appearance and gesture so necessary to mythology. Silver made by Revere grew rapidly in value, until a good piece fetched $5000; it was rumored that the late J. P. Morgan offered Mrs. Marston Perry $100,000 for Revere's famous "Sons of Liberty" silver punch-bowl. His engravings and caricatures were cherished. The folk mind, upon learning that Paul Revere made false teeth, and that George Washington wore false teeth, invented the well-known statement that Revere made a set of dentures for the master of Mount Vernon. In 1895 the D. A. R. made Paul Revere's house in Boston a shrine. It is now in charge of the Paul Revere Memorial Association. In the front room, beneath the Copley portrait of Revere in shirt-sleeves at his work-bench, one finds this inscription: "The plain, true patriotic type of American is our best example."

Nathan Hale is one of the most appealing American heroes. A

youth lately graduated from Yale, who seems to have heard the great stories of Greek and Roman history ringing in his ears, he undertook in September, 1776, the perilous mission of spying upon the British on Long Island. Crossing the Sound disguised as a Dutch schoolmaster, with his Yale diploma at hand as a rather curious credential, he met with success and was about to reach his own picket lines on Manhattan. According to family tradition, he was then betrayed by a Tory cousin. Upon capture he frankly declared his name and the object of his errand, and was hanged summarily the next morning, September 22. His last words, an echo from Addison's play *Cato,* were "I only regret that I have but one life to lose for my country." His old father, Deacon Hale, commented sadly, "A child I sot much by, but he is gone." Although his death caused some passing indignation among Hale's friends in the American army, he was not widely known. The later story which pictures Washington as inspiring him to the hazardous task is pure myth; there seems to be no evidence that the two ever met.[22] Not until the execution of the British spy André, four years later, was the memory of Hale revived to justify the reprisal; while comment was made upon André's more egotistic last words: "I pray you to bear me witness, that I meet my fate like a brave man." To the popular and sentimental imagination, André became a British aristocrat, while Hale was obviously a country boy. Even Hale's Yale friend Timothy Dwight, after paying passing tribute to his sacrifice, came to rest more lyrically upon the "graces" of André—

With soul too noble for so base a cause.[23]

In 1836 Doctor Eneas Munson, Jr., wrote to *The American Historical Magazine:* "Cannot you rouse the dormant energies of an ungrateful republic, in the case of Captain Hale, to mark the spot where so much virtue and patriotism moulder with his native dust?"[24] A strange sense of respectability, which did not operate in the case of André, caused a feeling even in Hale's native South Coventry, Connecticut, that his death by hanging had been something of a disgrace.[25] Finally in 1847, after long delays and the grant of $1200 from the State of Connecticut (following refusal of the Federal Congress to contribute anything), a modest shaft of Quincy granite was erected to Hale's memory at Coventry.

At last Hale found his laureate, in 1853, when at the centennial anniversary of the Linonian Society, at Yale, Judge Francis Miles Finch

read his poem which began to make the patriot known in school
readers thereafter:

> To drum-beat and heart-beat
>   A soldier marches by;
> There is color in his cheek,
>   There is courage in his eye,
> Yet to drum-beat and heart-beat
>   In a moment he must die.

. . . .

> From Fame-leaf and Angel-leaf
>   From monument and urn,
> The sad of Earth, the glad of Heaven,
>   His tragic fate shall learn;
> And on Fame-leaf and Angel-leaf
>   The name of HALE shall burn!

Some years later it was this poem which attracted a Connecticut schoolboy named George Dudley Seymour to think of Hale as "the ideal
youthful hero of the Republic."[26] Seymour, who became a successful
patent lawyer in New Haven, in 1898 began a movement to erect a
statue "for God, for country, and for Hale" upon the campus of the
patriot's *alma mater*. Distrusting as theatrical a statue which Partridge
had made in 1902 as a composite of "the typical Yale student," Seymour
at last found his ideal in the manly, homespun figure cast by Bela Pratt
in 1914. It is less dramatic than MacMonnies's Hale done for City Hall
Park in New York—"something," said MacMonnies, "that would set
the bootblacks and little clerks around there thinking, something that
would make them want to be somebody and find life worth living"[27]—
but it remains the classic though imaginary Hale. In 1925 Seymour persuaded Postmaster-General New to place this image upon the half-cent
postage stamp, of which almost three billion have been issued. Despite
some indifferent verse, and several cheap dime novels, and a stagey
drama by Clyde Fitch in 1898—with Nat Goodwin playing an ageing
and dissipated Hale—the fame of this lad has grown stoutly and well
with the passing years, since the tribute of Finch's poem.

Next to Washington the best-known soldier in America, at the outbreak of the Revolution, was Israel Putnam.[28] He had been one of
Rogers's rangers in the French and Indian campaign, had been captured by the redskins and tied to a tree with the faggots crackling when
he was rescued, had served as lieutenant-colonel in Pontiac's War, and

been active in organizing the Sons of Liberty in 1765–66. Rough and ready, utterly fearless, and possessed of miraculous luck, "Old Put" was the kind of man who attracted legends. Near Pomfret, Connecticut, it was said, in his youthful days Putnam had been lowered by a rope into the den of a savage wolf; flashing his pine-knot torch in her gleaming eyes he had shot her, and taken her by the ears, while his friends above, "with no small exultation, drew Mr. Putnam and the wolf both out together."[29] As late as 1828 it was reported that "travellers frequently go out of their way for the purpose of visiting Putnam's Cave."[30] During the French and Indian War, they reported, he had saved a gunpowder barrel from the burning barracks, though "blistered from head to foot."[31] Like a war-horse he smelled the Revolution afar off. Upon hearing the news of Lexington, in April, 1775, "he instantly unyoked his cattle, left his plough standing in the unfinished furrow, in the midst of the field, and without stopping to change his dress, immediately set off for the scene of military transactions."[32] Although Prescott commanded the redoubt at Bunker Hill, the lion's share of popular credit went to Putnam; he is supposed to have issued the famous command, "Don't fire until you see the whites of their eyes."[33] Stories continued to be told of his shrewdness, as when he deceived a British officer visiting the meager Continental forces at Princeton by placing a lighted candle in every college window; and of his hairbreadth escapes, notably his flight from the enemy by riding his horse down a steep declivity called Horseneck; it was sometimes said that he had hurdled "the Falls of the Hudson River." Putnam's immense popularity swept him to a military rank beyond his abilities, and his later career is one of ill-success and disobedience to the will of Washington. Paralysis ended his activity in 1779, when the War was still young.

In what has been called "the earliest history of America edited especially for American children," published in Philadelphia in 1792, he and General Montgomery—who fell upon the heights of Quebec—are the two Revolutionary heroes honored with short biographies; a woodcut shows Putnam taken prisoner by the Indians.[34] Cramer, the enterprising almanac publisher of Pittsburgh, had ready by 1816 popular lives of Putnam, Washington, Captain John Smith, and Columbus. Another project in the same decade, called *The American Nepos,* containing lives of great Americans which four clergymen and two scholars had certified "are fit examples for Youth," included Putnam cheek by jowl with the half-traitorous General Charles Lee. In the

1830's in vaudeville, in that curious type best described as the equestrian farce, General Putnam became a comic Yankee. His impersonator performed tricks on horseback, or acted out such a well-liked legend as that of Putnam's challenge to an angry British officer to join him in sitting on a powder-keg with a lighted fuse. After letting the fuse burn to its last inch, while the officer decamped in haste, Putnam calmly arose to show that the keg was full of Wethersfield onions.[35] After a time, his comic aspect was forgotten and Putnam returned as "the boys' hero for all time."[36] *The Uncle Sam Series* by Richard Henry Stoddard—who wrote for children and *Godey's Lady's Book,* and in private life was distinguished for his profanity—described Putnam as "a man that knew not fear":

> He looked the Great Commander,
> And was the Man of Men!

In 1876 Increase N. Tarbox wrote a full-length life of Putnam, ranking him next to Washington as the great man of the Revolution. When in 1888 an equestrian statue of him was dedicated at Brooklyn, Connecticut, Professor Charles F. Johnson of Trinity College wrote an ode:

> God sends our kings, Lincoln and Washington;
> Putnam is not of these. They stand alone,
> And solitary on their heights remain;
> He with his fellows on a lower plane.
> But on that plane of broad humanity,
> What stronger man or nobler soul than he—
> A nature on broad lines and simple plan,
> Type of the primitive American!

III

Ethan Allen and Francis Marion are the Robin Hoods of American mythology. Allen and his Green Mountain Boys—stalwart, deep-chested, fun-loving—were celebrated in a novel by Daniel Pierce Thompson which ran to fifty editions between 1839 and 1860. The chief of this merry clan, a preliminary sketch of Abe Lincoln the New Salem giant, is thus described by Thompson through the eyes of one of his "boys":

And when they tell you, as they truly may, that they have seen him bite off the heads of board nails by dozens,—seize by his teeth, and throw over his head, bags containing each a bushel of salt, as fast as two men could bring them round to him,—grasp two opponents who had beset him, one in each hand, and lifting them clear of the ground, hold them out at arms length, and beat them together till they cried for mercy,—engage alone with a York Sheriff and his posse of six common men, rout the whole, and leave them sprawling on the ground—you will probably allow that such a man will not be very likely to succumb to your hero [Benedict Arnold].[37]

Ethan Allen himself, in the account of his captivity among the British, boasted that he had bitten a ten-penny nail in two to show his contempt for King George.[38] It has remained ever afterwards a part of the fable. By his stubborn pride and appalling profanity, he asserted that as "a pioneer prisoner" of the Revolution he taught the redcoats to respect patriot captives. At the dawn of the Revolution he had become a hero in Vermont—by daring to visit Albany and drink a bowl of rum punch in a tavern, it was said, finishing with a hearty "Huzza for Vermont!" in contempt of the £100 price on his head. He had surprised Ticonderoga with the help of Benedict Arnold, and Arnold's later treason left him in sole possession of the glory. Later stories sprang up about his humanity—how he had rescued the "lost children" in the wilds of Sunderland, how he persuaded a timorous woman to have an aching tooth pulled by submitting one of his healthy molars to the operation and exclaiming "Now take courage, madam, from the example I have given you."[39] Yet despite his humanity Ethan Allen's return to Bennington in June, 1778—from his captivity and from dining with General Washington himself—had been celebrated with firing of cannon, deep drinking, and the spectacle of a patriotic hanging reserved for the occasion. Allen himself as special prosecutor helped override an appeal. The victim was one David Redding, found guilty of communicating with the enemy. As he was turned off, the crowd cheered wildly for "America, Vermont, and Ethan."[40] Perhaps it was just as well that these townsmen did not learn in July, 1780, that Allen himself had opened a correspondence with General Haldimand, commander of the British forces in Canada—attempting evidently to drive a bargain by which the 300,000 acres of the Allen family claim would be recognized by the Crown, and Vermont would desert the cause of rebellion.[41] The barter fell through, and Ethan Allen has remained to many people —who are only a little disturbed by his agnosticism—a conventional patriot. To some historians he looks to be one of the few black sheep that have slipped into the fold of American heroes.

In the Deep South it appears that Marion, Morgan, and Light-Horse Harry Lee are now well-nigh forgotten. Civil War idols are more vivid, and have largely supplanted them. If one dare propose a sort of Gresham's Law of hero-currency, it may be remarked that purely sectional heroes tend to drive out earlier ones which were shared more or less by the national sphere. Francis Marion was once the darling of South Carolina. He was a small, spare, dark man with a genius for guerrilla warfare and for rousing warm personal devotion. The Huguenot families, who felt indebted to England for many benefits, were slow in mustering until Marion called them. Gentlemen cheerfully served as privates in the ranks of "Marion's Men," and many soldiers rode blooded horses which had won a cup or bowl. Marion, it was said, never had to ask the government for arms or clothing for his men; plantation blacksmiths hammered swords out of scythes, and women spun and wove for the troops.[42] His camp at Snow Island, with its flickering fires lighting the gloom of giant cypresses and tangled vines, was "just such a spot as Robin Hood might have chosen in old Sherwood."[43] William Cullen Bryant wrote "The Song of Marion's Men":

> Our fortress is the good greenwood,
>   Our tent the cypress tree;
> We know the forest round us
>   As seamen know the sea.

But Marion's men were not plunderers. When after the War an act was introduced before the Legislature offering immunity for any illegal acts committed by his partisans, Marion rose indignantly and said if there were any, he and his men wished to bear the full penalty.[44] The essence of his legend was one of consideration for his soldiers, austerity for himself. The best-known anecdote was that of "the potato dinner," told in biography, folklore, and popular almanac, painted by John H. White, and repeated in most school texts today. A British officer arriving under a flag of truce was invited to stay for dinner; the meal consisted solely of sweet potatoes baked in ashes and served on pieces of bark. When asked if this were his daily fare, Marion replied that, having a guest, he was lucky in being able to provide a better dinner than usual. According to legend, the Briton was so impressed that he gave up his commission and returned to England, full of sympathy for the patriots.

Up to the Civil War the Swamp Fox (as Tarleton had called him) ranked next to Washington as the idol of the South. About 1810 Weems collaborated with Horry, one of Marion's comrades in arms, in writing a life of the hero—Horry supplying the facts, and discovering to his chagrin that Weems was padding them with fantasy. Weems's Marion indulges such sentiments as, "I am in love—and my sweetheart is LIBERTY!" The inevitable parallel is drawn with Washington: "They were·both born in the same year—both lost their *fathers* in early life—both married excellent and *wealthy* ladies—both left widows—and both died childless." Weems was delighted to find that, for a time, this book outsold even his life of Washington. When he boasted of that fact to Horry, the latter drily reminded him, "The price of the one is much less than the other—[that] is the reason."[45] The novelist William Gilmore Simms, who had breathed the hero-worship of Marion from earliest years, launched a saga of seven novels about Marion, beginning with *The Partisan* in 1835—novels of midnight marches, moonlight bivouacs, surprise and defense, flight and capture, showing, as Carl Van Doren has said, "a whole society engaged in Marion's task."

> We follow where the Swamp Fox guides,
> His friends and merry men are we;
> And when the troop of Tarleton rides,
> We burrow in the cypress tree.
> The turfy hammock is our bed,
> Our home is the red deer's den,
> Our roof, the tree-top overhead,
> For we are wild and hunted men.

The Baltimore writer John Pendleton Kennedy; the anonymous author of *Marion's Men,* a novel of 1843; and John Frost in a "pictorial life" of the hero in 1847, helped to feed the cult. Just after the Civil War, Marion was revived briefly along with Moultrie, Sergeant Jasper, Pickens, and Governor Rutledge, to show that Southerners had fought gallantly for the original Federal Union,[46] but his legend was already past its prime.

To call the roll of all popular patriots would take too long. Nathanael Greene, a humble Quaker who had to learn the arts of war from the beginning, in the closing years of the Revolution was thought by many to be Washington's ablest general. His modesty and manly simplicity were praised by poets like Freneau and Barlow, and he inspired five full-length biographies before 1868. Anthony Wayne was a more dashing, if egotistic, figure, "the hero of Stony Point." A march was written in his honor, and later apparently altered to celebrate Washington.[47] In Civil War times, "when we need to renew our love of country at the fountains of Revolutionary patriotism and faith," O. J. Victor—prolific in boys' books and dime novels—wrote a paper-backed life of Wayne, assuring his young readers that the epithet "Mad Anthony" meant only "impetuosity and a daring spirit." Similarly on the eve of the Spanish-American War those two fire-eating historians Henry Cabot Lodge and Theodore Roosevelt, in writing their *Hero Tales from American History*, ranked Wayne next to Washington, and held up to the admiration of youth "his eager love of battle, and splendid disregard of peril . . . his favorite weapon was the bayonet." Other partisans have their favorite heroes. The Friendly Sons of St. Patrick in 1907 erected a monument in Independence Square, Philadelphia, to John Barry, "the father of the American Navy." Jews take special pride in Haym Solomon, "financier of the Revolution." American Poles cherish Pulaski and Kosciuszko, and Germans von Steuben. Lafayette, "America's friend," was by far the most popular hero from overseas. His return in 1824 called forth the greatest American ovation of the age; the venerable patriot "was solicited to hold in his arms at the baptismal font all the infants born during his route, to listen on Sundays to as many different sermons as there were churches of various persuasions, to partake of as many breakfasts and dinners daily as suited the pleasure of the various societies and corporations to invite him to."[48] Lafayette, whose purse was small and who had returned to the New World with misgivings that he might not be able to travel far, was overwhelmed by his reception. To the public he was a *revenant* from the days of Washington, a living symbol of '76. Mrs. Basil Hall, a snobbish Briton observing the United States in 1827, was "sickened" at the eternal pictures—in inns, hotels, private dwellings—of George Washington holding a scroll and of Lafayette "looking like a farmer on a cold day."[49] But even she could not foresee that Lafayette would continue to be a potent symbol in American mythology, at so late a date as 1917.

Mrs. Hall's bitterness against American heroes sprang, to a degree, from her feeling about John Paul Jones. Her husband's grandfather was that Lord Selkirk whose family plate Jones's men had "stolen" in their descent upon the Solway. Jones's apologists have always noted that he restored the plate about eight years later, without damage, "even the tea-leaves remaining in the tea-pot," with a courtly letter of regret to Lady Selkirk. Even Jones, for all his service upon the quarterdeck, was a Revolutionist in the tradition of the embattled farmers. An early ballad shows him addressing his men, free lances like himself, as "we bold buckskin heroes."[50] As the son of a poor

Scotch gardener, who returned as master of a frigate to strike terror to the lords and ladies of his native coasts, he also partook of the Robin Hood motif in its democratic phase. "It is the war of the rich against the poor," he tells a friend in Allan Cunningham's novel *Paul Jones* in 1827, "a crusade for the purpose of enslaving people born as free and rocked in the same cradle as ourselves."[51] In the same book one of his henchmen tersely informs Lady Selkirk: "The proud people of your island, in spite of their long descent and their longer rent-rolls, will soon acknowledge the superiority of western virtue and valour." In a widely read dime novel of 1873, Frederick Whittaker's *The Sea-King,* the stripling Jones takes a brutal scolding from Selkirk, whose daughter he had dared to court, but turns upon his heel saying: "My lord, farewell. . . . You may think that there are no gentlemen but those born in the purple. Before many years are over, my lord, you will see a nation of gentlemen arise across the ocean, that never knew a lord. To that nation I will go; and you, my lord, who supported the stamp duties, will live to see the fairest jewel of the British crown wrenched from it by the hands of those whom you call plebeians. I shall be among them, my lord."[52] The same spirit touched even the sobriety of biography; O. J. Victor's life of the hero, issued in Beadle's Dime Biographical Library in 1861, tells how Jones after allowing the plunder of the Earl's silver by his marauders, captured some poor fishermen off Carrickfergus: "With them were also two infirm men found in one of the prizes, to whom he gave money for their expenses home. The fishermen were also paid for such losses as they had sustained. Such conduct proves that the American commander possessed a truly kind heart."[53]

The only adverse handling of Jones by a fiction-writer, in this respect, comes surprisingly enough from the pen of Samuel Spewack, co-author of *Boy Meets Girl*. In 1928, under the pseudonym of A. A. Abbott, he wrote a novel called *Mon Paul: The Private Life of a Privateer,* in which Jones appears as a rank social snob and toady. Almost all the historical facts are wrong, including the pig-Latin inscription on the sword which Louis XVI gives the captain.

Jones, a man of marked virtues and vices, has lent himself to both praise and blame. His highest virtue was what Americans have long admired as "grit"—sheer tenacious courage. His three-hour fight with the *Serapis,* in a sinking and burning ship with inferior cannon, and his legendary words "I've just begun to fight," make perhaps the most spectacular episode in American naval annals. Of course even this episode has its obverse side as propaganda. A rare volume called *Elegiac Epistles on the Calamities of Love and War,* published in London in 1780, claiming to be written by a seaman on the *Serapis,* tells how that ship—convoying a merchantman whose crew were bringing home tea and coffee-beans for "affectionate wives" and "to preserve an agéd mother's life"—was foully attacked:

> Paul Jones the ruler of the motley crew.
> Heavens! that a man, forgetting nature's laws,
> Should take up arms against his country's cause!
>
> .   .   .   .
>
> "Do you strike?" our gallant Commodore demands:
> No answer's made, and silent are all hands.

Thus the treacherous Americans decoy the British on board, and then assault them in "superior force." Naturally the British hated Jones, and a London biography of him which was reprinted in America and —enjoying the rewards of sensationalism, and at first a monopoly of the field—ran to thirty editions here by 1831, did much to damage his reputation: he seduced three girls in his early youth and made two of them pregnant, and his attempt upon a dairymaid of the Earl of Selkirk laid the basis for his later feud; "after a few more debaucheries and a few more rapes" he took to highway robbery and then piracy; upon the outbreak of war he became "the American corsair," and won his battle against the *Serapis* only because he was "totally ignorant" of the fact that he had been beaten.[54] The last is probably the truest statement in the book. His cruelty, concerning which there is a little sound but not very lurid evidence, is played up in early American biography; a Northern historian as early as 1823 found that it sprang from Jones's youthful service in the slave trade, "this horrid traffick, but it was subsequently ameliorated by association with humane and dignified Americans."[55] His boastfulness, "an inherent quality in great naval commanders," was conceded even by friendly biographers.[56] Also, most of them regretted that Jones after the Revolution had hired himself out to Catherine the Great, in Russia, and thus had lost his amateur status by becoming a mercenary.[57]

Yet in countless ballads, broadsides, chapbooks, and romances Jones flowered into the perfect hero. Cooper in *The Pilot* made him a brave, adroit, darkly brooding gentleman—so moody and taciturn that he seems to bring the sorrows of Werther upon the brine. Alexandre Dumas, Herman Melville, Sarah Orne Jewett, and Winston Churchill

lent him the homage of romance, sometimes revealing him as a
"dreamer," "a poor Scottish lad with a splendid vision."[58] In 1900
Augustus C. Buell published a much-quoted life of Jones, from "new
documents," showing that Jones was a Virginia planter who liberated
his slaves Cato Jones and Scipio Jones, and that in regard to shipboard
discipline Jones once testified "I never punished any man more than
talking to him like a father, or, in extreme cases, stopping his grog
for three days."[59] Six years later Mrs. Reginald De Koven showed
that the entire work was based upon non-existent documents, and
Messrs. Scribner promptly withdrew Buell's book from circulation.
In the meantime General Horace Porter, U. S. Ambassador to France,
had used Buell's fictions to inspire a new devotion to the memory
of this gallant tar. With ardor the Ambassador set to work to find
Jones's body, buried in a leaden coffin in the old cemetery of St.
Louis, somewhere beneath the tenements and drains of modern Paris.
On April 14, 1905, General Porter cabled the Secretary of State:
"Buried in shirt and wrapped in sheet; linen in good condition, bearing a small initial worked with thread, either a 'J' or, if read upside
down, a 'P.' "[60] Although experts have pronounced the identification
"not proven,"[61] General Porter was appointed as "special ambassador"
to bring the body to Annapolis—where it now lies in the crypt of
the United States Naval Academy Chapel. The tomb of marble and
bronze cost $75,000, and is one of the most ornate in America. Whether
the body is that of John Paul Jones or not, it remains as a permanent
inspiration to the midshipmen.

CHAPTER SIX

PRESIDENT WASHINGTON AND PARSON WEEMS

Perhaps the reason little folks
    Are sometimes great when they grow taller,
Is just because, like Washington,
    They do their best when they are smaller.
                                    —School recitation.

I

I N HIS early twenties George Washington began to be talked about in Europe. In London in 1754, when he was a militiaman of twenty-two, was published the report he had made to Governor Dinwiddie after his journey to Fort Le Bœuf, through a wilderness of snows and black icy streams. He had mapped the country, given a matchcoat and a bottle of rum to an Indian queen, to build good will for England and Virginia against France. Again, in August of that year, readers of the *London Magazine* perused a boyish letter this Washington had written to his half-brother from Great Meadow, after a first skirmish with the French and Indians: "I heard the bullets whistle, and, believe me, there is something charming in the sound." According to Horace Walpole, George II read this letter of his young subject with the comment, "He would not say so, if he had been used to hear many."

In fact, the green soldier's exuberance was short-lived. Before his words were printed he had already tasted the first of many defeats. To the flag of France he had been forced to surrender Fort Necessity, and to sign a paper in which his ignorance of French betrayed him into admitting the "assassination" of an ensign named Jumonville, supposedly a peaceful scout, in the earlier skirmish. Washington had taken no chances with Jumonville, and from a military point of view his act was not unjustified. But in Paris, with great éclat, his captured journal was published after a little judicious doctoring—and "le cruel Wasinghton" became a nine days' wonder. The British of course defended him stoutly, at least until the Revolution, when a Tory printer in New York named Rivington brought forth an epic poem recalling Washington's "assassination" of this fine young Frenchman. Propaganda is always a flexible sword.

The average American today has never heard of Jumonville, or how Washington at a precocious age provoked an international incident. The issue is too complex to fit readily into the Washington legend. Most people, however, know something of his next step into the limelight. That took place with Braddock's defeat in 1755. Popular tradition—always a little less than fair to a future hero's rivals—pictures Braddock as a fool in scarlet, swaggering through the forest, scornful of Washington's warning against ambush until too late. Braddock was a man of honest worth, and also very brave. But Washington, still weak from a bed of fever, was equally brave. Two horses were killed under him, and four bullets tore through his coat. Folklore says the Indians decided he was under the care of the Great Spirit; certainly Washington began to believe in his guiding Providence, holding fast to that faith through the Revolution's darkest days. At this early date, too, the exaggerations of myth entered Washington's life; promptly he had to write home to deny "a circumstantial acct. of my death and dying speech." A glimmer of the theatre already played about him.

Washington's part in salvaging Braddock's shattered troops left him with considerable prestige, especially among native Virginians. Here was a man who had come to the help of professionals from overseas. The Governor made him a colonel, and commander-in-chief of all Virginia troops—some 300 men, whose task was to defend 300 miles of frontier. He was clearly Virginia's best home-grown soldier, at a time when the military was supremely important. Thus responsibility settled early upon his manly shoulders, giving him sober ways. Henceforth, it seemed, he was duty's man.

The British regulars were prone to be jealous of this rising youth, in his spotless buff and blue uniform of militia. Some tried to snub him, overriding his authority. To get his rights, Washington had to travel on horseback to Boston in 1756. His budding fame made New Englanders like the Adamses put him down as a Virginian worth watching. Restlessness was in the air, and some day they might need a Southern ally who could fight. Years later, after that day had come, Tories and personal enemies of Washington recalled his youthful friction with the redcoats, and hinted it was the mainspring of his zeal for Independence. Near the close of his Presidency, the editor William Duane sneeringly observed, to Washington, "that had you obtained promotion . . . after Braddock's defeat, your sword would have been drawn against your country." It was the closest that foes could come to impeaching the motives of Washington as patriot.

This young man loved soldiering. The cavalier traditions of Virginia had prepared him for it, as well as the passion for discipline and precision in his own soul. His orders from booksellers, in the years between Fort Necessity and the Revolution, show that he read chiefly two classes of books—those about war and those about practical farming. Young Washington was no saber-rattler, but in the pattern of military life—with its sense of mastery, its quiet planning of objectives, its scrupulosity of code and dress—he discovered an æsthetic satisfaction which others found in music or mathematics. He had the serious-minded aristocrat's habit of taking charge of things, of looking after and worrying about those in his charge. Worry early became a trait of Washington's mind. But, with all his frosty young dignity and insistence on perfection, Colonel Washington inspired hero-worship among his men. When in December, 1758, they heard he was retiring, in order to marry Mrs. Custis, they drew up a "humble Address" from "your most obedient and affectionate officers," revealing the role of foster father which this stalwart of twenty-six had already established: "In our earliest Infancy you took us under your Tuition, train'd us up in the Practice of that Discipline, which alone can constitute good Troops, from the punctual Observance of which you never suffer'd the least Deviation." Such phrases, as well as the closing ones about "Sentiments of true Honor and Passion for Glory," are touched with the rhetoric of chivalry that Virginians have always loved. In his native province, therefore, and to lesser degree in the colonies at large, Washington early began to be admired as the perfect soldier.

But he was never the pure militaristic type. Even between youth and ripe age there was a marked difference—bridging the time when he assured Fitzhugh that "my inclinations are strongly bent to arms," and the later day when he told his countrymen that the deepest wish of his heart was to see the pestilence of war swept from the earth. Under success, he reached the disenchantment with his first love that another Virginia soldier, Robert E. Lee, discovered in defeat. But at all times Washington had other keen interests. One of them was politics. He had been defeated for the House of Burgesses in 1755 and 1757, but won out in 1758 and was re-elected steadily thereafter. With his sense of public responsibility, he served from 1764 to 1770 as a justice of Fairfax County. In public life, Washington won everybody's respect, although he lacked fluent and brilliant gifts, and as a speaker never outgrew a heavy, somewhat clumsy manner. But his consuming passion was the soil. As a boy of sixteen he had bought, with his first surveying fees, the "Bullskin plantation"—even as a lad in the machine age might acquire his first flivver—and in the course of his life went on to accumulate some 62,000 acres. Mount Vernon, which came to him after the death of his half-brother Lawrence in 1752, was the proudest possession he ever had.

Sowing and reaping, planting and grafting, riding over the springy turf or along fields of green tobacco and rippling grain—these too were æsthetic delights. "Agriculture has ever been the most favorite amusement of my life," he wrote after the Revolutionary campaigns were done, when visitors coming away from Mount Vernon were thinking that his chief pride was to be known as America's first farmer. A silver cup which he received at this time from an agricultural society in South Carolina, "as a premium for raising the largest jackass," is still displayed among his trophies in the museum of Mount Vernon. His tastes and sports—fishing, hunting deer and pheasants, riding to hounds, acting in amateur theatricals, eating watermelons on the veranda of Mount Vernon, dancing with a stamina that sometimes lasted for three hours without pause—were those of a leisured rural society. Washington to the American mind has long represented "the country gentleman"—whose portrait by Gilbert Stuart is the perennial trade-mark of a magazine by that name.

With the passing years, Mount Vernon and Washington's nostalgia for it came to symbolize the purity of his patriotism. From his colonial campaigns, from the Revolutionary War, from eight years of the Presidency, he quit the life of power—the career of professional soldier, of potential dictator—to go back to his farm. Even as his military policy of watchful waiting gave Washington the title of "Fabius," so his character of farmer-patriot stamped him for that classical generation as "Cincinnatus." The ancient Roman left the furrow to take up arms for his country, and then with the selflessness unknown to all dictators, with duty fulfilled returned to the plow. The idea appealed deeply to America's distrust of the military idol, and her frank liking for a man ready to bow before popular self-government. The renunciation crowned the finished task. In the Renaissance, Sir Thomas Elyot in *The Governour,* after meditating on the example of Cincinnatus had concluded that "nobility" is innate, that it is quite independent of election to office or the trappings of authority. This, Americans came eventually to feel about George Washington. Early and late, from the buckskin wilderness to the magistracy of a new republic, he showed that he used responsibility well. To its abuses he never succumbed. And thus—although the word "democracy" was foreign to his vocabulary—he set the pattern for romantic democracy in the United States. To a world which remembered other self-made leaders of empire like Alexander and Cæsar, and even then looked upon the rising star of Bonaparte, this fact made Washington unique. It was the cardinal fact in his herohood. Byron drew that contrast, in writing of

> the first—the last—the best—
> The Cincinnatus of the West,
> Whom envy dared not hate,
> Bequeathed the name of Washington,
> To make man blush there was but one.

II

Certain glacial traits made Washington a rather surprising hero for a race whom Europeans are prone to think nervous and mercurial. Emerson, in 1852, after studying for some days the portrait of Washington that he had hung in his dining room, wrote in his Journal of its "Appalachian strength": "The heavy, leaden eyes turn on you, as the eyes of an ox in a pasture. And the mouth has gravity and depth of quiet, as if this MAN had absorbed all the serenity of America, and left none for his restless, rickety, hysterical countrymen." No doubt, in the noon of Emerson's life America had grown more febrile than in the eighteenth century—but even among his peers Washington was singular in his massiveness of character, his static rather than kinetic energy, his patient endurance and fixity of aim.

Beside him, John Adams seemed fretful, Patrick Henry volatile, Thomas Jefferson impulsive. Like a glacier, Washington appeared at times to move slowly and also to be ice-locked in a reticence that inspired more admiration than love. To us, however, his reticence is more baffling than it was to his own time. Sentimentalists, cynics, and psychoanalysts have tried to penetrate Washington's "secret." This age of self-expression often mistakes reticence for apathy, assuming that Washington had no deep emotions or that he was hopelessly repressed. We fail to remember the standard of good form held up to eighteenth-century gentlemen, who practised certain arts of self-effacement now forgotten. And the Southern gentleman, like Washington, though less cramped in his social habits, was more shy of baring his soul than was the introspective Yankee.[1] His diaries—first published in 1925, to reveal the preoccupations of farm and social life, and an infrequency of church attendance that shocked some people—are quite different from the corresponding records of soul-probing, analysis of human motives, and eager pursuit of ideas penned by the great New Englanders. Spiritual nudism would have shocked Washington.

Because of his slow dignity, joined to method, efficiency, and punctuality, Washington never appeared to be hurried. Some thought him a plugger, or downright lazy. But in good time he accomplished all things, with the same irresistibility of a glacier. This shows clearly in his attitude toward the Revolution. Herbert Agar and other moderns have remarked that on May 30, 1765, the day of Patrick Henry's fiery tocsin against George III, in the House of Burgesses, Washington's diary offers only the calm remark, "Peter Green came to me a gardener," and the next day observes, "Cut my clover for hay." They fail to note the fact that he did not even hear Henry's speech, having placidly left Williamsburg for Mount Vernon. But, as his correspondence reveals, he had clean-cut opinions about issues of the day. The Stamp Act he opposed, as a method of picking the citizen's pocket without his consent, but upon the hysterical violence of the Boston Tea Party he looked with disapproval. Similarly in April, 1768, on the day of "the great remonstrance" Washington was absent from the meeting of the Burgesses; he and Posey and other jolly companions were riding after a fox. But ten days later he did set forth for Williamsburg, and in his mind soon crystallized the decision—with a clarity unknown to many of his fellow patriots—that compromise was futile. He was always an authoritarian, to whom the civil power came first. But with single-mindedness Washington changed his sincere allegiance to the King for an equally staunch devotion to American freedom. Abruptly convinced that the Crown no longer fostered liberty in America, he did not hesitate to scrap the lesser for the greater loyalty. In liberty he had a simple, elemental faith, which became inwoven with his religious ideas. It was approved by God, and therefore must prevail. Hence his serenity in disaster, and the morale that Washington —a leader who lacked eloquence and thrilling personal charm—could still infuse into a shaky cause, and into an essentially minority movement that never enlisted more than one-eighth of all able-bodied Americans.[2]

After serving as a Virginia delegate to the First and then the Second Continental Congress, this silent man who sat quietly in uniform was made Commander-in-Chief on June 15, 1775. The choice was inevitable. Unlike Israel Putnam and other local sons, he was there in the flesh, and Washington's presence was always compelling. He was known to be America's best soldier, a man of solid judgment. He had the prestige of wealth, gained by his own efforts and by marriage. His selection would also consolidate the South behind a cause in which New England lawyers, merchants, and politicians had taken perhaps a too conspicuous part. Tradition says that Washington remarked to Patrick Henry, "This day will be the commencement of the decline of my reputation." He knew how invidious his position was, how brief might be the honeymoon of any leader in a republic. But for the time being, everybody except the secretly envious John Hancock was delighted with this tall, handsome, reassuring leader. Most of the Massachusetts men worked hard for his election. They were impressed with his riches, and his refusal to accept any salary. "There is something charming to me in the conduct of Washington," wrote his nominator, John Adams. "A gentleman of one of the first fortunes upon the continent, leaving his delicious retirement, his family and friends, sacrificing his ease, and hazarding all in the cause of his country!" These words were addressed to Elbridge Gerry, who from far away began to write of him as "the beloved Colonel Washington."

"Under the old elm" of song and story, at Cambridge on July 3, 1775, Washington took command of his troops. The unknown Tory satirist who wrote "The Trip to Cambridge," tried his best to make fun of the new leader, "the country's papa," "all clothed in power and breeches" as he rode up on a dappled donkey. But the arts of caricature —successful enough with the eccentricities of later heroes like Andrew Jackson and Lincoln and Jefferson Davis—fell flat before the smooth, well-groomed dignity of Washington. His features offered as little opportunity to ribald distortion as did those of Robert E. Lee.

It was fortunate that the Massachusetts men who had sponsored Washington were not able to read the fastidious Virginian's opinion, in a letter to Lund Washington, that the New Englanders "are an exceedingly dirty and nasty people." (Yet strangely enough, on August twenty-second in his General Orders, Washington at Cambridge had to reprimand these sons of Puritans for their careless bathing, "running about naked upon the Bridge, whilst passengers, and even Ladies of the first fashion in the neighbourhood, are passing over it.") Later, in 1777, British propaganda produced some forged *Letters from General Washington* in which he was made to praise New England soldiers at the expense of the Southerners—"cool, considerate and sensible, whilst we are all fire and fury"—with the intent of breeding dissension. The other tack might have been far more successful, for the issue of Washington's snobbery toward Yankeedom smoldered through the later years of the War. Meanwhile, Washington's triumph in forcing Howe to evacuate Boston in March, 1776, confirmed him, for a season, as the idol of the Bay State. Harvard made him a Doctor of Letters, and the Massachusetts legislature gave him a public dinner, with an address of thanks, at the Bunch of Grapes tavern.

He began to figure in poetry and drama, with associations of Roman heroism not unlike those of Addison's *Cato*—Washington's favorite play in amateur theatricals, one whose rhetoric he loved to quote.[3] His stiff integrity had a Roman quality, as artists and orators quickly sensed. And the cause for which he fought recalled those patriots who cradled the republicanism of early Rome. Philip Freneau wrote of Washington,

> Bold in the fight, whose actions might have aw'd
> A Roman Hero or a Grecian God.

David Humphreys and Jonathan Mitchell Sewall rhymed in the same vein, their favored epithet being "the god-like Washington," their tone an insistence upon his antique dignity. In John Leacock's turgid play, *The Fall of British Tyranny,* written about the time of the fall of Boston, Washington is the majestic *deus ex machina,* though dull of speech in comparison with Ethan Allen, Putnam, and Charles Lee; only after five gouty acts does Washington warm to a little fervor and exclaim, "I have drawn my sword, and never will sheathe it, till America is free, or I'm no more." Patriot artists resented any lukewarm appreciation of Washington's excellence. A Boston play called *The Motley Assembly*, which has been ascribed to that republican bluestocking Mercy Warren, draws a scene from high life in which Mrs. Flourish bridles at Captain Aid's toast to "godlike, glorious Washington":

Mrs. Flourish. Why, he is no more than man, Captain Aid.

Aid. Then all mankind beside are less, madam.

Mrs. F. You have not seen all mankind, sir. I believe Mr. Washington, or General Washington, if you please, is a very honest, good kind of a man, and has taken infinite pains to keep your army together, and I wish he may find his account in it. But doubtless there are his equals—so say no more.

Aid. If you meant that as a compliment, madam, it is really so cold a one, that it has made me shiver. I will, therefore, with your leave, drop the subject, and take another glass of wine.

Similarly, Francis Hopkinson wrote of a Tory lady who loved to lisp the titles and dignities of the peerage, "whilst 'Captain A. the tailor,' 'Colonel B. the tavern-keeper,' and even 'General Washington the farmer,' only created contempt. But I am persuaded, if some Indian chief, with a long Cherokee or Mohawk name, had commanded our armies, she would have thought much more respectably of the American cause." Hopkinson himself, in January, 1777—after Washington had lost New York, but atoned by the brilliant victories of Trenton and Princeton—wrote of his idol:

To him the title of Excellency is applied with peculiar propriety. He is the best and the greatest man the world ever knew . . . neither depressed by disappointment and difficulties, nor elated with a temporary success. He retreats like a General, and attacks like a Hero. Had he lived in the days of idolatry, he had been worshipped as a God.[4]

Devotion to George Washington had already become a cult, a chip on the shoulder.

To the public at large, and to Congress, Washington's prestige fluctuated sharply. The withdrawal from Long Island in September, 1776, and the rout at Kips Bay—when, according to an unreliable tradition begun by the Reverend William Gordon, Washington in fury snapped his pistol and flourished his sword against the cowardly Americans, while his aides had to drag him back from advancing alone against the enemy—cost him some public confidence. The loss of Fort Washington, and the retreat through the Jerseys, added to the doubts of those for whom nothing succeeds like success. But through the gathering gloom, on Christmas night, 1776, Washington roused his dispirited army, crossed the Delaware, and fell upon the Hessians, reputed the best soldiers of Europe, with devastating effect. To clinch this victory of Trenton, he struck decisively again at Princeton, before settling into winter quarters. Trenton, though a battle of minor military results, has always stirred the American imagination. The true military hero, whether in success or failure, must have a sense of drama: Nelson and Napoleon both had it in transcendent degree, Lee had more of it than did Grant, Pershing has had almost none. Washington, at Trenton and at Yorktown, showed the careful preparation, electrified by audacity, of which he was capable at his best. An exultant country first sensed that a genius was in command. The ice and snow, the darkness and drunken stupor, the brilliant surprise attack, the panic of a thousand prisoners, make an incomparably good story. Poets quickly warmed to the occasion—

> Where the great chief, o'er Del'ware's icy wave,
> Led the small band, in danger doubly brave,

began the strains of Colonel Humphreys, while the Reverend Wheeler Case wrote:

> A storm of snow and hail the Lord sent down,
> A blessed season this for Washington:
> He now return'd, and thro' the storm he press'd,
> And caught twelve hundred Hessians in their nest.

Today, the episode is inseparable from Leutze's painting. Its accuracy, of course, leaves much to be desired. In 1932 the Bicentennial Commission published a catechism of "Questions and Answers" by Congressman Sol Bloom, which contained this comment:

Q. Is the Leutze picture of George Washington Crossing the Delaware, in the Metropolitan Museum of Art in New York, authentic?

A. This picture is not authentic because it shows the American flag which was not adopted until the following year. Also, it shows Washington standing in the boat. While there is no evidence available to prove that Washington did not stand in the boat, it is much more likely that he was seated.

This picture, which aptly furnishes the background to Grant Wood's painting, "Daughters of Revolution," belongs to the heroic sentimental. Even more unreliable, on the left-hand side of folklore, is a tradition about Washington and "the obscene anecdote he told that night in the boat crossing the Delaware."[5]

Washington's glory was now on the crest of the wave. Congress, regaining its self-assurance after a hasty evacuation from Philadelphia, gave him the powers of a dictator for six months. Recruits now began to arrive in a steady stream. Washington tried to season this green timber into hardiness during the winter and spring. But summer and early autumn brought the wane. In September, 1777—after Brandywine, most criticized of all Washington's maneuvers—his prestige plummeted to a new low. His temperament, like that of Stonewall Jackson and Grant and other born soldiers, had a curious rhythm: of inspiration and fierce energy followed by the doldrums, of magnetic rages succeeded by moods of numbness. That Washington could not always be at his best the public failed to understand. Washington himself, fortunately, made no fetish of success or omen of failure. He took both in his stride. Up to Yorktown, in fact, the successes in his life were outnumbered by the failures—as a young fighter in the French and Indian Wars who never won a real battle, as a man disappointed in his dream of empire-building in the West, as the loser of New York and Philadelphia during the first two years of the Revolution. But he had risen to prestige over failures. His doggedness, lack of bitterness against men and circumstance, and inner serenity were reassuring. Those who knew him best shared Washington's own faith in himself. But those who knew him little, or whose eyes were jaundiced by envy, began to doubt.

"O Heaven!" prayed petulant John Adams in his diary, "grant us one great soul! One leading mind would extricate the best cause from that ruin which seems to await the want of it." Even before Washington's defeats at Brandywine and Germantown, on the floor of Congress Adams had rebuked "the superstitious veneration that is sometimes paid to General Washington," with allusions to graven images that came naturally to any scion of the Puritans. Massachusetts, indeed, had heard whispers of Washington's private criticism of her soldiers. Now she turned against him. In the later autumn of 1777, after the contrast of Gates's lucky victory at Saratoga, Washington's standing dropped to the lowest in his whole career. Among his subordinate officers, in Congress, and in Anglo-American circles abroad, a dark intricate plot took shape, the so-called Conway Cabal. To some it meant the elevation of Horatio Gates to commander-in-chief, to others it hinted appeasement with England and a craven peace. And to all involved in these backstairs intrigues, Adamses and Lees and other names since revered in American patriotism, it promised the humiliation of George Washington. Eventually the scheme collapsed, through bungling and bad timing. But under fire Washington had remained as calm, almost as free from vindictiveness, as did Lincoln in the most crucial days of the Civil War. And Washington, it might be remembered, lacked the safety valve of Lincoln's laughter. In a spirit of ironic politeness he treated with his enemies. Washington's naturally hot temper—which a few men saw, and others inferred from his sandy red hair and steel blue eyes—had been sublimated in the same school of discipline that had changed his innate vanity into a passion for perfection.

Through this same winter of 1777-78 Washington and his men endured the ordeal of Valley Forge. Chilly smoky huts, half-starved and dying men, and bloody footprints in the snow make this episode unforgettable. Orators, artists, and pageant-makers cherish the name of Valley Forge, and visitors long ago made it a national shrine. Here, in Washington Chapel, services are always held on February twenty-second. The popular mind supposes that these hardships were necessary to the cost of the Revolution. But historians know better. Washington's soldiers starved and shivered, while food and clothing were abundant, largely because Congress quibbled with the Commissary Department.[6] The folklore of heroism is selective: it has chosen to forget the stupidity of Congress, as well as the very real but unromantic epidemic of the itch which plagued the Continentals even more miserably than the lack of shoes. The true story of Valley Forge is fine enough, but myth has chosen to embroider it. Washington's known acts at Valley Forge—such as taking great pains for the health and cleanliness of his men, ordering inoculation for smallpox in the winter and the shaving of beards in the spring, arguing his men's welfare in patient letters to Congress, encouraging amateur theatricals and playing at wickets with his officers—are far more characteristic of the man than the one story everybody knows. This is the yarn that a Quaker, named Potts, came upon Washington on his knees in the snow, and listened while the Commander prayed long and fervently. Parson Weems (whose veracity will be examined later) first told the incident in a newspaper article on March 12, 1804, in the Washington *Federalist,* called "The importance of religion." It caught the public eye, and was reprinted elsewhere. Seeing that he had a good story Weems incorporated it into the sixth edition of his life of Washington, in 1808. Henceforth it has been indestructible. That Washington apparently never knelt to pray even in church, but remained standing, did not affect the legend. It was carved in stone in a prominent place over the

old Sub-Treasury building in New York City, and only a decade ago a
Federal postage stamp showed Washington on his knees at Valley
Forge. On the latter occasion Doctor Isaac R. Pennypacker, chairman
of the Valley Forge Park Commission, made a public protest against
this commemoration of a falsehood—but it did no good.[7]

A revealing incident in the hero-worship of the living Washington
occurred on his birthday, at Valley Forge, in 1778. Knowing his love
of music, Procter's artillery band—really just a drum and fife corps—
trudged through ice and snow to serenade him. The General's popularity with his men grew with time and under adversity. Its evolution
may be traced from his assumption of command in 1775, when, as his
accounts show, the thieving soldiery began by stealing his pistols; up
through the mutual appreciation which men and Commander showed
for each other in the darkest days of the Revolution; and finally to
Washington's Newburgh address in 1783, when his opening words,
"Gentlemen, you will permit me to put on my spectacles, for I have
not only grown gray, but almost blind in the service of my country,"
drew tears from many eyes and won him an easy victory over their
discontent. His hatred of the cruelties of war, and reluctance to sacrifice the lives of his men, were known through the years. This does
not mean that Washington was an easy taskmaster. He drove his men
hard. In the frontier warfare of his youth, to discourage desertion, he
had erected a terrifying gallows forty feet high, on which he had
hanged two men—one a two-time deserter, and the other "one of the
greatest villains on the continent." He believed stoutly in flogging, and
practiced it throughout the Revolution. Two hundred and fifty lashes
were considered a fair dose. At Valley Forge, a lieutenant of artillery,
convicted of theft and absence without leave, was discharged after his
sword had been broken over his head—in Washington's opinion, "a
mild punishment."[8] By the military lights of his time, Washington
was severe but not cruel—neither so harsh a disciplinarian as Old
Hickory, for example, nor so gentle as Robert E. Lee. But he was just,
loyal to his men, ever ready to battle for their welfare and comfort.
Even his farewell to Valley Forge held a cheerful note. In May, the
news of the French Alliance arrived. The icy despair of winter was
broken. Washington ordered all military prisoners of the day pardoned, the firing of salutes, the decking of every hat with a nosegay
of blossoms, and the issuing of a gill of rum to every man. The Commander and his boys had endured together, and together they hailed
the sunrise of victory.

During the last phase of the Revolution, homage to Washington followed a rising curve. "Every lip dwells on his praise," wrote young Colonel Alexander Hamilton in 1778, "for even his pretended friends (for none dare to acknowledge themselves his enemies) are obliged to croak it forth." In that year, in Francis Bailey's *Lancaster Almanack* for the coming twelvemonth, he was first called "The Father of His Country." In 1780 in London was published, "under the express sanction of the Duchess of Devonshire," *A Poetical Epistle to George Washington, Esquire,* by Charles Henry Wharton, an American Catholic priest living in England. The proceeds were to go for the relief of American prisoners of war. To Washington it offered a manly if stilted tribute—

> Great without pomp, without ambition brave,
> Proud not to conquer fellow-men, but save. . . .
> Such be my country!—what her sons should be,
> O, may they learn, great Washington, from thee!

More remarkable than the poem was the fact of its publication in a hostile capital. In 1781, Washington's birthday was publicly celebrated for the first time, when the French army paraded in his honor. The capture of Yorktown, the following October, crowned Washington's military career. That historic surrender contains two touches characteristic of Washington, which painting and popular history sometimes remember. The first was his appointment of a substitute to receive Cornwallis's sword, when the British commander on a plea of illness sent it by a substitute. Knowing the value of what the French term protocol, in setting the dignity of the new Republic, Washington insisted always upon wringing the last modicum of respect from the reluctant British. The second was his command that Cornwallis's sword be returned to the defeated general—a touch of gallantry, as we shall see, which folklore later invented for Grant at Appomattox.

For the next fifteen years, very few words were printed or spoken in public, in the United States, against George Washington. "All panegyrick is vain, and language too feeble to express our ideas of his greatness," exclaimed the *Pennsylvania Journal* soon after Yorktown. Everywhere he was hailed as "The Saviour of His Country." Banquets, receptions, balls, triumphal arches, and the scattering of flowers followed him from Virginia to Philadelphia. In that city, where General and Mrs. Washington spent the winter, crowds cheered him through the streets whenever he left his door. Seeing too little of him, they gathered before Charles Willson Peale's house, where the painter had made an exhibit of "transparencies" to honor "the conquering Hero." Washington bore all with patience, dignity, and modesty—even at the Southwark Theatre, where he witnessed a garish illumination of thirteen pillars in honor of the new states. "On the middle column was seen a Cupid, supporting a laurel crown over the motto—'Washington, the pride of his country and terror of Britain.' "[9] Washington and Cupid were a strangely assorted pair. The idiom of the Washington cult is shown well enough in the Connecticut election sermon of 1783 delivered by President Ezra Stiles of Yale:

O Washington! how do I love thy name! How have I often adored and blessed thy God, for creating and forming thee the great ornament of human kind! . . . our very enemies stop the madness of their fire in full volley, stop the illiberality of their slander at thy name, as if rebuked from Heaven with a—"Touch not mine Anointed, and do my Hero no harm!" Thy fame is of sweeter perfume than Arabian spices in the gardens of Persia. . . . Listening angels shall catch the odor, waft it to heaven, and perfume the universe![10]

In December of that year, at Annapolis, on the night before Washington resigned his commission, the Maryland legislature gave a grand ball in his honor. Here Washington received a minor tribute—perhaps an anticlimax after the rhetoric of poets and divines—but one which a gallant Virginia gentleman, a lover of dancing and the company of fair women, may have found more to his taste. All the ladies asked permission to dance with him, and so, with each in turn, the tall grave soldier glided about the floor of the state-house—as an eye-witness says, so that every one "could get the touch of him."

III

One who dips into the panegyric of Washington, between the end of the War and his return to public life in 1787 as president of the Constitutional Convention, gains little impression of the man himself. All is unreal, nebulous, ecstatic. He remains "the godlike Washington."

> Yea,—Fame shall ope for thee her hundred Gates
> While at her Shrine the aspiring Hero waits.
>   E'en to the frigid Pole
> So far thy Deeds of Virtue shall extend,

he was assured in 1784 by a nameless poet whose tribute, in an unpublished manuscript, is now buried among the Washington Papers in the Library of Congress. Song-writers composed marches in his honor (one apparently converting "General Wayne's March" into "Washington's March"), and painters visited Mount Vernon constantly. In a well-known letter in 1785, Washington wrote philosophically to Francis Hopkinson, who had been the means of setting another portraitist on his trail:

> *In for a penny, in for a pound,* is an old adage. I am so hackneyed to the touches of the painter's pencils, that I am now altogether at their beck; and sit 'like Patience on a monument' whilst they are delineating the lines of my face. It is a proof, among many others, of what habit and custom can accomplish. At first I was as impatient and as restive under the operation as a colt is of the saddle. The next time I submitted very reluctantly, but with less flouncing. Now no dray horse moves more readily to his thill than I do to the painter's chair.

Houdon, Sharpless, Charles Willson Peale, Gilbert Stuart, and other artists tried to capture the Washington of these latter years. But even here, in the physical man, he began to suffer the distortion of art. Between 1756 and 1790 he was slowly losing his teeth (frequent toothaches adding to his irritability during the Revolution), until all were gone and artificial dentures took their place. Gilbert Stuart's Washington, by far the most familiar image, owes its pursed severity of lips to these false teeth and to the cotton padding by which the painter tried in vain to restore the structure of gums and mouth. In early portraits Washington was not so grim, even though less brilliantly drawn than by the pink and gray suavity of Stuart. His visage then lacked what a newspaper wag called "the letter-box mouth." The effect of these teeth, and of Stuart's style, upon the Washington of legend is hard to exaggerate. Was he, indeed, a dour man?

"Let your countenance be pleasant but in serious Matters Somewhat grave," Washington as a boy had written, copying in his meticulous hand the well-known *Rules of Civility,* the Emily Post of his day. Gravity, deepened by cares, did make up a large part of Washington's nature. His reserved air, like his big-boned and masterful appearance, stamped him in any company as a silent leader. In comparison with Washington, some other American idols seem almost frivolous—like Jefferson with his gossip, or Lincoln with his droll stories. Washington's majesty no doubt concealed a measure of shyness, even as his deafness in later years encouraged an aloofness of manner. There was a defensive touch in both. He was prone to be forthright rather than tactful, strong of will rather than flexible of mind. He was far less the expedient man, the politician, than were Franklin and Jefferson and even Lincoln.

Washington's rigidity sprang in part from his aristocratic frankness and in part from his scrupulous honesty. Nothing ever made him more furious than an anonymous charge, in February, 1789, on the eve of inauguration, that he had located and laid claim to some of the Fairfax lands as his own. Recent debunking biographers, with very scant success, have tried to make him out a sharp business man. The fairest evidence confirms Washington's aide Tilghman, who called him "the honestest man that I believe ever adorned human nature."

Most eulogists, in fact, have praised his character far more often than his intellect. With sincere modesty, Washington himself said he had inherited "inferior endowments from nature." In old age he tended to bore bright young men, even while they respected him deeply. Alexander Hamilton could not help comparing his own lightning calculations with the tortoise pace of Washington's mind. But, as in the fable, the tortoise had a will to get there. In 1814 that shrewd observer, if not steady friend, Thomas Jefferson, wrote a private estimate of Washington as he knew him. "His mind was great and powerful, without being of the very first order," said Jefferson. He described him as brave, calm, deliberate, prudent, and just; a man of action rather than of reflection; a fluent writer of letters but a poor speaker. And, Jefferson added, he was the possessor of a heart "not warm in its affections."[11]

About Washington's coldness there are several opinions. One often hears the myth that he had no friends, and that through the Revolution he never smiled. Fact contradicts these statements. They have arisen, no doubt, because his public life was and is much better known than his private life. His best friends—the Fairfaxes of his youth, Doctor James Craik and Benjamin Harrison in his middle age, Lafayette, Tilghman, Humphreys, and Alexander Hamilton as the protégés of his riper years—were men who shared something of Washington's personal reticence. More casual acquaintances he held at arm's length. Virtually nobody dared to call him George, up to the debunking biographers of the twentieth century. A familiar story tells that Gouverneur Morris in 1787 boasted to Alexander Hamilton that "he could be as familiar with Washington as with any of his other friends." To win his bet of a supper and wine, Morris walked up to Washington at the next reception, "bowed, shook hands, laid his left hand on Washington's shoulder, and said, 'My dear General, I am very happy to see you look so well!' Washington withdrew his hand, stepped suddenly back, fixed his eye on Morris for several minutes with an angry frown, until the latter retreated abashed, and sought refuge in the crowd. The company looked on in silence. At the supper, which was provided by Hamilton, Morris said, 'I have won the bet, but paid dearly for it, and nothing could induce me to repeat it.' "[12] Later times have felt a similar diffidence in striking an attitude of intimacy toward Washington. His awesome character has either frozen affection into icy admiration, or else has inspired, by way of relief, the folksy tales of Weems or the slanders of cynicism.

Yet in private life Washington played a different part, often ignored by legend. From camp in 1777 a Virginia lady wrote to one of her friends, that when "General Washington throws off the Hero and takes up the chatty agreeable Companion, he can be downright impudent sometimes, such impudence, Fanny, as you and I like."[13] An unpublished letter from Washington to General Walter Stewart, now in the possession of Mr. Philip Schuyler Church, closes with a typical bit of Washington raillery: "Compliments to Mrs. Stewart—tell her that if she dont think of me often, I shall not easily forgive her & will scold & beat her soundly too—at Picquet—the next time I see her." The badinage is not brilliant, but at least is meant well. It belongs to the informal Washington, who loved to play cards and tease the ladies decorously, who spent great sums on silver lace for himself and toys for his stepchildren, who had an epicure's palate for madeira and at one stage of his life smoked long white clay pipes. He was no Puritan, no humorless abstraction of virtues—although his clerical biographers, and the schoolmasters of New England, did their best to make him so for several generations.

An anonymous writer in 1790 found that Washington's smile "was extraordinarily attractive."[14] Of his laughter we hear almost nothing. His sense of humor was neither jovial nor rich in vein; Washington was no Ben Franklin. But the conventional portrait has robbed him of such as he possessed. Among the few contemporaries of Washington who guessed that he enjoyed comic stories, and wrote him the good ones that came along, was the Benedict Arnold of happier days; later, of course, there was no time for comedy. In letters to Joseph Reed and a few other trusted friends, Washington indulged the dry irony, sometimes curling into sarcasm, which best expressed the humor of his mind. "Valiant New Englanders" who aspired to be "chiminey-corner heroes," or the antics of George III, "the best of

Kings, so anxiously disposed to promote the welfare of his American subjects," were topics to which Washington's irony warmed. After the War, the one subject and virtually the only one upon which Washington wrote with humor was the breeding of jackasses. Like most agriculturists he had a Rabelaisian streak. In 1785 the King of Spain sent him a prize jackass, which Washington christened "Royal Gift." Through the months that followed, Washington regaled his good friends and relatives—Bushrod Washington, William Fitzhugh Jr., Richard Sprigg, and Lafayette—with amusing bulletins on the conduct of this animal. A typical passage is that to Fitzhugh, on May 15, 1786:

At present, tho' young, he follows what one may suppose to be the example of his late Royal Master, who cannot, tho' past his grand climacteric, perform seldomer or with more majestic solemnity than he does. However I have hopes that when he becomes a little better acquainted with republican enjoyments, he will amend his manners and fall into our custom of doing business; if the case should be otherwise, I shall have no disinclination to present his Catholic Majesty with as valuable a present as I received from him.

Similarly to Sprigg, on June 28, the solemn husband of petite Martha Washington wrote:

I feel myself much obliged by your polite offer of the first fruits of your Jenny. Tho' in appearance quite unequal to the match, yet, like a true female, she was not to be terrified at the disproportionate size of her paramour, and having renewed the conflict twice or thrice, it is to be hoped the issue will be favourable.[15]

But these aspects of Washington—the ironist on one hand, the broad jester on the other—are unknown to the average American, although he has some glimmerings of the same qualities in Franklin and Lincoln. Officially, then, Washington is denied a sense of humor.

With Washington's domestic relationships, folklore, rumor, and officious meddling began to deal as soon as he became famous. Curiosity has continued ever since. First of all, the public wants to know about his mother. Did he say that he owed all to her, was she proud of him, and did he pillow her declining years? Public interference with Washington's filial bond began as early as 1781, when her complaints of poverty reached the ears of the Burgesses of Virginia, and a movement was started to grant her a pension. Washington, who had not been consulted, was angry and humiliated, and sent word that his mother was well provided for. His only public reference to her occurred on February 14, 1784, in his reply to the Mayor of Fredericksburg, who had spoken of the town as "the Seat of your venerable and Amiable Parent." Washington's invariable custom being to respond to a welcoming address by review of the points it contained, he here acknowledged "the honorable mention w$^{ch.}$ is made of my revered Mother; by whose Maternal hand (early deprived of a Father) I was led from Childhood."[16] From this formal statement, sentimentalists have adduced that she was the guiding star of her son's life, that between them existed an extraordinarily tender love. Weems told how as a boy Washington gave up going to sea because *"she felt her heart would break if he left her.* George immediately got his trunk ashore!" Joel T. Headley, in a pictorial life of Washington in 1859, showed an engraving of "Washington receiving instruction from his mother," as a tiny lad at her knee, and another of "Washington taking leave of his mother" with many tears, when he went to assume the Presidency. In 1894 a monument to her, begun sixty years before, was finished by the women of Fredericksburg, with a dedicatory speech by President Cleveland; inside it were placed some letters, since proved to be unauthentic, describing her flaxen hair and "chekes like May blossoms." In the same generation a Richmond newspaper published a forged letter of George Washington, in which he was made to declare that he had taken his mother's portrait with him to New York and Philadelphia in his Presidency, as a most cherished possession, and had repaired a bullet-hole in the canvas. (No known portrait of Mary Ball Washington survives; it is probable that this letter was written to support the claim of an alleged one.) On Mother's Day, 1931, Congressman Sol Bloom, as impresario of the Bicentennial, broadcast from Arlington an address declaring that "The mothers of men are the link between heaven and earth," citing the highly apocryphal words of this "glorious" mother: "George was always a good boy and deserves well of his country."

Meanwhile, from the seat of the devil's advocate, Rupert Hughes was describing her as "a very human, cantankerous old lady, who, from being a fond taskmaster in her early motherhood, evolved into a trial for everybody. She seems to have smoked a pipe incessantly."[17] Her pipe-smoking, by the way, is an unsupported tradition. It belongs with other yarns from the folklore of Fredericksburg—such as her parsimony in slicing off the top crust of a leg of mutton to serve as a lid for many days thereafter, or Washington's oath after a violent quarrel with his mother that he would never spend another night under her roof (so that in later years he visited her, but always rode away by sunset). So far as is known, these are but the sweepings of local gossip.

The facts are simple and creditable, but not very satisfying to the sentimental. Washington's mother sprang from a less aristocratic and cultivated family than did her husband. A woman of small education who never learned to write or spell correctly, she lived a home-keeping life and probably had little influence on her famous son. After his father's death the boy seems to have passed most of his time with his elder half-brothers—who grew a little vexed at the "trifling objections" she raised when they wished to send him to sea. (If he had always remained the paragon of obedience to authority, praised by Weems, we should have had no Revolutionary leader.) Throughout life, Washington apparently had great respect for his mother, but there is no evidence of affection or love between them. When for example in the winter of 1757–58 the young man fell seriously ill of dysentery, seemingly she never made the short trip from Fredericksburg to Mount Vernon to look after him, though his friends the Fairfaxes were most attentive.[18] In his Revolutionary career she played no part. A tradition that, after Yorktown, a great "ball" was held at Fredericksburg, at which Washington seated his mother on a dais while his officers pressed forward and bowed low over her hand, is pure fiction. In later years, her worry about finances grew into a phobia. The distressful proposal about a state pension was its beginning. Washington's letters and accounts show the substantial sums he sent her, and how he tried to manage thriftily the affairs of her plantation. But, like a miser, she hoarded and complained, rather pitifully writing to her favorite son John Augustine shortly before his death in 1787: "I am borrowing a little Cornn—no Cornn in the Cornn house. I never lived soe poore in my life. Was it not for Mr. French and your sister Lewis I should be almost starved, but I am like an old almanack quite out of date."[19] On February fifteenth of that year, her application to George Washington for a large sum led him to reply sharply that "it is really hard upon me when you have taken every thing you wanted from the Plantation by which money could be raised," whereas he had not even received the nominal rents due him. He advises her to calm down, to give up housekeeping altogether and live with one of her three children. "Candor requires me to say," he adds, that Mount Vernon would not be a happy place for her. Its many visitors would compel her to be dressed all the time, or stay in her room, or else come down in dishabille, which "I should not like, because those who resort here are, as I observed before, strangers and people of the first distinction."[20] It is a sensible but stern letter, wholly out of key with the sentimental worship of Washington. As a contrast, one might glance at *The History of the Bicentennial Celebration* of 1932, which reproduces Ferris's idyllic painting "Washington's Farewell to his Mother," showing the President-elect kneeling for her blessing: "As he stooped for a parting embrace, she felt him slip a purse into her hand. She put it back, raising her head with the old-time pride. 'I don't need it!' she said, . . . 'My wants are few' . . . Time passed, but he lingered to plead tenderly, 'Whether you think you need it or not,—for *my* sake, mother!' "[21] Readers who used to enjoy passages of this kind no doubt were as trustful as those who in 1859 paid hard cash to P. T. Barnum to behold the colored nurse of George Washington, "aged 161 years."

The public also wants to know, who were the loves of George Washington? One painter, of the conventional school, shows Washington and the young widow Martha Custis in love at first sight, standing by the mantelpiece in sedate adoration of each other, while her two darling children play on the floor. But Washington's match in 1759 with her whom he called "an agreable Consort," the richest widow in Virginia as the realists never let us forget, is too bromidic for many tastes. Long ago it became sport to hang illicit passions upon him, the coldest and stateliest of American heroes. This began in London, in *The Gentleman's Magazine* for September, 1775. An authentic letter from General Benjamin Harrison to Washington, dated July 21, 1775, had been intercepted by the British and published correctly in the London *Daily Advertiser*. It was a dullish political news-letter, and some unknown writer for *The Gentleman's Magazine* decided to spice it up, for republication, by the insertion of a paragraph which is not found in the original text as still preserved in official British archives. This paragraph made Harrison tell how he had lately met "pretty little Kate, the washerwoman's daughter . . . and but for the cursed antidote to love, Sukey, I have fitted her for my General against his return." Later, she became an octoroon slave-girl, whom Jefferson or Hamilton was proposing to share with Washington. In still other versions, Washington offers her as a dainty morsel to Jefferson or Hamilton or Lafayette. Even today, many people claim to know somebody who has seen the original letter. Thus propaganda echoes along the whispering-galleries of time. One of the recent debunkers of Washington, the business man and amateur scholar William E. Woodward, swallowed this forgery—with the guileful comment, "Fitted her for what? for doing the laundry, of course."

In 1776 a pamphlet printed in London by one J. Bew, also grounded in forgery, stated that Washington had a Tory sweetheart named Mary Gibbons. She lived in Jersey, and the General was rowed across the Hudson every night by a discreet aide-de-camp. And there are at least three more canards, without the smallest benefit of proof. One declares that Washington at the age of eighteen left Virginia to go to Barbados with his consumptive half-brother because George was "in trouble." In his absence a neighbor girl bore his child, a boy whose surname was Posey. The proof is that Washington helped to pay the schooling expenses of a lad named Posey. But the case is somewhat weakened when we find that he gave such assistance to three Posey boys, and also to their sister Milly, as well as to at least five other deserving children. Were all these Washington's offspring? Then indeed, as has been suggested, a new meaning enters into the title Father of His Country. Still another yarn, often repeated but seldom printed, states that on this trip to Barbados in 1751 Washington, instead of running away from "trouble," ran into it. He had an affair with a married woman, and begat Alexander Hamilton, who, as every one knows, was a bastard. The fact that Hamilton was born at Nevis in 1757 is not easy to explain. Stories of Washington's illegitimate son or sons seem to be pure fabrication; they spring either from political malice, or from the circumstance that Lund Washington, sometime manager of Mount Vernon, did have an illegitimate son, who lived in another state, and was said to resemble the Washingtons.[22] Medical men are interested in a youthful attack of mumps which may have rendered George Washington sterile for life. A final story, perhaps the most wanton of all, states that Washington's fatal illness was the result of his assignation in the snows of December with an overseer's wife. It resembles one of the earlier innuendoes of General Charles Lee, about Washington's liberties with his underlings at Mount Vernon. General Lee, who was something of a traitor and a coward, and had borne Washington's searing rage at Monmouth, had good reason to dislike his commander.

Many admirers of Washington, while rejecting these scandals with a shudder, are romantic enough to play up other stories whose texture is thin as moonshine. In 1748 young Washington wrote a letter mentioning his attraction to some "Low Land Beauty," whose identity is unknown. But at least a dozen Virginia families claim her as ancestress, telling how Washington courted her in vain. His banter about a little girl named Betsy Fauntleroy, and his visit in 1756 to Mary Philipse among the Knickerbocker gentry, have been made into fervent love affairs. A supposed letter from Washington to Sally Cary Fairfax, wife of his best friend, dated September 12, 1758, has caused excitement for two generations. It was printed in the New York *Herald* on March 30, 1877, and sold at auction the next day. The manuscript has never been heard of since, and no competent scholar ever examined it. Its content is not very sensational. The writer makes "an honest confession of a simple Fact," namely that he is in love with a "lady known to you." Some have made the coy inference that this is the recipient herself, though others point out that he may mean his fiancée Martha Custis. Young Washington did admire the charming Mrs. Fairfax, and wrote her chatty letters from the frontier, touched here and there with a stiff style of compliment. And in old age, on May 16, 1798, when she had long been living in England as the toast of London and Bath, he wrote her a letter speaking of "those happy moments the happiest in my life which I have enjoyed in your company." This nostalgia for the old days of visiting between Mount Vernon and Belvoir has been translated, by the romantic, into a sunset avowal of his *grande passion*. It has not been noticed before that, some years earlier, on February 27, 1785, Washington penned almost the same phrase to the lady's husband, George William Fairfax:

> But alas! Belvoir is no more! I took a ride there the other day to visit the ruins. . . . When I viewed them, when I considered that the happiest moments of my life had been spent there, when I could not trace a room in the house (now all rubbish) that did not bring to my mind the recollection of pleasing scenes, I was obliged to fly from them.[23]

In the entire record of Washington's friendship with the Fairfaxes there is nothing more incriminating than the passages here cited. Yet Mrs. Sally Nelson Robins, National Historian of the Colonial Dames, has written: "I consider his early romances but zephyrs to this one crimson whirlwind passion of his life."[24] Bernard Faÿ, that versatile Frenchman, in 1931 wrote a life of Washington built largely around Sally, "the queen of his thoughts," who "could converse in French" and taught him grace. She coddled him in illness, met "the wild surge of his heart" with wise understanding and a little teasing, and remained always "the great love" of his life. Frustrated and ever dreaming of Sally, Washington became a man of immense reserves and silences. Rupert Hughes likewise made much of the heartstricken man who had fallen desperately in love with his best friend's wife. In 1932 a whole novel, Bernie Babcock's *The Heart of Washington,* was devoted to the subject. But it, at least, did not claim to be other than fiction. The apparent truth of the matter is that Washington enjoyed the society of pretty women, polished the art of courtliness like a true Virginia gentleman, and found a satisfactory though hardly inspiring wife in Martha Custis. In the major concerns of his life, it appears, Washington was not much influenced by women. But to some, this is a disappointing story.

About an equally personal matter, the religion of Washington, there was speculation in his lifetime and much fabrication afterward. A weakness for lying is the occupational disease of many clergymen—as the conduct of Weems, Jonathan Boucher, Bishop Meade, and others bears witness, regarding Washington. Such men may have thought that tinkering with truth, in a good cause, carried its own absolution. We shall see the same temptation in preachers who knew Lincoln, Grant and other unchurchly heroes. Many spurious prayers have been written for Washington.[25] Baptists and other sectarians have claimed that he was immersed in the Schuylkill, or sometimes the Delaware, River. One story tells how when the army was encamped at Morristown he called on the Presbyterian dominie, and asked to receive "the Lord's Supper" at its semi-annual observance: " 'Though a member of the Church of England, I have no exclusive partialities.' The Doctor reassured him of a cordial welcome, and the General was found seated with the communicants the next Sabbath."[26] Ironically enough, Washington seems never to have received the Sacrament even in the Episcopal Church. When his Philadelphia pastor scolded him indirectly in a sermon, for this omission, Washington never again "came on the morning of Sacrament Sunday."[27] Through all the trials of his life Washington steadily believed that Providence helped him. His diary shows that he attended church more often in times of stress than of calm. His sense of truth, honor, and justice were bound up with religion, although contrary to myth he appears not to have been a deeply spiritual man. Beyond these statements one cannot go. In public addresses he alluded to God, but never mentioned Christ. How much of orthodox Christianity he accepted or rejected is Washington's secret. Here again his reticence baffles curiosity.

He was, however, singularly tolerant for his times. In drawing up instructions for the expedition against Canada in 1775, he forbade any ridicule of "Popery" among the French Canadians, or indulgence in that favorite Protestant sport of burning the Pope in effigy. "While we are contending for our own Liberty, we should be very cautious of violating the Rights of Conscience in others, ever considering that God alone is the judge of the Hearts of men and to him only, in this case, they are answerable."[28] On various occasions he attended the worship of Catholics, Presbyterians, Congregationalists, Lutherans, Dutch Reformed, and other sectarians. Yet Washington's old-time eulogists, who worked so hard to make him by their separate lights an orthodox Christian, curiously failed to pay homage to Washington the liberal. Not until the Bicentennial speeches and pamphlets of 1932 was much appreciation given to this trait.

IV

So much for the character of the living Washington. The panegyrics, myths, and misstatements already sprouting about it help us, perhaps, to understand the last decade of his life. These years saw the extremes of apotheosis and abuse. Only Lincoln among American heroes can match the full diapason of public emotions, from an angelic choir to hymns of hate, which Washington inspired.

From the green acres of Mount Vernon he was called in 1787 to the Constitutional Convention in Philadelphia. As the First Citizen of the Republic, he was promptly chosen its President. Washington's immense weight of approval had much to do with the ratification of the Constitution. It was inevitable, too, that he should be summoned to fill the first Presidency of the republic. Years before, with horror, he had rejected Colonel Nicola's proposal of a military coup which should overthrow the politicians and give him a crown. To Washington, the civil was ever superior to the military power. Now, when the honor came in constitutional guise and with unanimous acclaim, he accepted it with the misgivings of a tired, ill, debt-ridden man. It was his purpose and duty to build prestige for the office. Washington's versatility was thus put to its final test. To his daring in planning the Revolution, and his tenacity in winning it, was now added the demand for his judgment and political skill in shaping the new nation. If he had failed at any of the three tests, his herohood would have been badly damaged if not destroyed.

With vast popular enthusiasm he was greeted en route to his inauguration, in the spring of 1789. Triumphal arches were erected,
roses strewn in his path by girls dressed in white, and lyrics sung to
Handel's "See the Conquering Hero Comes" and other tunes. The
capital, New York City, gave him the first great ovation of the many
in her history. When he took the oath of office, salutes were fired with
such gusto that broken panes jingled merrily from scores of shop-
windows. A silversmith named Forbes, whose thrift got the best of
him, ran from his shop and begged the captain of artillery to cease
firing. "Who," was the reply, "would refuse a salvo of artillery on
such an occasion for a few paltry squares of window glass?"[29] A Boston
girl wrote home:

I have seen him! and though I had been entirely ignorant that he was
arrived in the city, I should have known at a glance that it was General
Washington: I never saw a human being that looked so great and noble as
he does. I could fall down on my knees before him.[30]

A tour through New England in the autumn of 1789, and one through
the South in 1791, offered contact with popular opinion by "a swing
round the circle" such as later Presidents have made. Washington's
diary shows his imperturbable cheerfulness under mass greeting; but
in comparison with his notes on soils, harbors, and fortifications, little
space is devoted to the songs of welcome, poems, dinners, and flower-
strewings. Other things were more vital than the breath of cheers.
With more than a touch of the aristocrat's pride, he later described
himself as "a mind who always walked on a straight line . . . without
seeking any indirect or left-handed attempts to acquire popularity."[31]
His own gauge of perfection, for George Washington, was more ex-
acting than the public's.

As the first President, Washington was an object of curiosity. The
people did not know what a President should be like, and often referred to him as "His Majesty." Washington in turn tended to be
cold and stiff on state occasions; once, at least, he was publicly criticized for not bowing in the approved way.[32] His conduct of public
affairs—the Indian problem, the Whisky Rebellion, Jay's Treaty, and
other issues—was firm and generally sagacious. With more tact than
might have been anticipated, he maintained for several years the
equilibrium of two brilliant but mutually hostile personalities in his
cabinet, Jefferson and Hamilton. Later, the teetering balance was lost.
Jefferson secretly egged on Freneau and other journalists to attack

the President, who in Jefferson's opinion was growing rigidly conservative, yielding with age to a kind of spiritual arteriosclerosis. In
consequence, Washington began to lean heavily upon Hamilton as
the staff of his weary steps. He accepted Hamilton's financial views,
and ultimately submitted the draft of his Farewell Address to Hamilton's editorship. In a sense, he had become a partisan.

So-called liberals now felt that the Republic had outgrown Washington, that he was unable to keep pace with the march of democracy.
The French Revolution he detested. Its minister Genêt, arriving in
1793, stirred masses of Americans to such frenzy that, as John Adams
later recalled, "ten thousand people in the streets of Philadelphia day
after day *threatened to drag Washington out of his house* and to effect
a revolution in the government." Washington's second inaugural, in
that year, was almost scandalously flat in comparison with his first.[33]
Yet Washington, the supreme military hero, achieved probably the
greatest moral victory of his career in 1795 in resisting the foolish
war with Britain for which so many Americans were clamoring. He
knew how disastrous another war and a military dictatorship would
be to the fledgling nation. Needless to say, this act stirred none of the
old applause that had greeted Trenton and Yorktown. Only in
retrospect does it seem great. At the time it was charged, by Jefferson
and others, that Washington had sold out to England. Jay's Treaty,
whose shortcomings Washington saw as clearly as any but whose
benefits he appreciated, earned hisses for the Administration. The
President himself, bearing the brunt, wrote of "such exaggerated and
indecent terms as could scarcely be applied to a Nero, a notorious
defaulter, or even to a common pickpocket."[34] This was the ingratitude
of republics. In 1796 from Paris, Thomas Paine sent over his *Letter
to George Washington*. He ridiculed "the pompous encomiums he so
liberally pays to himself," and dismissed Washington's Revolutionary
services as "the Fabian system of *doing nothing*. The *nothing* part can
be done by anybody . . . he has not the talent of inspiring ardour in
an army." In public and private relations, said Paine, Washington's
chief traits were apathy and ungratefulness; the President was unwilling to help either France or Thomas Paine, who had languished awhile
in the dungeons of the Terror. Among the posthumous papers of this
firebrand was found "Advice to a statuary who is to execute the statue
of Washington":

> Take from the mine the coldest, hardest stone,
> It needs no fashion: it is Washington.

But if you chisel, let the stroke be rude,
And on his heart engrave—Ingratitude.

Benjamin Franklin Bache, inspired by family resentment of Washington's supposed coolness to Franklin, attacked the President viciously in his newspaper the *Aurora*. "If ever there was a period for rejoicing, this is the moment," he announced in March, 1797, when Washington retired from office. "Every heart in unison with the freedom and happiness of the people, ought to beat high with exultation that the name of WASHINGTON from this day ceases to give a currency to political iniquity, and to legalize corruption." On the floor of Congress, while a committee was drafting a graceful reply to the Farewell Address, a group of dissenters (including the newly elected Andrew Jackson) sturdily refused to vote their thanks to Washington, indulging remarks on his "royal progresses" and snobbish delusions of grandeur. With the exception of Andrew Johnson, says one historian, "no President ever went out of office so loaded with odium as Washington."[35]

With far more weariness than resentment Washington returned to Mount Vernon. He had always driven himself too hard, and was now worn out. It was the good fortune of Lincoln the hero to die in office, at the high tide of success; but Washington's good fortune was to survive past his eight years of office, so that none could ever accuse him of planning to be a dictator. He thus closed a career, as soldier, counsellor, and statesman, that has influenced the pattern of American life more than that of any other man in history. "I am not afraid to go," he whispered in the anguish of a hard death, on December 14, 1799.

The death of a hero generally silences his enemies, who have nothing more to gain from abusing him, and stirs the tardy appreciation of the masses. American practice reverses Voltaire, who said we owe consideration to the living, but only truth to the dead. Thus with Washington. Born skeptics, like his successor John Adams, suspected propaganda even in crape. Years later Adams wrote Jefferson a letter on the "abuses of grief":

The death of Washington diffused a general grief. The old Tories, the hyperfederalists, the speculators, set up a general howl. Orations, prayers, sermons, mock funerals, were all employed, not that they loved Washington, but to keep in countenance the funding and banking system and to cast into the background and the shade all others who had been concerned in the service of their country in the Revolution.[36]

The journalist-poet Freneau, who had roasted Washington as President, brought out two fulsome elegies on his death. Richard Alsop wrote a windy funeral poem of many pages, full of the mannerisms of Mr. Pope. An anonymous lament, "Immortal Washington," avowed

> Of all mankind, the greatest
> Was our beloved Washington.

Throughout the country marched funeral processions. A manuscript now in the Massachusetts Historical Society, a letter from Doctor John Warren to his son, January 11, 1800, sums up the national spectacle:

Funeral processions, Orations, and Eulogies, have every where spoken the anguish of our hearts, in the most impressive language that Sorrow could dictate— In some places an Urn has been conveyed on a Bier, with an Eagle dropping the laurel on the Urn; In others, a monument on a superb pedestal shrouded in black. In this town, the most numerous collection ever known in the place, was formed into a procession.

This was in Boston, home of many "hyperfederalists." In New York, the Masons, Tammany Hall, and the Cincinnati took charge of the great funeral parade on the fourth of January; their lament was printed as a broadside—

> Pious orgies, pious airs,
> Decent sorrow, decent prayers,
> Will to the Lord ascend,
> And move his pity, and regain his love.

The Government ordered a day of mourning in all Christian churches, between Washington's death and his birthday in 1800. Memorial services are known to have been held in nearly two hundred towns, from Maine to Savannah and as far west as Lexington, Kentucky. Hundreds of tributes—newspaper obituaries, orations, essays, acrostics —found their way into print.[37] Before the Massachusetts Legislature, Fisher Ames likened Washington to the purest and best heroes of antiquity. Seeking to crown him with martyrdom William Beers recalled, to the citizens of Albany, that Washington had once more accepted command of the American Army, in 1798, when trouble with France was brewing: "He came, my fellow-citizens—to die in your defence." Some praised him for "scrupulous accuracy [in] accounting for every cent that has ever passed through his hands"; others lauded his industry, his modesty, his selflessness in forswearing "the glow-worm glories of a Crown." The orator of Harvard College,

Doctor Tappan, proclaimed that he belonged to the company "of GODS UPON EARTH." Timothy Dwight of Yale praised his self-sufficiency, citing as a rather curious example that in dying "General Washington closed his own eyes." New England divines and orators, it appears, most often compared him with Moses, leader and lawgiver who died in sight of the Promised Land. Some could not resist the dithyrambs of the Old Testament. "From the blood of the slain, from the fat of the mighty, the bow of George turned not back, and the sword of Washington returned not empty," cried Eliphalet Gillet at Hallowell, Maine. A few touched cautiously on the subject of his religion. "He was a member of the Episcopal Church, consequently a believer in Christianity," announced John Brooks in Boston. In the South, the land of classical oratory, Washington was likened most frequently to Cincinnatus, less often to Leonidas and Fabius. At Alexandria his old neighbors assembled in church on his birthday. A stand of colors under the portrait of Washington received tributes of wreaths from sixteen girls, who as they bestowed their flowers uttered a kind of litany:

1. Thus we offer our tribute to the memory of Washington.
2. The Daughters of America shall long lament thy loss.
3. He was acceptable as the return of Spring.
4. He was ornamental as the flowers of Summer.
5. He was beneficial as the fruits of Autumn.
6. He was terrible to oppressors as the storms of Winter.
7. Washington was a stately oak.
8. Washington as a sun illuminated the Western Hemisphere.
9. The Sun set, and gloom overspread the land.
10. Washington sleeps with his fathers.
11. Let the willow shade his grave.
12. Let the grass mantle it.
13. Let the fragrant herb perfume it.
14. Let the birds of the wood serenade it.
15. Let human voice chant a melancholy dirge.
16. Let the sons of Columbia emulate the character of Washington.

Only a few dissenting voices were heard in the land. Seth Williston, a missionary from Connecticut to the Indians of western New York, preached a sermon on February 22 warning against the idolatry of Washington. And in Brookfield, Massachusetts, the Reverend Peter Whitney did the same, in a discourse called *Weeping and mourning at the death of eminent persons a national duty.*

V

It was inevitable that George Washington should become "forever the model boy next door whom we are urged to emulate and for whom, therefore, affection is difficult and whose conduct we regard with suspicion."[38] His qualities were those of high competence and perseverance rather than brilliance. In business or politics—yesterday, today, tomorrow—Washington's gifts are those which make for success. His achievement seems more logical and less mysterious than that of the poetic, erratic Lincoln. Washington offers us a somewhat attainable ideal. None of us, we know, could be Lincoln. But if we worked very hard and took infinite pains, and always did our duty, we might become little Washingtons. (Without a war and the foundation of a new republic we could not grow into great Washingtons.) He is therefore a silent reproach to our shortcomings. Some of us, especially in boyhood, were inclined to resent this fact.

Besides the perfectionism of Washington himself, there were other things that conspired unfairly to make him into a prig. His was an age of improving literature for the young. In England, books like Thomas Day's *Sanford and Merton,* the pious tales of Hannah More and Maria Edgeworth, the tearful romances of Henry Brooke and Henry Mackenzie, enjoyed an immense vogue. In France, Rousseau and Chateaubriand gazed fondly upon youth, with even more indulgence, as the pattern of moral beauty. Before the late eighteenth century, children had had scanty literature of their own and figured little in an adult world. Now, it was natural that the first attention paid them should be to harness their little lives in the leading-strings of morality. The good child and the bad child became stock types. Most people could not go all the way with M. Rousseau in avowing there was no such thing as a bad child, but felt that traits like truth-telling and cleanliness and obedience ought to be held up for admiration in the new literature. (It is significant that Parson Weems in 1791 began to introduce the books of Hannah More, Henry Brooke, Hugh Blair, and others to the United States; years later he wrote to his publisher, Carey, "Humanity and Patriotism both cry aloud, Books, Books, Books.")

Furthermore, the clergy—whose vital role in fanning the flames of the American Revolution must not be forgotten—were strongly on the side of Washington. He was a great patriot, and a "safe" man rooted deep in the economic and ecclesiastical *status quo.* And so he remained in later years, when Mr. Paine and Mr. Jefferson were airing heresies dangerous to church and state. Schoolmasters and textbook writers were also prone to be on the side of General Washington. Young Noah Webster in "The News-Boy's Address to His Customers," printed in 1790, praised him, "as wise as Solon, strong as Hector," in verses which sometimes gasped for rhyme:

> But soon a general States' convention,
> With much lov'd Washington the bench on,
> Proposed a federal government
> To all the States for their consent.[39]

The New England Primer of 1794 inculcated the letter *W* with

> By Washington
> Great deeds were done,

supplanting the earlier couplet

> Whales in the Sea
> God's Voice obey.

In other schoolbooks, woodcuts of King George disappeared in favor of George Washington or local patriots like John Hancock and Sam Adams. The new nation was forging new loyalties. A noted New York doctor, Samuel Latham Mitchill, later explained how he had revised his family's nursery rhymes by dropping all reference to the King, "with whom we have nothing to do," so that an old favorite ran—

> When the pie was opened
> The birds they were songless;
> Was not that a pretty dish
> To set before Congress?

Less innocently, it is reported, the Nazis today have revised the old fairy tales of German children, to accord with their race and national mythologies.

The Child's Instructor, published in Philadelphia about 1792, told of a five-year-old prodigy named Billy, who bidden by his mamma to say a speech for the ladies, began: "Americans! place constantly before your eyes the deplorable scenes of your servitude, and the enchanting picture of your deliverance. Begin with the infant in his cradle; let the first word he lisps be WASHINGTON."

In the spread of the new Washington lore there was still another factor. The cardinal acts of Washington's life—in the Revolution, the Federal Convention, the Presidency—were recent and fixed in sober history. Everybody knew them well. Moreover, Washington's deeds in battle or campaign were less spectacular than those of Greene, Wayne, or Marion. The embellishment dear to hero-legend had thus to seek other stuff than the *gestes* of a Charlemagne or Arthur. Instead, it turned to his childhood, the least known period of his life, and also to his character. Traits of honesty, truthfulness, courage, generosity, and piety as illustrated by anecdotes of youth made the ideal blend of myth and panegyric.[40] Hence, in the hands of a man like Weems, George Washington emerged not as a military idol or profound statesman, but as a Sunday School hero.

Mason L. Weems, the nineteenth child of a Scotchman who had come down in the world, had to make his own way in life and knew it. Profit was never long absent from his thoughts. At first he had taken the unpromising path of the Episcopal ministry. Itinerant in his clerical calling, as well as in the side-line of book peddling, he contrived to preach several times at Pohick Church, not far from the Washingtons. So far as is known, he never met Washington, although Weems did receive from him in 1799 a polite acknowledgment for the dedication, to the General, of *The Philanthropist; or, A good twenty-five cents worth of political love powder*. (Beginning in 1809, Weems styled himself "Formerly Rector of Mt. Vernon Parish." On July 10, 1816, from New Holland, Pennsylvania, Weems wrote his friend Carey that he had preached "to a host of good Dutch People, who are mightily taken with me for having been Chaplain to the Great Gen[l] Washington, and the writer of his wonderful Life.") A jack-of-all-trades with a hungry look, Weems lived by projects and enthusiasms. In 1792 he had drawn some notoriety to himself with his first tract, entitled, *Onania;* Weems had a penchant for addressing himself to the moral problems of adolescence. On his travels he carried a puppet show and a violin, and was in demand at country dances. Later he wrote a temperance pamphlet, and sold it "like hot-cakes" in tavern bars after imitating the antics of a drunkard.

The most profitable idea of his life came to him in the summer of 1799. He resolved to write a book about the greatest living American, "artfully drawn up, enliven[d] with anecdotes, and in my humble opinion, marvellously fitted ad captandum gustum populi Americani!!!" as he wrote the publisher Carey. He sketched a crude frontispiece, with the inscription:

> Go thy way old George. Die when thou wilt
> We shall not look upon thy like again.

Six months later Washington did die, and Weems hastily revised his manuscript, changing present to past tense. Promptly in 1800 it was published. "We may sell it with rapidity . . . it will be the first," he wrote Carey in January. With mounting excitement he saw it become a best-seller, and swing into edition after edition. "The people are tearing me to pieces," he wrote frantically to his publisher, later pausing to mourn: "You know I let my Washingtons escape me 50 pr cent shorn of their retail fleeces." On another occasion he wrote solemnly: "God knows there is nothing I dread so as Dead stock, dull sales, back loads, and blank looks. But the Joy of my soul is quick & clean sales —Heavy pockets, and light hearts."[41] In all, there were fifty-nine editions before 1850, and seventy-nine up to 1921. It became the second best-seller of its generation in the United States, and even Germany called for four editions.

Weems constantly tinkered with and amplified his text. The late Paul Leicester Ford showed how Weems tried out his Washington anecdotes in the newspapers—sometimes in advertisements for Chief Justice Marshall's ponderous four-volume life of Washington, which Weems boosted in the realization that it was no rival—and incorporated in the next edition those yarns which seemed to strike public fancy. Naïve though he was, Weems knew the ways of ingratiation. A letter from him to the master of Monticello, now among the Jefferson manuscripts in the Library of Congress, dated February 1, 1809, calls attention to the seventh edition: "Your Excellency should be pleas'd to find that I have not, like *some* of his Eulogists, set him up as a Common Hero for military ambition to idolize & imitate—nor an Aristocrat, like others, to mislead & enslave the nation, but a pure Republican whom all our Youth should know . . . I shall heartily thank you for a line or two in favor of it—as a School book."

In this classic he remarked that George Washington was the issue of a second marriage, "a circumstance which ought, in all conscience, to quiet the minds of those who have their doubts with respect to the lawfulness of second marriages." Without known proof, he told how young George threw stones or silver dollars across the Rappahannock. ("A physical impossibility," Congressman Sol Bloom announced at the Bicentennial, although Walter Johnson the baseball pitcher later convinced him he was wrong.) These feats—like Washington's taming of a wild horse, told in the doubtful memoirs of G. W. P. Custis— belong to the youth of any legendary hero. Hercules and Alexander were also stout lads. The mythical schoolmaster Hobby, who "between

his knees laid the foundation of George Washington's greatness,"
appears to be a joint creation of Weems and of Jonathan Boucher.
Boucher, a clergyman who held a grudge against the Washingtons
because of their refusal to send "Jacky" Custis on a grand tour of
Europe with him, added the detail that Hobby was a convict. Weems
loved sentimental stories. One of his vivid scenes tells how little
George's father reproved the boy for not sharing an apple with his
cousin, by showing him an orchard which God's abundance had
loaded with apples:

Poor George could not say a word; but hanging down his head, looked
quite confused, while with his little naked toes he scratched in the soft
ground . . . then lifting his eyes, filled with shining moisture, to his father,
he softly said, "Well, Pa, only forgive me this time; and see if I ever be so
stingy any more."

In harmony with the code of grown-ups in Weems's time, rather than
the boys' own code, the biographer told how George, when quite a
big lad (just before he quitted school), would tell the teacher on his
playfellows who got into fights. George would rebuke the fighters
themselves with these words: "And what must be the feelings of our
tender parents, when, instead of seeing us come home smiling and
lovely, as the JOY OF THEIR HEARTS! they see us creeping in
like young blackguards, with our heads bound up, black eyes, and
bloody clothes." Later generations, inclining to the boys' point of view
in regard to tattling, have contrived to drop this fable from the remembered myths of Washington. Truth-telling, on the other hand,
is perennially recommended; therefore Weems's most famous yarn
is still current.

This of course is the cherry tree story, which first appeared in 1806
in the fifth edition. In this edition, for the only time, Weems calls
the instrument of havoc a "little" hatchet. The boy did not fell the
tree, but "barked [it] so terribly, that I don't believe the tree ever got
the better of it." The scene between father and son is ever delightful:

"I can't tell a lie, Pa; you know I can't tell a lie. I did cut it with my
hatchet."
"Run to my arms, you dearest boy," cried his father in transports, "run to
my arms; glad am I, George, that you killed my tree; for you have paid me
for it a thousand fold. Such an act of heroism in my son is more worth than
a thousand trees, though blossomed with silver, and their fruits of purest
gold."

The source of this, the most popular story in American biography, is a puzzle. Weems states that he had it of an "aged lady," "a distant relative." Of its factual truth there is no evidence whatever, and even in the school exercises, pageants, and poems of the Bicentennial in 1932 it was carefully suppressed—save in a few verses by Lydia Chatton:

> Let others echo Rupert Hughes
>   And mix up motes and beams—
> The anecdotes that I peruse
>   Were told by Parson Weems.
> Above iconoclastic views
>   That little hatchet gleams!
> "I cannot tell a lie," I choose
>   The Washington of Weems.

Up through the Civil War era, the anecdote seems to have been universally relished, even though sober historians might skirt the issue of its truth. A very popular boy's life of Washington, for example, first published in 1863 by Morrison Heady ("Uncle Juvinell"), told the story in a form more rococo than Weems's—starting with George's prayer, "Good Santa Claus, be kind to me while I am sleeping peacefully," and building up a sub-plot about suspicions thrown on a pickaninny named Jerry. To the Puritan mind, the story was a very good one. Moreover, the real Washington's refusal to flinch from the responsibilities of manhood, under his supreme sense of duty, lent a touch of veracity to the absurd yarn.

But eventually the higher criticism began to laugh this fable out of court. Mark Twain said he was sure he was a greater man than Washington: Washington couldn't tell a lie, whereas Mark Twain could, and wouldn't. That Weems could, and did, grew increasingly plain. A grandson of Weems stated that the episode was probably suggested to him because one of the parson's own children had cut down a "Pride of China" tree, and manfully confessed. Another version calls it a rose bush; other descendants of Weems deny the incident altogether. To complicate the problem further, we hear of a mug made in Germany in the late eighteenth century, with pictures of the cherry-tree story and the inscription "G. W. 1776."[42] The facts about this mug are not verified; but at least we are left wondering if the anecdote is not a bit of folklore antedating Weems. It is also reported that an institution in the Middle West has the original iron hatchet—a claim which A. Edward Newton blandly challenged by suggesting that this was more apt to be America's second famous hatchet, that of Carrie Nation.

Weems's life of "the greatest man that ever lived" is filled with other revealing touches. He exaggerated Washington's poverty prior to marriage with rich Mrs. Custis ("Here was a proper rise for you!"), in the best traditions of the success story. His account of the Revolution had an enormous effect in shaping the heroism and jingoism of popular history, as Sydney G. Fisher pointed out some years ago. For generations, school texts were written (often unconsciously) in the shadow of this antic parson.[43] And his interpretation of the model Washington, from his cradle in Virginia to apotheosis in Heaven where seraphs embraced him with "tears of joy such as only angels weep," was powerful indeed in the making of American legend. "Let us believe as in the days of our youth," said one reader of Weems, Abraham Lincoln, "that Washington was spotless; it makes human nature better to believe that . . . human perfection is possible." The speaker could not foresee that after the Civil War new heroes would be made, with Lincoln himself as their captain, and that America's growing maturity would slowly put away the childish viewpoint of Parson Weems.

Until after the death of Lincoln, Henry Lee's claim for Washington, that he was first in the hearts of his countrymen, remained uncontested. For him were named uncounted thousands of Americans, ranging from the family intimacy of George Washington Parke Custis to the remoteness of Washington Roebling. The naming of places had begun in 1775–76, with the christening of Washington, North Carolina (present population: 7000). Washington Heights on Manhattan followed a few months later. In 1784 Jefferson proposed to create a State of Washington out of the eastern part of Ohio, but finally this region shrank to Washington County, Ohio. Not until 1853 did a portion of the Oregon Territory become the present State of Washington, giving the first President an honor unique among American heroes. In September, 1791, it was decided to call the unborn capital of the nation Washington City. The next year saw the naming of Mount Washington, in New Hampshire, thought to be the highest in the United States. Peaks in New York State, Montana, Oregon, Nevada, California and Alaska would later bear his name, and the sentimental would imagine "a wonderful likeness" of his profile in a great stone face near Harpers Ferry. In all, eight streams, ten lakes, thirty-three counties, nine colleges and universities, and one hundred and twenty-one towns and villages have been named for him. From a great bridge in America's metropolis to hills in Morocco and the Fiji Islands, the patronymic fame of Washington extends.

Paul Svinin, who published a travel book in 1815, reported that "every American considers it his sacred duty to have a likeness of Washington in his home, just as we have the images of God's saints." From about 1800 to 1850, scores of Washington almanacs bore his picture on their cover. Even the Franklin almanacs, a more prolific series, spread abroad the folklore of Washington; the *Franklin Magazine Almanac* for 1848 published in Pittsburgh, for example, gave a long narrative by a hero-worshiper who, as a schoolboy, had slipped into Congressional Hall and sat on a stove, "not much heated," in order to gaze upon the matchless President. His visage was everywhere, spread by the ardor of a young nation. It became a commercial, as well as a political and moral, device. Throughout the Ohio Valley and elsewhere numerous "Washington taverns" sprang up; some of their publicans were ex-soldiers of Washington, who indulged in endless reminiscence of him over pipes and ale, as his sign-board swung in the wind.[44] The potters of Staffordshire, gauging American taste from across the sea, turned out innumerable blue plates, mugs, and sugar-bowls bearing Washington's likeness. One prolific artisan, Ralph Wood, appears to have had an overproduction of Franklin statuettes, showing the homely sage with pink cheeks and blue coat, scroll in hand; with quaint impudence he labelled them "George Washington" and sent many to the United States.[45] From the hands of English craftsmen one also finds ceramic pieces showing Washington with his foot on the neck of the British lion, flanked by soldiers, cannon, a ship in full sail, and the motto "Success to America." The printed ware of Liverpool specialized in "Monument Pitchers," showing a fanciful pyramidal tomb with the legend "Washington in Glory."[46] Collectors of early American glass know that Washington topped all other favorites in the designs for whisky bottles; a recent catalogue lists some forty-nine different specimens blown from about 1820 to 1825.[47] (At the time of the Mexican War, Zachary Taylor briefly vied with him for this honor.) It was perhaps contradictory that the first great temperance crusade in America, started in 1840 by six liquor addicts of Baltimore and soon enlisting 600,000 members, called itself "The Washington Society." At its Springfield rally on Washington's Birthday in 1841 the chief speaker was an eloquent young lawyer named Abraham Lincoln: he paid tribute to "the mightiest name of earth," but sowed no doubts by mention of the seventy-six gallons of rum-punch by which Washington had assured his election as burgess in 1758, nor of the humorous contract Washington had drawn up with a gardener stipulating that the man be paid "four dollars at Christmas with which he may be drunk for four days and nights."[48] It may be worth noting, in the commercialization of American heroes, that, save for Paul Jones and Robert Morris, few indeed have been adopted as liquor trade-marks; such names of whiskies as "Mount Vernon" and "Old Hermitage" offer a more respectful approximation.

VI

The Washington cult, in its more literary aspects, seems to follow the contours of taste. An age of genteel romanticism decked the granite of his memory with violets. Catherine Maria Sedgwick, writing her novel *The Linwoods* in 1835, confessed that "whenever the writer has mentioned Washington, she has felt a sentiment resembling the awe of the pious Israelite when he approached the ark of the Lord." Samuel Woodworth, author of "The Old Oaken Bucket," in 1816 wrote perhaps the first romantic novel about him, called *The Champions of Freedom, or the Mysterious Chief*. The Mysterious Chief, tersely alluded to as "M. C.," is none less than the ghost of Washington, who fights through the War of 1812, and counsels a brave young soldier who has inherited the sword of Mount Vernon. This very sword, flashing fire in times of stress, has a life of its own. Even a good artist like Cooper in *The Spy*, drawing Washington as the portentous "Mr. Harper," showed him moving duskily like a demigod among the characters of flesh and blood. Washington's very presence congealed the imagination. When familiarities were attempted, they appeared to put the novelist in a posture as foolish as that of Gouverneur Morris slapping Washington's back. A novel of Braddock's campaign called *The Wilderness*, published in 1823, pictured the young Virginian as a "Romeo among the ladies," who comes upon two girls in the forest perusing Thomson's *Seasons* and supping on cakes and metheglin: "Ladies—forgive me, if I say my delight is equal to my astonishment!" Later, disguised in a suit of porcupine's quills and a beaver-skin cap, "a singularly beautiful and gaudy costume," he rescues the fair Maria from the French and falls in love with her. But renunciation is his keynote, and so he gives her up to her fiancé, whom Washington has just saved from being burned at the stake by the Indians.

In 1837 a Tennessean named Walter Marshall McGill celebrated his hero in a vast epic poem called *The Western World*. Ghosts, angels, supernatural voices encourage Washington throughout the Revolution, which is described battle by battle:

> Lo on the plains the great warrior awakes,
> The great Washington with valor shakes.
> At the fierce sound of the bugle's loud note,
> The old warrior awoke—he gave a shout.

Ten years later George Lippard published his *Legends of the American Revolution*. He told of a mystic who had heard the voice of God, "I will send a Deliverer to this land of the New World, who shall save my people from physical bondage, even as my Son saved them from the bondage of spiritual death!" This mystic came from Germany to the New World, and one midnight consecrated Washington with holy oil, a crown of laurel, and a sword. Lippard, an eccentric Philadelphia lawyer, three years later organized the Brotherhood of the Union, giving himself the post of "Supreme Washington." The purpose of this society was to assert the brotherhood of man and the hatred of capitalism. Lippard sought to make Washington's name a rallying-point for a great working-class movement such as Marx and Engels were dreaming of in Europe; but at the age of thirty-two he died of consumption.

Later and better artists emblazoned the name of Washington. At the Semicentennial of Washington's Inauguration, April 30, 1839, preceding a two-hour oration by John Quincy Adams, William Cullen Bryant's "Ode" was read. He compared Washington's strong but placid will to the "mighty Hudson" flowing beneath winter's ice:

> The wildest storm that sweeps through space,
>   And rends the oak with sudden force,
>   Can raise no ripple on his face,
>   Or slacken his majestic course.

Fifty years later, in all the pomposity of the Gilded Age, came New York's Centennial Celebration of 1889—which featured an impersonation of Washington taking the oath, by President Benjamin Harrison, while a crowd estimated at a million thronged Broadway and Wall Street. As an index of the age, the fever heat of excitement was reached over the glittering Centennial Ball and its quadrille danced by ladies with the best pedigree—into which had entered the social intrigues of

Ward McAllister and Mrs. William Astor. But the image of Washington, though overshadowed, was essentially unchanged. Whittier's poem read at this Centennial described his masterful serenity—

> Wise beyond lore, and without weakness good,
> Calm in the strength of lawless rectitude!

Oliver Wendell Holmes called him "the throneless Conqueror . . . ruler by a people's choice." The greatest poet of the age, Walt Whitman, saw him as a symbol above all partisanships, "a pure and august being," "the Beloved One." Strength of purpose remained to artists the dominant note of Washington. In a later generation Carl Sandburg would write, under the Washington Monument by starlight:

> The name of an iron man goes over the world.
> It takes a long time to forget an iron man.

Yet Washington, like another man of perfection, Robert E. Lee, never stirred the artists so deeply as did Lincoln. Perhaps he was too much of "a code man," as the late Carl Russel Fish called him, building a balanced life upon the accepted patterns of conduct, without having to strike out for himself as did Lincoln. Perhaps he was too self-sufficient or too rich to fathom the poetry of adversity. (A syndicated newspaper cartoon on February 22, 1940, showed a father with his hand upon his son's shoulder, pointing to Washington's portrait alongside of Lincoln's, saying, "And this one rose above riches.") And possibly, to the eyes of romantic art, Washington resembles too closely the average man, raised to the highest power by will and duty. In Washington's lifetime, Chateaubriand as an enthusiast of twenty-three had called on the President in Philadelphia, and come away trying to analyze the colorlessness—or better, the protective coloration—of his idol. "This man," he wrote, "who strikes the imagination little, because he is in proportion, has merged his existence in that of his country."

Under the hands of biographers since Weems and John Marshall, Washington has proved a difficult subject. The destruction of his world, the eighteenth century, by Jeffersonian and Jacksonian democracy, and the onrush of such tides as those of sentiment overwhelming the decorum of his age, and of industrialism destroying the old agrarian order, have swept away the landmarks by which he should be judged. To the average popular biographer Washington is a man uprooted, a legend without a background. He grows therefore more unreal. Most writers in the nineteenth century treated him with an awe that was stifling. A schoolmaster named Francis Glass tried to give him the true classical dignity by writing a life in Latin. Glass applied in vain to Thomas Jefferson for financial help,[49] but one of the schoolmaster's pupils, thrilled by the idea, worked for years to support Glass while this book was in the making. Published in 1835, it turned out to be no more than a literary curiosity. Then came the Unitarian clergyman Jared Sparks, writing a life and editing the writings of Washington in twelve tall volumes. For a few years his work was hailed with great applause, and on its strength he became professor of history and later president of Harvard. Then Lord Mahon and other scholars began to call attention to the liberties he had taken. In Sparks's effort to thwart the public's "prurient curiosity to see a great man in dishabille"—as a sympathetic reviewer phrased it—he had "corrected" Washington's spelling and grammar, altered sentences and inserted some of his own in the letters of Washington. Washington's gift of "a Bottle of Rum" to the Indian Queen Aliquippa appeared as "the more substantial token of a present." His approval, in writing to Colonel Bouquet in 1758, of "scalping parties of Indians" against the French, became "small parties of Indians." A small sum of money which Washington called "but a flea-bite at present," was rendered as "totally inadequate to our demands at this time." His friend "Old Put" became "General Putnam." Washington's harsh words about the "unaccountable kind of stupidity" of New Englanders were entirely cut out by this Harvard scholar, who also suppressed Washington's scathing remarks about the English and the Scotch, "those universal instruments of tyranny." (Sparks had made many British friends while searching London for manuscripts.) This editor also altered certain statements of Washington about religion and God.[50] Any flavor of skepticism, salt, or choler, or that plain speech which Sparks's generation feared as "vulgarity," stood condemned.

Washington Irving, the namesake of the hero who had given him an old man's blessing, published a five-volume life of Washington between 1855 and 1859. As literature, it is still the best book about Washington. Most of its facts are sound, and its cool dignity invites comparison with Gilbert Stuart's art. But a passion for "gentility" is taken over from Sparks, whose text Irving accepts with full faith. And, as a typical embellishment of his own Knickerbocker love for long pedigrees, he shows Washington's descent from a Norman baron of William the Conqueror, called William de Heartburn. (Some twenty years later a genealogist named Albert Welles proved Washington's descent from the Norse god Odin; in 1939, during the visit to America of King George VI and Queen Elizabeth, a British official of the College of Heralds showed with perhaps better evidence that Washington and Lee were both cousins to the present Queen of England.[51]) While Irving's biography was appearing in installments, Bishop William Meade of Virginia wrote at length of Washington's prayerfulness, as "the great high-priest of the nation." The Bishop cited Washington's orders against gaming, drinking, and swearing in the Army to prove —somewhat illogically—that the General himself never indulged in these things. Meade scouted all attempts to "bring him down to the common level, by representing him as passionately fond, not merely of the chase and much addicted to it, but also of the dance, the ballroom, and the theatre."[52]

After the publication of Washington's diaries in 1925, under auspices of the Mount Vernon Ladies' Association, it was no longer possible to deny that he loved hunting, dancing, and theatricals—as befitted a gentleman who had grown up in Virginia before the shadow of Victorian Puritanism had fallen across her green lawns and white mansions. Under the impetus of this discovery, which seemed so refreshingly novel to the 1920's, a flurry of so-called debunkery began. For a long time, as Philip Guedalla remarked, Washington's reputation had been lying in state. Even while Lytton Strachey was setting a new vogue in biography, Mr. J. P. Morgan and his librarian Miss Belle Da Costa Greene were buying at a fancy price and destroying several Washington letters which the latter was quoted as calling "smutty." Miss Greene cheerfully observed that such destruction was justified, "even if it only served to keep alive in our schools the fable of the cherry tree," which she judged to be more inspiring than the example of the real Washington. "Could we afford to pay the price and then destroy our investment? We could, and did."[53] This act of "whitewashing Washington" in the mausoleumlike depths of the Morgan Library set scholars' teeth on edge. Mr. Morgan and Miss Greene have steadfastly refused to tell what sort of letters they destroyed, and in view of the masses of forged Washington letters circulated in the last fifty years the presumption is strong that they were the victims of a little historical blackmail. But, whatever these letters contained, the facts are now no longer able to speak for themselves. This is unfortunate. When the late Mrs. Warren G. Harding told friends that she had destroyed the private papers of her husband to avoid impertinent public curiosity, they pointed out to her that President Harding had now lost all chance of telling his side of his story to posterity. Musty scandals generally survive in the correspondence of a public man's enemies, and it is unfair to give the man himself no opportunity for rebuttal. With Washington, no doubt, the case involves taste rather than morals; and what was "smutty" to the Morgan Library in 1924, may not have been so to Washington's franker day or to freer minds of recent times. But patriots in that decade, still nervous after the World War and the Red scare, were jealously guarding the citadel of American heroes—Mayor Hylan saying, of Washington and his circle, that "it will be a sad day if alien propaganda is permitted to alter the enviable record of their service and patriotism."[54]

Flight from scrutiny provokes attack, and this age of fearfulness naturally drew the notice of sharpshooters. In the end, Washington proved to be more invulnerable than the faint-hearted had supposed. In 1926 William E. Woodward published a book called *George Washington: The Image and the Man*. A South Carolinian and a hardheaded business man, in revolt against the New England passion for turning heroes into prigs, he stressed Washington's love affairs, his gaming and cursing and drinking, his insensibility to the world of ideas as that of a frontier rowdy. Woodward played up Washington's materialism, and told how he had ousted some poor squatters from his lands in western Pennsylvania. Thanks to their improvements, he was able to sell for $12,000 a tract for which he had paid $55 and surveying costs. Woodward's interpretation of the facts smacked of special pleading. His attempt to make Washington into a very shrewd customer, one of the great horse-traders of his time, recalls Wendell Phillips's remonstrance with a Negro orator who had denounced Washington the slaveholder as a scoundrel: "It isn't graphic. If you call George Washington a scoundrel, what have you got left for Frank Pierce?" Woodward's stress upon Washington's supposed vices also upset the equilibrium of his book. In eighteenth century Virginia, such vices were not news. But extreme conservatives of 1926, as was expected, were shocked by Mr. Woodward. About the same time, newspapers published Washington's recipe for brewing beer, discovered by a scholar of the New York Public Library, Victor Paltsits; and one Congressman, an ardent Prohibitionist, arose in his place and demanded its suppression from the public prints. Ere these shocks had been weathered, Rupert Hughes began to publish his leisurely life of Washington. Hughes's knowledge of Washington, and his conclusions, were better than Woodward's. His attitude, as its most teasing, was that which Emerson had expressed in *Representative Men:* "Every hero becomes a bore at last. . . . They cry up the virtues of George Washington—'Damn George Washington!' is the poor Jacobin's whole speech and confutation." Hughes was pleased to suggest that the monument to Washington's mother had been erected on the site of "an outhouse," and that the minister who christened the boy was likely drunk, because ministers often got drunk on such occasions. Sometimes Hughes had his facts scrambled, his references wrong. He quoted as evidence a letter written by Lord Fairfax to Washington's mother, although its source was a novel by S. Weir Mitchell. The true moral to be drawn from Washington's life, he concluded, "is that one should dress as magnificently as possible and indulge in every luxury available, including the dance, the theatre, the ballroom, hunting, fishing, racing, drinking and gambling, observing in all of them temperance, justice, honesty and pride, while avoiding excess and loss of dignity."[55] At such debonair statements, an outcry issued from the lovers of Weems. But, on the whole, the effect of Hughes's work was salutary. Washington could take it.

President Coolidge, asked what he thought about the new debunkery of Washington, swivelled his chair toward the window. "Well, I see the Monument is still there," he said. His address to Congress on Washington's Birthday in 1927 revealed how Washington was becoming all things to all men. "No great mystery surrounds him," declared Mr. Coolidge, ". . . he was a man endowed with what has been called uncommon common sense. . . . His estate was managed in a thoroughly businesslike fashion. He kept a very careful set of account books for it, as he did for his other enterprises . . . constantly on the outlook for sound investments and for ways to increase his capital . . . the first commercial American . . . the moral efficiency of an abiding religious faith." Of Washington, soldier and statesman, no more than a few words were said. Five years later, again before a joint session of Congress, President Hoover spoke on Washington's Birthday in terms of loftier generality: "Washington had courage without excitement, determination without passion." He was, in many respects, the great humanitarian and the great engineer. The reading of Washington's Farewell Address remains a solemn ritual in Congress every twenty-second of February—but since the advent of the New Deal, as will be noted later, Washington has received less oratorical praise from the White House than has Thomas Jefferson.

The Bicentennial of 1932 was the flood-mark of national homage to

Washington. George M. Cohan wrote "Father of the Land We Love"—

> Whenever drums begin to roll
> Within the nation's heart and soul
> A patriotic something seems to say—
> First in War, First in Peace,
> First in the Hearts of His Countrymen.

Boy Scouts gathered black walnuts from the trees of Mount Vernon and distributed them all over the country, for planting in parks. Major James H. Doolittle flew the great-great-great-grandniece of George Washington on a dawn-to-dusk journey over all the territory covered by the General in his travels (except for Barbados, which went unnoticed). Percy MacKaye wrote a folk-masque, *Wakefield,* with Washington as "the Imbruing Presence" mingling with Ethan Allen, Brigham Young, Davy Crockett, Pecos Bill, Paul Bunyan, characters from Shakespeare and the Bible, and the barons of Runnymede. Phyllis-Marie Arthur wrote "What He Means to Me":

> Oft as I work to fill the cookie-jar,
> I see his noble face there on the wall,
> Smiling upon the laundry calendar:
> Saying, it seems to me, "I've suffered all."

The Bicentennial Commission placed a poster-size reproduction of Gilbert Stuart's Athenæum portrait in every schoolroom in the United States. News releases by the Commission announced that Washington was the inventor of ice cream, and the first American to raise the domestic carrot. Sol Bloom, the envy of his Congressional colleagues, got dozens of hours of free radio time—on Mother's Day, Memorial Day, Independence Day, to the Farmers, from the home of Washington's mother, from Pohick Church, at the home of Francis Scott Key, "under the cherry blossoms at Washington," and before Congress on the anniversary of the death of Goethe ("No statesman was greater than Washington. No poet . . . was greather [*sic*] than Goethe").[56] Edwin Markham, in the official Bicentennial poem, recalled the majesty of Washington, "superbly lone . . . like far Polaris wheeling on the North." Mr. Laurance H. Hart of Queens, New York, whose impersonation of Washington has become his lifework, appeared before numberless school children in his white wig, knee breeches, and sword —answering questions and making speeches solely in Washington's vocabulary. New lives of Washington, for children, came from the press. Most of them long ago had dropped the cherry tree, the mettlesome colt, the tattling at school. To make the boy Washington appealing they often played up his awkwardness—the laughing-stock of girls, the hobbledehoy clumsy enough to "send a footstool careering into the silk-clad ankle of the master of Belvoir"—and how he mastered this trait. For adults, sober but not solemn scholars of Washington, like John C. Fitzpatrick and Nathaniel W. Stephenson, began to rewrite his life with fewer wisecracks and flat denial of the Fairfax love affair. American biography was coming of age, ceasing to thumb its nose at the great.

Voices were raised here and there against Washington's near-perfection. But in comparison with those of earlier years they were less flippant, more wary. Thus at the close of 1940 Bernhard Knollenberg, former New York lawyer and librarian at Yale, published a book called *Washington and the Revolution*. He admitted that Washington was a great leader but a hard one—with his "constant resort to the most brutal floggings," and a suspicious nature that has blackened, for all time, the honorable characters of Gates and Conway. The Conway Cabal, suggested Mr. Knollenberg, never existed save in the minds of pro-Washington historians: to give the hero all the perfections requisite for America's first superman—of patience, nobility, honor—and to show him in conflict with a whole nest of villains. General Washington, as Mr. Knollenberg saw him, hated to be found in the wrong, and would resort to deception or lies if caught in an embarrassing corner. The critic's method was that of a shrewd prosecuting attorney, marshalling the facts to obtain a conviction—facts which in themselves were a good deal less sensational than the inferences he drew from them. That his book would gravely alter the usual estimate of Washington's integrity, as tested by time, seemed unlikely. But it was worth a hearing.

Interest was quickening in the two great shrines of Washington. The first was Mount Vernon, whose shabby and weed-grown appearance under the later Washingtons had shocked European visitors in the 1830's, a decade which also saw a mysterious attempt to steal the hero's body. Soon a new tomb was completed, locked, and the key thrown into the Potomac.[57] In 1853 a South Carolina spinster named Ann Pamela Cunningham, whose mother had been thrilled by the ships' bells that tolled as sailors passed Mount Vernon, formed the Mount Vernon Ladies' Association to buy this estate for the American people. During the Civil War it was neutral ground: soldiers in blue and gray were asked to stack their arms outside the gates, and did so. Now, more than half a million people visit Mount Vernon every year—some tiptoeing through the mansion as if it were the house of God, others noisy and trivial, rushing through in order to say that they have been there. One souvenir hunter stole a plate from the kitchen, but returned it voluntarily after several years; another snapped off the head of a dog in the hunting-scene of the white marble and Syenite mantel, but the relic was confiscated and glued back in place. Not long ago the assistant superintendent was called on to settle a ten-dollar bet between two arguing men, as to whether the place were the home of Lee or of Woodrow Wilson. But the average American at Mount Vernon, though not the sentimentalist his grandfather was, shows at least a measure of appreciation and knowledge.

The second shrine of course is the mighty shaft of the Washington Monument in the National Capital. Begun in 1833, it provoked fifty years of bickering over design and expense. Congressmen who groaned at the cost were reminded that the salary which Washington had relinquished would, at simple interest, have built three such memorials. Eventually it became the people's project, but work was slow. Briefly in 1850 the Know Nothing Party took possession of the Monument, and in a burst of 100 per cent Americanism threw into the Potomac a stone from the Roman "Temple of Concord" which the Pope had contributed. The sculptor Robert Mills planned "a grand circular colonnade" round the base of the Monument, with a figure of Washington seated in a chariot being driven by Liberty or Victory. Luckily this plan was abandoned. The simplicity of the obelisk—which *The New York Tribune* in 1875 was deriding as "the big furnace chimney on the Potomac"—is now seen to be the perfect tribute to Washington. The Lincoln Memorial is a softly lit temple where tears and prayers have been offered at the feet of a beloved martyr; but, like Washington himself, this lofty impersonal shaft inspires lifted rather than moistened eyes. George Washington, the proud and shy aristocrat, no doubt would have preferred it so.

CHAPTER SEVEN

THOMAS JEFFERSON, THE GENTLE RADICAL

> This is an ignorant year
> Within a cruel time.
> If he were here
> We might rebuild
> The firm wall raised by him,
> The column felled.
>
> —LAWRENCE LEE, "The Tomb of Thomas Jefferson"
> (1940)

I

NATURE did not intend Thomas Jefferson for a hero. Temperament, physique, and background were all against it. If destiny had not plucked him from the ivory tower he built at Monticello, and hurled him into the thick of public turmoil, Jefferson would have lived and died a bookish, fastidious Virginia squire. He might have become, more easily than a hero, a writer of belles-lettres, a college don, or an amateur philosopher sunning himself on the leeward side of John Locke. He is like no other American leader, although there are faint resemblances in Woodrow Wilson and Franklin D. Roosevelt of which their friends have made the most.

Certainly Jefferson the idol was not hewn from the same stone as

148

Washington, Israel Putnam, Francis Marion. He had a sedentary man's shrinking from military discipline. The drums and trumpets passed him by. His only sight of advancing redcoats was through a telescope, from a knoll near Monticello called Carter's Mountain, in June, 1781, and in later years his enemies were quick to assert that his headlong flight after that vision spoke for itself. He was a man of exquisite perceptions, an artist with nerves attuned to the age of sensibility. At the death of his wife he fell into a swoon so deep that his life was feared for; those who disliked Jefferson did not hesitate to call him "womanish" and "feline."

Loose-jointed in appearance and in talk—lacking Franklin's homely vigor without achieving the majesty of Washington—"Long Tom" Jefferson wore his elegance of mind and raiment with an insouciance that some misjudged for sloppiness. As President he received a British Minister in slippers and dressing-gown (a democratic style that Huey Long once tried to copy, in receiving a German dignitary). Even at his inauguration Jefferson had quietly walked from Conrad's boarding-house to take the oath in the Senate chamber of the unfinished Capitol; though legend persistently repeats that he arrived on horseback, dismounted casually, and hitched his horse to the "palisades" of the Capitol fence. He owned ten thousand acres and two hundred slaves, and recoiled from courting the masses or playing the political bully-boy. Yet he became "the People's friend," a high-handed imperialist, and a saber-rattler before the Barbary pirates. For all his agrarian background, he was far less the full-blooded country gentleman than were Washington and Jackson. He raised tobacco but never used it, never kept a playing-card in his house, bred fine horses but never loved the race-track. Duelling did not tempt him. He drank no spirits, but was fond of French wines and cookery—one of those gentlemen, as Patrick Henry said, who "abjured their native victuals." He was virtually a vegetarian, as he told Doctor Ulley—and, like most vegetarians, proved to be a terrifying idealist, tinged with fanaticism. His mores were not those of the carnivorous mammal. And his mind was a brilliant, delicate, complex mechanism. In fact, as Henry Adams remarked, all our early Presidents save Jefferson can be drawn with "a few broad strokes of the brush"—but the master of Monticello, with his shifting lights and shades, nuances and translucencies, defies even the finest pencil. Did the People ever have a more extraordinary friend?

Let us see how Jefferson came to be a hero. Born in 1743 among the red clay hills of Albemarle County, Virginia, he sprang from good stock. His mother, Jane Randolph Jefferson, made him cousin to numerous purse-proud Tuckahoes. Jefferson affected to pass lightly over the old pedigree of the Randolphs, "to which let every one ascribe the faith and merit he chooses," and to stress the homespun simplicity of his father, Peter, whose "education had been quite neglected."[1] With this help, legend has made Peter Jefferson into a clodhopper, stressing the democratic rather than the patrician heritage of his son. Late research, however, has shown that Peter Jefferson owned a great acreage of rich land, had five overseers, served as vestryman and justice of the peace and sheriff, and displayed a skill in map-making that bears witness to his cultivation of hand and brain.[2] He was no Thomas Lincoln.

At William and Mary College young Thomas Jefferson was something of a bookworm, who as his classmate John Page recalled "could tear himself away from his dearest friends and fly to his studies." A century later, drawing heavily upon imagination, John Esten Cooke wrote a novel called *The Youth of Jefferson, or a Chronicle of College Scrapes*. Tom, or "Sir Asinus," here figures as a tall, freckled, sandy-haired lad with a prankish temper. Thinking he is pursued by the proctor, he flies down the corridor in a faded dressing-gown, and barricades himself gun in hand, crying out: "Beware! I am armed to the teeth, and rather than be captured I will die in defence of my rights—namely, liberty, property, and the pursuit of happiness under difficulties!" (The mature Jefferson did not include "property" among the inalienables; that belonged to Hamilton's point of view.)

"Under temptations and difficulties," young Jefferson wrote, "I would ask myself what would Doctor Small, Mr. Wythe, Peyton Randolph, do in this situation?" His three youthful heroes were a Scotch mathematician, a jurist and college tutor, and a tidewater gentleman of Jefferson's own blue blood. To the end of his life, indeed, Jefferson's ideal was blended of two types, the scholar and the intellectual aristocrat, which have rarely been popular with the masses of Americans. It was the dash of liberalism which Jefferson himself added to the *beau ideal* that made him an unforgettable favorite. Meanwhile, Jefferson gained notice at the Virginia bar and in 1769 was chosen by his native county for the House of Burgesses. He fell under the spell of Patrick Henry, who "appeared to me to speak as Homer wrote." Sympathetic with Henry's hostility to the Crown, Jefferson was still cool enough to perceive the orator's defects in logic and learning. Jefferson came early to distrust the spell of rhetoric. In part it may have been a rationalization: a weak throat and unconquerable diffidence in large groups kept Jefferson from ever becoming himself a spell-binder. His pen was mightier than his voice. Three silent men—Franklin, Washington, Jefferson—were the first great idols of the Republic: the age of silver tongue and spread eagle, of Webster and Hayne, Grady and Bryan, was yet unborn.

Quickly gaining note as a pamphleteer for Independence, Jefferson was sent as a Virginia delegate to the Continental Congress. New Englanders liked him as a penman, even as they admired Washington as a soldier. "Though a silent member of Congress, he was so prompt, frank, explicit and decisive upon committees and in conversation," wrote John Adams, ". . . that he soon seized upon my heart." This popularity was very important to Jefferson's budding career. In June, 1776, as a tribute to his fine literary gift, legal training, and eagerness to work, he was named first of a committee of five to draft the Declaration of Independence.

Jefferson was not then aware of the world-shaking import of his document. Later he took it retrospectively in his stride, as it were. In the face of contrary facts he stated so vehemently that the Declaration had been signed by Congress on the Fourth of July—even to the extent of imagining a "paper" draft signed on that date, when confronted with the parchment undoubtedly engrossed on August 2^3—that indulgent posterity, in the main, has let Jefferson have his way. With due respect to his fellow-committeemen, Jefferson was truly the author of the Declaration—the proud boast of his tombstone, and his supreme claim among the Founding Fathers. If he is something less than the Divinely inspired creator of this noble document—whose theories, spirit, and even phrases are the products of a long evolution—he is surely the amanuensis of Americanism. To Lee in 1825 he wrote that the Declaration "was intended to be an expression of the American mind." Its clarity, vigor, beauty, and fighting affirmation of the democratic faith endear Jefferson forever to his countrymen. No one else could have seen so well or expressed so finely the ultimate, as well as the immediate, aims of the new American spirit. It was addressed to the people. Hence it omitted a few underlying subtleties. Chief of these was the vital distinction Jefferson saw between *natural* rights (those which man can exercise "without the aid of exterior assistance," such as freedom of thought and speech) and *civil* rights (like gaining and holding property, in which men agree to abdicate a measure of individualism, and to act only "under the guarantee of society"). This was the reason why property was not one of the "inherent and inalienable rights," since it lay under the hand of social control. Jefferson's individualism was one of rights plus duties; Hamilton's tended to stress property rights above other matters, and paved the way for that ideal later called "rugged individualism"—a term, said Herbert Hoover in 1934, which "I should be proud to have invented," but which to others meant an industrial philosophy active in the creation of slums and economic misery, while it destroyed the green countryside and the domestic handicrafts that Jefferson loved. But Jefferson did not put his distinction into writing until after he had quit Philadelphia and gone back home, "being alone and wanting amusement," and it remained unpublished for more than a century after his death.[4] This was typical of the casualness of Jefferson.

After firing the salvo of the Declaration, Jefferson returned to Virginia, convinced that his next duty was to sow the liberal seed at home —by abolishing entails, revising the criminal code, setting up free schools, and cleaving Church from State. Jefferson had no stomach for soldiering; his aptitude lay in "mental fight." Certain keen partisans of Washington, Hamilton, and the Federalists have never forgiven Jefferson for failing to expose himself to hunger, frostbite, and bloodshed in the cause to which he had rallied his countrymen. The late Senator Beveridge, biographer of John Marshall, by playing up a phrase in one of Washington's letters, imagines the shivering soldiers in their smoky huts at Valley Forge thinking of the penman of their faith, asking each other with chattering teeth, "Where is Jefferson?"[5] Yet there is no real evidence that Jefferson was looked upon at this time as a quitter. He was craven only in the subtler sense of T. E. Hulme's saying, that "a non-muscular man is inevitably physically a coward."

In 1779 Jefferson succeeded Patrick Henry as Governor of Virginia. He did not make a good wartime governor, as even loyal Virginians admit. He was too timorous about overstepping his strict legal rights, even in an emergency, and in practical matters his judgment was undeveloped. And Jefferson had the sudden violence of the sedentary man. With his four thousand British prisoners he was alternately too soft and too hard—at first arranging musicales and philosophical causeries for them and opening his library to the officers, and then upon hearing of Americans abused on board British prison-ships, loading his captives with irons and preparing to treat them as common criminals until Washington intervened. In later years he showed the same bursts of violence: demanding that Aaron Burr be hanged out of hand, and in the War of 1812 proposing that if the British touched our coasts "we must burn the city of London, not by expensive fleets or congreve rockets, but by employing an hundred or two Jack-the-painters, whom nakedness, famine, desperation and hardened vice, will abundantly furnish among themselves." This is a strain in Jefferson's nature, supposedly mild and calm, which has never colored his legend and even been ignored by most of his biographers.[6] Hero-worship and symbol-making call for simplification, in dealing with a man so complex as Jefferson.

In the late spring of 1781, with Virginia's treasury bankrupt and the British overrunning the Old Dominion, Jefferson desperately prepared to resign in favor of a military governor. At that juncture, the redcoats swooped down on Monticello and would have caught him but for the warning of Jack Jouett, "the Southern Revere." The head of a government should avoid capture by the enemy if he can, as many European sovereigns and premiers have lately decided. A statesman who runs away may govern some other day. No discredit should arise if he has first done his best—as Tom Paine pointed out in 1805, in defense of Jefferson. It is true that after the invasion was over Jefferson had to face a charge of insufficient preparedness; on December 19, 1781, he appeared before the Legislature, was acquitted and voted thanks. But his prestige in Virginia was clouded by the disasters of his Governorship, and by his having given up the helm in a storm. Thin-skinned to criticism, Jefferson looked forward to "the all-healing grave." It was his first and last public failure. In Virginia its memory lasted until —during his absence as Minister to France—the progressives under Madison came into local power, and loyally rehabilitated Jefferson as their master. Many years later, in Jefferson's first term as President, when a rash of newspaper libels broke out against him, the facts were deliberately twisted to make it seem that Jefferson had been rebuked by the Virginia Legislature for his cowardice, in running away from the British! The charge was absurd, but strangely passed into common belief, especially in the North. Federalists dwelt upon the spectacle of this long-legged statesman leaving Monticello with more haste than grace. Even a generation ago, the great historian Edward Channing used to lecture vividly to his Harvard classes about the affrighted agrarian, "coattails flying in the wind." Chronologically, this is the first libel against Thomas Jefferson.

II

In France, Jefferson was overshadowed by the remembrance of Franklin. He lacked Franklin's easy bonhomie, and quaintly enough was more of a Puritan than the great Bostonian had been. Jefferson too was a widower, but no lovely ladies found him apt at flirtation and banter, nor did any crown him with laurel at *fêtes champêtres*. At forty-three he was older than Franklin at seventy-five. "A dozen years ago this scene would have amused me," Jefferson wrote to Mrs. Trist, "but I am past the age for changing habits!"

Abroad, Jefferson grew more aggressively American, seeing England as an aristocracy besotted with liquor and horse-racing, and France as a land where marital fidelity is "an ungentlemanly practice." He also loved to magnify the virtues of his native land, solemnly assuring Crevecœur that New Jersey farmers probably learned how to make "the circumference of a wheel of one single piece" from Greek epic poetry, "because ours are the only farmers who can read Homer." Jefferson fondly imagined himself the typical American farmer.

France also confirmed Jefferson's aversion to "priestcraft" and hereditary aristocracy. At the news of Shays's Rebellion at home, he rejoiced—believing in a little blood-letting at intervals for the health of the body politic. After his return to America the full fury of the French Revolution broke. At first Jefferson hailed it with almost fanatic tranquillity: "Was ever such a prize won with so little innocent blood? . . . rather than it should have failed I would have seen half the earth desolated."[7] Even today, conservatives who hold to "sound Jeffersonian principles" try to forget his reckless remark about watering the tree of liberty periodically with blood. Jefferson maintained that only the sickly timid tory fears the People, whereas the strong leader loves and trusts them. In later years Jefferson disliked the radial plan upon which L'Enfant had laid out the city of Washington—knowing it was designed to keep mobs from throwing up impassable barricades, while soldiers massed in its "circles" could command the approaches to the Capitol with artillery.[8] Let the People come, he said.

Yet in practice, Jefferson was the gentlest of Girondists. Upon the eve of the Revolution the French Foreign Minister had smiled upon meetings of the disaffected in Jefferson's house, "being sure," as Jefferson wrote, "that I should be useful in moderating the warmer spirits." After Jefferson's orderly election to the Presidency (which he loved to style "the revolution of 1800"), he reassured bankers and industrialists that he abhorred the spirit of unrest bred by the "blood and slaughter" in France, and was so temperate that radicals could hardly believe their ears. Out of office he was an idealist and revolutionary; within, a conservative and opportunist. Moreover, Jefferson the agrarian, urging that we "let our work-shops remain in Europe," had as deep a fear as did Hamilton of the mobs of Old World cities. Jefferson compared such mobs to "sores" on the face of a nation. Convinced that those who labor in the earth are God's chosen people, and that tillers of the soil have an instinct for order and justice, Jefferson was ready at any time to sign up with embattled farmers. A revolution with pitchforks he understood, but pikestaves unnerved him.

Returning from France to serve as Secretary of State, Jefferson came into collision with Hamilton, and soon retired to Monticello. Shy by nature, disliking to fight hand-to-hand, he tried to convince himself that he wanted nothing so much as to plant his corn and beans in peace. "I have no passion to govern men; no passion which would lead me to delight to ride in a storm," he wrote his friend Rutledge on December 27, 1796. But events helped to draft him. Leadership was needed in the fight for "republicanism," what a later age would call democracy. An immersed scholar like John Taylor of Caroline was no vote-getter, while an eager man like Patrick Henry (already hardening into reaction) had fallen into the mud too often while scrambling for prizes and profits. The younger generation in Virginia, Madison and Monroe, frankly looked to Jefferson as their master. And the Federalists, by training their guns upon Jefferson even out of office, roused his slow-kindling anger and also drew more public notice to him. He thus became the focus for discontent. At fifty-four—still protesting he preferred "the prattle of my grandchildren and senile rest" —Jefferson began to fight. He entered upon the Vice-Presidency, under John Adams. The threat of Aaron Burr's election in 1800 could be blocked only by a man like Jefferson. His duty was clear, and success followed. And so, like many other political leaders in a land where undue anxiety for office is bad form, Jefferson was carried forward upon the shoulders of his friends. Hero-worship was quick to respond.

The first *Jefferson Almanac* appeared in 1800, for the year 1801; its publisher, George Keating, guaranteed "to give the Purchaser an Almanac for 1802 in case Thomas Jefferson is not elected President of the United States." Campaign pamphlets and thumbnail biographies of Jefferson now poured from the press by dozens. Typical is J. J. Beckley's *Epitome of the Life & Character of Jefferson* (Philadelphia,

July, 1800), lauding the "ardent mind of Jefferson, eagerly pursuing the principles of the revolution" (trusting apparently that readers would assume he meant the American rather than the French one); calling him "a man of pure, ardent, and unaffected piety . . . the adorer of one God . . . the friend and benefactor of the whole human race . . . the MAN OF THE PEOPLE . . . the brightest luminary of the western world." Robert Treat Paine's lyric "For Jefferson and Liberty" was sung at innumerable Jefferson rallies and "festivals," along with Rembrandt Peale's song "The People's Friend":

> Devoted to his country's cause,
>   The Rights of Men and equal Laws,
>   His hallow'd pen was given:
> And now those Rights and Laws to save
> From sinking to an early grave,
>   He comes employ'd by Heaven.

Among the Berkshire hills of Massachusetts, Elder John Leland of Cheshire, who had preached electioneering sermons for Jefferson, conceived a magnificent victory tribute. To his Baptist flock he proposed that they should make the biggest cheese in the world in honor of Thomas Jefferson. An eye-witness reported:

Every man and woman who owned a cow was to give for this cheese all the milk yielded on a certain day—only no *Federal cow* must contribute a drop. A huge cider-press was fitted up to make it in, and on the appointed day the whole country turned out with pails and tubs of curd, the girls and women in their best gowns and ribbons, and the men in their Sunday coats and clean shirt-collars. The cheese was put to press with prayer and hymn singing and great solemnity. When it was well dried it weighed 1600 pounds. It was placed on a sleigh, and Elder Leland drove with it all the way to Washington. It was a journey of three weeks. All the country had heard of the big cheese, and came out to look at it as the Elder drove along.[9]

Upon his arrival in Washington, "Leland the cheese-monger," as scoffing Federalists called him, preached on Sunday before the joint Houses of Congress, from the text, "And behold, a greater than Solomon is here"—praising the President with such zeal as one might expect from a godly man who had driven for three weeks with the largest cheese in the world. A segment of this cheese was still uneaten in 1805; it was served at a presidential reception with cake and a huge urn of hot punch. This tribute was rivalled belatedly in 1837, when a New York admirer of outgoing President Jackson conveyed to the

White House, "with banners and bands of music," a cheese weighing 1400 pounds.

Although James Fenimore Cooper knew a Federalist parson who refused, at the font, to christen an infant "Thomas Jefferson," namesakes quickly began to appear. Among many namesake letters found in Jefferson's private papers, now in the Library of Congress, is one written with the painful care of a hand unaccustomed to the pen. The writer, Thomas Harris, says that he is "a free black man" of Sterling, Connecticut, and that his wife has

> presented me with a pair of *twin boys*. A pair of *black twin boys* are, Sir, I believe no common sight. Such a pair however claim protection and support from me, which I fear I shall not be able to afford them. But Sir, as a testimony of my gratitude, for those principles of Justice and humanity by you so boldly advanced and ably advocated, and of the very great respect in which I hold the Father of his Country, the friend of freedom and equal rights, the benefactor of mankind, and of people of colour in particular, I have named one of my twins *Thomas,* and the other *Jefferson.*[10]

In regard to Jefferson as the Negro's friend, one of the most popular stories circulated about him was that he had returned the bow of an old darkey, in order that a Negro "might not outdo him in politeness." Popular in school readers a generation ago, the anecdote usually went hand in hand with one about an old wayfaring man, wishing to ford a stream, who picked out Jefferson from a company of gentlemen on horseback as "the kindest-looking person." Jefferson's benevolence toward the poor and the slave was a legitimate part of his legend, though his attitude toward slavery—as the owner of two hundred blacks himself—was never quite clear to the public. For Jefferson himself (while favoring some gradual emancipation) was loath openly to endorse abolition when asked to do so by the French Society for the Abolition of the Slave Trade. It was another issue upon which the theoretical and the practical Jefferson never quite got together.

Jefferson's fan mail, as a later day would call it, is luckily preserved in the Library of Congress but of course unpublished. It reveals some interesting things. The President's known scientific bent, for example, attracted a host of letter-writers unknown to fame or to Jefferson. They send a sample of cotton wadding made by a new process, a bit of old Peruvian earthenware, "a plan of aerial navigation" which needs Federal support, a new type of loom, an apple-paring machine, "an invention for traveling under water." American ingenuity felt that a kindred spirit was in the White House. Sometimes Jefferson's humble admirers caution him to take better care of himself, hinting that he runs the risk of assassination. Sometimes he is told that a Jefferson debating club has been formed in his honor, or a play or epic poem dedicated to him, often with the proposal that he produce or print it.

That Jefferson was, in a sense unknown to Washington and John Adams, "the People's President," here stands revealed. A mechanic writes in to say that he and his wife have had "the fever," and need a loan of $500 which they are sure the President will supply. Another laborer writes that he is averse to hard work, and so needs money to get an education and become a literary man; all credit will then belong to Jefferson. A Kentuckian reports that a dislocated shoulder prevents his doing heavy labor, and therefore he wishes $2000 to finance him while he studies law; apparently getting no answer, he repeats his request six weeks later with growing irritation. The pastor of a flock of Baptist Republicans in Lebanon, Ohio, tells Jefferson that his church has lost money in a legal dispute and needs a loan; other letters, incidentally, testify to cordial relations between Jefferson and a number of Baptist preachers and congregations. Many petitions come from needy veterans of the Revolution, debtors, and petty offenders in jail. Perhaps the most singular demand is a letter to Jefferson from one William Esenbeck, January 11, 1806; as a citizen of the national capital, he wants the President to detail six Indians to help him hunt wild beasts around the city.

Although one finds the curious complaint, in a letter of January 25, 1801, that "you will carry on the Government in a most parsimonious manner," it is plain that Jefferson in his first term won vast popular favor by abolishing the excise (the cause of the Whisky Rebellion, in Washington's day), the land tax, stamp tax, and other direct levies which had been made during the war scare of 1798. This pruning won Jefferson an abiding place in the heart of the American farmer. But the most widely applauded act of Jefferson's regime was the Louisiana Purchase. It was a shrewd and simple bargain which everybody could understand, although Jefferson himself took little subsequent pride in the Purchase and did not number it among the great "works" listed by his epitaph—probably because he knew how unconstitutional his methods had been. But the average American, in an age of land-hunger and expansionism, felt no such misgivings, and was quick to approve Jefferson the empire-builder. A typical letter, from an unknown admirer, James Garner of Pendleton, South Carolina, June 7,

1807, relates that he has just been "taking a small view of the western Country, Natchez & Lower Louisiana":

I Returnd Home, & having a higher (if possible) Regard & Esteem for your Personal Qualifications, in that great Acquisition of the western world & Numberless Measures mild and Advantageous to the American People in General, Excites me to Write, to inform you that I never Expect to See you, & in order to Get as nigh as possible have Taken the freedom of Calling my Second and Last Son Th. Jefferson.

After Jefferson's sweeping re-election, carrying all states save Connecticut and Delaware, his reputation seems to have reached its peak. His Second Inaugural shows that Jefferson, like other great leaders in world history, had become the mouthpiece of his age. Here occurs his famous counsel of "commerce and honest friendship with all nations—entangling alliances with none." Unlike Washington, Jefferson was an adept literary artist, and it is significant that posterity has mistakenly put into the mouth of Washington one of Jefferson's most captivating phrases.

About 1806—when Jefferson the expansionist was laying claim, incidentally, to the Gulf Stream as an American preserve, "in which hostilities and cruising are to be frowned on"—his popularity was almost overwhelming. The Embargo had not yet reared its head. As early as November of that year, and increasingly through the next twelvemonth, letters poured in begging him to consider a third term. From Bergen County, New Jersey, he was told that "It is the duty of every man to submit his individual wishes to the general will"; "at a crisis when the flames of war are raging in Europe with unabated violence," added the Chenango County Republicans of New York. In Delaware the Kent County Republicans wrote: "Your services is [sic] necessary . . . men are ridiculing the Declaration of Independence." A few admirers dissented, one reminding him that "if JEFFERSON retiring with éclat enforces the principle of Rotation . . . what man would in future have the temerity to avow a contrary doctrine? He would be immediately and deservedly denounced, as an enemy to the sovereign People. . . . None ever can be more universally beloved."[11] But, whether tempted or not, Jefferson followed Washington's precedent.

Sensitive to censure, Jefferson also had the shy man's dislike of being lionized. Although a great democrat, he wanted to keep popularity at arm's length. This had been evident in earlier days—when in the late winter of 1797, approaching Philadelphia to take his seat as Vice-

President, he had tried to enter the city by stealth. As usual, American enterprise frustrated the scheme: "A body of troops were on the look-out for him and signalled his approach by a discharge of artillery, and, marching before him into the city, bore a banner aloft on which were inscribed the words: 'Jefferson, the Friend of the People.' "[12] As President he made it a rule to send back even small tokens offered by admirers, lest he be suspected of taking perquisites and bribes; near the end of his second term he meticulously returned an ivory cane to Samuel Hawkins, saying he desired no reward save the "conscious-ness of a disinterested administration." When Boston citizens sought to make his birthday a patriotic anniversary, he disapproved "trans-ferring the honors and veneration for the great birthday of the Re-public to any individual, or of dividing them with individuals." The Fourth of July was enough glory for Jefferson. At the zenith of his popularity Jefferson looked icily upon Sullivan's proposal that he take a swing around the circle, to let the provincials have a look at their beloved chief; the President declared himself "not reconciled to the idea of a chief magistrate parading himself through the several States as an object of public gaze and in quest of an applause which, to be valuable, should be purely voluntary."[13] For all his mastery of some political arts and his secret thirst for approval, Jefferson never over-came a feeling, like that of Shakespeare's Coriolanus, about cheapen-ing himself to court the mob, "the mutable, rank-scented many." Jef-ferson's self-knowledge—that kept him from any illusions about his power of oratory or his personal magnetism—may have added to this feeling. Yet it is safe to say that no man today, Democratic or Repub-lican, could become a major political hero who showed one half of Jefferson's aristocratic diffidence.

Still, he took a very human interest in what people thought about him. Jefferson kept a personal scrap-book, now in the University of Virginia Library. The first fifty pages are filled with political songs and verses, panegyrics and lampoons, accounts of dinners and Repub-lican picnics, bearing chiefly upon himself. One tells of a monster celebration on the banks of the Ohio near Cincinnati, on the Fourth of July, 1806, at which Jefferson was toasted as "the supporter of the rights of man . . . whose integrity and virtue will live in the remem-brance of a free and enlightened people, when calumniators are buried in oblivion," and cheered in the playing of "Jefferson's March" with a two-gun salute (George Washington received only one gun). Lyrics in praise of Jefferson are set to the tune of "Hail, Columbia" and

"Anacreon in Heaven" (subsequently that of "The Star-Spangled Banner"). In this album one finds "Original Thoughts on the Election of Thomas Jefferson—composed by an obscure Alien," in faltering meter but full of rhapsody. There is a satire sung at a Federalist rally on Independence Day in New Hampshire, which begins:

> Great Washington's hobby, from first dawning youth,
> Was virtue, and valor, and wisdom, and truth.
> While Jefferson's hobby, on Chesterfield's plan,
> Was to *rise* in the Statesman, but *sink* in the Man.

Beside this aspersion is the retort of a loyal Jeffersonian; he leaves the first two lines intact, but emends—

> And Jefferson's hobby (on Washington's plan)
> To unite in the Statesman, the PATRIOT and MAN—

for good measure adding that "John Adams's hobby is dullness profound."

Jefferson's album includes the verses of one brave poet who exclaims

> Huzza for the prudent Embargo!

Yet, as is well known, the Embargo Act of 1807 was the one keenly unpopular deed of Jefferson's eight years. High-handed, it infringed upon American trade, "making many smugglers and traitors, but not a single hero," as Henry Adams remarked. If this be thought New England prejudice, one may hear Mr. Albert Jay Nock, that warm Jeffersonian of our own day, call it "the most arbitrary, inquisitorial, and confiscatory measure formulated in American legislation up to the period of the Civil War."[14] Forbidding the sailing of American ships upon the high seas lest they fall into the clutches of warring Europeans, the Embargo was humiliating to patriots and disastrous to traders. Except for theorists who shared Jefferson's hope that "economic sanctions" might come to be a moral equivalent for the War of 1812, nobody loved the Embargo. Yet, as an experiment, much could have been said for it. At the end of his very successful administration Jefferson was left temporarily discredited. Many families in the South, as well as in the Middle States and New England, were ruined by Jefferson's prudential isolation; they never forgave him, and handed to the next generation their hatred along with their insolvency. Fredrika Bremer in 1850 on a railway journey through Georgia met a man "in person not unlike a meal-sack, whose father had lost $50,000 by the Embargo; he said 'I regard Tom Jefferson as the compound of everything which is rascally, mean, wicked, dishonorable.' "[15]

IV

Indeed, in speaking of Jefferson the hero it is necessary to take account of that obbligato of hatred heard throughout his Presidency. Some of the First Families of Virginia had detested him since the Revolution, because he fought to end aristocratic privileges like entail, and the Episcopal clergy because he divorced Church and State. In fact, parsons and "economic royalists" were Jefferson's born enemies. In Jefferson's day the charge of irreligion was a much more effective weapon of attack, before the eyes of the common man, than the charge of economic heresy. John Adams, although as much the skeptic as Jefferson, held economic views approved by the traders of New England, and hence was never set in the public pillory among the godless. A good many politicians who did not themselves give a rap for the divinity of Christ or inspiration of the Scriptures seized upon the theological brush with which to tar Jefferson. Jefferson avoided public utterance of his gravest doubts, but at heart seems to have been a deist. He disliked all sects, but came closest to being a Unitarian. He held vague hopes of immortality, but believed above all else in the religion of progress, of human betterment, "passing over us like a cloud of light." "It does me no injury for my neighbor to say there are twenty gods, or no god. It neither picks my pocket nor breaks my leg," he wrote in the *Notes on Virginia,* in tolerant words which irritated many. Although his views had been fixed long before he went abroad, Jefferson upon returning from France found he was suspected of being "Frenchified" or "contaminated" by alien nonsense. From Virginia the prejudice spread elsewhere as soon as Jefferson began to fill Federal office.

Doctor Timothy Dwight, president of Yale, "Pope" of Connecticut, and akin by blood or marriage to those Hillhouses and Wolcotts and Wadsworths who held the purse-strings of Southern New England, led the assault. In a typical *Discourse preached on the Fourth of July* he predicted in 1800 that under Jefferson all Bibles would be burnt, children "wheedled or terrified" into singing *Ça ira,* and "we may see our wives and daughters the victims of legal prostitution." The nationalization of women, as Doctor Dwight well knew, is always a clarion call. In his later book *The Character of Thomas Jefferson* Doctor Dwight charged that this heretic was also vain, insincere, double-faced, and "would descend to the low means and artifices of a practiced intriguer and demagogue to gain favor with the lowest classes of the community." To have become the People's President was, in fact, an act of perfidy! Stephen Cullen Carpenter announced that Jefferson had denied "the right of property, marriage, natural affection, chastity, and decency."[16] In New York the Reverend John Mason warned the American people against electing a President who "disbelieves the existence of an universal deluge."[17] Upon Jefferson's inauguration, it was reported, pious New England housewives buried their Bibles in their gardens to keep them from confiscation.

Assaults upon Jefferson continued to mingle economics with godliness. A parson significantly named the Reverend Cotton Mather Smith charged that Jefferson had robbed a widow and her fatherless children of an estate of £10,000, entrusted him as executor. The President calmly replied that his sister was the only widow whose estate he had ever administered, and that so far as he knew she had no complaints. In the days of Jefferson's Vice-Presidency the Reverend Jedidiah Champion of Litchfield, Connecticut, had prayed with fervor for President Adams, and added "O Lord! wilt Thou bestow upon the Vice-President a double portion of Thy grace, *for Thou knowest he needs it.*" But after Jefferson's accession to the highest office, the Reverend James Abercrombie of Philadelphia declared that on account of the incumbent's atheism he was "very reluctant to read the prayers for the President of the United States, prescribed in the Episcopal ritual." Whether it were better for God to give, or withhold, His grace from Mr. Jefferson was a puzzling question.

Jefferson received scores of anonymous letters about his religion, as his private papers show. They were far more numerous during his first than his second term, by which time most people saw the absurdity of burying their Bibles. A typical letter signed "A. B." and written on January 25, 1801, tells Jefferson he is rumored to be "a kind neighbour" and "certainly a Great Man," but, says the writer, "I am afraid of your Religion & your Politicks." He confesses he is not a pious man himself, but fears that if Christianity is uprooted in the United States "oaths will be nothing, and no one will be safe in his person or property." Probably the writer had never read Swift's dry remarks on abolishing Christianity in England. Another letter, signed "a poor Afflicted Sickly bruised Reed," written May 2, 1801, exhorts Jefferson to look to the Bible for wisdom, to pass more severe laws against swearing and Sabbath-breaking. A letter from "a Youth of fifteen," on March 10 of this same year, admits the alarm felt by those "who have some Regard for Religion, Liberty, and good Order," at Jefferson's efforts to destroy "the Constitution which was framed by our forefathers." That a man so near the fountain-head of our national life as Jefferson should have been accused of laying violent hands upon the "forefathers" is a fact worth noting.

The dwindling of such letters during Jefferson's second term sprang, in part, from a rather curious situation. The great mass of his followers were humble rather than rich, farmers rather than city folk. Tidings of Jefferson's deism reached them faintly. More surely they knew he had eased their tax burdens, and was opening to them a vast new frontier for settlement. In other words, he was their friend. And it was among these people, Baptist and Methodist, that a great wave of revivalism surged during the early years of Jefferson's Presidency—the Gasper River, Holly Springs, Red River, Flemingsburg, and other camp-meetings which excited nationwide comment. From the loneliness of back country and frontier they discovered the gregarious warmth of revivals. By the light of flickering lanterns, beneath the tents of Zion, in the muddy waters of a hundred inland rivers, men and women were washed in the blood of the Lamb. A generation later, in the backwoods of the Lincoln country, Herndon found them hugging each other and singing in ecstasy that was half religious, half sexual—

> I have my Jesus in my arms,
> Sweet as honey, strong as bacon ham.

At Newburgh, New York, *The Recorder of the Times,* August 29, 1804, like many another rural newspaper, remarked the incontestable fact that in Mr. Jefferson's "wise and virtuous administration" God Almighty has "poured out his spirit among the people in a manner before unknown in America." It was a mighty rebuke to Doctor Timothy Dwight and his chilly pewholders. In fact, it became common for the rank-and-file Jeffersonians—radical in politics, conservative in religion—to deny as calumny any doubts of their President's piety.[18] To many, Jefferson's stand against "priestcraft" struck a chord of Protestant sympathy loud enough to be heard above the thunders of Congregational and Episcopal pulpits. One of the worst poems ever written to praise an American hero, called *The Pudding proved by eating of it,* printed in Monroe County, Virginia, in 1804, declares:

> His States' Work doth not depend on any Clergy Whim,
> His Bus'ness hath naught to do with a Priest-Craft System:
> His religious Opinions is but between his God and him.

.   .   .   .

Better have Deist President that is of mild command,
Than a Christian one, that is for an overbearing hand.

The great mass of Americans, then as later, refused to pay attention
to the handful of militant freethinkers who tried to claim Jefferson,
or to the small band of parsons who refused to bury the hatchet. Even
today a few conservative Virginia dames—born and bred in a socio-
economic stratum whose prejudices are well-nigh immortal—think of
Tom Jefferson as the freethinker and dangerous radical, who made
the Episcopal Church in Virginia "just like any other church." But
in the main, Jefferson's reply in old age to a prying individual—"Say
nothing of my religion. It is known to my God and myself alone"—
has been respected by his average hero-worshippers.

Some charges made against Jefferson early and late by his enemies—
that he chattered like a French monkey, loved flattery, and practiced
vivisection for cruelty in the name of science—were such distortions
of a silent, dignified, kindly man that they had not enough vitality
to live. Even Washington Irving's portrait of "William Kieft" in his
Knickerbocker's History in 1809—dressed in "cocked hat and corduroy
small-clothes" and mounted on "a raw-boned charger," who invented
carts that went before horses and weathercocks that turned against the
wind, who lived in "a sweet sequestered swamp" on an estate "commonly known by the name of Dog's Misery," and who punctuated
counsels of state with thunderous blasts of his nose blown into a red
cotton handkerchief—is funny, but even more unrecognizable than
Maxwell Anderson's picture of Peter Stuyvesant as Franklin Delano
Roosevelt. *The Jonnycake Papers* later burlesqued such caricatures
by recalling that "Tom Jefferson . . . was nothing but a mean-spirited,
low-lived fellow, the son of a half-breed Indian squaw, sired by a
Virginia mulatto father, as was well known in the neighborhood
where he was raised wholly on hoe-cake (made of coarse-ground
Southern corn), bacon and hominy, with an occasional change of
fricasseed bullfrog, for which abominable reptiles he had acquired a
taste during his residence among the French at Paris." Such hostile
nicknames as "Thomas the Magician" or "Thomas Conundrum," seeking to suggest political skulduggery, never caught on. The public
indeed had decided that Jefferson's was white magic.

The rankest canard which flew about Jefferson was that his taste
ran to colored mistresses. It seems to have been invented in the North,
where to some Federalists the fact was perhaps incredible that a Southern gentleman might own a hundred female slaves without claiming

a *droit de seigneur.* In *The Portfolio,* issued in Philadelphia in October, 1802, one finds this lyric about the President of the United States:

A SONG

Supposed to have been written by the Sage of Monticello.

Et etiam fusco grata colore Venus.—Ovid.
"And Venus pleases, though as black as jet."

Tune: "Yankee Doodle."

Of all the damsels on the green,
On mountain or in valley,
A lass so luscious ne'er was seen
As Monticellian Sally.

Chorus: Yankee doodle, who's the noodle?
What wife were half so handy?
To breed a flock of slaves for stock,
A blackamoor's the dandy.

What though she by the glands secretes;
Must I stand shil—I, shall—I?
Tuck'd up between a pair of sheets
There's no perfume like Sally.

The little poet Tom Moore, visiting Washington in 1804 and presented at the White House by the anti-Jeffersonian Merrys, was irked by the tall President's failure to take special note of the greatest living Irish bard. To the joy of Federalists he published his verse epistle to Thomas Hume, describing the chieftain in Washington who

retires to lash his slaves at home;
Or woo, perhaps, some black Aspasia's charms,
And dream of freedom in his bondmaid's arms.

James Fenimore Cooper's old schoolmaster "cracked his jokes daily about Mr. Jefferson and Black Sal, never failing to place his libertinism in strong relief against the approved morals of George III."[19] The rumor has no known basis in fact. Jefferson, so scrupulous to answer charges which had a grain of truth, never troubled to quash this story.

Yet it had a long subterranean life. During the campaign of 1860 enemies of Abraham Lincoln, trying to damage him with the liberal as well as the Southern vote, claimed he had said Jefferson was a slaveholder who "brought his own children under the hammer, and made money of his debaucheries." Also that one of Jefferson's dusky daughters "was sold some years ago at public auction in New Orleans, and was purchased by a society of gentlemen who wished to testify by her liberation their admiration of the statesman who 'dreamt of freedom in a slave's embrace.'" Lincoln branded this supposed speech of his "a base forgery."[20] "Old Martin," who for many years rang the campus bell of the University of Virginia, proudly boasted that he was a great-grandson of Thomas Jefferson. Although some of the Jeffersonians of Charlottesville thought he might have been a wild oat sown by one of the statesman's "fast" Randolph grandsons, one suspects the projection in time of an old legend. The University founded by Jefferson has always been very proud of him, never prone to apologize for either his real or imaginary vices. In fact it is a roosting-place for the more fantastic rumors about him—such as, that he laid out its serpentine walls while drunk, and that he built a row of small houses back of the pavilions to serve as collegiate brothels. Quite without truth, it is sometimes said that in the charter of the University of Virginia Jefferson provided for licensed prostitution, upon the theory that such an outlet was better for young bullocks than vice without regulation. As recently as 1930 Mr. John Cook Wyllie of the University Library received a series of inquiries, asking for a copy or photostat of the charter, from the Public Library of St. Louis. After some coyness it came out that a patron of the St. Louis Public Library had been greatly upset by hearing this ancient rumor.

The remaining charges against Jefferson's morals stem from the year 1802 and the vilification of a Scotchman named James Thomson Callender. The facts are ironic. Callender, who had fled his own land after libelling the British Government, was first thought by the credulous Jefferson to be a misunderstood, mistreated democrat. So Jefferson gave him secret patronage. This journeyman of slander soon began to attack the Federalist Party, Adams, and Hamilton. His snapping at Hamilton's heels forced that statesman to clear himself of suspected unfaithfulness to public trust, at the expense of revealing his adultery with Mrs. Reynolds—a brave but most humiliating disclosure by Hamilton. The Jeffersonians were gleeful. Attacks upon President Adams, however, sent Callender to a Richmond jail for nine months. Upon Jefferson's inauguration Callender was pardoned and his fine of $200 was remitted. But a delay in the return of this money so angered Callender that he turned against Jefferson, and bedaubed him with the same mud with which he had spattered Hamilton. In 1802 in the Richmond *Recorder* he printed charges against

Jefferson whose stain can never be quite forgotten by those otherwise disposed to hate the third President. Callender was a maudlin drunkard who often threatened to commit suicide, and in 1803 was found drowned in three feet of water in the James River; but his work lived long after him. A swarm of pamphlets took up the charges, newspapers printed sniggering allusions to them, and early in 1805 they were aired upon the floor of the Massachusetts Legislature by Congressman John W. Hulbert.

The charge of cowardice in Revolutionary days, and Jefferson's alleged statement that belief in God was "of no social importance," were spiced with accusations of sexual error, in the Callender-Hulbert libels. Jefferson admitted the truth of only one charge—that as a young man he had made improper and unsuccessful advances to Mrs. John Walker, wife of a lifelong friend and neighbor. This memoir of his dead life must have caused exquisite pain to the sensitive aristocrat. It was singular to find him writhing upon the same barb, driven by the same hand, which had pierced Hamilton. Jefferson penned a confession "that when young and single I offered love to a handsome lady—I acknoledge [sic] its incorrectness," and circulated it among his intimate friends and cabinet officers, with denial of the other charges.[21] Jefferson had the misfortune at this time to become involved with the talkative, none-too-sympathetic Lees, Henry Lee serving as go-between for Jefferson and the unhappy husband—who in 1806 requested in Jefferson's hand a statement of "his, & his lady's entire exculpation" for publication if the scandal ever reappeared.[22] It is safe to say, as Douglas S. Freeman remarks, that Jefferson was no hero in the eyes of the Lee family or the idealistic Robert E. Lee; they and related Virginia families have tended to look upon Jefferson with contempt.[23] Americans at large, however, have long forgotten this episode, buried among the rotten timber of Callender's libels. It is probable that a score of modern Virginians have heard about Jefferson's mythical taste for octoroons to one who has heard the real story of poor Mrs. John Walker.

Critical students of Jefferson have long been troubled by an aspect of his personality which makes less inflammable tinder for scandal, but comes closer to the real man. It is akin to the only serious blemish of Franklin, a pliant expediency. Were it not for the stalwart example of Washington, cynics might conclude that the greatest heroes of the early Republic were men who succeeded because of their resemblance to Sam Slick. Washington alone towered above the fogs of opportunism, and did all his work without recourse to occasional backstairs stratagems. He alone had a scrupulous code beyond that of the practical politician, and deservedly is the greatest hero of our early Republic. Franklin and Jefferson generally contrived to compromise issues without compromising themselves, but here and there they slipped a trifle. Clearly below them, in a descending scale, were men like Patrick Henry—who, as Jefferson knew, was a rather shady individual—and Robert Morris, so-called "financier of the Revolution." (Although Morris is still in patriotic favor, with hotels and credit associations named for him, it is now clear, as Professor Abernethy remarks, that the Revolution financed Robert Morris, and that he embraced the cause of independence as a heaven-sent speculative opportunity.[24] But remarkably few, indeed, are the unworthies who have slipped into the fold of American hero-worship.)

The deeps of Jefferson's character are not easy to plumb. In the first place, he was a very amiable gentleman. He liked to please people. In the days of his Ministry to France he obliged a large circle of friends and acquaintances by shopping for them: even Mrs. John Adams wrote asking him to buy her daughter "two pairs of corsets," somehow assuming that Mr. Jefferson without being told would know the right size. Jefferson came close to being a born victim of that American phrase, "let George do it." He was a natural committeeman, and if destiny had not drafted him for a higher role he would have made the ideal Vice-President. He wished to say what people wanted to hear, and (despite his authorship of a great document of defiance) he dreaded to provoke criticism, offense, personal friction. The rigors of debate had no appeal for him. Although he might collect gossip about his enemies with the calmness of research, he was reluctant to make aggressive use of it. Only when goaded did he fight back; even then he was quick to offer the olive-branch. One of his most characteristic utterances was the statement of his First Inaugural, "We are all republicans—we are all federalists."

In his talk and his letters Jefferson usually let others set the topic and tone, often restating their opinions with his own greater literary finesse. Once this habit brought him to the brink of political ruin. This was at the time of his flowery outburst, in the Latin vein, to Mazzei on April 24, 1796, during Washington's administration and pointed at the President, about those Americans "who were Samsons in the field and Solomons in the council, but who have had their heads shorn by the harlot England." Jefferson was deeply shocked when this letter bounced back in the public eye, and did all he could to unsay it.[25] A little later, proof reached Washington that Jefferson's nephew living at Monticello had forged a letter of flattery, in disguised handwriting under the fictitious name "John Langhorne," hoping to trap Washington into private utterances which might be used against him politically. Whether Jefferson had a hand in this naïve ruse cannot now be proved, in black and white, but Washington himself and some of his later partisans have so believed.[26] Most people know nothing of this incident, and the biographers of Jefferson strangely do not mention it—though they like to tell how Jefferson, one later spring, placed upon the bust of Washington at Monticello a wreath of immortelles a French admirer had sent the philosopher to wear on his own birthday.

Jefferson the man was easy to know, but impossible to know well. Many called him "a trimmer." Sometimes it appeared that he steered a circuitous course, catching the prevailing winds as he went along, to reach in the end a wholly honorable port. John Quincy Adams, naturally inclined to overstate the case, said that Jefferson had "a memory so pandering to the will that in deceiving others he seems to have begun by deceiving himself."[27] More sympathetically, one must say that Jefferson had been forced to learn the arts of expediency. As a young Governor, his scrupulosity over legal points had been the prime reason for a failure he never forgot. Later he was prone to believe that the end justified the means. In his most important decision, the Louisiana Purchase—in which he privately admitted that he had "done an act beyond the Constitution" in not waiting for the cumbersome machinery of democracy—certainly the result was splendid, and vindicated by all patriotism and good sense. Justifying his high-handed methods in the Burr conspiracy, free to admit that democracy is too slow in crises, Jefferson the President wrote (in words so alien to Jefferson the Governor): "Should we have ever gained our Revolution, if we had bound our hands by manacles of the law?"[28] It was significant that President Roosevelt, in his message to Congress on September 3, 1940, apropos of the "swap" of fifty old destroyers for eight naval bases for defense of the Western Hemisphere, should have buttressed himself with the precedent of Jefferson's "unconstitutional" bargain with Napoleon—calling his exchange "the most important action in the re-enforcement of our national defense that has been taken since the Louisiana Purchase." The American people, it appears, approved both.

Jefferson's was a complex brain—the brain of a dreamer and idealist, trained by experience into a shrewd, adaptable, hard-headed politician —and it let him see all sides of a subject. His very penetration bred contradictions, and led him sometimes into passing inconsistency. (He has been quoted for and against states' rights and the right of secession, for and against restricted immigration, for and against the spoils system, for and against a big navy and preparedness.) Though some of these contradictions are more apparent than real, it must be admitted that Jefferson's intellect—far from being a single-track mind like Washington's—was a whole switch-yard. But the most vital fact remains to be added. Jefferson's devotion to the United States, above all other interests private or public, selfish or partisan, was superbly consistent. There he never wavered. Hamilton's intrigues with the British Crown in 1792, which carried him perilously near to treason,[29] have no counterpart in the Jefferson pattern. Only to political dogmas or exclusive economic interests did Jefferson fail to show a fixed loyalty. There he allowed himself to blow hot and cold, depending upon occasions.

Of course the average American on the basis of his vague knowledge, in early times as well as today, could not be expected to rationalize all these things. He was simply disposed to accept Jefferson as "the People's friend," and this trust was not ill placed. Jefferson's contribution to the United States, as statesman and President, was not an airtight or even very logical political system. It was chiefly a faith—faith in the long run in the dependability, wisdom, and honesty of the common literate individual, as represented in his day by the agrarian majority. Woodrow Wilson said: "The immortality of Thomas Jefferson does not lie in any one of his achievements, but in his attitude toward mankind." This verdict, whether endorsed by a great modern liberal or by the man in the street, is the core of the Jefferson cult.

V

Through the long sunset years between Jefferson's retirement in 1809 and his death in 1826, he became an oracle and patriarch. He was one of the last surviving symbols of the Revolution, the sage on the hill-top, who (as a visitor wrote in 1816), after "having filled a seat higher than that of kings, succeeds with graceful dignity to that of the good neighbor." A typical English visitor to America, Isaac Candler, grew bored with being told that Jefferson was "the most learned man in the world," and with hearing Jefferson's opinions on art and literature quoted to end all discussion. (The mantle of versatility was already being cast about the shoulders of great Americans.) Jefferson's growing financial embarrassments were neglected by his native state, but brought generous gifts from citizens of New York, Philadelphia, and Baltimore. In June, 1826, Jefferson declined on the score of health an invitation to become the city of Washington's guest of honor on the Fiftieth Birthday of the Declaration of Independence. His reply, traced with a feeble hand, but stating with his old fire the conviction that "the mass of mankind has not been born with saddles on their backs," was published immediately as a broadside. It was his last pastoral charge. Shortly after noon of that Fourth of July—the date upon whose prime validity Jefferson had so long insisted—the statesman breathed his last. Every schoolboy knows that John Adams, expiring on the same day in Massachusetts, faintly murmured, "Thomas Jefferson still survives." Many Americans felt a sentiment thus expressed by a Virginia newspaper: "In this most singular coincidence, the finger of Providence is plainly visible! It hallows the Declaration of Independence as the Word of God, and is the bow in the Heavens, that promises its principles shall be eternal." But at least one jealous Jeffersonian, who lived in Albemarle County, thought that John Adams's death on the same day "was a damned Yankee trick."[30]

In death, as in life, Jefferson remained second to Washington. Daniel Webster, in his great joint eulogy on Jefferson and Adams at Faneuil Hall in 1826, exclaimed: "Washington is in the clear upper sky. These other stars have now joined the American constellation; they circle round their center, and the Heavens beam with new light." It was plain that none could rival the glory of Washington, who had fought for and won the liberty that Jefferson and Adams had phrased. The first to hold highest office and the first to die, Washington was divorced more completely than they from sections and parties. It was also clear that to the country at large Jefferson was a greater hero than Adams. His single deeds—from the Declaration to the Louisiana Purchase—had been more splendid, and his policies had struck deeper root. The Adamses have always served America well, but their vanity, coldness, and knack of doing the gracious thing "in the ungracious way" have kept them in a class inferior to the heroes—the worthies.

It was Jefferson's good luck, and the nation's, that his loyal pupils Madison and Monroe for sixteen years carried on his will and testament. The liberalisms of later men, who in various ways tried to revive

the faith of Jefferson—Jackson, Lincoln, Woodrow Wilson—were uprooted more quickly by falling into hostile hands. Jeffersonianism
enjoyed a long fruitful summer of increase; it became a name and
philosophy of rich American associations. Even the Whigs, Jackson's
enemies and Webster's friends, who had taken all there was to salvage
from the shipwreck of the anti-Jefferson Federalists, in 1841 after their
Log Cabin campaign, as a New York newspaper noted, "have of late
years repeatedly declared themselves true Jeffersonian Democrats."[31]
Henry S. Randall, in a devoted three-volume life of Jefferson in 1858,
remarked that although Jefferson was still secretly assailed "by class and
hereditary hate," yet no orator dared publicly attack the two greatest
Americans, Washington and Jefferson, "the one who was the Sword
of his country, and the other the Pen."

Walt Whitman—who had younger brothers named Thomas Jefferson and Andrew Jackson Whitman—spoke of the two agrarian statesmen as "the sainted Jefferson and Jackson." In youth the poet of "the
Divine Average" had hailed Jefferson as "the Columbus of our political
faith," and in old age still cherished him as "among the greatest of
the great."[32] With the storm of Civil War darkening, Jefferson, as
author of the affirmation that all men are created free and equal,
began to receive fresh honor in the North. The new Republican Party,
dressing its ranks for a great crusade, looked to Jefferson the idealist.
Lincoln, replying on April 6, 1859, to an invitation to a Jefferson birthday rally in Boston, was moved to grave mirth by the shifting of old
party lines. He told the story of two drunks who got into a fight:
each fought himself out of his own coat and into that of the other
fellow. Lincoln remarked that Jefferson's land, the South, now held
that personal liberty was nothing in comparison with property rights,
while "Republicans, on the contrary, are for both the man and the
dollar, but in case of conflict the man before the dollar." That was
Jeffersonianism. "The principles of Jefferson are the definitions and
axioms of free society," Lincoln added. "All honor to Jefferson—to
the man who, in the concrete pressure of a struggle for national independence by a single people, had the coolness, forecast, and capacity
to introduce into a mere revolutionary document an abstract truth,
applicable to all men and all times."

Jefferson as hero waned somewhat after the Civil War. New idols
like Lincoln and Grant tended to dim the galaxy of the Revolution.
The unity symbolized by the amended Constitution now appeared
more precious than the ringing defiance of the Declaration. Jefferson's

memory had neither its Weems nor its John Hay: his very character was too deep an enigma for conventional biography. Orators, novelists, and poets seemed to pass him by; even Monticello grew shabbier, more neglected, with each passing year. His liberalism fell upon deaf ears in the era Vernon Parrington has called "the Great Barbecue." Only here and there were men to whom Jefferson was a magic spirit. The most ardent of them was Henry George, shocked over land-grabbing in the West and the growing slums of Eastern cities. Henry George believed in Jefferson's God—the Author of Nature who had created the earth for men to till, and to exercise the gift He had given them of life, liberty, and the pursuit of happiness. George conceived the Single-Tax as an offshoot of Jefferson's philosophy, as a safeguard against exploitation of the soil. But he was in the minority.

The Democratic Party, reviving slowly after the Civil War, made Jefferson its patron saint; but the national leadership of Jefferson's region, the South, had been shattered. The dominant party, the Republicans, had forgotten Jefferson since Lincoln's day. A semi-liberal like Theodore Roosevelt (who shared the historical loyalties of his Federalist friend Lodge) detested Jefferson. The only thing he could approve was the Louisiana Purchase; in all else Jefferson was a weakling. Roosevelt's most blasting damnation of Bryan was a comparison with Jefferson—well-meaning, shallow, cheap, vacillating, possessing "Jefferson's nervous fear of doing anything that may seem to be unpopular with the rank and file of the people." Thus he wrote to Taft on September 4, 1906. Indeed, Jefferson was out of fashion with more simon-pure liberals than Roosevelt. One of the most powerful books of that decade, Herbert Croly's *The Promise of American Life* in 1909, offered stinging epithets about "Jefferson's intellectual superficiality and insincerity." Even in his champions Jefferson was unfortunate: in the muckraking era, William Randolph Hearst took up "Jeffersonian democracy" as his favorite shibboleth.

Wilson had marked intellectual sympathy for Jefferson, but no warm personal admiration; he once told Colonel House that Alexander Hamilton "was easily the ablest" statesman of the early Republic.[33] After the Great War, Jefferson was often quoted on "entangling alliances," approved as an isolationist and lover of peace. In view of Red Russia, little was said of Jefferson the radical. Upon another tack, in 1928, it was asserted direfully that the election of a Catholic President would "roll back the progress of Democracy of Jefferson and Jackson."[34]

VI

Jefferson did not come into his own until the New Deal. Whether consciously or not, he has been built up to offset Lincoln, as a symbol of the Democratic Party, and to give the new liberalism its sanction by tradition. The great Jefferson Memorial now being completed in Washington, the reawakened cult at Monticello, the three-cent stamp, the new Jefferson nickel, and the massive face which Gutzon Borglum has carved upon Mount Rushmore—all proclaim that he is our newest Federal god in the highest degree. Some of these tributes might have come at all events; together, they show an unmistakable drift.

Franklin D. Roosevelt as candidate for President, at St. Paul in the spring of 1932, declared that Benjamin Franklin, Jefferson, and Theodore Roosevelt were the three great Americans who knew best the cross-currents of our folk life, the hopes and fears of the common people—"and of these three Jefferson was in many ways the deepest student. . . . His, after all, was the essential point of view that has been held by our truly great leaders in every generation." (The exclusion of Lincoln was perhaps a political one, since he, rather than the "progressive" Theodore Roosevelt, was embedded so deeply in Republican myth.) A few months later in San Francisco, making his notable speech on Progressive Government, Franklin D. Roosevelt ranked Jefferson first on the roll-call of American liberals, followed by Theodore Roosevelt and Woodrow Wilson. As President, on July 4, 1936, at Monticello, he glowingly praised Jefferson's "consecration" to social justice and to "the freedom of the human mind." Mr. Roosevelt has quoted George Washington a little gingerly, even on so safe a subject as popular education, lest he be contradicted by other passages "from the somewhat voluminous writings and messages of the First President"[35]—but of Jefferson's mind, which many regard as more perilously self-contradictory, Mr. Roosevelt has always spoken with assurance. In a more personal view, the parallel between the master of Monticello and the squire of Hyde Park, another gentle radical, is too good to miss. In July, 1937, it was reported that a portrait of Jefferson painted by the Polish patriot Kosciuszko, and carried at that time from the Polish Embassy to the White House, bore a striking resemblance to Mr. Roosevelt. Certainly the thirty-second President feels at home in the milieu of the third. At the University of Virginia on June 10, 1940, the day of Italy's entry into the War, the President welcomed an occasion to speak his mind in "this university founded by the first great American teacher of democracy." That Thomas Jefferson is Mr. Roosevelt's political hero one can hardly doubt, or that his ideals have tinged the philosophy of the New Deal.[36]

Claude G. Bowers, admirer and biographer of Jefferson, was made Ambassador to Spain by President Roosevelt in 1933. From Madrid, to the Democratic campaign of 1936, Mr. Bowers contributed his book, *Jefferson in Power: The Death Struggle of the Federalists*. It described the career of a liberal aristocrat through eight years of serene triumph, winning the people's love, engaging in vast public works, and readily crushing his enemies who had "fought with far-seeing cunning from behind the protecting shield of the Supreme Court." Mr. Bowers pointed his moral by saying, "the story is offered as a warning to all succeeding political parties and politicians that public opinion cannot be defied with impunity." (Dissenters remarked that Mr. Bowers had nothing to say about Jefferson's dictum that "the best government is that which governs least.") While Mr. Bowers, here and elsewhere, implies that Jefferson would applaud the New Deal, Mr. James Truslow Adams in *The Living Jefferson* (1936) states that Jefferson would have hated it. Needless to say, both men agree with Jefferson.

The enemies of Jefferson are dead, or in hiding. Nowadays no such words are uttered publicly as those of Bishop Henry Codman Potter, "shepherd of the Four Hundred," at the Washington Inaugural Centennial of 1889 in New York: "We have exchanged the Washingtonian dignity for the Jeffersonian simplicity, which was in truth only another name for the Jacksonian vulgarity." Under the new liberalism, the Federalist heirlooms of the Republican Party have been locked away in the cupboard. Since Andrew Mellon was called "the greatest Secretary of the Treasury since Alexander Hamilton," the name of Jefferson's bitterest enemy has scarcely been heard in American politics. Republicans, like the Whigs of Webster's day, now invoke "sound Jeffersonian principles." Nobody can raise many votes with sound Hamiltonian principles.

Conservatives may also claim the hereditary honors, as it were, in having among their ranks the lineal descendants of Jefferson, the Coolidges of Boston. This family presented Jefferson's writing-desk to the nation in 1880, has served on the trusteeship of Monticello and the new Federal memorial, and takes unfailing pride in Jefferson's memory. Thomas Jefferson Coolidge, banker and member of the Somerset Club, served as Under-Secretary of the Treasury early in the New Deal, but it was apparent that he was no scourge of the vested interests. Harold Jefferson Coolidge in 1937 published a slim volume called *Thoughts on Thomas Jefferson: Or What Jefferson Was Not*. He there pays his respects to " 'Jefferson Clubs' whose leaders are politicians of the type of 'Al' Smith, 'Jim' Farley, or James M. Curley. These are the men who talk most about Jefferson." Mr. Coolidge, one gathers, is a little irritated, knowing that by any other name the wild Irish rose would smell as sweet.

Today three great shrines to Jefferson are being repaired or built. The first is Monticello, where Jefferson lavished ingenuity over wind-vanes and double-action doors and experimented with new seeds and cuttings, and where, as he wrote, "all my wishes end." Thousands of pilgrims, in Jefferson's later years, called to pay their respects; the sage's hospitality to them helped to drive him bankrupt. After his death Monticello fell into strangers' hands; less reverent visitors, seeking souvenirs, broke open the high iron gates and chipped pieces from Jefferson's obelisk. At its lowest ebb the estate was bought by a Jewish commodore in the Navy, Uriah Levy. His nephew, Jefferson Monroe Levy, a New Yorker who had made millions in Canadian Pacific Railway and had a taste for politics, inherited it and took some pride in possession. In 1923 he sold Monticello for half a million dollars to the newly formed Jefferson Memorial Foundation—which immediately turned it into a national shrine. Only 19,414 visitors came in the first year, and the outlook, with a staggering mortgage, was not bright. But through the following years popular interest in Jefferson quickened; new biographies were printed, orators invoked Jefferson more warmly, magazines published articles on Jefferson and the New Deal. Last year more than 100,000 visitors paid a half dollar each for admission to the shrine—even though Monticello is more remote from large cities and major highways than are Mount Vernon, Franklin's grave, the Hermitage, or Grant's tomb. Chairman of the Foundation and most enterprising of Jeffersonians is Mr. Stuart Gibboney, a direct descendant of Patrick Henry, veteran of the Spanish-American War and the Boxer uprising, and New York attorney for Angostura Bitters. Mr. Gibboney, a good friend of the Jefferson Coolidges, takes pleasure in sending them—with something of a twinkle in his eye—copies of their great ancestor's more inflammatory utterances.

Jeffersonians have long regretted the lack of a great Federal shrine, comparable to the Washington Monument and the Lincoln Memorial. Through the efforts of Mr. Gibboney and the Foundation, aided by sympathy from the Democratic Party, Congress in June, 1934, created a Jefferson Memorial Commission. Its choice of a site is significant of Jefferson's new hero-rank. When the Lincoln Memorial was built to complete an axis running from the Capitol through the Mall, and past the Washington Monument to the river bank, it was seen that at some future date the general cruciform plan would be finished by an intersecting axis drawn from the White House through the Washington obelisk to the tidal basin, where hundreds of cherry trees bloom in the spring. This site, long awaiting some memorial to match Washington's and Lincoln's, is that of the new $3,000,000 shrine to Jefferson. A circular temple of white marble, in the Palladian style of dome and colonnade that Jefferson introduced to America, will house a heroic standing figure of Jefferson yet unmade. President Roosevelt broke ground in December, 1938, and in November, 1939, laid the cornerstone, saying, on the latter occasion: "He lived as we live, in the midst of a struggle between rule by the self-chosen individual or the self-appointed few, and rule by the franchise and approval of the many. He believed as we do, that the average opinion of mankind is in the long run superior to the dictates of the self-chosen."

The third project is in St. Louis. The state of Missouri has always had a special affection for Jefferson. Even though he narrowly missed having a state as namesake, when Jefferson Territory was rechristened Colorado, in Missouri Jefferson has received more official honors than in his native Virginia. Jefferson, it is not forgotten, bought from Napoleon the inland empire of Upper Louisiana, of which St. Louis was the capital, and described this commonwealth as "choice country with room enough." The St. Louis Exposition of 1904 was held to celebrate this Purchase and to honor Jefferson. Missouri's capital is Jefferson City, and the statesman's statue rises above the capitol steps. In 1883 the University of Missouri asked for, and received from the Jefferson heirs, the original tombstone discarded from Monticello; it has been ever since the most prized possession on that campus. (Some years ago, President Richard H. Jesse of the University of Missouri caused a furore among loyal Missouri Jeffersonians when, at a dinner of the Knife and Fork Club of Kansas City, he mentioned the old darkey who claimed descent from Jefferson, and other "intimate" rumors which Jesse as a Virginian was disposed to believe.) From Missouri Jefferson has received many miscellaneous tributes: In 1856 the Legislature commissioned the state's best artist, George Caleb Bingham, to copy the Stuart portrait of Jefferson for the senate chamber of the Capitol. In Missouri oratory, Jefferson's name has always carried something of the same finality as Webster's in Massachusetts or Lincoln's in Illinois; Senator George Graham Vest—greatest of Missouri spellbinders and best known for his "Tribute to a Dog"—once exclaimed, "For myself, I worship no mortal man living or dead; but if I could kneel at such a shrine, it would be with uncovered head and loving heart at the grave of Thomas Jefferson."[37] In 1931 Jefferson's birthday was made a legal holiday in Missouri. The Jefferson Highway, joining Canada and Louisiana, runs the length of the state, where an extensive new park has been reserved in Jefferson's honor.

In Jefferson's lifetime the city of St. Louis, in 1824, sent him an honorary membership in her Agricultural Society.[38] Later the city set up a Thomas Jefferson Museum. Pilgrimages from St. Louis to Monticello have been popular. In October, 1901, "the Jefferson Club of St. Louis" (organized in 1892, and soon counting 6000 members) invited "all those persons who believe in the principles and teachings of Thomas Jefferson" to go to Monticello on a chartered train and set up a block of Missouri granite near his tomb. On Jefferson's birthday in 1939 some 600 Missourians, headed by their Governor, called at Monticello. Early in the Depression, when PWA and WPA funds were flowing, St. Louis conceived a monster project to honor Jefferson the expansionist. Her politicians persuaded Congress to appoint a commission—which recommended that a tract of eighty acres, in the slums along the St. Louis waterfront, be bought and cleared as the site for a $33,000,000 "Jefferson National Expansion Memorial," with a great park, fountains, a dome-capped temple, and in the center a huge granite shaft. Today, in the colder light of economy, the project "is down to about $9,000,000, and the city of St. Louis is paying part of the cost," as Representative Cochran reported in 1939. Even so, the project was attacked by Congressman Schafer of Wisconsin: "The New Deal has strayed far from the fundamental principles and policies of government expounded and practised by Thomas Jefferson. Our New Deal friends, no doubt, ease their consciences by spending millions of dollars to erect a great memorial in honor of the man whose principles and policies they have repudiated."[39] A park has taken the place of the slums, but the fate of the Memorial as planned is still uncertain.

At all events the cult of Jefferson marches on. He has attracted the worship of more statesmen and political thinkers than of artists, dramatists, and poets. The absence from the halo of Thomas Jefferson of Washington's military glory, Jackson's rugged picturesqueness, or

Lincoln's tenderness and pathos, is responsible no doubt for the slower growth of his legend. Jefferson's greatest deeds—the Declaration of Independence, the abolition of class privilege in Virginia, the Louisiana Purchase, the fostering of secular education in America—grew increasingly less dramatic and pictorial. By no homely incident, no single gesture, can the maker of myths evoke for every man the essence of Jefferson. His appeal is more reflective, more intellectual. Doubtless this has handicapped the lovability of the man. In art, even Jefferson's arch-enemy Hamilton has fared better—in romantic novels of which Gertrude Atherton's *The Conqueror* is best, in John Drinkwater's play *Hamilton,* and in statues usually found among the marts of trade and finance. But, with his lack of glitter and "theatre," and his quiet life unmarked by Hamilton's aura of martyrdom, Jefferson is beyond question the greater American symbol. The drafter of documents and policies that stand beside the well-spring of our national life, Jefferson remains (as his most scholarly biographer Gilbert Chinard calls him) "the apostle of Americanism." He is the first great democrat, the people's friend. The stature of no traditional figure has grown taller than his, in the last generation. His fame is slow-ripening but solid. Undoubtedly, as John Adams said, Thomas Jefferson still survives.

CHAPTER EIGHT

WINNING OF THE FRONTIER: BOONE, CROCKETT, AND JOHNNY APPLESEED

Nothing can be more pleasant to the American boy than just such a life as that followed by Daniel Boone— wandering for hours through the wilderness, on the lookout for game, building the cheery camp-fire in some glen or gorge, quaffing the clear icy water from some stream, or lying flat on the back and looking up through the tree tops at the patches of blue sky, across which the snowy ships of vapor are continually sailing.

But any parent who would allow a child to follow the bewitching pleasures of such a life, would commit a sinful neglect of duty.—EDWARD S. ELLIS, *Life and Times of Col. Daniel Boone* (Philadelphia, 1884).

I

THE father of Abraham Lincoln—a relative by marriage of Daniel Boone[1]—liked to tell about a family who had moved so often that their chickens knew the signs of a new journey; the fowls would then walk up to the wagon, lie flat on the ground, and put up their feet to be tied for another trip. Restlessness has long been the keynote of life in the United States. The buckskin pioneer blazed the trail for forty-niners, railroad kings and empire builders, sooners, squatters, and migratory workers. Travel was an anodyne for loneliness, disappointment, maladjustment, and poverty; at the horizon, all skies appear to lighten. Even Napoleon, by some standards the most successful man of his day, felt a passing nostalgia for the prairies. To Las Cases he remarked that America "is an immense continent where there is an especial degree of freedom. If you are melancholy, you can get into a waggon and ride thousands of miles." The frontier took up the slack of discontent. Those seeking "something lost behind the ranges" pushed through the Cumberland Gap into the lush Kentucky grass with Daniel Boone or into the fertile reaches of the Ohio along the track of Johnny Appleseed, into the brawling Southwest behind Davy Crockett and Sam Houston, through the wind-whittled mountains of New Mexico with Kit Carson and Old Bill Williams, skirting the alkali flats of Wyoming and Utah where footprints of Jim Bridger were still fresh, and on to the Golden Gate with Frémont. The plodding horse and covered wagon roved ever westward, until the ocean halted their progress. Such was the drive of American life, as urgent as the heliotropism of sunflowers and bees. Even when old age overtook him, the pioneer sat in his rocking-chair—that American invention which Mrs. Trollope had noted with disapproval—and continued the rhythm to which his life was geared.

The winning of the West is the great fantasy of our Republic. It is the epic which the folk mind has looked upon as more truly American than the settlement of Jamestown and Plymouth, the spacious life of the old plantation, or the building of stone and steel. The rifle and the axe, which "made all men equally tall," were disciplines in the academy of Andrew Jackson and the nursery of Abraham Lincoln. Europe, as Emerson knew, stretched to the Alleghenies; America lay beyond. The American boy still dreams of Kit Carson, as personated by Daniel Beard and the Boy Scouts; the city-dweller loves movies of the hard-riding plainsman, of Gary Cooper and Gene Autry disappearing in a cloud of dust; Eastern trippers adore Indian reservations and dude ranches. The cult of the outdoors is here mingled with the appeal of adventure. Boone and Crockett are static heroes; it is indeed unlikely that they will ever become greater names than they are now, or that huge memorials will rise to them in Washington. More picturesque than our symbols of government, they do not carry the potential of emotion possessed by the Founding Fathers or our major Presidents. To some, they have the halo of rugged individualism; to a few others, they are emblems of expansion and imperialism; readers

of Cooper, a dwindling minority, think of their synthesis in Leatherstocking as the essence of old-fashioned American enterprise. The
literary mind of Europe inclines to this last point of view. A dispatch
from Paris to the New York *Times,* on April 6, 1917, commented
apropos of America's entry into the War: "Old Leather-Stocking still
slumbers in the depth of the American soul. Wait till the lion wakens.
Don't believe he will go at it half-heartedly; it is not his nature. Once
the game has been started, it must be won."

Daniel Boone, born near Reading, Pennsylvania, in 1734, was the
son of a Quaker blacksmith. It is very unlikely that he ever saw "the
Boone coat of arms" which English genealogists some years ago produced for the family.[2] A young peddler just able to write his own
name—and in later years to carve upon trees "D Boon cilled a bar"
—he quickly began to take an interest in hunting, and in exploring
as agent for the Transylvania Company. Folklore has made him "the
first white man of the West," "the Columbus of the land." But, as
the late Clarence W. Alvord pointed out, hundreds of people had
hunted in Kentucky before Boone set foot there in 1769, when get-
rich-quick schemes in Western lands were stirring many into speculative frenzy. Boone was but "one of the many pawns in the magnificent
game of chess being played on Kentucky territory," wrote Alvord, in
regretting that some more important symbol of flesh-and-blood, some
individual like Morgan or Henderson who set these mighty forces
in motion, had not been selected to typify that great adventure.[3] But,
better than his employers, Boone served as the apotheosis of the
common man, the free-lance frontiersman, "ordained by God to settle
the wilderness," and was seen by folklore as the new Moses leading
millions into the promised land. Land-jobbers have no heroic appeal.

Boone was a brave, kindly, honest soul, too simple for the com-
plexities and knaveries of civilization. Robbed, cheated, dispossessed,
he moved farther and farther west, pathetically seeking a fortune
with which he never caught up. His declaration that he wouldn't live
within "a hundred miles of a damn Yankee" was inspired less by the
spirit of Rousseau than by his experience with sons of the Puritan.
In 1783 he met a schoolmaster, John Filson, in search of literary
"copy"; in 1784 Filson brought out a purported autobiography of
Boone. In Filson's pages the pioneer talks like a pedant. He builds "a
shelter to defend us from the inclement season," and is "diverted with
innumerable animals presenting themselves perpetually to our view,"
and amid "sylvan shades" thinks of "the ruins of Persepolis or

Palmyra."[4] The book was rendered into French in 1785, showing
Boone, in elegant Chateaubriand prose, revelling among his "plaisirs
champêtres"; in 1790 it passed into German, and Boone became better
known in Europe than among his own woods. At last the fur cap of
Franklin was transported to its primeval setting. Boone, delighted
with Filson's rhetoric, acquiesced in this so-called autobiography,
stoutly maintaining in old age, "All true! Every word true! Not a
lie in it!"[5] He took less kindly to a grandiose epic written by one of
his wife's relatives, Daniel Bryan, in 1813—regretting "that he could
not sue him for slander." Boone's grievance was well grounded; *The
Mountain Muse: comprising the Adventures of Daniel Boone, and
the Power of Virtuous and Refined Beauty* is a monstrous volume. It
begins with the creation of the world, as seen over the shoulder of
John Milton. The Assembly of Seraphs in "a Firmamental Hall" elects
the fearless Boone, "who would not crush with wanton tread a fly,"
to conquer the West. A seraph bearing Boone's celestial commission
flies in search of the hunter, "whom he discovers on the Tower of
Ararat, immersed in patriotic meditations." Boone takes leave of his
tearful wife—   "My Boone!" she cried,

> And press'd him to her groaning breast; "My Boone!
> How can you leave your Home, your Wife and Babes,
> Your life in bloody woods to jeopardize
> Among the murdering Indians' cruel tribes?
> My God! the horrid thought I cannot bear!"

Boone goes forth to slay panthers, and to rescue the fair Melcena from
redskins whom our hero surprises "while engaged in the dissection
of a slaughtered buffalo." He explores the tributaries of the Ohio, and
"gives names to the Waters, &c.," like Adam naming the fauna of
Eden—all the while uttering such praises of solitude as

> "The Fashionable World's a Masquerade,
> In which the real character's concealed:
> Its smiles are like the fabled Syren's songs;
> Its pleasures are the painted pills of Death."

Boone did not live to see his next praise in poetry, in 1823, in the
Eighth Canto of Lord Byron's *Don Juan,* as the happiest of mortals:

> Boone lived hunting up to ninety;
> And what's still stranger, left behind a name
> For which men vainly decimate the throng,
> Not only famous, but of that *good* fame,

> Without which glory's but a tavern song,—
> Simple, serene, the antipodes of shame,
> Which hate nor envy e'er could tinge with wrong.

To Byron, the fretful poet in exile and connoisseur of solitude, the far-seen image of the backwoods hunter in Kentucky was romantic and compelling. These verses in one of the great poems of the day lent wings to the Boone fable.

The ageing Boone—so crippled by rheumatism that his wife had to go hunting with him to hold his gun[6]—fared less well at home. Bankrupt in Kentucky, he moved on to Missouri, impelled by hope and restlessness, rather than by the legendary sense of claustrophobia. To the last, he protested that he loved friends and neighbors.[7] Congress was slow in confirming his title to a Spanish land-grant, and even his countrymen began to forget the man whose fame overseas grew mightily. Chester Harding, who travelled one hundred miles to paint the old man shortly before Boone's death in 1820, reported:

> I found that the nearer I got to his dwelling, the less was known of him. When within two miles of his house, I asked a man to tell me where Colonel Boone lived. He said he did not know any such man. "Why, yes, you do," said his wife. "It is that white-headed old man who lives on the bottom, near the river. . . ."
> I found the object of my search engaged in cooking his dinner. He was lying in his bunk near the fire, and had a long strip of venison wound around his ramrod, and was busy turning it before a brisk blaze, and using salt and pepper to season his meat. I at once told him the object of my visit. I found that he hardly knew what I meant. I explained the matter to him, and he agreed to sit. He was ninety years old, and rather infirm.[8]

Yet when it was broadcast that Daniel Boone had died, the world remembered. In his honor the Legislature of Missouri adjourned, and his funeral was the largest the West had ever known. Boone was buried in the cherrywood coffin which he had kept under his bed for many years, in the manner of John Donne. In 1845 the State of Kentucky claimed the bodies of Boone and his wife, and with a grand procession had them re-interred at Frankfort. A handsome monument was there erected in 1862, but in the Civil War suffered defacement from Union soldiers—who possibly may have known Boone's opinion of "Yankees."[9] Years later it was restored by the pennies and dimes of Kentucky schoolchildren. In 1937 Missouri tried to secure the body of Boone for removal to its original burial-place; but Governor A. B.

Chandler stoutly refused, the state's attorney-general adding that if the Legislature gave up the remains to Missouri, "the lawmakers would be driven from the Commonwealth."[10]

Meanwhile the lore of Boone was built by the passing years. Stories were told of how he nearly shot his future wife, by mistake, on a panther hunt at night; how he owned a cow, "Old Spot," who learned to give Indian alarms, and was wounded in the siege of Boonesborough, where the good Lord had miraculously sent a heavy rain to put out the burning stockade; how Boone ran backwards in his tracks, and swung on grapevines for intervals of many yards, to baffle the redskins; how he led a party to rescue young Jemima Boone and her playmates from Indian kidnappers. In 1818 Boone was amused by the story, published in the East and abroad, that he had been found dead, kneeling by a stump, rifle in hand, and a deer dead some hundred yards away. After his real death two years later, in bed, the story was revived by even the sober British quarterlies. Audubon's *Ornithological Biography,* which reported a meeting with the great hunter, helped to keep his memory green. Audubon uttered no reproach for the man whose wastefulness—like that of all the early hunters—had done so much to exterminate the wild life of the Mississippi Valley, by slaughter of beast and fowl far beyond the needs of the larder. To Audubon, Boone was remembered as a man of vast muscular strength whose stature "appeared gigantic"—yet the hunter's relative Daniel Bryan related that he was five feet eight or nine, and slender. In anthropology Audubon, it appears, was a less accurate observer than in ornithology —and he already saw Boone refracted through the lens of legend. In similar vein, James Kirke Paulding had boasted that Boone and his fellows could "march to the north pole, and shoot out the wind's eye, if it were no bigger than the point of a needle."[11]

In five great novels, from 1823 to 1841, Cooper wove the character of Boone into Leatherstocking, Hawkeye, Natty Bumppo, or Deerslayer. Always he is tall, gaunt, leathery, with piercing gray eyes and shaggy brows, dressed in deerskin and moccasins adorned with porcupine quills. He never goes to church, and avows: "I am a plain, unlarned man . . . never so much as looked into a book, or larnt a letter of scholarship, in my born days . . . in my time have killed two hundred beaver in a season."[12] Without boasting he contrives to tell how good he is, as a marksman and a man. The real Boone deserted his wife for long intervals at a time—one legend, probably false as it is discreditable, telling how the wife in these absences took up with

Daniel's brother and bore him a child—but Leatherstocking lives under
the old knightly vow of celibacy. He is never domesticated. He shows
pride, courage, naïveté, honesty, patience, and justice. He rescues girls
from Indians, eludes pursuit, turns from hunter to trapper as sinew
and eye grow feeble. The inroads of civilization make him sad: "I
have lived to see what I thought eyes could never behold in these hills,
and I have no heart left for singing."[13]

To some, Boone came to be remembered as the great Indian slayer.
Causici's marble panel over the southern door of the rotunda, in the
National Capitol, shows Boone killing two Indians at once. Yet the
real Boone had never preened himself upon such exploits, telling his
son Nathan that he was sure of having killed only a single redskin,
namely a warrior at the battle of Blue Licks.[14] The perils of Boone's
life were stressed by the romancers. "Beauty came to him with Terror
looking over her shoulder," wrote William Gilmore Simms.[15] Timothy
Flint, a Massachusetts missionary who read Chateaubriand more dili-
gently than his Bible and spent his life searching for a savage earthly
paradise, in 1833 brought out a life of "the Achilles of the West . . .
as truly great as Penn, Marion, and Franklin." Flint was the Weems
of the frontier, and had equally few scruples about lying. When the
"impudent impostures" of his book on Boone were censured, he
replied that like Pindar's razors it was not made for use but to sell.
To review all his fantasies is impossible. But his kinship with Weems
is shown by one of the first episodes in the book—how Boone's brief
schooling ends when he prankishly puts tartar emetic in the Irish
schoolmaster's whiskey bottle—and by its closing pages, which examine the religion of Daniel Boone and conclude that "the creed of
the red men naturally became his. But such were the truth, simplicity,
and kindness of his character, there can be but little doubt, had the
gospel of the Son of God been proposed to him, in its sublime truth
and reasonableness, that he would have added to all his other virtues,
the higher name of Christian."[16] In 1847 Virginia named a county
in honor of the old hunter, and in 1851 George Caleb Bingham painted
a picture which has played a large part in popular visualization of the
hero, "Daniel Boone escorting a band of pioneers into the Western
country." The age of the dime novel, in 1873, brought forth Frederick
Whittaker's *Boone the Hunter; or, The Backwoods Belle,* in which
it is reported that Boone united "great shrewdness" to the goodness
of his heart, and that he "read and wrote with facility, the latter in
a clear and legible manner." "One of the simplest and grandest figures

in the story of American civilization," he is here led through the mazes of strange imaginary exploits—such as climbing a tree to see, through a second-story window, a villainous city slicker and fencing-master named Yelverton cheating at cards. Boone unmasks him and kills him with brilliant sword-play. "Sir, I apologize," are the dying man's last words, for having said that Boone was no gentleman. In 1904 Winston Churchill in *The Crossing* showed his young adventurer fired to great deeds by hearing Boone's story from the lips of the old woodsman himself—even as some boys who talked to the living Boone, it is said, ran away from home to become hunters and explorers.

Boone has long been the boy's own hero. In 1912, recalling it was 143 years ago that Boone first gazed upon the green valley of Kentucky, the Reverend Thomas B. Gregory wrote in a Philadelphia newspaper: "God never made a grander man than Daniel Boone, and in every public school in the land the story of his life should be made a regular part of the children's study. It would be a moral tonic. It would redden the children's blood and help to make them brave, honorable, and upright citizens."[17] A decade later, in a five-act play about Boone, Edward J. White declared in verses almost as bad as those of the hero's relative Daniel Bryan—

> His life it is well for our youth to note and con,
> And, making him their model, some of his virtues don.[18]

Less conventionally, William Carlos Williams, the physician-poet, in 1925 called Boone "a great voluptuary born to the American settlements against the niggardliness of the damming puritanical tradition."[19] Byron's hero-worship had almost come full circle, and Boone once more rejoiced, with a touch of misanthropy, in the "ecstasy" of solitude.

In 1940 a serial strip drawn by C. C. Cooper for the Sunday comics, "Fighting with Daniel Boone," retold the old stories for boys.

Kentucky has long commemorated June 7, when this wanderer entered her meadows, as Boone Day. In 1934 the state celebrated the two hundredth anniversary of his birth, selling Memorial Half-Dollars, planning parks and a highway in his honor, holding a Boy Scout pageant about him at Covington, and staging Boone Bicentennial Balls.[20] Elsewhere the name of this pioneer is not forgotten. In 1937 a defeated Republican candidate for councilman in the city of Buffalo listed, rather surprisingly, in his expense account: "Donations $40—including $10 from Adolf Hitler, $10 from Josef Stalin, $10 from

Daniel Boone."[21] A citizen of Pennsylvania named George S. Stirl calls himself "the reincarnation of Daniel Boone." With long white beard and dressed in buckskin, he sells photographs of himself at a dollar apiece; three years ago he startled the caretakers of Mount Vernon by appearing there on a crowded Saturday afternoon, with an Indian in tow.

II

Out of the War of 1812 and Andrew Jackson's campaign leaped the braggart of the canebrakes. In New Orleans theatres and music-halls, as early as 1822, "the hunter of Kentucky," "half a horse and half an alligator," becomes a stock character[22]—applauded because he speaks a comic lingo, tickles the American passion for rhetoric and exaggeration, and boasts about himself in a vein relished by the rising frontier democracy. Self-assurance in buckskin thus talked back to the highbrow and snobbish East. In 1831 Paulding described "Uncle Sam" as "a good hearty fellow, about half horse half alligator." Mark Twain fifty years later reported that a rough-and-tumble fighter of the western country announced himself:

"Whoooop! I'm the old original iron-jawed, brass-mounted, copper-bellied corpse maker from the wilds of Arkansaw! Look at me! . . . Sired by a hurricane, dam'd by an earthquake . . . I take nineteen alligators and a bar'l of whiskey for breakfast when I'm in robust health, and a bushel of rattlesnakes and a dead body when I'm ailing. I split the everlasting rocks with my glance, and I squench the thunder when I speak!"[23]

He was the type immortalized by Davy Crockett. The first Crockett book, published in 1833 probably with some help from the Colonel, has Davy describe a stop he made on his first trip to Washington, as Congressman from the sticks of Tennessee:

I was *rooting* my way to the fire, not in a good humor, when some fellow staggered towards me, and cried out, "Hurrah for Adams!" Said I, "Stranger, you had better hurrah for hell, and praise your own country." Said he, "And who are you?"
"I'm that same David Crockett, fresh from the backwoods, half-horse, half-alligator, a little touched with the snapping-turtle; can wade the Mississippi, leap the Ohio, ride upon a streak of lightning, and slip without a scratch down a honey locust; can whip my weight in wild-cats—and if any gentleman pleases, for a ten-dollar bill, he may throw in a panther—hug a bear too close for comfort, and eat any man opposed to Jackson."[24]

When Crockett stood up for a fight, folklore reported, he "would jump into the air and crack his heels and crow like a rooster, and neigh like a stallion." Yet in truth he was a lazy, easy-going, slovenly squatter, and one of the most peaceable men in "the Shakes"—his region in western Tennessee, where an earthquake had once disturbed the tranquillity of nature.[25]

In John Quincy Adams's administration Crockett had been elected to Congress—after he had become a militia colonel, and taught himself to read and write. People liked the way he signed documents with the motto, "Be sure you're always right, then go ahead." It seemed fitting to an up-and-coming settlement. They also liked his marksmanship, which enabled him to trim the wick of a candle with his bullet at a distance of several hundred feet. And the hospitable frontier knew that he was "the best fellow in the world," who would give you the shirt off his back. In running for Congress he let his rivals, he said, "wear the people out." He also boasted that their stump speeches had been drowned out by crickets chirping "Cr-k-tt" and bullfrogs croaking "Cro-o-ckett-tt." When his opponents had finished, Crockett would pass a horn of liquor among the voters. On election day he garnered his reward. In Washington he was just another Jacksonian, until out of sympathy for the small settler he ventured to disagree with Jackson's friendliness to land speculators. Quickly the breach widened, and Old Hickory's enemies the Whigs—seeking to bid for the frontier vote which they had hitherto neglected in favor of "the aristocracy"—saw that Davy Crockett was their man. He was a real frontiersman, yet announced that he wore no collar labelled "My dog—Andrew Jackson."

It seems pretty clear that the Whigs, with the ready co-operation of Crockett and the folk imagination, built him into a great legend. A "Crockett March" was composed in his honor, and about him Paulding wrote two plays, "The Lion of the West" and "The Kentuckian." Before a wildly cheering audience, the real Crockett in store clothes, and Colonel Nimrod Wildfire in buckskins on the stage, bowed to each other. Davy was persuaded to make a tour to the North and Down East, in 1834, and to write a book about it, always expressing diffidence at the huzzaing throngs ("This is all very well, but I most think I'd rather be in the wilderness with my gun and dogs than to be attracting all this fuss"). That the soul of honest Davy, susceptible to vanity and exhibitionism, enjoyed his new acclaim, can hardly be doubted. Philadelphia Whigs gave him a gold watch-seal with the motto "Go ahead," and a fine rifle to set beside his trusty "Old Betsey."

New York cheered itself hoarse, but he finally tore away and got aboard a steamship for Boston:

When I went on board, the captain showed me into a splendid stateroom, which I was to occupy for the voyage. So, when I had made my toilet (as great folks say), that is, combed my hair and taken a glass of brandy and water, I went on deck. . . . This brought me into new trouble; for the passengers found I was on board, and came round me, so that I missed seeing the city until we got past it.[28]

In Boston he was toasted at rallies of the Young Whigs, "the Champagne foaming up as if you were supping fog out of speaking-trumpets." He made speeches against his onetime commander, Andrew Jackson: "I helped to give him the name of 'Hero,' which, like the lightning from heaven, has scorched and blasted every thing that stood in its way." Taken to the wharf to see the old frigate *Constitution,* with Jackson's effigy as its new figurehead, he obligingly commented, "There's where he put himself—*before* the Constitution." Shown the happy mill-hands of Lowell, presented with "a dozen canisters of the best sportsman's powder" by Mr. Du Pont, and given a fine suit of domestic broadcloth, he was easily converted to industrialism and high tariff. The Whigs had never had a more obliging puppet.

At the next election his constituents repudiated him, and in a huff he wandered off to Texas—where celebrities were still sparse. Flags flew and cannon boomed, to greet him at San Augustine and Nacogdoches, and frontier belles who danced with Colonel Crockett never forgot that privilege. His life ended in a flare of glory at the Alamo, where, it was said, he sang to the Mexicans, "Won't you come into my bower?" as he greeted them with "Betsey"—and at last fell in the shadow of the Lone Star Flag. Folklore sometimes reported that he had been shot with a silver bullet, because none other could kill him. Sometimes it was said he had not really died, but was roaming the dusty plains with a bear named Death Hug, or jumping the Mad River on a wild stallion, or broiling buffalo meat in the van of a prairie-fire. Trappers in California saw him hunting grizzlies; sailors back from the South Seas related he was down there diving for pearls. Myth-makers told how in the Winter of the Big Snow, one morning when the sun was frozen fast, he had walked up Daybreak Hill and greased the axle of the earth with bear-fat—until the sun came up and he walked home "introducing people to the fresh daylight with a piece of sunrise in my pocket." Thus a great legend, bursting the bands of Whig politics, grew into the fire-bringer of old mythologies.

Stories, verses, and songs about Crockett are found in newspapers and "albums" of the pre-Sumter period. A song popular with Negro minstrels, "Pompey Smash," told how a braggart darkey had met "the Tennessee screamer"—

> We fought a day and night and then agreed to drop it.
> I was purty badly whipped—and so was Davy Crockett.
> I looked all around and found my head a-missin'—
> He'd bit off my head and I had swallowed hisn!
> Then we did agree to let each other be;
> I was too much for him, and he was too much for me.[27]

Beginning in 1835 and running to the eve of the Civil War, some fifty Crockett almanacs were issued—in New York, Boston, Philadelphia, Baltimore, Nashville. They were addressed chiefly to farmers, the profession Crockett himself had followed with scant success. Their comments on wind and weather were interlarded, not with Poor Richard's thrift, but with Davy's braggadocio—from babyhood when he was weaned on whiskey and rattlesnakes' eggs, to his prime when he strangled bears and rode gleefully on alligators. The infant Hercules grew up to be Baron Munchausen. In the main, the residue of Whig politics was forgotten; indeed, some of the tales were told interchangeably about Crockett and Old Hickory. He tended however to become an expansionist symbol. The *Crockett Almanac for 1845,* printed in Boston, renders this posthumous opinion:

"You see, feller citizens, I'm like my salt water friend, Ben Hardin, of the rale American grit, an like him, I go in for Texas and the Oregon, clar up to the very gravel stone; for they both belong to Uncle Sam's plantation, jist as naturally as a cabbage leaf belongs to a cabbage stalk."

And he threatens "to roast John Bull with gun lightenen," and "show his mother Vic, that although she may take tea in Canton, sugared with Chinese blood, she can't fodder her cattle in Oregon." And the next year's almanac, in this series, shows Crockett taking his pet bear and alligator out "under the old Liberty Tree to celebrate the Great Lord's Day of Freedom, the FOURTH OF JULY," and to cheer for "Texas and Oregon!" The Civil War seems to have choked this cockalorum; Crockett almanacs suddenly cease in the late fifties, and in 1862 Edward S. Ellis, writing the Colonel's life for the Beadle Library, says "his fame has subsided almost as rapidly as it arose," that now many Americans think no such person ever lived. Three dime novels gave him a *post-bellum* flurry of fame, but America had outlived its growing-pains and its buckskin naïveté. Davy Crockett was dead, killed by the silver bullet of the get-rich-quick era.

III

The frontiersmen of the West were wastrels. Crockett claimed to have shot one hundred and five bears in a season, and to have slain six deer in one day—leaving two hanging in the woods—while chasing other game. Clouds of pigeons and droves of turkey vanished along with the buffalo. No marksman could resist a good shot, no matter how full his bag. And they were a prodigal, shortsighted lot. Some Indian tribes decided that these lazy hunters lived upon the frontier because they could not get along elsewhere.[28] It was a shrewd judgment. Within their ranks, however, was a man of different stripe—not the destroyer, but the sower. To the nation at large he never became so familiar as Boone and Crockett, but among the farmers of the Ohio Valley three generations ago and to a band of poets and novelists since that time he has been held in deep affection. To an age of richer myth and more fixed anchorage in the soil, he might have become the rough draft of a fertility god. As it is, he survives in four monuments and in a few rhymes and stories. Some people think, wrongly, that the Jonathan apple is his namesake.

Jonathan Chapman, far better know as "Johnny Appleseed," was born in Massachusetts in 1774. About 1800 he is first sighted in the Middle West, floating down the Ohio with a cargo of rotting apples brought from the cider-presses of western Pennsylvania. It was his dream, later his benign mania, to sow seeds and plant saplings in the wake of the pioneers, so that orchards might burgeon in the wilderness. He would exchange a sapling for a "fip penny bit," some cast-off clothes, or an IOU which he never collected. To the poor he gave whatever he had. In frontier cabins he loved to stretch on the floor, and read the Bible or the mystical pages of Swedenborg aloud in tones of prophecy. His pacific heroism, like that of William Penn, consisted in going unarmed to meet the Indians, bearing with him the principle of love. The red men thought him big medicine, and told how rattlers would not bite him, while bears let him play with their cubs. In time he became a lay saint, a St. Francis of the frontier. In the War of 1812, when the British were inciting the Indians, he did his countrymen an important service. He travelled from the threatened village of Mansfield to Mount Vernon, Ohio, to bring help and to warn lonely settlements on the way. Some legends have him trudging the distance barefoot, as he often walked; others, as galloping on horse and blowing his blast of warning upon a converted powder-horn, under a midnight sky lighted to the rear with burning farmhouses. But his most famous words, which appear to be fairly well authenticated, were uttered years later at a revival meeting. The preacher—some have identified him with Peter Cartwright, who preached hell fire to Andrew Jackson, and ran a political race against Abraham Lincoln—asked from his pulpit, "Where is the man who, like the primitive Christian, walks toward heaven barefoot and clad in sackcloth?" In reply to this rhetorical question, a figure stepped forth dressed in ragged trousers and shirt of coffee sacking, with holes cut for neck and arms. He was barefoot, and wore a tin mush pan on his head in lieu of hat. "Here is your primitive Christian," said Johnny Appleseed. In the spring of 1845, making a long trip to repair a distant orchard which he had not tended for some time, Johnny caught pneumonia and died at William Worth's cabin not far from Fort Wayne, Indiana; there he was buried.

Upon news of his death, young William Tecumseh Sherman, the future general, is reported to have said, "Johnny Appleseed's name will never be forgotten in Ohio," while upon the floor of Congress General Sam Houston cried more dramatically, "Farewell, dear old eccentric heart. Your labor has been a labor of love, and generations yet unborn will rise up and call you blessed."[29] His figure, once familiar in country lanes of Ohio and Indiana, now cast the long shadow of myth. Little girls, for whom he cherished a special fondness, became mothers and grandmothers but never forgot the bits of ribbon or calico or home-made toys he had given them. They remembered he never sat as a guest at table until assured there was enough food for the children. A writer in *Harper's Magazine* in 1871 collected some stories about him—how he brought "some news right fresh from Heaven" to many a lonely cabin, how he thought that cutting down a tree was murder, how he quenched his camp-fire because it drew and burned the mosquitoes.[30] In 1895 appeared a volume called *Johnny Appleseed's Rhymes*. The author was another eccentric, Denton J. Snider, leader of "the St. Louis movement" in philosophy, who lived in the ghetto of that city but supported himself by lecturing to ladies' clubs. He had been born in Ohio in 1841, and claimed that as a small boy he saw Johnny Appleseed wander into his village playing on a fiddle, that he had given the old minstrel an apple and had seen him put the seeds in a battered wallet. Snider told stories he had heard—of people boasting they owned orchards planted by Johnny, of an old soldier who maintained he had been kept from starvation by coming upon a grove of peach-trees in the wilderness, of a young lady who said mystically, "Johnny Appleseed is still living, and I think I know where." But the rhymes he printed appear to have been chiefly Snider's own. A later Chicago historian who took them seriously was shocked by their "ribald and somewhat doubtful" tone, and suggested that the collector had confused Johnny Appleseed with Johnny Applejack—who seems to have been gusty and bibulous.[31] There are several quaint puzzles about the legend of Johnny Appleseed—including his only likeness, "A drawing made in 1850 by a student at Oberlin College who had seen him." As reproduced in one book, it shows Johnny wearing a long peaked cap; in another book the identical drawing is altered to reveal him in a huge straw hat.[32] Both portray him carrying a substantial pruning knife, although according to the earliest printed source Johnny thought it "wicked" to prune or graft trees.[33]

Although the grandson of the man who buried him said in 1901 that nobody could come within fifty feet of locating his grave,[34] in 1912 the Indiana Horticultural Society built an iron fence around one of the graves in Archer's long neglected burying-ground, and put up a tablet stating that Johnny "died 1843"—two years before the authenticated date. The cemetery is in a lonely spot, well off the highway, but in 1930 it was reported that some two thousand motorists each year were going out of their way to visit Johnny's grave.[35] In 1882 he was given his first monument, on the site of the Copus massacre in Ashland County, Ohio, in memory of his warning to other settlers which helped them escape a similar fate. In 1900, the Hon. M. B. Bushnell, whose father had known Johnny Appleseed, gave a marble shaft in his honor to the municipal park in Mansfield, Ohio. Fifteen years later, at the town of Ashland, a monument eight feet high made of native boulders was erected by efforts of Ohio schoolchildren; it is inscribed "An Ohio Hero, patron saint of American Orchards and Soldier of Peace." In his speech of dedication, Myron T. Herrick—future Ambassador to France in the Lindbergh era—rather curiously took this barefoot mystic as a symbol of how to succeed:

Johnny Appleseed personifies the two factors that always make for real success in life. He had an ambition to do one thing well, and he was imbued

with a resolute disinterested spirit. . . . He fulfilled his mission and we today
are bringing him belated recognition in this monument as one of the successful men of Ohio.[36]

No doubt it is difficult to address schoolchildren without becoming
inspirational. In 1916 Johnny received his fourth monument, in Swin-
ney Park, Fort Wayne, Indiana. It is a huge field boulder bearing a
bronze tablet, with an image in bas-relief of Johnny planting an apple
tree, and the erroneous dates of birth and death as 1776 and 1843.

An early writer said that Johnny chose for his orchards sites "such
as an artist or poet would select." Poets of varied quality have been
fond of him—Lydia Maria Child, William Henry Venable, Edgar Lee
Masters, Vachel Lindsay, Stephen Vincent Benét. Masters in 1918
thought of Johnny Appleseed chuckling over the little orchards he
had hidden, for later delight, in the midst of the wilderness—

> to make these places of worship,
> Labor and laughter and gain in the late October.

Vachel Lindsay in 1921, "In Praise of Johnny Appleseed," recalled him
as the orchard god of ripening America—carrying in a deer-hide sack
tomorrow's peaches and pears and cherries, and in his breast "the love
of the heart of man":

> Washington buried in Virginia,
> Jackson buried in Tennessee,
> Young Lincoln, dreaming in Illinois,
> And Johnny Appleseed, priestly and free,
> Knotted and gnarled, past seventy years,
> Still planted on in the woods alone.

More recently the Benéts have written:

> The stalking Indian,
> The beast in its lair
> Did no hurt while he was there.
>
> For they could tell
> As wild things can,
> That Jonathan Chapman
> Was God's own man.

Many Americans first learned about him from Eleanor Atkinson's
well-written novel of 1915, *Johnny Appleseed: the Romance of the
Sower*. He is "a little brother to wayfaring man and beast," whose
sainted loneliness flowers in love for all created things. In old age

he becomes "this dear visionary, who was 'not all here' because a good part of him was already in heaven." For an Illinois Woodcraft Council in 1926, "Donald Thistle" (a pseudonym for H. Clark Brown) wrote a sentimental play for boys and girls, in which Johnny utters such words as "I always think of my mother when I see apple bloom."[37] In 1940 a radio play, "Johnny Appleseed," by Bernhard C. Schoenfield, with Walter Huston in the role of narrator, proved so popular that it was twice rebroadcast on the Kate Smith hour, and will soon be sold in disc form by the Columbia Recording Company. Johnny, an orchardist in Pittsburgh, hears an angel with a nasal twang—really Johnny's inner self— calling him to a life work that makes him into "a Giant," greater than Paul Bunyan or John Henry, who were symbols of man trying to conquer the woods and rocks of early America by strength rather than tenderness. As artists have always felt, Johnny's was a social mission, the more rare because it was carried on amid the stark individualism and waste of the frontier. (All his hero-worshippers remember the apples, and kindly forget the dog-fennel, scourge of the Ohio Valley, which he also introduced to that region in the belief that it would cure malaria.)

Years ago folklore and fiction invented a sweetheart for Johnny: sometimes she jilts him, and thus impels his wanderings, but sometimes she dies on their wedding morn and upon her grave Johnny sows seeds which come up in the spring to spell "Apple Blossoms." In 1930 it is reported that Johnny was descended from George Chapman, the Elizabethan dramatist, that he graduated with honors from Harvard, and became a sort of scholar gipsy after being kicked by a horse.[38] This of course is the frankly literary touch. It is also related —by some one who must have had a dim memory of what Izaak Walton's Doctor Boteler thought about 'the strawberry—that Johnny said, "God might have made a better fruit than the apple, but he never did."[39] It has been claimed that he was a friend of Daniel Boone, of Logan the Indian chief, of William Henry Harrison, of Henry Ward Beecher—and that he saw young Lincoln splitting rails and said, "Keep it up, Lincoln, maybe you'll be President some day."[40] In 1904 Newell Dwight Hillis explained that Johnny first began to be eccentric and wear a tin pan on his head after an attack of "typhoid or malarial fever . . . he was dazed and out of his mind."[41] A generation later Henry Chapin presented his life story as the legend of a man who believed in service.[42] In 1931 William A. Duff, writing a voluminous history of North Central Ohio, observed that his appreciation "has steadily grown with the passing years, particularly in the last couple of decades."[43] In 1937 Walter Havighurst wrote a novel about him, *The Quiet Shore*. Today a scholar at Ohio State, Robert Price, is publishing new facts about Johnny Appleseed—who, a generation ago, looked so shadowy that he seemed no man born of sperm but of myth: sometimes rumored to be the son of a Calvinist divine or of a half-breed Indian, he now has a pedigree of stout New England ancestors and a father who fought in the Revolution.[44]

Johnny Appleseed, hermit of solitude, caught the popular fancy which might have belonged to a greater individualist of the outdoors, Henry Thoreau. Johnny's was a manual and material, rather than intellectual, service to his countrymen. Moreover, novelists and poets seem to prefer the praise of a man who cannot speak for himself.

CHAPTER NINE

OLD HICKORY

"It is very difficult to electioneer successfully against Genl Jackson—his character and his services are of the kind which *alone* the people can appreciate and feel— one cup of generous whiskey produces more military ardor than can be allayed in a month of reflection and sober reason."—JOHN OWEN to BARTLETT YANCY, 21 July 1824, North Carolina Historical Society MS.

I

ANDREW JACKSON is probably the only President of the United States who did not believe that the earth is round.[1] Fastidious men winced at the spectacle of this raw-boned Southwesterner in the White House, who admitted stable-boys, laborers in shirt-sleeves, and Negroes to his levees. Fortunately, they said, his wife who smoked a corncob pipe had been translated to a better world before she could become First Lady of the Land. But a man with his horse-racing, cock-fighting, pistol-duelling antecedents could not help attracting all the riffraff of the country. Emerson once remarked that if he ever found himself loving life unduly he would attend a caucus of Jackson men: "I doubt not the unmixed malignity, the withering selfishness, the impudent vulgarity, that mark those meetings would speedily cure me of my appetite for longevity."[2] To Philip Hone, silk-stocking mayor of New York, he was "this terrible old man." Yet no President of the United States, from George Washington to Franklin D. Roosevelt, has inspired while in office the intense personal popularity of Andrew Jackson or seen that acclaim swell so vastly while he was in power. In 1824 Jackson obtained the highest popular vote for President, although he failed to secure office when the electors fell to bargaining. Four years later he was swept into the White House—after a great cry of "Shall Congress or the People elect our President?" had rebuked the caucus system— by a vote four times as great as that of 1824.[3] And in 1832 his majority was even larger—so overwhelming that the editor of the anti-Jackson *Vermont Journal* confessed he had "no heart to publish election returns."[4] One of his opponents, William Wirt, wrote disconsolately: "My opinion is that he may be President for life if he chooses."[5]

Jackson was widely known, as no other President has been, by the simple title of "the Hero." The reasons for his glory are equally simple. Better than Washington or Jefferson, this battered old soldier —with his blazing blue eyes, sunken cheeks, and shock of white mane, his courage and his stubbornness, his rages and his tenderness—was the essence of Americanism. He was the kind of man whom the majority of Americans in his day imagined themselves to be—the magnification of a type which could not fancy itself, in its most expansive moods, as a Washington or a Jefferson. He never left the continent of North America; he never set foot on foreign soil except to conquer it, as in the Seminole episode in Spanish Florida.

Whether, in 1767, he was born in South or in North Carolina, is an old and bitter feud. His birthplace was somewhere in the Waxhaws, on the border of those two states—before their governors met to run the clearer dividing-line and to occasion the legendary remark, "It's a long time between drinks." Less amenity has entered into their rival claims over Jackson. In 1910 the North Carolina D. A. R. erected a stone monument in Union County, about three quarters of a mile from the state line, to mark the historic spot, and placed a sign-board on the highway: "Andrew Jackson, seventh President of the United States: Birthplace three hundred yards east of this place." A traveller who follows this road into South Carolina will come upon another marker: "Andrew Jackson, seventh President of the United States: Birthplace one hundred yards west of this place." These signs have been torn down by stealth, and replaced with tenacity, by partisans in recent years.[6] All through the controversy Tennessee newspapers have observed, with calm detachment, that of course Jackson really belongs to the state of his choice.[7]

Jackson, as a boy of fifteen, captured in a round-up of local militia, refused to black the boots of a British dragoon and was gashed with the officer's sword. The story admits no dispute. It is told in all the campaign biographies of Jackson's day, and in most schoolbooks of later times. When in 1834 a Congressman branded the story as false, Jackson roared "The damned infernal scoundrel," and demanded that any skeptic feel the scar on his forehead.[8] Anti-Jacksonians who grew tired of hearing about the episode could only point out, as one pamphleteer did, that any American boy would have done the same![9] Writers perhaps more sentimental than reliable have given us vignettes of young Andrew at his mother's death-bed, reporting how long afterwards, following the Battle of New Orleans, he said that all that he was he owed to her.[10] Other legends—which at least comport with the later Jackson—tell us that he "was the most roaring, rollicking, gamecocking, horse-racing, card-playing, mischievous fellow that ever lived in Salisbury." A few speak of mulatto mistresses, and of his inviting the only two white prostitutes in town to a Christmas ball, by way of fun.[11] In later years "the youthful indiscretions of General Jackson between the ages of sixteen and sixty" were often dished up to the public, but to the surprise of some New England Whigs it was found that the South and West admired him for them. (In appraising heroes, the North looked first to their morals and religion; the South to their financial honor and freedom from self-interest.)

After a casual apprenticeship to the law young Jackson packed his saddle-bags and set out for the new land of Tennessee—arriving, according to tradition, with two fine horses, gun, pistol, and fox-hounds. It became his standard equipment. Neither books nor wardrobe ever meant much in Jackson's life; of scholarship or dandyism he was never accused. But, eager to acquire status as a frontier gentleman, he fought his first duel not with fists but with pistols. In Nashville he courted the daughter of his landlady Mrs. Donelson, a family whose social rank helped him in getting on. However, nobody could deny that he married Rachel for aught save love. The passing years, none too kind to Rachel's dumpy figure, left her undimmed in Jackson's romantic eyes. The public knew little of Jackson's stiff buckram chivalry or his unexpected vein of tenderness. But it sensed that he loved children—adopting eleven, after his marriage proved childless, and in the

White House once postponing a council of state until a grandniece in his arms finished her nap—and that he was a family man. This was just as it should be. The public also knew that Jackson was ready to fight any man, anywhere, for "the sacred name of a lady." Through a misunderstanding of technicalities, he had married Rachel two years before her legal divorce from her first unhappy union, with one Captain Lewis Robards. When Robards professed to be aggrieved, Jackson threatened to cut off his ears and ran his thumb judiciously along the blade of his hunting-knife. In 1803, when Jackson's political foe "Nolichucky Jack" Sevier taunted him with "taking a trip to Natchez with another man's wife," Jackson stiffened with flashing eyes. "Great God! Do you mention *her* sacred name?" and he lunged at Sevier with his walking-stick. When friends parted them, Jackson sent him a blistering challenge. The duel ended with Governor Sevier hiding behind a tree to escape Jackson's bullet.[12] Three years later, in a duel which every Tennessee schoolboy still knows, Jackson killed a fellow-lawyer, Charles Dickinson, for a similar insult. After Jackson became a national figure, Whig pamphleteers and editors never tired of allusions to "a convicted adulteress and her paramour husband." Jackson's friends assured him that a prospective President could afford to fight no more duels, or add to the two bullets which he then carried in his gaunt physique. "How hard it is to keep the cowhide from these villains!" he boiled.[13] To voters at large the cry of "bigamy" did Jackson little harm. The motive was felt to be political cowardice and spite. A manuscript letter in the Massachusetts Historical Society, from Edward Everett to C. Foote of Charlestown, June 4, 1836, comments, in the old milieu of Puritanism:

I will not undertake to say that public sentiment is so corrupt that *no* exposure of private immorality will ever hurt a candidate, but the case must be rare & peculiar. Gen¹ Jackson was benefitted not injured by the exposure of the abduction of his wife & his connection with her before marriage. Such men as Gen¹ Hayne having wives & children got up in public meetings & pronounced eulogiums on Mrs. Jackson. The business of Mrs. Eaton injured neither Gen¹ Jackson nor Mr. Van Buren but it crushed Calhoun &c who tried to make it the instrument of subverting the administration.

The Eaton episode—centering about the less worthy wife of a Cabinet officer, whose snubbing, as a scarlet woman, by the respectability of Washington caused Jackson to espouse her cause, and insist in Cabinet meeting "She is chaste as a virgin!"—caused an instant projection of

Jackson's sympathy. He saw in her a second Rachel. To this rough border captain, all womanhood—outside the bordellos which he had long forgotten—was sacred. Many ladies thought that he had gone too far in championing voluptuous Peggy Eaton. But they had not yet been given the ballot. Hence their social taboo was politically unimportant.

Jackson's rise to fame and power came along the frontier. He gained judicial and military offices in a land where men of ability, and even modest education, were few. His business ethics were rough and ready. His "extremely equivocal" land speculations led even to an investigation before the United States Senate.[14] But that circumstance was largely overlooked, in later years, by the searchers after discreditable facts who eagerly seized upon his voting, as a fledgling Congressman in December, 1796, against a tribute of thanks to retiring President Washington. Jackson evidently thought Washington rather too pro-British, and too highfalutin' by frontier standards; but "this expression of his dislike to the father of his country" was never forgotten by Federalist propaganda.[15] In 1797 Jackson served briefly in the Senate, and then quitted Federal politics for many a year. In 1802 he was elected major-general of the Tennessee militia, by the narrow margin of one vote. Four years later he seemed to fraternize with Aaron Burr—another mistake of which his later foes made great capital—but when the "treason" became clear, hastily denounced it.

II

Jackson probably would never have become a national hero, or presidential timber, without the War of 1812. But in March of that memorable year he issued a call for 50,000 volunteers: "The period of youth is the season for martial exploits . . . how pleasing the prospect . . . to . . . promenade into a distant country. . . . To view the stupendous works of nature . . . Niagra [sic] . . . Montmorenci . . . carrying the republican standard to the heights of abraham."[16] He was a stern soldier, whom the perils of Indian warfare, wretched food, and dysentery did not daunt. Upon privations he throve, and with pride his men began to say that he was "tough as hickory." Shortly he came to be known as "Old Hickory."[17] After his victories over the Indians —made more glorious by the inefficient mediocrity with which the war at large was being waged—Jackson's good friend Judge Overton wrote to him: "I can but imperfectly communicate to you the feeling of the people. Your standing . . . is as high as any man in America."[18] But this was chiefly the judgment of Tennessee and of Nashville, where crowds lined the road to welcome the returning hero, and at a banquet gave him the first of many ceremonial swords which still deck the walls of the Hermitage. Jackson did not become America's idol, clearly and indisputably, until after he had whipped Pakenham and the red-coats at New Orleans on January 8, 1815. To military strategists this victory seems comparatively easy; all the advantage of terrain, and the knowledge thereof, belonged to Jackson; but his masterful leadership, in moulding an army out of wild frontiersmen, rowdy adventurers, lately converted pirates led by Lafitte, was the greater triumph. Some say the Battle of New Orleans was "unnecessary" because, unknown to Jackson and Pakenham, the Treaty of Ghent had already been signed to end the war. New England never liked the War of 1812, and the Massachusetts Legislature, piously thanking the Lord for its successful termination at New Orleans, made no mention of General Jackson. Hence, when the textbooks came to be written, the glory of Jackson's achievement was often belittled. After generations of chafing under this prejudice the Legislature of Tennessee in 1927 appointed a "Commission of Research as to the True Value of the Victory at New Orleans." Such stout Jacksonians as Reau E. Folk and Claude G. Bowers undertook to do right by Old Hickory. At length, in Nashville in 1935, they published *The Battle of New Orleans: Its Real Meaning. Exposure of Untruth Being Taught Young America*. It was there asserted that without Jackson's brilliant victory the British, upon capturing the city, would have laid permanent claim to it under their old refusal to admit the validity of the Louisiana Purchase. "The thin red line" which Jackson shattered might therefore have strangled the queen city of the Mississippi, and nullified the Treaty of Ghent, which was yet lacking ratification. This, then, is the true gospel in Tennessee —a state where orthodoxy is still an important touchstone of truth.

The populace of New Orleans then and later accepted Jackson in his full glory. On January 22, following the victory, he was crowned with laurel before the Cathedral door—while little girls in white, silver stars on their foreheads, strewed flowers in his path, and the great organ within thundered the "Te Deum."[19] A song honoring Jackson, to the tune of "Yankee Doodle," mingled with the stately liturgy. Rachel came down from Nashville to share the triumph, to dine upon "a gold ham" and dance with her haggard husband—among the kindly Creole aristocracy—"to the wild melody of *Possum up de Gum Tree*." Only

Judge Dominick Hall, sour and unpopular, fined Jackson $1000 for his
highhanded dealings under martial law. The crowd subscribed a purse
to pay the fine, but Jackson waved it aside. The only solace they had
was that of unhitching Jackson's horses and dragging his carriage amid
lusty cheers from the court to the Exchange Coffee House—where
Jackson made a short speech favoring "obedience to the laws, even
when we think them unjustly applied."[20] Many years later the fine was
remitted, when the capital plus interest proved a godsend to an impoverished ex-President. But his arbitrary behavior, in the days following the great victory, rose up in later years when politicians tried to
convince the electorate he was a cruel tyrant. In 1828 the famous "Coffin
Handbill" showed the six black coffins of the militiamen whom, in
January, 1815, Jackson had ordered shot for desertion. It was said that
one poor fellow did not suffer instant death from the fusillade of the
firing-squad, but writhed in agony upon the coffin where he had knelt.
Another broadside, published in James City County, Virginia, in 1828,
called Jackson "a man who is guilty of ADULTERY, ASSASSINA-
TION, and MURDER." Impartial people admitted that Jackson was
the sternest commander whom American irregulars had had since the
days of Steuben, but hardly the ogre of the Whigs. Jacksonites attempted to laugh it off by Taliaferro's "Supplement to the Coffin Handbill," which informed "the gentle reader that this monster, this more
than cannibal, Gen. Jackson, eat the whole Six Militia-men at one
meal!!! Yes, my shuddering countrymen, he swallowed them whole,
coffins and all, without the slightest attempt at mastication." Years
later, Harriet Martineau told of a New England Sunday-school teacher
who had asked the name of the slayer of Abel. "General Jackson,"
said a pupil.[21]

Congress voted Jackson a gold medal upon hearing the tidings of
New Orleans. But so little was he known to the country at large, that
the War Department had to write for a portrait before it could proceed
with the design.[22] The epoch when Ralph Earl, an itinerant painter,
was to settle at the Hermitage and at the White House for seventeen
years—doing almost nothing save portraits of the General, to meet
popular demand—was yet to come. Now the nation asked, who was
Andrew Jackson? One Kentuckian wagered "a considerable sum" he
was an Irishman; an Eastern newspaper informed its readers that he
was a native of Devonshire.[23] A correspondent named Andrew Barratt
wrote to ask if Old Hickory were not a relative of his, because his
father's half-sister had "married a Mr. Jackson." He would like to claim

kinship with such "a brave man" and "a hughmain [*sic*] man."[24] Apparently he was not daunted by the six coffins. In the autumn of 1815 various friends of the General wrote him that in Ohio, Kentucky, Pennsylvania, and Virginia "many . . . are solicitous that you should become a candidate for the next President."[25] The greatest general of the Revolution had been honored with that office; to some it seemed that the chief hero of the War of 1812 should follow in his steps. But Jackson himself, an admirer of James Monroe and grateful for Monroe's support at New Orleans, had no wish to press his claims at this season. As late as 1821 Jackson thrust aside a New York editorial, hinting at the still premature boom: "Do they think I am such a damned fool! No sir; I know what I am fit for. I can command a body of men in a rough way; but I am not fit to be President."[26] His reluctance, though said with uncommon bluntness, was in the approved American tradition. But he became riled by talk—begun by Henry Clay in 1819 after Jackson's hot-blooded conduct of the Seminole War, and amplified through the next five years by Clay men—that Old Hickory was purely a "military chieftain" itching for dictatorship. Jackson was finally driven to want the Presidency to show that he could fill it, and confute his enemies. The dilemma was not unlike that of Jefferson at bay before the Federalists. That opposition made these men into Presidents one cannot doubt.

Yet Jackson, for all his homespun qualities, had to make an about-face before he could become the people's candidate. In Tennessee he was a landowner and a "hard money" man, who in earlier days had represented the nabobs of the frontier against the leather-shirts of John Sevier. As early as 1815 he had held a few shares in the Nashville branch of the United States Bank. Up to about 1824 he tended to favor that bank as a bulwark against wildcat financing and printing-press currency, for which debtors and ne'er-do-wells were clamoring. But the proletarian movement, and growing hard times, converted Jackson in spite of himself. With apparent sincerity he began to hate the moneyed interests of the East, and soon his geographical loyalties inspired economic ones. He decided that democracy was a higher desideratum than "sound money." The spirit of the masses had captured Jackson and made him its mouthpiece. In April, 1824, for the first time, Jackson began to talk about "a moneyed aristocracy dangerous to the liberties of the country."[27] It was foregone that the West should become the new home of democracy, rather than the settled and urban East. As William Graham Sumner once observed, "When the earth is underpopulated and there is an economic demand for men, democracy is inevitable."[28]

Soon it was forgotten that Jackson's attitude upon economic issues had ever been ultra-conservative, and his boom as the people's candidate grew apace. All loyal Tennesseans, who best knew his change of front, were glad to cheer for a local son; those outside the state recalled only that for many years he had been known as a picturesque Indian fighter, frontiersman, and great general. With almost no censure for inconsistency, from a border conservative he thus evolved into a national liberal—reversing, as has been remarked, the career of Patrick Henry as youthful firebrand and later reactionary.[29] Needless to say, Jackson's was the course which endeared a man to the people.

A few churchmen were disturbed because Jackson swore copiously "By the Eternal."[30] Others had passing qualms over his horse-racing and cock-fighting and duelling. Jacksonians replied that his duelling days were over, and as for racing, Old Hickory himself was "the war-horse who . . . has won many a glorious purse for his country, and is not to be driven from the course by the shouts of defeat from the jockies in Washington."[31] A few hostile editors criticized Jackson in the late fall of 1824, as senator-elect, for setting out with his family for Washington in a morocco-lined carriage behind four blooded horses. Friends retorted that this equipage was taken for the sake of Mrs. Jackson's comfort, and not to put on airs.[32] Enemies regretted that the great military fervor created by the visit of Lafayette in 1824 "inflamed militia companies" and added to the applause for America's greatest living martial hero, the victor of New Orleans.[33] It was reported that Pennsylvania militiamen in the winter of 1825 talked of laying siege to the city of Washington if their beloved idol were done out of the Presidency by politicians.[34] Everybody knew that Lafayette, calling at the Hermitage, had recognized a pair of pistols he had given General Washington and said he rejoiced that they were still in worthy hands.[35] These military men understood each other.

Jackson did not cheapen himself with campaigning. In March, 1824, he wrote to a friend: "I have no doubt if I was to travel to Boston where I have been invited that would insure my election. But this I cannot do. I would feel degraded the balance of my life."[36] Not even to woo cold New England would this Democrat bestir himself. It was not unlike Thomas Jefferson's attitude two decades before. Jackson gallantly accepted his defeat by the Adams-Clay coalition in the winter of 1825, although, as the bargaining nature of the transaction dawned upon him, he and thousands of Jacksonians seethed with suppressed rage. Jackson quietly returned home, advised by John Henry Eaton to "say nothing and plant cotton." "Having lost many of my teeth" to the damage of his articulation, Jackson declined even to address a Bible society; adding that he might be charged with electioneering "under the sacred garb of religion."[37] For the time being he remained quiescent. He knew that no election bonfires blazed for John Quincy Adams, and that only the rainy weather had kept Jacksonians in Washington from burning Mr. Adams in effigy. Adams, with his sterling ability and a core of stubborn integrity—despite his "corrupt" election—would never be a hero. He had never fought either battle or duel, and as a British traveller complained, "Mr. Adams seems to have no reserve or mystery."[38] As a token of John Quincy Adams, one thinks of the time when as President of the United States he went swimming in the Potomac, and some rude boys "amused themselves with laughing at his bald head as it poppled up and down in the water, and, as they drew nearer, threatened to crack open his round pate if he came nigh them" —until the President had to "seek a more retired bathing-place."[39] If the bather had been Old Hickory, instinct no doubt might have warned the scamps that they would be thrashed within an inch of their lives.

Some truly felt that Jackson was too much the military tyrant for a nation's head. John Quincy Adams himself had suggested the old soldier for Vice-President, "a station in which the General could hang no one."[40] After Jefferson's death in 1826 it was reported that the master of Monticello had looked upon Jackson with misgivings. Daniel Webster said Jefferson had told him: "I feel much alarmed at the prospect of seeing General Jackson President. He is one of the most unfit men I know of for such a place. He has had very little respect for laws or constitutions and is, in fact, an able military chieftain. His passions are terrible."[41] Jefferson never liked soldiers, and to a man of Webster's known opinions, in the privacy of Monticello over a social glass, Jefferson had spoken his mind with perhaps a touch of over-emphasis. A pro-Jackson pamphlet of 1828 resented a garbled version of this opinion:

Scarcely had the venerated remains of Jefferson been consigned to the tomb, ere the coalition thought of the expedient of fabricating calumnies and charging them to the departed patriot. He was made to say, "you might as well make a sailor of a cook, or a soldier of a goose, as a president of Andrew Jackson." Such language and such a simile from President Jefferson, author of the *Notes on Virginia!* The very thought is sacrilege. Let us read what he has left on record, and mark the contrast. "Gen. Jackson," said Mr. Jefferson, "is a clear headed, sound minded man, and has more of the Roman in him than many now living."[42]

But Jefferson never said, or apparently thought, that this unvarnished old soldier was the man to carry on "Jeffersonian democracy" in the White House. Jefferson's models—the philosopher, the scholar, the liberal-minded planter—were not the ideals of Old Hickory, who in 1822 had written to his nephew: "I have always thought that sir William Wallauce [sic] . . . was the best model for a young man. In him we find a stubborn virtue, . . . too pure for corruption, . . . all-ways ready to brave any danger for the relief of his country or his friend."[43] The heroes of heroes are always a significant key. Courage, and loyalty to nation and friends (generally welded together in Jackson's mind), were his ruling passions. Over the retrospect of years Vachel Lindsay wrote—

> Andrew Jackson was eight feet tall.
> His arm was a hickory limb and a maul.
> His sword was so long he dragged it on the ground.
> Every friend was an equal. Every foe was a hound.

Yet even as the man on horseback, Jackson differed from the earlier pattern, that of Washington. With his shock of unruly hair and un-kempt boots that swayed about his bony knees—"an ugly old Kaintuck flat-boatman" as a sophisticated Creole hostess marked him down, with some disapproval—Jackson anticipated the sloppiness of Ulysses S. Grant. Albert Gallatin found him a "lanky uncouth-looking person-age," his "manners those of a rough backwoodsman." Even in the field his tactics were those of the tenacious guerilla fighter or bushwhacker. By the standards of Robert E. Lee, as well as those of Mount Vernon's master upon whom Lee had shaped his own life, Jackson would never have passed a dress-parade. By their lights it took a gentleman, in the stricter sense, to make war gracefully. But that he represented the cul-ture of the 1830s—with his preference for corncob and red clay pipes, for steel knives over silver, even his pampered "stomach trouble" and biliousness and his addiction to patent medicines—could not be gain-said. He was the epitome of a sickly yet vigorous generation, of pioneers beset with fevers and agues. The mother of President Garfield remem-bered, "We was sick every fall regular." Mrs. Trollope and other snobbish British visitors saw in Jackson the symbol of disintegrating social standards; that he represented also the intellectual and æsthetic backsliding of an epoch might have been a more serious charge. For in certain respects his age was as inferior to its antecedents as a portrait by Ralph Earl was to a Gilbert Stuart.

Meanwhile, Jackson was the man of the hour. The final burst of enthusiasm which carried him into the White House began in January, 1828, at a mammoth celebration of the thirteenth anniversary of the Battle of New Orleans. Jackson's trip to that city turned into a royal progress. "Jackson Clubs" in the North and East sent representatives; the entire jubilee was keyed to a presidential note. Jackson's private papers, now in the Library of Congress, show that for the first time he began to receive great quantities of fan mail—more than immediately after the battle itself. Acrostic poems, dedications of books, requests for help from old campaigners of 1815, reports of his immense popularity, flooded his desk. "The Jefferson Association of Baltimore" wrote in August, 1828, to inform him that it was one of four young men's clubs organized in that city to glorify the heroes of America—the remaining three being Washington, Franklin, and Jackson. Its favorite toast is "the Farmer of Tennessee—the army's boast—the senate's pride—the people's choice." Jackson replied: "I heartily approve of the plan of its orgonesation, as a means of cherishing a lively sentiment of national pride."[44] (Jackson's spelling was ever shaky; an ancient American tradition states that "o. k." originated from his attempt to abbreviate "all correct.") A citizen of Newtown, Kentucky, on August 30, 1828, invites Jackson to a great barbecue, "where we intend to give the Greatest diner that Ever was known in this State" and spike the guns of Henry Clay. The writer reports that he has a newborn son—

and he is named Andrew Jackson. I want you to present me with a Sword for him for as soon as he is able to understand Who he is named after I intend to Learn him the Military Deception and tutor him to follow the steps of his farther Ma. Gen. Andrew Jackson.

Through the following months a frenzy hitherto unparalleled raged about Old Hickory, who "has slain the Indians & flogged the British & therefore is the wisest & greatest man in the nation."[45] The methods of local frontier elections were for the first time tried upon a national scale. Militia companies drilled and paraded, orators thundered at fish fries and barbecues, whiskey flowed like water. Zeal for whitewashing led to solemn assertion by Jackson's friends that "Gen. Jackson does not at any time play cards. Neither does General Jackson swear," while the enemy camp went so far as to report that Jackson's father had been a mulatto and his mother a prostitute.[46] But his success this time could not be denied. He received 178 electoral votes to Adams's 83.

A band of Jacksonians in Berkeley County, Virginia, wrote on November 29 to congratulate him upon

the richest reward which has ever been conferred on the most fortunate, beloved and illusterous personage in ancient or modern times for meritorious deeds.—The idea of being chosen by millions of intelligent freemen to be the master pilot of this grand Republic is superlatively delightful and fascinating.

A score of letters from different states invite him to attend Jackson Balls, to review parades of Jackson Guards, or merely to stop for a visit on his way to Washington. A typical fan letter, from the postmaster of Fultonham, Ohio, December 9, 1828, begins: "Please excuse the liberty I have taken, which I presume you will, being the peoples president and myself being one of the people." Yet in this same month the sweetness of Jackson's personal triumph ceased, with the death of his faithful wife "Aunt Rachel"—caused in part by the late revival of the old cruel charges against her. His mail during these weeks reminds him that "Jesus Christ was persecuted & crucified for saving the world," warns him against assassination, offers the regards of "humble individuals" who "obtrude themselves on your notice," and presents clumsy condolence upon his loss ("a man or woman is hardly born, comparetively speaking, untill they are dead"). A hustling tombstone-maker in Kentucky, five days after Mrs. Jackson's death, says he has heard the news, and "I therefore tender you my servises in that line of biseness."[47]

III

With a heart of ashes Jackson set out for his Inaugural. But among his followers the chant of victory arose clear and strident. The capital was crowded with old soldiers, woodsmen in leather shirts, Irish immigrants, adventurers and office-seekers, newspapermen. "I never saw anything like it before," wrote Daniel Webster, a touch of derision in his ruffle-shirted bosom. "They really seem to think the country is rescued from some dreadful danger."[48] Lodging-house keepers stowed five in a bed and spread pallets on floors and billiard-tables. Barbers advertised "haircutting in the Jackson style," while haberdashers offered "Jackson stocks." Hickory canes were in evidence everywhere. On

Inauguration Day eager thousands stormed the Capitol to see their idol, erect, white-haired, sallow-faced, coming on foot from Gadsby's boarding-house. "It is beautiful, it is sublime!" exclaimed Francis Scott Key.[49] Few cared that Jackson's address was mediocre; hostile critics, in the main, had already decamped from Washington. As the old chieftain rode down Pennsylvania Avenue to the White House, a great crowd followed him. They made his reception a never-to-be-forgotten saturnalia—of chairs ruined by muddy boots in frantic efforts to see the hero, of broken china and bloody noses. Windows were shattered to allow needed ventilation, as white and black, frontiersman and farmer and day laborer, thronged the halls which they had never seen before. Even Jefferson, as an earlier "People's President," had been for them, but not of them—and an incursion such as this was unthinkable in his day.

Among Jackson's papers one finds a poem, dated February 16, 1829, to which "the writer is emboldened to add *confidentially* the name of Emily C. Stras." It begins:

> He comes the sacred oath to swear;
> Then seated in that awful chair,
> Higher than thrones—with Washington
> And equal fame and fate he's won.
>
> Our Jackson is coming, oh, ho! oh, ho!
> Our Jackson is coming, oh, ho! oh, ho!
> Our Jackson is coming, the far echoes swelling,
> Resound that he's coming, oh, ho! oh, ho!

Eight more stanzas follow, endorsed on the back in Jackson's hand: "Mrs. Emily C. Stras—'The Campbells are coming': a tribute of respect." Jackson's mail during the following eight years reveals not only tributes of poetry, and invitations to visit admirers or stop at hotels named for him, but also an unprecedented avalanche of presents. Many of them are offered with a devotion more impeccable than the spelling or grammar. There are barrels of scuppernong wine, hickory poles, carved pipes (Jackson still preferring his corn cob, "the sweetest and best pipe," as he told General Sam Dale), hats, canes, cheeses, and near the end of his regime a phaeton made from the timbers of the frigate *Constitution*. One donor calls him the man who "bestowed the Blessings of Government upon the Poor as well as on the Rich."[50] One J. B. Rose, an exile, "the only French Piano Maker in New York," begs him to accept a piano, in November, 1832; Jackson, with none of

Jefferson's fastidious reticence about gifts, accepts with hearty alacrity. During the same month, a typical pamphlet sent to the President, reprinting a speech at the Salem, New Jersey, Hickory Club, declares: "Since the days of George Washington, no man has enjoyed what may be called a personal popularity with the American people, save Andrew Jackson." This was on the eve of the "Nullification Crisis," when Jackson's firm stand against secessionist talk in South Carolina, his ringing declaration at a Jefferson birthday dinner, "Our Union—it must be preserved," plus a threat of military force, gained him more favor than he lost. He tested that popularity early the next summer by visiting Philadelphia, where his reception lasted four days, and New York, where he bowed to more than two hundred thousand cheering people upon arrival. Mounted upon a "white charger," he was hailed as "the savior of the Union." In Rhode Island his appearance set off so many cannon booming that "the State provided new glass for nearly every householder who asked for it."[51] Upon Boston Common he received salvoes of cheers, although Beacon Street was cold and it was said that only one little girl waved a handkerchief for him from an upstairs window.[52] Harvard College made him a doctor of laws, although John Quincy Adams protested "this insult to learning" in honoring a man who could "hardly spell his own name." "As the people have twice decided that this man knows law enough to be their ruler," replied President Quincy, "it is not for Harvard College to maintain that they are mistaken."[53] Later folklore, taking a hint from the humorist "Major Jack Downing," said that Jackson had replied to the ripple of academic applause in pure Ciceronian: "E pluribus unum; sine qua non." It was also reported that soon after this honor a New England spinster had sent him a proposal of marriage.[54]

Jackson's assault upon the Bank of the United States, and his routing of its arch-dragon Nicholas Biddle, was perhaps the most popular act of his Administration. In part it may have been inspired by the wily Van Buren—representing New York's ancient feud with Philadelphia—but fundamentally it sprang from Jackson's intuition of the people's will. It made him for all time the hero of the masses, the successor of Jefferson in the battle against privilege. A youthful liberal like Walt Whitman began to think of Jackson as a "noble yet simple-souled old man," a "massive, yet most sweet and plain character." In later years Whitman clung to the illusion that he had seen Jackson not once but many times, and "often talked with him."[55] The Good Gray Poet forgot, as his biographer notes, the flaws in Jackson the

Democrat—how he had manipulated electoral machinery even to the point of dictating Van Buren as his successor, how he had exploited patronage and frankly avowed the spoils system, how he helped to plunder the public domain and played into the hands of crooks and wildcat bankers, how he remained deaf to the claims of city workers under the new industrialism and hounded the Cherokees and approved the extension of slavery. Whitman's hero-worship was eclectic, as it seemed—like that of many thousands in Jackson's day, casting its eyes chiefly upon the homespun President himself and his overthrow of the Bank. The inconsistencies of Jackson, and his vestigial traces of the buckskin aristocrat, were pared away by the legend-makers. His lack of the deeper democratic logic which sustained Thomas Jefferson was seldom noticed, in approval of the roughly successful deeds of "King Andrew's Reign."

Jackson throve upon opposition. A valiant fighter and a good hater, he appeared at his best when courage was required—not only against the redcoats and Indians, the Bank and the Nullifiers, but in more casual combat. He enjoyed threats of assassination, and in the midst of his battle with Nicholas Biddle allowed the favored journalist of the Jackson press, Francis Blair, to publish some of them. Few remarked the dubious taste of this act, in applauding the President's valor. As early as 1828 he had received a letter, now in the Jackson Papers, signed "One of the People":

> You are now the only hope of the nation. . . . I pray you take care of yourself, & guard against poison and the dagger. Be always prepared to give yourself a vomit. The most speedy is 15 grains of white vitriol (sulphate of zinc) or 15 grains of blue vitriol (sulphate of copper). Remember that Henry 4th of France and William of Nassau founder of the Republic of Holland were assassinated.

When in May, 1833, in ailing health, Jackson started his tour of the United States, at Alexandria a discharged lieutenant in the Navy shook his fist violently in the President's face and began to threaten violence. He then fled, but Old Hickory's rage in trying to break down a door which barred him from his sudden adversary "seem'd to have put his blood in motion," as an onlooker reported.[56] The effect was salutary. On January 30, 1835, while Jackson was attending the funeral of a congressman, a crazed assailant named Richard Lawrence sprang in front of him and drew two pistols, but both misfired; Jackson lunged at him with a walking-stick, though a young army officer seized the man before the President could cane him. An expert on small-arms found both pistols in excellent condition, and calculated the chance of two misfires as one in 125,000. This appears to have been the first gesture of assassination toward a Chief Executive in America. Jackson's very callousness and lack of imagination heightened his courage. Sudden death and disaster were as foreign to his reckoning as the concept of failure. George Washington Parke Custis liked to tell how he had once sailed with Jackson down Chesapeake Bay, and under the threat of a storm which might have capsized the boat, Jackson—in words which Custis fondly supposed the President was garbling from Julius Cæsar—had said calmly, "My good friend, you never travelled with me."[57] Neither humility nor prudence played a part in the Jackson fable. In such respects he was in tune with his times.

When his "Reign" was over and Jackson bade a long farewell to Washington, a great crowd gathered at the Baltimore & Ohio station to see him off. His white hair streamed in the wind, and standing upon the rear platform—that rostrum of American idols from his day to the present—Jackson bowed stiffly as the train pulled out. When the smoke died away, one observer felt "as if a bright star had gone out of the sky."[58] During the last few years of life, among the quiet meadows of the Hermitage, Old Hickory was not forgotten. Up to the last he was swamped with requests for mementoes. Even in his White House days he had learned to save all the clippings whenever he had a haircut, in order to satisfy as far as possible the great demand for locks of hair.[59] At the inauguration of James K. Polk ("Young Hickory"), Commodore Elliott had his pocket picked of all his cash and a lock of General Jackson's hair. In the spring of 1845, when the old warrior was reliably reported to be dying, requests for hair and for autographs grew more importunate—some correspondents not troubling to conceal their apprehension that this was the last chance. And even as he lay mortally ill, Jackson remained a powerful symbol of American imperialism. At a Jackson Day dinner in Washington, one of his old campaigners, Auguste Davézac, lamented the cowardice of politicians while the annexation of Texas hung in the balance:

They forget that Jackson still lives! Even if the hero were dead, go to the Hermitage, ye men of little faith; Go! ask for that *old cocked hat;* it is still there; take it; raise it on the top of a long hickory pole! One hundred thousand American horsemen, rallying around that standard, will tread down Europe's or Mexico's mercenaries like the grass of the Texan prairies.[60]

It was one of the minor moments of historical drama that Jackson's protégé the greatest Texan, Sam Houston, arrived at breakneck speed after many a weary mile—just after the head of his old captain sank in death.

IV

After Jackson, the military ideal became a tool for political manipulation. In 1840 the People had turned against Jackson's heir, the sedentary Van Buren, in favor of the first synthetic publicity hero, William Henry Harrison. The aged Jackson, forgetting that he had set the pattern for Harrison's campaign, called him "the Mock Hero," and groaned in disbelief that the voters "can be led by hard cider, coons, log cabins, and demagogues. I have a higher opinion of the intelligence of the american people than this." In this same campaign William Cullen Bryant was remarking that the new military favorite, Harrison, has "animal courage . . . a very common and not a very exalted kind of merit," when unaccompanied by "moral courage." Emerson noted in his Journal: "Can one nowadays see a soldier without a slight feeling—the slightest possible—of the ridiculous?"[61] A few years later Abraham Lincoln in Congress would taunt the Democrats who had nominated Lewis Cass: "Like a horde of hungry ticks you have stuck to the tail of the Hermitage lion to the end of his life, and you are still sticking to it."[62] Yet Lincoln's own candidate was General Zachary Taylor.

The soldier as hero suffered a check with the defeats for President of Winfield Scott and Frémont, two of the politicians' least happy choices, but he returned with Grant and Garfield, men of marked personal mediocrity. Old Hickory, for all his faults, was the one successful soldier President of the nineteenth century. Behind the election of all these men lay a simple mass psychology. Aside from the wish to do honor to a public benefactor in uniform lay the American assumption of versatility—that a man of achievement upon the field of battle would succeed equally well in the councils of state. The other side of this coin is seen in the proposal of *The Chicago Tribune* in 1863, and of many Unionists impatient with the blunders of McClellan and Burnside, that President Lincoln take personal command of the Army in battle. Presidents and generals were somehow thought to be interchangeable. From heroes of the Spanish-American War, public opinion soon rejected the first sailor to stir widespread Presidential talk, Admiral Dewey, but favored Theodore Roosevelt, a fighting man but in no sense a professional soldier. Since that day the soldier President has vanished from the American scene. It would be rash to suggest that he is gone forever. Today, however, his type suggests to many American minds the dictator. Moreover the growing complexity of American government seems to have turned us further and further away from the qualities which made Old Hickory successful in his simpler milieu. Without another great war and its altered conditions, as well as its new crop of heroes, it is extremely unlikely that a military man will become a future President. He will never be picked from the routine ranks of West Point and the War College.

The tenure of Jackson's fame is more secure than that of a mere military man. He remains as a personality and symbol whose importance is but slowly declining. At the end of his public life his glory appeared very bright. The just verdict of William Cullen Bryant, "precisely the man for the period in which he well and nobly discharged the duties demanded of him by the times,"[63] seemed lukewarm to the ardent Jacksonian. Jackson's old adversary who had now made his peace, Thomas Hart Benton, reported that when the chieftain descended the Capitol steps for the last time, a great shout rang out, homage such as "power never commanded, nor man in power received . . . the acclaim of posterity breaking from the bosoms of contemporaries."[64] An unnamed senator in Washington told Francis Grund that "General Jackson understood the people of the United States better, perhaps, than any President before him," and that they believed in him "as the Turks in their prophet."[65] Upon Jackson's death his partisans are found asserting that "Washington & Jackson will always be linked together as the two greatest men & patriots of America."[66] Jackson, "an almost uneducated orphan boy of the wilderness" as one of his funeral eulogists called him, blended some of Washington's military glory with the self-made attributes of Franklin. The three were not infrequently bracketed together.[67] Under the shower of panegyric and public tears, few paused to analyze the reasons for Jackson's greatness. One of the few was Justice John Catron of the Supreme Court, who visited the dying General in April, 1845, and went home to think on the qualities which had made Jackson the leading American of his generation. His leadership, which came in part from magnetism and commanding appearance, and expressed itself in quick decision and prompt action, was the essence of Jackson's popularity. The people felt that he was working, and working effectively, for their sakes. "If he had fallen from the clouds into a city on fire," wrote Justice Catron, "he would have been at the head of the extinguishing hosts in an hour.

He would have blown up a palace to stop the fire with as little mis-
giving as another would have torn down a board shed. In a moment
he would have willed it proper, and in ten minutes the thing would
have been done. . . . He cared not a rush for anything behind: he
looked ahead." It was a little ironic that Catron should have addressed
these lines, on June 11, 1845, to a future President of the United States
whose lack of this promptitude and force made him perhaps the least
heroic man ever to fill that office. His name was James Buchanan.

Within two decades, Jackson began to be examined more critically
by his partisans. His first notable biographer, James Parton, in writing
three volumes in praise of Jackson's rude manhood and courage, concluded in 1860 that Jackson "was a fighting man, and little more than
a fighting man." Parton's attitude was divided; in a single chapter he
pronounced the General's election to the Presidency "a mistake," and
then like a good democrat was compelled to eat his own words. With
mingled idealism and shrewdness he wrote:

The instinctive preferences of the people must be right. That is to say, the
man preferred by the people must have more in him of what the people
most want than any other of his generation. . . .
The calamity of the United States has been this: the educated classes have
not been able to accept the truths of the democratic creed. . . . Hence, in
this country, until very recently, the men of books have had little influence
upon public affairs.[68]

The retreat of aristocracy from American public life was to a large
degree the work of Jackson and the spoils system. It was unfortunate
that the statesmanly training and inner cultivation which that aristocracy represented should be lost to American politics, that its best
endeavors should thenceforth be turned to the making of money and
the attempted recapture of government through "big business." But
that the people, lacking a second Jefferson, should have exalted Jackson,
was natural enough. That Jackson was followed by a line of super-
annuated soldiers who lacked his moral courage and of hack politicians
who lacked his integrity, was a greater tragedy. Not until the rise of
Lincoln did Old Hickory find a worthy successor—a successor so great,
in fact, that he has absorbed the best part of the Jackson tradition, its
homespun honesty, and left the General as a slowly waning symbol.
Yet, it is humorously said, a few old Tennessee counties are "still voting
for Andrew Jackson."

Although "The Old Hickory Division" in the Great War—recruited from Tennessee and the Carolinas—did valiant service, and was officially credited with having broken the Hindenburg Line in September, 1918, the cult of Jackson the soldier has long been fading. The spate of congressional oratory released in 1929, by the placing of Jackson's statue in the Hall of Statuary of the National Capitol, praised him as the scourge of privilege, and said almost nothing about New Orleans and the Indian wars. "Jackson's victory in the economic field to my mind far outranks his victories on the field of battle," declared Senator Brookhart, while colleagues like Fess, Bruce, Tyson, Heflin, and Mc-Kellar followed the same vein—some calling for a new Jackson to arise and chasten Wall Street.[69] Under the New Deal, Jackson Day Dinners evoked even more outspoken sentiments against "America's Sixty Families." Few even recalled that "Jackson Day" was the anniversary of the Battle of New Orleans. On that occasion in 1936, for example, President Roosevelt compared his own achievements to those of the seventh President, and added:

Our frontiers of today are economic, not geographic. Our enemies of today are the forces of privilege and greed within our own borders. May a double portion of Old Hickory's heroic spirit be upon us tonight. May we be inspired by the power and the glory and the justice of his rugged and fearless life.

In his third "Fireside Chat" Mr. Roosevelt sought to stiffen the resolution of America under adversity by telling the story of the small boy who, when asked if Jackson "would go to Heaven," answered, "He will if he wants to." Seventy-seven years before, Abraham Lincoln had told this story for a similar purpose—save that Lincoln quoted the reply in somewhat homelier words, "He'd get there if he had a mind to."[70] But Jackson, as an emblem of American tenacity, remained the same.

The Hermitage, visited by some ten thousand people every month during the summer season, remains a popular shrine. Since 1899 it has been under the care of The Ladies' Hermitage Association, composed largely of members from old Nashville families—Donelsons, Overtons, Caldwells—who have their private stock of Jackson anecdotes, manuscripts, and mementoes, even to a fan or piece of jewelry worn by some belle who danced with the General or his guest Lafayette. Here is the cradle of the Jackson cult. The Hermitage has known its vicissitudes: the advent of the Civil War cancelled a plan to make it a branch of the Military Academy at West Point, and in that War—despite the

Nullification sentiments of his namesake—Colonel Andrew Jackson III fought in the ranks of gray and returned to the Hermitage as a paroled prisoner. In 1894 "a professional body-snatcher" from New York visited the Hermitage one day, showed special interest in the tomb, went away in the afternoon to borrow a spade from the Donelson home at Tulip Grove, worked apparently all night to exhume the body but was stopped by the stone foundations of the monument. Months later he confessed the attempt upon his death-bed, but made no explanation of his purpose.[71] Two Presidents of the United States, since the Civil War, have visited the Hermitage and broken bread there. The first was Theodore Roosevelt, a staunch Jacksonian who years before had written, "With the exception of Washington and Lincoln, no man has left a deeper mark on American history,"[72] and whose next annual message to Congress drew forth a $5000 appropriation to restore the Hermitage. The second was Franklin D. Roosevelt, in 1934, who placed a wreath upon Jackson's tomb. But no President can forget his predecessor from Tennessee—for Clark Mills's masterpiece of 1853, the first equestrian statue ever made in the United States, is the most arresting object in Lafayette Square, facing the White House. Cast from cannon which Jackson captured at New Orleans, by a man who had seen neither Jackson nor an equestrian statue, it shows a frantically rearing horse—a veritable Bucephalus—upon whose back sits a cool figure of Old Hickory tranquilly lifting his cocked hat to the cheering multitude. The critical are reminded of an equilibrist in the circus, but this statue has always been immensely popular—and has helped set the style for heroes on horseback, who, at strategic points, still complicate the traffic of our greatest cities.

Jackson remains, in fact, the equestrian warrior—a bold, hardy, uncompromising man of steel. His "courage never to submit or yield" was the fiber of the Jackson legend even in Civil War times—when those distrustful of Lincoln's early diffidence grew fond of contrasting Jackson's crisp decisiveness.[73] But he has never been absorbed very deeply into the blood of American mythology. He is too simple; he lacks the spacious qualities which serve to make Washington the eighteenth-century gentleman an enigma to the public today, and the baffling lights and shadows of Lincoln play no part in his cult. For generations the literary men and textbook writers—in the East as well as in the Deep South, Massachusetts and Virginia alike—have regarded Old Hickory as an American worthy who was nevertheless a quarrelsome roughneck, tinged with the demagogue. Only in Tennessee does he have the folklore reality of the Bell Witch (whom by report he once encountered) and the vigor of a great political loyalty. And there, the local D. A. R. and The Ladies' Hermitage Association have helped to disembowel his legend by insisting that he was not "rough and uncultured," but a ripe scholar of the Monticello stamp. Textbooks which reveal that his spelling and grammar were faulty are frowned upon, and a movie like "The Gorgeous Hussy"—with Aunt Rachel and her pipe—are protested. If one removes the homespun fibers in Jackson's character, there is great risk that nothing will be left save an abstraction of hardihood.

CHAPTER TEN

LINCOLN: THE DEMOCRAT AS HERO

"I have often heard it remarked that Lincoln was the idol of the people. I fear this declaration was founded in truth. The people of this country are inclined to hero-worship. . . . God will punish idolatry."—The REVEREND HUGH P. McADAM of Troy, New York, in a sermon on "Black Easter," 1865.

I

THE Kentucky birthplace of Lincoln is an epitome, in architecture, of legend-building. The small log cabin at Hodgenville has been enclosed in a massive Greek temple. Into its granite has been cut an inscription which errs in the date of Lincoln's mother's birth, wrongly gives the names of her parents as Joseph and Nancy Shipley Hanks, incorrectly states that she was orphaned at the age of nine and reared by foster parents, and supplies false dates for Nancy's marriage to Thomas Lincoln and for their removal to Indiana. It seems a pity to carve so many misstatements, in a few lines, on so durable a medium as granite. Some of them spring from sheer carelessness, others from zeal in concealing Lincoln's own belief that his mother was an illegitimate child, sired by "a well bred Virginia planter" whose name research has never been able to discover.

Americans have a special fondness for the mothers of heroes. It seems as though the ancient cult of Mariolatry, choked by Protestantism, has flowered anew in this theme. More romantically than any other race, not excepting even the sentimental German, we are a folk with an Œdipus complex. Even our great desperadoes, as we shall see, the bold bad men of the West, were good to their mothers. We read of many famous Americans—from Daniel Webster to Bryan—that they never found anything equal to their mother's cooking. It is almost a touchstone of herohood. As for our national idols—whether lasting ones like Washington and Lincoln and Lee, or the ephemeræ of current political campaigns—we are quick to warm to the sentiments of silver hair, the lamplit home, and the little schoolhouse. These are the yardsticks of democracy and heart appeal.

Lincoln's law partner, William H. Herndon—a sentimentalist who prided himself on being a hard-bitten realist—is our best authority for the statement that Lincoln once said of his mother, "All that I am, or ever hope to be, I owe to her." They are words which any dutiful son might have said, with fond exaggeration, of a mother who had died when he was only nine. Eagerly accepting this statement, folklore has forgotten Herndon's eugenic explanation: that Lincoln believed that whatever spark of genius he had came through Nancy Hanks from her mysterious father the Virginia aristocrat. A biographer less reliable than Herndon, Josiah Gilbert Holland, gives the most popular version of Lincoln's words: "All that I am, or hope to be, I owe to my angel mother." Her death from "the milk sick" in October, 1818, in that half-faced camp at Pigeon Creek, Indiana, undoubtedly left a benign influence lingering about her son. But Lincoln himself might have smiled at a late "psycho-biography" by L. Pierce Clark, which interprets him in terms of "the Eden from which the infant Lincoln had been so ruthlessly expelled when he was weaned." Lincoln might also have been surprised to see the Hanks coat of arms as reproduced in Caroline Hanks Hitchcock's book Nancy Hanks in 1900; to learn there that "Hanks" derived from the Egyptian Ankh, meaning "soul"; to hear that his mother Nancy grew up in a Virginia milieu of "hunting, hawking, and fishing in the great estates of nearly a thousand acres." Similar myths have described how she taught her son to write and cipher, and read the Bible to him. Yet the late Senator Beveridge, after patient research, concluded that she was "absolutely illiterate."[1]

Her idealization had begun when Lincoln was President. William

M. Thayer in *The Pioneer Boy and How He Became President,* in 1863, drew upon imagination—probably with no violence to the lost facts—in describing her as loving, resourceful, far above her backwoods environment. Thayer was apparently the first to apply to the Lincoln saga the old methods of Parson Weems. Any invention, so long as the result was "inspirational," passed muster. Orville J. Victor in 1864, for the Beadle Dime Novel Biographies, and Horatio Alger in 1883, followed in his steps. Late in 1865, after Lincoln's death, when the public was tender with grief over its tardily appreciated loss, Holland described her as "a slender, pale, sad and sensitive woman," while Phoebe Hanaford told how the boy Lincoln had haunted her grave inconsolably, and as President was about to revisit the spot when Booth's bullet carried him to her on the heavenly shore.[2] (Of these details there was as little proof as there was justification, at the other extreme, of Edgar Lee Masters's sneer at Lincoln's callousness in failing to erect a tombstone over her grave, though he died "worth more than $100,000.") At the beginning of the twentieth century, the poet James Oppenheim had made her into a madonna:

> Frail Mother of the Wilderness,
> How strange the world shines in,
> And the cabin becomes a chapel
> And the babe lies secure—
> Sweet Mother of the Wilderness,
> New worlds for you begin,
> You have tasted of the apple
> That giveth wisdom sure.

While the oral myths of Kentucky and Indiana—eager, like most backwoods folklore, to touch the keys of sentiment—have favored her frail physique, and the story of Lincoln's birth in poverty while a blizzard raged outside the shack, there have been other versions. *The Matrix,* a novel by Maria T. Davies in 1920, pictured her as a dashing horsewoman, and "probably the first woman in Kentucky to enter trade and secure her own financial independence." William E. Barton in 1929 sought to link her blood with that of Robert E. Lee.

The father, Thomas Lincoln, has fared indifferently in myth. To the wife and mother he is always secondary. Many groundless traditions brush him aside in insisting that Abraham Lincoln's real father was Calhoun or Henry Clay or Patrick Henry (dead ten years before) or an obscure Abraham Enlow. In all, seven fathers and seven birthplaces have been assigned to Lincoln, recalling the seven cities of Greece that claimed Homer dead. One ardent devotee, Denton J. Snider, under the spell of miracle concluded that his hero was begotten "not of Tom Lincoln, but of God the Father."[3] Rarely does romance seek to clear Thomas Lincoln of backwoods shiftlessness: the contrast with his ambitious son makes a better story, and there is always a tendency to exaggerate the father's squalor. Neighbors remembered that he thrashed the boy severely, and was scornful of his book-learning. Beyond the tradition that Thomas Lincoln was a pioneer abolitionist, myth has done nothing to idealize him.

The widow Sarah Bush, whom Thomas Lincoln married a year after Nancy's death, has met with undeserved neglect. Her energy, cleanliness, and good sense revolutionized the Lincoln household, as Lincoln vividly recalled after thirty-five years. He called her "mamma," saying that "she had been his best Friend in this world and that no Son could love a Mother more than he loved her." Just before leaving Illinois for the White House in 1861 he found time to drive out to the old farm and tell her good-bye, with a fond embrace—although, a little while before, he had declined to make this trip to see his dying father. Yet the folk mind finds it hard to escape from conventional notions about stepmothers, the ogres of so many fairy-tales. Hence the glory which she might have shared with Nancy Hanks has all passed to the latter.

Lincoln's boyhood is rich in legends dear to America. He made possible the final romanticism of the log cabin—though some said he was great because of his background, while others believe he was great in spite of it. Certainly, from a soil of poverty on the prairies of Indiana and Illinois sprang his fierce ambition, his lack of conventional dignity, his sympathy for the common man, his humility which blended with a sturdy and serene self-confidence. But thousands of other lads, from the same environment, failed to be Lincolns. This paradox is one which never fails to fascinate the people. Lincoln himself was too good a politician not to make some use of his origins. In Springfield, after hearing his political rival Colonel Dick Taylor praise the plain people, Lincoln stepped to Taylor's side and opened the Colonel's coat to reveal a ruffled shirt and gold seals. Then, it was said, Lincoln made his own speech, recalling his boyhood and flatboat days and his single pair of buckskin breeches which shrank in time till "they left a blue streak around my legs that can be seen to this day." This was an *argumentum ad hominem* that surpassed logic. Later, in 1860.

when Lincoln's name was coming before the whole country, one of his politically wise friends, Richard Oglesby, had gone out to the old homestead and looked up John Hanks. He asked "what kind of work 'Abe' used to be good at." After scratching his head, Hanks replied, "Well, not much of any kind but dreaming, but he did help me split a lot of rails when we made the clearing twelve miles west of here." Hanks was then persuaded to carry two rails from the old fence into the Illinois State Republican Convention. They bore the punning slogan—

ABRAHAM LINCOLN
THE RAIL CANDIDATE
FOR PRESIDENT IN 1860.

Lincoln characteristically refused to guarantee that he had split these identical rails, but said he had cut many like them, or better. The rails did more than symbolize the self-made pioneer. As a warm Lincoln delegate wrote, they "were to represent the issue of the coming contest between labor free and labor slave, between democracy and aristocracy."[4] They confirmed, for all time, one aspect of his legend. The humorist Orpheus C. Kerr, during the Civil War, reported that "when Abe was an infant of sixteen, he split so many rails that his whole country looked like a wholesale lumberyard." This was the Paul Bunyan touch, the true epic flavor. Later, after Lincoln's death, old John Hanks toured the country in "the Original Lincoln Cabin" built in Illinois in 1830, charging twenty-five cents admission for adults and ten for children, and advertising he would "answer such questions as may be propounded to him."

Boyhood stories were told by simple folk who enjoyed the fame of having known Lincoln. If their memories were dim, their ideas in the main were strictly conventional. Through the mist of forty or fifty years they recalled that Abe was never late to school—in itself a modest record, in view of Dennis Hanks's testimony that Lincoln had only six months' schooling in Indiana. He was "very quiet during playtime, never was rude," and "noted for keeping his clothes clean." Like other heroes in minority, he was a great peacemaker and the scourge of bullies. He never drank, chewed, or smoked. He never swore—an aspect of the Lincoln legend which was sometimes carried to extremes. David Homer Bates, a former telegraph operator in the War Department, in 1926 published a book stressing the President's moral perfection. " 'By jinks,' Lincoln exclaimed one day, under pressure, in the telegraph office. Almost instantly he looked self-accused and apologetic. To the suggestion that 'by jinks' was not swearing, he replied that according to what his mother told him when a child, it was *swearing* and wrong."[5]

Dennis Hanks boasted about their common skill in shooting squirrels, and told how "Abe was tickled to death" when he shot a fawn. But others related how young Lincoln's tender heart made hunting and fishing distasteful. He could not bear the sight of rabbit blood, it was said, and kept cruel playmates from putting hot coals on a mud-turtle's back. Yet a more celebrated story told how Lincoln had proposed to his fellows that they sew up the eyelids of a drove of hogs that rebelled at being driven aboard the flatboat for New Orleans. Generations of Illinois farmers, sitting before the stove in crossroads stores, liked to argue about Abe's theory—whether a hog could be handled better with his eyes sewed shut. One version says Lincoln refused to do the sewing, but held the animals for this operation. Another, that he justified the act by saying—with the psychology of a wartime President—"In a battle with wild hogs we must use war tactics." Beveridge, most painstaking biographer of Lincoln's youth, rejects the story solely because of Lincoln's proverbial kindness to animals. A latter-day volume is called *Dogs Were Ever a Joy to Lincoln,* but the most trustworthy evidence shows Lincoln's great fondness for cats. He owned many throughout his life, and petted kittens wherever he saw them. He too was self-sufficient, and he walked alone.

Lincoln's life fulfills well enough his political nickname of "Honest Abe," which plain people have always liked. But two famous stories —how as a shopkeeper he walked several miles to return a few cents' overcharge, and how he closed shop to set right the short-weight of a quarter pound of tea—are sheer invention. Not even local memory supports them. But tales of Lincoln's long walks to borrow books are well attested. "My best friend is the man who'll get me a book I ain't read," he said. Fable shows him studying before the open fire, despite his stepmother's recollection that he "didn't [read] after night much, went to bed early, got up early and then read." Art and cinema picture him in a variety of uncomfortable postures, head resting on a log or feet propped high against a tree trunk, perhaps leaning upon a shock of fodder or stretched on the counter of Offutt's store, with book in hand. Surely, by the meager standards of his community Lincoln had a vast appetite for books: surveying, law, poetry, history, biography. Such a passion was then less typical of the prairies than of New England, with her learned blacksmiths and philosophical peddlers. It was Lincoln's good luck to best the Yankees at their own game of self-help, and become the great idol of that cult. As a remote example, some fifteen years ago the America-Japan Society offered prizes for essays on Lincoln by Japanese students; these compositions, in many styles and moods, had one common denominator, namely that Lincoln was a poor boy who became the greatest man in his country. The most extreme instance of Lincoln as the epitome of self-help is reported to the author by Professor Helen White of the University of Wisconsin. "Abraham Lincoln," wrote one of her freshmen, "was born in a log cabin which he built with his own hands."

Young Lincoln's most celebrated borrowing of a book was from his neighbor Josiah Crawford. It was Weems's life of Washington, which the boy left in the rain, but promptly confessed the damage and pulled fodder to pay for it. Folklore has fondly embraced the incident as a parallel of the cherry-tree story in the volume itself. At crucial times Lincoln often thought of George Washington, invoking the God of Washington for guidance, in the new President's farewell words to his Springfield neighbors, and a few days later reminiscing about Weems's book before the New Jersey Senate. Upon the eve of the great storm, the thoughts of Lincoln in the North and of Lee in the South ran much upon the supreme patriot-hero of America. To the former, nourished upon Weems and Ramsay and Grimshaw, Washington stood forth as the champion of democratic liberty. To the latter, breathing the air of Arlington and living among the Custis clan, Washington was par excellence the soldier aristocrat of his beloved Virginia. The deductions which these two men drew, therefore, were different.

Tradition has much more to say about the mental industry of young Lincoln than about his physical laziness. The sympathetic Dennis Hanks admitted that Lincoln "was lazy—a very lazy man. He was always reading, scribbling, ciphering, writing poetry." One John Romine, who hired the stalwart lad to work for him, testified: "He would laugh and talk—crack his jokes and tell stories all the time; didn't love work but did dearly love his pay. . . . Lincoln said to me one day that his father taught him to work, but never learned him to love it."[6] In a communal life of much toil and little bookishness, Lincoln's vagaries were probably exaggerated. But at any rate, his indolence of body, like his state of being chronically in debt (honorably enough, through the death of his shiftless store-partner Berry), have found no place in the inspirational legend.

But tales of his great strength were lovingly told, by old neighbors and later by popular biographers. Here he was the true frontier hero.

He could lift "1000 pounds of shot by main strength," and carry heavy posts that required the sinew of four average men. He chopped sugar trees and sycamores like "three men at work," and could sink an axe into hard wood deeper than any other man in Indiana. He was the champion corn-husker, the best wrestler and jumper in New Salem, Illinois. There he out-wrestled a local strong man, Jack Armstrong, to become the idol of a good-natured gang of rowdies called the Clary Grove Boys. "They were hero-worshippers," Beveridge writes, "as untamed human beings generally are—the type of men that conquerors have used to fashion invincible armies and politicians to shape formidable gatherings." Henceforth he became their umpire and their ideal. They were the charter members of the Lincoln cult.

These wild boys, like the "Wide Awakes" of later political campaigns, played no small part in the forging of loyalties. They were among the volunteers for the Black Hawk War of 1831-32 who unanimously picked Lincoln as their captain. This was Lincoln's only exploit as a soldier. It was a foray of marching and discomfort which Lincoln made fun of, on the floor of Congress fifteen years later, in ridiculing General Cass's pretensions to the Presidency:

By the way, Mr. Speaker, did you know I am a military hero? Yes, sir; in the days of the Black Hawk War I fought, bled, and came away. . . . If General Cass went in advance of me picking huckleberries, I guess I surpassed him in charges upon the wild onions. If he saw any live, fighting Indians, it was more than I did; but I had a good many bloody struggles with the mosquitoes.[7]

Lincoln's truthful humor kept him from laying claim to the honors of an Indian fighter. Yet biographers later tried to make him into a second Andrew Jackson, or on the other hand to illustrate his humanity with a story about how he saved an old redskin's life. Denton J. Snider in 1910 wrote a grandiose epic poem, "Lincoln in the Black Hawk War." If the public decides otherwise, it is futile for a man to deny his own heroship.

Back from this adventure, Lincoln entered politics as a candidate for the Illinois Legislature in 1832. "I am humble Abraham Lincoln," he is reported to have said in his first speech, while the Clary Grove Boys cheered him and got into a few fist-fights: ". . . If elected, I shall be thankful; if not, it will be all the same." His mingling of humility and detachment would often be the vexation, if not the despair, of his opponents in days to come. Just now he was defeated, but carried his own New Salem precinct by 277 votes out of 284. His power over men often varied inversely with his distance from them. Two years later he was successful, standing on a platform of opposition to Andrew Jackson and favor for the Federal Banks—a homespun candidate with a rich man's creed, a great democrat and a potential Republican. This paradox stemmed, in part, from his admiration for Henry Clay, the self-made "Mill Boy of the Slashes," and next to George Washington the idol of Lincoln's youth. Also, no doubt, Lincoln shared the feeling of many Western squatters that they had more in common with the industrial East than with the buckskin aristocracy of the Southwest which Jackson represented.

Other aspects of the young Lincoln were stored, unconsciously, with political ammunition for the future. A yarn which many people still believe is that on his flatboat trip to New Orleans Lincoln had visited a slave auction, and seeing an octoroon girl sold from the block, clenched his fists: "By God, boys, if I ever get a chance to hit that thing I'll hit it and hit it hard!" Certainly, from early times Lincoln like most squatters of the prairie wanted no extension of slavery into the Northwest, no competition from slave economy in that virgin territory. But this specific story rests on the testimony of John Hanks, who told it as an eyewitness, although in fact he did not go farther south than St. Louis.

Another youthful story concerned Lincoln and liquor. As a store-keeper, Lincoln liked to test his strength by lifting a whisky barrel by the chimes, until it reached his face and he could drink from the bunghole. It is likely enough, as is generally asserted, that he spat out the whisky. A more dubious tradition, favored by prohibitionists, reports that he always delivered a temperance lecture on such occasions: "As a good friend, without counting the distress and wreckage of mind, let me advise, that if you wish to remain healthy and strong, turn it away from your lips." Preachment did not run in Lincoln's character, as Herndon knew him. Although Nat Grigsby recalled that "Abe drank his dram, as well as all others did, preachers and christians included," the overwhelming evidence of Lincoln's life shows him a very temperate man—sometimes sipping a social glass, but having neither taste nor a "good head" for serious drinking.[8] The liquor license issued to Berry & Lincoln in 1833 has been facsimiled by Wets, and explained away by Drys, for several generations. Throughout Lincoln's life, his supposed stand on drink was fraught with publicity and myth. On May 19, 1860, two of his friends, thinking to win the temperance vote of the East, persuaded him to put away the brandy and champagne he was about to serve to the Republican committee of notification. The cold water that he substituted achieved national notice.[9] A year later, Southern propaganda kept falsely reporting that "Old Abe had been beastly drunk" since inauguration, to keep up his courage. In 1887 the liquor interests circulated among Georgia Negroes a handbill containing a forged speech of Lincoln against prohibition. Later, the prohibitionists turned the trick of falsification. In 1915 at the sixteenth convention of the Anti-Saloon League, an octogenarian named James B. Merwin flourished a gold watch given him after the bone-dry campaign in Illinois in 1854–55, "by the friends of temperance in Chicago. . . . Inscription written by Abraham Lincoln," and so engraved upon the dust-lid. Inquiry showed that such a watch had been presented to Mr. Merwin by the friends of temperance, but that Lincoln had taken no part in their campaign, as Merwin stoutly claimed. Moreover, the inscription did not contain the words "written by Abraham Lincoln." These had been added at some later date.[10]

II

The unfitness of Lincoln's wife—the plump, sharp-tongued, mentally unsound Mary Todd—to share his heroic niche has led to the exaltation of Ann Rutledge. In her, romance has discovered the spiritual mate he needs. Poetry, fiction, drama, and cinema have dowered her dim figure with all the glamour in Lincoln's life. She is his soul's affinity. As one casual example, the two streamlined trains of the Alton Railroad, from Chicago to St. Louis via Springfield, are named "The Abraham Lincoln" and "The Ann Rutledge." No train has ever been christened after Mary Todd.

Lincoln's partner Herndon—cordially hating Mary Todd and hated in return—was the discoverer of Ann Rutledge. During Lincoln's public life and the White House years no one had heard about her. But after the President's death, in the autumn of 1866 Herndon was collecting material for a lecture on Lincoln. One Sunday Herndon had driven in his buggy over New Salem way and talked with an old neighbor named John McNamar. Ann had been betrothed first to him, but by McNamar's long visit to the East he seemingly deserted her, and Lincoln began to pay court to the dejected girl. She had died of fever in August, 1835, before McNamar's return and before any known plighting of her troth to Lincoln. (Often folklore omits McNamar from the story, so as to draw no attention from Ann's devotion to Lincoln, and makes them engaged sweethearts.) Herndon, who had a sentimental streak not uncommon in hard-headed lawyers, seized upon the romance with delight. Travelling on to the Rutledge family, he found them of course eager to recollect the ardor of young Lincoln's wooing. Under Herndon's skill as a cross-examiner the story grew, and on November 16, 1866, he gave his lecture on the newly discovered tragedy of Lincoln's life. He put long frenzies of grief (with phrases borrowed from Hamlet and Lear) into Lincoln's mouth, and told how on a night of storm the stricken man had exclaimed, "I can't bear to think of her out there alone. . . . The rain and the storm shan't beat on her grave." Herndon turned a brief and perhaps tender courtship into the grand passion of Lincoln's life—dwelling upon Lincoln's undoubted gloom in the latter half of 1835, but saying nothing about the fact that a few months later Lincoln was paying vivacious court to another girl.

Ann Rutledge, whom some recalled as a brunette and others as violet-eyed and golden-haired, henceforth became a great legend. The incarnation of spiritual beauty, turning from a faithless fiancé to the protectiveness of Lincoln's love, only to be cheated by death, she appealed irresistibly to America. Novels and poetry in that Victorian age adored "the pangs of dispriz'd love" and passion purified in death. George Eliot, Dickens, and Christina Rossetti had rung endless changes on this theme. It is profitless to point out that nobody has ever shown that Ann preferred Lincoln to McNamar, or that Lincoln's devotion to her long survived her life and cast its shadow through the years. Lincoln's best friend, Herndon, had to hear of Ann Rutledge solely from the lips of sentimental neighbors thirty-one years after the event. Paul Angle of the Illinois State Historical Society, most scholarly Lincoln expert today, concludes: "Of reliable evidence touching upon the romance itself, there is not the slightest particle."[11] Mr. Angle has good reason to know the trickiness of the Rutledge legend. In 1929 he exposed as forgeries some tenderly illiterate love-letters between Ann and Abraham, the "discovery" of Wilma Frances Minor, which the *Atlantic Monthly* had published with pride and in good faith.

Dale Carnegie, author of *Lincoln the Unknown* in 1935, tells how he visited New Salem by moonlight in order to think properly of "young Abe Lincoln and Ann Rutledge." And "when I came to write the chapter dealing with the death of Lincoln's sweetheart, I put a little folding table and a typewriter in a car and drove out over country roads and through a hog lot and a cow pasture until I reached the quiet, secluded spot where Ann Rutledge lies buried." This is the original grave in Concord Cemetery, he adds, and not Oakland Cemetery in Petersburg—whence, in May, 1890, an enterprising cemetery promoter transferred "four pearl buttons and some dirt" which he had dug up from the Concord grave. Oakland Cemetery now advertises that it is the last resting-place of Ann Rutledge. There in January, 1921, a monument was erected, bearing the best lines of poetry ever written about her. They will be recalled from the *Spoon River Anthology,* by Edgar Lee Masters:

> Out of me unworthy and unknown
> The vibrations of deathless music;
> 'With malice toward none, with charity for all.'
> Out of me the forgiveness of millions toward millions,
> And the beneficent face of a nation
> Shining with justice and truth.
> I am Ann Rutledge who sleep beneath these weeds,
> Beloved in life of Abraham Lincoln,
> Wedded to him, not through union,
> But through separation.
> Bloom forever, O Republic,
> From the dust of my bosom!

Ten years later Mr. Masters published his sardonic book *Lincoln the Man,* the fullest attempt yet made to debunk Lincoln, by innuendoes against his honesty and decency. After these vibrant lines of poetry, there was some irony in the assertions of chapter four—that no true affection existed between Ann Rutledge and her suitor, who, concluded Mr. Masters, was a man of low sexual vitality.

Lincoln's marriage, which began in 1842, has never attracted romancers. Not even the decorous sentiment that surrounds George and Martha Washington has been created for the Lincolns. Artists like Carl Sandburg and Robert E. Sherwood, with an insight of realism, have seen the pathos of this ill-matched union, while psychoanalysts have been fascinated by it. But the folk imagination passes over it, baffled and silent. Convention demands that a hero shall be irresistible yet chivalrous to women. Lincoln often was neither. Of small talk and drawing-room graces he knew nothing, and piqued by his lack of success he took refuge in wry jokes about his homeliness, or else was prone to make fun of the women who had rejected him, behind their backs. Not many women saw the kindliness of his nature which was still deeper than these rocky strata. Asked why he had such scanty companionship with women, Lincoln told a funny sad little story about a poor boy who said mournfully, "I don't s'pose there's anybody on earth who likes gingerbread better'n I do—and gets less of it." Interpretation is too deep here for the folk mind, and this aspect of Lincoln has been left alone. Mary Todd, the Springfield aristocrat, the one woman whom Lincoln was able to win, jilt, and win again, because she believed he was going to have an ambitious career, is equally baffling to the legend-makers. Many people believe, rightly or wrongly, that Lincoln defaulted on his first wedding day, out of morbidity or fear. Indeed a deep melancholy, now impossible to plumb, settled upon him after some painful experience on the threshold of the year 1841. His best friends knew that suicide ran in his mind. But late in the summer of 1842 Lincoln and Mary Todd were drawn together again, over their anonymous ridicule in the public press of an inoffensive citizen named James Shields. Their gibes led to Lincoln's burlesque duel with Shields in September. The incident reflects no credit upon Lincoln, but it seems to chime with his saturnine moods of those days. Later he was ashamed of it—though "Abe Lincoln joke books" in the White House years recalled it as a "good-humored" episode of the national jester, and Thomas Dixon's novel *The Southerner* in 1913 romantically alluded to it as "a duel over a fine point of honor."

A few weeks later Lincoln and Miss Todd were married, in a strange spirit of desperation—the bridegroom saying that he was going "to Hell, I reckon." The best man, Matheny, called it "a policy match all round," and it took the plain people of Sangamon County a good while to forget that Lincoln had "married into the aristocracy." Unhappy years followed. Mrs. Lincoln, with her fetish of nice people, tried to break her husband of eating in his shirt-sleeves, using his own knife in the butter, or greeting lady callers in the parlor with the cheerful report, "She'll be down as soon as she gets her trotting harness on." And on the other side, there was Lincoln seen splitting wood at one o'clock in the morning to make a kitchen fire because his wife had driven him from the house without supper, or lunching meagerly at his office alone on grocery crackers and cheese—never daring to ask his friends home to dinner, but bearing with patience and often a touch of whimsical irony the tantrums which finally led to Mrs. Lincoln's insanity after her husband was in his grave. But patience will not always tame a shrew. And irony, an instrument distrusted by most women, was peculiarly ineffectual with Mary Todd Lincoln. In the public eye, neither in the President's lifetime nor later, was she assimilated to his great presence. The popular mind, while loving to dwell upon Lincoln the kindly bespectacled father holding Tad at his knee, has almost wholly forgotten the wife and mother. Long ago it was tacitly agreed that she was unworthy of Lincoln—whereas the associations of a henpecked hero could only be comic.

III

That Lincoln skyrocketed from total obscurity to the Presidency in 1860—summoned by "the Norn Mother" in "the Whirlwind Hour," of Markham's famous poem, or called miraculously by the voice of God—is more mystic than true. His build-up had been long, patient, far-sighted. After serving as an Illinois state congressman, he had finally gone to Washington in 1847 and sat in Congress for two years. Through the next decade he came to be known as one of the shrewdest members of the Illinois bar. Riding in his rickety buggy from one county courthouse to another, swapping stories in taverns, dropping into homes and saloons and crossroads grocery-stores, chatting with farmers in their dusty barns and with reapers under the blazing sun— Lincoln was becoming a familiar and lovable character in some fourteen Illinois counties. "Ain't ye glad to see me? Ain't ye glad I come?" he sometimes greeted his fellow-lawyers. And remembering his sense of fun and practical jokes, his tunes on the jew's-harp, and his hearty "double-handed handshake," they were undoubtedly glad. Most people who cared more for friendliness than style felt that Lincoln "belonged." With barefoot boys and toothless grandmothers he could joke in effortless fellowship. Gestures that professional politicians attempted, before and after Lincoln's time, came as naturally to him as a reflex. Yet he had unfathomable reserves. He did not give or receive slaps on the back any more than did George Washington. Neither his wife nor his intimates called him "Abe," though later that name made good political capital. To most of his old friends he remained "Mr. Lincoln," even after death and glory had given him a titleless immortality.

His appearance was unforgettable. In the end, it proved a greater boon than the sleek conventionality of politicians like Douglas and Seward. After he became a great local character, strangers on the Illinois Central called out, as he sat down in the coach, "Hullo, Abe;

how are you?" Most striking was his height, of six feet four. It was
the one eminence upon which a great democrat might flatter himself.
He liked to measure himself back-to-back with other tall men, and
did so at fairs and political conventions and in the White House.
With ever-original folk wit, people said to him, "You're a man to
look up to," or asked, "How's the weather up there?" They told he
had frightened a teamster, grudging to turn out on a miry road, by
rising up from his buggy inch by inch against the sunset, until the
driver cried, "Don't go any higher—I'll turn out." (It was a variant
of Davy Crockett's 'coon up the tree, saying in the fable, "Don't shoot,
Colonel—I'll come down.") On the way to being a great man, Lincoln
had no such handicap as his friend the future Confederate Vice-President, Alexander Stephens of Georgia, weighing ninety pounds and
almost a dwarf, who winced when men patted his head and called
him "my son." Lincoln's stature, like that of Washington, was an
intangible of leadership.

But like most very tall men, Lincoln stooped a little and walked
shamblingly. His large hands in cotton gloves resembled canvased
hams, one observer thought, and Lincoln's feet were encased in clod-
hoppers. He always needed a haircut, and in 1860 newsboys who sold
papers with the nominee's picture sang out, "Here's your Old Abe,
he'll look better when he gets his hair combed." His rusty dress-coat
with sleeves too short for the bony wrists, gray woollen shawl in lieu
of overcoat, his faded cotton umbrella with string around the middle
to keep it shut, his homely and sorrowful face sometimes lit with
mirth, and the note of his shrill high-pitched voice—this was Mr. Lincoln of Springfield. The result of nature, simplicity, and the habits
of youthful poverty and negligence, this image could not have been
bettered for caricature or immortality. Its stamp seemed peculiarly
American. And the man himself—like Washington, Andrew Jackson,
and Lee—never set foot outside the New World of his birth. In
retrospect James Russell Lowell would hail him as "New birth of our
new soil, the first American."

Lincoln's clean shaving and fresh linen redeemed the picture from
squalor—although people prone to snub or dislike Lincoln affected to
see a lack of fastidiousness. Edwin M. Stanton as an affluent lawyer
in 1854 first saw Lincoln in the McCormick Reaper Case. Never
dreaming that Lincoln one day would appoint him Secretary of War,
nor then suspecting that Lincoln "belonged to the ages," Stanton
privately called him "a damned gawky, long-armed ape" and noted

the blotches of sweat under the arm-pits of his linen duster. Hostile propaganda in the Civil War reported that Lincoln dined exclusively on fried liver and onions, that his lips were "pale and smeared with tobacco juice" and his teeth "filthy," that he changed his socks "once every ten days."[12] That Lincoln, unlike the average politician of his day, neither chewed nor smoked, did not matter to the enemy. In later times we find Edgar Lee Masters writing, of Lincoln at Springfield: "One wonders if he was not unwashed, in those days of the weekly bath in the foot tub, if a bath was taken at all." Such innuendoes, trivial in themselves but potent of suggestion, are based solely upon the phrase "one wonders."

But in ignoring personal aspersion, as well as hate, the living Lincoln had shown a serenity unmatched by any other great American. He had no time for them, realizing too how little they mattered in the final verdict of success or failure. If his ghost walks, no doubt it took little heed of the hot controversy that raged in 1917 over the Lincoln statue that America should give England, in token of the Hundred Years' Peace. The issue was that of the real versus the ideal Lincoln. Many artists joined Ex-Presidents Roosevelt and Taft in hailing as the true Lincoln a figure which George Gray Barnard had made for Cincinnati. Its face modelled from Lincoln's life mask, and its physique from a Kentuckian who had spent many years splitting rails, this statue was gnarled, homely, and toil-worn. The son Robert Todd Lincoln, Harvard man and Pullman Car executive who never relished the log-cabin motif, called it "defamatory," while others branded it as "a grimy-fingered clodhopper." Moreover, a poll showed that the American people disapproved of Barnard's statue, and favored most of all the gentle, wistful, lovable spiritualization that Saint-Gaudens had made for Lincoln Park in Chicago. A replica of the latter was therefore made for Parliament Square in London, while a copy of Barnard's statue was given to the industrial city of Manchester, where a toil-worn Lincoln seemed less of a scandal. Similar trends appear in the schoolbooks. William B. Guitteau's text, *Our United States,* for example, in its 1919 and 1923 editions read, concerning the Lincoln-Douglas debates: "Tall, gaunt and awkward, wearing ill-fitting clothes, his voice high and shrill, his dark wrinkled face clouded by a look of habitual melancholy, Lincoln suffered in comparison with his brilliant adversary." School patrons and patriots generally disliked this passage, and in 1930 Guitteau excised it from his book. This was the same psychology which had rejected, with some indignation, the

raw realism in biography of Lincoln's old Springfield friends Ward
Lamon and William H. Herndon.

But in Illinois, while Lincoln's star was rising, people came to know
and love the man in all his angularity. His homeliness was irradiated
by traits of mind and heart, then so warmly immediate but now grown
dim and formalized. It was known that he played marbles with boys,
cracked jokes with some young marauders whom he had surprised
robbing his melon-patch, and laughed at the Springfield urchins who
once hid behind a fence and knocked off his tall hat with a lath,
"Boys, you ought to be ashamed to impose on an old man." Casual
stories were told which legend later built into the epic of a Mr. Great-
heart: how he chopped wood for widows, and in surveying the site
of Petersburg laid out one street crooked in order to save the house
of a woman whose husband belonged to Lincoln's company in the
Black Hawk War. In his Sunday clothes he had pulled a hog out of
the mire of the prairie, and dismounting from his horse had lifted a
fluttering chickadee back on its nest. One anecdote told how he had
met a little girl in tears because her trunk had not been hauled to the
station, and train-time was near; Lincoln shouldered the trunk and
carried it himself. Sometimes the little girl became a weeping woman,
instead. Some of these yarns no doubt are apocryphal, or recollected
to order. But the fact remains that long before the professional sentimentalists went to work on him, Mr. Lincoln of Springfield was
known as the friend of children and a neighbor to distress.

Myth doubtless has exaggerated his role as the legal champion of
widows and orphans, the St. Michael of the Eighth Judicial District.
It is now forgotten that Lincoln was once criticized, as Henry Whitney
recalled, for appearing on behalf of "a great soulless corporation" like
the Illinois Central Railroad. Public opinion rushes between extremes.
Evidence shows Lincoln as an honest lawyer, skilled in chatting with
juries, and like all dutiful barristers trying to do his best for every
client rich or poor. He was as ambitious for recognition and political
advancement as he was careless about finances, and sometimes charged
absurdly low fees. Always Lincoln remained ingenuous in respect to
money, believing even as President that every dollar bill issued by the
Treasury was actually signed by the official whose name appeared
thereon.[13] His business methods were sloppy. His tall hat, inside
which he kept letters and memoranda, is famous; once in discarding
an old hat he overlooked an important paper. Whitney recalled an
envelope which Lincoln had marked, "When you can't find it any-

where else, look in this." He seemed a strange man to be the potential hero of a great business civilization, and of a great industrialist party in politics. His law office was littered with newspapers from which he read aloud, the first thing every morning, as he sprawled on the sofa with one leg over a chair. In 1859, starting to clean out his desk, he found some Government seeds, relics of his Congressional days, beginning to sprout in the dirt of one corner. In the White House, Nicolay and Hay were driven frantic by lack of method in the outward man. Inside, the organization was much better.

Lincoln's cool shrewd brain has been neglected, in the later hero-worship of his heart. But those who dealt with the man himself, in Springfield as in Washington, were less apt to forget the former. His process of thought was no brilliant flash in the pan, but the long-headed horse sense that Americans traditionally prize. To the canny temper of Franklin he joined the deliberation of Washington. "My mind is like a piece of steel," he told Josh Speed, "very hard to scratch anything on it, and almost impossible after you get it there to rub it out."[14] Lincoln's mind had something, too, of Franklin's speculativeness—trying to make a steam plow, inventing a river boat with "expansible buoyant chambers" to lift it off sand-bars, and in the war years passing from dismemberment of Tad's mechanical toys to a study of new patents in firearms. But circumstance turned this frontier mother-wit away from mechanics and science, into law and politics. He learned to move stubborn men instead of stranded boats.

One of the favored Lincoln episodes of these Springfield days was the "almanac trial." Lincoln, it was said, got "Duff" Armstrong, the son of old Clary Grove friends, acquitted of a charge of murder, by producing in the courtroom an almanac to show that the deed was not done in clear moonlight, as the state's chief witness had sworn. That other things—including Lincoln's summation to the jury, with tears running down his face—had played a main part in the acquittal, were forgotten in the story of Lincoln's supposedly preternatural cleverness. Sometimes it was said Lincoln had won his point by using an almanac for the wrong year, or had falsified the date, or pasted a bogus leaf into the right almanac. Wasn't he a caution? they asked. At one time, a doctored almanac alleged to have been used by Lincoln on this occasion was in the Chicago Historical Society; mysteriously it vanished more than fifteen years ago. A check by Harvard astronomers and others has cleared Lincoln of any falsification.[15] Edward Eggleston's novel *The Graysons* in 1888, and a recent cinema, left the impression that this trial came early in Lincoln's career, though it really happened in 1858 when Lincoln, in late middle age, was entering the national limelight. And from Virginia it is reported that the same almanac story is told there, but with Patrick Henry as its hero![10] The alchemy of time has made Lincoln's shrewdness into pure benign wisdom, but in his own day this quality was linked with his secretiveness. *Vanity Fair* during the Civil War called him "Fox Populi," and at much closer range Herndon described him as "the most secretive —reticent—shut-mouthed man that ever lived." When advice was volunteered, Lincoln listened respectfully, but seldom took it. His deepest problems and counsels he kept to himself. This trait has helped to make him the most fascinating of American enigmas, teasing the biographer and artist as simple heroes like Andrew Jackson and Grant have never done.

IV

In 1856 the Republican Party was formed, chiefly by small farmers and mechanics wanting Western homesteads and no expansion of slavery. In May of that year Lincoln addressed their first Illinois convention, at Bloomington, in a famous "lost" speech. But his words were such that delegates stamped, cheered, waved handkerchiefs, and threw hats. He spoke as man to man, without rhetorical folderol, and, whether they or Lincoln himself sensed the fact, he was already becoming a great artist with words. Straightway talk began to be heard of Lincoln for President. The Whig National Convention that year gave him 110 votes for Vice-President; he told Whitney it must be another man, "a big man of the name of Lincoln in Massachusetts." In June, 1858, nominated by the Republicans for United States Senator, Lincoln made his "house divided" speech, and became a truly national figure. Like the best words of earlier American heroes—Jefferson's Declaration and Washington's Farewell Address—it was not startlingly original, but said simply, yet with drama, what millions were ready to hear. Three months later the Lincoln-Douglas debates fixed the eyes of the nation upon two men—one who dressed with elegance and travelled in his private railway car, another who looked as if he slept in a hayloft and who rode in the caboose. Lincoln lost the election, even as he had failed years before in keeping a more modest seat in Congress. But like George Washington, Lincoln never lost his self-confidence and contrived to build prestige on failure. Not many knew that he was stalking his quarry with an art that concealed art, or that he owned one of the most influential German newspapers in the Middle West. Lincoln, having crawled one rainy day into an empty box-car with young Henry Villard the journalist, could mention rumors of the White House and say laughing, his arms hugging his bony knees, "Just think of such a sucker as me as President!"

Early in 1860 the triumph of his New York speech at Cooper Union made it possible for Lincoln to fuse the Western program with the business platform of the old Whigs. The factionalism which had bogged down wheel-horses like Seward and Chase did not cling to this new candidate out of the West. "He's the greatest man since St. Paul," exclaimed Noah Brooks of the *Tribune*. And he seemed to know what the people wanted. The politicians did not meditate on this mystery, from wonder or duty. But, with their perennial need to pick a winner, they could not ignore Lincoln. In May the National Convention opened in Chicago, with Lincoln's campaign in the hands of shrewd lieutenants less fastidious than he in respect to bargaining. While throngs of excursionists outside the hall shouted "the Lincoln yawp" and brought to bear their intangible excitement upon the delegates, Lincoln's name swept to victory on the third ballot. Murat Halstead saw a nameless Lincoln fan, hoarse and breathless, take a chair at the dinner-table of the Tremont House in Chicago: "Talk of your money and bring on your bullies with you!—the immortal principles of the everlasting people are with Abe Lincoln, of the people, by God!" A waiter came up to take his order. Glaring at the waiter, he roared: "Go to the devil—what do I want to eat for? Abe Lincoln is nominated, God damn it; and I'm going to live on air—the air of liberty by God." But in a moment he called for the menu and ordered a big dinner, swearing he could "devour and digest an Illinois prairie." Such was the intoxication of that great day.

On the sixth of November Lincoln was elected President. In ten Southern states he failed to get a single vote, and his popular vote was only 40 per cent of the total. Over cross-currents of sectional hate he sailed to victory. Several things conspired to make him President —the homespun pattern prepared by Jackson and Harrison and Taylor, the "availability" formula set by Polk and Pierce and Buchanan, plus exigencies of the moment and astute political planning—and "the Norn Mother" of the poets melts into myth. But, once the die had been cast, Lincoln rose to the opportunity.

As he set out for Washington in the late winter of 1861—wearing, in his growing patriarchal character, the new whiskers that a little girl in Westfield, New York, had suggested he raise—Lincoln gave little inkling that he would be America's supreme war President. As a congressman he had poked fun at his own military record. Later, during the Civil War, perhaps with mock frankness, Lincoln told a friend: "I am a great coward. I have moral courage enough, I think, but I am such a coward, physically, that if I were to shoulder a gun and go into action, I am dead sure that I should turn and run at the first fire—I know I should."[17] Lincoln had a knack of making sport of himself, in ways in which conventional gentlemen did not make sport of themselves—ways so alien to heroes who took themselves seriously, like Washington and Jackson and Lee and Grant and the Roosevelts. The imputation of physical cowardice, for instance, was no jest to Thomas Jefferson. But Lincoln seemed to lack a certain reticent pride, to be as heterodox about the gentlemanly code as he had been in the burlesque duel with Shields. Some Brahmins no doubt recalled Doctor Holmes's recent remarks in *The Professor at the Breakfast Table* that the President of the United States "has always been what might be called in general terms a gentleman," but that some day a democratic tide might sweep into the White House a man who would say "thinkin'" or pronounce "chair" as "cheer." This was exactly the way Lincoln spoke. At first, many failed to see a point made by the English newspaperman Edward Dicey—that just as one never thinks of beauty or ugliness in the presence of some women, so terms like gentlemanlike or ungentlemanlike had no relevance for Lincoln. That Lincoln had the core of the gentlemanly character, a deep integrity and kindness, is beyond dispute, but the codes of the gentleman so important to Washington and Lee mattered little to this man.

Sometimes this negligence led Lincoln into blunders in his public relations. Enroute to inauguration he had taken the detective Pinkerton's nervous advice, and slipped by night through hostile Baltimore to enter Washington incognito. Southern newspapers jeered at this lack of backbone, and a dishonest New York reporter, Joseph Howard, invented the yarn that Lincoln had disguised himself in a Scotch plaid cap and long military cloak. Some said Lincoln had donned his wife's bonnet or petticoat, and cartoonists helped the myth with biting caricatures. "The men who made the Declaration of Independence did not make it good in that way," said *The Louisville Courier*. "They fought for their rights; Lincoln runs for his . . . and leaves his wife." Several million people in the spring of 1861 believed that Lincoln had crept through the back door of the White House in a blue funk. This episode pointed up early criticism of Lincoln by Northern firebrands, who called him "wishy-washy," "namby-pamby," "a tortoise." His slowness and spirit of conciliation maddened them. Was he a man of courage? "Poor Lincoln, honest, hesitating, drifting, *feeble-minded* Lincoln—patriotic buffoon!" wrote a correspondent to Charles Sumner, apropos of kidnap threats from the South. "It would be no great pity if he were lugged off to Dixie, except for the name of it!"[18]

For Lincoln's real enemies, more blasting language was reserved. Promptly upon his nomination in 1860 the storm of party hate had burst about him. "Ape," "baboon," "a low-bred obscene clown" he was called, a bastard by birth, immoral in private life, the husband of a Copperhead spy. He was branded as "evasive" and "pettifogging" (a term immemorially linked with small-town lawyers). In the spring of 1861 Southern papers hailed him as "a cross between a sand-hill crane and an Andalusian jackass," "the abolition orang-outang that skulked to Washington the other day." *The New York Herald* advised him to resign as an act of patriotism, suggesting that otherwise "he will totter into a dishonored grave, driven there perhaps by the hands of an assassin, leaving behind him a memory more execrable than that of Arnold." As the War went on, hostile clergymen in the North spoke of him as "usurper, traitor, and tyrant," "the old monster" thirsting "for more blood." Pamphlets christened him "Abraham Africanus I," hinting at Negro blood, and showing him in close collusion with the Devil. No longer was he called "a simple Susan," but now was endowed with "Yankee shrewdness and cunning." Normally gentle men joined the chorus of Southern hate. Lee was never one of them, but the poet Lanier called Lincoln "the Great Apotheosis of the Great Hog," and even six years after the President's death Paul Hamilton Hayne could allude to him as "the gawky, coarse, not over-cleanly, whisky drinking and whisky smelling Blackguard . . . whose memory has been *idealized* by the Yankee fancy."[19]

Under abuse and vilification Lincoln showed an absence of bitterness which no other American hero—neither Washington nor Jefferson, Theodore Roosevelt nor Woodrow Wilson—has ever quite matched. The man seemed to have no personal resentment. "If the end brings me out all right what is said against me won't amount to anything," he once told Nicolay. "If the end brings me out wrong, ten angels swearing I was right would make no difference." He understood the unimportance of malice. At heart a man of good will, he refused to nurse grudges and feuds as luxuries too costly for times of crisis. And his strange quality of selflessness seemed to make him invulnerable to slander. Two generations later Herbert Croly saw Lincoln's magnanimity as "perhaps his greatest distinction"—remarking that, unlike the good-natured yet aggressive frontiersman who believed in an eye for an eye, Lincoln held to higher standards. A man like Old Hickory loved his friends and hated his enemies, thus being spiritually inferior to Lincoln. Lincoln yearned for public office and for victory in war, but never let ambition upset his mental stability. "With malice toward none, with charity for all," set up a code higher than that of most great soldiers, statesmen, public servants. He had the stuff from which spiritual heroes are made, and after his death men began to compare him with Socrates and Christ. This serenity in forgiveness is, to humanity, the final transcendent touch of greatness. Time and again Britons of our day have quoted with pride the words that made Edith Cavell the noblest memory of the World War: "Standing as I do in view of God and Eternity, I realize that patriotism is not enough. I must have no hatred or bitterness toward any one." One who compares Andrew Jackson with Lincoln, or Grant with Lee, in the final lists of American hero-worship, realizes that patriotism is not enough.

V

Lincoln had begun the Civil War with misgivings. "Suppose you go to war, you cannot fight always," he said in his First Inaugural. "And when, after much loss on both sides, and no gain on either, you cease fighting, the identical old questions as to terms of intercourse are again upon you." But behind these words, as behind his Cooper Union speech of the previous year, lay conviction that fearlessness for the right is better than fearfulness for peace. This is the approved American attitude, the state of mind in which, whether wisely or foolishly, we have undertaken all our wars. With grief undoubtedly sincere, Lincoln had decided some time before that the Civil War was inevitable. Soon, in April, 1861, came the Fort Sumter incident. Southern historians have lately appraised Lincoln's sheer diplomatic strategy in handling this episode—by maneuvering the Confederates into firing the first shot and thus putting themselves in the role of aggressors, whereupon Lincoln issued his call for troops and committed the North to a war "to save the Union."[20] Without subscribing to their cynical inference, that the war was designed to save not only the Union but also the Republican Party and Abraham Lincoln, one may credit Lincoln with greater finesse than either his friends or foes perceived in 1861.

To speculate about history as it might have been is often an idle sport. Yet one may ask whether, if without loss of principle Lincoln had been able to prevent the Civil War, he would be today a greater or lesser hero. Very likely the lesser hero. The arbiter, however skilled and wise, lacks the appeal of a champion who brings his cause to clean-cut victory. The greatest popular idols are partisans; their loyalties are sealed in blood and tears. The grand cause is glorified by the men who die for it in battle; and the hero who in turn gives his life, as the last sacrifice in the crucible of fire, is supremely great. King Arthur and Roland and Joan of Arc belong to this high company. Even more surely, if Lincoln had lost the war, had failed through lack of resources or military geniuses and through no flaw in his own nature, he would never have become a demigod. He rose upon failure, but ultimate success was vital to his legend as we now know it. If Lincoln had been rejected in the presidential election of 1864—as he thought "exceedingly probable" before Sherman's capture of Atlanta recalled public confidence—he would have been the same Lincoln, but a different hero. A South lastingly divorced from the Union under his Presidency, or reunited under some later chieftain, would never have paid his memory the smallest honor. A soldier like Robert E. Lee might come to be a noble legend in defeat, for he had met the enemy hand to hand and had done his best. But the President of a defeated Union could never hope for better laurels than the wilted ones that now rest upon Jefferson Davis.

In the red light of battle Lincoln appeared in three heroic roles. They were Honest Abe the democrat, "Massa Linkum" the emancipator, and Father Abraham the savior of the Union. All three have contributed something to the enduring epic of Lincoln.

Lincoln the democrat came first, for his roots ran back to New Salem and Springfield. Dennis Hanks and other old neighbors who called at the White House reported, with satisfaction, "Just the same old Abe." A story, told with many variations, ran that at a levee the President had interrupted a young English peer a moment after his introduction: "Excuse me, my lord, there's an old friend of mine"— and had stepped over to greet a bent Illinois farmer and his sunbonneted wife, come to see their wounded son in a Washington hospital. The President shook hands with engineers and firemen, saying, "I always want to see and know the men I am riding behind." He chatted with sentries on duty at the White House, sometimes greeting them in the wintry dawn with "That coffee smells good, boys. Give me a cup." A Kentucky farm-hand and his girl came unannounced to the White House and sent up word that they wanted to be married; "So you children want to be married?" Lincoln smiled. "Come right in and we'll get at the marrying." (The groom soon joined up with the boys in blue.) People loved to repeat his saying, "God must love the common people, he has made so many of them." And they were charmed with his supposed reply to a favor-seeker, "Why, I don't amount to pig tracks over in the War Department." Folklore told how Mr. Chase had come upon the President polishing his huge dusty shoes and reproved him: "Mr. President, gentlemen don't black their own boots." Looking up with innocence, Lincoln asked, "Whose boots do they black?"

"Anything that kept the people away from him he disapproved," wrote Lincoln's private secretary John Hay, who tried in vain to dam this flood of callers. At all hours, even as Lincoln walked along the street in talk with a friend, unknown admirers and cranks laid siege to him, men and women wanting something or merely anxious to tell their troubles. No chief executive was ever so accessible. Later fable might exaggerate somewhat Lincoln's patience and tact under all trials, but in truth those qualities seldom deserted him. "He did not 'put you at your ease' when you came into his presence," wrote Horace White of *The Chicago Tribune*. "You felt at your ease without being put there." Friendliness came naturally to Lincoln. Of political camaraderie he might have been accused, were it not for the plain fact that he had only one set of manners and used them all the time. The masses were learning to accept him as one of themselves, in nurture as well as in viewpoint. They had never dared do this with Jefferson or even Andrew Jackson, and would never quite feel the same about any successor of Lincoln. Hence the unique kind of love he inspired. "Mr. Lincoln is the only President we have ever had who may be said to be from the working class of people," wrote the editor of a Michigan rural weekly. "No other President has ever worked with his hands for a livelihood after arriving at the full maturity of manhood."[21] *The Chicago Tribune* quoted a Midwest farmer, "Old Abe Lincoln stands seventeen feet higher in Iowa than any other man in the United States!" Even from Boston, James Russell Lowell was thrilled by "the fireside plainness with which Mr. Lincoln always addresses himself to the American people." He decided that Lincoln was the first President who could use the capital "I" without egotism or apology. In his mouth it seemed to mean a collective multitude.

Toward his soldiers, Lincoln joined the democracy of a brother with the solicitude of a father. The President visited camps and battlefields with little evident regard for safety or formal dignity. Men liked his kindly smile as he rode past, long arms and legs pendulous "like a grasshopper's," no martial figure on horseback. (Only a Staffordshire potter, who had never seen Lincoln, produced, for the American market, an equestrian statuette of Lincoln with a bright red cloak and fierce sideburns, mounted on the identical horse that had been used for statuettes of the Duke of Cambridge.) Along rows of hospital beds Lincoln passed, shaking hands, asking questions, sometimes sitting beside the dying until breath failed. Noah Brooks, trailing him on such an expedition in April, 1862, saw "tears of gladness stealing down their pale faces." Deepened by compassion, it was the same Lincoln who had greeted his friends along the old Eighth Circuit, "Ain't ye glad I come?" Matthew Brady's photographs show, month by month, the lines that war was carving in his worn face. One or two heard him cry, "My God!" over the casualty lists, and the White House guard Crook often heard him moan in his sleep. Long ago Lincoln had made his decision, that the Union could be saved by blood alone, and if he was staggered by the price, or ever wavered into doubt, none but God knew.

An army nurse named Adelaide Smith later told how she persuaded one of her patients, a lad who had lost a leg before Petersburg, to go with her to a White House reception, after the Second Inaugural. The soldier had never seen Lincoln before, and was amazed when the President singled him out from the white-gloved throng, took his hand, and said, "God bless you, my boy!" On the way home the soldier said to his nurse, "I'd lose another leg for a man like that."

Two incidents helped to make Lincoln, in the public eye, the friend of poor soldiers and their kin. The first was that of Private William Scott, a Green Mountain boy, who in the late summer of 1861 was found asleep on sentry duty, and sentenced to be shot. Lincoln never saw him or sent any personal word, but arranged for a pardon. Seven months later the boy fell in action at Lee's Mill, and died in a coma without uttering a word. Newspapers recalled his name and began to weave a tissue of myth. They said Lincoln had driven at breakneck speed on the morning of Scott's doom, and leaping from the carriage had looked the lad in the eye and asked for a solemn promise that he would fail no more. Later, leading the charge at Lee's Mill, the boy had fallen and murmured with dying lips, "I wish you would tell President Lincoln that I have never forgotten the kind words he said to me. . . . I have tried to be a good soldier and true to the flag." Following this legend, a government clerk named Francis de Haes Janvier wrote a poem, "The Sleeping Sentinel," describing Lincoln's arrival in "a stately coach" before the firing-squad:

> He came to save that stricken soul, now waking from despair;
> And from a thousand voices rose a shout which rent the air!

In 1863 the elocutionist Murdoch recited this poem before an audience of three thousand in Philadelphia, and "few listened to the end with dry eyes." He repeated it throughout the North, and once gave it before President and Mrs. Lincoln "and a select party of their friends, at the White House." What the President thought of it is not recorded, but his own tastes in poetry ran to the sentimental, and doubtless he saw the myth could do no harm. Lincoln's clemency became famous as the war went on. It matters little that, as William E. Barton found, some of the time-worn anecdotes were sheer fabrication, or on the other hand that Lincoln concurred in the death sentence in 267 cases.[22] The President unquestionably had a tender heart, and in the midst of a cruel war did his best to ease the harshness which a professional military code imposed upon thousands of green volunteers. Emerson in March, 1863, commented on the loss of dignity which Lincoln showed in running to and fro overriding the judgment of courts-martial, but most of the people loved these tokens of mercy in the grim days when thousands were falling in battle. They applauded also his tenderness toward bereaved mothers and wives. Lincoln's letter to Mrs. Bixby, "the mother of five sons who have died gloriously on the field of battle," was really a message to all the sorrowing, and the press printed it far and wide. Unknown to Lincoln, only two of Mrs. Bixby's sons had died in action. One had been captured, and exchanged in good health; another after capture had gone over to the South, and been set down on the records as "deserted to the enemy"; and still another, who had given his age as eighteen, was discharged when his mother swore he was only sixteen and subject to attacks of insanity. Lately the authorship of this letter has been called into question. After Sandburg and other recent biographers had told with some wealth of detail how Lincoln wrote it, contrary testimony from John Hay came to light. It was given confidentially to John Morley, and passed on to Nicholas

Murray Butler, who related in his second volume of *Across the Busy Years* that Hay admitted "he himself had written the Bixby letter and that this was the reason why it could not be found among Lincoln's papers and why no original copy of it had ever been forthcoming." Hay as the President's secretary—in the days before typewriters—had learned closely to imitate the Lincoln script as well as the Lincoln idiom, and his claim is probably true. But the spirit of the Bixby letter, unimpeachable in its compassion and beauty, was Lincoln's.

Lincoln's second heroic role was that of the Great Emancipator, freeing millions by a stroke of his pen. Here the facts are often falsified. Lincoln disliked slavery and opposed its extension. But in places where it already existed he admitted that he did not know what to do about it, believing in all humility that it was a problem beyond the grasp of any single man. He had long favored gradual emancipation, with payment to slave-owners who would otherwise be ruined. The need of educating the Negro for freedom he also saw. With the fanatics of abolition Lincoln had little patience. In Worcester, Mass., in an impromptu speech in 1848 he had said almost callously of Lovejoy: "I have heard you have abolitionists here. We have a few in Illinois and we shot one the other day." This remark was omitted by the Whig newspapers of Massachusetts in reporting his speech.[23] Later, in December, 1859, upon the soil of Kansas, he condemned the "violence, bloodshed, and treason" of John Brown, and felt that his execution had been legally just.

It is somewhat ironic that Lincoln's soldiers marched to war chanting the song that immortalized "old John Brown," and that Garibaldi and other Italian liberals sent the President a flowery letter hailing him as "heir of the aspirations of Christ and of John Brown." John Brown is not the most satisfactory of American heroes. New England's literary men, coming out of their lamplit studies to see John Brown as he passed with glittering eye—sedentary men sharing the thrill of his distant enterprise—had called him "a pure ideal of artless goodness." They knew nothing of the Potawatomi massacre of 1856, when Brown and his boys at random had picked the family of a mild pro-slavery man, and killed five at midnight, splitting open heads and chopping off arms and fingers of their victims. That was an election year, and the Frémont newspapers and speakers agreed to suppress the incident in the interest of popular good will. For almost a generation people were able to deny that John Brown had had any part in these murders. At last, he undertook his coup at Harpers Ferry. There his boys began their stroke for black liberation, strangely enough, by killing a free Negro, a baggage-master who was minding his own business. Captured by Colonel Robert E. Lee's United States Marines, and sentenced to death, John Brown appealed to God as his judge. Governor Wise of Virginia ignored the affidavits proving the hereditary insanity of John Brown, and foolishly allowed the rebel to become a martyr. Thomas Hovenden's familiar painting in 1881, "Last Moments of John Brown," shows a kindly old man, arms pinioned behind, kissing a Negro baby held up by its mother, while sneering soldiers look on. The incident is pure myth, but true enough are the condemned man's last words: "I believe that to have interfered as I have done—in behalf of [God's] despised poor, was not wrong, but right." The hero-worship of John Brown, a man who advocated putting a gun into every Negro's hand, did much to madden the South against New England. Louisa Alcott called him "Saint John the Just." Thoreau, apostle of civil disobedience, rang with his own hands the bell that summoned his neighbors to Concord Vestry to hear his thrilling defense of John Brown. And Emerson foresaw that Brown "will make the gallows glorious like the cross." Yet he has never become a major American idol. His homicidal insanity is not easily forgotten. Stephen Vincent Benét has written well, but not worshipfully, of his legend seen through the smoke of Civil War; and John Steuart Curry has lately painted a mural for the Kansas State Capitol, "Tragic Prelude," showing a Michelangelesque John Brown of frenzied eye and streaming beard, a tornado of the Kansas plains. Modern Communists approve his philosophy of violence, while ignoring his Bible-reading. Earl Browder has called him "immortal," while Michael Gold wrote a play called *Battle Hymn* and a biography praising him as symbol of "the simple, obscure heroes who fight for freedom today in America." A more temperate Leftist, Oswald Garrison Villard, has written his most rational defense.

Lincoln, however, rejected the solution of violence. In his First Inaugural he said that he had "no lawful right" to ban the South's peculiar institution. When the war broke out, he promptly rebuked those Northern leaders who interpreted the conflict as primarily against slavery.[24] "My paramount object in this struggle is to save the Union, and it is *not* to save or destroy Slavery," his open letter to Horace Greeley declared, just a month before the preliminary Emancipation Proclamation. Against the shadows of folklore, it seems passing strange that the Civil War should have found its two great heroes in Lincoln, who was no abolitionist, and Lee, who was no secessionist. Both had

higher loyalties—Lincoln to the Union, Lee to his native Virginia—
which plunged them into the conflict.

"His tactics were to get himself in the right place and remain there,
until events would find him in that place," wrote Lincoln's friend
Leonard Swett, with fine insight. An instinct, deep in Lincoln's bones
as wood-lore, told him never to hurry events. Thus he delayed speaking
on emancipation, conciliating the border states and waiting for public
opinion to ripen. In late September, 1862, when the war outlook was
momentarily brighter, Lincoln warned the seceded states that if they
did not soon return to the Union he would proclaim their slaves free.
Presumably if they had heeded the call, all would have been forgiven
and the slaves retained. But they paid no attention. And so on January 1, 1863, Lincoln issued his final Proclamation. Once more, as over
the Fort Sumter incident of 1861, Lincoln had taken a trick in the
game of moral advantage. He linked his cause with a powerful dynamo
in nineteenth-century action—that new solicitude for human life and
suffering which the white race began to develop two or three generations before our Civil War.

Yet in fact, the Emancipation Proclamation, applying only to soil
disobedient to the Union, did not strike off any chains. Liberation of
the blacks did not become a legal reality until after Lincoln's time,
with ratification of the Thirteenth Amendment. Lincoln's act was a
notable *tour de force;* but it did not embody his chief policy respecting slavery, made no denunciation of slavery as an institution, and
above all did not solve the Negro problem. Paul Angle has lately remarked: "The conception of Lincoln as the Great Emancipator is
unhistorical, and insofar as his fame today rests upon it, the foundation
is insecure."

Legend of course has decided otherwise. A single man must be credited with this memorable work. The noblest candidate, unstained by
the vindictiveness of "the tragic era" when emancipation became an
actuality, was Lincoln. Another powerful argument was the adoration
of "Massa Linkum" by the Negroes themselves. His entry into Richmond in April, 1865, through a mile and a half of sobbing and exulting
blacks, shouting for the "year of jubilo," kneeling about him and
praying, could not be gainsaid. A dusky mother held up her sick
child: "See yeah, honey, look at the Savior, and you'll git well." Widely
quoted were the words of an old "praise man" in South Carolina to
his dusky flock: "Massa Linkum, he eberywhar. He know eberyting.
He walk de earth lak de Lawd!" No greater reverence than this, the

homage of a poetic and worshipful race, has ever been laid at an American hero's feet.

Lincoln's third great role is that of preserver of the Union, the patriarch of a reunited nation. In preparation for this part, his affectionate nickname "Father Abraham" could not have been bettered. He had been called "old Mr. Lincoln" when he was scarcely thirty, and like Washington could not resist some allusion to his antiquity whenever reading in public caused him to don spectacles.[25] In Springfield he had once caught a little girl in his arms, to save her from falling on the sidewalk, and upon asking her name let her go with a whimsical benediction: "Well, Mary, when you reach home tell your mother that you have rested in Abraham's bosom." Later, in the war years, the phrase struck a deeper note—a promise of safety, rest, infinite sympathy. To the music of Stephen Foster, thousands sang "We are coming, Father Abraham." In the summer of 1864 a newspaper sprang up at Reading, Pa., called *Father Abraham;* its faith and creed were simply Abraham Lincoln. His secretary John Hay called him "the Ancient," and Edwin Arlington Robinson in later times wrote of him as "ancient at his birth." The most popular statues of the President always show the bearded Lincoln, stooped with care, not the clean-shaved Lincoln of the first fifty years. The soul of wisdom and gentleness, the man who kept up the morale of war without the bitterness of war, seeking to rebind the broken Union, is "Father Abraham."

Lincoln saw that a common purpose was vital, and that the Northern majority, like himself, cared most about saving the Union. First he pleaded with the "departing sisters," and then when they refused to return he took the step of war to reclaim them. In 1861 he planted the struggle firmly upon the issue of national unity. Later, when this appeal had sunk deeply in, and the cause was ready for a new injection of morale, he consented to the Proclamation, which added the motive of humanitarianism. Thus, with excellent timing and a genius for reading the folk mind, Lincoln blended a majority with a minority group impulse.

At this point, a comparison of America's two great war Presidents is helpful. In a similar way, under Wilson, the national pride that had chafed at insults to American commerce and citizenship was fused at the right time with a larger idealism—and thus was forged the will to victory. In working out this vital statement of fighting faiths, both Lincoln and Wilson were superb literary artists and propagandists for democracy. Professor Randall of Illinois, one of the best Lincoln experts, finds him inferior to Wilson as an efficient war executive. Like any inexperienced man, Lincoln wanted to do everything himself. He lacked that respect for congressional consent which Wilson in 1917–18 was so careful to preserve. His arbitrary acts, suspending the writ of *habeas corpus* and ordering wholesale imprisonments, led many to call Lincoln a dictator. His draft system, encouraging the purchase of substitutes and the abuse of "bounties," and effective in raising only 2 per cent of the Union men under arms, was far less able and democratic than that of 1917. Lincoln's choice of political subordinates and of generals was repeatedly poor, and the early war years make a sorry record for the North. Only later did the discovery of Grant and Sherman redeem the blunders of Lincoln. As Paul Angle impartially says, "in view of these inadequacies, one can hardly call him a great executive."[26] In normal times, Lincoln's failings as an administrator might have stamped him with lasting mediocrity. Only to the ardent hero-worshipper like the late Nathaniel W. Stephenson does Lincoln appear among the "consummate masters of statecraft." Yet, awkward as he was in all techniques save tact, Lincoln was Wilson's superior in warm personal qualities. He was homely while Wilson was academic, humorous where Wilson seemed stiff, and lovable in lights that made Wilson appear the precisian. Lincoln's stature as a hero comes, not from efficiency as an executive, but from traits in the man himself which have little to do with diplomatic or military genius.

Even at his most arbitrary, Lincoln was working for the Union and, he felt, for democracy. Why did he want so desperately to save the Union? A critical Southerner has lately suggested that a great nation in fragments, no longer able to call itself "the United States of America," would have lost its physical pride: "Americans have been prone to boast of the size of their country. Is there some mystical, imponderable, but precious quality in mere bigness?"[27] However it may have looked to a jingo, this statement is hardly a just description of Lincoln's thoughts. Nor was the fetish worship of the Constitution—which the Union League and the old guard Republicans later built into the Lincoln legend—ever compelling to Lincoln's mind. There was a better reason for his devotion to the Union, as Alexander Stephens said, with "the sublimity of a religious mysticism." Lincoln held that national unity was vital to the health of democracy in America. He also believed that this Union stood as the great democratic experiment in the eyes of the world, and that with its failure the dawn would be blotted from other skies. "And this issue embraces more than the fate of these United States," he told Congress in his first message. "It presents to the whole family of man the question whether a constitutional republic or democracy—a government of the people by the same people —can or cannot maintain its territorial integrity against its own domestic foes." The Gettysburg Address (which Lincoln himself, and a good many newspapers, agreed was "a flat failure") has been worn so smooth by a million tongues that we are apt not to feel the edge of Lincoln's words "that this nation, under God, shall have a new birth of freedom; and that government of the people, by the people, for the people, shall not perish from the earth." But he meant just that. With passionate faith he believed that democracy was the best of governments, and in so far as he thought of himself in the White House it was in terms of its demonstration. "I am a living witness," he told an Ohio regiment, "that any one of your children may look to come here as my father's child has . . . that each of you may have, through this free government which we have enjoyed, an open field and a fair chance for your industry, enterprise, and intelligence."[28] By what he was, therefore, as well as what he stood for, Abraham Lincoln has become a world symbol to all who struggle for freedom.

VI

Lincoln's inner life remained a puzzle to his contemporaries. He was the saddest man, and the greatest teller of funny stories, who ever sat in the President's chair. To those who knew him least, he was a carefree joker who met every crisis with the words "That reminds me of a story." To his friends, the President often seemed to be a man trying to outjest the heartstruck injuries of the nation's bloodiest war. To posterity, the Lincoln of legend has been gently stripped of his motley, of the cap and bells that hardly go with a halo. His jokes, it is said, have all become parables, and his sadness no longer seems personal, but a sorrow rising from his contemplation of humanity, like Christ's tears over Jerusalem.

Humankind has always loved good stories. Lincoln, who once said, "I am only a retail dealer," drew some of his yarns from that folk humor old as Æsop—old, no doubt, as the camp-fires of the Stone Age, or whenever men first learned to ease the increasing tension of civilization with laughter. The frontiersman, the farmer, and other lonely Americans made "a good story" the small change of their rare social intercourse. Lincoln said that his best stories came from country folk.

To them, as to him, the wisdom of life ran in fables. With uncommon insight Sumner remarked of Lincoln, "His ideas moved as the beasts entered Noah's ark, in pairs."

Lincoln's stories, as Lamon said of the White House days, were "labor-saving contrivances," cutting through dialectic with the blade of good sense, deflating formalism and pretension with a minimum of hurt feelings. Humor was the great democratic solvent. A painter who lived for six months in the White House, Francis B. Carpenter, compared the President's high-pitched laugh to "the neigh of a wild horse on his native prairie." Lincoln's jokes, in fact, often rang with the peculiarly American tones of the horse-laugh, skeptical of convention, irreverent of pomp. His laughter turned flexibly against himself. Asked by an old Springfield neighbor how it felt to be President, Lincoln replied: "You have heard about the man tarred and feathered and ridden out of town on a rail? A man in the crowd asked him how he liked it, and his reply was that if it wasn't for the honor of the thing, he would much rather walk." He also told about a crusty old Democrat who stalked up to him and glared, "They say you're a self-made man." Upon Lincoln's assent, he observed, "Well, all I've got to say is that it was a damned bad job."

Even in his New Salem days, it was said, ailing men came to listen to Abe Lincoln's jokes, and found afterwards that their rheumatism was better. In the Civil War, Lincoln's humor was a real but imponderable factor. He gave the country not only his will to win, but his will to laugh under desperation. Told that McClellan was ready to advise him on how to run the nation, in its darkest days, Lincoln was reminded "of the man whose horse kicked up and stuck his foot through the stirrup. He said to the horse, 'If you are going to get on, I will get off.'" It was known that he had interrupted the business of a Cabinet meeting in order that a caller, named Orlando Kellogg, might come in and tell them all "the story of the stuttering justice." Men like Chase and Stanton were mystified, if not impatient. Sometimes Lincoln's humor was a safety-valve, releasing the high pressure of wartime idealism. He was supposed to have told how an old loafer said to him, "I feel patriotic." And when the President asked, "What do you mean by feeling patriotic?" the fellow answered, "Why, I feel like I wanted to kill somebody or steal something."

Some people objected to the gaiety Lincoln showed toward solemn subjects. When a committee called to inform him that the Union defeats were "the curse of the Lord" upon a drunken army, Lincoln couldn't resist the remark that this was "rather unfair on the part of the curse, as the other side drank more and worse whisky than ours did." *The New York Evening Post* reported a story which the straight-laced thought irreligious. To a general who told Lincoln that most people assumed he wanted a second term, the President mentioned an evangelist who asked permission from a Springfield official to lecture in the State House on "The Second Coming of Christ." "Oh, bosh," growled the official, "if our Saviour had ever been to Springfield and got away with his life, he'd be too smart to think of coming back again." On the eve of Lincoln's re-election in 1864, campaign propaganda circulated a story that while riding in an ambulance over the battlefield of Antietam, with the dead still unburied, the President called on his friend Lamon for "a ribald song." The story ran like wildfire, and Lincoln who at first had said quietly, "Let the thing alone," was finally compelled to state the facts under Lamon's signature. They revealed that Lamon had sung a minstrel ditty, "Picayune Butler," after seeing Lincoln's gloom upon hearing some tearful stanzas, but that the place was no battlefield and no corpses were near. But long after the Civil War this tale lingered on—sometimes giving the locale as Gettysburg, after Lincoln's Address, and sometimes showing Lincoln and Lamon sitting on a coffin as they burst into roaring song. It was the most vicious yarn ever invented against Lincoln the supposed buffoon.[29]

A more general charge is that Lincoln told dirty stories. That his humor was sometimes broad—in the company of cronies, fellow lawyers, tavern loungers of the Illinois days—seems highly probable. "The pity is that his funniest stories don't circulate in polite society or get embalmed in type," wrote Henry Whitney, who knew Lincoln well. But other witnesses were prone to exaggerate. Henry Villard, who met Lincoln in 1858 and admired him, regretted that "the coarser the joke, the lower the anecdote, and the more risky the story, the more he enjoyed them"—adding that Lincoln "never hesitated to tell a coarse or even outright nasty story, if it served its purpose," such as getting rid of a bore. It should be remembered that Villard was a naïve young Bavarian, over-serious, saturated with a Victorian prudery unknown to the insular American male of Lincoln's social and economic class. Touched with a kindred squeamishness, the painter A. J. Conant in 1860 heard Lincoln tell stories that seemed to him unprintable, but admitted that Lincoln's was not smut for smut's sake but for its "human point." During the Civil War, hostile papers made much of the

President's off-color stories, and before the election of 1864 anti-Lincoln parades carried transparencies reading "No More Vulgar Jokes." At all times, Lincoln's enemies forgot that he had his standards—in Offutt's store once thrashing a loafer who had uttered unseemly talk before women customers, and in his law office stepping to the door to see that no women were within earshot. Lincoln and Herndon had once undertaken the case of a woman charged with keeping a brothel. They asked for a change of venue, and Lincoln drove across the prairie from one town to another, with the madam and her girls. After the trial Lincoln's client was queried about his famous stories. She said Lincoln kept them laughing the whole time, but after a moment's hesitation added that all his yarns could be told "with safety in the presence of ladies anywhere." Her criteria may not have been quite those of Harriet Beecher Stowe, for example, but the evidence is worth weighing.

During Lincoln's Presidency, while he became known as "the National Joker," chapbooks like *Old Abe's Joker* in 1863 and *Old Abe's Jokes, Fresh from Abraham's Bosom* in 1864, foisted a great variety of yarns upon him—good, bad, and indifferent. Others, with a more gamy flavor, circulated from mouth to mouth. But after his death, most admirers came to deny that he had ever told jokes of belly-laughter, or even used earthy speech. Even the Lincoln who said, apropos of political hangers-on, that "there are too many hogs for the tits," was suppressed in favor of the stately Christian gentleman speaking the phrases of Gettysburg and the Second Inaugural. One phase of Lincoln the democrat thus began to be lost. Lincoln the backwoods Boccaccio was given even shorter shrift.

Mrs. Honoré Willsie Morrow, who has idealized Lincoln in five novels and in the pages of *Good Housekeeping,* states that Lincoln never told bawdy stories. Her proof is simple. She asked various men who had made a study of Lincoln's jokes to tell her the worst they knew—and the ones they told never really shocked her! A more subtle idealization of Lincoln's humor is seen in Edwin Arlington Robinson's poem "The Master":

> The saddest among kings of earth,
> Bowed with a galling crown, this man
> Met rancor with a cryptic mirth,
> Laconic—and Olympian.

Robinson's is a fine poem, but its Lincoln is a New England one—the son of the prairie swallowed up in Lincoln the Good and Lincoln the

Wise, a bloodless abstraction of nobility and suffering. Lincoln's gusty laughter, which battened upon stories about lizards in preachers' breeches and practical jokes on newlyweds, was "cryptic" only to the intellectual Yankee at King Arthur's Court. Even in the White House that mirth called for crackerboxes and glowing stoves. Artemus Ward, Petroleum V. Nasby, Orpheus C. Kerr—those humorists whom Lincoln quoted to his Cabinet even at such a moment as the reading of the Emancipation Proclamation, and who in turn stood loyally behind the President throughout the war—they best could have fathomed Lincoln's laughter. He was their fellow guildsman.

The other side of the coin was seen by those who knew Lincoln well. "Melancholy dripped from him as he walked," wrote Herndon. Lincoln called his dark moods "hypo"—hypochondria, that fashionable malady of the eighteenth century about which Pope and Boswell wrote, which strangely fastened itself upon this son of Western skies and wind. Lincoln's friend Robert L. Wilson recalled that he "told me that he was so overcome by mental depression that he never dared carry a knife in his pocket." Thus, in Lincoln's youth. Like pioneers, prospectors, cowboys, and men of hard lonely life, Lincoln loved melancholy and sentimental poetry. Everybody knows that his favorite was William Knox's "Oh, why should the spirit of mortal be proud?" He recited it and copied it so often that folklore often asserts Lincoln was the author. And he loved songs about the vanished happiness of childhood, though his own youth seems to have been bleak and harsh enough. Lincoln's gloom, like his mirth, was overwhelming and abnormal. From the heights to the depths was a swift cascade: one predicated the other. Sometimes friends thought Lincoln's mind was unhinged, not only in seasons like the hectic autumn of 1835 and the black winter of 1841, but in passing moods such as Henry Whitney describes from their circuit-riding days: "One morning I was awakened early—before daylight—by my companion sitting up in bed, his figure dimly visible by the ghostly fire-light, and talking the wildest and most incoherent nonsense all to himself."[30]

The root of Lincoln's lifelong pessimism can only be guessed at. Sentimental people hark back to Ann Rutledge, or less popularly to Lincoln's unhappy marriage. Yet, by all the evidence, Lincoln was not stricken for life by the loss of Ann, whereas, long before he took Mary Todd to wife, melancholy had settled upon him like an enveloping garment. His friend Stuart thought the trouble could be traced to Lincoln's sluggish liver and bowels. But when Herndon published this as his own diagnosis, too, the cult of Lincoln worship was shocked. Heroes may fade with consumption, or with their battles o'er be racked by gout, but chronic constipation is taboo. Psychiatry today, with its study of depressive types, may come closer to the heart of Lincoln's moodiness. But the essential puzzle remains.

Lincoln, Messianic in so many guises, has become "the Man of Sorrows." The jesting President, still widely admired in 1901 when Alexander McClure compiled a big book called *Abe Lincoln's Yarns and Stories,* began to wane under the deification of the Lincoln Centenary of 1909. A hero is always what the folk mind wants him to be. And the sadness of Lincoln held a more lasting, deeper appeal. It was a quality that had aroused the protectiveness of many who met the living man, even casually, in Springfield and in Washington. "You cannot help feeling an interest in him, a sympathy and a kind of pity," wrote Richard Henry Dana in 1864; "feeling too that he has some qualities of great value, yet fearing that his weak points may wreck him or wreck something." After these weaknesses were made perfect in martyrdom, Lincoln's melancholy stirred an even deeper pity. The loneliness, poverty, and weariness of his mortal pilgrimage were seen almost achingly in retrospect. "What is it that moves you about his simple, unprejudiced, unpretending, honest career?" wrote young William James in September, 1865. "I can't tell why, but albeit unused to the melting mood, I can hardly ever think of Abraham Lincoln without feeling on the point of blubbering." To the folk mind, henceforth, the sorrows of Lincoln were bound up with his grief over a nation of warring brothers, the yearning of his heart for the black man in chains, or the premonition of his own tragic end. "Strange mingling of mirth and tears," Colonel Robert G. Ingersoll said in a lecture, "of the tragic and grotesque, of cap and crown, of Socrates and Rabelais, of Æsop and Marcus Aurelius—Lincoln, the gentlest memory of the world."

VII

Lincoln's was a strangely dramatic death, at the high noon of victory, only five days after Lee's surrender at Appomattox. The President's words only a few weeks before, "with malice toward none, with charity for all," still lingered in the April air like a benediction. To Whitman, Lincoln's death was a climax on the stage of universal time, as the curtain was rung down to "close an immense act in the long drama of creative thought, and give it radiation, tableau, stranger than fiction." History had no parallel for this finale, tragic as it was grand. The rail-splitter, the self-made boy, the joke-teller, the aspiring country lawyer, were erased as the final lineaments were drawn, of prophet and sacrifice. A generation in whose blood lingered the heroism of Fox's *Book of Martyrs* saw him in sudden translation to glory. The pistol of a half-crazed, half-drunken actor, John Wilkes Booth, blazed in Ford's Theatre on Good Friday, 1865, and Lincoln the man became Lincoln the legend.

Upon Booth the deed fastened eternal villainy. Perhaps he would have chosen it rather than the repute of a ham actor which already belonged to him. He fondly believed the South would receive him with open arms. But the great majority looked upon his deed as criminal folly. Some foresaw the evils of reconstruction that Lincoln would have tempered. Others saw an act of blood; assassination is not the American way, as was remarked even in the case of Huey Long. The South loathed Booth instinctively, even though it might have to teach itself to love Lincoln. The murderer, quickly traced down and shot in a burning barn, became a myth of infamy, like the wandering Jew who had scoffed at Christ. Report had him fleeing to Oklahoma or Mexico, leading a furtive life. More than a generation later Finis Bates, sometime Attorney General of Tennessee, embalmed the body of a house-painter who claimed he was John Wilkes Booth and rented it out to carnivals—where it may be seen today, as an attraction in "Jay Gould's Million Dollar Spectacle." True to the Benedict Arnold tradition, Thayer's biography for youth, *Lincoln the Pioneer Boy,* reported that Booth at the age of ten "was disrespectful and saucy to his mother. . . . I am not surprised that such a boy should become an assassin." In the North, a few Copperheads who dared to praise the deed were tarred and feathered, thrown in jail, or killed. At Medway, Mass., a visiting clergyman who made no mention of Lincoln's martyrdom in his Easter sermon was "given fifteen minutes to leave town; he left instanter." A chorus of newspapers, critical of the living Lincoln, abruptly changed their tune. As one instance out of many, *The New York Herald,* which only a few months ago had called him "a failure," a tyrant who "has outraged the liberty of the citizen and of the press," in committing "criminal error," on April 17, 1865, reported: "The kindliest and purest nature, the bravest and most honest will, the temper of highest geniality, and the spirit of largest practical beneficence in our public life, has fallen a victim to the insane ferocity of a bad and mad vagabond."

The dying President, carried from the theatre to the house of a tailor across the street where a candle was seen burning, found rest upon the bed of a tiny room rented by one William Clark. His death brought magic to those dingy walls. Four days after the President's death, young Clark, a stenographer in the War Department, wrote his family:

The people are awfully indignant, hundreds calling daily at the house to gain admission into my room. . . . Everybody has a great desire to obtain some memento from my room, so that whoever comes in has to be closely watched for fear they will steal something. I have a lock of his hair which I have had neatly framed, also a piece of linen with a portion of his brain. . . . The same mattress is on my bed, and the same coverlid covers me nightly that covered him while dying.[31]

These were the people, who had shocked Lincoln at his Second In-augural reception by hacking large pieces out of the White House curtains as souvenirs, who even today in visiting the house where Lincoln died have tried so often to steal the tumbler from the wash-stand that the Federal caretaker has rigged up an electrical trap. Of them Walt Whitman wrote, as he meditated on the sacrifice for democracy that had cost half a million lives and the life of Abraham Lincoln—

. . . as one sees the shallowness and miserable selfism of these crowds of men, with all their minds so blank of high humanity and aspiration—then comes the terrible query, and will not be denied, Is not Democracy of human rights humbug after all? Are these flippant people with hearts of rags and souls of chalk, are these worth preaching for and dying for upon the cross? May be not—may be it is indeed a dream—yet one thing sure remains— but the exercise of Democracy, equality, to him who, believing, preaches, and to the people who work it out—*this* is not a dream—to work for Democracy is good, the exercise is good—strength it makes and lessons it teaches —gods it makes, though it crucifies them often.[32]

Lincoln, the crucified one who ran in Whitman's mind, had been convinced that to work for the democratic dream was intrinsically good. Whatever he may have thought of the people's ultimate worth, in their rights he believed undauntedly. He could not foresee the irony in store for much of his own work: that even today the Negro's problem would be largely unsolved, and that the poor white, supposed to benefit by emancipation of the black, would progress no further than the share-cropper. Or that the Fourteenth Amendment, while making a citizen of the slave, should by its "due process of law" clause afford more comfort to the gospel of wealth than to the poor black child—that, by a strange jugglery of words, Lincoln had lived and died so that the giant corporation, rather than the Negro, might become a person. Or that, in the age of Blaine and Mark Hanna, the tenets of Lincoln thought favorable to the new industrialism should be stripped of their Jeffersonian context and fitted into the mythology of big business, while his idealism was being laid under glass in the museum of oratorical glories. Even now, in the sermons of "Black Easter," 1865, New England and the East were beginning to refashion the prairie boy nearer to their hearts' desire—as the saintly austere Lincoln, who was also the prophet of industrial predestination. Later, with equal violence to the facts, the Communists would claim him, because Karl Marx had written him a letter and because in 1860 at Hartford Lincoln "thanked God that we have a system of labor where there can be a strike." The Leftists ignored his words spoken the next day in New Haven: "I take it that it is best for all to leave each man free to acquire property as fast as he can. . . . I don't believe in a law to prevent a man from getting rich; it would do more harm than good. So while we do not propose any war upon capital, we do wish to allow the humblest man an equal chance to get rich with everybody else." Some, therefore, would shut their ears to Lincoln's doctrine that capital was the fruit of labor, and inferior to it; while others would scrap his conviction that capitalism was part of the democratic system. Lincoln would become all things to all propaganda. Of these sequels, Lincoln had no prevision. After life's fitful fever he slept well. He had become a god.

A popular *carte de visite* picture showed Lincoln in glory, in Washington's bosom, while the first President crowned his peer with laurel. Had not Edwin Booth, brother of the assassin, declared, "Abraham Lincoln will be loved and honored hereafter not less than Washington?"[33]

> Heroes and Saints with fadeless stars have crowned him—
> And WASHINGTON'S dear arms are clasped around him.
> God of our Land! to Thee this pure oblation!
> Freedom's sweet blood, poured out for Freedom's Nation!
> Deign to behold our Cross and Crucifixion,
> And be HIS Martyrdom OUR Resurrection!

exclaimed a popular broadside, printed a few days after the assassination, by A. J. H. Duganne. Sermons called his murder "the worst ever committed on any Good Friday since the crucifixion of Christ." A few clergymen had qualms about his assassination in a theatre, "a poor place to die in," and a few others saw his death as God's punishment upon the idolatry of the American people.[34] But much of the grief was deep and sincere, without reservation. Lately loved and only half understood, Lincoln was gone forever. The nation's heart seemed broken. Lincoln's greatest elegist was Walt Whitman. This poet brought to his appreciation the immediacy of hospital cots, stretchers, and the loyalties of men who had died in the Captain's cause. In the simplicity of his grief Whitman would have understood those early morning passengers in a Philadelphia street-car who, upon learning of Lincoln's death from the first newspaper, wept into their hands or sat stunned with silence, while the driver took the bells off his horses. But none could express the depth of mass sorrow as did Whitman— to whom Lincoln was the ideal of virility tempered with gentleness, the answer to the poet's quest for a masculine hero, a great comrade-democrat.

> Coffin that passes through lanes and streets,
> Through day and night with the great cloud darkening the land,
> With the pomp of the inloop'd flags with the cities draped in black,
> With the show of the States themselves as of crape-veil'd women standing,
> With processions long and winding and the flambeaus of the night,
> With the countless torches lit, with the silent sea of faces and the unbared
>   heads . . .
> Here, coffin that slowly passes,
> I give you my sprig of lilac.

The funeral train of eight black coaches had wound from Washington to Philadelphia, through little towns blanketed in crape, farmers and wives and children anxiously holding up draped flags on the edge of the fields, old men carried in wheel chairs to see the passing train. New York City was showy in its hysteria—offering a giant hearse drawn by sixteen white horses, with a dismantled Liberty Temple on top amid nodding plumes. A price of $40 was paid for a single window on the street, to witness the parade in which 160,000 marched. Boys sold places in the funeral queue, reaching from City Hall to the Bowery, for $10. Tears mingled with garishness. Floral tributes of clocks, their hands stopped at 7:20 to mark the time of Lincoln's death, began two traditions: the first was an untrue bit of folklore asserting that all jewellers' clock signs are painted with their hands set at the time of Lincoln's passing, the second a passion for floral clocks commemorating the hour of decease which reached its height in the gangster era of Colosimo and Uale in the 1920's. The Lincoln cortège passed beneath innumerable arches of crape spanning Broadway—some Biblical, some rhetorical, one of the best declaring "The great person, the great man, is the miracle of history." A huge urn of incense smoked in front of Barnum's Museum. For some distance beside the hearse trotted a St. Bernard dog; his owner, one Ed Morton, told how Lincoln had once patted the dog's head, while reporters gravely noted "the peculiar instinct of the dog in recognizing Lincoln's hearse." While the body lay in state in City Hall, some 150,000 viewed it, and many women tried to break through the guard to kiss the careworn face.

Along the Hudson River in the dusk, as the train resumed its journey, crowds of country people lined the tracks with lanterns and torches. On the hilltops some acted sad pageants, such as a goddess of Liberty dipping a flag into a grave, against the sunset or by the light of bonfires. From Albany westward, hills bore arches and tableaux. Towns offered flowers brought by thirty-six girls invariably dressed in white, with black scarves, to represent the sorrowing states. Railway stations—"depots," Americans of that generation called them —echoed with the music of funeral bands and choirs. Mothers brought babes in arms to gaze for the first and last time upon Lincoln's face. Each town, reading in the papers what others had done, sought to outdo them in its dark pomp. Cleveland and Columbus offered Chinese pagodas to house the casket as it lay in state. Indianapolis built within the State House a great catafalque of black velvet and gold stars, "the most faultless display of elegance that has yet contained the remains." Even grief had its civic vanities. Roses were thrown beneath the wheels as they rolled their burden back to Illinois—the locomotive carrying pictures of Lincoln pasted beside the searchlight, and a black blanket sprinkled with stars thrown over the engine as if it were a hearsehorse. As the journey neared its end, mottoes cried poignantly "Come home." In Chicago 125,000 viewed the body within twenty-four hours. As soon as the hearse was empty, souvenir-hunters fell upon it and had to be scattered by soldiers with bayonets. The people, for whom Lincoln had toiled, displayed their heartbreak, their callous curiosity, their vulgarity. Even in Springfield, after the funeral, the red, white and blue blanket on "Old Bob," Lincoln's horse, was torn to pieces by relic fans.

In all, as Mr. Lloyd Lewis has computed, seven million people had seen the coffin or funeral train, and one and a half million viewed the corpse. Ninety funeral marches had been composed and played. Never before, or since, has a nation so prostrated itself at a hero's bier. Upon a few, the mass sorrow bore achingly and intolerably. A youth in New York City, one Charles Johnson, said "I am going to join Abraham Lincoln," and cut his throat with a razor.

The relics of that grief, as found in Lincoln museums today, reflect sincerity, fantasy, and bathos. Broadsides flooded the country: the Second Inaugural printed in gold letters with a black border was perhaps most popular, though Lincoln's Farewell to His Old Springfield Neighbors, the Gettysburg Address, and the Emancipation Proclamation were also favored. "Golden Sayings of Lincoln" bore his picture, with Chickering upright and grand pianos advertised on the back. A broadside now in the Library of Congress, acquired in 1866, is entitled "We Mourn Our Loss," and within a black border encloses "Our Own Social. Order of Dancing"—beginning with "Promenade" and ending with "Quadrille: Family Set—High Daddy." Handkerchiefs were embroidered with the motto "Lincoln ever Faithful," and many people had Lincoln's portrait painted or pasted on the dial of their watches. Statues first appeared in Washington and Chicago, and later throughout the country; but there were no toga-draped or semi-nude figures comparable to Greenough's "George Washington," for Lincoln did not belong to "the heroic antique." Years later, after Garfield and McKinley had joined the list of assassinated Presidents, a whole pictography of American martyrdom sprang up. There were paper-weights of "Our Assassinated Presidents," dinner-plates bearing the faces of "Our Martyrs," and a brand of cigars called Memorata which illustrated the three executives above the motto, in dubious Latin, "De mortibus nil nisi bonum."

The lore of superstition naturally added its tribute. Much was made of the report that Lincoln foresaw his death. He had told Mrs. Lincoln of a dream, in which he had seen a catafalque in the East Room of the White House. She also remembered the curious double image of himself he had once glimpsed in a mirror, saying that the shadowy ghost meant death during his second term. Most famous of all was the dream he related on Good Friday, 1865, to several Cabinet members; it concerned a ship "moving with great rapidity toward a dark and indefinite shore." Lincoln, child of wilderness and prairie, undoubtedly had a certain curiosity about dreams, although he never let them affect his action. Moreover, his death was seen in a cosmic setting. Witnesses testified that about ten o'clock on the night of his assassination the moon was seen to emerge from murky clouds, as red as blood. There were more coincidences. *The Chicago Tribune* related that, as the funeral train neared the Lake shore, "the waters of Lake Michigan, long ruffled by the storm, suddenly calmed from their angry roar into solemn silence." Folklore says that the brown thrush of Illinois stopped singing for a year after Lincoln's last homecoming. And the story is told of a phantom funeral train supposed to pass over the New York Central every year, on some night in late April; clocks and watches stop as the silent train sweeps by with its black-draped cars and a glimpse of blue-coated men guarding a long coffin.

VIII

In 1872 a man named D. B. Turney published a solemn parody of the "higher criticism" in its attack upon the historical Christ. This book, called *The Mythifying Theory, or Abraham Lincoln a Myth,* proved that Lincoln never existed at all. Likewise in 1894 a writer whose name, or pen-name, was Bocardo Bramantip produced *The Lincoln Myth.* From the year 3663 A.D. he looked back on the nineteenth century to discover that Lincoln—a shadowy figure whose reported life was too romantic, as his death was too dramatic, for the world of fact as we know it—sprang from pure allegory or a solar myth, invented by a wildly hero-worshipping generation, or else cooked up by politicians eager to extend the Chief Executive's powers. In such grave fun-making there was a grain of truth. Emerson, in his eulogy on Lincoln, had remarked that "in a period of less facility of printing, he would have become mythological in a very few years." He failed to see that the making of legends still goes on, in these days of the press and of floodlighting.

A small book might be made of Lincoln sayings that the man himself never uttered—jokes, proverbs, dicta on prohibition and protective tariff, and a speech on war profiteers and "corruption in high places" which first appeared in the Presidential campaign of 1888.[35] Innocent enough are the spurious words of Lincoln cut in stone over the entrance to the Museum of the City of New York:

> I like to see a man proud of the place in which he lives;
> I like to see a man live so that his place will be proud of him.

In 1909 the Reverend J. T. Hobson told how the President's son Robert always remembered a little "sermon" his father had preached to "the boys": "Don't drink, don't smoke, don't swear, don't gamble, don't lie, don't cheat. Love your fellowmen and love God. Love truth, love virtue, and be happy." This sermon attained wide circulation, until at length it came to the attention of Robert Lincoln himself. Whereupon he flatly denied that he had ever heard of it before.[36] Similarly, the President was quoted as saying, when he looked upon "the graves of our dead heroes" at Gettysburg: "I *do* love Jesus." Immense efforts have been made to prove that Lincoln was a Christian, and alleged confessions of faith have been put into his mouth. He is shown as praying with Henry Ward Beecher and other popular evangelists during the Civil War. A photograph of Lincoln and his son Tad looking at a photographer's album is widely known as "Abraham Lincoln reading the Bible to his Son," and was shown under that label at the Lincoln Exhibition of the Library of Congress in the autumn of 1939; ironically enough, Lincoln had told Noah Brooks he "was afraid that this picture was a species of false pretense" because somebody might mistake the album for a Bible.[37] In truth, Lincoln was no orthodox believer. In youth, like young Ben Franklin, he was prone to mock at churchgoers. Ripening years, the death of his little son Willie, and the cares of the Civil War softened the angularity of his skepticism. Like Washington he had always had an intuition of Providence, of a destiny shaping man's life but expecting him to do his best. Lincoln's has been called a creed of constructive fatalism. Among the many Lincoln stories, the President's favorite was that about two Quakeresses overheard discussing the wartime leaders, Davis and Lincoln:

"I think Jefferson will succeed."
"Why does thee think so?"
"Because Jefferson is a praying man."
"And so is Abraham a praying man."
"Yes, but the Lord will think Abraham is joking."

There is no sound evidence that Lincoln prayed, however, or that he believed in the divinity of Christ. With rare perception Mrs. Lincoln said of her husband: "He never joined a church, but still he was a religious man. But it was a kind of poetry in his nature, and he never was a technical Christian." Lincoln the religious man, like Lincoln the superb literary artist, was essentially a poet. Knowing the hungers of his own soul, and the will to believe among mankind, he instinctively clothed his speech and acts in a garb of idealism which many took for the raiment of orthodoxy. Lincoln's heart was Christian, although his brain probably was not. This statement will not content those who insist upon conventional perfection for their heroes. In preparing some notes for Herndon, that doughty champion of Lincoln's agnosticism, Leonard Swett wrote on August 30, 1887: "You will note that I have stricken out all allusion to Mr. Lincoln's swearing, and reading the Bible. . . . The public would believe I lied about it. . . . The heroes of the world are its standards, and in time . . . they become clothed with imaginary virtues."

At the other extreme are still a few violent dissenters from the Lincoln cult. Fierce Southerners like Archibald Rutledge, and Lyon G. Tyler the late President of William and Mary College, and to some degree the late Ambassador William E. Dodd, in idealizing the Old South, have seen Lincoln's gaunt hand crushing the flower of that culture. A generation ago, schoolchildren in the South habitually tore Lincoln's picture out of their history books. In 1931 there was a ripple of applause when Edgar Lee Masters "debunked" Lincoln. Several years ago the head of the Teachers Union in a large Southern city stated that legitimate grounds for dismissal included "mentioning Abraham Lincoln favorably in a history course."[38] In the fall of 1939, in driving on the highway from the lately restored village of New Salem to Springfield, the writer noticed that a handsome bronze plaque of Lincoln in bas-relief, set up by the D. A. R., had been defaced by two bullets, one deeply denting the cheek of the figure. Likewise, on the lawn of the Sangamon County courthouse is a small statue of the President, erected in 1932 by the Daughters of Union Veterans of the Civil War. Upon this same visit it was noted that some one had heavily rouged the statue's lips, and on its back was scrawled the word "sourpuss." It is possible that some average citizen of Springfield had grown tired of hearing about Abraham Lincoln. Lincoln himself no doubt would have understood. To the actor James Hackett, during the Civil War, he wrote: "I have endured a great deal of ridicule without much malice; and have received a great deal of kindness, not quite free from ridicule."

Among the moderate critics are several able Southern historians. They think the Civil War did little good, that the real development of America—expansion of the frontier, factories rising, railroads on the march, and the necessary wane of slavery—would have gone forward in much the same course without it. They deny the conflict was "irrepressible," and say that peace would have been better. They think that a wiser Lincoln might eventually have coaxed back the seceding states, without the tragedy of war. Hence they question the glory of Lincoln, sometimes hinting that his deification became necessary in order to justify, historically, the half million lives and billions of property wasted by the Civil War.

But to the average American, Lincoln is our greatest hero. About one hundred and thirty thousand pilgrims every year visit his tomb at Springfield, many kneeling to pray or cross themselves in the dimly lighted crypt. The tomb has been guarded with better care since 1876, when a plot was discovered to steal the embalmed corpse, by Kneally's gang of ten counterfeiters, who planned to hold it for ransom until their master engraver was released from prison. Folklore often whispers that the tomb is empty, a rumor such as clung to the graves of Old World heroes like Charlemagne and Barbarossa. But the body is now sunk in metal and concrete ten feet below the earth's surface. The second great shrine, the Lincoln Memorial in Washington, is visited by no less than a million people each year. "This lone white temple, a pantheon for him alone," was dedicated in 1922 by one of Lincoln's successors, Warren G. Harding, who, as *The New York Times* reported, appeared to take solace in describing Lincoln as "a very natural human being, with the frailties mixed with the virtues of humanity." Its reflecting pool, its colonnade of thirty-six marble pillars, its walls inscribed with Lincoln's greatest words, and its brooding statue by Daniel Chester French, make it probably the most unforgettable monument in the United States. "In this temple as in the hearts of the people for whom he saved the Union the memory of Abraham Lincoln is enshrined forever," reads the inscription above his image. A long-time ban against cameras has now been removed, and thousands of visitors now photograph each other against the background of this figure. Some, it is reported, try to climb the pedestal and seat themselves in Lincoln's lap. But this is forbidden by rule. The impulse, however, is significant.

The cult of Lincoln is by no means confined to America. Michael Pupin bore witness to the magic spell which Lincoln, along with Franklin, cast upon his boyhood in a Serbian village. Englishmen like Lord Charnwood in biography, and John Drinkwater in drama, have thrilled to his memory. And Carl Sandburg, greatest of Lincoln biographers, has lately recalled an episode in Tolstoy's life. The Russian artist while travelling in the Caucasus was the guest of a Circassian tribe. The chief gave him food and drink with royal hospitality, and then as they sat in talk of the great world beyond the horizon's rim, of Napoleon and the czars of Russia, he finally asked his guest:

But you have not told us a syllable about the greatest general and the greatest ruler of the world. We want to know something about him. He was a hero. He spoke with a voice of thunder, he laughed like the sunrise and his deeds were strong as the rock and as sweet as the fragrance of roses. The angels appeared to his mother and predicted that the son whom she would conceive would become the greatest the stars had ever seen. He was so great that he even forgave the crimes of his greatest enemies and shook brotherly hands with those who had plotted against his life. His name was Lincoln and the country in which he lived is called America, which is so far away that if a youth should journey to reach it he would be an old man when he arrived. Tell us of that man.

Deciding that "the greatness of Napoleon, Cæsar or Washington is moonlight by the sun of Lincoln," Tolstoy found that the Civil War President is the only national hero whose keynote is love. Likewise, E. W. Thompson's poem "We Talked of Lincoln," in 1909, tells of loggers, campers, adventurers—"ten fur-coat men on North Saskatchewan's plain"—who sat about a camp-fire under the Northern lights:

We talked of Abraham Lincoln in the night
Until one spoke, "We yet may see his face."
Whereon the fire crackled loud through space
Of human silence, while eyes reverent
Toward the auroral miracle were bent
Till from the trancing Glory spirits came
Within our circle round the flame,
And drew up closer-ringed, until we could
Feel the kind touch of vital brotherhood
Which Father Abraham Lincoln thought so good.

That Lincoln's matrix, the frontier, is gone forever, that the crisis which exalted him can never come again, take nothing away from Lincoln the symbol. To the folk mind his appeal is stronger than that of other heroes because on him converge so many dear traditions.

There is the log cabin theme and the pioneer boyhood, joined to the crackerbox sage. To some, he brings back the good old days when politics, Lincoln's prime intellectual interest, was the great national game, rather than baseball. He belongs also to the nationalist tradition of Old Hickory and Webster, for the Lincoln cult and Constitution worship grew together inseparably as tokens of our unity. To many,

Lincoln seems a greater democrat than Thomas Jefferson. He is the great-hearted father of his people, and of the world. His symbol is capable of almost endless interpretation—at once more flexible, more subtle, more human than that of Washington. And finally, the pattern of his life, from lowly birth and long apprenticeship to martyr's death, was fixed long ago in the tender, familiar contours of the Christ story.

"O Lincoln, come down from thy summit of bronze and march!" cried the chancellor of Lincoln Memorial University in the blackest winter of the Depression.[39] As other tragedies cast shadows, and armies once more sweep over the world, no doubt we shall have other poems like Vachel Lindsay's "Abraham Lincoln Walks at Midnight," written in the World War:

> He cannot sleep upon his hillside now.
> He is among us—as in times before!
> And we who toss and lie awake for long
> Breathe deep, and start, to see him pass the door.
>
> His head is bowed. He thinks on men and kings.
> Yea, when the sick world cries, how can he sleep?
> Too many peasants fight, they know not why;
> Too many homesteads in black terror weep. . . .
>
> He cannot rest until a spirit-dawn
> Shall come;—the shining hope of Europe free:
> The league of sober folk, the Worker's Earth,
> Bringing long peace to Cornland, Alp, and sea.

Whenever the American soul is troubled by doubt or disaster, wherever it begins to speak words of aspiration and idealism, Lincoln's memory returns like a tribal spirit. In this way heroes live forever. Just as the man himself was a reflector of the popular mind in his time, giving the image greater clarity by this reflection, so his legend has become a mirror for our national selves. When unclouded by political designs, the mirror is likely to show the best of these selves.

The Lincoln of flesh and blood, as we can guess at him, in a good many respects was not the Lincoln of lore. He was neither so solemn nor so infallible. He made mistakes, and sometimes changed his honest opinions—although such behavior is not granted to the deified hero. He inclined to be less the finished statesman and more the artist— pungent, unconventional, ironic. To his warm and sympathetic heart the legend is not untrue, although it slights a better brain than Washington and Old Hickory and Lee had, a keener political instinct than even the Roosevelts have possessed. "We never love cold intellect. We may admire it . . . but we never love it," said the Reverend John McClintock in preaching a funeral sermon on Lincoln in St. Paul's Chapel, New York. In legend, all else has been eclipsed by Lincoln's lovable traits. Out of the stuff of human nature, by the imagination of Americans and the world at large, a Lincoln has been hewn who is free from time, space, and every other limitation. Lincoln the epic, one of the finest pieces of folk poetry, thus becomes a universal.

CHAPTER ELEVEN

LEE: THE ARISTOCRAT AS HERO

Out of its scabbard! Never hand
  Waved sword from stain as free,
Nor purer sword led braver band,
Nor braver bled for a brighter land,
Nor brighter land had a cause so grand,
  Nor cause a chief like Lee!
—FATHER ABRAM J. RYAN, "The Sword of Robert E. Lee."

I

ONCE upon a time it was very desirable to be a gentleman. His outlines, as we now remember them, were etched by the Renaissance—notably in England in the sixteenth century. In those days no Oxford don would have ventured the dry joke of a Harvard professor of the last generation, to his two hundred students, "I suppose none of you young men has ever seen a gentleman." In those days, industrial science and specialization and the concepts of democracy had not appeared to unhorse the courtly ideal. To the English Renaissance the gentleman stood for the perfect man—what the philosopher was to ancient Greece, the orator and agrarian patriot to old Rome, the courtier to Castiglione's Italy, and the wit to Molière's France. The gentleman sprang from the medieval knight—not wholly losing his bravery in battle or chivalry at court, but adding talents and manners already shaping to meet the modern world. Able to fight when necessary for his country, the gentleman leaned more and more to the arts of peace. Like all prestige patterns and hero ideals, he was created by causes and for purposes which were but dimly perceived. The Tudor kings and queens, seeing how the Wars of the Roses had weakened the power of members of the old noblesse, took care to trim the spurs of these traditional game-cocks. Duels, tourneys, and the more personal appetites of blood lust were kept on a low diet. Meanwhile, a new secular education began to turn young aristocrats into literary and diplomatic careers—pen and portfolio gaining over the sword. Also, commerce and growing wealth among the middle class—exalting the Medicis, the Fuggers, the Cecils and Jacques Cœur—were blurring old marks of caste. The gentleman, with less clanking of armor, now moved easily in the halls of justice, parliament, foreign embassies, the universities, and even the counting-house. He was a compromise between the rigid fanatic ideals of chivalry and the workaday world.

Yet his tap-root was still the soil, in a chiefly agrarian order where land was the emblem of wealth and the first gesture of the parvenu was to buy an estate. And wealth, as always, meant power for a class, and culture for some individuals. In the Renaissance it was no disgrace for a gentleman to be a highbrow, at least an amateur scholar immersed in his Sabine farm. His sports, like archery and riding and hunting, arose from the soil. They were really his rehearsals for war, in an old aristocratic predilection which lingered down to the times when Thomas Jefferson wrote his young nephew: "Games played with the ball stamp no character on the mind." A man must be brave, truthful, just, and self-controlled. Beautiful manners, courtesy, and the generosity which flowered in hospitality and the liberal life, belonged to the gentleman against his background of leisure. "That gentleman that sells an Acre of Land, loseth an ounce of credite, for Gentilitie is nothing but ancient Riches," wrote Lord Burghley to his son. To be sure, one might continue to be a gentleman upon bannocks and cold water, but it was recognized that adversity to the second and third generation impoverished the soul—even as several generations of prosperity made boors into gentlemen.

Transplanted to the New World in the seventeenth century, the English gentleman found in the South his great good place. The land was fertile, the climate favored outdoor sport, the economy of tobacco and cotton raising seemed almost preordained, and soon "the saints of New England" (as William Byrd called them) helped the planters to black slaves and thus assured them a broad margin of leisure. It is untrue to say with the romantics, that Virginia was peopled by the British peerage, or with the cynics that it was settled by the jailbirds of London. Most of its later great families, like the Lees, came from rather obscure British origins. Many had followed the mercantile life. But under a new sun they bloomed into fine gentlemen, with a culture which mingled the current graces of Augustan England with the curious relic of medieval serfdom. Slavery taught the planters to command men. Surprisingly few seem to have become tyrants, while great numbers were thus trained for a leadership which they filled all the way from the Revolution to the Civil War. Many, like the ideal gentleman of the Renaissance, learned that self-discipline was the key to command of others. Thinking in terms of rule and obedience, and setting themselves to master a variety of practical arts from surveying to horsemanship, planters took easily to the military life as well.[1]

In a lull in his duties as military engineer, in 1837-38, young Robert Edward Lee studied the Lee coat of arms. Incidentally, with his sketchy West Point education, he made a mistake in Latin by rendering the motto "Non Incautus Futuri" as "Futurus." He explored a family tree which traced his descent from the Lees of Shropshire. No careful research has been able to confirm this pedigree, but to young Lee there was magic in the belief that he sprang from the blood of crusaders and plumed knights.[2] Indeed, genealogy is often more powerful as inspiration than as sober genetic fact. More vitally than most men, Lee lived in the nimbus of a great tradition. And even if his Old World origins were less glamorous than he supposed, he could take substantial pride in the Lees of Virginia. "I know of no country that can produce a family all distinguished as clever men, as the Lees," George Washington is reported to have said in 1777. The most flawless of the Lees, the hero of the Confederacy, had not yet been born. Some of these Revolutionary clansmen were all too human. William and Arthur Lee, associates of Franklin in Paris, were a contentious, scheming, time-serving pair, though undoubtedly clever. "Light-Horse Harry" Lee, Robert's father, was a brave and dashing soldier, devoted to Washington above all other loyalties. But his personal charm went hand in hand with fierce temper, gentlemanly vices, and carelessness with money which led to two imprisonments for debt and in 1813 a long farewell to Virginia. Five years later he died in bankrupt exile. By letters and precept he tried to teach his sons the self-control, prudence, and thrift which the ideal gentleman ought to possess—and which Light-Horse Harry so painfully lacked. The profession he loved best, soldiering, he even belittled in a letter written in exile to his eldest son, Carter Lee:

The rank of men, as established by the concurrent judgment of ages stands thus: heroes, legislators, orators, and poets. The most useful and, in my opinion, the most honorable is the legislator, which so far from being incompatible with the profession of law, is congenial to it. Generally, mankind admire most the hero; of all, the most useless, except when the safety of a nation demands his saving arm.[3]

Yet Light-Horse Harry, who wrote these lines, and his son Robert Lee, who edited them after the Civil War, were men whose lives emulated "the hero" of the sword. The former with sincerity also wrote: "Fame in arms or arts, however conspicuous, is naught, unless bottomed on virtue." His son, whose lifelong frugality and self-mastery showed how one might profit silently by the father's weaknesses, looked back upon Light-Horse Harry with the eyes of love and idealization. He was vastly proud of his sire. And in seeking to be worthy of him, Robert Lee surpassed his model.

Yet Robert Lee's most powerful inspiration came from George Washington. A born worshipper of great men, he found in Washington the perfect example. No illustrious American ever inspired another so deeply as Washington inspired Lee. "In the home where Robert was trained, God came first and then Washington," Douglas S. Freeman has written. The master of Mount Vernon had been the captain and idol of Lee's father. Among the Lees in Robert's boyhood the memory of Washington was no "steel engraving," no cloudy abstraction of a Gilbert Stuart face, no mere sentimental perversion of Weems. His footprints had not yet faded from the soil of the Republic, and hundreds of Virginians were alive who had seen the Commander plain. To Lee, he was as real as an ideal can ever be. And as the years passed Lee's own temperament and behavior and ways of thought blended with those of his hero. He came to resemble him, as men do who live long with an ideal. Lee's personal modesty saved him from too much self-awareness of this parallel; others saw it with greater clearness than the man himself. As a boy at the Alexandria academy and at West Point—where straitened family finances had conspired to send him—Lee developed a passion for perfection which was not unlike the mainspring of Washington's life. He loved the precision of mathematics, map-making, engineering, logistics, the strategy of the field. In doing his best, in "finishing up," as his old tutor called it, Lee took an almost æsthetic delight. System came naturally to him, as it did to Washington, for Lee too had a practical, simple, objective nature. He saw life in terms of action rather than thought, of space rather than depth, of outline rather than nuance. Yet microscopic routine bored him, as it did Washington; both needed good lieutenants.

Like Washington, Lee was a product of plantation aristocracy. He swam and danced, and even at the age of forty was able to compete in high jumps with his sons. His large muscular hands were expert in the manège of horses. He was an early riser—in this habit falling into the pattern approved for the Renaissance gentleman, who had looked upon much sleep as a waste of time, as Sir Thomas More said, "wherein almost half the lifetime of man creepeth away."[4] (In urban society, beginning apparently about the time of Queen Anne and continuing to the present day, sleeping late was regarded as an aristocratic privilege.) In common with the ideal gentleman Lee was no epicure for his palate's sake, though he wished to share good food and drink with others. But like Washington he could bear the hard military life —even as he bore all discomforts and disappointments—without complaint. Sometimes he slept on the ground when house and bed were near. "General Lee was never so uncomfortable as when he was comfortable," observed General Richard Taylor. Both prized the luxury of handsome, smart, well-tailored clothes and immaculate linen. "Cleanliness of person is not only comely to all beholders, but is indispensable to sanctity of body," Light-Horse Harry had written in his precepts. It was the mark of personal morale, of an inner fastidiousness. Even in West Point days Lee came to be called the "Marble Model," with something of the erect commanding dignity which had stamped Washington. Years and new responsibilities in the public eye, as well as disciplines of camp and field, heightened that dignity in both. Sometimes the marmoreal quality came to seem a little chilling. In social life both cultivated a touch of playfulness toward the ladies which belonged to the cavalier tradition, but their jokes were dull. The old-fashioned gentleman was not expected to be a wit. Even Chesterfield, "a wit among lords," a man who wrote about the gentlemanly ideal without ever quite attaining it himself, advised his son: "I could heartily wish that you may often be seen to smile, but never heard to laugh while you live." Laughter, it was said, distorts the face and also ruffles an inward decorum.[5] Lee the precisian had minor lapses—in youth when he gaily risked a military reprimand by "riding double" with a fellow officer down Pennsylvania Avenue in Washington, in the family circle when he loved to have the soles of his feet tickled, in old age when he failed to keep step in academic parades at Lexington as if to disavow all military ways—and in daily life was less ponderous than Washington. But nobody ever slapped his back, and his most familiarly affectionate nickname was "Marse Robert."

Lee resembled Washington in being almost primitive in his simplicity—direct, forthright, sometimes disconcertingly frank. Neither shared Lincoln's literary gifts of artistry. "I never did like adjectives," Lee once remarked to Alexander Stuart. Like most military men Lee could draw up a factual statement with clarity and force, but memorable phrases play little part in the Lee legend. The words most often quoted from him, which are inscribed beneath his bust in the Hall of Fame, are: "Duty is the sublimest word in our language. Do your duty in all things. You cannot do more. You should never wish to do less." Although the sentiment is true enough, no such sententious words were ever written or spoken by Lee. They are supposed to occur in a letter to his son Custis, but are really a "steal" from Immanuel Kant. It seems probable that some young officer in the Union Army whiled away an idle hour by forging them in the Lee papers, captured among the spoils of Arlington. As long ago as 1914 Doctor Charles A. Graves exploded this myth, and now the sponsors of the Hall of Fame are beginning to think of changing their inscription.[6] If Lee stands in sharp contrast to Lincoln the phrase-maker, he is also alien to Lincoln the secretive politician. The difference here is very similar to that which lies between Washington and Franklin. "Sincerity marks the aristocrat, and secretiveness the plebeian, simply because force—which need not be secretive—is the traditional weapon of the lord, and cunning—which must be secretive—is the traditional weapon of the peasant," Havelock Ellis has remarked.[7] Lee's instinct and training taught him to command men, more gently perhaps than did Washington; but neither learned the arts of indirect persuasion or expediency so typical of Franklin, Lincoln, and most self-made statesmen. Among the random jottings found in Lee's field valise after his death was this note:

Private and public life are subject to the same rules; and truth and manliness are two qualities that will carry you through this world much better than *policy*, or *tact*, or *expediency*, or any other word that was ever devised to conceal or mystify a deviation from a straight line.[8]

It is significant, also, that Lee shared Washington's Federalist bias and in the later alignment of parties followed the Whigs rather than the Democrats. His class and sectional prejudices were never expressed so bitingly as those of Robert Toombs of Georgia, on the eve of Civil War: "We are the gentlemen of this country." But for all his personal modesty, Lee was undoubtedly proud of being a Virginia gentleman. Such politics as he had were those of *noblesse oblige*.

Lee's marriage in 1831 to Mary Anne Randolph Custis, great-grand-daughter of Martha Washington, in the public eye made him the heir of the First Patriot's family. With his bride he settled at Arlington, a Washington shrine second only to Mount Vernon. For here were the family portraits, the lantern from the hall of Mount Vernon, the china presented by the Cincinnati, the bookcase and clothes and camp equipment of General Washington, and the bed upon which he had died. Lee's father-in-law, George Washington Parke Custis, "the child of Mount Vernon," was a living storehouse of Washington anecdote and hero-worship. Even on the verge of the Civil War, in January, 1861, Lee was absorbed for some days in the newest book about Washington, Edward Everett's mediocre biography. It is little wonder, then, that Lee's being was filled by the elixir he drank so eagerly. In one respect, at least, Lee himself came closer to the legendary Washington than did Washington the man. This was his deep spirituality. Whatever its significance, one may note that Lee's lifelong friend and religious counsellor was Bishop William Meade, the source of much true and false information about General Washington's piety. Certainly Lee's private devotions, morning and evening, throughout the campaigns of the Civil War, and his keen interest in the spiritual welfare of his soldiers, suggest the mythical Washington upon his knees at Valley Forge rather than the non-committal Washington of fact. Lee's concept of the gentleman was bound up with that of the Christian. The terms to him grew almost interchangeable, because the essence of each was duty.

Lee's devotion to duty was, indeed, the great lesson he drew from the worship of Washington. From a sense of high duty Washington had forsaken comfort and safety to lead a great rebellion. Similarly, Lee with no love for slavery or the theory of secession, felt that Virginia claimed his ultimate loyalty. Against the soil of Mount Vernon and Arlington he could not lift his sword. He did not hold with Lincoln that the majority should rule, but saw minorities have rights to be respected—as Calhoun claimed, and as Woodrow Wilson re-echoed in the day of "self-determination." Appearing before the Virginia Convention on April 23, 1861, to take command of the armed forces of that state, he was seen to look up at Houdon's shining statue of Washington as he entered the rotunda. And the president of the Convention, in charging Lee with his commission on this day, compared him to that earlier patriot of Westmoreland County—ready to draw his sword not in aggression but in defense of his native land, now "first in war" and later to become, in the fullness of Henry Lee's phrase, "first in peace, and first in the hearts of his countrymen."[9] Robert E. Lee thus made his choice, in the belief that Washington would have done the same. And having set his hand to the plow Lee never looked back. He prayed for victory, but when God willed defeat he was content. He had done his best, and with neither regret nor tears Lee accepted the result. After he had gone to Lexington to take up the presidency of an impoverished little college which bore the magic name of Washington, he wrote in October, 1865, to his old comrade-in-arms, Beauregard. Though usually reluctant to rake over the embers of the war, Lee here recalled that George Washington had once fought for his king, and then revolted against him: "He has not been branded by the world with reproach for this; but his course has been applauded." Lee had lately been threatened by Judge Underwood with criminal proceedings on a charge of treason, but with calmness he knew that no man who had followed duty as he saw it, as Washington might have seen it, would go down to history as a traitor. Three years later he wrote to Wade Hampton: "I did only what my duty demanded. I could have taken no other course without dishonor. And if it all were to be done over again, I should act in precisely the same manner."[10]

Lee's inner serenity and discipline made him resemble Washington in other ways. There was his superb self-control over a high-strung nervous system. "I cannot trust a man to control others who cannot control himself," Lee said in picking his military staff. In irritation his neck would redden and a few icy words might escape him, but Old Hickory's rage and bluster were foreign to his nature. If he had been unfair, Lee was quick and generous with amends. Only on the rarest occasions—as when in the tension of the engagement at Sharpsburg he ordered a straggler shot for finding and killing a pig, and Stonewall Jackson had to override the sentence—did he forget himself a little absurdly. Washington's sparing but magnificent gift for profanity might have been a healthy safety-valve for a temper such as Lee's. Emotion he seldom showed. "Coolness and absence of heat indicate fine qualities. A gentleman makes no noise: a lady is serene," Emerson wrote, in words which Lee might have endorsed. His suavity, his gentleness, proved to be the chief defect of Lee the soldier. Up to the Civil War, as Freeman has pointed out, Lee's chief contact had been with gentle people, who like Lee himself responded quickly to the rein of *noblesse.* "The forbearing use of power . . . is a test of a true gentleman," Lee had once scribbled in his memoranda. But in the war he had to deal with the surly, the jealous, the incompetent—men like Longstreet, Ewell, and Pickett in some moods, not to mention President Jefferson Davis—and Lee's detestation of squabbles led him to yield too much. After several failures, of which Gettysburg was the most costly, Lee developed a certain tough-mindedness which had come more easily to Washington. It is perhaps curious that Lee and Lincoln, greatest leaders of our bloodiest war, had to overcome the same weakness—a besetting amiability. Plainly, neither was cut out to be a dictator. Yet Lincoln became the dictator of the North; and late in the war it was proposed that Lee, who up to February, 1865, had not even had supreme military command, be made the Southern dictator.

Self-denial was also a part of Lee's character. It shows most simply in his refusal to use such stimulants as tobacco and whiskey. From the Mexican War, in which he had sustained a wound and immense fatigue, he came back with an unopened bottle of spirits which a friend had put into his knapsack. In the Civil War Lee's serving of buttermilk to the staff officers became something of a joke. His counsels of abstinence to his students at Lexington have been used time and again as propaganda by the W. C. T. U. But tolerance for others, by the light of the gentlemanly code, saved him from priggishness. He believed in the spiritual value of asceticism. "Teach him he must deny himself," he told a mother who brought her infant son for his blessing, in the last year of Lee's life when he was the patriarch and oracle of the shattered South. It was a philosophy which had prepared Lee for his destiny, as the symbol of graciousness in defeat, of "the good loser" dear to American traditions. Lee had learned to do without many things. His youth of threadbare aristocracy, his manhood of hard work and tediously slow promotion, an invalid wife who had succeeded an invalid mother in evoking all Lee's tender care, the death of a beloved daughter, the privations of many a hard campaign—these things had schooled him for Appomattox. Washington took the highroad to glory through victory; Lee's destiny sent him upon the shaded path of disappointment.

Upon others, Lee invariably left the impression of a great gentleman. To take a few out of many examples: Lieutenant Henry J. Hunt, who knew him well at Fort Hamilton when Lee was in his thirties, thought him "as fine-looking a man as one would wish to see, of perfect figure and strikingly handsome. Quiet and dignified in manner, of cheerful disposition, always pleasant and considerate, he seemed to me the perfect type of a gentleman." Charles Anderson, a Unionist who had seen Lee in Texas just before the Civil War, wrote:

And of all the officers or men whom I ever knew, he came (save one other alone) the nearest in likeness to that classical ideal, Chevalier Bayard. . . . And if these our modern, commercial, mechanical, utilitarian ages ever did develop a few of these types of male chivalric virtues which we attribute solely to those "ages of faith," Robert E. Lee was one of the highest and finest models.

In April, 1861, when Lee travelled to Richmond to take command, with crowds calling for him at every stop of the train, a fellow passenger thought him "the noblest-looking man I had ever gazed upon." To British military officers observing the Civil War, Lee was the most memorable man they met. "General Lee is, almost without exception, the handsomest man of his age I ever saw," wrote Colonel A. S. L. Fremantle, ". . . his manners are most courteous and full of dignity. He is a perfect gentleman in every respect. . . . He has none of the small vices, such as smoking, drinking, chewing or swearing, and his bitterest enemy never accused him of any of the greater ones." Lord Wolseley, the famous commander who as a young man of twenty-nine had visited Virginia in 1862, replied years later to a Southern woman who had sent him an autograph of Lee: "I have only known two heroes in my life, and General R. E. Lee is one of them. . . . I believe that when time has calmed down the angry passions of the 'North,' General Lee will be accepted in the United States as the greatest general you have ever had, and as a patriot second only to Washington."[11]

Lee the gentleman appeared on the stage of Southern history to redeem from bravado and flimsy sentimentalism the ideal of "chivalry" which had been created in the ante-bellum South. A generation which flourished between 1820 and 1850, reading the Old World romances of Scott and the New World novels of William Gilmore Simms, had sought to justify itself by this ideal. The anodyne of magnolias and moonlight, and the fragile minority culture of tidewater Virginia and South Carolina—never very robust or productive—had been used as an apologia for the whole South. Its none-too-solid economy and its "peculiar institution" of slavery were thus set in romantic contrast to the North and West. This flight from reality took several roads. Some built a neo-scholasticism of economic and political logic upon Dew and Fitzhugh and Calhoun. Others created a dream-literature—Edgar Allan Poe, Edward Coote Pinkney, Thomas Holley Chivers, Henry Timrod, and a little later Sidney Lanier—which, beside the flowers blooming in New England, resembled some exotic grown in the shade. Still others cultivated Corinthian rhetoric in the halls of Congress, or the art of paying compliments to the fair. Early in the century the duel flourished, later giving way to bloodless tournaments where horsemen rode at the ring and carried ladies' colors on their sleeve. It was a charming, naïve, theatrical world which might have grown patently ridiculous. But the Civil War taught it heroism, suffering, and patience. And, as the genius it evoked, stood Robert E. Lee the cavalier, the brilliant soldier, the Christian gentleman. He contrived to make its chivalry suddenly real and sincere. Better than any other great American he satisfied all requisites, as "the president of noblesse and of chivalree." Washington, by the most fastidious standards, was a slightly second-class Virginia gentleman; many Virginians of his day remembered that prior to the Revolution the Washingtons were hardly more than satellites to the Fairfaxes. Jefferson's heredity, like his opinions, mingled aristocracy with democracy. Andrew Jackson in the strict sense was no gentleman at all. But Lee had more generations of gentle breeding at his back than even Washington, and less competition from colonial English families. And he was a pure type, lacking the disturbing intellectual overtones of Jefferson, the personal aggressiveness of Old Hickory. Although a soldier, he represented essentially the moral ideal of which Emerson had written in Yankee New England:

It is a vulgar error to suppose that a gentleman must be ready to fight. The utmost that can be demanded of him is that he be incapable of a lie. . . . You may spit upon him;—nothing could induce him to spit upon you,— no praises, and no possessions, no compulsion of public opinion. You may kick him;—he will think it the kick of a brute: but he is not a brute, and he will not kick you in return. But neither your knife and pistol, nor your gifts and courting will ever make the smallest impression on his vote or word; for he is the truth's man, and will speak and act the truth till he dies.[12]

Lee the gentleman was no fire-eater. His appeal was deeper and broader, and in time even the North came to show interest and finally to adopt him. As for the South, he was the last and most perfect flower of that culture—which reclaimed her chivalry from bombast, and made into poetry the fact of her defeat. The South lost the war, but she still had Robert E. Lee.

II

The folklore of Lee is far scantier than that of Lincoln. The explanation no doubt is simple. In Lee's youth there was no obscure chapter, seen through the haze of backwoods epic-building, illiteracy, and superstition, or revised by the mythologists of "success." The main facts were clear and verifiable. From the utilitarian point of view—that of the success-story writers, who belonged mainly to the industrial North —Lee was a man who began in the lap of luxury and ended in failure. The stuff of Virginia plantation boyhood had already been quarried by Weems, and in post-bellum years the public-at-large, the Northern and Western majority in particular, was more eager to hear of log cabins. The mature Lee was a far simpler personality than Lincoln, with vastly fewer lights and shades, paradoxes and frustrations. His decision to fight against the Union, and certain debatable points of field strategy, are about the only acts of his life which stir excited discussion. And although he has been called "traitor" many times—the echoes dying away down the years—unlike Lincoln he has attracted neither psychoanalysts nor cynics. Lee's life as a whole, therefore, offers little soil for the growth of myth, speculation, invention.

The one persistent rumor runs that Lee's mother, Anne Carter Lee, was once buried prematurely. A slave, passing the burial plot, heard cries or sounds of knocking coming from the new-made grave. Overcoming his terror he began to dig, and soon brought her living from the coffin. This story has been told again and again. Early in 1939 it was repeated by *The New York American* and by Ripley's "Believe It or Not." Douglas S. Freeman, dean of Lee experts and author of the four-volume biography published in 1935 after a labor of nineteen years, calls it "preposterous." Neither family records nor newspapers of the time contain the slightest hint of it. It appears to have been started by a half-illiterate old man in Kentucky, who claimed but could not prove his kinship with the Lees. To those who love Poe's *Fall of the House of Usher* and other thrillers, the yarn has its fascination. (Shortly before the Civil War, an inventor filed at the United States Patent Office designs for a coffin containing a lunch box and flask of spirits, and a bell-rope which communicated with an alarm signal above the grave.) The second edition of Tebb, Vollum, and Hadwen's book *Premature Burial* (1905) told the Kentuckian's story about Mrs. Lee. Even today, Doctor Freeman tells the writer, he receives some fifty letters a year inquiring about the myth. As editor of *The Richmond News Leader,* Doctor Freeman does his bit for truth by printing what he calls "a biennial editorial" stating the facts.[13]

Mention of Lee's mother recalls that he, in the tradition of great Americans, used to say that he "owed everything" to her.[14] Genetically, women of the Carter strain seem to justify the devotion of their sons. It is curious that males who bore the Carter name seldom amounted to much in public life or by individual brilliance, whereas women who crossed the Carter stock with other clans—Randolph, Harrison, Braxton, Lee—bore famous sons.[15] On the other hand, it might be noted that Robert Lee's half-brother, "Black Harry" Lee—whose mother was no Carter but a Lee—appeared to have inherited in double measure the reckless prodigality of some of the elder Lees. He was the black sheep of the family, the silent disgrace of Robert Lee's life. He went bankrupt after deep financial involvements, lost possession of the Lee birthplace "Stratford," and the scandal of his adultery with his wife's sister became so public that the Senate refused to confirm his appointment to Morocco. He died in Italy, in shabby exile. These two Henry Lees, the wastrel father and the debauched half-brother of Robert E. Lee, certainly helped to confirm their kinsman in his disciplined, frugal ways, as well as his devotion to duty.

Lee's rise to herohood was almost as slow as Lincoln's, though the distance traversed along economic and social paths was not so great. At West Point, Lee graduated as No. 2 in his class, outranked by a Charles Mason unknown to fame. In neatness and aptitude for military studies Lee was a model cadet—unlike such successors as slovenly Ulysses S. Grant, who stood near the middle of his class, or boisterous George A. Custer, who graduated at the foot of a class of thirty-four. Lee loved the profession of arms; although in old age, with all his campaigns behind him, he began to wonder whether becoming a soldier were not the greatest mistake of his life. He served a long apprenticeship to hard work—clearing the channel of the Mississippi near St. Louis, repairing various forts, spending many months in dull barracks away from his wife and children. At the outbreak of the Mexican War, twenty-one years after his entry into West Point, Lee was still living on a captain's pay and had never smelled gunpowder. In that war, Lee won his spurs. His two trips in one night across the great field of broken lava before Churubusco were called by General Scott "the greatest feat of physical and moral courage performed by any individual, in my knowledge, pending the campaign."[16] Scott said Lee was the best soldier he had ever seen in action—and when there was talk of war between the United States and England, Scott remarked that this country might well insure the life of its most valuable officer for $5,000,000. But Lee the soldier was little known in Virginia. In his own bailiwick of Alexandria the politicians had to write to Washington to get his correct title and military record in Mexico, in order that Virginia might vote him an award. Gradually, however, his new fame spread to civilian circles. Cuban revolutionists in 1849 offered him the chance to become "the Washington of Cuban liberty," but Lee feeling that his duties lay nearer home declined.

In 1852 he became superintendent of West Point. The Military Academy drew its cadets largely from the South—despite the system of congressional distribution of appointments, and the fact that the South had her own academies in the Virginia Military Institute and the Citadel at Charleston.[17] The explanation, again, is bound up with the cavalier ideal of the South, as well as the incidental family tradition that younger sons should shift for themselves. Emerson noted in his journal for August 9, 1837: "The Southerner asks concerning any man, 'How does he fight?' The Northerner asks, 'What can he do?' " Upon the outbreak of the Civil War, the South had the cream of the military talent—and not until two or three years had passed, and war became the business of the North, did the tide of success turn and numerical strength begin to pull its weight.

At West Point Lee did his scrupulous best, as always, but with relief transferred from staff to line in 1855. Four years later he put down John Brown's insurrection at Harpers Ferry. It was all in the day's work. Lee himself, though a slave-owner, had no love of slavery as an institution. If he had had the power, he would readily have given up all the slaves in the South to save the Union.[18] To the end of his life Lee felt that tact and forbearance on both sides would have prevented the Civil War. "I must say that I am one of those dull creatures that cannot see the good of secession," he remarked to a druggist in Alexandria on April 19, 1861, upon hearing the news that Virginia had withdrawn from the Union.[19] The druggist jotted down these words in his account book, opposite the entry of Lee's payment of his bill. President Lincoln was ready to offer Lee, at General Scott's recommendation, the command of a large Federal army to put down the rebellion. The house in which this suggestion was made, by the intermediacy of Francis P. Blair, is now one of the minor shrines of Washington. But Lee had reached a different decision. Convinced that his first duty was to Virginia, he resigned his Federal commission. A few days later, hailed by his fellow citizens as the first soldier of the Old Dominion, Lee accepted the command of the Army of Northern Virginia.

But once the war had begun, Lee, like Abraham Lincoln, was slow in getting under way. His caution earned him the derisive nickname of "Granny Lee," and his passion for fortification-building led many to sneer at the one-time engineer as "the King of Spades." Reluctance to sacrifice human life was set down as Lee's weakness. "General Jackson's two maxims, 'to fight whenever it is possible,' and in fighting, to 'attack at once and furiously,' are worth all the ditches and spades that General Lee can display on the side of the Chickahominy," impatiently said *The Richmond Examiner* on June 17, 1862, thinking no doubt of Lee's failures at Cheat Mountain, Sewell Mountain, and Mechanicsville.

Stonewall Jackson, not Lee, was the great hero of the early Civil War to the South. His brilliance and audacity in attack had never been seen before on an American battlefield. Even more than Lee and "Jeb" Stuart, he was a praying man—in striking contrast to Sherman, Grant, Lincoln, and the generality of Northern leaders, who had no orthodox piety. From the soil of the South, land of camp meetings and revivals and neo-Puritanism, Jackson sprang. Those who disliked him called him "the Blue Light Elder"—after all a term less biting than "Fool Tom Jackson," as his cadets at V. M. I. had nicknamed this gaunt, angular, awkward man with his burning intensities. He was no surer than Lee about the wisdom of the war. But once it was begun, he discovered that he had been born for such a life. The rebel yell he called "the grandest music I ever heard." His Old Testament was always in his pocket. In its pages he found the models for his official reports. "Look, for instance, at the narrative of Joshua's battle with the Amalekites; there you have one," he would say. "It has clearness, brevity, fairness, modesty; and it traces the victory to its right source, the blessing of God."[20] Whenever Jackson washed himself, he thought of the cleansing Blood of the Lamb; in eating, he meditated upon the Bread of Heaven. But in battle he could issue such a crisp order as "Tell General Ewell to sweep the field with the bayonet," and could expose himself to withering fire, knowing that God's will would be done. Predestination made him incredibly reckless. If not the Puritan contrast to Lee the cavalier, Jackson was at least the covenanter. He was hardly aware that he was stealing the limelight from Lee, whom he adored and obeyed with the scrupulous devotion he expected from his own subalterns. "I have never seen such a fine-looking human creature," said Jackson on his first glimpse of Lee. When they learned their perfect collaboration—Lee planning, Jackson executing—the tide of Lee's success set in. After the battle of the Seven Days, Jackson said of his chief: "So great is my confidence in General Lee that I am willing to follow him blindfolded."

In May, 1863, at Chancellorsville, Lee and Jackson together reached the zenith of their military careers. Lee had planned this superb victory, of 57,000 Confederates over 97,000 Federals. As he rode toward the Chancellor House, through the ragged patches of battle smoke, Lee's men caught sight of him. A staff officer described the scene: "One long unbroken cheer, in which the feeble cry of those who lay helpless on the earth, blended with the strong voices of those who still fought, rose high above the roar of battle, and hailed the presence of the victorious chief. He sat in the full realization of all that soldiers dream of—triumph; and as I looked upon him, in the complete fruition of the success which his genius, courage, and confidence in his army had won, I thought that it must have been from such a scene that men in ancient times rose to the dignity of gods."[21] This was the apotheosis of Lee the soldier; that of Lee the man would come after Appomattox. But even in that hour of triumph Lee was handed a note fraught with disaster. It was from Jackson, tersely reporting he had been wounded. Lee dictated a reply: "Could I have directed events, I would have chosen for the good of the country to be disabled in your stead," and added that the victory belonged to Jackson. A few days later Jackson sank into the clutches of pneumonia, while Lee in his tent "wrestled in prayer for him . . . as I never prayed, I believe, for myself." Through the delirium of death Jackson murmured, "Let us pass over the river, and rest under the shade of the trees." Like Lincoln two years hence, Jackson died in the high noon of victory. He left behind the memory of a fearless soldier, whose brilliant Shenandoah Valley campaign is still known in its minutiæ to every Virginian who belongs to the R. O. T. C. Jackson was and is a soldier's hero. His cult is more special than that of Lee. And although he was a poor farm boy who made himself famous, he never received homage from the Horatio Algers of the North.

Among the living, Lee was now left to his lonely eminence. A few campaigns had made him the father of his men, the ideal warrior "that every man in arms should wish to be." Soldiers began to tell around their camp-fires stories of his kindness, simplicity, and goodness—what Doctor Freeman, borrowing Napoleon's phrase, has called the *causerie de bivouac* so needful to an army's morale. First of all, they believed he was the best general on either side in the Civil War. This judgment posterity has confirmed. Lee made some mistakes: sometimes he expected too much of his ill-trained and poorly equipped soldiers, or left too much to his generals of brigade and division. The disaster of Gettysburg, for example, is an endless debate. At the time, with usual magnanimity, Lee had said, "It's all my fault; I thought my men were invincible." Later he averred that if Jackson had been alive, Gettysburg would have been won. Whether Lee should have followed Longstreet's advice, in favor of a turning movement to get between the enemy and Washington, is a moot point. Colonel William Mitchell, editor of *The Military Engineer,* tells the writer that later generations of West Pointers in playing military games have followed Longstreet's plan and won the battle for the South. (West Point still regards Lee as her most brilliant soldier, although one of her graduates has lately called him "the most dangerous man that the United States ever produced"—in that his superb generalship prolonged the agony of the Civil War at least a year and a half beyond its rightful term.) But after all controversies have talked themselves out, Lee's military genius remains beyond question. His mistakes were fewer and less costly than those of any Union general. Like Lincoln, Lee had a first-class brain, and taught himself as he went along—adjusting, discarding, revising with fluent improvisation throughout the war. He too was an artist, in a different medium. Beside Lee and his finesse of swordwork, Grant was a butcher with a meat-cleaver. John Esten Cooke expressed something of the idea in his novel of 1871, called *Hammer and Rapier.* Lee's later campaigns, like those of Napoleon's, are classics of audacity. But they show a greater economy of life, indulging no such "heroic" gestures as the charge of the Old Guard at Waterloo. At Fredericksburg in 1862, watching the magnificent countercharge of the Confederates, Lee's eyes flashed, as he saved himself from a Napoleonic mood with the famous remark to Longstreet: "It is well that war is so terrible—we should grow too fond of it!" A British journalist, Francis Lawley, who overheard those words, described Lee at that moment as having about him an "antique heroism." Lee's campaigns, as is well known, have been studied by the best military minds of the United States, England, and Germany. The late Von Hindenburg knew them all by heart.

And unlike the Napoleon legend, the Lee legend did not stop with genius. While *The Boston Transcript* was regaling its readers with the fable that Lee had once flogged a Negro girl and poured brine into her wounds, his men were telling stories of his humanity. A few were almost as sentimental as the Springfield stories of Lincoln—one for example recounting how under hot shell-fire Lee had stepped out in the open to pick up a tiny sparrow and place it back upon the nest. Another told how he had stopped on the road, in his invasion of Pennsylvania, to put up the bars of a pasture gate that some careless soldier had left down. He rebuked a courier who sat on his panting horse after delivering a dispatch, and to make amends reached into the saddlebag on the back of his own immaculate mount Traveller and presented the weary horse with half a buttered biscuit. Like Lincoln, Lee seldom called his opponents "the enemy," but almost invariably referred to them as "those people"—adding on one occasion that he "wished they were all at home attending to their own business, and leaving us to do the same." At one rare juncture he lost patience with them, when the Federals began to fire into some buildings occupied by women and children. "These people delight to destroy the weak and those who can make no defense; it just suits them!" he exclaimed bitterly. On the eve of the Second Battle of Manassas a matron and her daughters came out in their family carriage to get sight of General Lee; they arrived too early, and their span of bay horses was captured by the Federals. Hearing the story when he came up, Lee called upon the matron to pay his civilities and express regrets. She was so charmed that she ceased to mourn her loss. If one could still be a cavalier in the thick of battle, that man was General Lee. His devotion to children was famous. Many were brought to see him in camp. But he reproved a five-year-old whose father had coached him to say, "General Lee is going to whip General Scott out of his breeches"—then, to make it up to the youngster, Lee rode him upon his horse and gave him a copy of G. W. P. Custis's *Recollections of General Washington.*

Most revealing of all were Lee's relations with his soldiers. Even as with Abraham Lincoln, the patriarchal role descended early upon Robert E. Lee. "I begin in my old age to feel a little curiosity relative to my forefathers," he had written at the age of thirty-one to a kinsman. And early in the Civil War, in the year 1861, Lee too grew a beard of gray and grizzled aspect, which added to his dignity of command. His men proudly called themselves "Lee's army," and as they grew more ragged and lean, punsters described them as "Lee's Miserables." In appearance and behavior they may have fallen short of the abstract model soldier. They carried frying-pans tied to their waists, and a Maryland boy who watched them pass in September, 1862, noted "they were profane beyond belief and talked incessantly." But he added that they rode like circus riders, and had a dash that the Northern soldiers lacked. And they could fight. Lee himself believed there was never such another army as that of Northern Virginia, while his men believed the same of their general. On the road to North Anna, in May, 1864, when Lee warned some stragglers to move on and avoid capture, they answered: "Yes, Marse Robert, we'll move on and go anywhere you say, even to hell!"

Lee and his men practiced mutual consideration. A noisy column moving along a Hanover road fell silent when they saw Lee resting under a tree, as if asleep. Similarly, Lee on the march to Frederick came upon some of A. P. Hill's troops lying prone in the road, waiting their turn to march; saying "Lie still, men," he rode around them. When he saw men drinking from a spring where the horses were watered, he insisted that they use another spring near his quarters. During one of the battles of the Seven Days he moved his headquarters in order to give place to the wounded. On a train nearing Richmond, Lee saw a crippled soldier struggling to get into his overcoat; when no one else got up to help him, Lee quietly did so. At Gettysburg he gave his handkerchief to a private who asked for "a rag or something to wipe the sweat out of my eyes." But when a North Carolina infantryman once requested from Lee a chew of tobacco, the General had to refer him to a staff officer who had the habit. If these seem trivial episodes, one must remember how often they were retold around camp-fires and after the war, how they added their part to the Lee legend as polyps build a coral island. Doctor Freeman tells the writer of a Confederate veteran—a lieutenant in Pegram's Battalion—who related in his hearing scores of times, and always with moist eyes, the story of a dispatch he had carried to Lee, and the grave courtesy with which the General said, "Lieutenant, may I give you a glass of water?"

By reason of this tender rapport between commander and men, Lee is a greater legendary hero than the stern Stonewall Jackson, the brusque Sherman, the stolid Grant who sacrificed his hecatombs at

Cold Harbor. Again, the only true analogy with Lee is Lincoln. The story of the sleeping sentinel had its Southern parallel. A private deserted the ranks to go home, after getting a distressful letter from his wife; he was arrested and sentenced to be shot. Lee pardoned him. And tradition said that the man later fell bravely in action, the last survivor at his gun.[22] This final detail cannot be proved, but the popularity of the story is significant. It reveals that Lee, like Lincoln, became a symbol of clemency softening the horror of war. To the General, military discipline was more important than to the Union President; it is probable that sentiment has tended to exaggerate the gentleness of Lee. In the main, he regretted "the sad necessity" of shooting deserters, but agreed to that punishment—and saw it meted out more and more often, from the autumn of 1864 to the end of the war. Yet Lee did believe in giving deserters the benefit of the doubt, and once got up at two A.M. to intervene with President Davis because it had just occurred to Lee that a German deserter might not have understood the published orders. Also, in the early spring of 1865, sensing the imminent close of the war, Lee held up indefinitely the execution of Federal spies.

Lee's men tried repeatedly to keep their commander from exposing himself to danger. There are at least four reasonably trustworthy incidents about "Lee to the rear"—when whole companies cried for him to go back, or when men interposed themselves between him and the thickest fire.[23] Such an episode in the battle of the Wilderness has been commemorated in painting, and in John Reuben Thompson's poem "Lee to the Rear":

> "We'll go forward, but you must go back"—
> And they moved not an inch in the perilous track;
> "Go to the rear, and we'll send them to hell!"
> And the sound of the battle was lost in their yell.

Lee, on the other hand, had a sense of humor keen enough to enjoy the reply of a black camp-follower, whom Lee had complimented on his ability to survive all perils: "Why, General, I ain't been shot 'case I stays back whar de generals stay." Lee, who was a born fighter and fought with an audacity born of desperation, seems to have taken far greater personal chances than Grant, for example. And the chivalry of legend has appreciated this fact.

In the dark winter of 1863–64 a man in the ranks wrote to Lee asking whether he knew of the privations—in food, clothing, shelter—

which the army was suffering; if Lee were aware of their plight, the writer said, his soldiers would be content, in the knowledge that there must be good reason for such sacrifices. Lee wrote no answer, but the next day he issued an order explaining the situation, and asking his troops to bear up as bravely as their forefathers had done in the Revolution.[24] Appomattox came, undoubtedly, when Lee saw that further sacrifices would be futile. After the last disastrous battle of Sailor's Creek, in April, 1865, Lee told General Henry A. Wise that he was loath to give up because of what the country might think. Wise replied:

You are the country to these men. They have fought for you. They have shivered through a long winter for you. Without pay or clothes, or care of any sort, their devotion to you and faith in you have been the only things which have held this army together. If you demand the sacrifice, there are still left thousands of us who will die for you. You know the game is desperate beyond redemption, and that, if you so announce, no man or government or people will gainsay your decision. That is why I repeat that the blood of any man killed hereafter is upon your head.[25]

With kindred thoughts in his own mind, Lee made his last military decision.

Folklore has taken some liberties with Appomattox. The best-known myth says that Lee tendered Grant his sword, and that Grant returned it gallantly to him. Both Lee and Grant denied the story. By the terms of surrrender, "officers' side arms" were exempt, and this touch of theatre would have been as superfluous as it was untrue. General Lee, ever immaculate, did wear his best uniform and his best sword on that occasion, but the sword had no hilt "studded with jewels," as alleged by fable.[26] Grant's terms, however, were generous enough, in permitting Confederate soldiers to take home their horses and mules for spring plowing, and in offering them rations from the Union supply. If Grant the President had been as magnanimous as Grant the victor of Appomattox, the spirit of Reconstruction might have been very different.

Lee's favorite quotation from Marcus Aurelius seems to have been, "Misfortune nobly borne is good fortune." To his men Lee never seemed more glorious than in defeat. Some, incredulous, had at first crowded around him and Traveller, asking for news or crying, "General, we'll fight 'em yet!" Many tried to touch Lee's uniform or bridle rein, or pat Traveller's flank for a last farewell. As Lee and his sometime enemy Meade rode together toward Confederate headquarters, the soldiers in gray began to cheer. Meade said to his color-bearer, "Unfurl that flag." At sight of the stars and stripes, a gaunt soldier exclaimed: "Damn your old rag! We are cheering General Lee." Sobs mingled with tears, and Lee's eyes were not dry as he rode slowly along. One man, stretching out his arms to the passing figure, cried, "I love you just as well as ever, General Lee!" To others it seemed like the end of the world. Pietists called the loss of the Civil War "a temporary interruption of the workings of Providence." In the South—to the second and third generation, as the writer can testify, from a boyhood spent in the house of a Confederate grandfather—the impression remained that General Lee and his army had finally just worn themselves out in whipping the Yankees. South of the Mason and Dixon Line, a mournful pride was long taken in the odds, of more than five to one, under which Lee surrendered. With a touch of exaggeration, the bronze plaque now at Appomattox states that "Lee surrendered 9000 men, the remnant of an army still unconquered in spirit, to 118,000 men under Grant."

III

As the gunfire ceased, and the smoke of battle drifted away, it was plain that Jefferson Davis was not and never would be the prime hero of the South. He was born in a log cabin, had fought with valor in the Mexican War, and possessed a noble head. But these assets did not balance his handicaps. He was a "highbrow"—full of high sentence and bookishness, sickly, egocentric, theatrical, querulous. A reputation for drunkenness, not wholly deserved, followed him from the near-dismissal of his West Point days, on to the post-bellum Northern caricatures of "Jeffie Davis, the Belle of Richmond," showing him in flight wearing his wife's hoop-skirt but carrying a bottle of "Old Rye." Robert Toombs and other Southerners called him "that scoundrel Jeff Davis," and knew that his election as President of the Confederacy had been something of a fluke. To some people he became a symbol of the Southern cause, and was praised or hated solely on that account. A notorious bad man of the West, Boone Helm, hanged at Virginia City in 1863, uttered these last words: "Hurrah for Jeff Davis! Let her rip!" As the head of the civil power, Davis was treated with great deference by Lee—except when Davis brought politicians out to the battle of Mechanicsville as his guests. And Lee did his patient best to humor the Southern President's delusion, that Davis himself was a great military genius. Most Confederate soldiers, however, had little love for Jefferson Davis. The President's unpopularity reached its full at the close of the Civil War, when he fled, but was captured in women's clothes. Nothing is so little heroic as transvestism. In Philadelphia, in May, 1865, Wanamaker's "Oak Hall, Popular Clothing Store," took occasion to issue a jolly broadside—

> Jefferson Davis took to the woods,
> With his wife, and his children, and portable goods—
>
> . . . .
>
> So we sing of the petticoat traitor's fall,
> But we mustn't forget the great OAK HALL,
> Where we purchase every conceivable thing
> We can possibly want to wear in the spring.[27]

About the unhappy Davis there were other broadsides in the same strain; but none, apparently, sought to ridicule General Lee. When, however, the fugitive President was put in chains at Fortress Monroe on May 23, 1865, a tide of sympathy set in. Newspapers at once reported the act; the South felt pity and indignation, and in the North the moderates felt that such treatment was undeserved. A Union physician, Colonel John J. Craven, soon had the irons removed because they chafed his patient's ankles; in the next year he published a book called *The Prison Life of Jefferson Davis*, which told how Davis had cried to the blacksmith, "Kill me! kill me! rather than inflict . . . this insult worse than death!" The book described Davis's later patience, in prison, under the pangs of neuralgia, bilious fever, and "what he called 'the American malady,' dyspepsia." Davis thus became something of a popular hero, "calm martyr of a noble cause . . . with Washington entwined," as a poet named Walker Meriwether Bell hailed him. "With fortitude he endured imprisonment and suffering," reads the impressive Davis monument in Richmond. In 1891 Florida made his birthday, June 3, a holiday to "perpetuate . . . the heroic fortitude, and the patriotic character of Jefferson Davis," and other Southern states have given him minor homage. But he has never rivalled Lee as a hero. He was neither a great fighting man nor a good loser. He lived too long and too bitterly after the war. And Southern conservatives—who set the tone for all Civil War nostalgia —could not forget that he and his purse-proud wife served champagne while Richmond was starving, or that he belonged by origin to what Andrew Johnson called "the scrub aristocracy."

The idol of the Confederacy, in defeat as in success, remained General Lee. His personal decision to let bygones be bygones reconciled the South to the Union as nothing else could have done. When in June, 1865, he asked for a pardon from the Federal Government, not as a confession of wrong but as a token of civil submission, all save a few diehards felt they could follow his example. Here and there, even a generation later, "unreconstructed rebels" blamed Lee for kissing the rod. "A great man, but he took the oath," they said. But most saw that he had chosen the only sensible course, for the good of the South swallowing the reluctance of pride. A Southern girl at the White Sulphur Springs, longing to snub the Yankee visitors, later asked Lee how he felt about the North. She received the solemn reply, "I believe I may say, looking into my own heart, and speaking as in the presence of God, that I have never known one moment of bitterness or resentment."[28] Others who penetrated Lee's reticence told similar stories, and these circulated through the South. An angry preacher, who had great difficulty in forgiving his enemies, told how Lee had said to him that "I . . . have never seen the day when I did not pray for them." The story was also told of a ragged stranger, a Union veteran, who had accosted Lee and been given financial help. On an earlier occasion a little boy, badly frightened by Richmond children who accused him of being "a Yankee," was rescued by the General. Lee might easily have become the storm-center of unreconstructed sentiment; instead, he gently rebuked the South for its smoldering anger. Ultimately, of course, this spirit made Lee into a Christian symbol comparable to Lincoln, "with malice toward none."

Lee taught the South another lesson. Declining an invitation from England to become the life-guest of a nobleman, and another, it is said, to take command of the Rumanian army, Lee saw that his duty lay elsewhere. Unlike some Confederate generals he neither pouted nor fled the country. He accepted the presidency of small, meager Washington College at Lexington, Virginia, at an annual salary of $1500. This mere fact helped his old soldiers to accept their lot and go back to rebuilding the South. The Lees had lost their estate, Arlington, in the vicissitudes of war and privation; they were not even able to reclaim the relics of George Washington, which were hawked about the streets of the Capital. Yet legend, in seeking to make Lee the complete symbol of the South, has exaggerated his poverty. He died worth some $88,000, after a generous loan to the institution which came to be known as "General Lee's college" and was later christened Washington and Lee. His acceptance of its presidency came not from need, but from his desire for public service. Washington too had laid aside his sword to practice the arts of peace. Toward money itself Lee showed the fastidiousness of the ideal gentleman. Offered $10,000 a year for the use of his name as titular head of an insurance company, Lee told the representative: "Excuse me, sir; I cannot consent to receive pay for services I do not render."[29] Nor was he interested in the presidency of the Chesapeake and Ohio Railroad. He lent no ear to proposals in 1868 from *The New York Herald* and other newspapers that he should become Democratic candidate for President, to oppose his old foe U. S. Grant; no doubt he foresaw the bitter futility which such a campaign might breed. To the South, the integrity of Lee's last days shone with brighter luster against the age of "Grantism," of post-war finance and bucket-shop politics—the era when Jim Fisk, after an uncommonly rank deal, sent his famous telegram, "Nothing is lost save honor." The average Southerner was no Lee, but in the midst of his blighted orchards and rotting fences—while his Northern cousins were growing rich—he could not help drawing a moral solace from the example of General Lee.

So powerful was Lee's example that the Ku Klux Klan, then and later, claimed it had received his sanction; but ways of illicit violence, of mobs and night-riding, were never those of Lee. Better authenticated are the facts that in 1866 Lee prevented the lynching of a horse-thief at Lexington, and in 1868 protected from illegal threats a Negro who had wounded the son of a local judge.[30] The dynamism of one man against a mob makes an excellent story—as a movie called *Young Mr. Lincoln* demonstrated, in inventing a myth of this kind about Lincoln in New Salem—yet these true episodes of Lee's life have never been seized upon by folklore and fiction. Perhaps the South has been too sensitive on the subject of mobs.

Lee remained the aristocrat to his last hour. To a new student at Washington College, asking for a copy of the rules, Lee said: "We have but one rule here and it is that every student must be a gentleman." His knightly aspect—which had led a Northern girl, seeing Lee on the road to Gettysburg, to exclaim, "Oh, I wish he were ours!" —did not desert him as college president. Some of his old soldiers enrolled as freshmen, following less the beacon of higher learning than the star of General Lee. Many admirers sent their boys to be under his tutelage, and in time the college collected numerous prodigal sons, who, one hopes, became better men from dwelling in the shadow of their family's paragon.

Carte de visite photographs by the score, buttons from his uniform, and other souvenirs were in great demand during these last years. His faithful "Confederate gray," the horse Traveller, who had narrowly escaped halters of floral wreaths offered by admiring ladies during the war years, was now turned out to pasture—but so many hairs were plucked from his mane and tail that he became suspicious of strangers at sight. Lee took his own lionizing with grim humor. When his daughter once urged that his hat was growing too shabby, he jested, "You don't like this hat? Why, I have seen a whole cityful come out to admire it." Wherever he travelled in the South there were crowds at the station, brass bands, and namesakes to be blessed. Young Thomas Woodrow Wilson never forgot an inspiring glimpse of him at Augusta, Georgia. A girl who saw Lee enroute to the White Sulphur Springs, in 1867, wrote sixty years later:

The man who stood before us, the embodiment of a Lost Cause, was the realized King Arthur. The soul that looked out of his eyes was as honest and fearless as when it first looked on life. One saw the character, as clear as crystal, without complications or seals, and the heart, as tender as that of ideal womanhood. The years which have passed since that time have dimmed many enthusiasms and destroyed many illusions, but have caused no blush at the memory of the swift thrill of recognition and reverence which ran like an electric flash through one's whole body.[31]

She remembered too, on this same visit, that when Lee walked into the hotel parlor at "The Springs" the company—which had just been debating the propriety of hand-clapping him—fell silent, and then, as if by common impulse, rose and remained standing until he had taken a seat. It was such a tribute as Charles Lamb imagined any roomful would have paid to the entrance of his idol, William Shakespeare.

The most glowing remembrances of Lee in his last years come from the pens of Southern women. Lee the warrior reached his zenith of hero-worship among the soldiers of Northern Virginia; Lee the white-haired aristocrat gained his deepest appreciation from women. Frankly delighting in their beauty and charm, Lee understood the old cavalier art of light banter, playfulness, platonic love-making. But neither puritans nor Freudians have been able to taint his behavior with scandal. On this score he is among the most invulnerable of American idols. To women who met or saw him most casually, grace, dignity, and thoughtfulness were stamped unmistakably upon his handsome face. Upon his last visit to Baltimore, he bore the ordeal of being kissed by feminine admirers *en masse* with an equanimity that his blushing lieutenant Stonewall Jackson could not muster in the presence of one little girl. Up to the day of Richmond P. Hobson and later of the matinee idol, Lee received more adoration from women than any other American in public life—and bore his honors rather better than his successors. He was the *beau ideal,* for whom their romantic feeling and education had prepared Southern women. And as the symbol of a cause for which they had worked and starved and wept, he was irresistible. For women, perhaps more than men, respond to the poetry of lost causes in preference to the utility of success. Recalling his visit in 1870 to Shirley, home of his kinsmen the Carters, a girl exclaimed: "We had heard of God, but here was General Lee!"[32]

Myth-makers, who are generally sentimentalists, have fostered the story that Lee died of a broken heart, in October of that year. Southerners say that he could not long bear the tragedy of the shattered South; Northerners maintain that his heart was never in the Civil War, that he loved the Union too dearly, and grieved over the frustration that followed. The facts as known, and as appraised from Lee's letters by Freeman and other experts, are against these sickly assumptions. Lee seems to have sorrowed over the broken homes, the personal disasters of the war, as they came almost daily to his notice. But over the cause itself he nursed no inner corrosion, and was at peace. His old ardor had led him to do his best, to fight with all the genius at his command, but it had now cooled like lava into stone. God had ruled otherwise. And Lee, with his simple old-fashioned faith, accepted the verdict. Thomas Nelson Page told how a sophomore at Lexington, restive under Lee's advice about industry for success, once blurted out: "But, General, you failed." With tranquillity Lee replied, "I hope that you will be more fortunate than I."[33]

The immediate cause of his death appears to have been angina pectoris. Lee's last words befitted the earthly bivouac of a soldier— for, like Stonewall Jackson, he returned in delirium to the field. "Strike the tent," he said. Portents, such as the superstitious always love, surrounded his passing. It was reported that his picture had fallen from the wall of his house, that an aurora borealis had streamed across the sky for several nights before his death. The flood-waters were out, and one myth reports that the coffin in which Lee was buried had come floating mysteriously down the river.[34] It was the last note of the King Arthur theme. His tomb in the chapel of Washington and Lee University, is often called "the Shrine of the Southland"; it is now visited by some thirty thousand e `i year. The recumbent statue in white marble by Edward Valentine is meant to recall—as it does

—a crusader home from the wars. Marble indeed is the medium of the Lee cult. Mr. Jonathan Daniels, in his book *A Southerner Discovers the South,* remarks that it is characteristic that a "people living in the hottest sun ever borne as native by a northern stock of people anywhere . . . should have chosen Robert E. Lee as our idol. This conjunction of a sun-warmed people and white marble hero has not always been entirely beneficial. It did not take us long to discover that few of us could approximate the elevated ethics of General Lee. And, not being able to approximate General Lee, we scorned any intermediary standards. Proudly Southerners held to Lee or nothing." Similarly, of the unattainable Lee, the poet of *John Brown's Body* has written—

> The head on the Greek coin, the idol-image,
> The shape who stands at Washington's left hand,
> Worshipped, uncomprehended and aloof,
> A figure lost to flesh and blood and bones,
> Frozen into a legend out of life,
> A blank-verse statue.

III

Lee's death helped to lift his legend above the storms of controversy, even as his acquiescence in the Union and his services for peace had gone far to mollify the North. Julia Ward Howe, who had seen the conflict as a holy war "to make men free," was led to write generously of Lee in 1870:

> A gallant foeman in the fight,
>   A brother when the fight was o'er,
> The hand that led the host with might
>   The blessed torch of learning bore.
>
> .   .   .   .
>
> Thought may the minds of men divide,
>   Love makes the heart of nations one,
> And so, thy soldier grave beside,
>   We honor thee, Virginia's son.

Up until the beginning of the twentieth century, however, the cult of Lee flourished chiefly in the South. His old staff officers wrote most of the histories of the War between the States, from the Southern point of view, and inevitably in their pages Lee moved as the magic figure. At Confederate reunions his memory was kept ever green. Obscure young officers or stripling privates who had seen Lee only once or twice dwelt for life under the spell of his kindness, of some passing courtesy he had shown them, or of his distinguished bearing. The loyalties forged in battle-fire lasted forever. And these young men lived longest, told most of the stories, added the last words to memoirs of the war. "I was with him," they liked to say, with shining faces. They remembered, or thought they remembered, every word they heard him utter. In 1919, on Lee's birthday, Doctor Freeman addressed the three hundred inmates of the Soldiers' Home at Richmond—now reduced to seven survivors—and asked how many had ever seen General Lee. A few held up their hands, but most of them, as if to do his memory greater honor, rose to their feet, shoulders squared with pride. Among the officers who wrote books or letters or engaged in newspaper controversy, there were a few dissenters. Longstreet never forgot that Lee had overridden his advice at Second Manassas and at Gettysburg, as his military autobiography published in 1896 revealed. The fact that after the War Longstreet joined the Republican Party, and accepted a number of Federal sinecures, estranged him even more from orthodox Confederate veterans. Pickett, who had led the gallant fatal charge at Gettysburg, was another who sulked upon the outskirts of the Lee cult. The personal reason for his attitude— that Pickett knew that Lee knew of his occasional lapses with the whisky-bottle—was suspected by few Southerners. But they sensed that he was not on the side of the angels, and of Lee.

The church helped to foster Lee's hero-worship. Ever reverent of tradition, of moral values, he had grown more religious with the passing years. Somewhat late in life, in 1853, he had been confirmed in the Episcopal Church. The war deepened his spiritual nature, making him *par excellence* the Christian soldier, and when the struggle was over this faith sustained him—as it did the humbler Baptists, Methodists, Presbyterians of the South—in the shipwreck of a lost cause. Lee's old army chaplains invariably said, "He was a man of God," and often used him in their sermons for precept and illustration. The first biography of the true Lee cult was published in 1874 by the Reverend J. William Jones, "the fighting parson" of the Confederate Army. Jones served after the war as pastor of the Baptist Church at Lexington, where he virtually became Lee's Boswell. In 1906 in old age he brought out still another biography of his hero. A kindly, bearded figure familiar to soldiers' reunions, Jones was chaplain for nineteen years of the United Confederate Veterans. As the author of *Christ in the Camp; or, Religion in Lee's Army,* describing the revivals which swept through the ranks in the winter of 1862–63, and as the compiler of a *School History of the United States* widely used in the South, Jones played an important part in tracing the popular pattern of Lee the Christian patriot.

Under poverty and discouragement, with little else to boast of, the South found in Lee the splendor of a great symbol. His perfection was read into the whole Southern cause and character, by a half-conscious appropriation such as the North had used in respect to Lincoln. Lee's military counterpart, Grant, like Lincoln's administrative rival, Davis, lacked this potential in idealism—and both were rejected at last as flawed idols. While Lincoln remained the answer to America's dream of romantic democracy, Lee was the embodiment of a vanishing aristocracy. His kindliness kept his legend from the taint of personal snobbery, and his losses in the war drew the sting from any imputation of economic privilege. Idealists took comfort, too, from the fact that in the midst of the war he had freed the Custis slaves. His Federalist bias—less important to his legend than it would have become had Lee been a statesman—was forgotten in his assimilation by the region of the Democratic vote. In 1928, however, just after the Hoover election, a resolution was introduced in the Mississippi Legislature to move Lee's body from "Republican" Virginia to "Democratic" Mississippi. In general, party lines tended to drop away from his memory as they did from that of Washington; not to cling as they did to the names of Webster and Calhoun and Jackson and even Jefferson. Nobody tried to quote Lee on protective tariff or internal improvements. His words, in fact, were less important than his deeds —and his deeds ultimately less important than his character.

The North, however, did not begin popularly to adopt Lee until Reconstruction was over, the new loyalty was assured, the generals in blue began to die off, and the Spanish-American War (whatever its follies) brought the North and South into battle under the same flag. In 1900, in the first roll-call of the Hall of Fame, Lee was chosen by a nation-wide board of electors—authors, college presidents, historians, jurists, scientists, men and women in public life. He received only 68 votes out of a possible hundred, while Grant was given 93. Newspaper readers in the South thought that the jury was recruited rather too heavily from the highbrows of New England, who had given Daniel Webster an even more thumping majority of 96—outstripping Jefferson's 91, tying Lincoln's score, and surpassed only by Washington's 97. But some editorial writers in the North, engaged at this time in waving the last shreds of the "bloody shirt" over the Bryan-McKinley campaign, professed to be shocked that Lee was chosen at all. Under the title "Should Lee be in the Hall of Fame?" *The New York Sun* on October 18, 1900, printed a letter from "An Old Soldier": "What did he ever do to make his name famous, outside of being a traitor to his country? . . . Are the American people to understand that Lee, the commander of the Confederate forces, is to be named with such men as Washington and Lincoln?" *The Sun* agreed that Lee's case was "peculiarly flagrant," because he had been educated at public expense, and sworn an oath to the United States. "That his was a capital crime, a crime against civilization, cannot be denied," said *The Sun,* adding that despite his "otherwise exemplary and even beautiful life" his election to the Hall of Fame sprang from "a false and mushy sentimentality." Six days later this newspaper reported that it had been swamped by letters of approval and protest. To "a Savannah gentleman" it replied loftily:

> Up here we look at the Civil War dispassionately. We have no "lost cause" to mourn or keep alive in the thoughts of the children under our training. . . . If eleven Southern States had any justification in seceding or any right to secede because Lincoln was elected in spite of their opposition, they can go off now in a like huff when McKinley is elected.

Among the unpublished correspondence of Theodore Roosevelt now in the Library of Congress, one finds a letter to Roosevelt from John R. Procter, president of the Civil Service Commission, dated October 30, 1900:

> If you happen to meet any of the staff of *The New York Sun,* please say for me that if the democrats carry West Virginia, Maryland, or Kentucky, it will be largely due to the recent indecent attack made by *The New York Sun* on the memory of Robert E. Lee. The democrats have had the wisdom to republish this by the thousand and scatter it in those States. I hope I may some time meet the writer of those editorials so that I may have the pleasure of telling him face to face what a detestable sneak he is.

More generous feelings, meanwhile, were stirring in the North. Charles Francis Adams—who as a youth had commanded a Negro regiment from Massachusetts in the war, while his father served as Lincoln's Minister to England—came notably to Lee's defense. In 1901 before the American Antiquarian Society he read a paper called "Lee at Appomattox," which soon saw national publication. Therein Adams avowed his belief that Lee's absolute loyalty to the terms of surrender, and the example of his nobility, saved the post-bellum era from far greater vindictiveness. In the next year Adams gave the Phi Beta Kappa oration at the University of Chicago, "Shall Cromwell Have a Statue?" Recalling that Senator Sumner had said of Lee, "I hand him over to the avenging pen of History," Adams observed that Lee belongs technically to the great traitors of history, like Cromwell, Hampden, William of Orange, and George Washington, but not to the company of Catiline and Arnold, who were led by ambition rather than duty. Even as Cromwell now has his proud statue in the yard of Westminster Hall, where once his skull bleached on a pole, so Lee some day will have his national monument in Washington: "When that time comes, Lee's monument will be educational . . . it will symbolize and commemorate that loyal acceptance of the consequences of defeat, and the patient upbuilding of a people under new conditions by constitutional means, which I hold to be the greatest educational lesson America has yet taught to a once skeptical but now silenced world." Adams, like most Northern admirers of Lee, stressed his hero in defeat rather than upon the battle-field—making him a symbol of union rather than defiance. But his appreciation of Lee's character was so warming to the Southern heart that Adams was asked to deliver the Lee Centennial Address, on January 19, 1907, at Washington and Lee University. In that speech Adams said, that "if in all respects similarly circumstanced, I hope I should have been filial and unselfish enough to have done as Lee did." "Show me the man you honor," he quoted; "I know by that symptom, better than by any other, what kind of man you yourself are. . . . Whom do you wish to resemble? Whom you set on a high column, that all men looking at it, may be continually apprised of the duty you expect from them." No nobler ideal than Lee, he concluded, could be found in America.

The age of big business felt, perhaps, that it could use a great gentleman in its national pantheon, like a buffalo in a museum of vanishing Americana.

The Lee Centennial of 1907 marked, in fact, a new milestone in his hero-worship. It was observed throughout the South and in several Northern cities. Revival of interest in Lee had come just three years before, with the publication by Captain Robert E. Lee of the life and letters of his father—pages filled with the simple unassuming charm of Lee which had begun to be lost in the windy, formal biographies of a somewhat earlier time. After the Centennial, Lee's birthday came to be set aside as a legal holiday in most Southern states; it is often called "Lee-Jackson Day," although Stonewall Jackson's birthday is really two days later, on January 21. Religious services frequently accompany it, with the United Daughters of the Confederacy in charge. Members of this organization are spiritual custodians of the Lee shrine. Many have joined the Lee Memorial Foundation, begun in 1928 to rehabilitate the birthplace, Stratford. Among other observances in his honor, the U. D. C. annually awards "the Robert E. Lee Sword" for proficiency in mathematics, to the ranking senior at West Point. Annually, also, the cadet who is in line for this award receives letters from an aged spinster in Ohio, sternly advising him to reject "the sword of treason." Thus battle the vestals of the Republic.

Lee, unlike Washington and Lincoln and Grant, has never been "debunked" in biography. His ingenuous life, that of a well-balanced extrovert, is strikingly free from financial, sexual, and religious aberrations. The psycho-biographer of New England, Gamaliel Bradford, wrote a book of praise for Lee. He began with a mild protest against the legendary perfection of Lee, and then wrote three hundred pages subscribing to it. The past five years have seen the publication of appreciative essays, in the wake of Freeman's life of Lee; perhaps also the recent years of economic depression and worldwide gloom have made popular, by a kind of personal transfer, the catastrophe of the South as shown in fiction and cinema. Novels by Margaret Mitchell, Stark Young, Clifford Dowdey, and others offer the romance of an *ancien régime* as one escape from the proletarian problem. Yet Lee himself, as distinguished from his cause, has inspired less good art than Lincoln. The novels of Mary Johnston are now tarnished by time, while no great poet has appreciated Lee as Whitman took Lincoln's measure. In 1923 the British dramatist John Drinkwater, in his play *Robert E. Lee,* attempted a companion-piece for his *Lincoln.* But the result is inferior. Through the opening scenes of the play Lee appears as stiff, awkward, egotistic, while everybody waits for him to make his decision, like a much-courted belle. He utters sententious remarks, such as "War is the anger of bewildered peoples in front of the questions that they can't answer"; reveals his humanity by tossing an apple to his aide; and calls Stonewall "my man Jackson." No happier is Edgar Lee Masters's ambitious *Lee: A dramatic poem,* published in 1926. Lee rants in the vein of tragedy, about his "imperial" duty and his Revolutionary sire, but foresees his fate:

> I am a trump not to be blown
> True to the triumphant chord.

After his surrender at Appomattox, shadowy personages called the Republic and the South engage in a scolding-match like two fishwives. More recently, Donald Davidson has written a shorter and better poem, *Lee in the Mountains,* about the Lexington years—

> It is not General Lee, young men . . .
> It is Robert Lee in a dark civilian suit who walks,
> An outlaw fumbling for the latch, a voice
> Commanding in a dream where no flag flies.
>
> .   .   .   .
>
> The Blue Ridge, lapped in a haze of light,
> Thunders no more. The horse is at plough. The rifle
> Returns to the chimney crotch and the hunter's hand.
> And nothing else than this? Was it for this
> That on an April day we stacked our arms
> Obedient to a soldier's trust—to sink, to lie
> Ground by heels of little men,
> Forever maimed, defeated, lost, impugned?
> And was I then betrayed? Did I betray?

The scarcity of good poetry, of good art, about Lee as contrasted with Lincoln is an interesting problem. The post-war collapse which made Southern literature negligible for two generations no doubt explains much. Also, perhaps, the very simplicity of Lee offers no mystery to the interpreter. As a symbol, he is much less flexible than Lincoln.

Lee still lacks his national monument, despite repeated proposals in Congress offered by Representative Hamilton Fish, grandson of Grant's Secretary of State. The latest tribute was that of the Robert E. Lee Memorial Statue in Dallas, Texas. At its unveiling on June 12, 1936, President Roosevelt said: "All over the United States we recognize him as a great leader of men, as a great general. But, also, all over the United States I believe that we recognize him as something much more important than that. We recognize Robert E. Lee as one of our greatest American Christians and one of our greatest American gentlemen." These are the recurrent notes of the Lee legend, in phrases which have grown hackneyed. Of the pure military man, Lee is America's last great example. Later wars have not given him a rival. But his emotional hold upon the South, and to a less degree upon the nation, springs from qualities of mind and conduct. As a hero, Lee has one noteworthy handicap. His perfection is cool and unapproachable.

CHAPTER TWELVE

GENERAL GRANT AND THE GILDED AGE

"I remimber Grant f'r what he done ar-round
Shiloh whin he was young, but Hogan remim-
bers him f'r what he done ar-round New York
whin he was old. . . .

"Th' hero sthruts through histhry with his
chin up in th' air, his scipter in his hand an' his
crown on his head. But behind him dances a
boot-black imitatin' his walk an' makin' faces
at him." — FINLEY PETER DUNNE, as "Mr.
Dooley."

I

To UNLOCK the heart of General Grant's era a golden key is
needed. Grant himself, though a victorious general, failed
to sustain the dazzling role of Alexander, Cæsar, Napoleon.
His abiding interests and admirations were elsewhere, turning ever to the cult of material success. Even by the time
of his inauguration as President, the popular fervor which won the
Civil War had run to other channels. Wheels were turning, and great
fortunes were being harvested. To many, Grant in the White House—
the tanner's son who had made good—fittingly served both as example
and as Chief Magistrate of America's Gilded Age.

"Success has no more eccentricity than the gingham and muslin we weave in our mills," Emerson wrote in one of his practical moods. On another occasion he preached to America in his generation: "Don't be a cynic and disconsolate preacher. . . . Nerve us with incessant affirmatives." Emerson's day saw the beginning of boosting and hustling in our Republic.

The green youth of the success cult has already been glanced at. New England, with its Puritan philosophy of work and its barren soil which encouraged the arts of trade, cradled this cult. The curious bond between success and supernatural sanctions lasted for a long time. Early in the nineteenth century, universities like Columbia and Brown had chairs significantly called "the professorship of moral philosophy and political economy." At Yale President Timothy Dwight preached that "the love of property to a certain degree seems indispensable to the existence of sound morals," anticipating by two generations the remark of Darius Ogden Mills: "The most wasteful and extravagant people in the world today are the poor of our American cities."[1] The new drift in hero-worship was plain. The Reverend Mr. Dwight lauded "the Hero, the Statesman, and the Patriot" as higher types than the mere artist and thinker, since action "fills a nobler sphere of being than . . . thinking." Practicality was the test.

Clergyman and capitalist in those days understood each other. The vision, the energy, the constructive enterprise of the latter often received pulpit praise. Horace Bushnell, in a sermon called "How to Be a Christian in Trade," compared the vocation of merchant prince—carrying goods from wholesale to retail shops, thence to consumer—with the Divine task of the rain-clouds, "the merchants of the sky."[2] The esteem was mutual. John D. Rockefeller faithfully taught a Bible class. Two of his associates in the new oil monopoly, J. D. Archbold and Harry M. Flagler, were sons of missionary preachers, and carried a certain grim Calvinism into life and business. The latter once announced: "Sunday is to be kept at Palm Beach. Its observance is one of the features of the place." Occasional friction between the church and big business men arose, less over the fundamental moral law than over minor folkways, and solution was not too difficult. As an example, Trinity College in North Carolina looked briefly askance at the princely endowment offered by the tobacco kings, the Dukes, because Methodist Church rules forbid preachers to use the weed in any form. But these scruples were soon overcome, and today in front of the gray Gothic chapel of Duke University, the scion of Trinity, stands a statue of "Buck" Duke holding between his fingers a large cigar with its cone of ash about to fall.

With time, this cult grew more pagan—losing much of its ancient faith save that in the innate desirability of success, and here and there a superstition about keeping on God's side. Daniel Drew, in his day, prayed and founded a seminary apparently on the same impulse which leads the gambler to cherish his rabbit's foot. But Drew's younger rival, Jim Fisk—who flaunted his mistresses in open carriages and opera-boxes—dared to parody the attitude by asking that "divine services" be celebrated on Boston Common for his benefit and that of his regiment.[3] Regarding the decline of the great Christian business man, Lowell observed that "Protestantism had made its fortune and no longer protested." Such ideals as could be salvaged from the old tie reappeared in New Thought, the gospel of Elbert Hubbard, Bruce Barton's attempt to make Christ the archetype of Rotary, and the late scented snobberies of Buchmanism. But in the main, during the era called "Grantism," prayers ceased to mingle with invoices, as they had done among Puritan merchants.

A great deal of American success literature has been addressed to youth, in the attempt to build up a mercantile hero-worship. One of the earliest books printed for children's amusement, by that enterprising Yankee Isaiah Thomas, in 1787, was the Old World classic *The History of Little Goody Twoshoes,* written "for the benefit of those

> Who from a State of Rags and Care,
> And having Shoes but half a Pair,
> Their Fortune and their Fame would fix,
> And gallop in their Coach and Six."

The story stresses piety and industry, wisdom and prudence. Numerous editions of *Sir Richard Whittington and His Cat* were published, from Philadelphia to Charleston, during the early nineteenth century, to tell of "a poor country boy who attained great riches." Unlike Cinderella, the success heroine of little girls, Whittington owed less to magic than to perseverance. Also popular, after publication in Boston in 1793, was the fable of Mr. Charles Worthy, "who, from being a poor orphan, rose, through various scenes of distress and misfortune, to wealth and eminence, by industry, economy, and good conduct." In Washington in 1834 was brought out a little book bearing the cover-title *A Spur to Youth; or, Davy Crockett Beaten.* It told the life of "Paddy O'Flarrity, who, from a shoe black, has by perseverance and good conduct, arrived to a member of Congress . . . calculated to improve as well as divert the youths of America." The most prolific author of inspirational books before the Civil War was Timothy Shay Arthur. Like many others of the tribe, he failed at every pursuit other than the writing of success manuals. As a boy he had been removed from the Baltimore public schools at the teacher's request because of his extreme dullness; poor sight then caused him to give up an apprenticeship to the watchmaker's trade. He joined a temperance society, wrote *Ten Nights in a Barroom,* and scores of books on the theme of morality and industry as the key to success. A novel like *The Two Merchants; or, Solvent and Insolvent* in 1853 held up for admiration "a merchant of the old school . . . [with] the strictest principles of mercantile honor." Arthur's chief rival was a Massachusetts temperance clergyman, William Makepeace Thayer, who wrote *Success and Its Achievers, Men Who Win,* and *The Poor Boy and Merchant Prince.* The last was a life of Amos Lawrence, who started as a threadbare clerk but died a millionaire, upon whose coffin children scattered flowers. Success was largely a matter of abstinence, Amos Lawrence was quoted as affirming:

I decided not to be a slave to tobacco in any form, though I loved the odor of it then, and even now have in my drawer a superior Havana segar, given me not long since by a friend, but only to smell of. Now, I say, to this simple fact of starting *just right* am I indebted, with God's blessing on my labors, for my present position.

He also repudiated drink, card-playing, and gambling, while forging ahead with frugality, punctuality, and the reading of improving books. Nothing is here said about the practical technique of business methods; or about the element of genius, on the one hand, or luck upon the other. These topics are almost never mentioned in success literature. Is it possible that the common reader would become either shocked or disheartened? The bright boy, however, was able perhaps to read between the lines; the late Samuel Insull for example stated that he got his start from reading Samuel Smiles's *Self Help.*[4]

"I would have you believe that success in life is within the reach of every one," wrote L. U. Reavis in 1871, in a book bearing the impressive title *Thoughts for the Young Men of America, or A Few Practical Words of Advice to Those Born in Poverty and Destined to be Reared in Orphanage.* From rags to riches became the theme of innumerable books, by hack-writers and by those bearing such famous names as Horace Greeley, James Parton, and Harriet Beecher Stowe. The trust which some humble readers must have placed in their mentors is pathetic. The Marquis de Chambrun, visiting hospitals in company with President Lincoln during the last week of the Civil War, talked with a nurse who had just taken from the pocket of a dead German soldier—a recent immigrant to the land for which he died—a book called *How to Make One's Way in the World*. Hundreds of thousands heard the inspirational sermons of Russell H. Conwell, holding up to admiration the career of Jay Gould, who "has his seventy or eighty millions now, but he made the most difficult part of his progress in the little country village." President Grant, too, thought that Jay Gould was a fine fellow, who served excellent champagne and French brandy and talked sensibly in the summer of 1869 about keeping all the gold locked in the Federal Treasury.

But the two bees who carried the pollen of success most industriously through the land were William Holmes McGuffey and Horatio Alger. The McGuffey Readers, used in thirty-seven states of the Union from 1836 down to the close of the nineteenth century, sold the fabulous number of 122,000,000 copies. It is hard to exaggerate their effect upon the mind and culture of America. Their historian, Harvey Minnich, has lately reminded us that among famous Americans who studied them were Mark Twain, Lew Wallace, McKinley, Taft, Harding, Beveridge, Borah, James Whitcomb Riley, Gene Stratton Porter. Henry Ford is the dean of living devotees. The reader of McGuffey was taught scrupulous honesty, by the story of a chimney sweep who resisted stealing a gold watch he had found, and as reward was adopted by its owner. One learned obedience to parents from the fate of Frank Brown, who loitered with a "bad boy" near a pond, and so fell in and drowned. McGuffey, a Scotch-Irish schoolmaster who admired and borrowed freely from Poor Richard, taught thrift by means of proverbs, as well as stories about a boy who saved all the string from packages and was thus able to spin his top and to win an archery contest while his shiftless brother went discomfited. "Lazy Ned" and "Idle Jane" proved the moral that "There is no excellence without great labor." Mingled with these fables are stories about the Puritans of New England, Lafayette, and George Washington—praised for his piety, dignity, and generosity to an unknown Philadelphia boy with a sick mother. As a distillation of McGuffey's teachings about success, one may take his *Fifth Eclectic Reader* of 1879. There we learn that too much native talent is a handicap, because it tends to laziness. Most worthwhile deeds are wrought by the diligent rather than the brilliant.

"Tact, push, and principle"—in Thayer's phrase—make up McGuffey's formula as well, in the guise of politeness, perseverance, honesty. Punctuality is also stressed, at school as in business, and the story is told of an innocent man hanged because the governor's messenger had a slow watch. Duty is a concept hinging upon filial obedience, while charity consists in giving alms to the poor—"bread and cheese," or "a bit of cake to eat and some milk." It need hardly be said that no definite codes of conduct in economic life are laid down.[5] One could still follow McGuffey and be a robber baron.

Whereas the dime novel dealt with adventure, the Alger novel looked to success, and hence parents came to regard the latter as more moral. "Work and Win," the title of an Alger book, was the simple refrain of them all. Alger, nicknamed in school "Holy Horatio," was the son of a bullying Unitarian clergyman, who broke up the boy's first romance and sought to dominate him throughout life. Timid and neurotic, Alger was the arrested adolescent hero of his own books. On the subject of sex purity he had a "Joseph complex"; as a freshman at Harvard he had changed his lodgings after his landlady stood at the door in negligee, "and I might have seen her bare but I did not look," he confided to his diary. Later in Paris, like a true Anglo-Saxon among the French, he enjoyed a complete moral collapse. A café singer seduced him, taught him to sing and dance, and stirred him to such bravado of spirit that he wrote in his diary: "I want to live to be great. Suppose it is vain—all great men are vain. What have they got that I need, to be like them? Whatever it is I will see." Success became the quest of his life. Resolved to enlist in the Union Army, on the way to the recruiting-station he fell and broke his arm. He quit the ministry to write boys' stories for William T. Adams ("Oliver Optic"), and soon took up his abode in the Newsboys' Lodging House in New York. Newsboys liked him, but saw in him an easy dupe who believed everything he heard and emptied his pockets at every plea. In their parades he loved to beat the drum and march up Broadway, indulging a naïve exhibitionism. In the serial *Ragged Dick,* in 1867, he glorified the newsboy—tattered, barefoot, with a heart of gold— as perhaps the noblest type in young America. He was spared the recent statistics of Warden Lawes, compiled when opponents of child-labor legislation were still insisting that many American worthies began life selling papers, showing that over 69 per cent of Sing Sing's 2300 inmates had been newsboys in their youth.[6]

Alger's was a dream-world. He was fascinated by the extremes of poverty and wealth, haunting the slums of Chinatown and also the lobby of the Astor House, where he tipped the desk clerk to point out the celebrities to him. Like his own heroes, he never drank or smoked, but candy was his habitual vice. He also delighted to play with building blocks, and was never more excited than when following the clangor of a fire-engine. In a mood of depression he scribbled in his diary, "Am I, dear God, a failure?" Yet his stories for boys, 119 titles in all, enjoyed a popularity never matched before or since. "Making His Way," "Try and Trust," "Jed, the Poorhouse Boy," "Grit, the Young Boatman of Pine Point," "Slow and Sure," "Andy Grant's Pluck," "Strive and Succeed," "Tom Thatcher's Fortune," "Bound to Rise," "Wait and Hope," "Tom the Bootblack," "From Farm to Fortune," "Falling in with Fortune," "Luck and Pluck," "The Making of a Man"—these were the multiple images of Alger's own dream. Herbert Mayes in his book called *Alger: a Biography without a Hero* suggests, no doubt with truth, that Alger wrote for boys because he could not write for men. He enjoyed the immense fan mail, from youths and their parents, which these novels brought him. Sometimes his advice took lyrical form. To a boy on his birthday Alger wrote:

> To man's estate you'll soon succeed;
> As a man, strive to lead.

Yet Alger's own life continued to be bound in shallows and in miseries. When we observe that his heroes tend to be handsome, clean-cut lads, with sturdy bodies and manly voices, we need hardly to be told that their creator was sallow, pale, shy, and quavering in speech. The final irony of Alger's celibate life came over his infatuation with a well-to-do woman named Mrs. Russel Garth. Writing "Frank and Fearless" to raise money to pay for the trip, Alger followed her and her husband to Paris, and there tried piteously to engage her in a liaison. His rejection brought on a fit of insanity from which he never wholly recovered.

Alger wrote boys' biographies of three self-made Americans—Lincoln, Garfield, and Daniel Webster. Webster was the special hero of Alger's youth, and William Jennings Bryan of his later years. Intoxicating rhetoric he loved above all things. But without doubt Alger's greatest power over his generation came from his stories of pluck and fortune. As with Thayer and Arthur and McGuffey, his ideals are nebulous, sentimental, unreal. Like them, he taught a doctrine of morality as the way to wealth, and of wealth as a buttress to morality.

A scene in *The Store Boy* is revealing. This book tells of noble Ben Barclay, whose example reforms a shiftless tramp. This vagabond mends his ways, and when offered a bribe by the wicked squire he answers manfully: "You can't tempt me. If I were as hard up as when I called upon you before, I might not be able to resist you; but I am worth over ten thousand dollars." In the character of "Fred Fearnot" created by Hal Standish, and in the pages of a magazine published from 1900 to 1909 called *The Successful American,* one found popular continuations of the Alger gospel.

Ambitious boys and poor people found inspiration in such books; rich men, by the instinct of every type to glorify itself, applauded them as uplifting. Many relished Gerald Stanley Lee's *Inspired Millionaires.* Upon visiting the Vanderbilts, E. C. Stedman found them reading a book called *Successful Business Men.* Curiously enough, Napoleon figures as the hero *par excellence* in a great deal of this success literature; his care for detail, brilliant audacity, and mastery over men are held up as the perfect go-getting ideal.[7] "If I had read the life of Napoleon when I was a boy, my own life might have been different. It would have filled me with the ambition to make the most of myself," an "eminent man of middle age" was quoted as saying, in Tilley's *Masters of the Situation, or Some Secrets of Success and Power,* in 1887. But there were inspiring examples nearer home. "As rich as Jay Cooke" became a byword after the Civil War. The way in which he sold wartime bonds to the country showed that he was the first psychologist of mass salesmanship. Afterward, he demonstrated that in more personal contacts his touch was no less sure. He showered President Grant with twenty-five-cent cigars, and sent little Jesse Grant a fishing-rod and creel. The rewards of thoughtfulness came as unerringly as in the pages of a moral story, when he received millions of acres in Western lands for the Northern Pacific. The hero as empire-builder flourished. People read eagerly of A. T. Stewart, department-store owner whom the Civil War had made fabulously rich; Grant had tried to make him Secretary of the Treasury, in ignorance of Alexander Hamilton's law of 1789 which disqualifies a man engaged in mercantile pursuits. Fewer had heard of wealthy Adolph E. Borie, retired from the East India trade, who was as surprised as the public when Grant named him Secretary of the Navy. But everybody knew of William Henry Vanderbilt, who damned the public but lent Grant $250,000 as a personal favor when the bucket-shop of Grant & Ward was collapsing in 1884—a loan which the General did his best to repay by giving Vanderbilt his swords and war relics, and also the Grant farm near St. Louis. Other men who got their start in this era began to be called "kings of fortune," who ruled "the empire of business": Rockefeller, Armour, Crocker, Stanford, Huntington, Russell Sage, Henry Phipps. Almost all, as Carnegie remarked, "started as poor boys, and were trained in the sternest but most efficient of all schools —poverty." The steel master of Homestead, who ultimately sold out to Morgan for two hundred and fifty millions, was himself the envy and admiration of thousands. Carnegie's writings on business, with a dash of homely common sense, a bit of personal experience, and a philosophy about the social obligations of wealth, were to the later nineteenth century what Franklin's had been to the eighteenth. He was an immigrant Poor Richard, now giving his largesse of libraries and hero-medals to the world. In the complacency of the 1880's Carnegie shared when he wrote: "If asked what important law I should change, I must perforce say none; the laws are perfect." Mr. Dooley observed drily that Carnegie must be a happy man. "He has money, he has fame, he has Andhrew Carnaygie, and he's a little deaf."

The lineaments of the ideal business man were in some respects clear enough. He worked hard, kept certain moral laws, but lived by the code of "enlightened selfishness." Fiercely independent, he rode rough-shod over competitors and all minor checks—owning allegiance to the Constitution alone. Ambrose Bierce in compiling *The Devil's Dictionary* set down a definition which may have been suggested by his long association with Hearst: "*Impunity,* n., Wealth." At times, the self-sufficience of the business man overflowed the narrow bounds of the Alger pattern—as in Judge Elbert H. Gary's recollection of his schooldays: "I never allowed a teacher to punish me if I didn't think I deserved it." Moreover, while the Alger and Thayer romances stressed thrift, a penny-pinching which easily shaded into miserly accumulation, the greatest heroes among captains of industry—from Commodore Vanderbilt to the senior J. P. Morgan—were men of spectacular achievement, if not outright gamblers. Money was less intriguing than the romance of making it. (Even Cicero, in his time, had said that the souls of wholesale merchants were more apt to be noble than those of retailers, because the latter must lie in petty and sordid ways.) Honesty, for the business man, was an urban rather than an agrarian ideal—dealing more with the fulfillment of contracts and payment of debts than in the humane, generous concepts of "neighborliness." Even when certain approved virtues were lacking, they were read into his character. "The moment a man is known to have acquired a little property by his own industry, he receives credit for ingenuity and perseverance, and is trusted on account of these virtues," wrote Francis J. Grund in 1837.[8] Just a hundred years later, the Lynds in appraising Middletown in transition found that if a man is successful in business he can win approval more easily than the average man, in the face of such handicaps as snobbery, rudeness, cynicism, or overbearing ways. His dictatorial manner is thought to be "forceful," his cynicism is "shrewdness," and if he is cold one assumes "a concealed tenderness of character."[9] A history of the business man, through world history, was published in 1938 by Miriam Beard; it suggested that the merchant prince is a type immemorially old. Just now he is on the wane in America, as an inspirational name and paragon. Miss Beard noted specifically that the "two-fisted business man, educated in the university of hard knocks," is now old-fashioned. But the flowering of his glory had been the age of General Grant. Then even Walt Whitman, sitting on his steps at Camden through the long summer dusk, talking to a young disciple named Elbert Hubbard, was saying, "Business shall be, nay is, the word of the modern hero." In such a mood Whitman wrote, by invitation, his "Song of the Exposition"—imagining a great cathedral of the New World, built not as a shrine to outmoded faiths or to house the bones of military conquerors, but in the name of "sacred industry," with bays, wings, and "large calm halls" to illustrate not dogma but technology. In other moods, of course, Whitman exclaimed, "How I do love a loafer!" and girded at the fat plutocrats and lean misers, "all with close hard faces." He could never quite make up his mind about cheering for the merchant prince, and the formula of pluck, luck, and plunder. One snuffed vitality, exhilaration, poetry in the building of an empire. But when the yes-sayer yielded to the philosopher in Whitman, he began to ask whether the empire-builder's works were not more impressive than his soul.

It was a dilemma which the poet shared with the American mind. Was the merchant prince truly a hero? Material success looked good, but was the stuff durable enough for a pedestal? The cult held more sincere envy than pure admiration, and in seasons of depression it turned quickly sour. The strain of idealism—attracted so often to the hero of self-sacrifice, privation, tragedy—was wholly absent here. The rich man had his own reward, and whatever good he did for the country was incidental to his prime pursuits. No self-made millionaire was ever honored with the Presidency, and his birthplace or tomb made into a holy spot. Even the gospel of self-help, lacking the salt of Franklin's humor, came in time to seem pretty cold porridge. "The churlish curmudgeon who, by sharp practice and avaricious dealing, has amassed a fortune, should not be permitted to cajole his fellows by boasting of his early privations and sordid self-denial," wrote Grover Cleveland with gusto in *Success Magazine* for July, 1902. The great American habit of hustling, in the eyes of some, appeared to be little more than a nervous tic. Even in the heyday of the Grant era—when a great soldier's frank admiration for business, and wish to help it in every way, lent it a kind of pontifical prestige—America never surrendered all the corners of its soul to the evangel of getting on. A variety of prophets, from Henry George to Washington Gladden, sought to crack the hard crust of national self-satisfaction and found a multitude of fellow iconoclasts. As for hero-worship itself, the memory of Lincoln should have been (though it sometimes failed to be) an antidote to materialism in the North; that of Lee in the South was an even more powerful specific. Neither of these men belonged to the hustlers of Wall Street. Grant himself, as will be seen, ceased to be a hero when he threw himself wholly into the trade of piling up dollars, and regained his glory only by bravery in the face of bankruptcy and slow death.

There is a touch of parable in the role of Rip Van Winkle which Joseph Jefferson created in 1866, played to uncounted thousands, and made even in the Gilded Age the most popular character ever known to the American theatre. Jefferson, as Rip, was the beloved vagabond and dreamer, whom time passes by. He, like Whitman, loafed and invited his soul, and awoke from his long sleep to look with surprise upon the hustling civilization which had grown up about him. Was he not a symbol of escape from the grim cult of making money?

II

On the centenary of Grant's birth, April 27, 1922, a celebration was held at Point Pleasant, Ohio. Agnes K. Wagner sang:

> In this quiet country town, on the O-h-i-o
> Stands a cottage with walls snowy white:

Grown famous the whole world o'er, for it was here
The Fear-less Grant first saw the light.[10]

Romance has not been able to do very much for Grant's parents. His father, Jesse Root Grant, was a lean hard-bitten tanner and dresser of hides. He quarrelled with most of his neighbors, but was a good business man. He was mortified by Ulysses's repeated failures to earn a living as a young husband and father, but quickly adjusted himself to the son's success in the Civil War. During the war years we have glimpses of General Grant checking his father's roving eye in the direction of Army contracts—before the General became President and lost his scruples about nepotism—and rebuking the old man for writing letters to the newspapers defending the son's military strategy. "I have not an enemy in the world who has done me so much injury as you in your efforts in my defense. . . . Do nothing to correct what you have already done, but for the future keep quiet on this subject," ordered the General.[11] Grant's mother was equally recalcitrant material for folklore. She was a close-mouthed, religious woman who showed no visible affection for her son, or he for her. The only well-known story of mother and son tells how anxious neighbors rushed to her with the intelligence that her son was swinging on the tails of horses in the barnlot. "Oh, 'Lyss will be all right," she said without dropping a stitch. After the Civil War she greeted him, "Well, Ulysses, you've become a great man, haven't you?" During the White House years, when Washington was filled with Grant's kin—Old Jesse bickering with the patriarch of the in-laws, "Grandpa" Dent the professional Southerner, over his juleps and newspapers—the General's mother was his only relative who never set foot in the White House. Under these circumstances not even legend has dared to conjecture Grant's debt to his angel mother.

The folklore of Grant's boyhood flourished during the noon of his fame, sprouting from rather unpromising soil, but it has not lasted so well as the lore of young Washington or Lincoln. William M. Thayer, in his "Log Cabin Series," compiled *From Tannery to White House: The Life of Ulysses S. Grant.* He tells us that at the age of two, Grant fired off a pistol, "one of the lookers-on remarking, as he saw the coolness of the child, 'He will make a general.'" Thayer does not mention his boyhood nickname of "Useless Grant," or the unpopularity among schoolmates of this dull, bashful boy. He does however contrive to suggest the ill success of Grant in his studies:

"Some boys are too large to be squeezed into the narrow limits of a school curriculum. Their great natures protest against it." Edward Willett, in a *Life of Ulysses Sydney* [sic] *Grant* written for the Beadle Library of dime biographies in 1865, reports that as a boy Grant found that the word *can't* was not in the dictionary. Seemingly a paraphrase of the passage about failure not being found in "the lexicon of youth," in Bulwer's *Richelieu,* the story grew famous. Willett also related the best-known yarn of Grant's youth, that of the horse trade. Grant himself told in his memoirs that at the age of eight he wanted a horse, owned by a neighbor. With money in his pocket, and in his head parental advice about driving a bargain, he appeared at the neighbor's door to declare: "Papa says I may offer you twenty dollars for the colt, but if you won't take that, I am to offer twenty-two and a half, and if you won't take that to give you twenty-five." Campaign biographers, thinking the story did little credit to Grant's brains in an age when horse-trading was the touchstone of American business, added the clause, "but since I have seen the horse, I shall not offer more than twenty."[12] Willett, in the book for boys cited above, lends the transaction an air of bigger business by raising the ante to $60, but showing how Ulysses got the horse at last for only $50.

It was a happy accident that Grant bore the name of Ulysses, craftiest of Greek warriors. The drawing of names out of a hat, by the Grant and Simpson families, had given him a cognomen which—according to Sterne's theory of christenings in *Tristram Shandy*—the boy had to grow up and justify. Even better, the mistake of Congressman Hamer in appointing him to West Point in 1839, changed his name from Hiram Ulysses to Ulysses Simpson. "U. S. Grant" might mean "United States," or "Uncle Sam" as his fellow-cadets called him, but after the capture of Fort Donelson in 1862 it meant to the public, forever after, "Unconditional Surrender." The old epithet of "Useless" was dead and buried. (Only his wife, who called him by such pet names of glory as "Victor" and "Cæsar" which she had taken from applauding newspapers, sensed the inferiority complex which was never quite interred.)

Grant's West Point days were not distinguished. In the privacy of his room he consumed novels—Scott, Cooper, Bulwer—with the aimlessness of a hammock reader. He was a good horseman, but slovenly in personal appearance and bored with his studies. He was homesick, and later confessed that he had hoped a talked-of plan to abolish West Point would succeed. In these four years he never went to a dance, had a date with a girl, or was a guest in a private house. Toward women he was as diffident, and apparently felt as loutish, as young Lincoln. But Lincoln's intellectual curiosities he wholly lacked. He lacked also Lee's interest in the science of war. The choice of West Point had been his father's decision, not his own. "The truth is I am more of a farmer than a soldier," Grant told Bismarck, when a glittering review was staged for the ex-President at Potsdam. "I take little or no interest in military affairs." On this same tour, to make after-dinner conversation, he had uttered an astonishing remark to the second Duke of Wellington: "They tell me, my Lord, that your father was also a military man." The classics of military literature he never read. After the Civil War, a delegation from Boston sent to examine his library with a view to making handsome additions was surprised to find no books about war on his shelves; his collection consisted chiefly of patent-office reports. For military engineering he had some aptitude, but his knowledge of tactics was simple, self-taught, and often faulty.

From the retrospect of old age he thought the Civil War was "necessary." But about the first struggle in which he engaged, the Mexican War, Grant held a different opinion. "I do not think there was ever a more wicked war than that waged by the United States on Mexico," he wrote. "I thought so at the time, when I was a youngster, only I had not moral courage enough to resign."[13] Competently enough he served as regimental quartermaster, but gained less spectacular glory than did Lee and Jefferson Davis. At the war's end he married Julia Dent, sister of his West Point roommate. Through the years ahead, from rags to riches and back to poverty, they remained in love with each other—holding hands like an engaged couple whenever they were reunited after a few days' absence, shy prosaic people whose romance was the only lyric passage in their lives. The notion of infidelity was too absurd for serious attention, from even the bitterest of Grant's enemies.

The Mexican War, however, brought out one weakness of the flesh which looms large in the Grant legend. This was an appetite for strong drink. He first found this avenue of escape, it seems, from the sultry boredom of a soldier's life in Mexico. Evidence suggests that he never drank the oceans of fiery spirits with which political slander credited him. He had apparently a very weak head, and a sniff of the cork— as the phrase runs—carried him from torpor into exhilaration. After marriage, he helped organize a chapter of the Sons of Temperance and solemnly told his fellow pledgers: "There is no safety from ruin by liquor, except by abstaining from it altogether." Sent to California, homesick for wife and children, he lapsed sadly—at Fort Humboldt, according to memorable tradition, once driving three horses tandem at breakneck pace, with their three buggies careering behind. The behavior of Grant sober was so unlike that of Grant in his cups that nobody ever forgot these purple moments. They led to his forced resignation from the Army in 1854, and his return home on borrowed money, in disgrace. In times of discouragement—the following days of farming and shabby clothes and tramping the streets of St. Louis— he returned to the bottle. But when fortune smiled, banishing boredom and inferiority—during most of the Civil War and all through the Presidency—Grant was able to resist this appetite. True to the Alger formula, success made him a better man. Folklore, denied by Lincoln himself, said that the wartime President had dismissed rumors of Grant's alcoholism with the famous words: "Well, I wish some of you would tell me the brand of whiskey that Grant drinks. I would like to send a barrel of it to my other generals." This story was invented by a reporter on *The New York Herald,* and first appeared there on November 26, 1863.[14] Sounder was the testimony of Hamilton Fish to a Southern inquirer in 1872, respecting Grant's habits in the White House. The Secretary of State denied that he had ever seen the President "in the most remote degree under any excitement from wine or drink of any kind."[15] Not even biographers for boys, like Thayer, made an effort to conceal the reason for Grant's youthful resignation from the Army; the contrast to his later "total abstinence" and success in life was thought to point a moral. That success was the cause, not the effect, of Grant's temperance was a subtlety that they missed.

Desperate days followed Grant's return to civilian life. He plowed the acres of a little farm which he had aptly named "Hardscrabble," near St. Louis. On the streets of that town he peddled wood. He tried to collect rents for a real-estate house, but his seedy appearance and defeated air told against him. Julia Grant's family, the Dents, despised him and grew increasingly reluctant to support the brood of children he was begetting. Acquaintances from whom he tried to borrow small sums took to crossing the street at his approach. Just before Christmas Eve, 1857, he pawned his watch for $22, a fact of mute eloquence. He tried to sell, or hire out, two slaves owned by his wife; later eulogists sought to conceal the fact that she had ever owned slaves. Finally he moved his family to Galena, Ill., which the more prosperous Grants called home—"the place," as Robert Frost defines it, "where when you have to go there they have to take you in." His brothers gave him a job clerking in their leather store.

This is the story of Ulysses S. Grant before the Civil War, a disheartening chapter worthy the early pages of an Alger novel. It explains also why the later Grant loved to warm both hands before the drawing-room fires on Fifth Avenue, sampling the Havanas and brandy of A. T. Stewart, Edwards Pierrepont, August Belmont, and Jay Gould; why he adored to have Julia call him "Victor."

Upon the outbreak of hostilities he offered his services to the War Department. There was no answer; years later his letter was found in the dusty files. Soon, however, he was taken on as a drillmaster near Springfield. He had no uniform nor the wherewithal to buy one; a rusty cavalry saber, which he had found in the state arsenal and strapped about his waist, was his only insigne. They laughed when he was given command of a regiment of farm boys. "One of them, to show off to the others, got behind his back and commenced sparring at him, and while he was doing this another gave him such a push that he hit Grant between the shoulders," recalled General John E. Smith.[16] Stumpy and always badly shaved, Grant did not inspire respect at first sight. He was never very popular with his men, and soldiers never cheered him spontaneously. But he knew something about drill and discipline, and his will was stubborn as nails. His dogged brand of tenacity, frustrated before the war and a liability afterwards, was at its best in the field. He began to develop qualities of command and decision which neither Grant nor others suspected he had. A Galena businessman put up money to buy him a uniform and equipment, and he was off to the wars.

Into Missouri he marched, mopping up bands of secessionists, learning something about fighting guerillas. Thanks to his old friend Congressman Washburne—asked by Lincoln to nominate a brigadier general from Illinois—Grant was promoted far more rapidly than the lock-step system of the regular army would have countenanced. Success at Belmont encouraged Grant to press on against Fort Donelson. His reply to General Buckner, "No terms except an unconditional surrender can be accepted. I propose to move immediately upon your works," was thought "unchivalrous" by the Southerner who had lent Grant his fare home in 1854. But these words, backed up with victory, thrilled the North, passing into phrase and fable. Newspapers reported the coolness with which Grant had ordered the attack, a cigar in his mouth. He later remarked that Fort Donelson made him a heavy cigar-smoker for life; hitherto a light smoker, he could not resist the victory tribute of some 10,000 boxes of cigars. On the battlefield, tobacco was his one indulgence. The profanity, for example, which distinguished most officers of the war who did not belong to the school of praying generals, was no trait of U. S. Grant. He said that he never felt the urge. Later, in the Wilderness campaign, he was heard several times to say "Confound it!" and "Doggone it!" But a phlegmatic nature craved no further relief.

Two months after Donelson, the battle of Shiloh brought Grant a taste of public fickleness. General W. T. Sherman, whom he admired as a more brilliant man than himself, had assured him that the Confederates would not attack. Grant was therefore taken by surprise. Although he recovered his losses after hard fighting and the arrival of help, Grant received bitter blame in the newspapers. Drunkenness, inefficiency, even treachery were laid at his door. But Lincoln never wavered, liking what he called Grant's bulldog grip: "I can't lose this man. He fights." Lincoln perhaps did not know of Grant's lifelong "superstition" against retreating or retracing his steps: even as a young man, Grant in looking for a house and overshooting the mark, would go on until he came to a crossroad, and then work his way back over a new path. As a commander he knew how to fight in only one way. He waged a war of movement, always advancing upon the enemy, too "superstitious" to retreat. To Lincoln and to the North, weary of cautious, blundering, wavering generals, Grant seemed the veritable answer to prayer. His ablest campaign, against Vicksburg, redeemed him with the newspapers. In March, 1864, he was called to Washington, made lieutenant general, and pitted against his greatest opponent, Robert E. Lee.

The public began to enjoy his matter-of-fact colorless ways—because they were so unlike the drum-and-trumpet airs of military heroes. Hotel clerks assigned him to an attic room, until he signed the register. At his first attendance on a White House levee, he was crushed and elbowed until tall Mr. Lincoln spied him and Mr. Seward persuaded him to stand on a sofa so that people could get a look at him. His half-buttoned coat, straggly beard and clothes smelling of rank cigars, and false teeth which had been made in haste to replace a pair thrown out with the wash-bowl water by an orderly at Vicksburg—these incongruous notes blended the hero with the common man, and other common men were pleased by the paradox. He was not scintillating, but methodical; he made war in a cool, tenacious way which businessmen could understand. One job at a time sufficed. To proposals that he run for President in 1864, against Lincoln, he was deaf. "I should like to be mayor of Galena," he told a political delegation, ". . . to build a new sidewalk from my home to the depot." This dry comment, like those of Calvin Coolidge sixty years later, passed for the essence of Yankee wit. Similarly his determination at the Potomac, "to fight it out along this line if it takes all summer," passed into folk speech. Grant's phrases never sparkled, but by their very bromidic quality steadied the panic of war psychosis. He gave the impression of having situations well in hand.

When others were bewildered or excited, Grant was calm—normal save that his powers of perception and judgment were heightened by crisis. That he knew little of the science of war hardly mattered. As Winston Churchill has written of his ancestor, the Duke of Marlborough, "the success of a commander does not arise from following rules and models" but from an immediate grasp of each situation as it arises. Grant saw simple but essential facts that others, in the multiplicity of detail, missed. He understood, for instance, that the taking of Chattanooga would close the gateway of the South and seal her doom. A certain genius Grant undoubtedly had. It appeared more strongly in the Mississippi Valley campaigns (when he had fewer advantages in men and resources) than in the last assault upon Virginia. Grant in fact looked most admirable when fortune did not give him all the trumps, and he had to work shrewdly for victory. Lacking extraordinary stimulus, he did little.

In these days, as later in the White House, Grant relied upon advisers more than seemed possible for a man of superficially stubborn will. Adam Badeau told young Henry Adams: "For stretches of time, his mind seemed torpid. Rawlins and others would systematically talk their ideas into it, for weeks, not directly, but by discussion among themselves in his presence. In the end, he would announce the ideas as his own, without seeming conscious of the discussion. . . . They could never follow a mental process in his thought. They were not sure that he did think."[17] During the war years, with Lincoln, Sherman, Meade and others at his elbow, Grant overheard better advice than later reached his ears in the White House. Also, the wearing down of Lee's army by "attrition" was a problem which suited Grant's mind and temperament. In the North, many were aghast at the cost of his grim bludgeoning. Foes of Grant always called him "the Butcher," recalling the 7000 men he lost to less than 1000 Confederates at Cold

Harbor, on June 3, 1864—when Federal soldiers, under the hopelessness of the impending attack, pinned strips of paper, giving their names and addresses, upon their coats. Others recalled the slaughter of 4000 in the crater at Petersburg, by a singularly bad error in Grant's judgment. On February 25, 1867, *The New York Tribune* described "the face of the only man in America, perhaps, who could make the calculation of the multitude of lives necessary to blot out a multitude of other lives, and could work out the bloody sum of its accurate terrible results." It was well for the North, no doubt, with its vast resources of man power that Grant was a "doer" rather than a thinker—dogged, objective, plodding, haunted by few dreams or regrets. (Only his close friends knew how Grant hated cruelty to animals, especially horses, and had been sickened by a bull-fight in Mexico.)

Success, crowned by Appomattox, made him not the butcher but the savior. An index of his new fame is an advertisement which appeared in *The Washington Evening Star* on April 14, 1865:

> LIEUT. GENERAL GRANT, ARRIVED
> in town last evening, on his way to Philadelphia
> will visit Ford's Theatre THIS EVENING, in
> company with President and Mrs. Lincoln.

Thus, despite a poor play and the inauspicious day of Good Friday, a full house assembled to see General Grant—who unexpectedly changed his plans, and went on to Philadelphia—and they remained to witness the deed of Booth. If Grant had been present in the box, and had received a mortal wound from Booth's dagger, he would have shared the grand apotheosis of martyrdom. Instead, Grant lived through years whose best description seems to be in Housman's lines about

> Lads that wore their honors out,
> Runners whom renown outran
> And the name died before the man.

III

In the months that followed Appomattox, the tides of applause and ovation eddied about Grant. He had received Lee's surrender; he was the commander-in-chief of a victorious army, and soon by appointment from Congress became the first full general since George Washington. William Tecumseh Sherman was his only possible rival, but Sherman hated ovations and had the gruff good sense to steer clear of political publicity. "I never see my name in print without a feeling of contamination," Sherman once remarked. When told that three members of the press had been killed by a bursting shell before Vicksburg, he replied, "Good! Now we'll have news from hell before breakfast." Up to the times of Colonel Lindbergh, no potential hero dealt more rudely with the newspapers than did Sherman. Among Civil War idols, he was unique in the sincerity of his determination never to be President. None could mistake his rejection of the nomination offered in 1884. He scorned to play to the galleries, though in old age he succumbed to a weakness for making after-dinner speeches. Sherman's correspondence, now in the Library of Congress, reveals an almost complete absence of popular fan-mail. His efficiency as a soldier never captured the true fervor of hero-worship. The South—remembering words he did not say, "I will bring every Southern woman to the washtub," the March to the Sea, and later the scolding tone of his memoirs—made him into a villain. The North recalled that he said, in effect though not exactly, that "war is hell." But these seemed strange words from a professional soldier. And, like Farragut's "Damn the torpedoes," they were expunged from biographies for the young.

But Grant placidly accepted ovations, presents, intimations of the Presidency. His own youthful model, in war as in dress, had been Zachary Taylor, "Old Rough and Ready," whose reward had been the White House. Like him, Grant was now ready. Meanwhile he received more cigars, swords, horses, medals, and honorary degrees. Galena welcomed him home with a flower-decked arch, "General, the Sidewalk is Built"—and it led to a new $16,000 house filled with plush furniture, a gilt clock, a pyramidal what-not, a steel engraving of the Stag at Bay, and in the kitchen a Big Acorn cooking-stove. But this tribute was wistfully provincial in view of things to come. The Union League Club of Philadelphia presented him with a "mansion," containing according to the press "rich but not gaudy furniture," and in the parlor a bust of the General himself "resting on a richly carved pedestal." Bands, parades, and fireworks followed him everywhere. New York raised a sum of $100,000 for him, and "fifty solid men of Boston" bought Grant $75,000 worth of books, as seemed fitting in contrast to the gross materialism of Manhattan. Greeley's *Tribune* remarked on February 23, 1866: "Since Richmond's capitulation the stern soldier has spent his days, and eke his nights, in conjugating the transitive verb *to receive*." But of course *The Tribune* was biased, taking occasion five days later to rebuke America's "pitiable taste" in her selection of heroes, and adding: "There is every reason why we should honor those who survived the great battles. . . . But is it this we do when we give gifts and receptions to one man?" (Indeed, for the common soldier, *kudos* and pickings were slim. For instance, a few months later a magazine called *The Soldier's Friend* was offering small prizes in a handwriting contest for "soldiers and sailors of the Union who lost their Right Arm by disability or amputation in the late War." Grant, however, did give one of his horses for auction at a soldiers' benefit fair.)

Grant seldom had anything to say in response to ovations, being, as he said, "entirely unaccustomed to public speaking and without the desire to cultivate the power."[18] Once, as Badeau recalled, when crowds at a station shouted for a speech and Grant remained tongue-tied, little Jesse Grant, aged seven, stepped forward and recited "The Boy Stood on the Burning Deck." To an age of fulsome oratory, Grant's "reticence, modesty, and unostentatious simplicity" were enchanting. Here was the strong silent man—who like the proverbial owl gained a reputation for wisdom by saying nothing. Thomas Nast pictured a rugged soldier inscrutable as the Sphinx. "He spoke no word, but saved the State," Thomas Bailey Aldrich wrote; later, James Russell Lowell composed a poem "On a Bust of General Grant"—

> Strong, simple, silent . . .
> One of those still plain men that do the world's rough work.

Of course there were dissenters. "The Lively Life of U. S. Grant, the Dummy Candidate," a pamphlet published in 1868, remarked that he "has nothing to say and keeps on saying it day in and day out." But this was a scurrilous satire, which sneered at him as "the Uncle of his Country," and alleged that "several Temperance societies have offered him flattering inducements to become a frightful example in the interest of the cause." Milder critics noted that he conserved his verbal resources; having said something that pleased him, he repeated it. To his Galena neighbors, assembled to congratulate him on his election to the Presidency, Grant had said, "The responsibilities of the position I feel, but accept them without fear." He liked the sentence well enough to incorporate it into his First Inaugural speech, where some thought it displayed a touch of swagger. Still others opined that he did not always live up to his words. Upon the threshold of the Presidency he had said, "Let us have peace"—a declaration which rang through the land, and is now engraved over his tomb in Riverside Park, New York. Yet he refused to ride in the same carriage with Andrew Johnson, at his inauguration, and his policy of Reconstruction lacked much in charity.

Grant had been swept into office without scrutiny of his qualifications. The public, like Grant himself, thought of the Presidency as a reward rather than a responsibility. As early as August, 1867, Gideon Welles, Secretary of the Navy, confided to his Diary that he had found Grant "severely afflicted with the Presidential disease . . . vastly less informed, than I had supposed possible for a man of his opportunities." There was a whirlwind campaign. Grant clubs were called "Tanneries." Veterans of the Blue paraded with "Grant uniforms" and "Grant bands." They sang

> Oh! God was kind and heaven was true
> When it gave us a man like U—
> —lysses Grant
> When it gave us a man like you!

An even more popular lyric echoed through Grant's first and second campaigns, and the attempt to give him a third term in 1880:

> And if asked what State he hails from
> This our sole reply shall be,
> "From near Appomattox Court House,
> With its famous apple tree."

His plain and simple annals were too brief to offer much foothold to his assailants. But some regaled the public with old Jesse's cotton speculations, while others dug up Grant's order removing Jews from his department in 1862. He was elected, however, by a majority of 300,000. Disgruntled Democrats pointed out that he had received approximately 400,000 Negro votes, and that Horatio Seymour was really the white man's choice.

Grant began to appreciate his role as a public character. As one indication, soon after the election of 1868 he told Sherman that he was taking up horses as a hobby, remarking that it was "wiser to choose one's own than to leave the newspapers to affix one less acceptable."[19] In truth, Grant had always been fond of horses, and they responded to his skill—though we are told that dogs disliked him. Everybody in the country came to know about Grant's horses, especially "Cincinnati" and "Butcher Boy," and admirers gave him many more. He was also presented as a family man—who even in the stress of Appomattox had caught up a little girl and "smothered her with kisses, saying, 'This reminds me of my little girl at home, and makes me homesick.'"[20] His younger children—Julia, who later shocked Democrat dowagers by leading the cotillion and staying up all night at the age of sixteen, and Jesse, who on the Grants' world cruise put Queen Victoria in her place—also became public characters. Adult Grants and Dents, including the General's shady brother Orvil and the eleven others whom he appointed to public office,[21] added rather less to his popularity. Before the Senate in 1872, Charles Sumner alluded to "a dropsical nepotism swollen to elephantiasis."

Idealists had looked with anticipation upon Grant's entry into the White House. "No man ever had a better chance to be a great magistrate than he," wrote Lowell to Sir Leslie Stephen. Oliver Wendell Holmes sensed his modesty and power, "entire loss of selfhood in a great aim." "So long as we produce such a man as Grant, our republic is safe," the historian Motley declared to the Duchess of Argyll. (This was before Grant fired Motley as Minister to England, in 1870.) Some hailed him as the greatest President-to-be since Washington; before the first year was out they began to wonder if he were the greatest since Lincoln.[22] Andrew Johnson, the tailor from Tennessee, had had his faults. But he was nobody's fool, and he was a hard worker. These things could not be said for Grant.

"Somehow Grant the General, as first beheld in military dress, appeared to me quite a different person from Grant the President, rigged out at a ball in white tie and black suit, or when seen standing alone in early dusk at the White House gate, with glossy top-hat, smoking a fragrant cigar." Thus wrote James Schouler the historian, who with awe had first beheld the General at army headquarters.[23] Another young historian, Henry Adams, sounded greater depths of disillusion. He found the Grant administration "one dirty cesspool of vulgar corruption." "The moral law had expired—like the Constitution," he decided, and to a young idealist the scent of Washington was sickening. Adams's faith in evolution, in the perfectionism of democracy, took a wound from which it never recovered; and he wandered forth on a skeptic's pilgrimage to the thirteenth century, looking for some principle of spiritual integrity that the unmannerly West had lost. Liberal editors like Samuel Bowles, Godkin, and Bryant soon gave up hope in Grant, and joined Horace Greeley among the ranks of discontent. Of course, as Allan Nevins has lately observed, the common man knew and cared little about the inside story of the Grant régime. To his eyes Grant was already lodged in the cloudy Valhalla of myth—the will of the Union cause, even as Lincoln had been its brain. His services had already been rendered, and all the exactions of peace seemed trivial in comparison. Only after the multiplication of scandal, and the post-Presidential affair of Grant & Ward, did the average man begin to rub his eyes and take notice. But soon thereafter Grant's heroic death reclaimed all, and to old admirers he resumed the place in which Whitman's tribute placed him—

Man of the mighty days—and equal to the days!

Years before, Whitman had called the victor of Appomattox "the good, worthy, non-demonstrative, average-representing Grant," and was proud of exchanging silent salutes with him on the streets of Washington. Hence there were always two sharply different opinions about President Grant—the difference being that between sentimental devotion to a military hero and the realistic appraisal of a chief executive.

What were Grant's virtues and faults in the White House? On the credit side, let it be said that he was personally honest. He was often a dupe, but never a knave. From the various machinations which made his Presidency the most corrupt in American history—more versatile in its graft than even the Harding régime—Grant seems not to have made a penny for himself. His most critical students of recent date, like Woodward, Hesseltine, and Nevins, give him a clear bill of health in this regard. Among honest men who knew him best, and saw the unclean hands which pulled the strings about him, Hamilton Fish called Grant "the most scrupulously truthful man I ever met," while Horace Porter termed him "tediously truthful." (Porter had grown bored by Grant's total recall in telling his favorite stories or in relating conversations.) Grant was also a very loyal man. Starved of affection in boyhood, and immersed by forty years of failure, he looked hungrily for friendship, from men he could trust implicitly. For past kindnesses he was grateful. Folklore told how he had given the postmastership of Nashville to a St. Louis butcher who had "furnished meat to my family on credit"—saying, "I intend to appoint this butcher if it bursts the Republican Party." Another story reported that Grant bestowed office upon a St. Louis Democrat, with the remark, "Oh, damn the politics," in remembrance of the firewood that this citizen had bought, out of pure charity, in Grant's peddling days.[24] The public liked this loyal, democratic twist to the spoils system. Its dangers they did not foresee. They failed to understand that Grant, in his myopic search for friendship, would be taken in by flattery, costly presents, and bonhomie. Hail-fellows-well-met, with the joviality of saloon and billiard parlor —Ben Butler, Orville Babcock, Henry D. Cooke, Jim Fisk—knew how to twist Grant around their pudgy fingers, at least to a dangerous degree. His credulity could not quite stomach Fisk. For even though Fisk in his "admiral's uniform" of gold lace and stars had wined and dined the President, and persuaded Grant to accept indiscreet favors of railway and steamboat accommodations *de luxe,* there was never much trust between them. After the gold scandal of Black Friday, Grant announced to the newspapers that he had long known Fisk to be "a man . . . destitute of moral character."[25] The puzzle of Grant's association with him was left unexplained. But, with this solitary exception, Grant was never able to believe that any man who had befriended him could be a scoundrel—or, on the other hand, that any man who opposed him could be honest.

Grant's partisanships explain most of his tragic blunders. Feeling that all men were either violently for or against him, and must be treated accordingly, Grant as President bore grudges and hates with an intensity none had suspected before. He revelled in his loathing of Andrew Johnson, and could not pass the windows of Charles Sumner's house without shaking his fist at them. Having come under the sway of Whig Republicans, he pursued the issue of Reconstruction in the South with a vindictiveness as hard to reconcile with Appomattox as with Ambrose Bierce's later lines, in "The Death of Grant":

> His the soft answer that allayed
> War's giant animosities.

Thanks in part to Grant, "the poor man's fight" (as some had called the conscript system of the North) ended as the rich man's peace. The South groaned beneath carpetbaggers and scalawags, the North under Tweed rings and the profiteers of "shoddy," the West in the grip of hulking empire-builders—and in the White House was a man who looked upon big business with the awe of a neophyte for the Eleusinian mysteries. Making money was an arcane art which Grant never understood, but of which he heartily approved. He was plain as an old shoe, himself, but like his generation he was hungry for the luxuries of life, a parvenu to whose soul materialism meant happiness. His Cabinet of rich men, and the erratic changes which brought twenty-four men to occupy its seven places in the course of his administration, did not inspire much confidence. His second Secretary of State, Hamilton Fish, upheld whatever dignity and consistency there was behind the scenes. Fish saw, but kept loyally to himself, the ignorance of his superior. Unlike most Presidents, Grant had no knowledge whatever of law or diplomacy, and took no interest in learning. He was, in fact, lazy—calling Cabinet meetings and then failing to appear himself, leaving upon his desk important letters of state unopened for days, refusing to answer mail which intruded upon his summer peace at Long Branch. Fish's only thought was of concealment from "the Democratic papers," while he attended to the needful work himself.[26] In time, he understood the long stretches of torpor, broken by sudden spasms of violence, which was the rhythm of Grant's temperament. But the public knew little of these things. Whenever Grant made obvious mistakes, he was after all "a blunt, simple soldier." Misplaced loyalties and hates merely proved that he "had his mind poisoned." And if he were remiss, and took long vacations such as no earlier President had enjoyed, he was but resting on his well-earned laurels. It was an age of charitable excuse, in which success granted a plenary indulgence.

The chief scandals of the Grant administration were the Crédit Mobilier, the Gold Conspiracy, the Salary Grab, and the Whiskey Ring. The first, a swindle associated with the building of the Union Pacific Railroad, cannot fairly be blamed upon his administration. The fraud antedated his Presidency, although disclosure came during his re-election campaign of 1872. It did implicate two American heroes now tarnished, Garfield, and Blaine "the Plumed Knight," and an exceedingly crooked politician named John A. Logan—a strong Grant partisan—whose name is still sung with reverence in the state anthem of Illinois:

> On the record of thy years
> Abra'am Lincoln's name appears,
> Grant and Logan—and our tears,
>   Illinois, Illinois,
> Grant and Logan—and our tears,
>   Illinois.

In the Gold Conspiracy of 1869, Grant's prestige suffered because he was shown to have hobnobbed with tricksters like Gould and Fisk and Grant's own brother-in-law A. B. Corbin (who, as Fisk told *The New York Herald*, "married into Grant's family for the purpose of working the thing in that direction"). Tardily the President had broken up their scheme, but not until much damage had been done. The "Salary Grab," by which Grant kept abreast of salary increases that Congressmen had voted themselves by allowing his own stipend to be doubled, was a minor episode of 1873—but it angered the country. In the aftermath of the Whiskey Ring, Grant was far more culpable. Nevins calls this "the darkest single page in the history of the Presidency."[27] Grant's secretary and intimate friend Orville Babcock in 1870 conspired with a group of distillers in St. Louis to defraud the Government of the taxes on their product. The scheme began for the purpose of raising money for the Grant wing of the Missouri Republican Party, but soon proved too profitable to be kept for such impersonal uses. Other distillers throughout the Middle West joined up, or were forced into "the Ring" by blackmail—after being snared into some technical trespass against the law. High Treasury officials in Washington worked hand in glove with local politicians. In 1874, the St. Louis distillers alone bilked the Government of $1,200,000. In that same year President Grant and his party were entertained at the Lindell Hotel in St. Louis, for ten days, by the local arch-swindler. The following spring the scandal broke. With great difficulty Grant was dissuaded from going half across the continent to testify on behalf of his guilty "friend" Babcock. The President did everything possible to hamper his conviction. And when at last Babcock's guilt was proved, Grant set out to dismiss and ruin every official who had had a hand in exposing him.[28] Before all the dirty linen in this basket had been aired, another scandal broke. Grant's Secretary of War, W. W. Belknap, was found to have taken bribes from men who wanted Indian post-traderships. The President was indignant, not at Belknap, but at this disturbance raised for "partisan purposes." He was also annoyed by the disclosure that he himself had given four trading-posts to his brother Orvil, and that Orvil had farmed them out. General Custer's testimony on this point led Grant to deprive him of his command, as *The New York World* reported under the headline "GRANT'S REVENGE." Every season brought new cause for vexation to the simple, blunt soldier in the White House.

In 1872, when the need for a campaign chest drew Grant into still closer rapport with the rich, his administration shelved the Federal income tax. The prime tax burden was thus returned to the farmer and laborer, while Grant became for all time the hero of the Union League Clubs. It was perhaps unconsciously symbolic that, upon his visit to Central City, in the Colorado Rockies, a few months later, the path from his carriage to the hotel door was paved with silver bricks worth $15,000 apiece. In the next year President Grant's only daughter was married to an Englishman, and the presents in gold and silver and crystal and lace which flooded in from brokers and merchants of the East bore eloquent tribute to a certain popularity. These gifts, the cynosure of all eyes, "were arranged by a special agent from Philadelphia," reported *The New York Tribune,* "who attractively classified them in accordance with the stores from which they were purchased."

Grant's second term was less popular than his first. To the public at large, the honeymoon was waning. Somewhat disappointed that he was not drafted for a third term, Grant went out of office in 1877 and embarked for Europe. His grandiose reception abroad was the pride of loyal fans at home. The Army of the Potomac, in convention assembled, cabled him a message "in care of Queen Victoria, Windsor Castle, England." (That dawn of cynicism was not foreseen when the label, "late General Grant," like "late Victorian," should stand for ostentation in taste and hypocrisy of conscience.) Books, brochures, and innumerable newspaper articles were published about Grant's Grand Tour. The devout traced it through the pages of the Rand-McNally gazetteer. Even Thayer, the boys' biographer, gives an exhaustive account of it—including Grant's visit to Westminster Abbey, where Dean Stanley referred to him in the sermon, Thayer commenting proudly that Grant's honors "grew on every tree. . . . Even in the house of God they fell at his feet without shaking the tree!" Grant's sojourn in Venice inspired his famous remark to a young woman, that "Venice would be a fine city if it were only drained." This was the era of innocents abroad. After a triumphal entry into Jerusalem, with the blowing of shawms, and a leisured sampling of the Orient, Grant and his family returned home late in 1879.

Politics once more buzzed in the air. Grant was eager for a third term; he had come to like the White House very much. With the same old songs and slogans his name was presented to the Republican National Convention. But after an agony of thirty-six ballots he lost the nomination to Garfield, and with no word of congratulation sulked in his tent all summer. He still could inspire poetry. In the Grant miscellany, in the Library of Congress, is a large silk handkerchief on which is printed a poem to "Ulysses the Silent," in honor of his visit to Oshkosh on June 14, 1880:

> Oh! say, have ye heard it, the news that is flying
> Abroad in the land that the Hero is near?

The Hero, to honor whom, nations are vying,
Is coming, is coming, he soon will be here!

Afar in the north is a rush and a tremble,
As onward the iron-horse speeds in his glee;
Ye old men and matrons, assemble, assemble,
And young men and maids, it is he! it is he!

. . . .

Pass on, as thou must, to renewed acclamations;
But ever shall Oshkosh remember and say
How Grant, the World-famous, the Wonder of nations,
Came into her borders, one genial June day.

For fifteen years, now, Grant had been the familiar of rich men, without being one himself. In imitation, Grant as President had given dinners for thirty-six, which, with costly wines, ran to $1500 or $2000. It was natural that without public office his thoughts should now turn to wealth. Knowing that Grant wished to live in New York, and needed more income, *The New York Times*—with the help of John W. Mackay, William H. Vanderbilt, and that embarrassingly faithful Grant admirer Jay Gould—raised $250,000 as a trust fund for him. Grant then entered into partnership with a plausible young broker named Ferdinand Ward, becoming the first ex-President to join the ranks of Wall Street. Ward seemed to Grant to have the touch of Midas. Into the firm went all of Grant's savings, with those of his wife and sisters and $12,000 inherited by Grant's little niece. The General's old soldiers and their widows sent in all they could scrape. Profits of several hundred per cent within a few months tempted the most innocent, who like Grant himself had an immense respect for the Eleusinian mysteries. Behind Grant's back Mr. Ward used the General's great name, the legend of his invincibility, to the full. He whispered of Government contracts pouring in from Washington. The sentiments of a later rhapsodist, that "America is where General Grant is buried," were anticipated in lifetime by the feeling that the United States Government was where the General hung his hat. When skeptics asked for a sight of these contracts, Mr. Ward looked wise and said that the most important ones were in the General's possession, and that, as every one knew, the General was a close-mouthed man. But Ulysses the Silent held all the trumps. Sometimes Mr. Ward produced a few specimen contracts; regrettable to state, they were forged. Of these things Grant knew nothing. He had early brushed aside the suggestion that he try to angle for such contracts. His simple faith was fed by the falsified books of Grant & Ward, the assurance that he was now worth over $2,000,000, the glittering carriage which conveyed him downtown every morning, the twenty-five superb Havana cigars which Mr. Ward thoughtfully laid each day upon his desk. The years 1881 to 1884 marked the nadir of Grant's popular fame. Many suspected that all was not well with Grant & Ward, but did not know whether the General were naïve or a guilty accomplice. The common man, though lacking inside information, felt it was somehow undignified for a great military hero to be scrambling with the speculators in Wall Street —a name ever in bad odor to provincial nostrils. Grant's Mexican Railway schemes also sounded shady. And it was known that he had tried to interfere with the patronage under President Arthur. Ulysses S. Grant, supposedly pulling wires and raking in the dollars, began to seem less noble than the soldier under "the famous apple tree" of Appomattox or even riding in a barouche down Pennsylvania Avenue.

Then came disaster. Overnight, in May, 1884, the firm collapsed. Ward had reached the end of his rope, with liabilities of $16,792,640; within a few weeks he was on his way to the penitentiary Grant was bewildered, then remorseful. He offered everything he had to satisfy creditors, but even his trust fund had ceased to pay dividends. He lacked the hard cash to pay grocery bills of his household, until a few unknown admirers sent gifts (which he accepted as loans) of a few thousand dollars. The public began to pity him. And then, as if this were not enough, a gnawing pain in his throat was diagnosed as cancer. At bay, the old soldier faced death and the prospect of leaving his family unprovided for. For *The Century Magazine,* whose offers he had turned down in palmy days, Grant began to write articles on his campaigns, and Mark Twain—analyst of the Gilded Age and its expansive follies—offered him a generous contract for his Memoirs. Again Grant began to fight it out, pitting himself against time with the old resolution. He dictated until his voice gave out, then scribbled on a pad with shaky fingers. Pages of plodding, dogged, honest writing came from his pencil, recollections of a soldier which later admirers were to call the greatest since Cæsar's *Commentaries.*

Crowds began to gather before his New York house, asking for news which soon took the form of bulletins posted on the door. Sometimes, on his good days, the General would drag himself to the window and bow gravely to them. He hoped they understood about Grant & Ward, and attempted to explain the matter to Mark Twain, saying Ward was "an offending child." To the last, he could rouse no bitterness against associates proved unworthy of his trust. At times, too, he showed a sense of humor, though this vein had never run deep in his character. He told Doctor Shrady how, years ago, in a shower he had shared an umbrella with a stranger. Both were going to a reception in honor of General Grant. "I have never seen Grant," the stranger said, "and I merely go to satisfy a personal curiosity. Between us, I have always thought that Grant was a very much overrated man." "That's my view also," answered the guest of honor.[29] The reply was not insincere: for years Grant had been dwelling in the wonderland of his own success.

Publicity was mobilized around the dying General. Reporters occupied the windows across the street; one newspaperman made love to a chambermaid in order to get a good second-floor view. One day when his doctor let the tobacco-starved man take a puff or two on a cigar, great headlines appeared: GRANT SMOKES AGAIN. The Reverend J. P. Newman, a popular Methodist pastor, was encouraged by Grant's family to visit the bedside of a man who had never shown interest in religion. To the incredulity of Mark Twain, Mr. Newman was soon quoting for the newspapers Biblical remarks which Grant uttered about "the Valley of the shadow of Death." In April, when the General was unconscious and apparently sinking fast, Mr. Newman sprinkled water over him and told the press that Grant had been converted and baptized. After the baptism, as Grant revived while the doctor worked over him, Mr. Newman exclaimed, "It is Providence. It is Providence." "No," said the physician, "it was the brandy." In June the stricken man was carried to the cooler air of Mount McGregor, near Saratoga. Crowds of tourists followed him, gazing silently from the road. He was deeply touched when old Confederate generals— Forrest, Longstreet, Buckner to whom he had sent the famous terms of "unconditional surrender"—came to see him. He was also pleased when Congress, Democrats voting with Republicans, restored him to the rank and pay of General. Such tokens of reviving popularity, of sympathy, were precious. A week before his death, bundled under shawls and blankets, working under alternate phases of morphine and excruciating pain, torpor and hæmorrhage, he brought to a close his recollections of the Civil War: "I hope the good feeling inaugurated may continue to the end."

IV

Issued posthumously in 1885, these Memoirs won even greater popularity than Mark Twain had hoped. He paid Mrs. Grant some $450,000 in royalties. The fact was symbolic. Once more General Grant was a great American hero. Suffering had clothed him in ideality. As he lay dying, on March 14, 1885, *The New York Tribune*—which once had reproved the "pitiable taste" of homage to Grant—published Robert Buchanan's poem "Ulysses," comparing him to a weary eagle flying into the sunset, and to Ulysses the wanderer:

> What tho' a little space, when homeward sailing,
>   Thou saw'st the treacherous Isles where Syrens dwell?
> The sweetest songs they sang were unavailing
>   To keep God's warrior underneath their spell.
>
> *Thou* wast not made to herd with things polluted,
>   Grasp dust of gold, and fawn at Circe's knee,
> Thy flight was sunward, not thro' chasms sooted
>   With leaves that fall from Mammon's upas-tree.
>
> Rest, Wanderer, in the sun, Columbia kisses
>   Her soldier's honor'd brow, and clears its gloom—
> And this white lily of love she brings, Ulysses,
>   Was pluck'd upon thy brother Lincoln's tomb.

With less suavity of phrase, Edward J. Virtue composed and printed in Washington a broadside, "In Memoriam Gen. U. S. Grant," with a woodcut of his face:

> He was an honest, sturdy, hard-working "Tanner,"
> And a brave defender of his Country's banner.
> For the Mal-Acts of others—he was not to blame,
> Should not reflect on Our Second Washington's name.

A popular song, "Heroes who have lately passed away," called the roll of Garfield, McClellan, Hancock, John A. Logan, and of course Grant. The sword myth was refurbished:

> As a man of honor too, his equals they were few,
> For when Lee surrender'd, back his sword he gave.
> U. S. Grant! that was his name! Death at last to him came,
> A harmful word against him none can say.

Among the souvenirs of Colonel Fred. Grant, now in the Library of Congress, is an autographed song by Elizabeth Hancock—

> Our hero is dead, Oh Mount of Ascension,
>   MacGregor! thy heights shall be shrine to our feet;
> From thy top he went up to that grandest convention,
>   Where justified ones with the glorified meet.

The McGregor cottage in truth became a shrine. By Joseph W. Drexel it was given to the G. A. R., who formed a Mount McGregor Memorial Association. They preserved the chairs in which Grant slept when he was not able to lie down, the fans that cooled his brow, the tumbler from which he drank, the pencils and pads of his last messages. Also kept were the floral pieces—crosses, hearts and anchors, pillows, and a "Gates Ajar" from Mr. and Mrs. Leland Stanford. And, with the inevitable commercial touch, the Mt. McGregor Railroad issued a souvenir time-table, announcing that the spot is now "of historic interest to all." A postcard in the same collection, called "The Hero's Welcome," is a photograph of "Homer Henderson's famous allegorical painting, valued at five thousand dollars." It shows "our Hero's welcome in the Land Beyond. . . . Lincoln and Garfield, with an angel escort, have been awaiting him upon the other shore, and thus are the first to welcome America's greatest Ambassador to the Celestial world. Among the great departed may be recognized Washington, Jefferson, Franklin, Adams, Webster, Jackson, Clay, Douglas, Sumner and Lafayette who hasten with rejoicing to the scene." In Heaven or elsewhere Grant no doubt would have been astonished to find his arch-enemy Charles Sumner among the welcoming committee —Sumner the skeptic, whose infidelity had led Grant to make one of those unexpected and famous sallies which anticipate Coolidge. Told that Sumner did not believe the Bible, Grant remarked: "No, he did not write it."

Grant's memory has never inspired the sentiment of tenderness of Lincoln's or the majesty of Lee's. His character held rigidities and limitations which the artist realizes. His career, signally illustrating both the virtues and pitfalls of the success story, follows no crescendo of drama—to the tragedy of Lincoln or the tranquillity of "all passion spent" with Lee. Its first act is bleak with failure; its second, with the obbligato of fife and bugle, is the climax; its third, with the bustle of high office, is sadly undistinguished; its fourth, with ticker tape and the cries of newsboys, is shabbiest of all; and the last act, of pain bravely borne, is far better, but lacks the redemptive dignity of a willed sacrifice. Parts of the second and third acts are suppressed by conventional hero-worship. As one example out of many, a school text by the historian Muzzey saying that "A clique of Wall Street bankers practically managed the country during Grant's Presidency," has been banned by patrioteers. One American city expelled this text from its high school because this school was named for Grant, and it was felt embarrassing to offer the pupils an "unfavorable picture of Grant."[30] Grant is conventionally recalled as one of America's greatest soldiers, and war tends to revive his cult. Thus in the World War of 1917–18 George Morrow Mayo wrote—

> Here's to the Blue of the wind-swept North
> When we meet on the fields of France,
> May the spirit of Grant be with you all
> As the sons of the North advance.

And Edmund Vance Cooke numbered him among the inspirations of youth:

> Back of the boy is Wilson,
> Pledge of his high degree,
> Back of the boy is Lincoln,
> Lincoln and Grant and Lee.

In 1940 Helen Todd wrote, within the framework of his life, a sympathetic novel called *A Man Named Grant*.

But, save for sculptors, few artists have turned their hand to the Grant saga. He has his bronze and marble Memorial in Washington, on the axis of the Mall, done by Henry M. Shrady and unveiled at the Grant Centenary in 1922. The equestrian figure, with shoulders bowed and firm-set jaw, is good pictorial art but it offers no shrine or thrill to the pilgrim. Grant's tomb on Riverside Drive, above the city which saw his most prosperous and least happy days, is rather too Napoleonic for the man. Adjoining its site is a more modest grave, commemorating a lad named St. Clair Pollock, who died at the age of five, long ago on July 15, 1795. Save for the rare moods of petulance in Grant's temper, the character of him who sleeps under tons of granite—a character of simple virtues, of bewilderment and complaisance—is described well enough in the quaint epitaph of this neighboring stone:

> "Erected to the Memory of an amiable Child."

CHAPTER THIRTEEN

THE DIME NOVEL AND BUFFALO BILL

"Gosh! the things they write!"—COLONEL WILLAM F.
CODY, upon reading a Beadle novel about himself.

I

AT ONE TIME it seemed dangerously probable that the model
American boy would be a sissy. Nathaniel Willis in 1827
had founded that blameless guide *The Youth's Companion.* About the same season, Peter Parley was telling
his improving tales to boys and girls, with the air of a
eunuch uncle. Jacob Abbott in 1834 launched the first among those
paragons of priggishness, the Rollo Books. "Be good, sweet maid, and
let who can, be clever," was the accepted dictum to young ladies, and
even their brothers were expected somehow to emulate "the colorlessly
perfect and docile youth" whose existence T. B. Aldrich came to doubt,
a generation later, in writing *The Story of a Bad Boy.* Aldrich's generation had seen the coursing of red blood through the veins of fictional
youth.

The lurid adventure story began, it seems, as a yarn for adults in
the era of Jacksonian democracy. The common citizen, gaining the
reading habit under the sway of popular education and the newspapers,
liked tales of men against the sea, the forest, or the frontier. They not

only thrilled the dweller in humdrum life, but also fed his sense of self-reliance. They glorified the resourcefulness of the plain man against redskins, swindlers, pirates. Their heroes were neither rich nor intellectual, but men who hobnobbed with danger, lived with breath-taking freedom, and won out by bravery in action. Such a world of primitive struggle the average citizen could understand better than the archaic chivalries of Scott and Simms, the horrors of Poe, the thoughtful Calvinisms of Hawthorne. Here, as Merle Curti has said, was the real "proletarian" literature of America—"Ned Buntline's" rowdy yarns of the brine, Emerson Bennett's melodramas of the prairie, tales of tears and valor from the pens of George Lippard and Joseph Holt Ingraham. The hero was the man who dared. "Always do what you are afraid to do," preached Emerson in his lecture called *Heroism,* in praise of those who have "broken the monotony of a decorous age."

The Civil War, shattering the decorum of the sentimental years, made national this thirst for adventure. To be sure, the first dime novel —from the press of Erasmus and Irwin Beadle—appeared in June, 1860. Its title was *Malaeska,* and its authoress Ann Sophia Winter-botham Stephens, who helped edit *The Ladies' Companion,* held a tea-drinking salon in New York, and was acquainted with Thackeray and Dickens. Despite these unlikely antecedents, her hero was a white hunter, stern and steely, with less than Leatherstocking's compunction about taking human life: "Many a dusky form bit the dust and many a savage howl followed the discharge of his trusty gun." These brac-ing words would soon be rewritten hundreds of times. Edward S. Ellis, a young schoolmaster, promptly wrote a yarn about Seth Jones, scout among the Green Mountain Boys and foe of the redskins; its public called for more than 600,000 copies. The American Revolution was, in fact, the first favored theme of dime novelists. The Civil War, popularly styled "the second American Revolution," carried readers back to the spirit of '76. The publishers of a Revolutionary thriller by N. C. Irons, in 1862, announced that "in these stirring days when the Old Continental spirit is being reawakened, it will give particular satisfaction to the readers of fiction." Beadle published dime biog-raphies of Anthony Wayne, Lafayette, Paul Jones, Daniel Boone, and others; paper-backed lives of Washington and his generals were in new demand. Dime-novel glorification of the Revolution fell off after the Civil War; villains were no longer Tories, but Indians and West-ern bad men. But the first love of dime novelists was never wholly forgotten, and just after the Spanish-American War it quickened into life once more with "the Liberty Boys" series of Harry Moore, which ran to 1249 titles—including *The Liberty Boys' Neatest Trick, or How the Red Coats were Fooled; The Liberty Boys at Saratoga, or the Surrender of Burgoyne; The Liberty Boys and the "Swamp Fox," or Helping Marion; The Liberty Boys' Sharpshooters, or The Battle of the Kegs.* How much the popular hero-worship of the Revolution owes to such books is not often pointed out.

But, whether written about patriots in buff and blue, or the buckskin rangers of the West, or the jolly tars of the American navy, Beadle dime novels played a real part in the wartime psychology of the North. They were sent to camps by the millions, it is said, often bound in bales. Soldiers read them, silently or aloud, by the dim and flaring lamps, and passed them from hand to hand. They were swapped, says tradition, between Yank and Rebel on the battle line. Many boys were buried with dime novels in their pockets.[1] From news-stands and cross-roads stores these short novels in salmon-colored paper covers circulated almost as briskly among the civilian population of the Union. The American News Company had a standing order for 60,000 copies as each new issue rolled from the press. In fiction, they were the perfect expression of the Age of Barnum. Dime novels have been compared to the numberless herds of buffalo and clouds of passenger pigeons over the Western prairie which they often described; by reason of their abundance they too were seldom preserved, and now collectors of Americana pay from five to fifty dollars for a paper-backed Beadle of the early series.

At first, these cheap adventure-stories received more praise than blame. Even Lincoln, grateful for the anti-slavery propaganda of their chief editor, Orville J. Victor, bestowed some words of encouragement upon his work. They "do not even obscurely pander to vice or excite passions," said William Everett in 1864. Others saw that the novels were grounded in rugged individualism, exalting the poor against the rich, the self-made against the silver spoon, the purity of the country against the shame of cities. The books of Thomas C. Harbaugh, for example, favored as hero the good-humored, self-reliant lad who lived in the forest, and knew how to hunt moose and wolverine, to thwart fur-thieves and teach many a lesson to the cocksure New York boys who ventured into the wilderness of *Snow-Shoe Tom.* Charles Morris and others showed the country youth "adrift in the city," repulsing hoodlums, resisting vice, reading his mother's

Bible, and at last proving to be heir to a fortune. Dauntless Dick the privateer sails the ocean, and then settles down to riches and respectability. Above all, the frontier is regarded as the proving-ground of Americanism, of courage and adventure and occasionally romance. The dime-novel milieu is a man's world—but, here and there, blushing beauty requires a rescue, and love comes to hearts of oak. The Indian is ever treacherous and cruel; the Negro, who appears less often, is sentimentalized but revealed as helpless and essentially inferior; the foreigner, whether as dude Englishman, comic Dutchman, or Chinese cook, serves as the butt of practical jokes. The hero is Nordic, strong, stalwart, blue-eyed, utterly fearless and a chevalier to all in distress. Sometimes, in the "Westerns," he is allowed to drink but never to lose his self-possession. Major Hall's novel *Giant George,* showing the Giant giving his burro a drink of whiskey, shocked Beadle. The hero may take a hand in a poker-game, but chiefly to show up some despicable cheat. With "soiled and draggled girls"—absent from the pages of early dime novels, but insinuated later into the "Westerns" —he has naught to do, save to give them a helping hand when they are down and out, and point the better way. Heroines, on the other hand, stand in peril of redskins' tomahawks, but never of rape. The stock heroine of *Seth Jones* is captured after she decides "to take a little run to ease my limbs." Editors like Orville J. Victor deleted all profanity that fell under their eye. Even the word *devils,* so valuable in describing Indians and villains in general, was taboo in the Beadle novels because of its "religious associations."

But upon bloodshed there was no ban. Multitudes of redskins bit the dust, and the smell of gunpowder drifted on every breeze. When Beadle's output was challenged in 1866 by the more lurid publishing house of Munro, as the editor testified, "we had to kill a few more Indians than we used to; we held our own against them." The novelist's mind often revelled in sadisms. As a single instance, one may take Ned Buntline's account of young Buffalo Bill as a Union soldier in the Civil War. His motive, it is said, was to avenge the murder of his father—an abolitionist and friend of John Brown, according to Buffalo Bill's publicity, but unknown to history—slain by "Jake M'Kandlas." (As a matter of fact, Buffalo Bill's father died in April, 1857, after catching a heavy cold in the lungs; moreover, McCanles had been killed in a gun battle by Wild Bill Hickok in July, 1861, two and a half years before Buffalo Bill awoke one morning, "after having been under the influence of bad whiskey . . . to find myself a soldier in the Seventh Kansas."²) But Ned Buntline pictures young Buffalo Bill musing, to Wild Bill, upon the fate in store for the villainous "Reb" McCanles:

"I want to take him back to the spot where he murdered my father, and roast him there over a slow fire. Death—a mere man's death—is too good for him. He wants, and shall have, a taste here of what he'll get when he is dead!"

"Mate, you're as bad as the reds, by thunder you are!" said Wild Bill.

"Yes, when I think of him and his gang, I am. . . . Bill, I could glory in every pain that racked his frame. I could see his eyeballs start in agony from his head—the beaded sweat, blood-colored, ooze from his clammy skin —each nerve and tendon quivering like the strings of a harp struck by a maniac hand. Oh, how I could gloat over his howling misery! And it is coming, it is coming—his time. When it does, mercy will not plead to me —not a throe, not a pulsation would I spare for the wealth of all the world!"³

In time, such sanguinary appetites and deeds of gore brought the dime novel into bad odor. It came to be the yellow-backed thriller which boys sneaked into their attic bedroom, or read in the hayloft—a stimulant, said *The New York Tribune* early in 1884, which had led scores of boys to rob their parents before they "started off for the boundless West." It was ironic that this was Horace Greeley's paper, in which his celebrated editorial had appeared, advising young men to go in that direction.

Inevitably, like any stimulant, the dime novel added to its dosage. From Revolutionary patriots to Indians and frontiersmen, the evolution thence proceeded to two-gun men like Wild Bill Hickok and Texas Jack. Then came the era of the desperado, centering about Jesse James and Billy the Kid, in the late seventies and early eighties. Soon, by the same sequence which later brought in the gangster and his nemesis the G-man, arrived the avenger, the detective as hero— Deadwood Dick, a cool unkillable gentleman who wore kid gloves and "a thick black veil over the upper portion of his face," uttering "a wild sardonic laugh" and nursing a Byronic sorrow because his girl Calamity Jane would not marry him. As "Prince of the Road" he righted wrongs, and left behind the sobriquet "dick" for all detectives. Under his spell, wrought by a journalist named Edward L. Wheeler, a generation of American boys formed secret clubs, slipped down the drain-pipe at midnight for conclaves, and wore fruit-knives in their belts. Less dashing was his contemporary "Old Cap Collier," prolific of disguises and muscular enough to beat evil-doers "to a jelly." But he drank and gambled, even while shielding innocence and routing crime. He was therefore a rougher jewel than Jack Harkaway, fashioned by Bracebridge Hemyng along the lines of the ideal English public-school boy, or Nick Carter, created by half a dozen hands, who never touched cigarettes or the bottle. Nick detected crime all over the world with modest ingenuity. He solved train robberies on the New York Central, the work of resurrection men in New York graveyards (inspired by the kidnapping for ransom of A. T. Stewart's body in 1878), murders in San Francisco, the betrayal of state secrets in Japan. In this last, the Mikado told Nick: "An emperor can have but few friends, and I would consider it a privilege to count you as one of mine." In the nineties, and through the first decade of this century, came those youths Frank and Dick Merriwell—inheriting the manliness of Buffalo Bill, and the resourcefulness of the detective, but adding the flavor of prep school and 'varsity. The writer was Gilbert Patten. His publishers picked Yale University—future alma mater of Stover and other athlete heroes, the place where dime novel readers believed that men like bulldogs were bred—for Frank Merriwell's finest exploits. Frank was always kidnapped by villains before the Harvard game, but escaped in time to score the winning touchdown. In baseball he threw a mean curve, but was also ventriloquist, scholar *summa cum laude,* and a merry joker who put turtles in the beds of his nervous friends. He roamed over the West, South America, and Africa, foiling plots. He never smoked or drank, but his reasons were hygienic rather than ethical. In his heyday, it is estimated that half a million boys read about him every week; later he became syndicated as a comic strip.[4]

These novels and the men who wrote them—some of them travellers and hard-bitten soldiers of fortune, others parsons and schoolteachers and semi-invalids who dreamed the epic of the West—are now buried in the dust of time. The movies on the one hand, and pulp magazines on the other, have stolen their audience. Yet for more than a generation they held the mirror up to hero-worship. "First God, then Country, then Friends," was the motto of William T. Adams, one of the best of the tribe, whose pen-name was "Oliver Optic." Their plots were often absurd, their characters pasteboard, their code a quaint mixture of bloodshed and Victorian prudery. But upon the young mind their effect was not too baleful. They taught loyalty, courage, and patriotism. The ideals of chivalry, dying in the New South, revived among the cowboys of Western thrillers—even as many Civil War

veterans, after being uprooted from monotony and craving fresh hori-
zons, took to the West and helped to found its legends. The evolution
of the ideal cowboy proceeded from "Young Wild West" to Owen
Wister's "The Virginian," and then to the cinema fables of William S.
Hart.[5] Even though the frontier is gone, and the tempo of romance
now follows wings in the blue rather than the galloping hooves of
the prairie, the cowboy remains to many young Americans the hero
par excellence.

II

The years after Appomattox saw the rise of new folk legends, about
men like gods. Daniel Boone and Davy Crockett gave place to myths
of the industrial age. There was Paul Bunyan, lumberjack of the North
Woods. He was rocked in a floating cradle, and whenever he became
restless it raised a sixty-foot tide in the Bay of Fundy. Later he moved
to Michigan and finally to the Pacific Northwest, where he hollowed
out Puget Sound by using a glacier for a scoop. He was so fast that
he could blow out the light and get into his bunk before it got dark.
To sharpen his axe he invented the grindstone; his was so big that
every time the wheel made a single revolution it was pay-day. He
once hitched his blue ox, Babe, to a crooked road and pulled until it
was straightened out. Paul was hired by Jim Hill to build the Northern
Pacific Railroad. Jim Hill always got the best of Paul at bargaining,
but Paul was so strong that all jobs were done more quickly than he
had figured, so that he always won out in the end. In running the
right of way, Paul had all the beavers cutting down his logs, and the
gophers digging the post-holes.

If Paul Bunyan could best the empire-builders as a track-layer, then
John Henry the black Hercules could lick a steam drill. He quarried
stone for the Big Bend Tunnel in West Virginia:

> John Henry hammered in the mountains,
> It sounded like an earthquake in the ground.
> He said, "Don't go away, nobody,
> Just my hammer falling down,
> And just my hammer falling down."

He had a stroke like an Alabama mule, and it took six men just to
carry his drills back and forth to the sharpener. His foreman once
laid a big bet that John Henry could outdrill one of those new-fangled
steam drills. Before a great crowd he did so, then dropped dead in

his tracks. He killed himself to prove the power of brawn versus the machine, of sheer racial strength pitted against the ingenuity of the whites. John Henry's reality is buried deep in legend—and a late effort in 1940 to disinter him for the Broadway stage, with the art of Roark Bradford and Paul Robeson, ended in failure. But to thousands of Negroes who have never heard of Booker T. Washington, John Henry is the supreme hero of their race. Dozens of ballads relate his story.[6] And any Negro working man will tell you: "He's man beat the steam drill."

Another hero, enmeshed with the industrial age, is Tony Beaver. He was a giant logger who lived up Eel River in West Virginia. He raised watermelons so big that old Mr. Studebaker made a super-wagon for him, but it held only one of the smallest melons. Tony was also a builder, on behalf of flood control once making a dam of peanuts and molasses across Eel River—and, incidentally, inventing peanut brittle. One part of Tony Beaver's cycle holds more poetry and magic than these tall tales of utilitarianism. It tells how, early one morning when his fellow lumber-jacks were snarling at each other and looking at the world with sour-dough faces, Tony went out to watch the sunrise. He told his fiddler to play a loud merry tune, and suddenly they busted through the surrounding stillness and "let the big music through." Trees and stones, haystacks and rail fences, possums and rabbits, began to dance as they were swept along on the rolling floods of the big music. Even a little cripple danced and was healed. Only a grim old preacher, Brother Moses Mutters, who believed in sin and thought dancing was sinful, refused to join in, and held on to a pine tree with his coattails gyrating. The legend of Tony Beaver, then, is poised somewhere between the times of Orpheus and those of the TVA.

These heroes and others like them—Old Stormalong on the sea, Kemp Morgan in the oil fields, Pecos Bill the cowpuncher who in idle moments invented the lariat and the six-shooter and the Gatling gun, Casey Jones the peerless engineer of Memphis—reflect a struggle of which the myth-makers were perhaps seldom aware. This was the struggle of the hero, in the integrity of his self-assertion, to rise above the anonymous efficiency of the machine age. In these legends, giants still walk the earth, playing scornfully with machines like toys or outstripping them at their own game. Such giants, with all their exaggerations of power, humor, and sentiment, proclaim the dignity of man's naked strength. Sometimes the machine proves to be the death of the hero—as with John Henry and Casey Jones—but, contemptuous of prudence and faithful to his trust, he rises supreme in his death. Later, when the tall timber and frontier had vanished and there were no more regional heroes, a new breed arose who had made its truce with the machine—who became, in fact, wonder-workers of science and masters at the controls. They will be spoken of later, in the company of inventors, engineers, aviators. But here, in the waning nineteenth century, America's folk heroes—stronger on brawn than brains, on courage than ingenuity—had more in common with Boone and Crockett, when lone man was grappling with the frontier and keeping up his courage by telling tales of supermen.

III

Beyond these fictions of Beadle and figments of the folk mind, are certain men of flesh and blood who fitted this vogue for rough-hewn heroes. They may be sorted into those who kept to the leeward side of the law, and those who sailed against it. The latter became desperadoes, who "went bad" by a process which the West regarded as respectfully as it did religious conversion. They robbed banks and trains, "shot it out" with sheriffs, and died with their boots on. They were symbols of a predatory age no less valid than Jim Fisk and Jay Gould, but rather more easily sentimentalized. Admirers believed that these outlaws, like the Robin Hoods and Rob Roys of earlier fame, robbed the rich to give to the poor. A folk ballad about Quantrill, freebooter of the Missouri and Kansas border—who under the guise of helping the Confederacy stole horses, fired villages, and murdered women and children in cold blood at the Lawrence massacre—piously declared:

> Oh, Quantrill's a fighter, a bold-hearted boy,
> A brave man or woman he'll never annoy,
> He'll take from the wealthy and give to the poor,
> For brave men there's never a bolt to his door.

Sam Bass, another outlaw who was killed near Round Rock, Texas, in 1878, is hero of a ballad which used to be sung to soothe cattle along the old Chisholm trail—

> He first went out to Texas,
> A cowboy for to be;
> And a kinder-hearted fellow
> You'd scarcely ever see.

But Billy the Kid, who lorded it over the land-grant potentates of New Mexico, and Jesse James, who robbed the robber barons of Midwest banks and railroads, were greatest among proletarian heroes. They too showed that the individual was greater than a "combine" of regimentation. The folk mind, with scant knowledge of the facts, liked to believe they were inspired by a noble rage against economic inequalities. Billy the Kid was born as William Bonney, in New York City, in 1859. His mother, widowed and remarried, kept boarding-houses in New Mexico. According to fond tradition, Billy at the age of twelve killed his first man, a blacksmith who had passed some flirtatious remark on his mother. "Like all the noted killers of the West, Billy the Kid was of the blond type," wrote a sentimental biographer, Walter Noble Burns, some fifteen years ago. Burns, draw-ing upon the ballads sung by Mexican girls with guitars, saw him as a knight-errant—acting out a gallant drama of Death, like that of the matador. When a bullet knocked a cigarette from between his lips, Billy exclaimed: "Now that's too bad. I'll have to roll another." Besieged in a ranch-house, he saved the piano of his protectress from the flames, while she in turn played upon it "The Star-Spangled Banner" to inspire him "to still more heroic courage." He killed twenty-one men in the course of his twenty-one years, "not counting Indians," but all richly deserved their fate. To the poor and defense-less he was ever true.[7] In 1881, while visiting his sweetheart, Billy was shot by Sheriff Pat Garrett. (Theodore Roosevelt, who admired men with "guts," as President appointed Garrett to the collectorship of customs in El Paso, in 1901; but he failed to renew the appointment when Garrett brought a saloon-keeper as his guest to a Rough Rider reunion in San Antonio.[8]) Legend said that Billy had never been killed, but was alive in Mexico. It was a rumor like those which circulated about Davy Crockett, Jesse James, Buffalo Bill, through the reluctance of popular imagination to admit that its strong men could ever die. The memory of Billy the Kid evoked dime and half-dime novels in the Beadle and Wide Awake Libraries, songs that mourned him with the lugubrious keening of folk balladry, a road-show that flourished in the 1900's, and a cinema of 1935 which was endorsed by the Governor of New Mexico. In 1939 he was treated with better art and less sen-timent in Aaron Copland's "character-ballet" *Billy the Kid,* presented by Lincoln Kirstein's Ballet Caravan. But that Billy is unworthy of his heroic aura few can doubt. Historical evidence shows that he was a hardened criminal, casual in his blood-lust and of the treacherous type whom the West calls "a dirty little killer." His one authentic photograph, reproduced in Emerson Hough's *Story of the Outlaw,* dissipates the legend that he was a dapper man of steel. He there appears as an adenoidal farm-boy with a rifle.

Jesse James, son of a Baptist preacher, joined the church in youth and considered himself a Christian all his life. In the Civil War, from Quantril's guerillas he learned the cheapness of human life. He and his family always maintained that "persecution"—the refusal of Unionists to grant him an amnesty—drove him to a career of crime after the war. Apparently he invented train robbery when, on July 21, 1873, he held up a train of the Rock Island Railroad. Sometimes he stopped the locomotive by a danger signal; at other times he derailed it. He called such hold-ups "educational enterprises," it is said, and was proud of his ability to rifle a baggage car without waking up the passengers in the coaches. Bankers through the Middle West came to fear his name; and his escapes, even from the disastrous Northfield bank robbery of 1876 in which his accomplices were killed or captured, seemed like miracles. A familiar ballad tells that

> Jesse was a man, a friend of the poor,
> He never would see a man suffer pain;
> And with his brother Frank he robbed the Chicago bank,
> And stopped the Glendale train.

Stories were related of his friendly acts to poor squatters—buying coffins for those who had died of the fever, bringing food to the starving, paying off mortgages held by carpetbaggers. Though sentimentalism, no doubt, has multiplied these deeds, the fact remains that Jesse James while alive was a hero to Jackson County and other "unreconstructed" districts of Missouri—where the robbing of Yankee banks and trains was regarded with something like equanimity. Here local loyalties shielded James from capture for almost fifteen years. In 1882, while living quietly incognito in St. Joseph, Missouri, he was shot by a trusted accomplice, the "dirty little coward" of the ballad. By a quirk of folklore that invites comparison with the degradations of Robin Hood, Jesse James on the fatal day is shown drudging as a henpecked husband—

> Jesse was in his cabin one day all alone;
> His wife had left him there to clean up the home.
> He was scrubbing out the kitchen when the door-bell rang,
> And in walked Ford, a member of the outlaw gang.

Another ballad has him "talking with his family brave" on the night when the assassin called. Some traditions state that he was shot while hanging on the wall "the picture of his dog-gone wife," or a motto saying *God Bless Our Home.* The incident has been illustrated in a score of dime novels. Some of these yarns portray him as a killer who bore a name of terror, corresponding to the ballad which tells how men and women

> used to read about him in their homes at night;
> When the wind blew down the chimney they would shake with fright.

J. W. Buel's dime biography reports that Jesse spent his boyhood in the pastime of "burying small animals alive." But the majority, apparently, play him up as a romantic figure. He "came from a solitary race," and was beyond conventionality. He was the daring young man with the Colt .45, who once rode with a posse in his own pursuit. In the nineties, The Log Cabin Library published a "James Boys Series," describing the *gestes* of the gang; here a masked figure named Mysterious Ike invariably turns up to show Jesse and Frank James a short-cut out of the woods or a passage through the limestone caverns, and at last is revealed to be a woman in love with Jesse. Through the next decade, W. B. Lawson wrote a series of thrillers about the bandit; typical is one called *Jesse James and His Demon Horse; or, A True Pard to the Outlaw King.* Between 1901 and 1903, Street & Smith published 121 James novels, running to an estimated six million copies. According to the granddaughter of Jesse James, Miss Jo James—an employee of the Bank of America, in Los Angeles—some seventeen impostors through the years have claimed to be the real, and still unscathed, outlaw. In the winter of 1938–39 his memory enjoyed revival in a play on Broadway and a movie in technicolor said to have cost $2,000,000. The latter showed Jesse James as a brave though amiable gentleman, devoted to an aged mother, as required by the age of sentiment. The press quoted a comment by the hero's granddaughter, after a preview in Hollywood: "About the only connection it had with fact was that there was once a man named James and he did ride a horse."

The strong man and the desperado, as folk heroes, recall Machiavelli's distinction in *The Prince* between the lion and the fox. The latter gained his ends by swiftness and cool cunning. He was blood brother to the road-agent, the dapper gambler, and the faro expert who figures often in Western pulp fiction and in the stories of Bret Harte. He also blended easily into the free-lance "plainsman"—of whom Wild Bill Hickok is the most famous example. Wild Bill gained his reputation as a killer in 1861, in shooting out his feud with the McCandles clan in Kansas. According to Hickok's own story, his assailants in this battle were outlaws and secessionists; with incredible bravery and patriotism he killed six of them and wounded four more who managed to crawl away. Thus the episode has passed into myth, into the eulogies of Buel and Western fiction, and into the idealizations of William E. Connelley—patriarch of Kansas historians—in his worshipful book *Wild Bill and His Era*. Other and seemingly more trustworthy sources deny this story. They state that in this brawl he killed only three men, all of them unarmed, and that he often shot his victims because of nervous cowardice.[9] They also explain how Hickok, whose real name was James Butler Hickok, came to be called Wild Bill. In allusion to a deformity of the upper lip, which Hickok concealed by a flowing mustache, McCandles had given him the contemptuous nickname of "Duck Bill." Those who feared Hickok's anger at this slur called him "Dutch Bill" instead; after he had embarked upon a career of homicide, "Wild Bill" followed logically. Legends of his generosity are also common: it was said that he always paid the funeral expenses of his corpses, and that he supported the widows for life. It is certain that he contrived more often to be on the side of the law than against it, and in 1871 served as city marshal of Abilene, Kansas. Briefly he entered the Wild West show business with Buffalo Bill, appearing in Chicago and on Broadway before a public eager to see an authentic killer of the West—blue-eyed, long-haired, soft-spoken, and grim. Ned Buntline, Prentiss Ingraham, and other dime novelists made him into a great myth—"as brave as a lion, and as tender-hearted as a woman"—before he was shot in 1876 in a poker game in a Deadwood saloon, clutching a pair of aces and a pair of eights, which in the West ever afterward were known as "the dead man's hand." He also received the tribute of a cinema, in 1937, called *The Plainsman*. By grace of Cecil De Mille, Gary Cooper as Wild Bill was shown romantically in ·love with Calamity Jane— purged of her oaths and tobacco-chewing—and acting as a sagacious big brother to Buffalo Bill.

IV

But in the eyes of the world, the greatest idol out of the West was Buffalo Bill. Being a hero, in fact, grew to be the prime vocation of his life; he professionalized the role more than any other American in history. For almost fifty years, in more than a thousand dime novels, in melodramas, and in his own Wild West Show, Cody remained "the finest figure of a man that ever sat a steed." The moderns have a word for Cody: photogenic. He loved cameras and the theatre and the roar of applause, better than the thundering herd of the prairie. He connived benignly at most of the yarns told about him, including the 137 wounds he had received from the Indians. (His wife in her old age, somewhat disenchanted with her hero, revealed that he had suffered only one casualty, a scalp wound in his skirmish with the Sioux.)

William Frederick Cody was born in Scott County, Iowa, in 1846, son of an unprosperous farmer. Later he made the most of his barefoot boyhood, and the prediction of a fortune-teller that he would become President. Later, too, Colonel Prentiss Ingraham regaled dime novel readers with Billy's capture, at the age of eight, of four horse-thieves in a lonely cabin during a thunder-storm; one outlaw, trying to draw a gun, "fell dead at the flash, shot straight through the heart." Soon the Cody family moved to Kansas. To warn his abolitionist father of a murder plot, little Billy arose from a bed of fever with a handker-chief about his brow ("Tie it tight around my head, mother, then it won't ache so hard"), and rode seven stormy miles. When his father died, Billy became the sole support of his mother and sisters. He joined up with the wagoners, potted his first redskin, and at eleven was known as "the youngest Indian slayer on the plains." For these incidents there is no sound basis in fact. They bear the stamp of the Beadle workshop.[10]

Alfred Bronaugh Taylor, in a very popular dime novel called *Buffalo Billy, the Boy Bullwhacker; or, The Doomed Thirteen,* describes the youth as "frank, fearless, and handsome enough for an artist's study." Seeing a herd of wild buffalo, stampeded by savage Indians, sweeping full tilt upon him, Billy exclaims "Whew!" and "By the Rockies!" He climbs a tree, then jumps astride a huge bull buffalo charging past and gallops away—firing over his shoulder at the redskins. Ingraham told the same story, adding: "From that day, the boy was known as Buffalo Billy, the letter *y* being later discarded."

In the Civil War, Cody first became a Northern jay-hawker, stealing horses from slave-owners. Sentiment asserts that his mother was loath to see him join the Army, but gave consent on her death-bed in 1863. According to his own account, a drunken spree led him to join up. Cody did, however, state that he became an officer—although the records show him as a private throughout the war—and in pathetic old age, when his glory was fading, he endorsed all the lurid spying exploits that the penny dreadfuls had claimed for him.

Buntline told how young Cody the soldier rescued his future wife, then a schoolgirl of sixteen with a satchel of books on her arm, from a drunken artilleryman and his cronies:

But before he could again bend his hot, sensual face toward her pure lips, a horse and rider came rushing down the street with the speed of a winged bird. . . . "Oh, sir, you are so brave and so good! . . . I would have died before they should kiss me," said the lovely girl.

Louisa Frederici, who married Cody in 1866 when she was twenty-two—nearly three years his senior—recollected nothing of this, but only that her cousin had introduced him to her, and that through some casual misunderstanding she had slapped his face.[11] Later, his wife had to take in sewing to support herself and the growing family. Buffalo Bill in the heyday of success began to look upon her as dowdy, and never took her upon his European junkets. But these things the press-agents never mentioned.

Cody won his name shooting buffalo for meat, under contract to the Kansas Pacific. Out on the prairies a jingle ran—

> Buffalo Bill, Buffalo Bill,
> Never missed and never will;
> Always aims and shoots to kill,
> And the company pays his buffalo bill.

There were other rivals for the title. One of them was William Matthewson of Wichita, Kansas, whom the newspapers smoked out in the zenith of Cody's fame, thirty years later. In an interview Matthewson said: "I never was any hand to wear my hair long and go swaggering around the country blowing about what I had done. Cody knows he had no real right to the name, but if he wants to show off as a dime novel hero, I have no objection." As a matter of fact, Cody seems to have had a sound claim to the title. As a young purveyor to the railroad he won buffalo-killing contests over rivals—in the reckless prodigality of that day—while a gallery of excursionists followed in his wake, and toasted him in champagne.[12] Furthermore, as early as February 17, 1868, a St. Louis newspaper was referring to him as "Cody the noted guide." As a civilian scout he did assist Sheridan, but his later grandiose claim that he had been "chief of scouts in the U. S. Army under General Phil Sheridan" was untrue.

Under the sun of local publicity Cody began to bask. He now wore his hair long, to his shoulders, and cultivated a silky flowing mustache and tiny goatee. These had become the approved embellishment for scouts, as set by Wild Bill Hickok, General Custer, and others; nothing so enraged them as to have the ignorant mistake long locks as a badge of effeminacy. Such hair, they said, was a taunt to the scalping-knife of the Indians—to come and get it. The covers of Beadle novels invariably showed the scout with tresses rippling in the prairie breeze. Of Cody's encounters with the Indians much was made, and also imagined. He usually claimed that he killed the famous chief Tall Bull, but kept changing the details. In his first autobiography Cody shot him at a range of 400 yards, but in his old age in *True Tales* reduced it to 30 yards. Yet his show program carried a picture of the scout killing the Indian with a knife. Moreover, in *True Tales* Cody quoted a dispatch from *The New York Herald* of July 20, 1869, reporting that the red chief was "killed by Cody, chief of scouts." A comparison with the original, in *The Herald* files, shows that these words were not in the reporter's story. To add to the confusion, in 1897 *The New York World* printed an article over Cody's signature stating that Tall Bull—whose name modern slang may interpret in its own way—had been slain by Lieutenant Hayes. Still other sources report that his killer was Major Frank North.

Major North, "the white chief of the Pawnees," in 1869 was very close to becoming the dime novel idol, in place of Buffalo Bill. In that year Ned Buntline, in search of copy, had travelled out to the prairies and picked on North as his likeliest hero. But the Major, shy of publicity, told Buntline that Cody was his ideal man to exploit in fiction. This act moulded Cody's future career. Buntline's real name was E. Z. C. Judson. He was a battered customer, who had weathered adventures as fantastic as his own novels: he had run off to sea as a cabin-boy, rescued drowning people in New York harbor, fought seven duels in the Navy, captured two murderers single-handed, killed a husband who accused him of adultery, been hanged by a mob but cut down before the breath was out of his body, led the Astor Place riot of 1849, explored the caverns of Kentucky, entered with adolescent zest into the Know Nothing Party and other secret societies, claimed to have sustained twenty wounds in the Civil War but was cashiered from the Union Army, and carried several bullets in his body. It is an anticlimax—in view of Voltaire's famous remark, that "marriage is the only adventure possible to cowards"—to add that Ned Buntline had been married four times, but was still undomesticated. Now he became the creator of Buffalo Bill.

Since 1846 Buntline had supported himself by writing lurid fiction. In old age he achieved his *chef d'œuvre*. Cody let him ride the trusty Powder Face on a scouting trip, and the horse along with his master appeared in the next Buntline thriller. Cody delighted him with riding tricks, such as picking up a hat from the ground while going at full gallop, and blossomed more and more into a show-off. He told, for example, how he chased two Indians who had stolen Powder Face, killed both with a single bullet and scalped them on the spot. Buntline, returning to New York, dipped his pen into that mixture of tears and blood which was the ichor of his muse, and set to work.

"Better son never blessed a mother, wild as he was," said Mrs. Cody with love in every tone, as her glance followed his form. "Rough he may be to the others, but to us he is kind and gentle as the breeze of a summer eve."

"Yes, ma'am, Buffalo Bill is just as good as was ever made, no matter whar you find him," said Wild Bill. "There isn't a bit of white in his liver, nor no black in his heart."

Buntline, who enjoyed a good drink and also temperance lectures, made the ever bibulous Cody into an inspiration to youth—quoting him as saying:

There is more fight, more headache—aye, more heartache in one rum-bottle than there is in all the water that ever sparkled in God's bright sunlight. And I, for the sake of my dear brothers and sisters, and for the sweet, trusting heart that throbs alone for me, intend to let the rum go where it belongs, and that is not down my throat, at any rate.

Cody himself never spoke in this vein, informally or in print, but liked to make a joke of his Gargantuan appetite for fire-water. His ideas and Buntline's, concerning the ideal Western hero, did not always agree.

Among the "dudes" who came out West to hunt with the now celebrated scout, the junior James Gordon Bennett, editor of *The Herald,* was most potent in fostering his legend. *The Herald* began to call Cody "the beau ideal of the plains." Bennett sent him $500 to come to New York—largely, it appears, as a publicity device for the newspapers and dime novels, and for the opening of Fred G. Maeder's play *Buffalo Bill, the King of Bordermen,* in February, 1872, based on Buntline's stories. This melodrama showed him fighting a hand-to-hand duel with knives said to have been three feet long, against that reliable villain Jake McCanles, and also courting a "fair Kitty Muldoon" unknown to history. No secret was made of the real Cody's presence in the theatre, and the audience called for him and cheered him. He was wined and dined on Fifth Avenue, but after failing to turn up for a dinner given in his honor by Bennett, explained that he had grown "badly demoralized and confused," "been out on a scout and got lost." Otherwise his behavior satisfied his sponsors. It is said that he and Ned Buntline, in full cowboy costume, often rode down Broadway eight or ten times a day, and dismounted at the door of their publisher.[13]

Soon Buntline persuaded Cody himself to go on the stage. While plans were pending, the scout's Nebraska neighbors elected him to the state legislature; the election was contested, and Cody resigned, but ever after he was billed as "The Hon. W. F. Cody." Fifteen years later, in 1887, Nebraska once more added to his titles when the Governor made him a colonel in the National Guard, or "the National Army" as Cody preferred to call it. (Once, in 1890, when Cody used that phrase in reply to an inquiry about his military status, from one of his show Indians, the simple red man exclaimed: "M'lish! Oh, hell!")[14] Meanwhile, on December 16, 1872, Buffalo Bill made his theatrical début in Chicago, in Buntline's *The Scouts of the Prairie.* The great scout forgot his lines, but ad libbed throughout, and slew Indians in every act. The reviewers, hearing that the play had been written in four hours, queried "Why so much time?" But to the public it was a great success, though some complained of being strangled by the smoke. Cody reaped $6000 for the season—but thought he should have had more, and broke with his creator Buntline. Henceforth for life, through the fat years and the lean, his press-agent was Major John M. Burke, known as "Arizona John" though he came from the District of Columbia. He too wore his hair long, traded (as his best friends said) in "brass and wind," but for that naïve epoch was a magnificent publicist. Burke—who said solemnly, in his first season with Cody, "I have met a god"—adored the swagger, the grand manner, and the childlike heart of Buffalo Bill. In a thousand newspaper and theatrical offices over the world, for forty years, he built the great legend that Ned Buntline had sketched out.

Although spotlight and sawdust and grease-paint became increasingly the media of Buffalo Bill, he was wise enough not to lose touch with the West that had nourished him. In the early summer of 1876 newspaper readers were thrilled by the story of "Custer's last stand"

on the Little Big Horn. Custer, like Buffalo Bill, was a man who had
lived the epic of the West, with more than a touch of exhibitionism.
He was proud of his yellow locks and flamboyant costumes, carried a
newspaperman on all his expeditions, and wrote of "trusty rifles,"
"gallant comrades," and "noble steeds." A harsh commander and
vindictive enemy of the Indian, Custer like so many Western heroes
was a man of sentiment—weeping over plays and music, and, as his
adoring wife testified, "sobbing like a child" whenever he told his
mother good-bye to go soldiering. His death—soon to be celebrated
by Longfellow and a score of dime novelists—set the whites on the
war-path. In one of the minor skirmishes of 1876, Buffalo Bill fought
his much publicized duel with young chief Yellow Hand. The scout
advanced upon his foe wearing a Mexican suit of black velvet, with
silver buttons and lace and scarlet slashings. First he shot the brave,
then drove a knife into his heart: "Jerking his war-bonnet off, I scientifically scalped him in about five seconds . . . and shouted, 'The first
scalp for Custer!'" Major Burke and the reporters at once put the
story on the wires; in New York the trusty *Herald* gave the duel
nearly a column. It was an episode re-enacted a thousand times in
Buffalo Bill's later Wild West shows. He proudly carried Yellow
Hand's scalp with him for many years, and exhibited the chief's war
bonnet on his next tour, to advertise his new play *The Red Right
Hand; or, Buffalo Bill's First Scalp for Custer*. Only in New England
did press and clergy protest "the blood-stained trophies of his mur-
derous and cowardly deeds." Certainly it appeared that the hero had
grown more sanguinary since his encounter with Tall Bull, when,
as Buffalo Bill stated with graceful amenity, "after the fight I enter-
tained the chief's wife and family at tea . . . [she] esteemed it quite
an honor that her husband, a great warrior himself, should have met
his death at my hands."[15]

Buffalo Bill was not the greatest scout, soldier, or gun-fighter of the
plains. Nor did he take part in the really important Indian battles
of his time. But two immense advantages were his. He looked every
inch the hero, and his publicity men were by far the best. In addition
to Ned Buntline and Major Burke, the most popular of all dime
novelists began to exploit him from about 1876 to 1883. This was Prentiss Ingraham, a Southern colonel with slouch hat and walrus mustache, who had been a soldier of fortune in Mexico, Austria, Crete,
and Africa. In all, Colonel Ingraham wrote more than two hundred
paper-backs on Buffalo Bill. They bore such titles as *Buffalo Bill at*

Bay; or, The Gold Seeker's Doom; Buffalo Bill's Boys in Blue; or, The Brimstone Band's Blot-out; Buffalo Bill's Red Trail; or, The Road-Rider Renegade's Run Down; Buffalo Bill's Grip; or, Oath-Bound to Custer; and *Buffalo Bill and His Merry Men; or, The Robin Hood Rivals.* Seeing how easily the trick was done, Cody began to write dime novels, often about himself and his friends. Two popular numbers were *The Dead Shot Four* (which later became *The Dead Shot Nine*); or, *My Pards of the Plains,* and *Wild Bill the Wild West Duellist; or, The Girl Mascot of Moonlight Mine.* Once Buffalo Bill wrote to his publishers: "I am sorry to have to lie so outrageously in this yarn. . . . If you think the revolver and bowie-knife are used too freely, you may cut out a fatal shot or stab wherever you deem it wise." In 1879—when his stage appearances had already brought him $135,000—Cody added to his income by launching his first autobiography. Like the books of Mark Twain, it was sold by a house-to-house canvass, and proved vastly popular.

In 1882, plans for the great Wild West Show took shape. Nate Salsbury, a superb showman, assumed charge of the spectacle for which a dime-novel reading public was hungry. They got the Deadwood mail-coach, relic of the woolliest Dakota days when gold dust was pouring from the Black Hills. Deadwood, where Hickok had been shot and Calamity Jane had bearded his murderer, was a name to make spines tingle. The show promised well, even though Buffalo Bill was drinking more heavily now, and once remained "confused" for five consecutive weeks. He also wanted to introduce gambling as a side-attraction: "Write me and tell me what to do—and if we don't get that *money* what in K Christ are we to do?" he anxiously wrote Salsbury on April 12, 1884. But Salsbury, taking the longer view and knowing that the show must be kept clean for American boys, vetoed the idea. St. Louis, Chicago, and New York loved the spectacle—with its hard riding, straight shooting, and blood-curdling whoops. At last the Wild West had escaped wholly from the trammels of the theatre, and was under a big top. En route to New Orleans the river boat sank, but the Deadwood coach was saved, to be attacked for twenty years more by painted savages and to count the future Edward VII among its passengers. Cody's most popular feat was the shattering, from his saddle, of innumerable glass balls. It is now known—as was sometimes suspected by an unfriendly press—that he used not rifle bullets but shotted shells, in these acts of sharpshooting.[16]

More attractions were added, with the passing seasons. They included Annie Oakley, "Little Sure Shot," and Sitting Bull, whose profile, as the publicity pointed out, resembled Daniel Webster's. One feature, doubtless seldom seen in the West, was billed as "Football on Horseback, between Indians and Cowboys." Later came equestrians of other nations—Cossacks, gauchos, Arabs, chasseurs, lancers—and "Rossi's Musical Elephants," and, in sum, "More Ladies, Gentleman and Beasts than ever seen in one exhibition." In 1887 Europe was first treated to the spectacle. A command performance was given before Queen Victoria, who bowed to the Stars and Stripes as a color-bearer galloped around the arena; to Annie Oakley the Queen said, "You are a very, very clever little girl." The American Minister, James Russell Lowell, wrote somewhat acidly to Charles Eliot Norton: "I think the true key to this eagerness for lions—even of the poodle sort —is the dullness of the average English mind." But France and Spain warmly applauded "the World's Rough Riders" (as Cody's troupe was known, years before Theodore Roosevelt's regiment was built upon a similar hero-worship). Buffalo Bill, crossing into Italy, wanted to stage his show in the Colosseum of the Cæsars—but found it too shabby and small.

In the mid-nineties Buffalo Bill's celebrity reached its high noon. He was one of the great attractions of the Chicago World's Fair in 1893. Two years later, his posters compared Napoleon, "the man on horse of 1795," with Buffalo Bill, "the man on horse of 1895." In 1896, while Cody was playing 132 towns and cities in America, the faithful Major Burke reported that he was being "mentioned" for President. Cody himself relished the conundrum, "What is the difference between Buffalo Bill and Bryan?" Answer: "Buffalo Bill has a show." When the clouds of the Spanish-American War began to gather, evoked by that assiduous rain-maker William Randolph Hearst, Buffalo Bill eagerly scanned the sky. "I am ready to leave at any time," he kept saying to the newspapers. Was he not America's greatest scout and finest marksman? The press of 1898 called him "never a greater hero than he is today." While the bugles sounded, Buffalo Bill's farewell tour packed in the crowds. But somehow he never finished saying good-bye. Then, at the war's end, a surprised public learned the truth. From Ponce his friend General Nelson A. Miles had cabled: "Would like you to report here, taking first steamer from Newport News." In reply, Cody had grumbled at the cost of $100,000 which closing his show would entail, had suggested that peace was near, and asked whether after all he shouldn't wait? Miles answered by a single word: "Yes." At this disclosure the public was startled.[17]

Henceforth Buffalo Bill's luck began to turn. His press was no longer so good. Growing old, he became more nervous and irritable, and his marksmanship suffered. Privately he began to say: "I do not want to die a showman. I grow very tired of this sort of sham hero-worship sometimes." He bought much land in Wyoming, where the town of Cody was named for him, and there built a luxury hotel. He also had a fling at gold-mining, but his investments turned out badly. In 1904 he began divorce proceedings against the wife he had long neglected, alleging that she had tried to poison him and talking scandalously about her to the newspapers. She in turn charged him with illicit loves, with lavishing $50,000 upon an actress. Howard Gould named him as co-respondent in a divorce suit. As a last indignity of circumstance, Buffalo Bill began to grow bald; soon a flowing white toupee added its touch to the aspect of an old stager, with fine wrinkles about his weary eyes and an intangible seediness clinging to his once stalwart physique. The legend of the boy's own hero was beginning to crack.

In 1910 he began to advertise farewell tours, not for the wars, but a long good-bye. "On my honor as Buffalo Bill, my present visit will positively be my last hail and farewell in the saddle, to you all." Ever generous, in the open-handed style of the West, and indiscreet in business, Cody had spent his immense earnings like water. Now the box-office was dwindling, and he began to face an old age of poverty. In 1911, in order to keep his pledge never to appear again "in the saddle," he repeated his tour but entered the ring in a phaeton. Yet in 1913, too poor to be proud, he was back in the saddle. With his show heavily mortgaged, and soon lost to him forever, Cody fell into the financial clutches of a shrewd Denver newspaper publisher, H. H. Tammen. For a time he was virtually Tammen's bond slave. "This man is driving me crazy. I can easily kill him but as I avoided killing in the bad days I don't want to kill him. But if there is no justice left I will," he wrote to a friend, with the pathetic impotence of age. Buffalo Bill and his wife were now reconciled, drawn together by a poverty like that under which they had begun life together. By various shifts he tried to provide for her and himself. He joined up with the Essanay Film Company to make movies. (In 1913 that syndicate had recaptured, for a new generation of youth, the thrill of the old Wild West, with a juvenile series about "Broncho Billy" the cowboy; news-

papers that summer told of a little girl named Dorothy who rebelled
against a major operation until her mother cried, "Remember Broncho
Billy! You know Broncho Billy is brave . . .") But for Cody himself
the cinema held nothing but a mirage of hope. Soon he hit the road
with the Sells-Floto Circus, swallowing his chagrin that the admission
was only twenty-five cents. He tried dude ranching. He sought to get
a mail-order house interested in selling prints of the oil painting that
Rosa Bonheur had once made of him on horseback. He applied for
the monthly dole of $10 to which every holder of a Congressional
medal was entitled. The medal, awarded for scouting in 1872, was
soon to be withdrawn from him in a general clearing of the roster
of medal holders; as a civilian, he had never been eligible for it in
the first place. At the age of seventy-one—with a bravery under misfortune that was the least publicized but perhaps finest thing of Cody's
life, he gave his last performance in the ring. A few weeks later, on
January 17, 1917, he died in bed, while greater events were happening
and the bugles were beginning to blow once more.

Yet, when his body lay in state under the gold dome of the state
capitol in Denver, Colorado, thousands came to view it. In June it
was carried up to the crest of Lookout Mountain, facing the plains
and foothills of the West. There today a museum, Pahaska Tepee,
contains his boots, guns, and saddles. The town of Cody boasts an
equestrian bronze statue by Gertrude Vanderbilt Whitney, with Buffalo
Bill flourishing his rifle skyward; and Wyoming, jealous that Colorado
has claimed his body, keeps his birthday as a state holiday. His name is
still used in circus publicity, and railroads beckon tourists to "the Buffalo Bill country." But his legend fades like a tintype, or the yellowing
pages of a Beadle novel. And, with some irony, E. E. Cummings celebrates the eternal adolescent in a vein of poetry that Cody would have
been the last to understand—

> Buffalo Bill's
> defunct
>   who used to
>   ride a watersmooth-silver
>   stallion
> and break onetwothreefourfive pigeons justlikethat
>   Jesus
>   he was a handsome man
>   and what i want to know is
>   how do you like your blueeyed boy
>   Mister Death

CHAPTER FOURTEEN

COMMONER AND ROUGH RIDER

Where is Roosevelt, the young dude cowboy,
Who hated Bryan, then aped his way?
Gone to join the shadows with mighty Cromwell
And tall King Saul, till the Judgment Day.

*   *   *   *   *

Where is that boy, that Heaven-born Bryan,
That Homer Bryan, who sang from the West?
Gone to join the shadows with Altgeld the Eagle,
Where the kings and the slaves and the troubadours rest.

—VACHEL LINDSAY, "Bryan, Bryan, Bryan."

I

FOR almost five years young William Jennings Bryan had hoped to represent his school, Illinois College, in the annual inter-collegiate oratorical contest of the Middle West. This was the silver age of oratory, in the 1880's, when it was said that speakers kept the American eagle so constantly in flight that its shadow wore a trail across the Mississippi Valley. The Mid-West style of eloquence owed less to Demosthenes than to Dwight Moody; even its figures of speech were imbrued with the Blood of the Lamb, the metaphor of cross and crown. As a boy, Bryan had found religion under the heady spell of a Presbyterian preacher. Now, apropos of the oratorical contest, he wrote to his best girl, Mary Baird: "I prayed that humility might be given with success." To this young couple it was an immensely serious matter. He had signalled to her the news of his first success, in winning the right to represent Illinois College, by dragging his cane against the picket fence of the Jacksonville Female Academy at three o'clock in the morning as he went homeward flushed with triumph. But in the finals, alas, he was only runner-up. He wrote her of a dream in which his fate had been forecast: "I could see my name very distinctly occupying the second place, but I could not make out the name of the man who was awarded first prize."[1] In miniature, it was the story of his whole career.

After they married and moved out to Lincoln, Nebraska, on the lean fees of a struggling lawyer, Bryan began to attend political rallies as other young men might slip off to prize-fights. Once, at a little town named Gordon, the scheduled Democratic speaker failed to arrive. Almost at random, Bryan was asked to pinch-hit. He did so. In the early dawn he got home, and sitting on the edge of the bed said solemnly to his wife: "Mary, I have had a strange experience. Last night I found I had power over the audience, I could move them as I chose. I have more than usual power as a speaker. I know it. God grant that I may use it wisely."[2]

He looked the part of "The Boy Orator of the Platte"—with his string tie and black alpaca coat, brilliant eyes and luxuriant black hair flung back from an earnest forehead, and the thin lips of a zealot. A few years later, Stone of Missouri would find him "beautiful as Apollo." Nebraska sent Bryan to Congress in 1890. Four years later he failed of election to the Senate, but became editor of an Omaha newspaper and lecturer on the Chautauqua circuit. He had a message for the age. This era, the discontented nineties, a little later would discover its poetic hero in "The Man with the Hoe." With bitterness many were finding that the West was not golden for them, as it had seemed to the dawn of '49 and in the romance of the dime novel. Free land had given out, and other natural resources were seen to be limited. Those who had land suffered from overproduction and falling prices: Mary Ellen Lease from Kansas was exhorting them to "raise less corn and more hell." Many, without a stake in the riches pre-empted by the mining barons and the Union Pacific, eyed the empty cupboard as hungrily as Mother Hubbard's dog. Trusts and monopolies had arisen, and the smoke of factories stained the air that Daniel Boone and Jim

Bridger had once breathed. A panic of economic claustrophobia set in. The power of wealth was everywhere; in 1896 the Supreme Court declared illegal the existing income-tax law. Populism and the Greenback movement had crumpled in defeat. To Bryan, who had much idealistic hope and a great ignorance of money, a panacea lay in the fact that more silver than gold poured from the West. If only the ratio could be fixed to favor silver, say at sixteen to one, would there not be more wealth for everybody? The phrase "free silver"—like "free wheeling" in a later day of automobile advertising—had a real selling potency. It seemed to promise something for nothing. And in the winter of America's discontent, a vast popular naïveté about finance, typical of Bryan himself as well as of leaders from Jacob Coxey to Doctor Francis Townsend, swept an eager throng behind him. In retrospect, it seemed a pity that Bryan stressed the cause of silver more persistently than the case for social justice.

Bryan was still almost unknown to the average American in July, 1896, when a leaderless Democratic National Convention met in Chicago. Legend has long asserted that his "Cross of Gold" speech was extempore. As a matter of fact, he had rehearsed its thrilling close in Congress two years before, and polished its phrases "scores of times" before crowds in small Mississippi Valley towns.[3] Now, speaking for "the toilers everywhere," he thundered: "You shall not press down upon the brow of labor this crown of thorns, you shall not crucify mankind upon a cross of gold." The speech mixed platitudes and bad logic with a Christian symbolism that his enemies were quick to stamp as blasphemous. But it was sonorous, delivered in a voice magnificent as the music of a pipe-organ; at the moment it sounded irresistible. It brought tears to the eyes of many delegates, and even hysteria to women in the galleries. "When I neared my seat, somebody near me raised a shout, and the next thing I was picked up—and bedlam broke loose!" Bryan said later. An ovation, variously described as lasting from thirty-five minutes to an hour, paved the way to Bryan's nomination for the Presidency. Some hours after he had received the news, Bryan was found by a throng of admirers in a barber-shop, getting a shave; through the lather he smiled at them, and then began to cry. He wept in public on other occasions—at the tribute to Woodrow Wilson in Martin Glynn's keynote speech at the Democratic Convention of 1916, at his own words over the ceremonial funeral of John Barleycorn in 1920 in the First Congregational Church in Washington —with a fluency that betrayed his emotional nature. It was not strange that Billy Sunday looked upon Bryan as his fellow worker in the vineyard.

The campaign of 1896, when Bryan himself was only thirty-six, marked the flood-tide of his hero-worship. The first fine careless rapture was never quite repeated. Travelling 18,000 miles, he addressed an estimated five million people. Sometimes he made thirty-six speeches a day, but never spoke on Sunday. From the rear platform of trains he talked to farmers and "dear old ladies in sunbonnets," while the sun blazed over the cornfields and picked out the brasses of bands that had greeted him with Sousa's new march, "El Capitan." Then he would retire to the depths of his car, hang his wilted shirt to dry, and rub his neck and arms with the gin that he never applied in any other way. One newspaper correspondent regretted that the orator smelled "like a wrecked distillery," but the criticism seemed as trivial as Bryan's own objection that the private car which bore him was named "The Idler."⁴ Accused of lacking dignity, he retorted that the same charge had been made against Jefferson, Andrew Jackson, and Lincoln. At Fredericksburg, Virginia, he made the most of the legendary silver dollar that Washington had thrown across the river. In the metropolitan East his magic somehow evaporated. His acceptance speech in Madison Square Garden was a disappointment to the faithful, but a great comfort to the bankers—whom he had taunted by remarking that the only Bible text they knew was, "Then came wise men out of the East." *The New York Times* published alleged reports of alienists saying that he was insane, suffering from a disease called "querulent logorrhea." *The Tribune* echoed young Theodore Roosevelt's conclusion that Bryan resembled that traitor to true Americanism, Jefferson Davis. In New Haven the orator was drowned under lusty Bronx cheers—an episode which so scandalized the Cherokees and Seminoles of Oklahoma that in a mass meeting they resolved: "We admonish all Indians who think of sending their sons to Yale that association with such students could but prove hurtful alike to their morals and their progress toward the higher standard of civilization."⁵ Eastern critics sneered at Bryan's youth, as the Boy Orator of the Platte—"a river," as Senator Foraker reminded the public, "six inches deep and six miles wide at the mouth." Through the years that followed, Bryan's enemies never stopped calling attention to "his old complaint, hoof-and-mouth disease." Succeeding to the old feud between North and South came the new quarrel between East and West, now that post-Civil War days had re-routed the circulation of the

nation's lifeblood of commerce. The East could no more see the
heroic aspect of Bryan than the West, a generation later, could feel
the magnetism of Al Smith.

But to Bryan's own region, and to many humble admirers scattered
through the land, he seemed in 1896 to be the champion of God
against Mammon. To the despised "hayseeds," as William Allen
White remarked, "it was a fanaticism like the Crusades." His cause
undoubtedly had its pathos, and its frustrated justice. Coming home
from Chicago, Bryan found his house in Lincoln festooned with
streamers of bunting, the yard filled with crowds bearing armfuls of
flowers, and small boys sitting in rows along the roof. Presents began
to arrive—scores of rabbits' feet and horseshoes, a stuffed alligator so
long that its tail stuck out of the express wagon, silver watches to
replace his gold one, four live eagles, one mule, one pair of suspenders,
four volumes of Jefferson's works, canes made from Washington's
cherry tree and Andrew Jackson's hickory and wood from the house
where Patrick Henry made his first speech, an eggshell marked with
his initials, and fungi which resembled his face.[6] A Japanese boy
named Yamashita came all the way from his native land, despite all
Bryan could do to dissuade him, to put himself under the care of the
Commoner and to be educated as a member of his family.

The Bryan Papers, now in the Library of Congress, vividly mirror
the cult just before and after his defeat on November 3, 1896. He is
called "the new Christ of Humanity, to loose the chains of plutocracy
from the people, to fetter the dragons, owls, serpents, moths, ravens
an [sic] vampires." "You are the star of Independence and Sandow
of liberty." "A Solon and a Jackson." A New Orleans admirer writes
in to tell a joke about two darkeys: one insisted that "Genl Washington, Mr. Lincum, or Genl Grant warn't knee high to Mr. Bryan." The
other asked, "Well, how about God?" After scratching his head the
first replied, "Well, nigger, you must remember that Mr. Bryan is
young yet." A farmer from Creston, Iowa, promises that he will go
back to work if Bryan is elected: "you are the first big man that i ever
wrote to." A woman in Greenpoint, New York, asks for a ring "or
a little pair of ear rings": "how i came to write this letter is some of
the republicans neibors said to me if you met either Mr or Mrs bryan
on the street they would not let on to see you." Mrs. M. A. Cess of
Anderson, Indiana, writes on November 2:

Dear father of our Country . . . God has sent you amongst our people to
save the poor from the starvation and we no you will save us . . . my

husband would not give his support to McKinley . . . and concequencly he was turned out of work but he says he will trust to your being elected our children which is six says when Bryan is in mamma we can get work may God help you on to victory . . . I want you to send me something that I can keep we are poor but any thing would be worshiped that come from you . . . I wish you was welthy enough to will me A farm I would keep it for A place to gather at and worship in like our Savior we would take you for him.

In one packet of the Bryan Papers are 701 letters written between midsummer 1896 and the beginning of 1897, informing Bryan that babies have been named after him or asking his permission for such naming. Most of the writers are humble people, small-town merchants, dentists, tradesmen, manual laborers, and farmers; the majority come from the Middle West and Southwest. "I take my pencill in hands," writes an Indiana mother, "to let you know that I have got a baby 6 weak old and he is got your Name and I thought I would write and see wether you would send him a pressing [present?]." A citizen of Rusk, Texas, writes: "I have named my four months old boy for you. . . . He is physically a little Hercules and we hope he may be a Bryan morally and intellectually." In one letter Bryan is saluted as "My Dear Leader of the Poor"; many hope that their child named after him will be "as true to his country and the principles of Democracy" as "the biggest man in the U. S." Some misspell the name as "Bryon"; a namesake in Camden, Illinois, is called "Bryen" ("if he can't vote for you he can holler for you"); and a mother in Jamestown, North Carolina, requests "a present for Xmas" for "William Bryne Johnson." Professor J. R. Herrin, Teacher of Hypnotism, Pesotum, Illinois, informs Bryan that "a baby carriage for your namesake would be treasured in our family as a souvenir as long as we shall live, not for its intrinsic value, but for our esteem and reverence of the giver." Professor R. Maurice Adams, Teacher of Dancing, St. Louis, who styles himself "A father of 7 (seven) boys consecutively (no girls)," christens his seventh son William Jennings Bryan, and reports that on the eve of the election he stood near "the McKinley Parade and gave out 5000 badges—and I was fearless." (The badges read: "Call on Prof. R. M. Adams for dancing lessons, vote for BRYAN—Then you can wear diamonds and be HAPPY.") A citizen of Fauquier County, Virginia, reports "a Bran new Baby at my House . . . we had hoped to call it *Bryan* . . . it being a girl, we would like to know the full name of your wife." Twins are named for both the Bryans, and a girl at Dalesburg, South Dakota, is christened "Bryanette, in honor of your part taken in the greatest political conflict of modern times, which again will be refought untill the farmers voice is heard instead of plutocracy."

The number of letters Bryan received from children is probably unmatched in the fan mail of political idols before 1896. Until the Lincoln Papers are open to inspection one cannot speak with finality, but certainly no other favorite comes within hailing distance of Bryan as the children's hero. "We have McKinley pitcher in our schoolhouse I dont think he is very pretty do you. . . . I think you are the stuff," writes a little girl of ten from Glasgow, Kansas. A letter written "in the hayloft" by four grammar-school girls of Sonoma County, California, signed "The Bryan Quartette," addresses him as "Your Majesty." A schoolgirl in Trinidad, Colorado, writes: "The proudest moment of my life was when I shook hands with you and heard you speak. I will remember it forever. . . . I don't think I can ever find any one as noble and good as you are." A little boy in Rock Valley, Iowa, reports that he is trying to brush his hair to look like Bryan's, "only it is not black." Nicholas Theodore Bell, eleven, of St. Louis, relates that he marched in the Bryan parade "several hours"; he says he and his younger brother and their chum "are going to Washington to spend a while with you but you need not go to any trouble to fix for us, how long would be convenient for you to entertain us?" A Detroit child of nine complains that "at Recess the other girls wont let me play with them because they are for McKinley." A Maryland girl of the same age says that on the way from school she always sings "We'll hang Bill McKinley on the sour apple tree." A small boy in Paris, Kentucky, writes: "I took some ink and printed your name on a large piece of paper and pasted it on the fence between us and a Republican." "I am for free silver," writes Renzilla Seguine, aged nine, of Washington, New Jersey, "and my papa is too, he don't talk about it but I do . . . the reason papa don't talk about it he is a Prudential man and has to visit all classes of people." Some say they are praying for him, and a little Catholic girl offers her intention at mass for his election. Others write him poems, or draw his picture surrounded by colored flags.

In the days after Bryan's defeat, letters from children increased rather than waned. "We thought you were the grandest man in the United States. . . . Even if you were not elected we will still keep your picture in our parlor and I will still wear your button," writes a twelve-year-old girl from Memphis. Another, aged eight, from Farmville, Virginia, tells him: "I wore your badge & trimmed my hat with white chrysanthemums & hurrahed for you." "It is with a depressed heart I pen my regrets that you are not to be our next President," writes Carrie May Erd, twelve, of Lexington, Kentucky. "I have studied deeply and firmly believe you to be a second George Washington. . . . Far away in old Kentucky there are two children a boy & a girl, praying every night for the success of our Silver King." A schoolgirl in Sherman, Texas, assures him: "You are no less our hero, because you failed to receive your just dues." Roscoe C. Huffman, nine, of Virginia, Illinois: "I was so sorry you were not elected that I just had to cry. I felt so bad I did not go to school yesterday." One little girl tells him "I too am just dying to see you," while another invites him to Thanksgiving dinner in Ohio ("will meet you at the station"), and a third comforts him with the thought that "if all the girls could vote you would be elected." May Huey, a schoolgirl of Rockville, Indiana, writes: "I was in two Silver Demonstrations, once with my wheels decorated and once in a large wagon with 16 to 1 girls." A girl of thirteen, in Austin, Illinois: "The other night I said to myself, 'If I only had the money, and could get there somehow, I would go to see Mr. Bryan, for he will think no one cares for him, because he wasn't elected.' " "A little blue-eyed girl seven years of age" assures him that "I still holler for you," but that Santa Claus will not be able to bring her a Christmas doll because times are hard: "I know he could if you had been elected." One small boy reports that he failed to get a piano, another a Newfoundland puppy, promised in the event of a Bryan victory. A pupil in "Miss Mamie Alderman's Select School" in Wilmington, North Carolina, reports that "we had your name written all over our desks, doors, chairs, black-board's and also on our shoes. . . . I just wanted to let you know that there was one little girl that thinks about you a great deal." A boy from the same state who signs himself "William Bryan Meacham" but crosses out the middle name with an "H" (perhaps through belated honesty) commiserates with him on being "defeated by that rascal Maj. McKinley. . . . P. S. if I was you I would have felt like sending Fitzsimmons up to Canton instead of sending congratulations."

Bryan's failure—by some 600,000 out of a total of 13,600,000 votes— lent him a comradeship with defeated men such as success could never have given. It was felt that the insurance companies by threatening to foreclose mortgages on Western lands in case of a Bryan victory, and employers by promising to cut their pay-rolls if this fanatic were elected, had exercised unfair pressure. A townsman of West Sonora,

Ohio, reports coercion placed upon local factory workers, but adds: "i have been working for the farmers since July at 60 cents a day my bred will be corn bred this winter but would rather live on corn bred and [than?] to voat in favor of mark hanna and the rail rodes." A campaigner for Bryan in Indiana says that the mortgage on his house is about to be foreclosed by a Republican "because i voted for you." Another writes that he had bet his cow on Bryan's election, and now his children have no milk. Still another has lost on Bryan the money he intended to use in mending his roof: "My house is leaking badly. Please send the money at once." Since Bryan had requested his admirers not to bet, he owed these men no more sympathy than he gave others who had to roll peanuts great distances, trundle Republicans in wheelbarrows, or cross the continent riding donkeys. One may also assume that he did not pay a bill for $87 sent him by a farmer who had lost that sum when a charge of gunpowder, exploded to greet Bryan, had ruined some eggs in an incubator. An admirer in Spokane, Washington, sent a clipping, under the headline "NEWS KILLED HER," describing how Mrs. Mary V. Marvin dropped dead upon learning of Bryan's defeat. Some quoted "truth crushed to earth," while others took solace in Ella Wheeler Wilcox's poem on Bryan's defeat with its refrain—

No question is ever settled
Until it is settled right.

Unknown people, under the compassion of Bryan's defeat, wrote him the story of their own frustrated lives—of toil and heartbreak and hope. "Defeated, you are the grandest man in America," said one. John P. Altgeld wrote him a letter of comradeship, while Champ Clark declared: "You made a campaign that will live long in song & story. You set the high water mark for all who shall come after you." If Bryan had been able, henceforth, to live up to the prevailing dignity and composure he showed upon most occasions in 1896, and with increasing wisdom to champion the poor man, he might have become a very great hero.

But the rest of Bryan's life was an anticlimax. In the Spanish-American War the Governor of Nebraska made him a colonel, but the conflict was over before Bryan's regiment got ready to sail for Cuba. In 1900 he was renominated, but received fewer votes than in 1896. Passed over in 1904, he was given a final chance in 1908 against Taft, but failed. Many recalled the rule in baseball, "Three times and out." If a man is kept too long in the wings of the stage, waiting for his big moment, after awhile people begin to snicker at his thwarted hopes or grow bored with him. A hero must follow an ascending curve, even when turning defeats into moral victories. This Bryan could not do.

His following always came from centrifugal minorities—some against gold, others opposed to corporations and trusts, still others against imperialism in the Philippines—with little in common save their discontent. But they never pulled in unison, and at last it was clear that they could never give him anything but love. He was doomed to be the leader of lost or stillborn causes: the fading frontier and rural life against the city, pacifism in an age of expansion and military tension, fundamentalism in an epoch of doubt, and prohibition in the night-club era.[7] At times, to those who admired him, he seemed to be the Good Shepherd—but in fact he was only one of the flock, often as pathetically bewildered as the rest. Time and again his show was stolen by other men of greater ability—his progressivism implemented by Republican opponents like Theodore Roosevelt and Taft or rephrased by rivals like Woodrow Wilson and La Follette. Unperceived by the country at large, Bryan was at his heroic best in 1912, when he declined to spoil Wilson's chances for the Presidency by intruding his own candidacy. But, as Secretary of State, he frittered away his energies by Chautauqua lecturing, drew ridicule by serving grape-juice at state dinners ("because the glasses for plain and mineral water looked a little lonesome"), and resigned rather than send a sharp note to Germany over the sinking of the *Lusitania*.

The Boy Orator grew fat and flabby, the victim of an insatiable appetite for hot biscuits and fried chicken and green corn. The palm-leaf fan, and handkerchief tucked into the collar, completed the picture. With gusto he entered into the Florida real-estate boom, sprinkling his lectures on "The Prince of Peace" and "The Value of an Ideal" with such queries as, "What is our vision of what Magic Miami should be?" Many newspapers commented adversely when he became a rich man. Theology had long clouded his political views: he had opposed the appointment of President Charles W. Eliot, a Unitarian, as Minister to China, under the theory that it would nullify the work of Christian missionaries; whereas Bryan endorsed Warren G. Harding as a believer in the Scriptures. He temporized with the Ku Klux Klan because most of its members were Fundamentalists. By the standards of the Middle West, Bryan at heart was a moralist and militant preacher, even as was Theodore Roosevelt by the far more sophisticated standards of the East. And Bryan too battled at Armageddon for the Lord, not as a political reformer, but as the champion of Biblical literalism at Dayton, Tennessee. He still had his partisans. "I have many friends who would die for me!" he had cried, with tears in his voice, after resignation from the Wilson Cabinet.[8] Now, at the Scopes trial, he received messages of cheer from hundreds—including Billy Sunday, Aimee Semple McPherson, and an admirer in Smackover, Arkansas:

MY DEAR BROTHER BRYAN FIGHT THEM EVOLUTIONS UNTIL HELL FREEZES OVER AND THEN GIVE THEM A ROUND ON THE ICE GOD BLESS YOU IN YOUR TIME OF TRIALS AND GIVE YOU WISDOM AND GRACE TO DO WHAT DEAR JESUS WILL SMILE UPON   YOUR UNACQUAINTED BROTHER

HAPPY GORDON MEAD.[9]

It mattered little that Clarence Darrow seared him with the ridicule of a shrewd lawyer's skepticism, that Henry L. Mencken reported to the country at large that "there was a vague, unpleasant manginess about [Bryan's] appearance . . . the hair was gone from the dome of his head, and it had begun to fall out, too, behind his ears, in the obscene manner of the late Samuel Gompers." Young Scopes was convicted, and fined $100, for teaching the animal origins of man. And on the next Sunday afternoon in his sleep Bryan was called to his long home. As he had requested, the great pacifist was buried with military honors in Arlington Cemetery. Many choirs sang Bryan's favorite hymn, "One Sweetly Solemn Thought," and in Dayton, Ohio, a fiery cross was burned "in memory of William Jennings Bryan, the greatest Klansman of our time." It was an unfair tribute to a rather remarkable American who had gone wrong.

II

The life of Theodore Roosevelt, it has been said, was the dream of every typical American boy: he fought in a war, became President, killed lions, and quarreled with the Pope.[10] In many respects, he was youth's own hero because he never grew sedate. In 1904, the year of his triumphant election to a second term in the White House, Roosevelt's favorite Englishman, Cecil Spring Rice, was writing: "You must always remember that the President is about six." On his forty-sixth birthday that October, Roosevelt received a message of congratulation from Elihu Root: "You have made a very good start in life, and your friends have great hopes for you when you grow up."[11] Roosevelt's world, like the world of adolescence, was a place of high adventure, swagger, conspiracies with a touch of melodrama, fierce loyalties and equally fierce hates. And, sometimes, a boy's will was the wind's will —blowing and veering unaccountably. To politics he became what Buffalo Bill had been to the big top. But in his whole life of sixty years there was never a dull moment. He established a family tradition: that under a Roosevelt administration, whatever its faults, ennui is banished from public affairs.

In 1906, in the "Log Cabin to White House" series for young readers, that veteran dime novelist Edward S. Ellis brought out *From Ranch to White House: The Life of Theodore Roosevelt.* "He was heavily handicapped at the beginning," wrote our trusty author. "He was born into a 'blue blood' family without the necessity of toiling for a living." But as a near-sighted and asthmatic boy he refused to be pampered. He swung dumb-bells and took boxing lessons. At Harvard "one of his first steps . . . was to seek out a Sunday School in which he could do work for his Master"; learning that one of his pupils had blacked the eye of a bully who had pinched the boy's sister, Roosevelt "took out a dollar bill and handed it to the astonished lad with the remark, 'You did right.'" Shocked, the authorities of this Episcopal Sunday School dismissed the young teacher, who went over to a Congregational church—where, we gather, muscular Christianity was more admired. This legend is not wholly accurate; the chief reason for Roosevelt's retirement from his Sunday School class was his refusal to subscribe to Episcopalian doctrines.[12] Equally untrue is Ellis's assertion that Roosevelt's first race in politics was for the United States Congress, against "the dainty aristocrat William Waldorf Astor." (Whereupon, it is said, "the defeated Astor shook the dust of his country from his feet, and sailed for Europe, where he has lived ever since"—a rather startling sequence, that would place upon Roosevelt's shoulders the responsibility for the present Lady Astor, the policies of *The London Times,* and other transatlantic phenomena.)

As a matter of fact, Roosevelt was elected to the New York Legislature in 1881 against a Democratic opponent named Doctor W. W. Strew, some nine years before Astor's expatriation. But Roosevelt's strenuous Americanism, in days when other blue bloods were being pierced by what Henry James called "the sharp outland dart," lent a spirit of truth to the myth. To his generation, Roosevelt seemed to be the first American since the spoils system began who brought inherited wealth and background into the hurly-burly of politics. He lent a forgotten prestige to public life. In an age when the leisure class was devoted either to making money, with the Vanderbilts, or to the nerve-less disillusion of Henry Adams, Roosevelt proved that there were scores of things more exciting than making money—reform, ranching, hunting, fighting, building ships and canals, travel, exploration, even reading Tacitus—while boredom was a personal disgrace. And, as the late Stuart Sherman remarked, "whatever delighted him he sought to inculcate upon the American people, so that Rooseveltism should be recognized as synonymous with Americanism."[13]

When he first appeared at Albany, eager, earnest, nervous, with curly sandy hair and prominent teeth anticipative of the famous grin, the professional politicians took him for a dude. In noting his eye-glasses on a black silk cord, they failed to see that the nearsighted eyes behind them were as blue and pugnacious as Old Hickory's. They also failed to see that, like a later Roosevelt, he had magnificent talents as his own press agent—careful from the start that the newspapers got his side of every story, skilled in building his first crusade, for the reform of the New York City Board of Aldermen, into a drama of light versus the powers of darkness. One foolish satirist wrote:

> His strong point is his bank account,
> His weak point is his head.[14]

Roosevelt toughened himself by becoming a Dakota cowpuncher in his summer vacations. He was the original dude rancher. Soon, he had invested $52,000 in land and cattle, with a carelessness about money, an impulse to live beyond his income, that was perhaps his most aristocratic trait. He bought imprudently, and eventually aban-doned the whole enterprise. But the gains in morale were great. Cow-hands looked with astonishment upon "Four-Eyes," whose favorite oath was "By Godfrey!" whose exhortation to one of his men, "Hasten forward quickly there," became a Western classic.[15] His love of flam-boyant clothes led him to fancy sombreros and beaded buckskin shirts. Yet he was a likable fellow and hard worker, and won the hearty respect of his hands. Roosevelt's *Autobiography* tells of one or two encounters with "bad men," in which he displayed real physical courage. The somewhat synthetic nature of this courage, however, is best shown in an incident apparently never published. As a youth in search of health, Mr. Frederick Badger of Boston went to Roose-velt's Dakota ranch, and had a room separated by a thin curtain from the rancher's bedroom. In March, 1883, three thieves stole Roosevelt's boat and took it down the river. The aggrieved owner organized an expedition to retake it. During the night, before they set out, Badger was awakened by the sound of boots pacing the floor of the next room, and a voice saying over and over, with shrill determination: "I've got the gun on you. I know you stole my boat and I'm here to claim it." It was Roosevelt rehearsing an act that he carried out to the letter next day, in confronting the thieves and regaining his property.

An unsuccessful candidate for mayor of New York in 1886, Roosevelt soon received his first appointment to Federal office as a civil service commissioner under President Harrison. It soon became clear that new vitality, as well as new publicity, had been injected into a minor job. Roosevelt's genius was such that whatever he undertook appeared to be exciting fun as well as important. He began also to write books about history—the War of 1812, the winning of the West —with a sparkle unknown to college professors, that race of caged song-birds, as George Santayana has called them, who prefer fidelity to adventure. Roosevelt collaborated with Henry Cabot Lodge in writing *Hero Tales from American History,* a book whose moral they tersely expressed: "America will cease to be a great nation whenever her young men cease to possess energy, daring, and endurance, as well as the wish and the power to fight the nation's foes." (President Eliot, shocked at their proposals in the press that "this country needs a war," their suggestions for conquering Canada if Britain behaved badly in the Venezuela boundary dispute, called them "degenerated sons of Harvard," "a ruffian and a bully." They in turn thought him "flabby, timid."[16]) In 1895 Roosevelt enjoyed a new job, as president of the board of police commissioners of New York City. Leaving dinner parties to prowl in a black cloak through midnight streets, rebuking policemen who slept on duty or chatted with prostitutes, he won national fame as "Haroun-al-Roosevelt."

A vigorous stump-speaker against Bryan in 1896, after much wire-pulling he was rewarded by McKinley with the post of Assistant Secretary of the Navy. With McKinley's caution, and the pudding-like quality of his administration, Roosevelt had scant patience. On February 25, 1898, while the Secretary of the Navy was out of town for the afternoon, Roosevelt sent a cable to Dewey in the Pacific to stand by for action in the Philippines. Under the gathering war clouds, he thus made possible the Battle of Manila Bay. As soon as the war broke, Roosevelt prepared to resign and seek active service. He had been spoiling for "a bully fight," and here it was. "We will have a jim-dandy regiment if we go," he exclaimed. In April he had telegraphed Brooks Brothers in New York for immediate delivery on a "blue cravenette regular Lieutenant-Colonel's uniform without yellow on the collar and with leggings." He also ordered a dozen steel-rimmed spectacles, and stowed them in various parts of his uniform and luggage. "It will be awful if we miss the fun," he exclaimed in anxiety, while recruiting a regiment from the dude polo-players of Meadowbrook and cowboys of the plains. The term "Rough Riders," originally applied to the Pony Express, and borrowed later by the dime novels of Major Sam Hall and the circus of Buffalo Bill, crystallized a hero concept. It mattered little that the men themselves rode no horses into battle. The prose bard of the Rough Riders—the Taillefer of Theodore the Conqueror—was young Richard Harding Davis, "knight errant of New York of the Nineties," reporter and story-writer, the original of the firm-jawed Gibson man· with a dimple in his chin who set the pattern of virility for that generation.[17] Roosevelt fought and returned to write, himself, of those adventures. "If I was him, I'd call th' book 'Alone in Cubia,'" observed Mr. Dooley.

"San Juan was the great day of my life," Roosevelt recalled in 1918, a few months before his death. The attack at Kettle Hill, which he called "the San Juan charge," Roosevelt led under a rain of bullets —shouting encouragement to his men, crying to the laggards, "Are you afraid to stand up when I am on horseback?" A blue polka-dot handkerchief fluttered from the brim of his sombrero: to camouflage he made no concessions. The atmosphere of an *opéra bouffe* which memories of the World War have since lent to the Spanish-American sally, should not obscure the fact of Roosevelt's undoubted· bravery. His love for fighting was no bluff. Later he told Lodge: "Did I tell you that I killed a Spaniard with my own hand . . .? Probably I did. For some time . . . you will hear from me a great many . . . anecdotes of this war."[18] His boast in *The Rough Riders* of having killed "his Spaniard" provoked some newspapers to charge him with "bloodthirstiness."[19] Privately, in July, 1902, Roosevelt wrote his German friend Speck von Sternberg that he was "not in the least sensitive about killing any number of men if there is an adequate reason."[20] One looks in vain for an expression of like sentiment in the letters of better American soldiers, such as Washington or Lee. Grant, though less prone to swashbuckling than Roosevelt, probably shared his callous point of view; but certainly Lincoln did not. Roosevelt's attitude about killing men should not be mistaken for the ruthlessness of a Napoleon or a Hitler; read in the whole context of his life, it is essentially as naïve, as remote from real mass slaughter, as a small boy's cruelty with a beetle. But it reveals something of the ultimate flaw in Roosevelt's hero-character, a lack of the ingredient of magnanimity.

Roosevelt was, however, the most durable idol of the Spanish-American War. His few rivals soon faded out of the public mind. Richmond P. Hobson, whose sober and godly character at Annapolis had earned him the nickname of "Parson," met an ironic fate. After his attempt to bottle up the Spanish fleet by sinking a collier in Santiago Harbor, he returned to New York and was kissed by two girl cousins. Within a few weeks, on a countrywide tour, he had been kissed by an estimated ten thousand women, while confectioners were marketing a new candy called "Hobson kisses." The rage was not entirely new. In the 1840's Calhoun, travelling up the Mississippi from New Orleans to Memphis, was told "that it was a custom established in the river by Mr. Clay that they had the right to kiss any great man who chanced to be passing by."[21] But under the spotlight of national publicity in 1898 Hobson was made to seem faintly ridiculous. Regarding him and Admiral Dewey, a rhymester was soon reflecting in *Life:*

> These heroes—erst extolling—
> A fickle public drops;
> Folks chase a ball that's rolling,
> And kick it when it stops.

George Dewey, the victor of Manila, in the early autumn of 1899 had been given a New York ovation that cost $150,000. A triumphal arch, the work of thirty architects, spanned Fifth Avenue; made of lath, wood, and plaster, it was designed for translation into marble. At this time Dewey might have had the Presidency from either party "by simply holding his peace," observed *The Nation* on April 12, 1900, ". . . there has been no hero as popular, no idol so worshipped, since General Grant received the surrender of Lee's army at Appomattox." But within a few months Dewey maneuvered himself outside the Valhalla where he had suddenly found himself. Without reading it, he signed a jingoistic report of the Philippine Commission late in 1899; that finished him with the more liberal intellectuals. The people raised a sum to buy him a house in Washington; and although "simplicity" was part of his legend, when his tastes were consulted it was found that he would accept a house only in the most fashionable district, with a dining-room that would accommodate "at least eighteen" guests. Then the veteran married a Catholic widow, and deeded the people's gift to her—while rumor reported that the house would soon be the seat of a Papal legate. Then, in response to his presidential boom, Dewey made a genially bewildered statement on April 3, 1900: "It's easy enough to be President; all you have to do, I see, is to take orders from Congress, and I have been obeying orders all my life." The next day scores of editorials said that he had "cheapened the Presidency," while a typical front-page story, in the Atlanta *Constitution,* was headlined: "Leaders Laugh at Poor Dewey." Among others, Roosevelt looked upon Dewey's wane with express satisfaction. A few years later his triumphal arch, cracked and peeling, was removed as a hazard to traffic.

Roosevelt meanwhile had stumped New York State as a candidate for Governor. He wore his jaunty sombrero, and his special train carried seven Rough Riders in uniform, with a bugler who appeared on the rear platform to sound the cavalry charge before each speech. "You have heard the trumpet that sounded to bring you here," he told the voters of the small upstate town of Fort Henry. "I have heard it tear the tropic dawn when it summoned us to fight at Santiago."[22] Many applauded Roosevelt to the echo. His crusade of he-men against mollycoddles—the great theme that, mixed with a dash of the later Roosevelt's socialism, was just beginning to make Jack London popular —caught on. The redundant energy of the man, his bared teeth and flashing spectacles, dominated the political issues of which he spoke. Profiting by the crass political blunders of Tammany Hall, Roosevelt sailed to victory. A slight touch of radicalism began to cling to him. "How I wish I *wasn't* a reformer, oh, Senator!" he wrote to Chauncey Depew, refusing the hospitality of a pass on the New York Central. "But I suppose I must live up to my part, like the Negro minstrel who blacked himself all over!"[23] He wished to better the lot of the workingman; he sponsored a civil service law and a tax on corporation franchises. But at heart he was no Governor Altgeld; as Henry F. Pringle remarks, Roosevelt "seemed to be radical because his roar was so loud." Nevertheless Tom Platt, the Republican boss of New York, grew anxious to be rid of this strenuous young man and boomed him for Vice-President. A feud between two other Republican bosses, Matt Quay and Mark Hanna, did the rest, and assured his nomination to that office of eminent obscurity in 1900.

Roosevelt's Papers, as preserved in the Library of Congress, show no such outpouring of hopes and fears, of heart-throbs from the humble, as do the Bryan Papers. Here and there we find a letter like one in the fall of 1898 from Mrs. W. S. Miller of Atoka, Indian Territory: "What advice would you give to young boys about chewing tobacco—you are the Idol of every small boy in the country. A word from you now would be worth all the lectures on this subject till the end of time." Rare indeed is a message such as Roosevelt received from New York City in 1900, when he was Governor, written on a yellow ruled sheet torn from a copy-book:

Thursday June 21st
West Side Italian School
Grade 2 B

You are a good gentleman to us. Your are nice.
You have a pretty looking face. I love you.
Your girl
Rosie Biorno

There are a few letters from city boys who want to go out West and live on a ranch, and ask Mr. Roosevelt's advice. And there are a great many from Rough Riders, telling of children named for him, asking for jobs, or requesting help in trouble. "A bugler in your Regiment in Cuba, has been arrested upon a charge of shoplifting at Wanamaker's . . ." "Unable to work I held up a Gambler, and was sentence to Yuma, Ariz. Territorial Prison . . . I beg to have your aid . . . Mr. Roosevelt you know every one of your men loved you when you were Captain and expect your love in return, how well I remember the battle we had in Elcaney by the big Block House on the little river half a mile from the town, and how easily we won the Battle, by having you at our head, to lead us on." Major W. H. H. Llewellyn sent more or less regular bulletins: "I have the honor to report, that Comrade Ritchie, late of Troop G, is in jail in Trinidad, Colorado on a charge of murder . . . that Comrade Webb, late of Troop D, has just killed two men at Bisbee, Arizona. Have not yet received the details of our comrade's trouble . . . but understand that . . . he was entirely justified in the transaction." Roosevelt, telling his men goodbye in September, 1898, with perhaps less grandeur than the farewells of Washington and Lee, had warned them against the backwash of strenuousness: "Don't get gay and pose as heroes. Don't go back and lie on your laurels, they'll wither."[24]

His own laurels were still burgeoning. Elected to the Vice-Presidency in 1900, he found himself President the next September, after McKinley's assassination. Here and there, conservatives gloomed over "this crazy man" in the White House. The great public, however, was delighted to share in the family spectacle of the Roosevelts, including "Princess Alice" and the five children of the President's second marriage. Their clothes and sports, Alice's daring cigarettes and her marriage in the White House to Mr. Nicholas Longworth, held the people enthralled. Some grew excited, in the South indignant, when the new President invited Booker T. Washington to his dinner-table. The President's tennis drew much comment, on the whole more favorable than that attendant later upon Taft's golf—which seemed a more plutocratic game. Roosevelt's boxing lessons from Mike Donovan also captivated a public used to fat, sedentary men. in the White House. Later, Donovan wrote a book called *The Roosevelt That I Know,* and testified: "Had he come to the prize ring, instead of to the political arena, it is my conviction he would have been successful. The man is a born fighter." A memory that often played Roosevelt false in the direction of goals he wanted, but failed to reach, convinced him that he had once been lightweight champion· at Harvard.[25] According to impartial accounts, as a boxer Roosevelt had pluck but not much skill; legend however has magnified his ability. But on occasion he startled the public by a real exhibition of stamina. One of his last acts in office, early in 1909, was to ride horseback one hundred miles over rough Virginia roads, in order to shame grumblers in the Army over his recent order that all stout officers be able to ride a certain stated distance.

Roosevelt's theme song, played in the Cuban war, in swings around the country and on campaign, and at the inaugural parade in 1904, was "There'll Be a Hot Time in the Old Town Tonight." Big business began ·to wonder if there were not something ominous in that lyric pledge, but the people loved it as an index to the man whose exuberance was speeding the tempo of public life in the United States. He was a man of pure action, preaching a less selfish gospel of work than that of the success cultists. One worked for patriotism, for the State —and in the 1900's the specter of fascism had not arisen to haunt this doctrine. His scorn for the slacker, the cynic, and the "cultivated, ineffective man with a taste for bric-à-brac," served as a tonic to that generation. The first Boy Scouts would soon listen with awe to his advice: "Don't flinch, don't foul, hit the line hard!" While the adult public delighted in his apothegm, that he said was "a West African proverb: 'Speak softly and carry a big stick.'" The most famous demonstration of the latter saying, if not of the former, occurred near the close of his first term, in the taking of Panama. The building of a canal across the isthmus he regarded, with undoubted wisdom, as a national necessity. But his methods caused some criticism. Informally he called the Latin-Americans "Dagoes," remarking that "we may have to give a lesson to those jack-rabbits." He gave a benign wink to Panama, which revolted from Colombia on a prearranged date, while the American Navy stood by. "I took Panama without consulting the Cabinet," Roosevelt wrote breezily in his *Autobiography,* which appeared in 1913. At the University of California in 1911 he had recalled: "I took the canal zone and let Congress debate, and while the debate goes on the canal does also." Biographers have noted that this speech cost the United States $25,000,000. It so shocked the idealistic stratum of public opinion that, when Wilson became President, a treaty was drafted offering Colombia this sum and an apology. Furious, Roosevelt and his friends blocked this treaty. Not until 1921 was the sum paid, without the apology, in order to smooth the way for Colombian oil concessions in which the Harding Cabinet was interested.[26] Certainly, in comparison with the motives of Albert B. Fall, those of Theodore Roosevelt appeared not too unsavory—and his seizure of the Canal Zone did no damage to his popular repute. Americans felt, with some truth, that Roosevelt's personality and acts were making the United States into a first-class power.

Here and there one heard demur at the new militancy of America. In 1902 Ernest Crosby, pacifist and Tolstoyan, published a book called *Captain Jinks, Hero.* Jinks, having fought for his flag in the "Cubapines," yearns to be the perfect soldier. But in trying to convince himself that, on command, he would shoot his wife, he worries himself into an asylum where he is last seen playing with lead soldiers. Such criticism naturally focused upon the bellicose man in the White House, "as sweet a gentleman," wrote Colonel Henry Watterson, "as ever scuttled a ship or cut a throat." More genially, McLandburgh Wilson wrote:

> Our hero is a man of peace,
>   Preparedness he implores;
> His sword within its scabbard sleeps,
>   But mercy! how it snores.

That Roosevelt loved moments of fondling the big stick, such as sending the Navy round the world, cannot be denied. But Roosevelt in office was less the fire-eater than Roosevelt the private citizen. He was not unmindful of responsibility, and did everything in his power to quench the jingoes of America and Japan in 1906, when hard

feelings over immigration laws led to war talk. And, as the arbiter of
- Japan's war with Russia, he was the first American to receive the
Nobel Peace Prize. For all his emphatic motions toward imperialism,
as toward reform, Roosevelt often arrested his hand in the midst of
a gesture. Even in ordering the public printer to adopt simplified
spelling, he added that if the changes were not popularly approved
they would be abandoned—disclaiming his intention "to do anything
far-reaching or sudden or violent, or indeed anything very great at
all."[27] He liked to deliver thumping opinions upon any subject that
crossed his mind—including birth control versus the "full baby carriage," divorce, the novels of Dickens and Zola, the private life of
Gorki, and nature-faking—for, as he once said, "The White House
is a bully pulpit." And he also loved power. But he was saved from
being a dictator, political or moral, because he either took the popular
side of an old issue or else listened anxiously for the public's reaction
whenever he committed himself on a new one. He could be as angry
as a later Roosevelt over what he regarded as interference between
himself and the people, chiefly from the courts, but to the murmurs
of the ground-swell he hearkened almost timorously. "No man values
public opinion or fears it as much as Theodore Roosevelt," wrote a
shrewd politician, spying out the field for Standard Oil in 1905. "No
man seeks popularity as much as he. Mild reproof or criticism of his
policy would nearly paralyze him. Today he hears only the cries of
the rabble and thinks it is public sentiment."[28] Rightly, the public
never looked upon his toothly grin as the baring of dictatorial fangs,
but took to their hearts the "Teddy-bear," symbol of his ferocious
playfulness.

His election to the Presidency in. 1904, "in his own right," by a
majority of two and a half million, vastly heightened his self-confidence. (His only error, in that moment of exuberance, was in dis-
avowing any future plans for a third term: "under no circumstances
will I be a candidate for or accept another nomination." In 1912 he
had to eat these words.) He had been "dee-lighted" by the campaign
and the thunderous applause that reached his ears—except, as he told
Lodge, that he was irked by the "outrageous lie that I had been kissing babies." Mr. Dooley in an aside remarked that a baby kissed by
Roosevelt knew it had been kissed, and would bear the honorable
scars for life—that in fact a generation would grow up among us
looking like German university graduates. Whether a kisser of babies
or not, Roosevelt was a born politician. He had found his ancestors,

Dutch, Scotch, English, Welsh, and Huguenot, so useful in stumping for votes, that a popular anecdote claimed he had instinctively greeted a Jewish caller with a crushing handshake, "Congratulations! I am partly Jewish, too."

And the people were enchanted, too, when he stood up in his carriage and waved to admirers on the way to his inauguration. His frank delight in the presence of Rough Riders on this stately occasion, and the fact that he bent his knees in time to the band playing "There'll Be a Hot Time in the Old Town Tonight," were equally reassuring. Roosevelt had created a character, and lived up to it with winning consistency. And the crowd, as Samuel G. Blythe noted, "cheered the flag and cheered the Rough Riders, and felt that America was indeed a country which had licked Spain with . . . facile ease, and that they, being component parts of it, were not half bad themselves." The nubbin of the Roosevelt cult was seized upon by one of his old New York police captains: "It was not only that he was a great man, but, oh, there was such fun in being led by him."[29] Somebody compared his irresistibility to that of a circus parade led by a steam calliope.

Roosevelt never tried to conceal his opinion that Bryan was a kindly but cheap demagogue—to Roosevelt's eyes, not unlike Thomas Jefferson. But with the passing years Roosevelt came more and more to adopt Bryan's dreams, and, as Bryan could not do, to realize them in action. When at the Gridiron Dinner of 1905 a debate between them was proposed, one member of the club cried out, "What's the use? They're both on the same side."[30] Roosevelt launched the trust-busting era, and so successfully stigmatized "malefactors of great wealth" that for the next generation very rich men had to hire public relations counsels, like the late Ivy L. Lee, to whitewash them with human interest stories about dimes given to small boys and millions to churches and medicine. Roosevelt's attacks undoubtedly enhanced the endowment of many colleges and universities, including his own alma mater Harvard. A moderately rich man himself, Roosevelt had none of the veneration for a brahmin caste felt by most of the self-made Presidents from Grant through McKinley. Moreover, in the coal strike of 1902, after dealing with George F. Baer and other thick-witted industrialists, Roosevelt saw that his future adversaries were more foolish than fearsome. With no very clear program in view, but a sincere wish to gain popular approval, Roosevelt set forth to correct certain crying abuses. He attacked the railroads for their discriminatory rates and secured passage of the Hepburn Act in 1906; he had a

measure of success in enforcing the Sherman Act against huge industrial combines like Northern Securities and in threatening Standard
Oil; he did much for public health in reforming the meat-packing
industry and sponsoring the Pure Food and Drugs Act; and he helped
the cause of Western land conservation and irrigation. But he was
careful time and again to veer to the right, to praise "real conservatism." And in 1906 he tried to call a halt to sensational exposure of
graft in high places by his lecture "The Man with the Muck-Rake,"
with strangely little perception that the muck was worse than the rake.
As a liberal, Theodore Roosevelt was a house divided.

Nevertheless, Wall Street and the railroads began to curse him. In
words reminiscent of those later hurled at Theodore Roosevelt's fifth
cousin, Jim Hill of the Northern Pacific wrote bitterly: "It seems hard
. . . that we should be compelled to fight for our lives against the
political adventurers who have never done anything but pose and draw
a salary." The rich looked upon him reproachfully as a traitor, and
the self-made charged him with having no conception of the practical rules of the game. So long as he had confined himself to preaching the Darwinian philosophy of imperialism, with its stress upon the
survival of the fittest, they had no quarrel with him. Now they began
to fear that a radical was at the helm. They breathed a sigh of relief
in March, 1909, when he quitted the White House. Roosevelt, who
always loved the larger vertebrates, had picked genial and able William
Howard Taft as his successor. And though Taft owed his nomination
and election to the still potent magic of "TR," Wall Street was reassured. Taft's face, as well as his waistline, promised that the strenuous
age was over.

Roosevelt's announcement that he was bound for Africa to hunt
big game was one more fillip to his adoring public. Within a few
weeks' time he received more souvenirs than had been given to any
President before. There were rifles and cameras, walking-sticks and
shooting-sticks, kits and mosquito netting, and innumerable toy elephants and lions. Potteries sold the public a vast number of toby jugs
showing Roosevelt's grinning bespectacled face, a gun at his side, and
the handle of the jug shaped like an elephant's trunk. (From the
portraiture of toby jugs, it is said, "mug" came to mean face.) Roosevelt's had come to be the best-known face in the world. In an age
of cartoons it was the caricaturist's answer to prayer—so compact,
mobile, expressive. A later decade would see it carved, pince-nez effect
and all, upon the cliff of Mount Rushmore, as the companion of

Washington, Jefferson, and Lincoln. The five-cent stamp also would send his image on foreign-borne mail throughout the world. Meanwhile, his face was remarkably popular on cigar labels—ranging from a brand called "TR" to one captioned "U. S. Bouquet," featuring him alongside his peers Washington, Jefferson, and Lincoln. That Roosevelt himself never used tobacco in any form did not matter. Roosevelt's one-time Republican boss Tom Platt also had his namesake among cigars, sold chiefly around New York City; the discontinuance of this brand in the 1900's was an index of that politician's waning popularity. Roosevelt's opponent for the mayoralty of New York, Henry George of the single tax, also had his cigar—which bore the tag "By permission of." A similar tag was attached to a cigar honoring "Uncle Joe" Cannon, who had put through the bill appropriating $50,000,000 for Roosevelt's war in Cuba, and who tyrannized over the House of Representatives during the President's administration. And the Colonel's fellow-soldier in Cuba, Confederate General Fitzhugh Lee, had his cigar, as later did the Colonel's successor in the White House, with the "Judge Taft" brand. There was also a "Hobson's Choice," after 1898. The iconography of cigar labels reached its peak early in the twentieth century—and the preponderance of statesmen, symbols of mellow wisdom, with a sprinkling of military heroes as tokens of virility, is a fact worth noting.

Roosevelt's big-game hunt was a great success. King Edward VII, sharing perhaps the jealousy of those who lack the fluency and journalistic verve of the Roosevelts, remarked to Spring Rice that it was "a great pity" the Ex-President sold his experiences in advance to *Scribner's Magazine* for $50,000. But, before Roosevelt's grand tour was over, King Edward was dead and Roosevelt as representative from the United States had a decorously jolly time among the kings and maharajas at his funeral. Pageantry had a habit, it seemed, of dogging Roosevelt's steps. Wherever he went interesting things happened, and he kept Germany, France, and Italy excited with his speeches and controversies. He was the mad American of that generation. In June, 1910, he came home to find a great naval parade being held in his honor, a medal struck, and immense grandstands erected at the Battery. "Certainly the first citizen of the world today," wrote Major Archie Butt. Roosevelt was not so sure. After getting his bearings he commented a few months later: "I think that the American people feel a little tired of me, a feeling with which I cordially sympathize."[31] But like Buffalo Bill he could never resist farewell appearances. Soon he was touring the country, making speeches to say "I stand for the Square Deal," and daring to ride in an aeroplane at St. Louis while thousands held their breath.

The Square Deal was lightly tinged with a paternal socialism of which Roosevelt himself was hardly aware—the result partly of his revulsion against the blandness of Taft, and partly from a Roosevelt habit of growing imperceptibly more radical after years of keeping an ear to the grass-roots. His feud with Taft, like his growing bitterness toward Woodrow Wilson, cost him something in prestige. It revealed a subconscious rivalry in Roosevelt's spirit, a lack of generosity toward those who came after him. Again, it was the fatal flaw springing from his lack of magnanimity. His postponement of announcing his candidacy as a leader of the progressives left La Follette's aspirations to wilt on the vine. "I do not wish to put myself in the position where, if it becomes my plain duty to accept, I shall be obliged to shirk such duty because of having committed myself," he said.[32] The bolt of the Bull Moose faction made him of course a drafted candidate, as he had foreseen. Prone to be as gloomy about the future, in private, as he seemed optimistic in public, Roosevelt anticipated defeat. Nonetheless he began a brisk campaign, advocating recall of judicial decisions, social welfare legislation, farm relief, workmen's compensation, health insurance in industry, heavier taxes upon wealth, and limited injunction in labor disputes. Enemies, like Frank I. Cobb in *The New York World,* said Roosevelt sponsored "the state of mind that wants a Little Father, that wants Federal interference with every form of human industry and activity."[33] A great surge of popular sympathy went out to Roosevelt in October, 1912, when on his way to speak in Milwaukee he was shot in the breast by a fanatic. "I will make this speech or die," Roosevelt told friends who tried to rush him to the hospital. "It is one thing or the other." In this spirit of quixotic courage the speech was made; the country rang with applause. Here was the great Roosevelt tradition. The wound was superficial, but Roosevelt's campaigning days were almost over. In the November election he surpassed Taft, but fell before Wilson and "the New Freedom." A later day would see the Square Deal and the New Freedom fused as the New Deal.

Once more, in the spring of 1913, the Hunter left for the hills. Roosevelt plunged into the jungles of Brazil to explore the River of Doubt. With an injured and abscessed leg, and stricken with tropical fever, Roosevelt made another of his Boy Scout gestures, at once so absurd and so appealing. "I want you . . . to go ahead," he said to his son Kermit. "We have reached a point where some of us must stop. I feel I am only a burden to the party." Of course he was not abandoned to die, but brought home, never to be physically fit again.

He fumed against the dilatoriness of Wilson in plunging the country into the Great War, accusing the President of schoolmasterish cowardice, sneering at his "weasel words," saying cruel things about the shadows at Shadow Lawn, the summer White House—"the shadows of the men, women and children who have risen from the ooze of the ocean bottom . . . the shadows of the tortured dead." In March, 1916, there was talk of Roosevelt's renomination. "It would be a mistake," the old lion said, "to nominate me unless the country has in its mood something of the heroic." Feeling unsure of the war sentiment, his party picked Charles Evans Hughes. A few months later, with war declared, Roosevelt with desperate politeness to Wilson and alternate bluster and humility to the War Department, begged to lead a division of volunteers to France. From overseas Clemenceau sent an eloquent appeal to Wilson: "You are too much of a philosopher to ignore that the influence on the people of great leaders of men often exceeds their personal merits, thanks to the legendary halo surrounding them. The name of Roosevelt has this legendary force in our country . . . you must know, Mr. President, more than one of our *poilus* asked his comrade: 'But where is Roosevelt?' "[34] Hero-worship has seldom been paid a higher tribute. Another distinguished foreigner, visiting the United States, exclaimed: "It may be that Mr. Wilson possesses all the virtues in the calendar; but for my part I had rather go to hell with Theodore Roosevelt."[35] Perhaps he had never heard the song that Roosevelt's legions had sung, at Armageddon, in 1912:

> Follow! Follow!
> We will follow Roosevelt,
> Anywhere! Everywhere,
> We will follow on.

The essence of the Roosevelt worship was always loyalty to his person, rather than to his shifting ideals. But Woodrow Wilson, more fond of efficiency than glamour, and doubtless human enough to recall the shadows at Shadow Lawn, turned a deaf ear. In the one great war of his time, Theodore Roosevelt gave his sons but was unable to give himself. When his youngest, Quentin, fell in a burning aeroplane within the German lines, the father wrote his last vibrant words: "Only those are fit to live who do not fear to die; and none are fit to die who have shrunk from the joy of life. Both life and death are parts of the same Great Adventure."[36] Less than six months later the writer was dead.

The world of Woodrow Wilson went to war in an idealistic mood, not in intellectual sympathy with the imperialism of Roosevelt. After that war came a mood of disillusion and cynicism that was even more alien to his spirit. During the economic depression he faded rapidly as a symbol, the Square Deal which he never had a chance to attempt being forgotten in a widespread impression that he was merely a "warmonger." Both conservatives and liberals were apt to shelve his claims to supreme herohood, while keeping a sentimental fondness for the most picturesque American of his generation. The final appraisal of Theodore Roosevelt is yet to be made, with his virtues of strength and courage, his vast energy and consuming patriotism, and his generally beneficent effect upon American life, set over against a few flaws that are so obvious as almost to disarm criticism. Although he and Bryan were both, in a sense, immature, and sprang from an America which seemed to have grown younger and more awkward since Washington's and even Lincoln's time, it is clear that Roosevelt had a far better head than Bryan. He undoubtedly left a deeper impress than Bryan was able to do, upon the ways of American leadership. In his legend there was something more heroic. He was our last great American on horseback—as an epic bronze statue of him on a charger, unveiled before the American Museum of Natural History in New York, on Roosevelt's birthday in 1940, bears witness.

In 1921 the present Senator Arthur Vandenburg submitted to some fifty "representative Americans" the query, "Who in your opinion is the greatest American?" A clear majority—ranging from Samuel Gompers to Edison, from John Spargo to John D. Rockefeller, Jr.— unequivocally voted for Lincoln. A substantial minority—including most Democratic leaders and such members of Wilson's Cabinet as Lansing, Josephus Daniels, Newton D. Baker, and Franklin D. Roosevelt (cautiously eliminating "the great names from 1850 on," which "cannot be considered final")—chose George Washington. These results are such as one might expect. Likewise, some said the three greatest were "Washington, Lincoln, and Cleveland," "Washington, Lincoln, and Roosevelt," or "Washington, Lincoln, and Wilson." A good many echoed the judgment of William Allen White: "If I were speaking of the most typical American, it would be Theodore Roosevelt. But he is not our greatest American, nor does he approach the American ideal so nearly as Lincoln." Said Professor Charles M. Andrews, Yale's distinguished American historian: "If you are searching for the most typical American . . . I should name Roosevelt." More boldly wrote Henry C. Wallace, agricultural journalist of Des Moines and father of Henry A. Wallace: "I say without hesitation that in my opinion Theodore Roosevelt is best entitled to be called The Greatest American, because he exemplified in his own life the qualities we value most in an American citizen." An equally strong partisan, Gifford Pinchot, declared:

I believe that Roosevelt could have done everything Washington did and a good many things that Washington could not have done. That leaves Lincoln and Roosevelt. Between the two I confess I am in doubt. Roosevelt, I think, could not have played the part that Lincoln did in humanizing the relations between the North and South. Lincoln, I think, as a pure, intellectual force did not equal Roosevelt, nor could he in my judgment have grasped great international problems with the clear definition which so remarkably characterized Roosevelt's mind in action. My answer must be Lincoln or Roosevelt; which, I do not know.

Similarly, Professor Van Tyne of the University of Michigan, after polling his class in American history on Senator Vandenburg's question, reported 119 votes for Lincoln, 57 for Roosevelt, 18 for Wilson, 10 for Washington, 4 for Franklin, 1 each for Jefferson, Bryan, and Edison.[37] (College students are prone to vote for the more contemporaneous.) Qualities of cheerful aggressiveness, energy, decisiveness, love of adventure and daring, and a basic honesty and simplicity, were doubtless those which caused Theodore Roosevelt to seem, if not the greatest American, then perhaps the most typical.

The verdict of 1921 was probably more enthusiastic toward Roosevelt than that of a decade later. His present standing, as a national symbol, is difficult to gauge. But if America ever enters upon another era of expansion, of taking up the Anglo-Saxon's burden in Latin America or the Orient, his legend will be burnished anew. Whether he will become *the* Roosevelt of American hero-worship depends upon our future national policies.

CHAPTER FIFTEEN

THE UNKNOWN SOLDIER: HERO OF THE WORLD WAR

> Unnamed, unknown, remain, and still remain, the
> bravest soldiers. Our manliest—our boys—our hardy
> darlings; no picture gives them. Likely, the typic one
> of them (standing, no doubt, for hundreds, thousands,)
> crawls aside to some bush-clump, or ferny tuft, on
> receiving his death-shot . . . and there, at last, the
> Bravest Soldier crumbles in mother earth, unburied
> and unknown.—WALT WHITMAN, *Specimen Days.*

I

THROUGH 1918 and the early months of 1919 it looked as if
America and the human race had discovered a new idol
of titanic size. His promise of mercy and justice for all
recalled Abraham Lincoln, but his sphere of influence was
even more international than Cæsar's or Napoleon's. He
had spoken not to a section or nation in terms of "malice toward
none," but to a battle-weary world urging that hate be laid aside in
a "peace without victory"—or rather, the victory of brotherhood. His
presence brooded over Washington and Versailles, London and Rome.
From a Polish village came a delegation to Paris to see him; they
were dressed in cloaks of red-embroidered wool and Cossack caps,

with a priest as interpreter, and as guide a sheep-herder "who knew the stars, and the way to go."[1] Even farther away, in Asia and Africa, submerged minorities, awaiting the magic of "self-determination," looked hopefully to the Messiah in the West. Simple folk had believed for four terrible years that the war would end only by the advent of the Prince of Peace. Here, among living men, he was—the shadow of a great rock in a weary land. Wherever his long thoughtful head, graying hair, and resolute jaw were seen—on platforms high above cheering thousands, from automobiles and carriages flashing through the streets of American cities and European capitals, behind the windows of trains speeding across the Italian campagna and the vineyards of France—there were frenzied shouts and often tears of joy. Lincoln Steffens heard of "peasant families . . . all along the way kneeling beside the track in the dark to pray for him and his mission." Even in revolutionary Germany, idealists began to catch fire from him. Here at last above the surging tides of loyalty and hate was one whose sweet reasonableness seemed to offer all things to all men. That one man's self-determination might be another man's bondage was not yet perceived. The golden age, a millennium of peace, was at hand. The very coolness of the man himself, and the touch of his dispassionate logic, fell gratefully upon a fevered world. He was an American—and the Western ingenuity that had fashioned the aeroplane and machine-gun and submarine might also heal the havoc they had wrought. He was a man of ideals, who, as he often declared, wanted nothing for himself and his people. He was an umpire from the cloudland of Olympus.

And yet, with this matchless opportunity to become one of the great legends of mankind, Woodrow Wilson apparently failed. Within a few years, abroad, and within a few months, at home, he ceased to be the supreme hero of the World War. His own mistakes tell part of the story; the rest may be told in terms of a world unable to live up to a dream. Neither the ultimate success of Washington nor the martyrdom of Lincoln came to save a man whose sincerity and intelligence made him their not unworthy successor, even though he lacked Washington's strength through restraint and Lincoln's strength through patience.

Of Scotch-Irish blood, Wilson was born in 1856 in a Presbyterian manse, on a hillside in Staunton, Virginia. (Long afterwards, in 1918, at the Mansion House in London, he spoke of "the stern Covenanter tradition that is behind me"; we need hardly to be told that Wilson, whose boyhood heroes were Oliver Cromwell and Stonewall Jackson, at times seemed grim and fanatic to men who opposed him.) His birthplace is not yet a great American shrine, comparable to other Virginia spots like Mount Vernon, Arlington, Monticello, the birthplace and the tomb of Lee, or St. John's Church in Richmond associated with Patrick Henry's challenge of "Liberty or Death." Not until 1931 did Mary Baldwin Seminary buy the austerely charming old manse and open it to the public. It is now owned by the Woodrow Wilson Birthplace Foundation, an organization whose president is Mrs. Cordell Hull, a native of Staunton. Some five years ago, only six hundred visitors came annually to the spot; the number has now grown to about two thousand. The custodian reports that last year pilgrims from such remote lands as Armenia and Belgium "were as reverent in their praise of Mr. Wilson as a Nazi from Germany was insulting."[2] She also states that interest in the birthplace has quickened since the outbreak of war in Europe—some remarking that if Wilson's plans had been carried out the new conflict would have been impossible, others admitting that until now they had not been in sympathy with Wilson.

Wilson's boyhood, spent chiefly in post-bellum Georgia, has not attracted the myth-makers. Hardship and adventure played no part in it. Wilson himself testified that he was "a laughed-at 'mamma's boy.' "[3] He remained always a sedentary individual, to whom books and ideas held a vicarious thrill. He loved sea yarns and later detective stories, but under his father's tutelage learned to delight in history and biography. Boyhood health as delicate as Theodore Roosevelt's did not make him, by revolt, into a boxer and muscle-builder. As a student at Princeton and the University of Virginia—where, incidentally, he never climbed the hill to visit Monticello—Wilson studied law and political history, making himself into a sound though never deep or original scholar. Soon, as a young professor at Bryn Mawr, Wesleyan University, and Princeton, he was speculating upon other methods of moving the world than by the fulcrum of a big stick. In 1897 to a friend he wrote his thoughts about "a man who wishes to make himself, *by utterance,* a force in the world." Later, as President, he aspired to "wield the sword of penetrating speech." Henceforth, ideas and words would trace the career of Wilson, even as deeds had marked that of Theodore Roosevelt and welling emotions that of Bryan.

In 1902 Wilson became president of Princeton. Hearing his inaugural address, Colonel George Harvey is supposed to have said: "A man who could make an address like that could move the masses of the common people." Harvey, editor of *Harper's Weekly* and friend of Wall Street, was then in search of a safe Democratic rival to Bryan. Later, after booming Wilson for high office and seeing "Boss" Smith make him Governor of New Jersey, Harvey discovered Wilson had a will of iron that defeated the purposes of bosses and kingmakers. Their friendship ended in a bitter feud, while Wilson found a more disinterested adviser in Colonel House.

Meanwhile, Wilson's Princeton battles with Dean West and the clubs, over the issue of campus snobbery, gave him nationwide publicity as a champion of equalitarianism. A current joke said that Harvard with her electoral system offered education à la carte; Yale a substantial table d'hôte; Columbia a quick lunch; and Princeton an elegant picnic. Wilson sought to make it a democratic cafeteria, specializing in plain living and high thinking. He was already embarking upon the paradoxical crusade of his life, a fight for democracy waged somewhat in the temper of an autocrat. He imagined that all who opposed him were evil, replying to their opposition with rigidity, and sometimes a cold scorn, that locked the door upon conciliation. His longtime comrade, and successor at Princeton, John Grier Hibben, suddenly found the door bolted forever. Thin-skinned, Woodrow Wilson never sought to charm those who were critical of him, or unbent to them—as he did so admirably in the presence of friends.

Yet Wilson's faith in ideals, especially that of democracy, was deeply sincere. Before ideals he was as humble as he was arrogant before individuals who seemed to contest those ideals. "I believe, as I believe in nothing else, in the average integrity and the average intelligence of the American people," Wilson asserted at the start of his White House years, when with the New Freedom he sought to sweep aside "all forms of unjust handicaps against the little man," forerunner of the forgotten man. Dramatizing the sinister economic control of American life as an "invisible empire . . . above the forms of democracy," Wilson set forth the challenge of a progressivism better reasoned than that of Theodore Roosevelt's last phase. Even as the bugles of Europe were blowing, to drown shortly his call to domestic reform, Wilson began to summon Americans to "some upland where the air is fresher," and a future "in comparison with which the present is nothing." This was the note upon which he had served briefly as Governor of New Jersey, and upon which he had been carried to the

Presidency in 1912. Idealists, liberal editors, and those like Lincoln Steffens and Ray Stannard Baker whom Roosevelt had repudiated as muck-rakers were thrilled by "the old-fashioned liberal" who had declared at his Inaugural: "This is not a day of triumph; it is a day of dedication." (An echo was heard in the opening inaugural words of the next Democratic President, in 1933, later dropped from the revised text in Franklin D. Roosevelt's *Works:* "This is a day of national consecration.")

Yet in action, whether upon a college campus or in the national forum, Woodrow Wilson's democracy always looked a little "academic" in comparison with Andrew Jackson's and Lincoln's. Perhaps the naïveté of their times, which now lingered chiefly among the grass-roots, was as outmoded as the warm hospitality of the frontier. But if Wilson had been able to recapture a little of their heartiness, to tell a few salty stories instead of reciting the Anglo-Victorian limericks that he most relished, to dismiss his donnish eye-glasses and the white piping on his waistcoat, and either to joke his enemies out of court as did Lincoln or even spar boisterously with them as did "TR" instead of staring over their heads (as Wilson said) "at a star," he might have found the going easier. Born politicians like Franklin or trained ones like Jefferson might have taught Wilson the give-and-take, the yielding of minor objectives to secure major ones. Perhaps the very imputation of being a sedentary man steeled him against softness. "Toleration is an admirable intellectual gift," he wrote, "but it is of little worth in politics. Politics is a war of causes; a joust of principles. Government is too serious a matter to admit of meaningless courtesies."[4] This touch of harshness and imperious will was no doubt responsible for Charles W. Eliot's remark that "like most reformers, Wilson had a fierce and unlovely side." Of Savonarola and John Knox and Jonathan Edwards, other "stern Covenanters," the unconvinced had spoken in the same way, giving them admiration but no affection.

To say with the hostile, that Wilson was "a mere idealist," is far less than the truth. He was an expert on practical government. He was no dreamer. His Scotch economy came to the fore in his impatience with time-wasters. He was if anything too brusque and efficient with those hangers-on who always frittered away Lincoln's energy. Wilson could never suffer fools gladly. He admired strong leadership; as a historian he had remarked that "Presidents were leaders until Jackson went home to the Hermitage." Yet Wilson at his best handled Congress and Cabinet with considerable finesse, and with more respect for the machinery of constitutional government than Lincoln had shown. He was a master of publicity, both for the New Freedom and for the war aims of 1917-18.

Why then does Wilson the statesman seem "academic"? It is perhaps because his allegiance to democracy was so purely intellectual. In tastes, personality, and habits he was instinctively the aristocrat. In 1912 a certain Democratic Senator, acquainted with Wilson's early writings on constitutional government, refused to support him under the assumption that he was a disciple of Alexander Hamilton. By logic rather than intuitive sympathy Wilson was a democrat, and even though logic with Wilson himself was far more compelling than with most men, it did not win over the critical so easily as did Lincoln's double handshake. Apropos of other matters, a later Princeton professor, J. Duncan Spaeth, has well observed that, among the faculties of man, the heart is the democrat, the intellect the aristocrat, and the will the autocrat. In Wilson's make-up, brain and will predominated. Wilson espoused the heart's cause, but with inescapable reservations of temperament. The warmth in his soul he saved for his family and a few intimate friends (who still vigorously deny the charge that he was a cold man). But the public at large saw in Wilson none of Father Abraham's spontaneous humanity, or even the cheerful impulsiveness of the two Roosevelts. So greatly did frigidity come to dominate the Wilson legend, that some of the absurd stories spread by his enemies—that he waited at stage doors to take soubrettes off to midnight suppers, that his devotion to Mrs. Peck was so romantic as to brand him with the label of "Peck's bad boy"—did him less harm than good with the public. They suggested a Gulf stream beneath the polar ice. On the other hand, his supposed callousness in remarrying fourteen months after the death of his first wife in August, 1914, did his popularity a great deal of illogical damage.

Equally unfair was the assumption that Wilson lacked courage. In May, 1915, speaking to a group of naturalized citizens in Philadelphia, Wilson alluded to the peaceful ideals of our tradition: "There is such a thing as a man being too proud to fight. There is such a thing as a nation being so right that it does not need to convince others by force that it is right." The cartoonist Rogers, in *The New York Herald,* drew a backbone and captioned it "Lost! Somewhere in Washington." The historian William Roscoe Thayer made pointed reference to "moral eunuchs," and Theodore Roosevelt bewailed our national disgrace. The phrase "too proud to fight," coming only a few days after the sinking of the *Lusitania,* was thrown repeatedly into Wilson's teeth until he was made to look like both a prig and a coward—a sissy rebuking his manly schoolmates for their bloody noses. No foe troubled to quote the phrase in its context. Six years later Tumulty's memoirs told how he, reading a copy of Wilson's speech en route to Philadelphia, had scented trouble over "too proud to fight." But Wilson had refused to change it, believing, he said, that "self-mastery is sometimes more heroic than fighting." Wilson was no coward. His admission a few months later, in January, 1916, that his earlier opposition to preparedness had been wrong—that "I would be ashamed if I had not learned something in fourteen months"—took fully as much moral courage, from a stiffly proud man, as Theodore Roosevelt's clamor for war. Wilson's courage was the kind Emerson had described in "The Scholar": "The speculative man, the scholar, is the right hero. He is brave, because he sees the omnipotence of that which inspires him. Is there only one courage and one warfare? I cannot manage sword and rifle; can I not therefore be brave? . . . Is an armed man the only hero?"

Another aspersion that still passes for truth has to do with Wilson's re-election. It states that his return to office in November, 1916, under the slogan "he kept us out of war," was a piece of trickery in the light of his call for war against Germany six months later. In weighing this charge one should remember that Wilson was never an unconditional pacifist; even during the season of greatest scorn toward a man "too proud to fight" Wilson was protesting so vigorously to Germany over the *Lusitania* that his Secretary of State resigned in protest. At length, from May, 1916, to January, 1917, Wilson won a bloodless victory over Germany in keeping submarine warfare within the limits he had proposed. Early in 1916 Wilson began to sponsor rearmament, marching in preparedness parades, warning the United States of a day when a choice between peace and honor might be necessary. Meanwhile his opponents the Republicans took no stand for getting the country ready for war, while the pro-German or "hyphen" vote swung steadily toward the anti-Wilson camp. And finally, Wilson made no promise to keep the country, at all costs, out of war. Germany's declaration of unrestricted submarine warfare in January, 1917, the sinking of American merchant ships, the Zimmermann note seeking to involve Mexico, and other episodes, brought such pressure upon Wilson that he finally concluded war was the people's will. That Wilson in calling for war somehow betrayed a popular mandate will not stand up under scrutiny. Yet it figured largely in the Harding campaign of 1920, was revived by isolationists in 1939 and 1940, and has tinged Wilson's reputation with a curiously jesuitical color.

With equal lack of evidence, Leftists in the age of disillusion tried to impeach Wilson's motives. He herded the country into war, according to the more romantic cynics, at the behest of munitions-makers, the "merchants of death." Others say he was pulling Mr. J. P. Morgan's chestnuts out of the fire. From the work of scholarly biographers like Charles Seymour and exhaustive ones like Ray Stannard Baker, as well as from a great deal of collateral testimony, it is clear that Wilson was singularly untouched by the financial interests. He was far more innocent of friendships in and pressure from Wall Street than were his twentieth-century predecessors, including the "trust-busting" Roosevelt. With those whom he had branded as the invisible empire he had no backstairs traffic. At the beginning of the war the State Department virtually prohibited loans to belligerents, but the spirit of so-called profiteering got out of hand in the war industries trade and at length nullified the financial ban of August, 1914. Whatever handicap inexperience may have put upon Wilson, in this unprecedented crisis, he was in no sense the puppet that hostile propaganda has sometimes made him. Neither was he a war-monger, as the American Youth Congress and similar organizations now profess to believe, in casting scorn upon the spirit of 1917. With startling realism Wilson foresaw the tragic cost of war, and its aftermath including the ruin of his own reputation and the corruption of the Harding era. To Frank I. Cobb of *The New York World,* in the late watches of the night before the President's message to Congress on April 2, 1917, Wilson spoke, sitting with sleepless eyes before the typewriter on his study table. Every loophole of escape, he said, had been tried and found blocked by German action. Short of spineless submission, nothing remained. War, bitterly inevitable, would levy its price upon ideals as well as men; "he said when a war got going it was just war, and there weren't two kinds of it."

"Once lead this people into war," he said, "and they'll forget there ever was such a thing as tolerance. To fight you must be brutal and ruthless, and the spirit of ruthless brutality will enter into the very fibre of our national life, infecting Congress, the courts, the policeman on the beat, the man in the street." . . . He foresaw too clearly the probable influence of a declaration of war on his own fortunes; the adulation certain to follow the certain victory, the derision and attack which would come with the deflation

of excessive hopes, and in the presence of world responsibility. But . . . it
was just a choice of evils.[5]

Likewise, to Tumulty that evening, after the speech had been made
and greeted with a wild ovation—Chief Justice White, tears streaming
down his face, leading the applause—Wilson observed sadly: "My message was a message of death to our young men. How strange it seemed
to applaud that."[6]

Yet knowing the spirit in which wars are won, as well as their toll,
Wilson gave the United States a fighting faith. He hoped against hope
that this would not be "just war." That memorable address to Congress
set the pitch: "We have no quarrel with the German people," but solely
with "Prussian autocracy." (British statesmen in 1939–40 took this leaf
from the Wilson notebook.) "We desire no conquest, no dominion";
our purpose has to do with "the rights and liberties of small nations."
"The world must be made safe for democracy." This, he said, was
America's task. And he closed with words that few recognized as a
paraphrase of Martin Luther's ringing declaration: "God helping her,
she can do no other." Then and later Wilson made the nation feel that
this was a war of the people, for humanity's sake. In this light, no
sacrifice seemed too dear.

The importance of leadership, even in a constitutional democracy,
was never more clearly demonstrated. To a surprising degree, as Allan
Nevins has suggested, the American people derive their tone from the
man in the White House—morally easy-going under a Grant, strenu-
ously ambitious under a Theodore Roosevelt, idealistic under a Wilson,
slothfully materialistic under a Harding and a Coolidge. The popular
choice of a given candidate, for President, is doubtless some index of
the age to come. But Roosevelt and Coolidge succeeded to office by
accident, while it is highly doubtful whether the voters who elected
such men as Grant and Harding peered with any deep insight into
their true nature. A President undoubtedly helps to set the moral pace.
The course of Wilsonian idealism was unforeseen in 1912 and even
in 1916; if, in the former year, Theodore Roosevelt had been elected,
it is almost certain that America would have joined in the European
War, but in a temper very different from Wilson's. The prime defect
of Wilson's leadership was not the declaration of war, or his masterly
waging of that war with the help of good men whom he picked for
military and administrative posts. It lay in his assumption that the
idealism, the spirit of internationalism, which he had infused into the

United States would last indefinitely. To his grief he found that it did not last much beyond the Armistice, when the rebuilding (that interested him far more than did the destruction) was barely begun.

With Allied victory certain, in the early autumn of 1918, Wilson made the first of three mistakes that have cost him, at least temporarily, his herohood. In October of that year he appealed to the country to elect a Democratic majority to Congress on November 6, so that he might be "your unembarrassed spokesman at home and abroad." This act on the eve of the Armistice demoted him from a national to a party leader. It irritated many by its unfair inference that the Republicans had not done their bit to win the war. Its results were even more disastrous than Washington's veering toward Federalist partisanship in the last years of his Presidency. For, like several other great Americans, Wilson had his obtuse moments, his susceptibilities to fatigue and excitement, from which perhaps only Lincoln was immune. Wilson should have been warned when the country responded to his words by electing a Republican majority to Congress. More astute politicians, like Jefferson and Theodore Roosevelt, would have seen the storm signals and tried to regain their nonpartisan prestige. Instead, Wilson went on to his second mistake—by appointing a Commission to go with him to Europe, but leaving out any representation from the Senate and from the Republican Party. (The aged Henry White, a career diplomat and technically a Republican, was no sop to the opposition.) The humorist Will Rogers observed: "Wilson says, 'I tell you what, we will split 50–50—I will go, and you fellows can stay.'" Wilson's third error, according to Colonel House, was the determination to sit at the peace table himself: "He was the *God on the Mountain,* and his decisions regarding international matters were practically final. When he came to Europe and sat in conference with the Prime Ministers and representatives of other states, he gradually lost his place as first citizen of the world."[7] The staff of experts Wilson took with him—recalling the *odium scholasticum* that Wilson should have played down—was a minor blunder in comparison with these. (William Allen White wrote of "the Yankee knight errant followed by a desperate crew of college professors in horn-rimmed glasses carrying textbooks, encyclopædias, maps, charts, graphs, statistics, and all sorts of literary crowbars to pry up the boundaries of Europe and move them around in the interests of justice as seen through the Fourteen Points.")

In the first rapture of Wilson's reception abroad it seemed as if his decision had been wise. Hundreds of thousands thronged the streets of Paris, while banners and transparencies proclaimed "Vive Wilson" and "Honor to Wilson the Just." A boulevard was christened after him —perhaps a more impressive honor than that bestowed by an American mother who had lately named her triplets Wood, Row, and Wilson —and Warsaw prepared to erect his statue in her central square. To the peasants and shopkeepers and weary soldiers of Europe, his advent, as William E. Dodd observed, was like the Second Coming of Christ. He was the symbol of a better life. At first, the chancelleries of Europe were awed and not a little frightened. At one point, Wilson's threat to sail home on the *George Washington* and leave them to their bickerings, put the fear of popular revolution into their souls.[8] Soon however they recovered their grip, and under French leadership settled down to outwit the Yankee schoolmaster. Clemenceau, who had never troubled to read the Fourteen Points until after he had agreed to the Armistice supposedly based upon them, remarked privately: "Mr. Wilson bores me with his Fourteen Points; why, God Almighty has only ten!" Wilson's second trip to Europe, after a flying visit home in the early spring of 1919, was less rapturous, more beclouded with fickleness and dissent. Under pressure from selfish groups with their prearranged treaties, in an atmosphere of semi-secrecy that denied the first of the Points ("open covenants of peace, openly arrived at"), Wilson was beguiled into yielding bit by bit. His Covenanter rigidity seemed to forsake him, now in his greatest need. He was harried, tired, and ill—but clung to the hope that his most cherished plan, the League of Nations, would set right all temporary wrongs. Jerusalem could still be builded here, among these dark Satanic mills.

Then he came home in midsummer, 1919, to learn that the devil of discord had found work for idle hands, for hands he had not summoned to the task overseas. America was turning against him. At first he felt that this was the politicians' doing. With probably a fair chance of success, he determined to carry the issue to the people. He embarked on his trip to the West, explaining the League to Americans— seeking to remove the alleged curse of Washington and Jefferson by calling it "a disentangling alliance." In his wake everywhere travelled Borah and Hiram Johnson and other adversaries laboring to undo his spell. At Des Moines, with an invective that Lincoln would never have permitted himself, as a luxury too costly, Wilson described them as "jaundice-eyed bolsheviks of politics." Here and there Wilson recaptured the old magic: at the Palace Hotel in San Francisco, for example, a great crowd in lieu of applause after one eloquent passage rose in silent concert to their feet, and thus remained a long moment —as if he had lifted them physically toward the heights. And then on this hardest campaign, on September 26 at Pueblo, Colorado, in the midst of his speech Wilson broke into tears, tears of utter exhaustion and collapse. A few hours later while his train crossed the dusty prairies of Kansas, Wilson found that his face and left side were paralyzed. His speech at Wichita was cancelled, even while Wilson protested to Doctor Grayson that "Senator Lodge and his friends will say that I am a quitter . . . and the Treaty will be lost." With drawn blinds his train sped him back to Washington, and a seclusion that would never end until his death in 1924. It was Wilson's tragedy, and perhaps that of the world, that for many weary months he neither died nor got much better. If he had died, Wilson would have joined the company of Lincoln and those fortunates who had fallen like Bunyan's Valiant-for-Truth: "My sword I shall give to him that may succeed me in my pilgrimage . . . my marks and scars I carry with me, to be a witness for me; so he passed over, and all the trumpets sounded for him on the other side." But Wilson's sword did not fall from his now nerveless hand. A successor might have made the necessary compromises, apparently not too damaging, for which Lodge and his friends at first held out. Even Wilson in health might have yielded the smaller for the greater good, or else bent the nation wholly to his will. But with the grim petulance of a very sick man he refused to bate a jot, cutting himself off from the country at large, from even the friendliest contacts like those of House and Tumulty, and dismissing Lansing who had dared to call a Cabinet meeting when the President lay prostrate. The public, noticing for the first time the iron bars that had been placed upon White House windows in the days when Theodore Roosevelt's children played ball on the lawn, spread the rumor that a madman lived within. A more cruel slander whispered something about the ravages of tertiary syphilis. There was neither king nor regency. And the League was doomed.

By a majority of seven million votes Warren G. Harding was elected in 1920. On Armistice Day at Brownsville, Texas, in the first formal speech after his victory, he announced that the United States "did not fight to make the world safe for democracy . . . nor . . . for humanity's sake . . . no matter how much beautiful sentiment has beclouded our purposes in the World War"; we had merely fought for ourselves, and now the time had come to turn our back upon Europe.

On the same day, en route to Washington, Senator Hiram Johnson gave a *New York Times* reporter a " 'poem' written in his own hand":

> Because Wilson kept us out of war
> He kept us out of peace.
> He kept us out of clothing,
> He kept us out of booze,
> He kept us out of sugar,
> He kept us out of beer,
> And made America safe
> For rent hogs and profiteers.

School readers which, during the war years, had begun to place "Woodrow Wilson's love of freedom for all mankind" side by side with "the wisdom of Benjamin Franklin, the patriotism of George Washington, the rugged honesty of Abraham Lincoln, the devotion to duty of Robert E. Lee,"[9] to glory in the fact that "we seek nothing for ourselves but what we shall wish to share with all free peoples," and to praise our spirit in the World War as that of "Crusaders of old,"[10] had suddenly grown out of date.

The last three years of Wilson's life did him much credit. They were years of quiet dignity, of reticence in concealing a broken body and spirit. He declined to write for pay, or to quarrel with the times. "I am showing President Harding how an ex-President should behave," he said when a friend asked how he was occupying himself, in his modest house on S Street. William Allen White observed that the world "had never seen before so inspiring a spectacle, so triumphant a climax to a bitter tragedy." Not everybody had forgotten Wilson. His last great day came on November 11, 1921, when in his carriage he rode from the Capitol as far as the White House behind the body of the Unknown Soldier. President Harding, ex-President Taft, General Pershing, Briand, Balfour, Foch, Lord Beatty, walking behind the flag-draped caisson, drew no cheers from a crowd well aware that one does not applaud at a funeral. "But when they saw this stricken man who had been Commander-in-Chief of the forces with which the Unknown Warrior fought they broke into cheers," related *The New York Times* next day. "It was apparent that the sight of Wilson, his once strong body broken by ill-health, his limbs too frail to permit his marching with the other great men who followed the Unknown caisson on foot, was a grim reminder that he had been an outstanding figure in the world conflict. . . ." He seemed grateful too, almost to the point of tears, when some six thousand men, women, and children after the services at Arlington gathered in the street before his house, acclaiming him "as one of the soldiers wounded in the war," and when he stepped briefly to the door, putting flowers into his hands and cheering him as "the greatest man on earth." But these were only six out of the hundred thousand at Arlington, where a quiet announcement of the impromptu pilgrimage had been made.

At large, the nation was forgetting Wilson, and he knew it. On rare occasions, riding through the streets of the Capital, or slipping into a seat in the theatre, Wilson tried to keep the withered left side of his face from view and confessed that he shrank from crowds "as from a blow." When George Creel assured him that spectators had "only friendship and devotion in every eye," Wilson shook his head sadly: "No, just curiosity."[11] He did not believe that his cause was lost forever—"that we shall prevail is as sure as that God reigns" he told a little band of impromptu serenaders before his door on Armistice Day, 1923—but Woodrow Wilson, he knew, had been defeated. In the parallel lives of Lincoln and Wilson, it is the final irony that Lincoln's cause should have been lost but the man himself triumphant.

As Charles and Mary Beard have pointed out, Woodrow Wilson was the first President officially to proclaim the United States a democracy —even though the concept had rooted deep in the minds of Jefferson and Jackson and Lincoln. But Harding, Coolidge, and Hoover did nothing to "refurbish the symbol under which Wilson's war had been fought."[12] No statues, parks, stamps, or other memorials paid tribute to him in those times. The Great War was unofficially admitted to have been a mistake, except in so far as its revulsion contributed to normalcy and the great barbecue of the twenties. In 1920 Senator Brandegee had remarked that these days did not need "first-raters." Calvin Coolidge, the divine answer to this specification, once said with a touch of complacence: "It is an advantage to a President to know he is not a great man." Sinclair Lewis's novel, *The Man Who Saw Coolidge,* reflected the bathos of the new hero-worship. But even before Coolidge had passed from office, the tide of iconoclasm had already engulfed his predecessor: the Teapot Dome scandals and *The President's Daughter* had caused many an institution of learning to change its name from the Warren G. Harding High School. And even Hoover, a man of vastly greater ability and integrity, was discredited because—like James Buchanan—he could not vindicate democracy by rising to a challenge, as Jackson and Lincoln and the true heroes had done.

Almost the first kind words for Wilson spoken in many a year by a statesman of national stature were those in Franklin D. Roosevelt's acceptance speech at Chicago on July 2, 1932—invoking "the great indomitable, unquenchable, progressive soul of our Commander-in-Chief, Woodrow Wilson." Later in San Francisco that September, the Democratic candidate pointed to Jefferson and Wilson as the pillars of American liberalism: "Where Jefferson had feared the encroachment of political power on the lives of individuals, Wilson knew that the new power was financial." Despite these occasional words of President Roosevelt, Wilson the liberal—a man of peace whose absorbing interest lay in the domestic problems of America, who tried at first impatiently to brush away the intrusion of a European War—has not yet come into his own. Most people have forgotten the program of his first term. If our democracy is streamlined for survival—the only chance apparently that it has for survival—then Wilson's New Freedom may be seen at last in a less crowded perspective. To that view it will probably seem more significant than the tardy progressivism of Theodore Roosevelt, perhaps more calmly planned though less ripely fulfilled than the New Deal of Franklin D. Roosevelt.

So far, Wilson the War President has overshadowed the earlier Wilson. The rise of Fascism, the ironic sneers of Hitler and Goebbels at the bankrupt idealism of "self-determination," and the late repatriation of the shattered League of Nations to Wilson's old home at Princeton, have helped us recently to appreciate the battle of ideologies that Wilson waged. But American sentiment concerning our participation in the World War is still divided. The age of disenchantment, of recriminations over war debts, of *What Price Glory* and *Road to War,* lingers in the public mind. It is especially strong among a generation who might otherwise applaud the liberalism of Wilson—the youth who have grown up to look upon 1917–18 as the emotional debauch of their fathers, and who often blame Wilson rather than the collective will which he tried with painful honesty to gauge. In 1937 and again at the close of 1939 the Gallup Poll reported that approximately 68 per cent of public opinion regarded our entry into the World War as a mistake—since, as they commonly expressed themselves, "it accomplished nothing, not even permanent peace." But with the outbreak of total war in 1940, the tide of opinion began to run another way. Sympathy was rekindled for our old allies, especially for England. More Americans began to feel that the World War had been fought for real issues; that it had won for us all the temporary security we had enjoyed, and wasted, in the two decades of peace. In mid-December, 1940, a new Gallup Poll reported 42 per cent as believing we did right in 1917, and only 39 per cent still sure our entry into the War was wrong. The World War is so intimately bound up with the legend of Wilson—even though he, above all others, foretold its futility without the bulwark of the League—that so sudden a reversal of public opinion augured a new attitude toward his memory. In the latter half of 1940, when old newsreels of Wilson were flashed on the screen, in *The Ramparts We Watch* and other films, the applause was noteworthy. Henceforth if America should again go forth to war in the spirit of Wilson's day, it seemed almost certain that better justice would be done him.

II

Were there others, more fortunate than Wilson, whom one might call great American heroes of the World War? Every previous war in our history gave us a few idolized generals and admirals, soldiers and sailors of single deeds that thrilled the nation. Each earlier war had given us at least one military President. The World War was different. Instead of plumes and epaulettes and chargers there were grim new media of destruction which depersonalized war—tanks, planes, machine guns, gas, grenades, and artillery of enormous range. New tactics called for a war of defensive position. There were no charges up Cemetery Ridge or San Juan Hill. Even generals like Haig, Pétain, and Pershing had only a designated sector, not a truly independent command. The tactics of a Turenne or a Stonewall Jackson would have been impossible. Teamwork rather than individual brilliance was the new order of the day.

General John J. Pershing, as commander of the American Expeditionary Force, was therefore its most famous soldier. Slow and deliberate in his major decisions, with a dogged efficiency, he dominated his troops like Grant, rather than led them dashingly like Sherman. He was a crisper disciplinarian, a more fastidious soldier, than Grant, but equally effective in whipping into shape the raw material from which the bulk of American armies are always made. Pershing's insistence that his divisions should not be turned into replacement depôts for the French and British forces—his assertion "I am going to have an American army, led by Americans"—endeared him to his countrymen. In military circles in Europe he was regarded as a very obstinate man, and even as late as 1931, when his memoirs were published, they received acid reviews by such officers as Liddell Hart and General

Frederick B. Maurice.[13] They concluded, as Lloyd George had said, "You cannot budge him." Americans, naturally, have seen eye to eye with Pershing. They agree that he did a first-class job.

But like Grant, Pershing lacks glamour of the traditional military sort. He is deficient in the personal magnetism of an Andrew Jackson or a Lee. He was never a good mixer, in the political sense, and in the years after the war his rare public addresses were described as even more laconic than Coolidge's. His radio address in August, 1940, in opposition to isolationists of the Lindbergh camp, was the most effective he has ever made, in logic and sincerity. It was delivered with failing strength, reportedly against severe doctors' orders. But Pershing has never been an orator. Almost everybody now knows that he did not say, in 1917, "Lafayette, we are here"—in his memoirs he confesses that he would have been glad to do so, had the words occurred to him. They were really uttered by a nephew of Edwin M. Stanton, Secretary of War in Lincoln's Cabinet. (This elder Stanton, by the way, liked to foster the myth that at the moment of Lincoln's passing he had murmured the fine words since carved over the crypt at Springfield, "Now he belongs to the Ages," although it seems probable that they were an afterthought.[14] Thus are great sentences put into the mouths that should have said them.)

Pershing's excellence as a soldier, demonstrated in the Philippines and in France, needs no fictitious embroidery. But occasional attempts, during and after the Great War, to romanticize him have fallen rather flat. In 1917 and 1918 old neighbors at Laclede, Missouri, began to recollect the classic stories—how he was a bright boy and hard worker whose success they had foreseen, how "John always was good to his mother." Old ladies recalled "giving Johnny Pershing pieces of pie," and would even supply the recipe while reporters gravely copied it.[15] Later biographers for boys, with a good deal of imaginative license, told how the future General at the age of four, and his mother, had taken part in a Barbara Frietchie incident during the Civil War.[16] The most popular story, apparently true in its essentials but varied as to details, related how as a young schoolmaster of seventeen Pershing whipped the bully of the school "for brutally kicking a small stray dog" and then settled victoriously with the boy's father, "a big farmer with red sideburns," while the school gazed at him with new respect. At West Point, according to another tale, he "knocked the stuffing out of three rowdies" who tried to haze him. His taste of Indian fighting and his campaign against the Moros were also retold, during the

Great War, in many juvenile books and magazine articles. *The Ladies Home Journal* featured "The Romance of General Pershing," of how he had fallen in love at first sight with Frances Warren, who had heard her father, Chairman of the Senate Committee on Military Affairs, praise Pershing's valor in the Philippines. A Fox cinema, "Why America Will Win," re-enacted the principal events of Pershing's life. Orators at large, and Missourians in particular, recalled that he was the fourth American since George Washington to hold the rank of full general—his predecessors being Grant, Sherman, and Sheridan. Upon Pershing's return to his native state a medal was struck in his honor, while bands played, inevitably, "When Johnny Comes Marching Home Again." A cigar, a streamlined train, and squares in New York and Los Angeles have been named in his honor. He was once boomed briefly for President, but did not lend himself to the political mould. Some, in the A. E. F., still think of him as a martinet; in contrast to Joffre, it has been said of Pershing that "Nobody will ever call him 'Papa.'" His one nickname, "Black Jack" Pershing, is said to have arisen because at various times he commanded colored troops; but of its origin nobody is quite sure. Now at eighty he is America's most distinguished living soldier. But he is not the hero *par excellence* of the World War.

Gresham, Enright, and Hay, first soldiers of the American Army to die in action overseas, were heroized in newspaper poetry and Liberty Loan posters in the winter of 1917–18; but they were given no individuality. Major Whittlesey, leader of the "Lost Battalion" cut off for five days in the Argonne Forest early the next October, caught popular imagination at once. The bitter fight of his men against the encroaching Boche, as they lived without food and drank from a creek of green-coated water, and lost half their numbers before rescue came, made a thrilling story. The fact that his battalion was recruited largely from Yiddish and Polish push-cart men, sewing-machine operators and buttonhook workers from New York's Lower East Side showed that bravery was no monopoly of Colonial pedigrees. Later, Major Whittlesey, broken by the ravages of incurable disease, committed suicide on a trip to Bermuda. The greatest individual hero of the war was a Tennessee mountaineer, Sergeant Alvin C. York. On October 8, 1918, in the Argonne he fought a German machine-gun battalion single-handed, and with the help of 7 privates rounded up 132 German prisoners. The American public, ever eager to glorify the amateur as against the professional soldier, relished the fact that York had begun

his career as something of a conscientious objector against war, and
that after his fêtes and decorations he went back contentedly to the
life of a hillbilly. The record of Sergeant Woodfill was almost equally
good. Other wars had glorified the man who said some courageous
thing, and then lived up to it: "I haven't begun to fight yet," or
"There, my boys, are your enemies; you must beat them, or tonight
Molly Stark sleeps a widow," or "Damn the torpedoes; go ahead!"
The most unforgettable gesture of the World War was that of Sergeant
Daly leading his devil-dogs into a rain of bullets with the shout, "Come
on, you sons of bitches—do you want to live forever?" (Almost certainly he did not know that a Confederate colonel had uttered the
same words at Malvern Hill.[17])

Among the American heroes of the World War, "non-coms" were
more numerous than generals. In the Revolution there was only one
Sergeant Jasper, but in France recognition was won repeatedly by men
like him. The thoughts and deeds of men in the ranks received new
attention. Was not this an avowed war for democracy, in a world waking to consciousness of the common man? The art produced by the
Great War—poetry, drama, novel—spoke far less of martial glamour,
or trumpets and gold braid, than of the homely bitter detail, the simplicity and vices and courage of an average man. W. W. Gibson, John
Dos Passos, and Arnold Zweig did not write about the *gestes militaires*
as Homer and Tasso had done. Painting and sculpture mirrored a new
attitude. The epoch of the equestrian general, in Europe as in America,
was over. Monuments were now communal. Whatever dubious peace
and victory had been won seemed to belong to the rank and file, and
especially to those who had given their blood. As a war memorial for
the Widener Library at Harvard, Sargent painted a mural showing
Peace springing from the unburied bodies of the dead; for the impressive Elks' Memorial in Chicago, Eugene Savage painted two epic
pieces, "The Armistice" and "Paths of Peace." Battle scenes, with
streaming flags and defiant gestures, had grown strangely out of date.
A new anonymity and sickening reality had mastered the spirit of
modern war. Whatever good or evil the diplomats might make out of
this sacrifice of seventeen million lives, its patient helpless heroism
remained.

The Dean of Westminster, visiting the War Office in July, 1920, is
credited with the suggestion that an unknown soldier from the battlefields be buried in Westminster Abbey.[18] It was a proposal that appealed, quickly and irresistibly, to the democracies that had fought in

the World War; although Germany and Austria rejected the idea. On Armistice Day, 1920, Britain buried her Unknown Warrior in the Abbey, and France her Poilu Inconnu under the Arc de Triomphe. Italy likewise interred her anonymous hero within the Victor Emmanuel Monument in Rome. In 1921 Portugal buried her Unknown Soldier in the Pantheon in Lisbon, at the same time that America brought back her nameless son to Arlington. There were some racial differences shown upon these occasions—in London a solemn hush as the casket with a battered tin hat lying on the crimson of the flag was borne to the Abbey, where a king, princes, archbishops, and generals saluted the Unknown and laid flowers at his feet; in Paris a dramatic procession bearing the heart of Gambetta beside the body of the Soldier, while Royalists and Socialists clashed over the republican aspect of this rite; in Rome the hysterical shriek of a woman crying "My son! My son!" as she fainted before the coffin, while candles burned through the incense-smoke of a hundred churches for the repose of the souls of the war dead. The ceremony in Westminster Abbey, it was said later in Parliament, "touched the hearts of the people" more deeply than any other commemoration of the war. For once, there had been no order of social precedence. The first seats of honor were given to those women who had lost husbands and all their sons in the war; next came those who had lost all their sons or their only son; and then those who had lost husbands. Peeresses sat next to charwomen, as newspapers noted. It was observed also that the Unknown Warrior was buried within the west door of the Abbey, so that henceforth every king of England going up to be crowned must step over the grave of this man who died to save his kingdom. "He is himself the greatest of all," wrote Sir Philip Gibbs of the Unknown, "because remaining forever in our history as the chosen dust, round which is gathered the memory of all those thousands of Britain's youth, who like him suffered the agonies of the greatest war, and proved the quality of the common man who gave us victory."

Of the 50,000 American dead in France, some 1900 remained unidentified. Most of them had fallen in October, 1918, in the Argonne Forest, some at Belleau Wood and along the Somme, others along the salient at St. Mihiel. On October 24, 1921, from these four cemeteries, four earth-stained coffins were brought to the City Hall of Châlons and laid upon trestles. While a small company of French and American soldiers stood at attention, Corporal Edward Younger of the 59th Infantry—who had fought in all the American offensives and wore two wound stripes—was asked to make the final choice. It had been announced that General Pershing or Major General Henry T. Allen would select the body of the Unknown Soldier, but upon further thought it seemed more fitting that a comrade of the Soldier himself should do so. Corporal Younger walked past the four coffins, turned, passed again, then gently placed a bunch of white roses upon the coffin farthest to the right, looking from the door. The soldier witnesses stood at attention as six "non-coms" shouldered the grimy coffin and deposited it in a casket brought from the United States, and inscribed "An unknown American soldier who gave his life in the Great War."

In the cruiser *Olympia,* Dewey's flagship at Manila, the body was brought home. On November 9 the ship came up the Potomac in a misty rain, the guns saluting fort by fort as she passed. Thousands stood in the rain to see the flag-wrapped caisson pass along the avenue to the Capitol, the march led by another hero from the ranks, Sergeant Woodfill. Until Armistice Day the body lay in state under the dome of the Capitol, where only the bodies of Lincoln, Garfield, and McKinley had lain before. Some ninety thousand filed past the catafalque on Armistice eve, and even more assembled for the funeral march on Armistice Day—now first declared a national holiday by Congress. There were flowers from the President and from Congress, a wreath of red English roses from King George V inscribed in his hand

> As unknown and yet well known;
> As dying, and behold, we live,

a white pillow sent by an ex-service group bearing in purple flowers "Our Pal," wreaths preserved in ice from France and other foreign countries, and many flowers from Gold Star Mothers to "my boy." An Indian chief placed his war-bonnet on the coffin. And the Unknown Soldier received the highest decorations of the late Allies—the Congressional Medal and the Distinguished Service Cross, the Croix de Guerre and the Medaille Militaire, and the Victoria Cross never before given to one not a British subject. And millions throughout the United States paid the tribute of two minutes' silence.

Stripped of ancestry and name, of rank and calling, of home and friends and creed, the Unknown Soldier became a pure symbol of devotion to country. "Yet by sacrificing his identity," wrote an editor (probably the late Doctor John Huston Finley), "not only has he shared it with every American who lies in France, and indeed with every American who perished on land or sea in the Great War, but he has let every American at home find his or her hero in the casket of the Unknown."[19]

Causes had already begun to appeal to him—perhaps the surest of all tests of herohood. The Limitation of Armaments Conference, then taking shape, caused Percy Mackaye to write in the name of "the Unknown Dead"—

> Masters of life! On your decree,
>   Unknown and numberless, I wait:
> From war's earth-blind captivity
>   Untomb me! Let your love be fate
> And crown my risen youth with timeless victory!

Yet the hates of war, even the smaller ones, were not dead. A few weeks later the President sent a Christmas release to Atlanta penitentiary, to ailing and gentle Eugene V. Debs, the pacifist. Straightway, a man signing himself "The Father of Three Soldier Sons" sent a metropolitan daily a poem in which the Unknown Soldier was made to say:

> Today my worst detractor lifts his head
> And spurns me with his foot, a free man midst the free.
> Why bring me here except it was in mockery?

And still a few weeks later, on February 9, 1922, an acrimonious discussion broke out in the Senate when Senator Ashurst of Arizona bitterly charged the War Department with having "insulted" the Senate by relegating it to the rear in the Unknown Soldier's funeral procession. Soon, in the age of disillusion, a flippant story would tell of a naïve society matron who remarked wonderingly, when some one referred to the tomb of the Unknown Soldier, "What! haven't they found out who he was, *yet?*" And soon, in 1924, Edgar Lee Masters in his *New Spoon River Anthology* would be writing the epitaph of "Unknown Soldiers":

> Stranger! Tell the people of Spoon River two things:
> First that we lie here, obeying their words;
> And next that had we known what was back of their words
> We should not be lying here!

Belatedly, in 1929, one hundred years after the discovery in the churchyard of the Presbyterian Meeting House in Alexandria, Virginia, of a wooden ammunition box holding the body of a man dressed in Continental Army uniform, a marble monument to "the Unknown Soldier of the American Revolution" was erected. Sponsored by the Children of the American Revolution, this memorial bears the inscription: "Here lies a soldier hero of the Revolution whose identity is known but to God." It has become a popular shrine, chiefly by analogy with the tomb at Arlington.

General Pershing dedicated his war memoirs, in 1931, "to the Unknown Soldier." This Soldier has become a jealously guarded symbol of American patriotism. In early February, 1939, a good deal of popular resentment was caused by an Associated Press Wire photo showing a group of Italo-American World War veterans giving the Fascist salute over the Unknown Soldier's tomb. After viewing this picture, authorities denied a permit to Americans who fought in Spain—a nucleus of the "Lincoln Battalion"—to hold a ceremony at the tomb the next Sunday, Lincoln's birthday. When in September of that year, war once more broke over Europe, it was reported by the press that "twice as many Americans as usual walked, hushed and hatless, to stand in sombre silence by the white marble Unknown Soldier's Tomb." What may be the sequel of his sacrifice none can tell.

CHAPTER SIXTEEN

GODS FROM THE MACHINE: EDISON, FORD, LINDBERGH

> A worship new I sing,
> You captains, voyagers, explorers, yours,
> You engineers, you architects, machinists, yours.
> —WALT WHITMAN.

I

IF THE axiom of the ancient Greeks was "Know thyself," that of Americans is more likely to be "Know thy stuff." Instinctively we admire the doers, "habile" men, vigorous practical minds—Franklin, Washington, Andrew Jackson, Theodore Roosevelt in public life, and Fulton, Morse, Bell, Burbank, the Wright brothers in science. The American Dream is one of improvement. Lincoln is supposed to have told about a Massachusetts baby, "only six months old, sitting in its mother's lap, viewing its own cradle, to see if it could not invent a better one." This trait has become a source of national pride. A typical schoolbook, Willis M. West's *The Story of Our Country,* remarks that "the American invents as the Greek chiselled, as the Venetian painted, as the modern Italian sings." The steamboat, the cotton-gin, the sewing-machine, the typewriter, the telephone, the linotype, the gramophone, the incandescent lamp, motion pictures, the aeroplane, the machinery of agriculture, the vulcanizing of rubber, and much of the credit for the automobile, must be assigned to American ingenuity.

Romantics say that America, a land of immigrants, was peopled by the enterprising. Others more soberly point out that the Yankee ideal of self-help and self-support—unknown to a slave system or the stratified society of the Old World—bred a pride in working with the hands, a passion for efficiency, that came to be recognized (almost unanimously after the Civil War) as "American." Furthermore a chronic shortage of labor, in an era of expansion, led us to put machines to work. We had the land and mineral wealth that made machines practicable. From the apple-peeler, egg-beater, and clothes-wringer in the home, to the great dynamo which Henry Adams saw as the demigod of the United States, this impulse advanced. In time it shaped our national character. Americans liked to do things for themselves. To the bewilderment of Europeans, American wives often preferred the latest in vacuum cleaners and electric dishwashers to a servant in the house. And their small sons longed to become locomotive engineers and oil-well drillers and aeroplane pilots rather than field marshals, like German youth, or admirals, like young Britons. A couple of generations ago, the stream of pseudo-scientific fiction for boys began—in Norman Munro's weekly *Golden Hours,* and in the *Frank Reade Weekly.* Frank Reade, with his "gravity nullifiers," electrical aeroplanes, and rockets to the moon, was a lad moulded from the heroic aspects of Edison and the Wright brothers. He flew 25,000 miles over Central India and the Sudan, looking for jewelled temples, "lost savants," and other interesting objectives. Later came Buck Rogers and Superman, joining the strength of Tarzan to the brains of the machine age. The cult of the G-man, at its peak from about 1935 to 1937, was a kindred passion. Inspector Drane Lester of the F. B. I., who has lectured to innumerable boys' clubs, tells the writer that he is most often asked about scopolamine or "truth-serum," the polygraph as a lie detector, and the use of infra-red rays in laboratory work on criminal clues. Even the great heroes of sport—Jack Dempsey, Gene Tunney, Babe Ruth, Bill Tilden, Bobby Jones—were supposed to be men who united "scientific" skill with muscle, and were constantly interviewed about the secrets of their mastery. Science meant success.

Our accent upon deeds has made us neglect the ideal of inner perfection, represented by the philosopher and the saint, along with that of creative discovery for its own sake, known to the artist and pure scientist. "The greatest synthetic philosopher since Newton," as Euro-

peans called Josiah Willard Gibbs, pioneer in thermodynamics and
vector analysis, died in the year that Henry Ford's new automobile
started to become a household word. At Yale, where most of his quiet
life was spent, Gibbs once had a small brick cottage, housing the offices
of the graduate school, named for him; it has since been demolished.
To the average American he is quite unknown. But Edison requires
two movies, with Mickey Rooney and Spencer Tracy, to tell the story
of his life; his is the greatest trade-name in American and world industry; the invention of the incandescent light was celebrated by a Golden
Jubilee in 1929; Henry Ford has set up Edison's original laboratory at
Greenfield, Michigan, while another lifelong admirer, William Slocum
Barstow, has erected at Menlo Park the Edison Tower of bronze, steel,
and concrete, surmounted by a light bulb thirteen feet eight inches high
that illuminates the night sky, for miles around, with its 5200 watts.
In 1937 the Lynds, studying Middletown in transition, found that
Edison was sometimes linked with Washington and Lincoln as the
third greatest American.

The mainspring of Edison's life was utility. "Do you want to know
my idea of a successful invention?" he once asked. "It is something so
practical that a Polish Jew will buy it."[1] Edison did much for his country and the world. In his heyday, under the spell of such marvels as the
improved telegraph and the carbon telephone transmitter, the phono-
graph and the moving-picture camera, Edison was the American boy's
special hero. Every youth with a work-bench in the barn, or an evil-
smelling chemical set in the cellar, adored him. His work was the
apotheosis of "tinkering." The inventive vein that ran through Franklin and Jefferson and Lincoln, but was submerged by public duties,
bubbled to the surface in the industrial age, and, in the person of Edison, shot skyward like a geyser of spectacular achievement.

Boys read books that somewhat exaggerated Edison's youthful
struggles—against poverty (his father was a substantial citizen of Port
Huron, Michigan) and the ill appreciation of an adult world (known
chiefly because a school inspector pronounced him "addled"). Readers
liked his undoubted enterprise in selling candy, fruit, and newspapers
on the train, and in printing his own sheet of Civil War bulletins in the
baggage-car—in order to buy more chemicals. Here was the Alger story,
streamlined to scientific purpose. They liked the anecdote, contradicted
by Edison himself, that a box on the ear from a trainman, enraged by
his inflammable experiments, had deafened him for life. They enjoyed
the yarn, also denied by Edison, that in absorption in his work he had

forgotten about his wedding-day. They delighted in his saying, "Genius is one per cent inspiration and ninety-nine per cent perspiration" (though Edison's own creative genius waned about his thirty-ninth year and was never regained, despite the dogged persistence with which he worked until his death at eighty-four). Most boys' biographies, like the cinemas of 1940, did not quite do justice to the full-bodied Edison— a man of brilliant "hunches" in the fields he knew best, who called himself "the chief mucker" in his laboratory and sported working-clothes so grimy that his assistants daubed theirs with grease to convince him they were hard workers too, who told funny stories and reeked of plug-tobacco and rank cigars. He was a likable man, an authentic American, if not the disembodied symbol of scientific curiosity into which legend has made him. Somewhat refreshing is the Edison described by M. A. Rosanoff, who upon joining the laboratory in 1903 asked about the rules. Edison "spat in the middle of the floor and yelled out, 'Hell! there ain't no rules around here! We are tryin' to accomplish somep'n!' "[2] Self-taught, Edison was scornful of academicians and conventional culture, strangely ignorant of pure science, as well as of art, literature, music. In time his second wife, like Mark Twain's helpmeet, served to tame his robust philistinism and make him acquiesce in the social graces. This later phase of Edison, like that of Mark Twain, marked a slipping in his essential genius. But years before, thanks to a flame of undoubted brilliance, Dutch pertinacity, and a Puritan conscience that made him fear to be idle, Edison had become the world's greatest inventor. Some people began to call modern times "the age of Edison." America was justly proud of him. Even George Bernard Shaw, an Edison employee in London (in the same office with Samuel Insull), was inspired to idealize the American inventor type in his first published novel, *The Irrational Knot,* contrasting this hero— of many virtues and a few crudities—with an effete British snob, whose background was Eton rather than the work-bench. A generation later, at the time of the Golden Jubilee, the poets were paraphrasing Pope on Newton—

> God said, Let Edison be! And there was Light.

Like one of the mighty bridges of steel and re-enforced concrete that his own skill had made possible, Edison's legend spanned three channels: the success story, the ideal of "service," and the conquest of nature by industry. He marked the road of a new hero-homage.

"Edison was already, to my mind, the greatest man in the world,"

wrote Henry Ford, describing his meeting with the inventor in 1896
and the encouragement Edison gave him in perfecting the gasoline
engine. In his book, *Edison as I Know Him,* Ford recalled that, as a
boy, he had most admired the inventor's "gift for hard, continuous
work," and later decided that the greatest boon of the incandescent
light was that it had increased consumption, by multiplying the number
of daylight hours for mankind. Ford was a duller Edison, less versatile
in his mechanical knack but more dogmatic in his opinions. His early
life on a Michigan farm was not so rich in enterprise, in the stuff of
myth, as young Edison's. But like Edison, who hated "hoeing corn in
a hot sun," Ford was attracted to mechanics and the career of journeyman inventor, in a spirit of revolt against farm drudgery. Even more
than Edison, Ford was bored and unhappy away from his tools. These
heroes of the machine age were geared to incessant productiveness. Like
a Calvinist who believed that work was the original curse laid upon man
after Eden, yet preached the gospel of work even after one could retire
comfortably, Henry Ford drove himself hard to save labor. Of Ford on
a camping-trip, John Burroughs testified: "Mr. Ford was so restless that
if he could find nothing else to do he would clean out springs, or chop
wood, or teach a young lad to run the car."[3] And he skated in order to
keep physically fit, to do better work.

In the first decade of the twentieth century Ford built the cheapest
practicable automobile in the world. It was made in his own image, a
masterpiece of gaunt utility, pandering neither to the beauty nor comfort that his Puritan soul distrusted. ("They can have any color they
want, so long as it's black," became an American classic.) Its sale made
him a very rich man. He invented the technique of mass production, the
assembly line. After two decades he had become a billionaire, and a
household word. But he continued to order his life upon the principles
of his boyhood. "I have tried to live my life as my mother would have
wished," he told Eddie Guest, who understood such things. His philosophy was a strange blend of Ralph Waldo Emerson and Ralph Waldo
Trine: with the latter he collaborated on a book called *The Power That
Wins.* He believed in "service," and also vaguely in reincarnation—a
mystical doctrine about "little entities" floating in from the cosmos
and building up human personality, as Edison himself had believed, in
the cloud-land of his hard practical mind. The common man listened
to these ideas with distant respect, because they came from a very rich
and successful man, and because he rode in Mr. Ford's automobile and
felt *en rapport* with its manufacturer. The average man was inclined

to applaud many of Mr. Ford's tastes and opinions—his crusade against cigarettes in a tract called *The Case against the Little White Slaver,* his liking to take children on bird walks, his distrust of Wall Street and international Jewish bankers. Ford kept the common touch. Asked on his fiftieth birthday by a reporter, what was the greatest handicap of wealth, the industrialist had looked out of the window and said reflectively, "Well, for me I guess it was when Mrs. Ford stopped cooking." Many Americans agreed with him that "History is bunk," and shared his feeling that "I don't like to read books; they muss up my mind."

Ford became a great industrial hero in January, 1914, when he announced a minimum wage of five dollars per eight-hour day. Socialists denounced his "paternalism" and the dehumanizing effect of his assembly line; cynics suspected a move for free publicity, as effective as the "Ford joke" that had carried his product over the world. Certainly a great many people who had worked for Henry Ford did not look upon him as a hero. But the average American, in a thousand villages and on numberless farms, felt that Ford was the workingman's friend, since he paid five dollars to those whom he might have hired for two. Henceforth, his acts made headlines. His Peace Ship, two years later, had overtones of comedy—William Jennings Bryan, with a squirrel cage that some one had thrust into his hands, waving bon voyage; an eloping couple being married in the dining saloon; clergymen obligingly posing for photographers, playing leapfrog on deck. When Ford himself developed cold feet, and came home leaving his fellow-pacifists stranded in Norway, the metropolitan press hailed him with derision and delight. But in the Middle West, thousands of farmers and small-town citizens felt that his gesture to "get the boys out of the trenches by Christmas" had been a noble one, balked only by the obstinacy of kings and generals. A year later, his patriotism was cleared of suspicion when he proposed to the government to build "1000 small submarines a day and 3000 motors a day." (Similarly, in September, 1939, he told reporters: "They don't dare have a war and they know it. It's all a big bluff." But these words—as well as the old myth that Hitler has a framed picture of Ford over his desk, and the undisputed decoration that Ford received from the Nazis—were forgotten in the summer of 1940, when the industrialist offered to build "1000 planes a day" in a factory in Louisiana. Americans learned long ago to accept Henry Ford as the erratic harbinger of crises.)

To a good many people, Ford is a major idol. In the early stages of

Soviet collectivization, it is reported, peasants placed Ford's photograph beside that of Lenin, in the icon corner where the Holy Family and Saint Basil used to live.[4] He is the god whose paraclete is the tractor. One recalls Aldous Huxley's *Brave New World,* with its regimented supermen of the future who cross themselves with "the sign of the T," and date their letters "in the year of Our Ford." Political honors have narrowly missed the magnate of River Rouge. In 1918, he would have been elected to the Senate save for wholesale bribery on behalf of his opponent, Truman H. Newberry; the guilty were certain rich men bitter in their hatred of Ford. Early in 1923 a poll by *Collier's* and various newspapers showed that Ford was leading Harding almost two to one, as a favorite for President in the next election. Chauncey Depew commented: "After seventy years of political experience I can't understand the psychology which makes Ford a Presidential candidate." From the club windows of New York and Washington Depew could not realize the power of the Ford legend, of beneficent common sense, prosperity, high wages, water power, and the scattering of industry among the small towns of the hinterland. Most of the men and women who had bought his output of 1,332,209 "tin lizzies" in the previous year felt— save perhaps on cold winter mornings—like potential voters for Henry Ford. Even though he had never shared great slices of his wealth with philanthropy in the manner of Rockefeller and Carnegie, but plowed it back into the making of more cars, Ford had won his billion in a simpler, more tangible way than by the mysteries of high finance. Common people who looked on speculation as black magic could approve of Ford. "The best use I could make of my money is to make more work for more men," he had said. In some ways, he seemed to be the twentieth-century Franklin; a favorite adage, which he had carved over his fireplace, ran "Chop Your Own Wood and It Will Warm You Twice." Such advice atoned for a remark he made, to the great annoyance of bankers, in their thrift campaign for the masses: "No successful boy ever saved any money. They spent it just as fast as they could for things to improve themselves." (No doubt Mr. Ford knew that a dollar saved will not help buy an automobile.) Poor Richard in his more reckless moods, preferring an egg today to a hen tomorrow, had given similar advice. Even though Mr. Ford lacked Franklin's humor and his intellect, he was an inventor, organizer, efficiency expert, and super-salesman whom many Americans admired and quoted.

But he did not become President. Harding died, leaving his office to a New England Yankee who was even shrewder than the Michigan

Yankee in the school of self-help. Mr. Coolidge invited the motor-maker to the White House, told Mr. Ford he approved his ambitions regarding Muscle Shoals (though Congress saw that nothing came of it), and soon, in December, 1923, Ford announced that Coolidge was his choice for President in 1924. It was a quiet triumph for the sage of Northampton. Since then, Ford has not been mentioned seriously for the White House. He has been fading slowly from the American scene. Other manufacturers have rivalled and surpassed his output of low-priced cars; the comedy and mythology of the Model T have gone forever, and "Ford" is just another trade name. The magnate himself, growing old, has become a symbol of reaction, rather than of the progress so vital to his legend. Ever ready with advice, he found no magic formula for the depths of unemployment. As John Dos Passos wrote, in *The Big Money*—

> But when the country on cracked shoes, in frayed trousers, belts tightened over hollow bellies, idle hands cracked and chapped with the cold of that coldest March day of 1932, started marching from Detroit to Dearborn, asking for work and the American Plan, all they could think of at Ford's was machine guns.
> The country was sound, but they mowed the marchers down.
> They shot four of them dead.

Ford's early cars are now in museums, artifacts as rare as the Wayside Inn and the Little Red Schoolhouse, the square dances and the blown glass, which he cherishes—as if to make amends to that old-fashioned America which the motor-car helped destroy. Henry Ford, with his crotchety integrity, his farm-boy prejudices, and his genius of sorts, has watched the world go by.

II

Edison and Ford, "the wizard of Menlo Park" and "the flivver king," are true American folklore—the light-bringer and the charioteer among the myths of the machine age. But the story of Icarus, the boy who sought the open sky and had his wings melted by the jealous sun, offers a deeper view into the vicissitudes of hero-worship.

The flight of Charles A. Lindbergh, in May, 1927, was a moment built by the drama of circumstance. In 1919, Raymond Orteig had offered a prize of $25,000 for the first non-stop aeroplane flight between New York and Paris. Six men had died in an attempt to capture this purse. In the spring of 1927 the French ace, René Fonck, had failed through an accident to his plane in the take-off; upon the eve of

Lindbergh's attempt, Nungesser and Coli had met their death some-where over the North Atlantic. Richard E. Byrd, reported again and again about to try the crossing, but waiting for ideal conditions of weather, represented to the popular mind an attitude of extreme cau-tion. (Byrd was also a Virginia patrician and a man who obviously loved the limelight—both facts handicapping him for herohood.) Public anticipation, lately keyed up by the tragedy of the French flyers, looked upon the venture as both an achievement in science and a sporting event. Here was a spectacle of hidden death, like the drama of the Spanish bullfight, but waged for more tangible purpose, it seemed, than the empty daring which has never appealed much to Anglo-Saxons.

At this juncture the real hero entered, unannounced. He was a youth of twenty-five, and this detail converted the trial into an issue between Death and the boy. He was unmarried, but had a mother—the ideal situation for young heroes. He had made his own way, and into the venture had put all his savings of barnstorming and mail-pilot years. An inquiry into his record showed that he had coolly faced death before, four times having bailed out of disabled planes—once chased to earth by the spirals of his abandoned ship as it circled his parachute. He lived upon sandwiches and chocolate bars and water from a thermos flask; he repaired his own machine with the affection of a born mechanic, and regarded it as a partner in the enterprise. "We" took the edge off egotism. But it was very important that he proposed to fly alone. Other men had flown the Atlantic before, with assistants and crews—Robert Ripley announced in "Believe It or Not" that Lindbergh was the sixty-seventh man to fly this ocean—but none had followed the rules of the prize competition, and none had tried it solo. "The heroes, the saints and sages—they are those who face the world alone," Norman Douglas had written in *South Wind*. By the mathematics of hero-worship, a single-handed victory is far better than the combined efforts of two. The public was deeply, if sentimentally, touched by Lindbergh's refusal to take on his hazardous flight a kitten that had adopted him at Curtiss Field, Long Island; humane societies sent him their thanks. His sole companion, *The Spirit of St. Louis,* was a happy augury for France. To the public it was quite unknown that when Lindbergh first planned his flight, desperate for funds, he had approached the American Tobacco Company with an offer, in exchange for backing, to name his plane "The Lucky Strike." But those business men, dubious of the re-sult if he crashed, declined the offer.[5]

Bad weather delayed the flight, heightening suspense but not stretching it too far. The debonair touch in Lindbergh's preparation was exaggerated by the press, now grown tired of other competitors' squabbles over equipment and meteorology. They sensed that the public admires impulsive courage more than cold calculation. (Hero-worship ever tends to the heart rather than the head.) Therefore Lindbergh's months of hard concentration on this flight, his physical training for staying alert forty hours at a stretch, the excellent maps and adequate instruments with which he flew, were overshadowed in the nickname—justly hated by the man himself—of "The Flying Fool." The press made him into a golden-haired boy from Minnesota, son of the Vikings, who couldn't resist a sudden urge to fly the Atlantic. Newspapers reported that he had dropped into a movie the night before his flight; had gone to bed for a couple of hours, and after being called by the room clerk, came downstairs looking like "a sleepy tousle-haired boy." Lindbergh's book later stated that he had spent the evening at the airport, gone to his hotel room to finish preparations, but had no sleep at all. As he winged his way over Long Island Sound and up the coast, that May morning, newspapers told millions—asking over their breakfast tables, "Will he make it?"—that Lindbergh was flying with only a small magnetic compass and a map torn from a school geography.

Lindbergh's flight along the Great Circle, the report of his plane over Nova Scotia and Newfoundland, an unexpected zone of fog and sleet in mid-ocean which he must have encountered, and the many hours of silence that followed, drew taut the nerves of uncounted multitudes in America and in Europe. Thousands, who ten days before had first heard the name of Lindbergh, eagerly bought newspapers and scanned bulletin boards and listened anxiously at their radios. His safe arrival at Le Bourget, shortly after 10 P.M. on the second day, was greeted with hysterical joy. His reported words, "I did it," echoed the relief and pride of his countrymen. The public approved other reported words, "Somebody cable Mother," and the immemorial classic of Americans, "So this is Paris." A hero must be simple, not sophisticated—for even sophisticates in the blasé Twenties wanted simplicity in a hero—and Lindbergh's letters of introduction to Paris, along with Ambassador Herrick's loan of a pair of pajamas, enchanted millions. Of Lindbergh's personality little was known. But his clean-cut face and boyish grin, windblown hair and ill-fitting blue serge suit that he wore through the ovations, were enough for creation of a role. Perhaps, before May, 1927, he had been a small-town boy with a good mind, self-respect, and a fine mechanical knack. Now, during the day and darkness of his flight,

the imagination of the world, helped by the powerful resources of publicity, had made him into a young god. Some called him Mercury, shod
with wings; others saw him as the New World Galahad, brave, modest,
pure of heart. Henceforth his life would be tinged with unreality.

Certainly he had done an act of rare skill and courage. His victory
was not an invidious one; nobody had been defeated. The results
seemed altogether good. The frenzied applause that France gave him
did something, momentarily, to ease relations that had lately grown
strained over war debts. This episode was pitched upon a romantic, if
not a mystic, plane that made old quarrels sordid. "I am not a religious
man," said Ambassador Herrick at the reception given Lindbergh by
the city of Paris, "but I believe there are certain things that happen
in life which can only be described as the interpretation of a Divine
Act. . . . Lindbergh brought you the spirit of America in a manner
in which it could never have been brought in a diplomatic sack." Herrick, one may add, was the best public-relations counsel that Lindbergh
ever had. A few weeks later, President Coolidge would call the young
flyer "our Ambassador without portfolio." Lindbergh's reception in
Europe, before premiers and kings and flag-waving crowds, enhanced—
if it were possible—his standing in American eyes; every ovation sought
to outdo the previous one. Lindbergh wished to go on his way, to visit
his grandfather's home in Sweden, but the voice of the United States
and the presence of the cruiser *Memphis* ordered him home; he discovered that the public was already beginning to possess him.

One incident of his return voyage revealed the power of myth, in
the interpretation of a hero's character. It is true that he was quickly
made a colonel in the Air Corps Reserve, in which he had previously
held a lieutenant's commission, and that a colonel's uniform was sent
out to him some three hundred miles off Nantucket. According to the
accepted story he declined to put it on, feeling in the simplicity of his
heart that he ought not to pose as a military man, but return wearing
the mufti in which he had set out. In June, 1927, his appearance in
civilian's clothes, the famous blue serge, to receive the President's greeting in the shadow of the Washington Monument, was widely praised
by the press. Later, in 1930, when the first feud between Lindbergh and
the newspapers was rife, Morris Markey reported in *The New Yorker*
that Lindbergh on the *Memphis* had thrown the proffered uniform
over a chair, with the caustic remark, "I didn't notice that the Army
took much interest in me before the flight." Still later, in *The Saturday
Evening Post* for October 21, 1933, Lindbergh's press agent, Harry A.

Bruno, from direct knowledge gave what is no doubt the true version of the rejected uniform. (In denial of the myth that Lindbergh had no press agent on his Paris flight, it should be noted that the Wright Aeronautical Corporation in early May, 1927, had presented him with the services of Bruno and Richard Blythe, Manhattan publicists whom Lindbergh came to value as friends.) Blythe was present in Lindbergh's stateroom when the flyer unpacked and donned his colonel's uniform. Standing before the mirror, with boyish pleasure, he pronounced it "Pretty swell!" Blythe told him: "Slim, you can't wear the uniform. It's bad medicine." He explained that the aviator should keep himself free of "labels," as a plain civilian who had done a civilian's job. Somewhat stubborn, Lindbergh proposed to wear the uniform beneath an overcoat, even though the season was mid-June. Then Blythe sought to convince him that the coat did not fit in the back, saying "You look terrible." With a good-natured grin Lindbergh laid away the uniform. The episode is trivial, but the misconceptions it led to—on the one hand a proof of his fine simplicity, on the other of his intrinsic bitterness—are rich in comment upon hero-worship and hero-hate.

Lindbergh's return called forth the greatest national ovation ever given an American. Washington crowds broke through a cordon' of marines to reach him; the exuberant cheered and threw hats in air, while the sentimental wept. His few modest words, in reply to Coolidge's presentation of the Distinguished Flying Cross, were likened to Lincoln's Gettysburg address. But New York, under Mayor Walker, specialized in mammoth ovations. A crowd estimated at four million people lined the streets from the Battery to Central Park. A snowstorm of confetti, ticker tape, and shredded telephone books fluttered down the canyons of Manhattan; it cost the city $16,000 and the services of 2000 "white wings" to remove some 1800 tons of paper. (Later, in May, 1931, in the wane of Mayor Walker's glory, the New York Board of Trade would adopt a resolution rebuking such extravagant bad taste: "It is a poor tribute to a great person to empty a wastebasket over him.") At the week's end the city of St. Louis, which felt a proprietary interest in his flight, gave Lindbergh an equally frenzied greeting. Later, when he toured the country for the Guggenheim Fund for the Promotion of Aeronautics, other cities eagerly followed suit. The services of Ivy Lee, as manager of Lindbergh publicity on this tour, seemed quite gratuitous, except in so far as they protected the hero from the mobs that had begun to get on his nerves. The public, with terrifying adoptiveness, had begun to claim every moment of his life.

The newspapers had forgotten to be cynical. Few indeed were the journalists so hard-bitten as not to hymn the Lindbergh cult. "Romance lived again in him," said *The New York Evening Post.* "A hero is not elected on the basis of miles flown or any adding machine basis," observed *The Herald Tribune.* "He is a work of art, and like a picture or a poem, he either thrills you or he doesn't. Personality is of his essence; you must read his quality in the swing of his shoulders and the cut of his smile." And W. O. McGeehan of that newspaper, inured as sports editor to that burly realism which bred Ring Lardner and Westbrook Pegler, felt moved to reprove those who wondered at Lindbergh's calm assurance: "They forget that young Lindbergh has been up among the gods while the world spun beneath him." *The Washington Post* compared his spirit with that of the Pilgrims, George Washington, John Paul Jones, Farragut, and Dewey: "Lindbergh personifies America." "Every parent sees in him an ideal son," said *The Philadelphia Inquirer,* sensing the impulse to "mother" him, which stirred so many middle-aged people. With high approval *The St. Louis Star* remarked that, unlike the caricature of Americans overseas, Lindbergh was neither a boaster nor a money-grabber: "The last man of his type that Europe knows anything about was George Washington." "Lindbergh," declared *The Springfield Republican,* "flew like a poem into the heart of the world." He "has done more to arouse a common spirit of hero worship than any man of modern times," said *The New York Sun.*

The first man to fly from New York to Paris and capture the Orteig Prize, particularly if he did it alone, was bound to be cheered and fêted. But Lindbergh was more than the idol of a day—much more, for instance, than Gertrude Ederle or Bobby Jones, whose Manhattan receptions after victories abroad were almost as delirious. It was not merely that the ingredient of "science" lifted his venture beyond the realm of sport and skylarking. It was because Lindbergh had a symbolic aspect, that the public could not get enough of him as weeks and months went by. First of all, he seemed to be typically American, with a wholesomeness that the Jazz Age and Night Club Era had forgotten. His family, Swedish immigrants, had come to America in 1860 and settled at Sauk Center, Minnesota—the original of Sinclair Lewis's *Main Street,* a book that had held up to the world the spectacle of Midwestern village life stripped of its spiritual idealism. Young Lindbergh in fact was a quiet rebuke to the Lost Generation. He had visited Paris only to come home. A serious-minded, hard-working lad who had done his best on a shoestring, who had the American passion for tinkering with machines, but who neither smoked nor drank, bragged nor lost his head under the adulation of the Old World—Lindbergh did much to reassure the 1920's that youth was not going to the dogs. Basically America was sound, despite the reports of F. Scott Fitzgerald and Percy Marks and John Held, Jr., if it could still breed a specimen like Lindbergh. He brought back a touch of "the verities," in which everybody had been reared, but some had forgotten in the overt cynicism of the times. He was stalwart, modest, and shy. He implied mother and home and fundamental decency—in an age when to sophisticates mother suggested an Oedipus complex, home was the place where you slept off a hang-over, and decency was lost in the new paganism of petting-parties and rubber goods for sale at every gas station.

He was supposed to be girl-shy, and hence as eligible as that perennial favorite the Prince of Wales. From the 3,500,000 letters which Lindbergh received between May 21, and June 17, 1927, letters from girls and women outnumbered those from men by about four to one. Many enclosed their photographs. "I like your looks and believe you would like me," "We might hit it off; who can tell?" were favorite sentences. American girlhood momentarily lost its heart to this engaging youth: later, when his betrothal to Anne Morrow was announced, a popular cartoon showed a sentimental little maid in the kitchen, gazing sorrowfully at Lindy's picture under the clock, a crushed newspaper in her hand.

> Lad, you took the soul of me
> That long had lain despairing,
> Sent me Heaven-faring,
> Gave me wings again.
>
>   *   *   *   *   *
>
> All the world is blessing you
> For what your faith has done—
> Godling that you are, lad,
> Riding to the sun!

wrote one of the better poetesses, Angela Morgan; while the child prodigy, Nathalia Crane, won a prize with her precocious tribute. In Lindbergh, whose reticence toward women fitted the ideal of strength and boyish bashfulness, the American girl found her perfect hero, in revolt against the jelly-bean and the sheik. That he offered a worthier ideal there was no question. Just nine months before Lindbergh's flight, Campbell's mortuary parlors in Manhattan had been stormed by an hysterical mob trying to gain access to the body of Rudolph Valentino.

Valentino, it will be remembered, was a young Italian who had begun his metropolitan career with a police record of petty thieving and pimping, but rose to fame as "the world's greatest lover." He was supposed to have introduced the slave bracelet, and the powder-puff for men, into the United States. Many thought him effeminate, and at the time of his death Valentino's box-office power was on the wane. But the shock of his sudden death from peritonitis appealed to the sentimental. Maidens wept over him, as, in ancient days, they mourned the slain Adonis in the spring. Moreover, the star's manager, S. George Ullman, confronted by Valentino's staggering debts, stimulated the cult in order to dispose of the actor's two last pictures, released posthumously, "Son of the Sheik" and "The Eagle." Mr. Ullman sent some 40,000 appeals to those Valentino fans whose letters to the star he had graded "A" on the basis of literacy, asking them to help keep alive Valentino's memory. So successful was he, that Valentino clubs sprang up all over the world; they still see films and hear recordings of his voice on the anniversary of his death, while in Hollywood Cemetery feminine admirers bring flowers and swoon before his crypt, and reporters look for a "lady in black" invented long ago as a publicity gag. To the American majority, after Valentino, the romantic aspect of Lindbergh seemed fine and salutary.

And certainly Lindbergh had nothing to sell. After the Paris flight he received offers in excess of $5,000,000. He was asked to endorse scores of products, and turned them all down (privately it was said that he considered briefly endorsing a cigarette, to show the old ladies he was not a goody-goody). A talking-machine concern offered him $300,000 for a recording, in his voice, of the story of his flight, to be sandwiched between "The Star-Spangled Banner" and "The Marseillaise" as played by a top-flight orchestra. Perhaps the most extraordinary offer came from a movie company, proposing that he "appear in a film in which he would actually be married, the stipulation being that there be close-ups of his face when he first met the girl that appealed to him, and at the moment he was pronounced her husband. For this unique study of emotion it was said he would receive $1,000,000."[6] One of the humbler bids came from a man who offered him a partnership in a small chain of stores, proposing that Lindbergh's picture be featured in the window of each, and adding: "You will find me a good fellow to deal with. I don't get angry very often, and when I do I usually go away, so will not fight." He was offered a promotional share in hundreds of inventions for stabilizers and parachutes and automatic control of aeroplanes; and his interest bespoken in schemes to extract gold from sea-water, communicate with Mars, or reach the moon in a rocket. A retired mariner wrote Lindbergh about a device he had invented to prevent horses from running away: a boat davit, attached to the shafts of the carriage, would hoist the runaway animal off the ground.

At first, Lindbergh attempted to answer all his mail; a few days convinced him that it was a labor of despair. But he accepted none of these offers, profitable or fantastic. He was well paid for a series of articles he had contracted previously to write for *The New York Times,* but refused a larger bid from a rival. From the book *"We"* he received upwards of $100,000 in royalties; an enthusiastic collector paid $15,000 for the pencilled manuscript. Lindbergh accepted a salary of $25,000 a year as adviser to the Guggenheim Fund, and the same stipend as technical consultant to Transcontinental Air Transport and Pan-American Airways (advised in the early fall of 1929 to sell his stock in these companies, he refused, because of the bad effect such selling might have upon the popular status of the industry). Lindbergh accepted those offers which were consonant with dignity and with his keen desire to promote the cause of air travel in America. But his refusal cheaply to commercialize his success, to go into the movies and lend himself to trade-names, delighted the public as much as the flight itself. Again, his ideals had dealt a tacit rebuke to the cynical Twenties, when oil scandals in the President's Cabinet were still fresh, when everybody was playing the market and making money for dear life in every wildcat venture. Lindbergh's stubborn integrity became part of his public character.

He received the inevitable tributes. There were letters of pure, if fulsome, adoration. "Fair-haired Apollo," one of them began, "your meteoric traverse of the sea, your transcendent victory over boundless space, shall thunder down the avenues of time." And there were the ever-present letters of petition: "A little money will do, maybe ten or fifteen dollars. That will give me a chance to get new curtains for the room in which I have lain so many years," wrote an invalid. A small-town garage owner wrote that he was having trouble with valves, and "you are just the fellow to help me out. . . . I have ground the valves with carborundum dust . . . but they seem to leak. . . . I have had a good deal of trouble lately. We live with my wife's mother. She bothers Minnie (my wife) a little, especialy in the evenings. So next morning I haven't got my mind on my job. Better write me direct to the shop, and don't mention the mother-in-law. What I want is advice on valves."

Some four hundred Lindberghs wrote in, asking the hero's help in establishing their family trees. There were more letters in pencil than in ink, more in longhand than in typescript, more from small towns than from either city or country. Youths and adults were almost equally divided among the mass of correspondents. There were some 14,000 parcels of gifts and samples. Many, apparently, sent him the rarest thing they owned. He received a Persian manuscript of the Koran, an airship cut from a single diamond, pieces of tapestry, a pair of bedroom slippers embroidered with scenes from Lindbergh's life, a washcloth made by "a lady over eighty," crucifixes and boxing gloves, and a ten-pound twist of chewing tobacco from Springfield, Tennessee: "You Flying Fool. Chas do not know about your habits but a fellow flying like you should chew Tobacco."

Lindbergh's flight, it was estimated, caused newspapers in the United States to use 25,000 tons of newsprint beyond their regular consumption. Some 5000 poems, according to estimates no doubt very rough, were written in his honor in the summer of 1927. The French poet Rostand the younger, on the very field of Le Bourget, had written the first metrical paean of his flight. The American muse was not slow to follow. *The New York World* calculated its takings, alone, at two and one half bushels of poems. A poetry competition sponsored by "Charles Vale" (pseudonym for Arthur Hooley) drew four thousand entries; the hundred best were collected in a volume called *The Spirit of St. Louis*. Their authors call Lindbergh "golden Apollo," Columbus, Lochinvar, Bayard, Prometheus. Jean Batchelor prefaced her verses with Psalms 8:5, "For thou hast made him a little lower than the angels." The poetry of flight, of being nearer Heaven than the generality of mankind who crawl about like worms, was a dominant theme. Bliss Carman contrasted "the clean soul of youth . . . speaking the language of the open smile," with our sordid "moneylust . . . in the land of the Pilgrims." Similarly John G. Neihardt set "the Beast of Gold," "venality and greed," against the "lyric deed" of Lindbergh. One poet, Juline Comstock, told of a little boy who now pretends every night that he is "Lucky Lindy"—

> We sail the dark Atlantic,
> My little plane and I;
> For Lindy flew in darkness,—
> So I never never cry.

(One may note that in 1929 Evelyn Hood brought out a reader for beginners, entirely about Charles Lindbergh—including the favorite story that he once mounted his bicycle in a tree and pretended he was flying. A poem by Anne Lloyd, "The Tree-Top Child," told the same anecdote.) Oliver Herford wrote a poem of "Wings and the Boy." In the vernacular, I. J. Kapstein sent in a soliloquy that reflected the suppressed envy of thousands:

> What's this guy got that I ain't got?
> Why the hell am I here shipping out dry goods,
> while this guy ships himself over the Atlantic,
> and gets a big hand from all the big-timers
> with all them French broads
> falling all over themselves
> trying to kiss him? . . .
> He's in the same class with Steve Brodie
> jumping off Brooklyn Bridge,
> or like the guy that went over Niagara Falls in a barrel,—
> nervy guys but daffy as hell.
> . . . not that I'm knocking him,
> but there's plenty like him in Bellevue.
>
> Yeh, I'd give my right arm
> to do what this guy Lindbergh did.

A peak in Colorado was named Mount Lindbergh. The grandson of the President of Panama and numberless other children were christened for him—as were styles of dress, trains, boulevards and, notably, public schools. One of his English instructors at the University of Wisconsin, named Brosius, published some of Lindbergh's old themes that he had saved; his alma mater gave the flyer an honorary degree. One hundred thousand school children of San Francisco signed a petition asking him to visit them. It took a large room in the Jefferson Memorial Building, St. Louis, to contain a permanent exhibit of the medals and trophies he received. A short-lived political party called itself the "We" party. Lindbergh, honored by an air-mail stamp, broke the longstanding precedent that stamps do not commemorate living men. To suggest that it was indiscreet to canonize one whose career was just begun, not ended, would have seemed ungenerous. The public felt sure they could never love Lindbergh less. As Marquis Childs wrote in *The Herald Tribune* in 1929: "Five centuries have been required to make a saint of Joan of Arc, but in two years Colonel Charles A. Lindbergh has become a demigod." Whatever Lindbergh did was good. The public chuckled over the rather unfunny practical jokes that the flyer related, in *"We,"* which he had played upon friends and roommates at flying school—filling mouths of sleepers with shaving cream and hair grease, or putting a dead polecat into a pillow-case. The way in which Lindbergh liked to trip up friends, sending them tumbling over unseen wires, or flooding their bunk with ice-water as they slept, delighted his public as much as it did the perpetrator. These jokes seemed to fit into the boyish legend, to offer him the equivalent of a sense of humor which, in the adult sense, he apparently did not possess. Other facets of his character—a proud secretiveness, sudden anger, streaks of prim and even grim purposefulness, and a certain dullness of social personality which often appears in the mechanically-minded—these details were rejected, as misfit timber, from the Lindbergh legend. Later, their suppression exacted its revenge, and these traits were played up to the limit of malicious caricature.

Meanwhile, there were many brave airmen but only one Lindbergh. A card game called "Aviation," invented in 1928 by Edna K. Barker of Berkeley, California, and sold nationally, offered a crude quantitative test. The Lindbergh "book" counted 20 points in scoring; Byrd, 15; Chamberlain, 10; Lieutenant Maitland, 10; Amelia Earhart, 7; Balchen, 8; Acosta, 8. (An honor card commemorated Eddie Rickenbacker, greatest war ace of the air.) Other men received ovations for brave deeds, like Wiley Post; for scientific planning, represented for example by the young millionaire Howard Hughes; but again and again the public returned faithfully to Lindbergh. His good-will tour of Central America, his dawn-to-dusk flight across the continent, his voyage north to the Orient, were followed with more popular interest than any other flyer has ever commanded. Foreign lands struck off medals and issued stamps in his honor, again shattering precedent. Small boys, white, black, brown, and yellow, wanted to grow up to be Lindberghs. The Boy Scout Handbook showed a clean-cut Scout with the phantoms of Lincoln, Daniel Boone, Theodore Roosevelt, and Lindbergh marching beside him; a pamphlet by James E. West, Chief Scout Executive in the United States, carried this little preface:

Every man longs to be the hero to some boy.
Overnight Charles Lindbergh became the hero of ten million American boys.
The lone Pathfinder, blazing a trail through the arch of the sky, called to the
    blood of the pioneer in every American boy. . . .
He spoke of his plane as an equal partner in a great enterprise, and found
    a million echoes in the hearts of boys who know that things of wood
    and steel can live.
He walked with modesty in high places and courtesy in low. . . . And

America made him not only its hero, but the Symbol of its Idealistic Youth.

At least two questionnaires of the time, which have been recorded, showed the power of Lindbergh over the minds of youth—always readily swayed by the hero of the moment as against the historical one. In 1928 George R. Gerhard, supervisor of schools at Belleville, New Jersey, asked the boys of that town whom they most wanted to be like. Lindbergh received 363 votes; Coolidge 110; Ford 66; Edison 27; Alfred E. Smith 16; Pershing 14; Gene Tunney 13—and at the foot of the list stood J. P. Morgan, Mussolini, and "My Dad," with two votes apiece. Reporting this poll, *The New York Times* commented that Lindbergh's "influence is better than such heroes of youth as Napoleon or Buffalo Bill." In 1929 David Spence Hill from the University of Alabama tested 8813 urban public school children in that state with the question: "Of all the persons of whom you have heard, or read about, or seen, whom would you most care to be like?" Forty-seven per cent of the girls, but only 20 per cent of the boys, chose their ideal from home surroundings— father, mother, relative, friend, teacher. (This type of admiration ebbed rapidly from ages eight to fifteen, as one might expect with the growth of self-reliance and an expanding world.) Three per cent chose fiction characters, and 2 per cent religious personages. An even smaller number wanted most to be "like myself." But a majority of 57 per cent—divided between 71 per cent of the boys and 45 per cent of the girls—picked historical or public characters. Out of 2821 boys, 725 chose Washington, 608 Lindbergh, then a very steep drop to 154 for Lincoln, 145 Lee (in the Deep South, but one must not forget the influence of national textbooks), 107 Wilson, 80 Edison, 65 Babe Ruth, 53 Henry Ford, 38 Tom Mix, 35 Thomas Jefferson, 33 Tunney, 27 Theodore Roosevelt, 19 Franklin, 18 for Richard E. Byrd and also for Daniel Boone, 16 Longfellow, 13 John D. Rockefeller, 12 Jack Dempsey, 11 Stonewall Jackson. In the votes of 1837 girls, Washington and Clara Bow led the list with 367 and 207 respectively, and Lindbergh third with 169. Then came Billie Dove with 118, Ruth Elder 108, Clara Barton 64, Lincoln 60, Betsy Ross 57, Lee 42, and Mary Pickford 39. (One girl alone named a recently escaped convict, whom she would like to resemble because "no prison bars or laws could hold him.") However fickle the mind of youth, and whimsical its choices, Lindbergh's challenging position on all lists is the most striking fact in these polls. In that day he was youth's great hero.

Indeed, his fame appeared in distant places, in unexpected connections. At the Baden-Baden music festival of 1929 a cantata for radio, written by Paul Hindemith and Kurt Weill, dramatized Lindbergh's flight and his victory over such adversaries as Sleep, Fog, and Snow. In reviewing this performance, *The Musical Courier* spoke of the chief character as "quiet, matter-of-fact," a type of the unrhetorical twentieth century, adding: "Pathos is completely lacking in this cantata of the American hero." Pathos was yet to come.

III

To his first unsought publicity men, Bruno and Blythe, Lindbergh is reported to have said in early May, 1927: "Don't bother about getting publicity, because it doesn't interest me. Just make the newspapermen let me alone." Whether Lindbergh hated or secretly wanted publicity is an old puzzle; it has been threshed out hundreds of times in recent years, over Scotch-and-sodas in the bar of the National Press Club in Washington and in scores of village barber-shops. Some say he always managed to do the spectacular thing—such as starting late, when he set a transcontinental record, in order to reach New York at midnight, with searchlights playing on his plane. They also point out that hiding invites pursuit, and that his apparent loathing for publicity is by far the best way of gaining it. Ironically, if he had acquiesced in his glory, the public might soon have dropped him, as with Admiral Dewey and Admiral Byrd. Newsmen in the Middle West recall, on the other hand, that in his mail pilot days young Lindbergh was friendly with the press —told his stories to reporters without coaxing, and posed obligingly for his picture (once asked to smile, he inquired "At what?"). Through his first ovations, in Europe, Washington, New York, St. Louis, he kept the same cheerful patience. Then, with the almost senseless repetition of these frenzies in dozens of inland cities—mobs rushing down upon his plane and sometimes damaging the fabric in the quest for souvenirs, hoistings on shoulders, punchings, and back-slappings—it was rumored among newsmen, in the argot of the circus, that Lindbergh had begun to grow "sucker-sour." Lindbergh's modesty and shyness, for which he had been so justly praised, was calloused by contact into a hard glum reticence. He came to loathe the nicknames "Lucky" and "Lindy," and to hate the sight of a camera. It is a very understandable conversion. This analysis gives him at least credit for speaking the truth, and seems fair to a character elsewhere marked by sincerity rather than subtlety.

From the beginning of his fame, Lindbergh gave indications that he would not be a plastic hero. Before his flight to Paris, he refused to kiss his mother, the Detroit schoolteacher, for the benefit of photographers. Upon his return, on June 13, 1927, he gave an interview to newspapermen and answered many questions. Finally, Oliver Garrett of *The New York World* asked him, "Will you be at the station tonight to see your mother off?" Perhaps a little tired of Mayor Walker's repeated unctuous references that day to "your glorious mother," and the exploitation of a normal, undemonstrative relationship, the aviator suddenly froze. "Gentlemen," he said curtly, "if there are no more questions, I think this interview is over." The tendency to sentimentalize Lindbergh's bond with his mother had its natural reaction: it was soon reported, in a whisper of apprehension, that there had been an estrangement between them. The reason, apparently, was that in December, 1927, Henry Ford, on behalf of the kindly sentimentalists of America, had financed Mrs. Lindbergh's trip to Mexico City to spend Christmas with her son, in a plane which the Mexican Government instantly asked to buy as a souvenir; the whole proceedings, a little lush with the atmosphere of Mother's Day, were more fervent than the matter-of-fact comment of her son on the proposed trip, "It is entirely up to her." One is sure that, under other circumstances, Henry Ford would have chartered a plane to allow Mary Ball Washington to spend Christmas with George, or Nancy Hanks Lincoln with Abe. It was Lindbergh's misfortune to meet in his youth the hero-moulding processes which had worked posthumously, and painlessly, upon the personal relationships of Washington and Lincoln. The public created an ideal Lindbergh, more conventionally tailored and more sentimental, than the lad himself. They had done the same thing, over longer spaces of time, for all the traditional heroes of America. But with Lindbergh, this shadowy ideal, the *doppelgänger*, constantly crossed the path of the living person. It was embarrassing for both.

The newsmen—who from the start had laid aside their customary cynicism and flippancy to give the legend an unparalleled "break"— early began to look upon Lindbergh the golden boy with the possessive fondness of creatorship. It was an unhappy situation. Lindbergh soon grew to resent their fatherly intrusiveness, just as he came to recoil from the mothering of the public. European royalty are trained from infancy in habits of patience toward the People, even as their great-grandmothers bore children and their great-grandfathers died before an assembly of courtiers; they, moreover, inherit certain conventions which control publicity. But these things a Minnesota aviator of twenty-five did not have. At St. Louis, as he left an outdoors table, frenzied women fought for the corncobs he had left on his plate. At dinner in a hotel restaurant, it was reported, a well-dressed woman of middle age stopped before his table and tried to look in his mouth, to see whether he were eating "green beans or green peas." Soon, it was said, he could not send his shirts and handkerchiefs to a laundry without losing most of them.

Lindbergh's feud with his public began to take visible form. An oft-repeated story of the 1930's said that the break came in December, 1927, on the eve of his "good-will tour" to Mexico, when at Bolling Field in Washington he let the slip stream from his motor spatter with mud a group of photographers and admirers.[7] This incident did not occur so early in Lindbergh's public career. A dispatch from Washington on April 12, 1929, to *The New York Times* dates it correctly; it occurred that day, when Lindbergh, en route from Mexico to meet the body of Ambassador Herrick at the port of New York, stopped for twelve minutes at Bolling Field to see Major Lanphier, operations manager of Transcontinental Air Transport:

The small crowd had been waiting for several hours on the water-soaked field. . . . The crowd rushed toward the plane and when the leaders had nearly reached it, Colonel Lindbergh suddenly raced the motor and swung the plane around and out into the field, the strong slip stream from the motor throwing up mud and water.

Major Lanphier drove out to the plane and clambered upon a wing. When the photographers and some of the more courageous of the crowd drew near again, Colonel Lindbergh raced the motor, for a second time, driving the plane across the field and spattering the crowd once more. The photographers, deserted by the crowd, made one more attempt and suffered a third time.

Brief criticism flared in the Washington press, which had perhaps forgotten the hero's knack for sadistic practical jokes. But the public turned indignantly upon the most outspoken newspaper, which, it is reported, suffered many cancelled subscriptions; some of the mud-stained spectators even wrote in denials that the incident was Lindbergh's fault.[8] Coney Island went ahead with its plans for "Lindbergh Day" in May. For the time being, the public forgot this episode. In this same spring newspapermen were seething with resentment, whether justified or not, over snubbings they had lately received from Lindbergh; but they wrote only of his grandeur. Morris Markey recalled that at this time he saw Lindbergh, with his fiancée and Mrs. Morrow, land briefly at Portland, Maine. A group of reporters and cameramen, standing by, sent one of their number to ask for a picture. Lindbergh curtly refused. Then, in attempting to take off, Lindbergh got the wheels of his amphibian stuck in the mud. Instead of giving him a helping shove, the spectators jeered at him, and he was not able to get under way until after an hour's delay. But next day's newspapers recorded amiable little stories about his stop at Portland for refuelling.

Newspapermen at this time did not dare to crack the Lindbergh legend. The public had discovered a new, if wistful, affection for its hero. He was in love. His wedding occurred in May, 1929. The conduct of the press at this time increased the aviator's bitterness. It appears that from his first entry into the limelight, Lindbergh sincerely wanted publicity for the cause of aviation rather than for himself—that he could stand, with a touch of impatience, the great popular curiosity about himself, but extension of that curiosity to include his nearest relatives, first his mother, now his bride, and henceforth his children, he met with cold rage. By the sad irony of the case, the public was far less interested in aviation than in the aviator, less in his official than in his private life. The best-selling biographies of that date—Strachey on Victoria, Maurois on Shelley, Woodward (who in 1923 had invented the verb "to debunk") on Washington and Grant—showed preoccupation with what celebrities ate and wore, and how they made love. The old reticences had crumbled. At Sing Sing a famous murderess was photographed as she expired in the electric chair. Lindbergh was the living victim of the new curiosity. The honeymoon is best described in his own words: "For eight straight hours [newspapermen] circled about our boat at anchor in a New England harbor in a noisy motor boat, and occasionally called across the water to us that if we would pose for one picture they would go away."[9] At his first press interview, a few weeks later, he was asked if Mrs. Lindbergh were pregnant, and turned away in white anger. A Lindbergh servant was offered a bribe of $2000 by a reporter, to "betray the secrets of the household."

The relations of Lindbergh with his public grew increasingly confused. Some comment was caused by a newsreel, taken a short time after the honeymoon, which showed Lindbergh cold and unsmiling standing beside his plane, while his wife struggled out of the cockpit and carted their luggage off the field.[10] Lindbergh, it should be remembered, was the ideal of the Boy Scouts. Through the last week of August, in 1929, the Lindberghs had gone to the National Air Races in

Cleveland and the aviator had "stunted" each day with a group of Army and Navy flyers. As if resenting a transport plane's crossing the field, Lindbergh had flown close and caught the ship with its thirteen passengers in the slip stream of his engine. The ship rocked furiously, but the pilot brought it down safely. He came out of the cockpit, according to report, "white and sobbing with fury. He was placated by field officials. There was talk of an official investigation which never, of course, materialized, and the editorial columns of the press maintained a cautious silence."[11] Yet, before the close of the week's races, Lindbergh "astonished" cameramen on August 30 by walking the length of the field to meet them, and offering to pose, with an apology that he had forgotten to do so earlier.[12] Upon the threshold of the 1930's, Lindbergh's status wavered between crowd adoration and its only possible sequel, crowd hate. Even as fame lit up his most trivial acts with a significance well-nigh grotesque—the humane societies that in May had commended him for not risking a cat's life with his own, in December scolded him for attending a Mexican bull-fight—so the smooth success of his career carried a sting of hidden envy. A certain mass jealousy at length begins to dog a man who wins applause, high office, wealth, the companionship of kings and presidents, who has discovered, in short, that the world is his oyster. A name and face grow intolerably familiar, and begin to be resented. In the mill of modern publicity, heroes are worn out quickly. A veteran idol might have been unnerved by the impossible position in which this youth found himself. Upon one of Lindbergh's Central American trips, a New York editor, tired of cables reporting perfect landings and cheering crowds, had at last shot back an order: "No more unless he crashes."

The tragedy of Lindbergh's life fell in March, 1932. A great wave of public sympathy, of tenderness such as he could never have won by success, went forth to the stricken young father. A nation and the world again waited breathlessly for Lindbergh news, and this watch was as grim as the other had been joyous. Some, who thought they could have arisen above emotion to principles, felt in April that he had taken an unwise course in paying ransom to the kidnapper of his son. Perhaps the majority of Americans forebore to judge him. But all were deeply shocked by the tragic sequel in May. Then for a time, it seemed, the public mercifully let a curtain of reticence fall upon the little family at Hopewell.

In February, 1934, Lindbergh returned to the front page when he sent a telegram of protest to President Roosevelt, over the cancellation

of air-mail contracts. His repeated refusal to serve on the Dern Committee, investigating the Army's operation of the air mails, and his
strongly partisan testimony before the Senate Committee on behalf of
the air-lines which had employed him, did considerable damage to
Lindbergh's popularity among the admirers of Mr. Roosevelt. They
felt that the aviator had become a special pleader for "the interests."
The dispute however was too complex, and too quickly forgotten, to
leave much lasting effect upon the Lindbergh legend. Heroes stand
approved, or condemned, upon simpler issues.

A few months later the arrest and identification of Hauptmann
brought Lindbergh back into the major news. Throughout the trial
he was still a superman, in the public eye; his reticence, and his firmness without vindictive show, won him continued sympathy. Only in
certain German-American circles (where, ironically enough, Lindbergh was to become an object of praise four years later) were there
mutterings of discontent about the rich man versus the underdog. But
beneath the surface there had been no improvement in Lindbergh's
relations with the press. It has been stated, without proof, that two
cameramen forced their way into the Trenton morgue, in an attempt
to photograph the body of the murdered child. Certainly, a car of
photographers once crowded the Lindbergh automobile off a New
Jersey highway, trying to take a picture of the second son Jon, and on
another occasion a car with movie equipment was found parked in
front of the Lindbergh house. Probably the mass of Americans were
shocked by such persecution, and remorseful of their own curiosity that
was basically to blame, when in December, 1935, the Lindberghs sailed
quietly for England. That Lindbergh had a very real case against the
press, the Hearst papers in particular, one cannot deny.

But as the months and years passed, and the Lindberghs did not
return, the public mind began to feel that they had taken the easiest
way out, had chosen the too human and somewhat selfish rather than
the courageous course. Again, it appeared that the hero had snubbed
his throng of anonymous admirers. Doubtless sentiment rather than
logic dictated this verdict. Popular curiosity, of a favorable sort, about
the "mechanical heart" being devised by Lindbergh and Doctor Carrel,
was cancelled by political developments in the latter half of 1938. Upon
his European travels Lindbergh had decided, apparently with excellent
confirmation to come, that the German air force was much superior
to the Russian, and was in fact the strongest in the world. Rumor
invented a dinner of "the Cliveden set" in which he aired these find-

ings, and thus paved the way to Munich and appeasement. The melodrama of the incident, and Lindbergh's personal responsibility for
Chamberlain's policy, were no doubt exaggerated. But his acceptance
in October, 1938, of the Order of the German Eagle from the hands
of General Goering, at a dinner at the home of Ambassador Hugh R.
Wilson, to the public eye took on the aspect of a reward. It has been
said that Lindbergh could not have refused the decoration without a
breach of diplomatic manners; that it was given solely because of his
services to aviation; that upon its presentation "he flushed, smiled, and
seemed obviously flustered." Whatever the truth of the matter, the
Lindbergh legend had been stamped with a swastika. And as usual, the
flyer himself had too much pride to explain anything. The incident
had its curious minor effects: the lending library of a small New
York State town withdrew Mrs. Lindbergh's *Listen, the Wind* from
circulation, and in the *Official Aviation Guide* for December, 1938,
the T. W. A. dropped its sobriquet "The Lindbergh Line," in favor of
"The Sunny Santa Fé Trail." Charted by Lindbergh in 1928, the
route was now advertised with a different credit-line: "Nature made
it." And some people now liked to recall Corrigan's recent flight as a
jolly burlesque of the Lindbergh saga: William Powell, deputy commissioner of New York, had reported that quantitatively Corrigan was
the greater hero, with his 1900 tons of ticker-tape. (Whether consciously
or not, Corrigan had imitated Lindbergh when, after the ovation of
his home town, Los Angeles, he had snapped at photographers: "I'm
tired of looking at you.")

In spite of all these rifts between Lindbergh and his public, the latchstring still hung out for him. His return to the United States in April,
1939, to become technical adviser without pay to the Air Corps, was
hailed with a burst of the old applause. Most of his critics looked upon
him as a prodigal son who had come home to do his patriotic bit, under
the growing world tension. When Mrs. Lindbergh and the two children followed in May, the Hearst press and its affiliate International
News Service suppressed valuable photographs that had been taken on
shipboard—as if to make amends for old times. Several national magazines published friendly feature articles on the aviator, reviewing his
career and forecasting his service to America's rearmament program.

Two weeks after the outbreak of war in September, 1939, Lindbergh
made his first radio plea for isolation. His superiors in the War Department requested him not to enter this controversy. But when the speech
was made he was no longer under their authority; he had been relieved

from active duty in the Air Corps. His apparent refusal to be a "good soldier" caused another set-back to his reputation. To many, it seemed that he had shown an inability to play ball, to carry on the sportsmanship so essential to the old Lindbergh legend. Others felt that his boldness in taking up the role of national oracle was the boldness of ignorance; that he should stick to the controls of his plane, but leave the helm of state to statesmen. The late Heywood Broun suggested that Lindbergh was once more wearing the borrowed pajamas of an ambassador. (In justice to Lindbergh, it might be recalled that other gods of the machine age—notably Edison and Ford—had pontificated on war and peace, education, art, dietetics, fashions, the immortality of the soul, and many other topics. The illusion of versatility was a very common mirage against the American sky.) And still others applauded what seemed to them his courage and common sense: the Young Republicans of Hudson County, New Jersey, promptly formed a "Draft-Lindbergh-for-President Club."

Lindbergh had suddenly become articulate. Other broadcasts followed, and articles in magazines. In *The Reader's Digest* for November, 1939, in a curiously florid style that seemed out of character, Lindbergh wrote strangely of aviation and ethnology. The skill of machines, aeroplanes in particular, he called "almost a gift from heaven" which would enable us "to build our White ramparts again." Only white men understand machines, can use the powers of the air to "guard our heritage from Mongol and Persian and Moor." Aviation, he said, was "a scientific art which others only copy in a mediocre fashion, another barrier between the teeming millions of Asia and the Grecian inheritance of Europe—one of the priceless possessions which permit the White race to live at all in a pressing sea of Yellow, Black, and Brown." A certain mysticism about race purity, bound up with what Henry Adams would have called the worship of the dynamo, seemed to be the conclusion that Lindbergh had reached after long years of self-communion. Intellectuals supposed his doctrines came from Madison Grant, Lothrop Stoddard, or perhaps Alfred Rosenberg. Probably a greater number of Americans suspected that Lindbergh's ideas were a mixture of native horse sense with the ill-digested memory of dicta he had picked up for three years around the most brilliant dinner-tables of Western and Central Europe.

Meanwhile, Lindbergh's speeches on international affairs continued. It was widely reported that these speeches were written for him by men representing interested groups, but that Lindbergh read them with entire sincerity admitted no doubt. His father, the pacifist Congressman of 1917, author of *Why Is Your Country at War and What Happens to You after the War,* had held similar views about isolation: that volume, published during the World War, had borne a frontispiece, in one edition, showing father and son posed shoulder to shoulder. A stubborn and crotchety streak ran through the Lindbergh men. A tincture of the La Follette radicalism of the wheat belt, of Scandinavian isolationism, and of an anti-Briticism fairly common among the younger "liberals"—all entered into the state of mind which applauded Lindbergh the second, and which he in turn mirrored. And never to be forgotten was the long-smoldering fire of his resentment against the laxity of laws and disciplines in a democracy. A democracy, once calling him her first non-official citizen, had been powerless to protect the privacy of his life, the security of his home; and the residue of his memories was bitter. His tones of cynicism, recognizing no spiritual stake in the present European War, nothing worth fighting for except the right to be let alone, reflected a deep personal disenchantment. At Chicago on August 4, 1940, in urging America to learn to live amiably with a Nazi-dominated world order, Lindbergh observed that "co-operation is never impossible when there is sufficient gain on both sides, and that treaties are seldom torn apart except when they cover weak nations." In these days he was rebuking not American materialism but American idealism.

Americans who disagreed with him again washed their hands of the Lindbergh cult. The sharp dissent of his mother-in-law, acting president of Smith College, caused satisfaction to many. He was called "the chief of the Fifth Column," "the American Moseley" or "American Quisling." As 1940 ran to its close, it was doubtful whether the 6.7 per cent of the population (women predominating over men) which a *Fortune* poll at the beginning of the year reported as favoring him for President, still held to its modest loyalty. Lindbergh's honorary membership in the Lafayette Escadrille was rescinded in May, 1940, by officials who stated they "believe that Lindbergh's words are an insult to the memory of their comrades who fell on the field of honor." Proposals were under way to alter the names of various Lindbergh public schools; in Buffalo, Poles petitioned that Lindbergh Drive be renamed Adam Plewacki Drive, after the first resident of Buffalo to die in the World War. Brownwood, Texas, in December, 1940, changed its Lindbergh Avenue to Corrigan Street.

What the future held for the Lindbergh legend none could tell.

Certainly the fervent worship of 1927 and the vast pity of 1932 were alike forgotten. Boys were probably Lindbergh's staunchest admirers, because to many he still represented the most fascinating invention of modern times. At successive stages of our history, every boy wanted to grow up in a hurry and become an Indian scout, a buffalo hunter, a Rough Rider, a big business man, an engineer, a G-man. (Pessimists think the present hero-ideal is bankrupt; when the writer asked Mr. Henry Mencken what the average young American now makes haste to become, that observer answered, "a Government job-holder.") But ever since Lindbergh's flight to Paris, the aviator has had an enduring vogue, clearly ahead of any other occupational type for boys; for girls, the present vogue, thanks to Sue Barton and Penny Marsh, inclines to the trained nurse. Adults who believe that ideals forecast reality must prepare themselves for a generation of lone eagles who, when they crash in demonstrations of pluck, will be tended back to health by ministering angels in starched caps. Lindbergh undoubtedly has had a greater share than any other individual in shaping the boy's hero-type in this era. The explanation springs partly from the thrill of the machine, and in part from certain boyish qualities in Lindbergh himself which were once his greatest asset and now are perhaps his greatest handicap. For, like most prodigies, he has never grown up.

Yet, after thirteen years of stormy hero homage and distrust, the public is loath to ask for an absolute decree of divorce. The very tradition of a willful favorite has an appeal, all its own, to Americans. Not until the public is bored with Lindbergh will his cult be over. Possibly, in the future, he will redeem himself and silence the voices of criticism now so loud. Perhaps, like his ancient Greek forerunner, he may entirely come to grief when his wings of glory have melted. But that he can never wholly live up to the shining, absurdly splendid myth of May, 1927, seems clear enough.

In 1936 a young aviator-poet named John Williams Andrews projected an epic about Lindbergh. So far he has published only a fragment, called *Prelude to Icarus*. It tells of man's age-old dreams about the poetry and ecstasy of flying. Some of its verses, perhaps, are prophetic of the hero who does not yet appear:

> Who does not long for wings?
> Who does not know
> That never on this unavailing earth
> Is anything that can go free of it?

CHAPTER SEVENTEEN

CHAMPION OF THE NEW DEAL

"Posterity don't begin to vote till afther th' polls close."

—MR. DOOLEY.

I

I AM MAKING a strange wish for you, little man," President Grover Cleveland is reported to have said in 1887 to a lad of five, son of his friend James Roosevelt of Hyde Park, "a wish that I suppose no one else would make—but I wish for you that you may never be President of the United States."[1] Some years before, Horatio Alger had remarked that nine out of ten American boys, according to his observation, were exhorted to grow up and be President—although, under the ideal of worldly success that Alger himself was fostering, many bright boys now began to decide they had rather be rich than be President. This Knickerbocker lad in his sailor suit, brought to see Cleveland, did not need to wish for wealth and probably had no dreams at this time about the White House. Nevertheless he was destined to play a large part in upsetting, not only President Cleveland's well-meant wish, but also the mythologies of that era. He would come to symbolize the new forces opposing "rugged individualism" and the old-fashioned merchant prince, converting him into a diehard Tory. Rejecting Cleveland's method of dealing with labor unrest with a strong repressive hand, this thirty-second President would come to be admired and hated, upon a national scale, as only John P. Altgeld —among Cleveland's contemporaries—had been admired and hated within narrower regional limits. He would help to scrap the long-standing tradition that the poor man's hero springs from a log cabin. And, as for the legend of boy-into-President, he would inspire such a letter as one published in 1940 in a Western newspaper, signed "An American Mother":

I am a mother and am therefore opposed to the Third Term for President Roosevelt. I have a son and have the natural ambition that some day he will be President of his country. I think every American mother sees in her son a potential President. Of course the odds against the fulfillment of my hope are tremendous, but there is no reason why these odds should be increased by the breach of an American tradition. . . . If Franklin D. Roosevelt should be elected again, the odds against my son's election to the Presidency will be increased 33⅓ per cent. I ask that this letter be published so that all American mothers shall have their attention drawn to this invasion of their rights of entry in the Great American Futurity—the Presidential Race.[2]

The partisans of Mr. Roosevelt praise him for having traced out the success story, as it were, with reverse English—in overcoming the handicap of hereditary rank and riches to become the forgotten man's friend. Campaign biographies of 1932 presented him to the country as the holder of an old Dutch pedigree on his father's side, and (no offense to the Irish, German, and Italian vote) "equally fine colonial ancestry" on the distaff side. Unlike his running-mate, John N. Garner, he was not born in a log cabin, but "in a fine old home overlooking the Hudson River." He was neither a gilded idler nor a bookworm, but loved farm life and "at school he broke athletic records." Today, his friends (we read) "often wonder that one man can so perfectly understand the viewpoint of the dirt farmer and the city laborer."[3] Thus we are offered the Jeffersonian pattern of herohood, rather than the Lincolnian.

Mr. Roosevelt is aware of the solid Dutch connotations of his name— soundness and thrift, with a touch of stubborn testy integrity—and his admirers have delighted to send him wooden shoes and miniature windmills. But, as a genealogist, he knows the very small fraction of Dutch germ-plasm he possesses, while as a liberal and a politician he inclines to the cosmopolitan claims of his fifth cousin Theodore. Asked about the Semitic strain which friendly Jews and hostile Nazis,

GENIUS OF THE NEW DEAL

alike, have fancied in him, he replied on March 7, 1935, to the editor
of *The Detroit Jewish Chronicle:* "In the dim distant past [my ances-
tors] may have been Jews or Catholics or Protestants. What I am more
interested in is whether they were good citizens and believers in God.
I hope they were both."[4] Mr. Roosevelt's patroon descent, and the moderate fortune he thus inherited, have often been turned against him in
his role of liberal. The Oyster Bay Roosevelts branded him as a
"maverick" of the family when in 1920 he ran for Vice-President on
the Democratic ticket—despite the fact that Franklin D. Roosevelt's
father and immediate relatives were Democrats long before Theodore
entered politics as a Republican. Like Thomas Jefferson, the second
Roosevelt has often been called "a traitor to his class," a Benedict Arnold
in the economic ranks of Groton and Harvard. His friends have inquired, in return, whether poor boys who become rich and harden into
conservatism, like Herbert Hoover and Alfred E. Smith, may not with
equal justice be called traitors to their class? On March 2, 1938, the
House of Representatives was thrown into a furore when Congressman
Rich of Pennsylvania declared that the President "never did a day's
work in his life." (Congressman Bulwinkle of North Carolina, rushing
to the defense, pointed out that "before the President was stricken in
1923"—an error for 1921—"he was vice president of an insurance company.") Even Herr Hitler, replying to Roosevelt's peace plea of April,
1939, could not forbear pointing to himself as the model of self-made
men: "I, who twenty-one years ago was an unknown worker and
soldier of my people, have attained this [leadership] by my own
energy." Much has been made of the fact that the President's Phi Beta
Kappa key was not won in college, but presented to him later; that he
flunked a course in the Columbia Law School and failed to graduate,
but after passing the bar examination found a place—supposedly from
family influence—in the excellent Wall Street firm of Carter, Ledyard
& Milburn. In the 1940 campaign, friends of Mr. Willkie spoke of
New Deal attempts "to smear the ideals of success," and pointed to
their candidate's working his way through school, harvesting wheat,
puddling steel, husking corn, picking fruit and vegetables, running a
tent-hotel and teaching in a Kansas high school. In American politics,
the legend of Poor Richard was far from dead.

Mr. Roosevelt's boyhood offered none of the hero-tales that still
appeal to the grass-roots. His mother, in her book *My Boy Franklin,*
published in 1933, attempted to serve as his Parson Weems. Some readers enjoyed her maternal touches, which carefully avoided the sug-

gestion of nurse-maids: "At the very outset he was plump, pink, and nice. I used to love to bathe and dress him, although I took the responsibility of lifting and turning him rather seriously." She glanced defensively at stories of his youthful extravagance by writing that, "for a boy who never heard money discussed at home, I must say Franklin had a pretty conservative sense of values." She also recorded her observation that his sense of leadership developed early—a trait, as we have seen, fondly remembered about Benjamin Franklin and Washington and Lincoln and Buffalo Bill:

Franklin had a great habit of ordering his playmates around, and for reasons which I have never been able to fathom, was generally permitted to have his way. I know that I, overhearing him in conversation one day with a little boy on the place with whom he was digging a fort, said to him:

"My son, don't give the orders all of the time. Let the other boy give them sometimes."

"Mummie," he said to me quite without guile, lifting a soil-streaked face, "if I didn't give the orders, nothing would happen!"[5]

The best-known story of the President's boyhood, which she tells here, concerns a gold-decorated life-membership card in the Museum of Natural History that his father had given him, and how on a visit to London the boy used it to crash a garden party at the South Kensington Museum in honor of the future King Edward VII. The story, at least, served as an emblem of enterprise.

Nor have Roosevelt's school and college days yet collected the patina of legend or anecdote overlaying Daniel Webster's or T. R.'s. "I knew him when" say many old Grotties or members of Alpha Delta Phi or *The Crimson* staff at Harvard. But those who reminisce are not Abe Lincoln's neighbors along Pigeon Creek, eager to put in their ha'pennyworth of hero-worship. In the main they are gentlemen who stand on the other side of the barricades from the President. Their recollections, whether true or false, tend to be of a handsome, amiable, unstable youth who inspired liking but little trust, and whose family shrewdly kept him from throwing his money about. It is too early to say whether these legends will become a permanent part of the Roosevelt saga.

Some may discern unconscious symbolism in his mother's statement that when he entered political life in 1910, in candidacy for the New York State Senate, he elected to "jeopardize his chances by choosing a bright red open model . . . car instead of the conventional horse and buggy." In this fashion, a born campaigner, the young lawyer covered his district, and won by a margin of 15,708 votes to his Republican opponent's 14,586. A persistent rumor says that he had thirsted for political power ever since his wedding to Theodore Roosevelt's niece in 1905—when the reigning President, who gave the bride away, had stolen the show from the young couple, while seventy-five policemen kept order and small boys fell off a neighboring fence (as *The New York World* of March 18 reported) in their excited cries of, "Three cheers for Teddy! Ain't he the real thing?" while "the President shook his fist playfully at the boys." Partisans of Theodore Roosevelt seriously believe that Franklin Delano Roosevelt, then and there, resolved to outdistance his kinsman.

Franklin Roosevelt's political beginnings were auspicious. In the State Senate he came to be known as a stout foe of Tammany, in blocking the ambitions of "Blue-Eyed Billy" Sheehan to succeed Chauncey M. Depew in Washington. His constituents, country squires and farmers, liked this independent young man. He was returned to office in 1912. Even then, an aura of luck and drama seemed to follow him willy-nilly. One evening during his re-election campaign, after he had left the Dutcher House, in Pawling, to drive home, a fire broke out in the hotel. To his surprise, it is said, he read in the next morning's headlines: "Dutcher House practically burned to the ground. Senator Franklin D. Roosevelt hero of the hour. Rescues women and children by carrying them out of the flames."[6] Even better luck followed his admiration for Woodrow Wilson, and the campaign he had waged in New York State on behalf of the New Jersey candidate for President. Wilson appointed him Assistant Secretary of the Navy. Although roundly defeated in 1914 for United States Senator in the Democratic primaries by James W. Gerard, Roosevelt was becoming known and well liked in Washington. As a lover of boats, and an inheritor of the Roosevelt tradition in the Navy Department, he favored a big navy. The World War appeared to vindicate him; and it certainly enhanced the prestige of his office. Some men now hostile, who knew him then, insist that he was a pleasant gentleman who promised everybody anything, but did nothing. Others avow that, in the landlubberly régime of Josephus Daniels, crisp and decisive young Roosevelt *was* the Navy Department; they point to such a daring achievement as the bottling up of the North Sea by a mine-field which Roosevelt planned, from Scottish to Norwegian waters. Henceforth, at every stage of his life, Roosevelt is described by friends and enemies in terms that are flatly contradictory. His good looks, his charm, and his infectious laugh are about the only points of agreement. Shortly after America's entry into the war, Ralph Block wrote in *The New York Tribune* under the title "Another Roosevelt": "Roosevelt has a bearing that even William Faversham might envy. His face is long, firmly shaped and set with marks of confidence. . . . A firm thin mouth breaks quickly into a laugh, openly and freely." Borrowing Conrad's phrase in *Lord Jim,* "unobscured vision and tenacity of purpose," Block said that he began to "wonder how a democracy of opportunity can afford to leave him subordinated."[7]

Nominated for the Vice-Presidency in 1920, Roosevelt joined Cox in carrying to the country Wilson's hopeless fight for the League of Nations. He made some eight hundred speeches, and apparently gained the ease and polish of public address which has since made his voice the most masterly in American politics. The Roosevelt name was an incalculable asset to him and the Democratic Party. It carried magic, even for those who knew of the very distant relationship going back to the year 1690. Even Emil Ludwig, a more or less "official" biographer of 1938, writes repeatedly and carelessly of "the name and the shadow of that popular and legendary uncle," Theodore. In the campaign of 1920, newspapermen noted that hayseeds would call out, "You're just like your Old Man," or "I voted for your Pappy, and I'm going to vote for you too." (Franklin Roosevelt admires T. R. the progressive; he has described Theodore as one of the five moderns who interest him most, the others being Jefferson, Franklin, Napoleon as planner and reorganizer, and that American exotic Count Rumford. Rumford, it might be noted, as chief minister of Bavaria from 1784 to 1798 ran soup-kitchens and model workhouses, saying that, in reversal of the usual theory of his times, he proposed to make the poor "first happy and then virtuous.")[8]

After Roosevelt's crushing defeat, beneath the wreckage of the League, he became an insurance company executive. For eight years, apart from his sponsorship of Al Smith for President in 1924, he took no active part in politics. His critics, like John T. Flynn in a recent book, are pleased to point out the ill-success of the business and speculative ventures he undertook in the interim—the Consolidated Automatic Merchandising Corporation, the International Germanic Company, the American Investigating Corporation, as well as the $90,000,-000 deficit which he later left as Governor of New York. His friends point to Roosevelt's consistent record as a liberal. They, far more than his enemies, incline to give weight to the most important thing that happened to Roosevelt during these years—his illness with infantile paralysis. His courage under this blow of fortune, and the silent cheerfulness with which he mastered it, apparently served to deepen his character and to give him new sympathy for others in distress. Of this transformation, sympathetic biographers like Lindley and Ludwig have much more to say than has Flynn in his *Country Squire in the White House.* The theme was doubtless overplayed by Will Durant, in his dispatch to *The New York Herald,* June 29, 1928, describing Roosevelt's appearance at Houston to renominate Al Smith:

A figure tall and proud even in suffering; a face of classic profile; pale with years of struggle against paralysis; a frame nervous and yet self-controlled with that tense, taut unity of spirit which lifts the complex soul above those whose calmness is only a stolidity; most obviously a gentleman and a scholar. A man softened and cleansed and illumined with pain. What in the name of Croker and Tweed is he doing here? Nothing better could be said for the Governor of New York than that Franklin Roosevelt loves him.

Meanwhile the Republican press, as if intuitive of the future, rebuked Smith for "drafting" Roosevelt to succeed him as Governor of New York, for making "this most loyal of friends agree to serve his ambition at a price that is beyond all reason," calling the nomination "both pathetic and pitiless," "unfair to Mr. Roosevelt."[9] Reports were then spread, and re-echoed nationally in the campaign of 1932, that Roosevelt was physically unable to meet the requirements of high office. In the latter year, having forgotten his urgency in 1928, Al Smith wrote in *The Saturday Evening Post* for June 11: "It requires a man of great vigor and bodily strength to stand the physical strain of it, to make no mention whatever of the tax he has to put upon his mental qualities to permit him to conduct the campaign intelligently over so long a period." (Later, Emil Ludwig would remark that Roosevelt the courageous invalid had described Smith as " 'the happy warrior,' a phrase which he had perhaps applied inwardly to himself and transferred to his friend." He was clearly unaware that Judge Proskauer had suggested it to Roosevelt in 1924 for the nominating speech for Smith at Madison Square Garden. Thus the wishfulness, on all sides, of political biography.)

To the public at large, ever since Roosevelt's re-entry into the arena in 1928, his combination of mental vigor and crippled physique has been the best possible recommendation. He has not asked for sympathy, and in the 1932 campaign made only one ironic reference to the subject—remarking at Syracuse: "Well, here's the helpless, hopeless invalid my opponents have been talking about. I have made fifteen speeches today. This will be the sixteenth." But undoubtedly he has benefited by the public chivalry which has sent cripples to municipal and state office, and two blind men within the past decade to the United States Senate. It was the first fact about him which drew national solicitude. When in Georgia he once slipped and fell on the speaker's platform, and was helped to his feet to resume the speech without a break, the anxious audience broke into ringing applause. No cartoonist has ever dared to picture his canes or braces, and a few unsporting references in the press in 1934 to his "hobbling" gait were cried down by popular indignation. The success of the President's birthday parties for the Warm Springs Foundation, and of "The March of Dimes" to the White House, was an annual gauge of sympathy. With the passing of time, this aspect of Mr. Roosevelt grew less important to the picture. There were other reasons for admiring or distrusting him.

II

His nomination in 1932 owed much to the slowly ripening plans of Louis Howe, since Senatorial days in Albany the most devoted hero-worshipper of Roosevelt. The letters Howe wrote to politicians and useful citizens all over the country, and the wide contacts which Farley's friendliness and generalship established, were invaluable. Like most political favorites, in the age of publicity—when "linage" is as powerful a fillip to hero-hood as military glory once was—Roosevelt was fortunate in the lieutenants and press-agents who introduced him to the country. He was also supremely lucky in the timing of his appearance. Unlike Bryan and Smith, he did not blunder upon the stage when the audience was crying encore to the previous act. Instead he arrived when Hoover was being pelted off with hoots and jeers, when an almost intolerable situation demanded change. Walter Lippmann's famous criticism of him, on January 8, 1932, that he "is no crusader . . . no tribune of the people . . . no enemy of entrenched privilege . . . a pleasant man who, without any important qualification for the office, would very much like to be President," Roosevelt soon belied as quickly as he downed the imputation of a physical weakling. Every act was decisive. He flew to Chicago, battling head-winds, to accept his nomination with the words: "This is more than a political campaign. It is a call to arms." One rumor said that he had written this stirring speech during the flight; another, that he had found it too long and revised it, flinging page after page out of the speeding plane. Apparently the real story of that speech has lately been told by Raymond Moley—how Roosevelt brought from Albany the text in which Moley had had a major share, and how on the platform Roosevelt had interwoven it with the first page of a rival speech by Louis Howe which the candidate had not even seen before.[10] It seemed to be a symbol of Roosevelt's love of compromise, of reconciling opposites.

Moley, with the indiscretion of the disillusioned, also claims credit for "the Forgotten Man" (remembered from William Graham Sumner, it would appear) and for the "the New Deal" (which others have ascribed to Mark Twain).[11] In January, 1933, in an article on Mr. Roosevelt, Robert S. Allen had declared: "The actual writing of his speeches was done by himself. No one ghosted for him."[12] From time to time, however, it appeared that the group whom James M. Kieran had christened "the Brains Trust" had as much to do with Roosevelt's speeches as Alexander Hamilton with Washington's Farewell Address and John Hay with Lincoln's letter to Mrs. Bixby. Their more intricate collaboration was not without its embarrassments. On April 22, 1932, *The New York Evening Post* discovered that Roosevelt and Al Smith had in part made the same speech, by incorporating a statement on the tariff written for both by Lindsay Rogers of Columbia. And at San Diego on October 2, 1935, the President borrowed a phrase from "the greatest writer of history," meaning Shakespeare, on "malice domestic and fierce foreign war." It was soon discovered that the greatest writer of history was really Raymond Moley, whose creative powers were better than his memory.[13] Only the naïve, with little idea of a modern statesman's life, are shocked by the charge of ghost-writing. Grammarians who have spent time in analyzing Roosevelt's style, and in counting the Anglo-Saxon as against the Latin derivatives, for *The Quarterly Journal of Speech,* may be forgiven a sense of futility. The President never denies that he employs ghosts. With more admiration than disapproval, General Hugh Johnson has called him an expert at "picking other men's brains." "I can see," he writes, "no fault in national leaders—whether George Washington with Alexander Hamilton or Franklin Roosevelt with Tommy Corcoran—using ghost writers. After all, the speaker makes their words his own and is thereafter forever responsible for them. It is a lot better that they should be craftsmanlike words than political illiteracy."[14] Yet, in justice to Mr. Roosevelt, it should be said that, unaided, he expresses himself much better than any other President has done since Wilson, with something of a great artist's feeling for style.

Whatever the background, of fact-finding and phrase-polishing, in Roosevelt's first campaign speeches, he delivered them with fluent force. Everywhere great crowds turned out to see him. There were cheers, and sometimes frantic gestures of approval: in San Francisco, for example, admirers mobbed his automobile on its way to the hotel, one devotee nearly wrenching off the candidate's arm by clinging to his hand as the car moved on. His self-confidence, vitality, and enthusiasm were a tonic in that season of despair. Yet as Ernest Lindley, Roosevelt's favorite newspaperman, has said, he was "no great popular idol during the Presidential campaign of 1932." He did not look like a Messiah or even a Bryan; he was too worldly, too urbane, to be a voice crying in the wilderness. Of "class war" he said little, talking chiefly of good neighbors, our pioneer forefathers, the Constitution, and the Boy Scout manual. The hostile legend lingered here and there of a pleasant ineffectual gentleman. The country liked Roosevelt, yet was skeptical about his ability to deliver. But under the misery of depression, and the panic that crept even into higher financial circles, the nation decided by nearly twenty-three million votes to sixteen, to give him a chance. Since he had not been extolled as a Messiah, his quick decisive measures upon entering the White House were thrilling and reassuring. Roosevelt's real popularity began with his inauguration.

"This nation asks for action, and action now," he said in taking office. He added some dark words about "unscrupulous money-changers" who "stand indicted in the court of public opinion." But those money-changers, with two-thirds of the country's banks closed by previous official proclamation and the R. F. C. apparently powerless to help them, were too sorely bruised to lift the head of resentment. Henceforth Roosevelt played a dramatic role, such as Americans always love in their heroes. (Tyrone Power, visiting America in the 1830's, had remarked that we were a histrionic race—fond of oratory and the theatre, apt to strike attitudes against the backdrop of our brave new world. The hero envisages his era as a crisis, a drama of good versus evil, and himself as the man of destiny. In a sense, he must be a hero to himself before he can command that worship in others.) Roosevelt's magnificent calm at Miami shortly before the inauguration, when faced with an assassin's pistol, was a prelude of courage to the first political act. Now, with his call for "broad executive power to wage a war against the emergency," he captured the imagination. He called

Congress into special session, invoked the power of the Trading with the Enemy Act, and summoned the nation's leading bankers to a Sunday conference. Over the Bank Holiday, plans were laid for immediate rehabilitation. On the following Sunday, March 12, he addressed the country by radio, in "An Intimate Talk with the People of the United States on Banking." Roosevelt's old chief, Woodrow Wilson, had shattered precedent by speaking to Congress in person ("Why didn't I think of that!" T. R. was said to have exclaimed regretfully); now a President carried his voice directly to the nation. The press dubbed it a fireside chat. Speaking not of "the Administration" but of "I" and "we," he explained the reasons for the Bank Holiday. He asked the people to put their money back into the banks: "Confidence and courage are the essentials of success. . . . It is your problem no less than mine. Together we cannot fail." For the first time in history, the American people felt they had been admitted to an inner council of state. And his reassurance, his attitude of the doctor or the super social-worker, his promise that no one would starve, was immensely grateful to that weary and harassed time. A sacrificial, if not penitential, challenge is one to which any healthy nation quickly responds—as England has found under Winston Churchill.

Harold Laski has lately drawn the distinction between "dull" government, acquiescing in the status quo, daring no affirmations, and "thinking" government, active and bold, which a thriving democracy seems miraculously to bring forth in crisis. This expresses the difference between Hoover and his successor. The New Deal seemed to rescue the nation from a lag in the reform movement which had lasted since Wilson's New Freedom was swallowed up by the war. Experiments good, bad, and indifferent were begun, in a spirit of sudden enthusiasm. We went off the gold standard. Repeal was soon under way. The N. R. A. was set up, to the cheers both of big business and of left-wingers. Farm relief was undertaken with the A. A. A. The C. C. C. took care of jobless youth on the brink of starvation or defeat. As in all democratic crises, a program of action too complex for easy popular assimilation was epitomized in a paternal leader—Jefferson, Jackson, Lincoln, Wilson, Franklin Roosevelt—personalities who were conceived as fathers of their country, friends of the people, or at least avuncular good neighbors. Never before had a peacetime leader commanded more unanimity than did Roosevelt, temporarily, in the spring of 1933. "The house is burning down, and the President of the United States says this is the way to put out the fire," the Republican leader in Congress had declared, when the emergency banking bill came up for debate. Playing with the same image, Will Rogers wrote of the President: "The whole country is with him. Even if what he does is wrong they are with him. Just so he does something. If he burned down the Capitol, we would cheer and say, 'Well, we at least got a fire started anyhow.'"

In some ways it was Roosevelt's misfortune that, as President, he started at the top. Liberals like Jefferson and Jackson had harder sledding at the beginning of the course, and later began to enjoy the sensation of coasting. But it was clear that, whatever the future held for Franklin Roosevelt, he could never again in times of peace so benefit by the support of an unbroken nation—of all sorts and economic conditions—as in the honeymoon of his first term. In August, 1933, scattered talk of "coercion" in respect to the N. R. A. began to be heard, chiefly from the smaller businessmen restive under the codes with which big business (unforeseen by the President) had saddled them. Within the next six months, distrust of Roosevelt had shifted from this group to Wall Street—suspicious of the President's leaning away from the "sound money" philosophy of Carter Glass toward inflationism and the Warren heresy, enlivened by a brief flirtation with the silver states and an attitude toward international stabilization which swung from rejection in July, 1933, to ultimate acceptance three years later. Meanwhile, Congress had broken its resolutions of economy. It began to restore salary cuts, to put veterans back on pension rolls and soon to vote a bonus—choosing the easier, more expedient way, in which the President after some dissent appeared at last to acquiesce cheerfully. Soon the "pump-priming" theory of spending developed. The President and Congress grew less stringently sacrificial; while on the other hand, the bankers, having caught their second wind, used it to talk back to their erstwhile savior. The spirit of mutual forbearance, of high dedication, was too good to last.

Yet to the President as hero, minority opinion was comparatively unimportant. Through the following seven years, the people—the middle class, and even more markedly "the third of a nation" mired in poverty and unemployment—gave him an affection that was singularly steady. Whatever his mistakes, they felt that he was doing his best for them. In August, 1934, returning from Hawaii, he landed at Portland, Oregon, and made a leisurely progress to Chicago. E. D. Canham, chief of the Washington bureau of *The Christian Science Monitor,* who has covered the President's numerous swings around the country, states that this trip marked the highest point of cheering in Roosevelt's career.

In every city he received mammoth ovations; at crossroads people drove many miles and stayed up all night to see his train go by, with no expectation of glimpsing the man himself unless they supposed he remained on the rear platform waving all the time. (In strict realism one must take account of the passion, among rural Americans, for watching trains go by.) Through the following winter, solaced by the President's budget message in January, 1935, promising no increase in taxation, conservatives breathed more freely and again inclined to join the average man in praising Roosevelt. The visible collapse of the N. R. A. cracked the early myth of Roosevelt's infallibility, and a good many people with middling incomes who prided themselves on "common sense" rather than brain-truster theory began to question the President's economy of scarcity—of plowing up corn, and paying farmers for not raising pigs. "Impractical" came to be a more frequent epithet about the man in the White House.

On May 31, 1935, after the Supreme Court unanimously invalidated N. R. A., Roosevelt expressed his sarcasm about "the horse and buggy days" in a press conference that lasted an hour and a half. To some, it became clear that the President was less impartially serene than Washington in his heyday, less patient with dissenting opinion than Lincoln —in other words, that he was more the human being, the partisan, like Andrew Jackson. On June 19, as if to steal Huey Long's thunder, he sent a surprise message to Congress calling for "Soak-the-Rich" taxation. But Congress, restive under the charge of being a rubber-stamp, failed to do his bidding. Confident that the people were still with him, the President addressed the next Congress on January 3, 1936, in a fighting speech broadcast to the nation's firesides, deriding "entrenched greed" and "our resplendent economic autocracy."

Meanwhile, the rich began to speak of "that Man," to retail ribald stories about him and Mrs. Roosevelt, with adolescent snickers, in the bars of country clubs. Indeed, as Elmer Davis pointed out, hatred of Roosevelt became a substitute for responsibility, an enduring alibi. (One story from the other camp told of a broker who, after losing his bet on a favorite race-horse, bitterly exclaimed, "Damn Roosevelt anyway!") Carbon copies of poems, wisecracks, Biblical parodies were passed from hand to hand by normally dignified men—who found in underground humor the same relief which, it was said, Europeans gained from telling at much greater risk jokes about Hitler and Stalin. A resident of Park Avenue, proved to be insane, was institutionalized for sending threats to the President. In general, however, the group from whom his enemies were recruited was not machine-gun conscious. They adapted old myths to the Roosevelts, such as, that the President and his wife were about to be divorced but had patched up their feud for the duration of the White House (also related of Wilson and Harding). The divorces of the younger Roosevelts, as well as their tickets for speeding, their scuffles with cameramen, and the numerous money-making activities in which they engaged (from James's insurance and Elliott's radio chain to Anna's book *Scamper: the Bunny Who Went to the White House* written for the delectation of Sistie and Buzzie Dall), were greeted with derision among the rich, and wide-eyed wonder among the poor. It was remarked, with a variety of sentiments, that the younger Roosevelts had not married forgotten women.

Through the latter part of 1935 and during the next two years, one heard increasingly that Roosevelt (whom some had feared, under the N. R. A., as a potential Fascist) was really a Communist. Nobody remembered a quaint little episode in 1923, when a New York urchin of eleven, named Leo Granoff, had been arrested for wandering about late at night after his mother had gone to a movie and forgotten to give him a key to the house, and upon whose person was found a membership card in the Young Workers' League; Leo was released by the police, but as Norman Hapgood ironically observed, "his heresies were made the basis of a very touching appeal for the Boy Scouts signed by Franklin D. Roosevelt."[15] Diplomatic recognition of Russia, under Roosevelt, confirmed the first forebodings of Park Avenue. There were other whispers about him. He was ruled by the Elders of Zion, a "cabal of Morgenthaus, Lehmans, Frankfurters, and Cohens," as the charge was expressed in *The Highland Post* of Ulster County, New York, by Howland Spencer, "the squire of Krum Elbow," who later sold his estate bordering Hyde Park to Father Divine.[16] A handbill claiming circulation of 700,000 accused Roosevelt and the Department of Justice of shielding the real kidnappers of the Lindbergh baby "under the direction of leading American multimillionaire bankers and lawyers." This seemed to spring from cranks rather than from the camp which Roosevelt—irritated by the rising tide of hatred—began in 1936 to call "economic royalists," "economic dynasties thirsting for power," "the resolute enemy within our gates."

There was no doubt of the quarter from which blew the fiercest winds. *The New York Times* of December 11, 1935, told of a dinner of public utility men at the Biltmore, at which a toast to the President, proposed by the toastmaster, Thomas N. McCarter, had been "greeted with general laughter." Increasingly, as the 1936 campaign drew on, a yarn was told that Roosevelt caused the Government to pay $100,000 annual rent to his mother for the use of Hyde Park as a summer White House. Most members of the Liberty League believed such things. Rumors multiplied about the President's health. In the summer of 1935, the analogy between Roosevelt touring the country (after the wreckage of N. R. A. and the tax drive) and Wilson's futile campaigning for the League in 1919, led to gossip that the President was breaking physically. In May, 1937, a "Confidential: Not for Release" report distributed by the McClure Syndicate told how Roosevelt was found in a coma at his desk, and how he had been carried on shipboard for recuperation at sea, under heavy naval guard.[17] Thus was Roosevelt's fishing trip to the Gulf of Mexico given a lurid tinge. Prosperous physicians, over their after-dinner coffee, told one of megalomania or delusions of grandeur as a complication that often followed the onset of infantile paralysis. "I understand all the phases of poliomyelitis," they would say. "Now let me explain. . . ." As a matter of fact, one of the chief symptoms which led to their diagnosis was Roosevelt's attitude toward socialized medicine.

Under these criticisms and whispering campaigns, and as he watched the Supreme Court in 1935 and 1936 nullify much of the New Deal, Mr. Roosevelt grew more bellicose. The Liberty League, no less than certain Leftist advisers, goaded him into more aggressive attack upon those whom the first Roosevelt had branded as "malefactors of great wealth" —a phrase revived for the Democratic platform in 1936. In 1932 Franklin Roosevelt had sought to please everybody; in 1936, in his speech on October 31, he called for war to the knife:

Never before in all our history have these forces been so united against one candidate as they stand today. They are unanimous in their hate of me —and I welcome their hatred.

I should like to have it said of my first Administration that in it the forces of selfishness and of lust for power met their match. I should like to have it said of my second Administration that in it these forces met their master.

Conciliatory talk the previous autumn, about "a breathing spell" for big business, was heard no more. The American people at large are not radical, in the Union Square acceptance of that term, but they have an ingrained suspicion of Wall Street, a sympathy for "the little fellow" and his right to a more abundant life. They also relish drama, and enjoy a good fight. Mr. Roosevelt gave them these things in his 1936 campaign. Actually, his appeals and threats were vague, exciting, exhilarating, but not at all specific. A man of sincere solicitude for the underfed and homeless, and of equally sincere vexation against the forces opposing him, Mr. Roosevelt was neither a Machiavelli nor a trained economist. His grasp of first principles, of steady objectives, seemed, even to his friends, less marked than his talent for brilliant improvisation. His thunders on the left were not necessarily a prelude to bloodshed, although some critics began to wonder if he were not using the class war with as keen an eye to politics as his fifth cousin had employed the Spanish-American War. A hero has to have something to rescue. The people thought he could give them the fruits of a revolution without a revolution; the bankers believed that he was giving them a revolution with all its imminent horrors. These apprehensions, in 1936, were enough to bring hundreds of thousands flocking into the streets to see him wherever he went, bowing and smiling from open cars, while cordons of motorcycle police, the outriders of modern times, swept past. Meanwhile, somewhat ludicrously, rich men trembled in their clubs. A *Fortune* survey announced in October, 1936, that among those favoring Roosevelt, a majority of nearly 60 per cent expected him to remain as before and some 17 per cent anticipated that he would grow more conservative; whereas, among those opposing Roosevelt vehemently, about 57 per cent thought that he would become more radical and only 5 per cent thought he might turn conservative in a second term. "There is one issue in this campaign," Roosevelt told Moley. "It's myself, and people must be either for me or against me."[18] A clairvoyant politician, he knew that the battle would be decided, not on policies and issues, but upon his personal appeal; he also sensed, as the Gallup and *Fortune* polls constantly revealed, that in this circumstance lay his strength. Roosevelt the man was clearly more popular than Roosevelt the policy-maker, the economic planner, the sometimes headstrong statesman. And he was vastly better liked than any of his colleagues identified with the New Deal—Ickes, Wallace, Madam Perkins, Harry Hopkins, Jackson, Corcoran and Cohen—or even than the New Deal itself. Opposed to "the Kansas Coolidge" Alfred M. Landon, whose speeches were as flat as a Midwest plain, Roosevelt could not fail. His victory in forty-six states was the most decisive since James Monroe's in 1820, in the "era of good feeling."

Roosevelt's exultation savored less of the era of good feeling than of the stormy times of Old Hickory. The tutelary genius of Roosevelt's first term might have been Jefferson, a bookish liberal who proved, as the squire of Hyde Park remarked at Monticello, that it is possible for a great gentleman to be a great commoner. The genius of the second term, at least at its beginning, seemed to be the more pugnacious democrat from the Hermitage. On Election Day, 1936, for luck, Roosevelt wore Jackson's heavy gold watch-chain. A few days later Mr. Hearst with grudging admiration wrote: "Jackson is the only man in American history who had an equally overwhelming popular appeal and popular victory." At subsequent Jackson Day dinners Mr. Roosevelt himself has suggested the parallel, and he provided that the reviewing stand for the 1937 inaugural parade should be a replica of the Hermitage. Only Lincoln, greatest of war Presidents, was left for purposes of analogy.

III

With an unquestioned mandate from the people in his hands, Mr. Roosevelt now might have surveyed his stature as a hero. In one of his later speeches he spoke of keeping "faith with those who have faith in me." Between Mr. Roosevelt and his public, it was a true-love match, faithful, charming, possibly a little irrational on both sides with its trust in mutual infallibility—but love, after all, transcends logic. The poor and debt-ridden looked to him as their deliverer, while the farmers and urban middle class liked him as their cheerful, confident leader. Not yet did he have monuments of stone or bronze. But the casual memorials of that hero-worship ranged from a granite boulder on a mountain ridge near Park City, Utah, which some F. E. R. A. workmen early in the New Deal had inscribed "In memory of Franklin D. Roosevelt: 1932–36" (meaning, as Commissioner E. J. McPolin explained, "in appreciation of"), to a sentence which this writer saw scrawled in chalk on a box-car in the Denver freight yards, probably by some passing hobo: "Roosevelt Is My Friend."

He was an aristocrat, and yet he knew how to speak to the people—even more tellingly by radio than upon platforms—in a warm, persuasive voice of marvellous color and clarity. A Dutchess County and Groton accent carried into every home able to afford a radio a sense of comradeship such as no other recent President had possessed. Coolidge and Hoover, no aristocrats, had given forth an atmosphere of icebergs. (In the winter of 1932–33 one of the most revealing signs of Republican decrepitude had been a news item telling that Postmaster General

Brown had ordered himself a new automobile with a higher top, so that he could wear his silk hat while driving—an incident that gave Mr. Roosevelt the chance to inform Mr. Farley of his intended portfolio in the Cabinet by the comment, "I see your predecessor is having difficulty with his hat.") Mr. Roosevelt belonged to the tradition of the Tory liberal in nineteenth-century England, the "toffs" who with a touch both sentimental and humanitarian had carried through the great reform movements of that era. As early as the campaign of 1920 he had begun to use "My friends" in preference to the more stilted "Fellow-citizens."[19] He was a master of immediacy. When in his first fireside chat of 1934 he asked the average man, "Are you better off than you were last year?" Joe Zilch believed that the President was talking straight to him, as thousands of replies to the White House bore witness. Speaking of mortgages, the President asked that those in distress telegraph the credit department in Washington "or write to me personally in the White House." Thousands took him at his word, and the letters of course were sent on to the proper bureau. In November, 1937, in his chat about the forthcoming unemployment census the President said: "The postcard we are sending you on Tuesday is a direct message from me to you."

Later that month, recalling the President's last western trip, an educator at Columbia named Janet R. Aiken rebuked the grammar in his Cheyenne speech, "Engineers are human just like I am," observing that he should have said "as I am"; she also took him to task for saying at Boise, "Just like the plain folks, like all of us are." Did he learn such speech at Groton and Harvard? she inquired primly.[20] Whether seriously or with his tongue in cheek, the President said he had been misquoted, while newsmen rejoined that the Cheyenne speech, at any rate, had been reported as given. To the people it did not matter. A touch of solecism makes the whole world kin, and in both cases the sentiments expressed were above reproach.

In May, 1934, a report on Roosevelt's first year of fan mail quoted I. R. T. Smith, executive mail clerk at the White House since 1897: "I have never seen anything like it. I used to be able to get along with two or three assistants. Now I have twenty-two and they are all overworked."[21] At that time, letters averaged 7000 a day including Sunday. After fireside chats the number always rose sharply, up to a maximum of some 48,000 per day. One hundred poems daily, most of them addressed to or celebrating the President, along with dozens of musical compositions in his honor (often with the request that they be played by the Army or the Marine Band), were a not uncommon harvest. A typical poem from a child began:

> The greatest man in all the land
> The leader of our big brave band
> Is President Franklin Roosevelt.

In late September, 1939, when the present writer was permitted to glance through a portion of the White House fan mail, the President's files contained approximately 7,000,000 items. The second term had shown a slight falling-off from the first, as happens invariably when a public man ceases to be a novelty; but from year to year the stream was remarkably steady, running from three to four times the annual volume of letters received by Presidents from Taft to Hoover. Much of the mail has been shipped to the Roosevelt Library at Hyde Park, where it will be open to future students, and much has been routed to other offices such as P. W. A. and W. P. A., but the remainder fills all the filing cases of the White House secretariat. All are answered, except crank letters and certain communications filed in a large case labelled "Criticism." The latter almost invariably are typewritten, on business stationery or embossed letter-paper; whereas considerably more than half the fan mail appears in longhand, and much of it on ruled tablet-paper or sheets torn from composition books.

The President is addressed as "our dear Lifesaver," "our greatest President since George Washington." "Dear Mr. President" is the most frequent salutation; virtually nobody attempts the familiarity of "F. D." or "Franklin," though Henry F. Pringle in 1934 reported seeing a letter from a Midwestern farmer's wife which began—

Dear Frank:
Our neighbor, Pete Smith, loaned us $25 on our team. He says he'll take the mules unless he can come to see me when my husband is away. How can I save the mules?[22]

One suspects humorous intent. Certainly the average petitioner writes in a different tone. "Dear Mr. Roosevelt, you are our Hero; you have fought for us against the Banks," a typical letter begins. A mill worker who lost his job because he joined the union writes to the President about it. A butcher says that a W. P. A. job in his neighborhood is not being done as he thinks the President wanted it. A young housewife tells him that "poor people are being subjected to a series of examinations, at the whim of an unseen bureaucracy," and complains about the maladministration of relief in her town. Another housewife addresses

"Our President, Franklin Roosevelt," to say that her husband, working on a Federal project, never brings his money home, and she would like to know the reason why: "I'm praying to God that this will be answered for me, through you." A migratory worker whose application for relief was denied tells the sequel:

Dear Friend:

I was told to write to you about my case and you would do something. . . . After four days without food I went to the relief commission . . . got no action. . . . I was so hungry I was forced to do something. So I got my landlord's cat and chopped off its head. I buried the head and then skinned and boiled the cat and ate it. . . . The Society for the Prevention of Cruelty to Animals called on me. That seemed kind of funny to me. Please do something.

A Washington boy of fifteen, a runaway stranded in Kansas, asks for a loan to get home: "I'm one of those boys that thinks he knows it all and found out different." On March 12, 1937, the President had to settle an argument between two farm boys of Granton, New York, as to whether he knew how to milk a cow; Mr. Roosevelt's son James replied:

Dear Cecil and Robert:

The President has asked me to answer your letter of March 3 and to tell you he has milked a cow, having learned when a small boy. However, he would like to emphasize that he never claimed to be an expert at it and is considerably out of practice.

A letter from a farmer who says he received a Government check "for not raising pigs" poses a question regarding the best-laid schemes under an economy of scarcity: he built a pen for his sow, but in heat she escaped and has now presented him with the litter he promised not to raise. "Now I do not intend to deceive Uncle Sam as you can see. . . . As wife says, can I be blamed for the secret love life of my sow?"

Many thousands, it seems, feel confident that the President alone can solve their troubles. "Now, Mr. Roosevelt, you read this yourself," a sample letter runs. "Don't leave it up to some secretary." Another correspondent writes a postscript: "One thing I forgot to say in the letter I wrote you last week. Get it out, and put this on the paper right after. . . ." "I'm counting on you for help," is a frequent avowal. "I'll be down in Washington to see you next month some time, and then no doubt we can work this out together." Some write to tell him they *are* better off than before: "a few lines to let you no that I am working now. Sense I rote to you I have went to work." "A poor collored man" assures the President that "the country blooms again." (Another colored man, in Alabama, once called him by long-distance telephone and actually got through to the President.) "Your radio talk filled me with new faith in God and in our dear Country," says one letter, while another, written early in the Administration, praises Roosevelt ardently, and adds: "And God bless dear Mr. Garner too who is doing all he can for the White House." Many letters in 1934 sent him bits of old gold, including a pair of spectacles: "I'm getting too old to read much anyway, and you need the gold."

Often he is thanked for benefits received. "I do not know if Our dear President has anything to do with my troubles but I have been helped quite some, especially today. I have received a blanket, nightie, 8 towels (different kinds), and for my 13 yrs. old girl I got pajamas, panties, and a slip." A "poor man . . . sick for 5 years with Rheumatism" says, "have been blessed by you and the good Lord." On a scrap of yellow paper one reads: "The man you sent found our house all right and we went down to the bank with him and the mortgage can go on for a while longer. . . . I never heard of a President like you, Mr. Roosevelt . . . we are joined with millions of others in praying for you every night." That the President is told so many intimate problems—distressing, pathetic, sordid, and comic by turns—ceases to surprise after one has come upon the statement, uttered scores of times, that "I just seem to know you so well, like I might have known you all my life." A newspaperman who sampled opinion in the West in 1938 recorded the words of "an insurance man, of humble origins": "My mother looks upon the President as some one so immediately concerned with her problems and difficulties that she would not be greatly surprised were he to come to her house some evening and stay to dinner. She almost regards him as one of the family."[23] That the squire of Hyde Park and the Governor of New York, upon his election to the Presidency, had much foresight of the problems and anxieties he would be asked to share with the Forgotten Man, or how as the good neighbor he would become confidant and confessor to unseen millions, is highly improbable. Not since Bryan in 1896, apparently, had so many pens been taken into unaccustomed hands, so many tales of frustration and hope poured out to a national statesman.

To judge by White House files, there are at least three thousand namesakes of the thirty-second President who will burst upon a future generation. Unless, perhaps, some parents will be as fickle as Mr. and Mrs. H. K. Jones of Durant, Mississippi, of whom *The New York Times* told on November 6, 1932. A son born to them during the 1928 campaign was christened Herbert Hoover Jones, but four years later they filed a court petition "desiring to relieve the young man from the chagrin and mortification which he is suffering and will suffer," and requesting that his name be altered to Franklin D. Roosevelt Jones. In 1933 the new President's namesakes included Franklin Delano Blue Eagle Knapinski (who may indeed have suffered some mortification after a Supreme Court decision in 1935), a Franklin Garner Roberts, and triplets at Cave City, Kentucky, called Doris Franklin, Doris Delano, and Dallas Roosevelt. Whether namesakes or not, the most loyal young henchmen of the President seem to have been the numerous children who in 1938 stopped eating "Wheaties" because Boake Carter's broadcasts attacked the man in the White House—a boycott so severe that General Foods took their commentator off the air.

And, as testaments of esteem, uncounted presents have flooded the White House basement since March, 1933. An old seaman, flat on his back in a charity hospital, built an intricate ship's model inside a flat pint whisky bottle, and sent it in, "from one sailor to another." One finds the façade of a cathedral built of cigar-box wood; a chair with Roosevelt's image on the back in encaustic; embroidered portraits of the President, generally in gold thread; an Indian blanket interweaving a detailed likeness of Roosevelt, complete with Phi Beta Kappa key; a huge sword made of bone, inscribed with Roosevelt's name in gold German script; an Armenian rug bearing the President's face; a cowboy hat covered with one hundred autographs from a precinct that had gone solidly for Roosevelt in 1932; a "gray human hair" upon which a Cuban boy had written a message of felicitation on the Fourth of July, 1938, with a microscope for reading the message. There are canes without number, bronzes of Jefferson and equestrian statuettes of Jackson, donkeys, clocks, and desk ornaments—for it is widely known that the President is a lover of gadgets. In the 1936 campaign, during a wild demonstration in formerly staid and Republican Philadelphia, after Roosevelt's car had been filled with flowers, Secret Service men were startled when an excited individual ran past their guard and tosssed his gold watch into the President's lap.

IV

Mr. Roosevelt's second term was not without its ups and downs of popularity. Early in 1937, exultant over his victory before the people, the President proposed to pack the Supreme Court. With far less than his usual political skill, he handled the issue in a spirit of mingled flippancy and evasiveness that shocked many of his friends. Suddenly "the nine old men," who symbolized the Constitution and the fundamental law, aroused a sense of national sympathy and protectiveness. Whether logically or not, the great middle class felt that the President had slapped the Founding Fathers. Polls showed that six out of every ten Americans disapproved of his methods, and that for the first time Roosevelt had squarely collided with public opinion. Academic liberals (of the kind Mr. Roosevelt had called "the 'yes-but'" school) expressed misgivings of his technique as reformer. They wondered if it were another proof of the world-wide drift away from the hard-won ideals of constitutional government, the triumph of nineteenth-century liberalism, back to government by personalities, by supermen and heroes. Even the average citizen seemed to feel that Roosevelt had lacked something in patience and sportsmanship, that his determination to have his own way was a secret motive outweighing the alleged inefficiency of the Court. Many who shared his aims disapproved of his methods. At all events, he could have dealt with his public more frankly.

While the issue was pending, the writer of these lines happened to call upon George Santayana in Rome. Mr. Santayana, no partisan of politics, when asked how he sized up his onetime student in philosophy at Harvard College, smiled reflectively. "Roosevelt," he said, "is not yet a true philosopher. He has never learned that what he wants, and what is good for him, are not always the same thing."

On June 14 the Senate Judiciary Committee crushingly condemned the Court plan, "presented to the Congress in a most intricate form and for reasons that obscured its real purpose . . . a proposal that violates every sacred tradition of American democracy . . . a measure which should be so emphatically rejected that its parallel will never again be presented to the free representatives of the free people of America." The sequel left Roosevelt with a residue of personal bitterness toward his enemies, *i.e.,* those Democrats who had opposed him on this question. In 1938 the purge that failed demonstrated, as a Gallup poll had suggested, the stubborn independence of an electorate in the face of demands for "100 per cent loyalty to Roosevelt." In the interim, also, there had been much unfavorable comment over the Klan affiliations of Roosevelt's new appointee to the Court, Senator Hugo Black. Time and again, jubilant foes of the President announced that his popularity was breaking. Such thinking was wishful, as the President's swing around the nation in the early autumn of 1937 revealed. Reporters noted the cheering thousands, certainly cheering for Roosevelt the man rather than Roosevelt the foe of the Court. At Boise, the late Senator Borah, who had written some of the sternest phrases about "every sacred tradition" into the report of the Judiciary Committee, but who had since returned home and laid his ear to the grass-roots, introduced the visitor as "our great President" while Mr. Roosevelt beamed. A reporter, writing an article called "Roosevelt Rides Again," said that on this visit the President "made the people of the vast rural areas feel that it was them he preferred to be among, and that his presence in Washington arose from necessity rather than desire."[24] Ever skilled in addressing his hearers' interests and making them his own, he chatted of crop reduction benefits, irrigation dams, hydro-electric power rates. And above all was that suave charm which even his bitterest enemies admit. Average men who found fault with aspects of the New Deal were prone to blame his subordinates, saying they had "deceived" the President. Roosevelt the man was undimmed. In his own mind, apparently, Mr. Roosevelt began to rationalize his late painful defeat. Soon, in his collected papers, he would entitle the 1935 volume *The Court Disapproves,* and that for 1936 *The People Approve.* The joint disapproval of 1937 was forgotten, while the thawing liberalism of the Court during the next two years would cause him undoubted satisfaction. It was possible, too, that his decision in 1940 to seek a third term arose from a further wish to test his strength. Statesmanship, solicitude for the New Deal, vanity, and a hunger for power and vindication were perhaps fused, in a baffling complex, within the most intricate mind exercising itself upon modern American politics.

"Our President is the greatest American since Lincoln," a wheat farmer in the Pacific Northwest told Richard L. Neuberger in 1938. "Who else would take the abuse he takes and still go down the line for the people in the face of it?" That journalist, sampling the opinion of ranchers, lumberjacks, electricians, brakemen, salmon fishermen, about Mr. Roosevelt, found an overwhelming agreement that Roosevelt had made his mistakes; had sponsored good laws that were badly drawn, in respect for example to social security; had been unduly led astray by Leftists seeking to discourage business enterprise, and had been too tender in handling agitators like Harry Bridges—but, nevertheless, that he was the people's sincerest friend. "Since Lincoln," many added. Hatred of Roosevelt by the rich, often unreasoning and invariably selfish, had endeared him to the common people no less than had his friendly voice and his experiments in reform. Hatred invariably makes heroes, if not martyrs. "Our President is for the little fellow, and I'll string along with him," they often said. He was "our President." A conservative newspaper editor growled: "That 'our President' stuff is something new in politics. Some of the farmers and other people I know must think Mr. Roosevelt belongs exclusively to them—and maybe they're right."[25]

In August, 1938, a *Fortune* survey submitted the statement that ten years from now "Roosevelt will be regarded as a national hero." True, answered 41.9 per cent; while 35.6 per cent disagreed, and the rest had not made up their minds. But when asked whether they hoped Roosevelt would become a hero, about 50 per cent replied affirmatively, showing that hope was stronger than assurance; and only 21.7 per cent hoped not. As one might expect, more of the poor than of the rich thought he would be remembered as a hero, more in the Southwest than in the Northeast. Polls found repeatedly that he was more popular with youth than with their elders. In 1937 the freshmen of Princeton, a rich man's university, had given Chief Justice Hughes 70 votes as "greatest living American," to 56 votes for Roosevelt, 30 for Ford, and Lindbergh in fourth place. But in 1938 another generation of Princeton freshmen, along with the seniors of Hunter College, chose Roosevelt as "the greatest living man." That Roosevelt himself, with keen ambitions and a marked historical sense, was not indifferent to the verdict of posterity one could well believe. The Franklin D. Roosevelt Library at Hyde Park, which he had created in the midst of his second term as a permanent repository for the papers of his public life, revealed a concern, such as no other American leader had had, to tell his story to posterity. His ultimate standing would test the truth of an interesting but dubious suggestion made in 1928 by William E. Woodward, in a life of General Grant: that public opinion in America is made by the upper classes.

In the present year of grace there are many legendary Roosevelts. There were many Lincolns in 1865: time has sifted them to only two, the real, dimly discovered in his papers and in the pages of Herndon, and the myth, in the Valhalla of our national symbols. With Franklin D. Roosevelt, as with Woodrow Wilson, the real man is not yet apparent through a thicket of praise and blame. Mythical Roosevelts, mirrored in books, newspaper articles, and talk ranging from Workers' Alliance meetings to Union League Clubs, are easy enough to discover. One of them may be the real Roosevelt, or else he may be a composite of them all:

Roosevelt is a superman of social miracles. With ripe wisdom, far-seeing eyes, and a heart bleeding for those who labor and are heavy-laden, he works incessantly to build a more glorious America. The bold dragons of finance have discovered in him their St. George; the poor have found in him a gentle St. Francis. On Roosevelt's birthday in 1934, a sports-artist on *The New York Journal,* Burris Jenkins, Jr., drew him as "The Champion"—a great shadowy face furrowed with lines of suffering, lit with the soft radiance of a smile, promising hope and good cheer, shining through the background of a tenement home or share-cropper's hut, while the ragged family gather about a little birth-day cake with its single candle and toast him in a cup of cold water. Some believe that at heart he is a very sad man, disillusioned by the greed and selfishness of this possessive world, while outwardly he re-mains serene and cheerful, trying to do his duty with profound humility before God. Marquis Childs in *The Survey Graphic* last year described this concept of Roosevelt. This picture owes something to Lincoln lore, to the man of sorrows, with "time for all who need me." He is the great emancipator, striking off economic shackles, remoulding the Union in terms of social justice. Like Lincoln, he has been called a deeply religious man. Among present souvenirs in the White House is the replica of a bronze plaque: "In commemoration of Roosevelt's visit at a church on the way to his Inauguration 1933—Written at Natick Massachusetts July Anno Domini 1936—William McCarthy." It bears a bas-relief of Franklin D. Roosevelt, as if bowed in prayer, while above are two small pictures of George Washington, "Valley Forge 1778," and of Abraham Lincoln, "Gettysburg 1863." Below we read:

> This is the story of Franklin
> Whom men shall acclaim some day
> In meeting his nation's affliction
> He stopped for a moment to pray.

As a matter of record, Mr. Roosevelt attends church less regularly than most of our Presidents have done. Nominally he is an Episcopalian: a poll in 1936 among religious groups, however, found that his popularity was lowest with Episcopalians (58.4 per cent), Christian Scientists (52.5 per cent), and Presbyterians (52.3 per cent), and highest among Bap-tists (79.2 per cent).[26] In September, 1935, he sent out a circular letter, under his signature or its facsimile, to thousands of clergymen, asking them to write him of conditions in the nation, and soliciting their ad-vice on how "our government can better serve our people." Newspapers quickly discovered that this letter was almost identical (some sentences *verbatim*) with a letter that Governor LaFollette had sent to the clergy of Wisconsin the previous March. Under the attendant publicity, Roosevelt was called a flatterer and plagiarist by his critics, and by way of answering his circular a good many preachers wrote replies that were far from complimentary. A good political stroke had miscarried.

"In such a make-up," Emil Ludwig wrote of the President, "art and philosophy and religion have nothing to do; in a certain sense there is no room for them amid such stormy power of action and joy of life. When as a young father he was asked by his wife whether the children ought not to go to church, he answered: 'I really never thought about it. It is just as well not to think about things like that too much.' "[27] Ludwig, in this semi-official biography, interprets Roosevelt as "a study in fortune and power." He creates a hero of superabundant vitality, mental energy, and cheer. Roosevelt is both masterful and wise, but worldly. Ludwig asserts that "he writes his speeches himself," and that he is the strongest statesman of the modern world. He laughs at the "legend that a man sacrifices himself in office in order to carry a burden . . . power is pleasurable." He does not propose to share his goods with the poor, in a Tolstoyan sense, but addresses himself to the reform of principles in our economic structure. As for millionaires, he frankly prefers their company and the luxury of their yachts, to association with the poor and illiterate; "he does not hate [rich men], he only wants to shear them." At bottom, Roosevelt is a sincere man, a man of good will:

When the Negro comes into the spacious, homey bedroom to waken him, a man who is at peace with himself opens his eyes, to greet the morning and the park across the windows. And if it is raining he smiles happily and thinks what a pleasant sound the rain makes on the panes.[28]

There are other comradely touches: he is jolly, gay, fond of jokes and witticisms, a lover of stamp albums and naval prints. His laugh rings richly through the White House. He is a man's man, loving comfort and old clothes: "his outraged sons removed from his wardrobe an old suit which he inherited from his grandfather and still wore as President." (One hopes that this was not the paternal grandfather, Isaac Roosevelt, of the class of 1808 at Princeton; a more plausible rumor, often repeated, says that as Governor, F. D. R. had loafed about Hyde Park in one of his father's old suits until young James Roosevelt hid it. It might also be noted that in February, 1937, the Merchant Tailors' Designers Association picked Mr. Roosevelt as "the best-dressed American," outranking Fred Astaire and Lucius Beebe, commenting that he was the only well-dressed President in the past twenty years, the only one "whose formal clothes have not looked moth-eaten." Here, at least, he was no Lincoln.)

There are other Roosevelts. One is essentially a man of action, no deep thinker. An optimist and pragmatist, confident in his own judgment, he does the best he can and then refuses to worry. Physically he is a vigorous animal who works, relaxes, sleeps, and laughs readily. He does not vex himself with dark thoughts and hesitations. This evidently is the Roosevelt of the President's friend and biographer, Ernest K. Lindley. Mr. Roosevelt is a charming, witty, seemingly frank man—who delights in practical jokes and comic valentines, keeping his associates busy and happy with a buoyant *esprit de corps*. He is the answer to a journalist's prayer. Knowing that reporters need "stories" he does his best for the "boys." He has cut through such official subterfuges as "the White House spokesman" of the Coolidge era and the written questions and answers demanded by the suspicious Hoover. His press conferences are the best drama in Washington, pointed by a jaunty cigarette in its holder, an engaging grin and a sly malice pitched somewhere between Bernard Shaw and Noel Coward. Newspapermen, to whom charm is an old story, still find themselves fascinated by him—and, in spite of their editors, keep on presenting him to the country in a good light. He can no more help making news than an oyster can resist secreting a pearl, especially under irritation. He is more sensitive to personal criticism than to criticism of his policies (here quite the reverse of Lincoln, and more like Jackson). In fact, he thinks of issues in terms of personalities rather than of logic, and sees problems as differences of opinion to be settled rather than as principles to be reconciled. He dislikes hand-to-hand fighting and all unpleasantness (including the thought of poverty in the world), but is fond of shadow-boxing. Mr. Roosevelt likes men, almost all of them, but at the thought of vague groups he can wax militant. To argue with a single adversary is as unpleasant to him as is the firing of a subordinate: hence he is prone to surround himself with competent yes-men. He does not like to be drawn into debate. H. G. Wells found him "a ganglion for reception, expression, transmission, combination and realization," a rare seismograph for the social tremors of his time. Wells found him "unblinkered," a man of singularly open mind (Roosevelt's enemies have quoted Shaw's saying, about "a mind so open there is nothing left but a draft"). In sum, he is a man of real courage, a kindly liberal with the best intentions—but not farsightedly sure of his course, plan, or policy. He trusts in the future and in his own resourcefulness. As the late Speaker Rainey said, early in the New Deal, "We're on our way, but we don't know where we're going."

Mr. Roosevelt has sometimes been called "the smartest politician who ever became President"; Arthur Krock in 1936 termed him "the best showman the White House has lodged." One legendary Roosevelt is a brilliantly superficial man, making an often discordant mosaic out of others' ideas and contriving to hold it together by sheer political genius. He failed to reform the banking system in 1933, when he held it in the hollow of his hand, because he didn't know enough, or perhaps because he wasn't interested in permanence but only in the selfhood of popularity. He basks in the glow that his charm produces in others: he lives before the glass of his socially mirrored self. He is the prima donna of American politics. Even his mother has written that "Franklin never has been able to resist an opportunity of going anywhere on a destroyer."[29] So intent is he upon appearing well before others, of winning their suffrage, that he promises much and performs little. Of Franklin Roosevelt, as of an earlier statesman, it has been said that "when his friends set out to follow him, they met him coming back." This, according to Mr. Raymond Moley, is the true Roosevelt. He is accessible to crackpot schemers, and kindles quickly at their ideas; but, luckily, the next set of schemers nullifies the first. He is stronger on tactics than theory, on learning from others than in creating or thinking; he is at his best in improvising, under a controlled atmosphere of crisis. He has hunches rather than plans. But essentially he is a pleasant, garrulous man much too haphazard to be a statesman. According to these memoirs of his first brain-truster, Mr. Roosevelt's genius, in fact, departed with Mr. Moley.

There are still other Roosevelts. There is the charming ineffectual idler, a weakling of mind and body, seen by Walter Lippmann in 1932; and the ruthless dictator, malign and strangling in his hold, foretold by the late Ogden Mills in 1934 and feared by many old-guard Republicans in 1936 and 1940. At times, the latter is indistinguishable from "the paranoic in the White House." His most extreme enemies say, as they had whispered of Wilson, that a madman is at the helm of state.

In 1939–40 Roosevelt "the war-monger" emerged, the bogey of isolationists. They sneered at his vision of submarines off the Atlantic coast, which happened to coincide with the movement to repeal our Neutrality Act. Through the next twelvemonth, his sponsorship of preparedness and conscription alarmed them. Other critics blamed him for lack of preparedness, shutting their eyes to the fact that he had led rather than lagged behind public sentiment for at least four years. In general, however, Mr. Roosevelt's foreign policy and his trenchant stand for democracies abroad won him fresh applause. For the conservative upper classes, sharing his admiration for the British Empire and having, in international affairs, a longer range of vision than other economic groups, at last had something in common with the President. By and large, the more articulate Americans felt proud of their leader as he faced toward Europe. The more grudging said, "It took a new world war to save his face," with a certain awe contemplating the "Roosevelt luck."

That the European crisis, like the domestic crisis of 1933, brought out the best in Roosevelt and also heightened his prestige, impartial observers admitted freely. Likewise, under the new tension, the Republicans were compelled to match him with an opponent who promised a closer race than Hoover and Landon had given him. The nomination of Wendell Willkie, in turn, assured the recall of Roosevelt, as "the only man who could beat him." The stage-management of the third nomination, at Chicago in July, 1940, was less happy than Roosevelt's previous accolades as candidate. Unquestionably the choice of his party, as the Gallup poll revealed, the President entrusted his case to lieutenants who overplayed the scene: "the Voice of the People" crying into the microphones was identified, by the Republican press, as belonging to the local commissioner of sewers, a Kelly-Nash man. Long ago, in the days of his political apprenticeship, Mr. Roosevelt had said: "No one ever willingly gives up public life—no one who has tasted it."[30] So his fifth cousin had felt, in 1912. Both Roosevelts were born for public life, and stood ready to acquiesce in their destiny.

In 1940 the Champion met a younger campaigner, an "amateur" who had never held public office—a vigorous, earnest, intelligent Hoosier with a somewhat heavy touch. Mr. Willkie's progressive leanings, in endorsing much of the New Deal while claiming he could have done the job with less waste and friction, helped to show how far political thought had swung from the old river-bed of the 1920's. He began well, in announcing on the eve of nomination that his only campaign management was "under his hat." Americans like the amateur attitude, as we have seen many times; and samplers of opinion, in midsummer 1940, found a tide of approval running in his favor. But a few weeks later Mr. Willkie began to make the mistake of playing ball with the old guard—holding council with Hoover and Landon, being photographed with faces that the public had long tired of, and for the sake of Western votes buttering up Senator Hiram Johnson. Soon his bandwagon attracted the isolationists and John L. Lewis. Yet Mr. Willkie's early approval of conscription, and of the fullest aid to Britain and China, showed real flashes of courage in his daring to agree with the President rather than pander to anti-Administration sentiment as such. He thus curbed some of the bitterness latent in this campaign. Yet his campaign united the avowed political innocence of the Children's Crusade with the frank affluence of the Field of the Cloth of Gold. The President, winning by a popular majority of nearly five million, easily carried the industrial areas, all large cities save Cincinnati, the South and the Far West. In some ways the fact seemed remarkable. If Mr. Willkie was clumsy where Mr. Roosevelt was smooth, assuredly the Republican campaign had been waged as briskly and professionally as the Democratic campaign through the country at large had seemed haphazard. Just after the election, Mr. Harold Ickes, a master of invidious facts, pointed out that Roosevelt "was supported by less than 23% of our daily press." In view of the enormous resources of publicity, billboard advertising, and radio time, and the overwhelming support of industrialists and businessmen, in favor of the Republican candidate, the average Roosevelt fan might have reflected with satisfaction that all the mobilized powers of super-salesmanship—whose profession it was to sell automobiles and tooth-paste to one hundred million Americans—could not move him to accept a substitute.

"Safe on Third," proclaimed a banner in the torchlight parade of Hyde Park neighbors, on election night. The result was an unparalleled tribute to an American hero. That is, of course, as a *fait accompli*. For Washington and Jefferson certainly could have had a third term; almost as surely, Old Hickory could have won it in 1836. Among later Democratic liberals, Cleveland (who gained his second term precariously, after defeat) probably would have failed; Wilson undoubtedly would have come to grief in 1920. A National Press Club dinner on November 9, 1940, displayed a cartoon facing the President's plate: it showed him clutching a loving-cup in the shape of the United States, with the caption: "I won it three times—don't I get to keep it now?" Others saw that democracy had once more vindicated itself, as in the past, by finding its great man in the hour of crisis. That Mr. Roosevelt, under the lowering skies of the future, had a solemn and continuing debt to pay to the American people, who had voiced their faith in him by this unmatched tribute, was clear to all.

CHAPTER EIGHTEEN

HOW AMERICANS CHOOSE THEIR HEROES

*Times of heroism are generally times of terror, but the
day never shines in which this element may not work.
. . . But whoso is heroic will always find crises to try
his edge.*—RALPH WALDO EMERSON, "Heroism."

I

ANY roll-call of America's heroes invites one last question.
Whom do Americans most admire? What are the signs
by which they may be known? No doubt they stand for
qualities that seem precious for the group good. Yet
scores of worthies, men of high intellect and character,
have missed the magic ranks of those—in uniform and buckskin, on
horseback or trudging afoot or spanning the sky, at statesman's desk
or inventor's work-bench—whom Everyman takes as his heroes.

One is struck by a few exclusions, of sex and type and profession,
from the calendar of greatest Americans. Women have had a curiously
small share in the major hero-worship of America—a land which most
Europeans believe is a matriarchy. (Although women are among the
most ardent hero-worshippers, as all mothers and some wives know,
the cynical may suggest that no woman is ever a heroine to any other
woman.) The United States has had no Joan of Arc, Elizabeth of

England, St. Catherine of Siena, Cleopatra or Semiramis. Even Florence Nightingale appeals to American cinema and fiction more than the equally remarkable Clara Barton. Our history has had its heroic women. But Anne Hutchinson, who had more charity and good sense than the Puritan Fathers, does not match them in symbolic appeal. And the pioneer woman, who with a child at her breast and rifle in her hand stands in bronze in many a municipal park, is as anonymous as the Magna Mater of ancient mythology. Molly Pitcher carried water to the soldiers at Monmouth and manned the cannon of her dead husband; she has inspired the modest fame of a monument at Carlisle, Pennsylvania, the naming of a Pullman car, and the organization in 1940 of "the Molly Pitcher Rifle Legion" to pick off descending parachutists on our soil. In 1782 Betty Zane bore a keg of powder in her arms, under a fusillade of Indian arrows, to the stockade of Fort Henry; her kinsman Zane Grey wrote his first novel about her. These women became heroic by imitation of the stronger sex. Betsy Ross—whose present namesakes seem to run to tea-rooms—is much better known today than she was in her own time. Not until 1870 did her grandson William Canby publish a family tradition, now judged to be doubtful, that she made the first Stars-and-Stripes. Barbara Frietchie, immortalized by Whittier, also fades into heroic fiction. More brilliant women—Mercy Warren, Abigail Adams, Lucretia Mott, Mary Lyon, Maria Mitchell, Alice Freeman Palmer—have had smaller fame than these. None can truly be called the idol of millions. In our own time the greatest popular heroine without doubt has been Helen Keller, who typifies upon a high plane the American success story. Yet no woman has been hailed with the admiration given to Washington and Lincoln and Lee, or even Daniel Boone and Edison and Lindbergh. A tissue of causes—biological, economic, political—will occur to all. The most basic reason is simple. Joan of Arc, Elizabeth, "the queens and cave-women of ancient earth," were not, in the stricter sense, ladies. Whereas, during the greater span of our national life— that span which saw the creation of Little Eva, Elsie Dinsmore, and Pollyanna to match the typical American boy of Mark Twain and Howells and Tarkington—the dominant ideal has been the perfect lady. Some say that times are changing.

Certain professions have yielded few national idols. The artist, admired so keenly by another business civilization, the Renaissance, has not met with much popular honor in America. Old Masters have been prized, thanks to the timidity of American culture, more than have living artists. National traditions like those of Dante and Michel-angelo, and national shrines like Weimar and Bayreuth and Stratford, are unknown with us. For too many generations, art meant Europe. No American writer has received such homage as did Voltaire in Paris in 1778, when he was crowned with laurel in his box at the theatre, while people of quality disguised themselves as tavern servants to gain the privilege of bringing him a bottle of wine or smoothing his pillow. Edgar Allan Poe—who wrote, "I love fame . . . I would have incense arise in my honor from every hamlet"—died in poverty, in delirium, in a Baltimore hospital. Longfellow, as the voice of sen-timent, enjoyed a cool decorous popularity. Mark Twain, the voice of comedy, whom Howells called "sole, incomparable, the Lincoln of our literature," was one of the most picturesque Americans of his time and reporters followed him everywhere. But few understood his art, and those who did were often troubled by the depths of irony and darkness: in truth it was Mark Twain's personality, his white suit and flowing hair, rather than his literature, that made him known to millions. Later, Will Rogers, with more good humor and less of irony and art, came to fill the old bill of crackerbox philosopher, and join it with that of matinée star. But the pure artist in America has had much harder sledding. Emerson was best known to the crowd as a lyceum lecturer; Melville and Hawthorne drudged obscurely in customs houses; Walt Whitman in 1940 at last won the modest popular recognition of a commemorative postage-stamp. Generations which have sung the songs of Stephen Foster know or care little about the man. To the man in the street, Sargent and Whistler are merely names —though the latter is vaguely linked with that sentiment fostered each May by florists and confectioners.

The scholar, as he was acclaimed in the day of Erasmus and Scaliger or even in Germany before the first Great War, as a type has never kindled American imagination. And this in spite of our passion for literacy and higher education. Van Wyck Brooks has seen, in the splitting of Puritanism in the eighteenth century, a division of per-sonality into two directions unknown to the earlier day when the man of action had been also the man of God. Now one was the highbrow, the man of pure cold intelligence or holiness, typified by Jonathan Edwards, or else the lowbrow, the materialist or business man follow-ing the lodestar of "policy," represented by Benjamin Franklin. Thanks to Franklin's charm, humanity, and international fame, and to the climate of enterprise that came after him, the latter type came to be admired and cherished more than the former. He seemed a little more "American." The highbrow in politics, like John Taylor of Caroline and John C. Calhoun, has never been able to hold a candle to the Jacksons and Lincolns. Lord Bryce in his day observed that "the ordinary American voter . . . does not value, because he sees no need for, originality or profundity, a fine culture or a wide knowledge." An unexpressed American belief holds that wisdom must be practical, that it is best built not upon elaborate philosophies but on a few homely principles of common sense, buttressed with the lore of proverb and fable. It is simple, earth-born. Lincoln's statesmanship walked in the garb of "good stories" and pithy sayings, not intellectual profundities. More recently, "the brain trust" was unpopular. The scholar lies under the same prejudice as the highbrow. He has enjoyed a certain burlesque fame—as the Ichabod Crane of our literature, or the absent-minded professor of the comics—but his height is hardly heroic. The average American is prone to believe that nobody becomes a teacher who can succeed at any other trade. The leadership of Woodrow Wilson was surprising, like the more recent legendary fame of Albert Einstein (which owed much to the repeated newspaper announcement that "only twelve men in the world understood him"). At one point, Big Business smiled upon the scholar, as it endowed universities and enjoyed the sensation of multiplying the amount of knowledge in the world. But since then the axe of taxation has fallen, and Messrs. Tugwell, Warren, and Thurman Arnold have helped to breed a new suspicion of college dons. Sometimes, to the impartial, it seems that the American public has been shabbily neglectful of its great men when they happened to be academics: on August 23, 1926, for example, Doctor Charles W. Eliot was given a dozen words of obituary notice by the popular press while the death of Valentino swept the headlines. But as for the type in general, much fault lies with the scholars themselves. About one of them, Emily Dickinson wrote shrewdly: "He has the facts, but not the phosphorescence of learning."

The saint, in the Middle Ages, rivalled the soldier-king for supreme honors as hero; even modern France in St. Thérèse of Lisieux has given the world a holy legend of great power. But the United States has not had a single individual to be canonized by the Catholic Chuch, and the whole Western Hemisphere only three. The Protestant faith among us can boast neither a Luther nor a Calvin. The Western world is diverse in its beliefs and skepticisms; contemplative quiet is rare;

and the heroic age of theology passed before our nation began. A recent American essayist has called the saint "a tenth-rate sort of man." Even the clergyman as a type lacks the dignity given him in England under an established church. It was not always so. To the Puritans —who had few heroes because their accent on human frailty left only God as the ultimate hero—the holy man enjoyed the highest recognition among his fellows. The parson was the *person* of his village. Scholars of divinity were the models of prestige. Their pulpits were aloft and away from the congregation, they walked the earth with a certain majesty of port, and it was believed that comets or blood-red sunsets often appeared when they lay dying. But time and the changes in American thought have dealt rudely with them: the Mathers are popularly remembered for witch-hunting, and Edwards for his hell-fire sermons. More to the current taste is Roger Williams, whose most admiring biographer is a Jew, Oscar Straus. As a believer, not in "religious toleration"—with its implied snobbery—but in pure freedom of conscience, and as the planner of Rhode Island who tried to prevent exploitation of the land, Roger Williams is our nearest approach to the holy man as Protestant hero. His halo, unlike that of St. Augustine or St. Francis, is secular and negative. The American saint is apt to be a heretic. His vows, at best, are those of a monasticism like Thoreau's practising poverty, chastity, and civil disobedience beside Walden Pond. As still another paradox, our dynamic religious leaders who reached thousands or millions—Brigham Young, Henry Ward Beecher, Dwight L. Moody, Billy Sunday, Mrs. Eddy, and the cultists that modern California has spawned with the fecundity of a salmon—have been organizers, orators, miracle workers, but not in any traditional sense saints.

No physician, for his work in medicine, has ever been elected to the Hall of Fame in New York City. No doctor has ever become a first-class hero to the American people. Walter Reed and William Gorgas as victors over yellow fever, Osler as a brilliant adopted son, Harvey Cushing as the pioneer of brain surgery, and among the older generation even Oliver Wendell Holmes as the innovator of asepsis to check puerperal fever—these men have received less personal adoration than Lindbergh or Jack Dempsey or Babe Ruth. At the close of the World War *The Ladies' Home Journal* printed an article under the patronizing title, "The Returning Doctor: He can now become one of the most potent assets of American life." The most eloquent apprevication of the modern doctor, describing him as "the flower of our civilization," was written not by an American but by a Briton, Robert Louis Stevenson—in dedicating his *Underwoods* to Doctor Willey of San Francisco, as Stevenson left for Saranac to put himself in the hands of an even greater American healer, Trudeau, "the beloved physician" of that day. Yet as a nation we make a fetish of health and sanitation, give our front-page newspaper headlines to discoveries in medicine, and eagerly buy books about international surgeons or horse-and-buggy doctors. Several reasons may be offered for our neglect of the individual doctor as hero: The physician, like the scientist, usually shuns publicity in proportion to his greatness; if he lacks modesty, the American Medical Association is likely to supply it. His discoveries come to be better known than the discoverer —witness the millions who have heard about insulin to the thousands who know something of Banting and Best. And finally, the routine of healing seldom offers the sensational possibilities of a war or a piece of statesmanship or even a world's series; while the trivial often makes better news than the scientifically valuable. The doctor is a man who does his best work quietly.

The law has trained more American heroes and leaders than has any other profession. Jefferson, Andrew Jackson, Daniel Webster, Calhoun, Clay, Lincoln, Cleveland, Bryan, the Roosevelts, and many lesser men show the natural affinity, in a democratic state, between law and politics. (In the day of John Marshall's America, De Tocqueville keenly noted that "the profession of the law in the United States serves to counterpoise the Democracy.") But the lawyer *qua* lawyer, in America as elsewhere, has never been able to match the soldier or explorer as an inevitable hero type. In 1734 Poor Richard impudently observed, "Lawyers, preachers, and tomtit's eggs, there are more of them hatched than come to perfection." In colonial times lawyers were generally unpopular. The plain man thought of them as quibblers and trouble-makers. The rising tide of the Revolution swept them into better standing. In the town meetings of New England and the burgesses of Virginia, lawyers took the patriotic leadership. Keen-witted but unprosperous men bred to argument and oratory, like John and Sam Adams and Patrick Henry, quickly became the firebrands of rebellion. As the colonies settled down and became a nation, lawyers became statesmen. The analytic, contentious genius of America—the nay-sayers whom Emerson loved, poised between abstract logic and practicality—took naturally to the bar. Certain moulds appeared: the great constitutional lawyer of New England, the Southern orator with white stock and flowing hair, the frontier attorney with black string tie and long coattails, and later the railroad and corporation lawyer. Today specialization has destroyed the old spell-binding glamor of the bar, while popular hero-worship—during the gangster era—passed to a new type, the crusading district attorney. The isolation of the Supreme Court, along with its collective function, hampers popular hero-worship of its individual members. The Court, rather than its justices, is a great American symbol. Yet, by a curious paradox, the early idols of the Court, men like Marshall and Taney, were noted conservatives; whereas in the twentieth century, the lion's share of glory has gone to liberals like Oliver Wendell Holmes and Cardozo. Holmes—who may be one of the great American memories of the future, if democracy survives—took his seat on the Bench in 1902 in much the same spirit he had faced the bullets at Antietam forty years before. Bidding good-bye to a group of Massachusetts friends he said quietly: "To have a chance to do one's share in shaping the laws of the whole country spreads over one the hush that one used to feel when one was waiting the beginning of a battle. . . . We will not falter. We will not fail. We will reach the earthworks if we live, and if we fail we will leave our spirit in those who follow, and they will not turn back. All is ready. Bugler, blow the charge." Such, in any calling, is the heroic temper that always stirs some response from the depths of American idealism. Its comparative rarity in the profession of law is perhaps the chief reason why the lawyer, as such, has remained a pattern of prestige rather than a hero.

II

The sort of man whom Americans admire, trust, and are willing to follow can be sketched with a few lines. East and west, north and south, his portrait is familiar. At the basic level he must be self-respecting, decent, honorable, with a sense of fair play; no Machiavelli nor Mussolini need apply. He must be firm and self-confident in leadership: Davy Crockett's "Be always sure you're right, then go ahead!" is approved American doctrine, whether in the headstrong and cocksure types we sometimes follow, like Old Hickory and Theodore Roosevelt, or in the great characters of our imagination like Paul Bunyan and Huckleberry Finn. Mother wit and resourcefulness we love. But a reputation for "genius" is unnecessary and may do the hero harm. Brilliantly clever men like Alexander Hamilton and John

Randolph of Roanoke, and pure intellectuals like John Quincy Adams (by the guess of educators given the highest I. Q., 165, of all Americans in the Hall of Fame), are not major idols. An able man must not glory in his cleverness. By our standards one is sometimes allowed to "put over a fast one"—Benjamin Franklin and Abraham Lincoln did, repeatedly—but he must not appear to relish the coup for its own sake. Art must conceal art. Jefferson understood this restraint just a little better than does his disciple Franklin Roosevelt. A clodhopper politician like Huey Long, boasting "There are not many people in the United States who are smarter than I am, and none in Louisiana," did not understand it at all. Long's scornful assertion that he could buy votes in his Legislature "like sacks of potatoes," to the country at large was equally bad politics. Uncle Sam allows his favorites to be shrewd in a good cause, but there must be no avowal of cynicism in principle. (In modern movies, the hero may pull a fast one for the sake of his mother, or his girl friend, or some worthy ideal, but not for himself.) The backwoods always has a certain admiration for rustic rascality, and the metropolis loves a flippant wisecrack— but in America at large there is a pretty strong prejudice against the wise guy.

Vanity or personal arrogance in any form is taboo. The dandy in public life—accepted more tolerantly in the England of Disraeli and Lord Curzon—is disliked by Americans. Meriwether Lewis, a great explorer of the West, was handicapped by the nickname of "The Sublime Dandy" and his manners of a Beau Nash. William Pinkney, one of the most brilliant lawyers of a century ago, was ridiculed because of his fawn-colored gloves and corsets, and the vanity that led him to begin a speech all over again when he saw ladies enter the visitors' gallery of the Supreme Court. Effeminacy is fatal. Martin Van Buren failed of reelection in 1840 after the public had grown tired of his lace-tipped cravats and morocco shoes, and a ribald Whig politician had exposed his use of a lotion called "Essence of Victoria." In the West, the dude was a traditional villain. (Ironically, in 1860 Lincoln's campaign manager worked hard to get him photographed in a boiled shirt with pearl studs, to make a better impression in the East.) The arrogance of caste is equally deadly in American hero-worship. Hancock, Jay, Gouverneur Morris were snobs who never won the sway, with even a seasoning of popular admiration, that some Tory statesmen have enjoyed in England. The public can never forget that Hamilton once exclaimed, "Your people, sir, is a great beast!"

(These words, quoted in the second decade of this century in school-texts on American history by William B. Guitteau, McLaughlin and Van Tyne, and Albert Bushnell Hart, were omitted after protests from school boards and patrons, from subsequent editions in the 1920's, when the Hamiltonian philosophy was in favor during the era of Republican prosperity.) Harding paid Hamilton the dubious compliment of saying, in 1921, "No man's life ever gave me greater inspiration than Hamilton's"; and bankers have often praised the first Secretary of the Treasury. But the people at large have repaid his scorn with neglect. Even Daniel Webster—for all his adoration in New England and among the propertied classes—has failed, for like reasons, to make the upper rungs of hero-worship. All else favored him: a head so noble that it was often said "no man could be as great as Webster looked," a record of success from barefoot boy on a New Hampshire farm to the United States Senate and Cabinet, a superb voice that made the blood pound in men's temples. But he was known as "the pensioner of Wall Street," who spent his days so exclusively around mahogany tables in clubs and directors' rooms—where the smoke of Havana cigars hung blue, and "mountain dew" Scotch regaled his fine palate—that in the end he became not the idol of the People but of the Best People. There are apparent exceptions. The rich man's friend is sometimes elected President—as in the days of McKinley, Harding, and Coolidge—when the voters look upon themselves as potential rich men, but his popularity strikes no roots in the substratum of affection and legend.

Within limits, the mores of the hero may vary with his times. Emerson, living in the day of Old Hickory, Clay, and Webster, remarked that to the great man, "doing for the people what they wish done and cannot do, of course everything will be permitted and pardoned —gaming, drinking, fighting, luxury . . . everything short of infamous crime will pass." Hadn't Jackson run off with another man's wife? Didn't he and Clay fight duels and bet on race-horses? Weren't Clay and Webster notoriously heavy drinkers—even though Webster was said to concede enough to appearances on the platform to refresh himself with white brandy out of a water-glass? Emerson's conclusion was probably too sweeping: in the first place he forgot that the capital of Puritanism had already moved from New England into insular America, and secondly he failed to reckon with the merely regional popularity of Clay and Webster which even then was fading. Only Jackson endured, a greater democrat as well as a man of higher personal integrity. The hero of a democracy—unlike the Stuarts, Bourbons, and Napoleons of the Old World—cannot invite public opinion to go to hell. He must pay tribute to conformity. Through most of our cultural history, for the average man sex and religion have been life's two most serious subjects, and irregularity even in the mighty leader must not go too far. Aaron Burr's "one hundred bastards" belong to the legend of villainy, along with Thaddeus Stevens's alleged mistresses white and black; while Tom Paine's agnostic mockery made him in spite of his great patriotic services an object of folk hate. As for the hero, debunkery by sensational writers has usually addressed itself to secret nips at the bottle, failure to attend church, or flirtation with a neighbor's wife—rather than to matters of rightful public concern, like soundness of military strategy, foresight, or statesmanly wisdom. The great man who wins acceptance as a hero will find his vagaries and skepticisms trimmed down by convention. Nevertheless, it is surprising how few of the American great, in comparison with those of the Old World, have cultivated lush private lives, though their individual views on religion have often shown more independence than orthodoxy. To a man's man, the sturdy profanity of Washington and Old Hickory, like the earthy jokes of Franklin and Lincoln, will be forgiven and, in the main, forgotten. Fundamentally the hero is required to be chaste, loyal, honest, humble before duty and before God. He is apt to have a dash of Puritan conscience, but the beauty of holiness is no more expected than is a sense of poetry.

The people's choice of heroes for America has been prevailingly sound; our major favorites are those any nation might be proud of. They go far toward vindicating the whole democratic theory of careers open to talents. We believe that character is more important than brains. Hard work, tenacity, enterprise, and firmness in the face of odds are the qualities that Americans most admire, rather than originality or eloquence of tongue and pen.

The hero must be a man of good will and also a good neighbor, preferably something of a joiner. Of the solitudes and lonely isolations of a great man like Lincoln the public has little conception. It likes to think of its idol as simple in greatness. Manliness, forthright manners, and salty speech are approved. Love of the soil, of dogs and horses and manual hobbies and fishing, is better understood than absorption in art, literature, and music. (The public distrusts Presidents who are photographed fishing in their store clothes.) The hero must not lose

486 THE HERO IN AMERICA

touch with his birthplace and origins, however humble; the atmosphere of small towns and front-porch campaigns, cultivated by so
many candidates for President, pays tribute to this demand. "I really
believe there are more attempts at flattering the farmers than any
other class," Lincoln as candidate for President remarked at the
Wisconsin State Fair, "the reason for which I cannot perceive, unless
it be that they cast more votes than any other." Also, the touch of
versatility and homely skill is applauded in a hero. Thomas Jefferson
is remembered less as the eighteenth-century virtuoso than as an
inventor of gadgets from which he plainly got a great deal of fun.
"Tinkering" is American. European lads—like Henrich Steffens growing up in Denmark, and Michael Pupin in a Serbian village—have
testified to the fascination that Franklin, "wiser than all the wise men
of Idvor," held for them. The hero must do things better than the
common folk, but his achievements (unlike those of the artist, philosopher, and pure scientist) must lie open to everyman's comprehen-
sion. It is well, too, that the labels of the hero conform to those of the
group, so that identification between him and the majority can more
easily be made: for example, all of our major idols have been both
Anglo-Saxon and Protestant.

Bravery, honesty, strength of character are the stuff for hero-worship. At the boy's level, this worship gravitates toward the doer of
spectacular deeds; on the average adult level, toward the wielder of
power; and in the eyes of a more critical judgment, toward idealism
and moral qualities. The most universal hero is he who can fill all
these specifications. This, by the many shapes of their courage, integrity, and strength, Washington and Lincoln and Lee are able to
do. But Jefferson the sedentary man, Franklin the opportunist, and
Andrew Jackson the rough-hewn soldier fail to satisfy everybody.
Upon a still lower rank, men like Daniel Boone and Crockett and
Buffalo Bill and Edison remain almost juvenile heroes. They do not
have all the dimensions of our few supreme symbols. Was it not
Emerson who suggested that we Americans were the shattered pieces
of a great mould?

Our most powerful hero epics center about our leaders. What, then,
in the final analysis do Washington, Franklin, Jefferson, Jackson,
Lincoln, and in a provisional verdict Wilson and the Roosevelts have
in common? Among them lie many differences. In heredity, economic
origins, training, skill, temperament, party affiliations, and attachment
to specific policies they may seem as diverse as we could find by sifting

the nation from Atlantic to Pacific. All save perhaps Washington were "liberals" by the gauge of their times—and Washington, one must not forget, was an arch political rebel, who even in old age sought to balance his conservatism by an honest effort to be nonpartisan. (And even Washington has slowly waned before the warmer humanity of Lincoln.) What is their common denominator?

All of them, the people believe, loved America more deeply than any selfish consideration. The hero as made in America is a man who has the power and yet does not abuse it. He is the practical demonstration of romantic democracy. Washington is most sublime because, after winning our freedom, he refused a crown, military dictatorship, and every personal reward. Lee is grandest because he did what he thought was his duty, failed under heartbreaking odds, and then with gentleness did his best to repair all hate and malice. Lincoln is most appealing because, in the conduct of that same desperate war which gave him the power of a czar, he never forgot his love for the common people of North and South. More clearly than the great heroes of Europe, military and political, ours stand for a progress concept. They spring from stock that has bred schemes both wise and foolish—with its talk about the pursuit of happiness, the more abundant life, and the American Dream. None of these epic leaders left the Republic as he found it—although to avoid disturbing a single stick or stone seems to have been the policy of men like James Buchanan, Chester A. Arthur, William McKinley, and Calvin Coolidge. At times, to be sure, the people themselves have wanted no change, felt no urge to take on fresh responsibility in the national sphere. In eras like theirs, nothing is added to the stature of American ideals—such as civil liberty, equality of opportunity, faith in the average man, social justice, respect for the rights of weaker nations and for the good estate of democracy throughout the earth. A Chief Executive may then be called to office who rules as a minor Augustus over a gilded age, or serves as the genial host at a great barbecue. But ten years hence he is not likely to be remembered as a great man, or even as a symbol worth keeping.

Our heroes, we believe, are cast in a different mould. Their ruling passion, as we see it, is a sense of duty, alert to the best among the stirring impulses of their time, and able to make that impulse effective. They translate the dream into act. The supreme leader is he who can hitch the great bandwagon to the star of American idealism.

III

Men become tribal heroes when the voice of a nation says to them, "Well done, thou good and faithful servant." Usually this happens in a man's lifetime, though an occasional minor figure like Paul Revere owes his fame to the postscript of poets, orators, or biographers. In general, futurity concerns itself not with discovering new heroes but with seeing old ones in a more symbolic aspect or hewing them to new requirements. Of the major symbol, the Lincoln or the Washington, it may be said—as the skeptic said of God—that he is the noblest work of man.

In a democracy, where the favorite should rightly be the people's choice—and not the elect of hereditary honors or of a myth-making "party" leadership—he is an index to the collective mind and heart. His deeds and qualities are those which millions endorse. He speaks words that multitudes want said; he stands for things that they are often willing to spill their blood for. The hero is he whom every American should wish to be. His legend is the mirror of the folk soul. Of course that mirror is sometimes clouded by the breath of fame, by sheer publicity. In this age, above all others, newspapers and newsreels and radio and the mechanisms of ovation have such power, in making or breaking the idol of the moment, that fresh irony has been given the old saying, "Heroes are not born but made." Yet, in the long run, their power is less than is often supposed. The tumult and the shouting dies, the captains and the kings depart—and posterity, across the dusty valleys of time, will probably deal out fair justice to those who served their day with honesty and strength, along with those who served only themselves and the baser instincts of their time. Lincon fares better than Napoleon, in satifying the eternal human hunger for a man to admire. Over the centuries, the Galilean is far greater than Cæsar.

The foreground of our history is still shifting, uncertain. Washington and Franklin and Jefferson and Lincoln remain giants, symbols so durable that they could be broken only by an America which deliberately renounced its great past, its independence and democratic faith, in favor of alien mythologies like those of Marx and Hitler. The approval of these American symbols is clear. What hero-worship of the future will say about Woodrow Wilson and Edison and Lindbergh, about Theodore and Franklin Roosevelt, is far less certain. In the changing skies of our republic some stars will set, while other

lights seen to be planets will glow more brightly as the heavens become bare around them. Meanwhile, today seems always less heroic
than yesterday. "In those days there were giants," men keep saying,
curiously blind to the fact that human potentiality remains much the
same, and that so long as a nation has a faith worth fighting for, new
crises will breed new champions. Carlyle, sweeping the sky of history
for great men ancient and medieval, overlooked the nearer phenomenon of Abraham Lincoln. The Scottish sage's American friend, Emerson, another philosopher of hero-worship a little dazzled by Napoleon,
did not begin to take the measure of Lincoln's greatness until it had
been given perspective by a martyr's death. It usually happens thus.

Also, over the longer reaches of our history, there are visible changes
of taste and spirit in our hero-worship as well as in our patriotism.
In the era of oratory from Patrick Henry to Webster, and of biography
from John Marshall's *Washington* to Randall's *Jefferson,* our heroes
were treated with grandiosity. This was the Silver Age of our patriotism. Forum and pulpit, Fourth of July and school declamation,
poetry and fiction, the art of battle-scenes and equestrian statues and
pioneer memorials, enshrined them in a vaguely classical and nebulous
respect. One could hardly see the hero for the incense. Then came the
age of sentiment, anticipated early by Weems but not reaching its
flower until the 1840's and after—"the sentimental years," as Douglas
Branch has called them. The Lincoln cult, sprouting after the Civil
War, drew much sustenance from it. The mothers and the infancy
of heroes, their domestic lives and their tender hearts, supplanted the
old accent on grandeur. Patriotism as taught by the McGuffey readers
and by children's lives of the great, stressed homely simple goodness.
This idealization marched abreast of the humanitarian spirit in Victorian times: heroes were good to the poor, they cherished children
and dumb animals. The great man entered, not to the fanfare of
trumpets, but to the still sad music of humanity. Love of country and
its traditions blended into the love of home. Longfellow became our
greatest patriotic bard, while across the pages of Josiah Gilbert Holland and other Lincoln biographers sometimes one could not see the
hero for the tears.

Meanwhile, in the workaday world, in the long fat years of peace
that followed Appomattox, the high inspiration of patriotism and
hero-worship began to ebb. Politicians and schoolmasters continued
to pay it lip-service, but there were too many distractions to keep it
at the pitch of intensity a new nation had maintained for a generation

after the Revolution. Our frontier was gone, and our expansion completed; of the international scene we were not yet aware. Jefferson's "choice country, with room enough," occupied us, rather than Jefferson's idealism. A nation building railways and dams and factories tended to forget its heroic temper. We neglected even to idealize the White House and its prerogatives of leadership: in this era Lord Bryce, writing his *American Commonwealth,* penned a chapter called "Why Great Men Are Not Chosen Presidents." Our most exalted soldier, General Grant, was drowned in materialism. At the end of the century the Spanish-American War, a kind of military *fête champêtre,* gave us a few easy heroes but stirred no more than a ripple on the surface of our national life. Here and there, in the first decade of a new century, the torpor was broken by the demands of a rather naïve imperialism and of an equally naïve (though more lastingly significant) crusade toward social justice. Then the World War brought back a breath of our strenuous past, and for two or three years we tried to remember the idiom of a nobler language. Song-writers and poets and "four-minute men" called for high endeavor. Many Americans, like Rupert Brooke in England, thanked God that the old smugness was gone, and with T. E. Hulme thrilled to "the long note of the bugle."

But more quickly than ever before, under the post-war disillusion, we renounced all that we had fought for. Turning to normalcy, we felt ashamed of a tingle in the spine at the invocation of Washington and Lincoln or a catch at the throat upon seeing the Stars and Stripes. Justifying ourselves for deserting a world not yet made safe for democracy, we began to debunk our heroes and their traditions. Some followed the path of sheer cynicism. Others—led by social historians, explaining that there were no great men but only movements, and by "progressive educators" filled with what Professor George S. Counts has lately and ruefully called "irrational optimism"—eased us away from the concept of patriotism. Patriotism was nothing but a conditioned reflex. "O beautiful my Country" was nothing but a form of "institutional behavior." It had been taught us, subtly, by various groups—chiefly the patrioteers who were buttressing the capitalist system. Patriotism was class propaganda, or, as Ambrose Bierce had defined it in the days when he worked for Hearst, "combustible rubbish ready to the torch of any one ambitious to illuminate his name." Any one who gave an arm or leg for his country was, as a nationally-spread poster proclaimed, "a sucker." Heroes were bunk. There was no glamor in American history, only class struggle. These teachings had a powerful effect upon at least two groups. The first were immigrants, or the children of immigrants, whose feeling for American heroes and American tradition was naturally undernourished. The second were boys and girls of high school and college age, who decided they would never fall for the bait of nationalism as their fathers had fallen. If the world in general, and America in particular, came to grief, it was no skin off their backs. Today a new phase of the cycle has begun. Many of the elder social historians are growing aware, as Walter Lippmann observes, that they have been sentimentalists, "men who wanted to enjoy the good life without earning it." Their hope in the Soviet experiment, for example, has been utterly destroyed. They are beginning to grope for the traditions of our great past. They are about to decide that the heroes bred by that tradition are not jingoist symbols. They wonder if something is not to be said for the bitter, but tonic, taste of sacrifice. The prophets of intellectual youth have done some recanting: Walter Millis has concluded that there are roads to war not paved by Morgan dollars, while overseas John Strachey has enlisted in the R. A. F. in the coming struggle for power. Youth is still critical of war hysteria—and indeed would one wish to exchange youth's new sense of realism for the provincial innocence of 1914? But, if sacrifice is needed for democratic liberty, youth will probably die just as certainly as it did a generation ago. England has demonstrated that fact. And one who dies for his cause in cooler blood is a greater hero than one who dies intoxicated by hysteria.

In his day Walt Whitman saw the United States as a citadel "invincible to the attacks of the whole of the rest of the earth," because it was "the new city of friends." A nation of good will and brotherhood, seeking neither territory nor sovereignty over its neighbors, it was also the land of Washington and Lincoln—its "saints," as the poet called them. Such memories were a vital part of its great tradition, its moorings of idealism that he believed would strengthen in tautness and hold fast in any storm.

NOTES

HEROES IN WAR AND PEACE

1. F. J. Grund, *The Americans in Their Moral, Social, and Political Relations* (London, 1838), I, 263.
2. David Hume, *Essays, Moral, Political, and Literary,* ed. Green and Grose, II, 328.
3. Described in *The New York Times,* 25 February 1924, and cited with more material on the same topic by Carlton J. H. Hayes, *Essays on Nationalism* (1926).
4. Earl Browder, *The People's Front* (1938), p. 166.
5. Merle Curti, "Reformers Consider the Constitution," *American Journal of Sociology,* May 1938, and "Wanted: a History of American Patriotism," *Proceedings Middle States Association of History and Social Science Teachers,* 1938; see also Conyers Read, ed., *The Constitution Reconsidered* (1939).
6. Charles W. Ferguson, *Fifty Million Brothers* (1937), p. 212.
7. R. W. Emerson, "Heroism," in *Works* (Cambridge, Mass., 1904), II, 250. T. E. Hulme, in *Speculations* and in *The Cambridge Magazine* for 4 March 1916 set down some interesting thoughts on the irrationality, the absolute good, of heroic sacrifice in war, "as negative, barren, and as necessary as the work of those who repair sea-walls." The doctrine, like any attempt to divorce ends from means, of course has certain dangers.

CAPTAIN JOHN SMITH AND THE INDIANS

1. James Kirke Paulding, *Letters from the South* (1817), I, 18–19.
2. Anon., *Biographical Sketches of Great and Good Men, Designed for the Amusement and Instruction of Young Persons* (1828), p. 27; and W. Hunt, *American Anecdotes* (1830), I, 96.
3. *Cf.* Albert Keiser, *The Indian in American Literature* (1933).
4. Jarvis M. Morse, "John Smith and His Critics: A Chapter in Colonial Historiography," *Journal of Southern History,* May 1935, pp. 124–25. Wesley Frank Craven, *Dissolution of the Virginia Company* (1932), pp. 12–21, reviews the "John Smith Controversy" as begun in 1859–60 and continued after the Civil War, involving the New England scholar Deane, the Southern historian Alexander Brown (who came to regard Sir Edwin Sandys rather than Smith as the true hero of Jamestown), and on the Smith side ex-Governor Wyndham Robertson of Virginia, who claimed to be a descendant of Pocahontas.
5. W. Strachey, *The Historie of Travaile into Virginia Britannica* (Hakluyt Society ed.), p. 65.
6. M. C. Tyler, *History of American Literature of the Colonial Time* (1897), I, 29–30.
7. C. M. Andrews, *The Colonial Period of American History* (1934), I, 142 n.

8. See Joseph H. Ingraham, *Leisler; or, The Rebel and King's Man* (1846), and William H. Carpenter, *Claiborne the Rebel: A Romance of Maryland under the Proprietary* (1845).
9. Mary N. Stanard, *The Story of Bacon's Rebellion* (1907), p. 48.
10. *William & Mary Quarterly*, IX, 4–5.
11. Stanard, p. 119.
12. Gustavus Myers, *The History of American Idealism* (1925), p. 23.
13. Charles Campbell, *History of the Colony and Ancient Dominion of Virginia* (1860), I, 317.
14. Peter Force, *Tracts and Other Papers* (1836), I, no. 8, p. 4; although the letter is not signed by Jefferson, its contents plainly imply that he wrote or dictated it. See also C. M. Andrews, *Narratives of the Insurrections* (1915), pp. 11 ff.
15. J. Burk, *History of Virginia* (Petersburg, 1805), II, 160 and 194.
16. Andrews, *Narratives of the Insurrections*, p. 76.
17. Specimen novels are Emerson Bennett's *The Fair Rebel: A Tale of Colonial Times* (1853), John Roy Musick's *A Century Too Soon: A Story of Bacon's Rebellion* (1893), Frederic J. Stimson's *King Noanett* (1896), Hulbert Fuller's *Vivian of Virginia: Being the Memoirs of Our First Rebellion* (1897), Alice Maude Ewell's *A White Guard to Satan* (1900), Maude Wilder Goodwin's *White Aprons* (1901; presenting Bacon as "the hero of the 17th century in the Southern colonies"), John Lane's *The Birth of Liberty: A Story of Bacon's Rebellion* (1909), William Sage's *A Maid of Old Virginia: A Romance of Bacon's Rebellion* (1915), and Clifford M. Sublette's *The Bright Face of Danger* (1926).
18. Stanard, p. 167.
19. Louisa Coleman Blair and Robert F. Williams, *Nathaniel Bacon* (Richmond, 1907).
20. Edward S. Ellis, *The Cromwell of Virginia* (1904).

THE PILGRIM FATHERS AND THE AMERICAN WAY

1. John Smith, *Generall Historie* (1907 ed.), II, 182.
2. For an analysis of this topic, reflecting the writer's Harvard training and point of view, see Evarts B. Greene, "The Place of the Pilgrims in American History," *University of Illinois Celebration of the Pilgrim Tercentenary* (Urbana, 1921), p. 23.
3. John Robinson's *Relation, or Journal*, reprinted by Edward Arber, *The Story of the Pilgrim Fathers* (London, 1897), p. 421.
4. *Massachusetts* (Federal Writers' Project, 1937), p. 327.
5. H. R. Shurtleff, *The Log Cabin Myth* (1939), p. 9.
6. John Foster, *Essays* (Andover, 1826), p. 111.
7. S. E. Morison, *Builders of the Bay Colony* (1930), p. 13.
8. V. L. Parrington, *The Connecticut Wits* (1926), pp. 187–88.
9. W. Bradford, *History of Plimmoth Plantation* (1912), I, 301.
10. R. C. Winthrop, ed., *Life and Letters of John Winthrop* (1864–67), II, 237 and 430.
11. F. J. Turner, *The Frontier in American History* (1920), p. 293.
12. *Narragansett Club Publications*, VI, 133.
13. Perry Miller and T. H. Johnson, *The Puritans* (1938), p. 5 and n. To this volume and to Miller's *The New England Mind* (1939) I am indebted for various suggestions in this chapter.

14. Cotton Mather, *Two Brief Discourses* (1701), pp. 37–38.
15. John T. Flynn, *God's Gold* (1932), p. 306.
16. Bishop W. Lawrence, in *World's Work*, I, 286–290.
17. Q. by Everett Dean Martin, *The Behavior of Crowds* (1920), pp. 158–59.
18. A. E. Alden, *Pilgrim Alden* (1902). Such romantic accounts of John Alden as those found in Jane Goodwin Austin's novels *Betty Alden* (1891) and *Standish of Standish* (1895) might be compared with the more soberly factual account by C. M. Andrews, *The Colonial Period of American History*, I, 269–70 *et passim*.
19. B. Tompson, *New Englands Crisis* (1676).
20. The quotation is from Thomas Prince, *Chronological History of New England* (1736), I, 86. Compare Solomon Stoddard, "An Answer to Some Cases of Conscience," in Miller and Johnson, *The Puritans*, p. 457.
21. Henry Cabot Lodge's account of this development will be found in *The Story of the Pilgrim Tercentenary Celebration at Plymouth* (1923), p. 19. See also *The New English Dictionary*, s. v. "Pilgrim."
22. *Massachusetts* (Federal Writers' Project), p. 320. Other data from William De Loss Love, *The Fast and Thanksgiving Days of New England* (1895), ch. XXVII.
23. Q. by L. S. Mayo, *John Endecott* (1936), pp. 285–86.
24. *The Story of the Pilgrim Tercentenary*, pp. 15–16.

POOR RICHARD: THE BOY WHO MADE GOOD

1. *Works of Benjamin Franklin*, ed. Jared Sparks (1836), III, 123. Franklin himself wrote only a small portion of "The Historical Review of the Constitution and Government of Pennsylvania," but the ideas there expressed are his own; see A. H. Smyth, *Writings of Benjamin Franklin* (1905), I, 137–38.
2. J. Francis Fisher, *A Discourse Delivered Before the Historical Society of Pennsylvania, 9 April 1836*, pp. 23–24.
3. S. G. Fisher, *William Penn* (1932), pp. 242 ff.; also W. I. Hull, *Eight First Biographies of Penn* (Swarthmore College, 1936).
4. George L. Harrison, *The Remains of William Penn* (priv. printed, Philadelphia, 1882).
5. *The William Penn Memorial* (New York, 1911), pp. 39–40.
6. *An Oration on the Life and Character of Benjamin Franklin, Delivered Before the Franklinian Society of William and Mary College, 17 January 1840*, p. 26.
7. *Memorial of the Inauguration of the Statue of Franklin* (Boston, 1857), p. 108.
8. James Parton, *Life and Times of Benjamin Franklin* (1864), II, 585.
9. This translation from Morellet's *Mémoires* will be found in *Cozzens Wine Press*, a monthly magazine published by the New York vintner of that name, for 20 April 1855, pp. 84–86.
10. *Benjamin Franklin Gazette*, January 1928, pp. 1 and 4.
11. *Writings*, ed. Smyth, X, 58–60.
12. *Benjamin Franklin Gazette*, May 1938, p. 1.
13. Julian P. Boyd, *Pennsylvania Magazine of History and Biography*, LXI (1937), 233–34; and Charles A. Beard, *Jewish Frontier*, March 1935.
14. Paul Leicester Ford, *The Many-Sided Franklin* (1899), p. 314.
15. *Ibid.*, p. 426.
16. Parton, II, 599–600.

17. Ford, p. 52.
18. *Writings*, ed. Smyth, VIII, 59.
19. Franklin to Cadwallader Colden, 29 September 1748.
20. Parton, II, 546.
21. Bernard Fay, *Franklin, Apostle of Modern Times* (1929), p. 504.
22. H. W. Schneider, *The Puritan Mind* (1930), p. 256.
23. *Writings*, ed. Smyth, IX, 665.
24. This phrase is quoted from the *Franklin Magazine Almanac for 1828*, published in Pittsburgh.
25. *Biographical Stories for Children* (Boston, 1842), pp. 135-37.
26. Samuel Johnson, *Taxation No Tyranny* (London, 1775), p. 68, and Horace Walpole's letter of 27 February 1777 to the Rev. W. Mason.
27. *A Present from New York* (New York, 1828).
28. *Memorial of the Inauguration of the Statue of Franklin* (Boston, 1857).
29. Cadwallader Evans to Franklin, in Sparks, VII, 283.
30. *Writings*, ed. Smyth, X, 226-27; and Parton, I, 464.
31. T. P. Abernethy, *Western Lands and the American Revolution* (1937), pp. 54, 57, and 111; for a less academic appraisal of Franklin's opportunism, Ford, *op. cit.*, pp. 442 ff.
32. *Writings*, ed. Smyth, V, 133; and Franklin to John Hughes, in S. G. Fisher, *Pennsylvania: Colony and Commonwealth* (1907), pp. 313-14. Franklin was referring mainly to British citizens at home, in connection with the Wilkes agitation.
33. W. Strahan to W. T. Franklin, Franklin Papers, American Philosophical Society, XLIV, 21; noted by Abernethy, *op. cit.*, 206 n.
34. See Verner Crane, "Benjamin Franklin and the Stamp Act," *Transactions Colonial Society of Massachusetts*, May 1933, and also Crane's *Benjamin Franklin, Englishman and American* (1936); Bernhard Knollenberg's review of Van Doren's *Franklin*, in *Yale Review*, Winter 1939; Dixon Wecter, "Burke, Franklin, and Samuel Petrie," *Huntington Library Quarterly*, April 1940; and Conyers Read, "English Elements in Franklin," *Pennsylvania Magazine of History and Biography*, July 1940.
35. *Pennsylvania Packet*, 8 May 1775.
36. Parton, II, 85; *cf.* Franklin article in *Dictionary of American Biography*, VI, 597.
37. Fay, p. 405.
38. E. E. Hale and E. E. Hale, Jr., *Franklin in France* (1887), I, 80.
39. *New Jersey Gazette*, 31 December 1777.
40. Mme. de Campan, *Mémoires de la vie privée de Marie-Antoinette* (Paris, 1822), I, 233-34.
41. William Lyon Phelps, *Scribner's Magazine*, May 1928.
42. Note his relations with Ingenhousz as described by Abernethy, pp. 276-77.
43. Ford, pp. 12, 14, 28, 33, 36; T. P. Abernethy, "Commercial Activities of Silas Deane in France," *American Historical Review*, XXXIX, 477-85, and "The Origin of the Franklin-Lee Imbroglio," *North Carolina Historical Review*, XV, 41-52.
44. *The American Herald* of Boston, 14 January 1788.
45. Ford, p. 17.
46. *Writings of Thomas Jefferson* (Washington, 1905), X, 421.
47. *Ibid.*, X, 55; see also XIX, 38. The second part of the tribute is from Jefferson's message to the American Philosophical Society, 28 January 1797, in *Early Proceedings of the Amer. Philos. Soc.* (1884), p. 251.

48. J. M. Stifler, *The Religion of Benjamin Franklin* (1925), pp. 37–38.
49. David Williams, "More Light on Franklin's Religious Ideas," *American Historical Review*, July 1938, pp. 803–813.
50. George P. Fisher, *Life of Benjamin Silliman* (1866), I, 88.
51. *Writings*, ed. Smyth, X, 84–85.
52. *Eulogium on Benjamin Franklin Before the American Philosophical Society, Delivered March 1, 1791*, printed by B. F. Bache (Philadelphia, 1792), p. 38.
53. See for example James Austin Richards, D.D., *Benjamin Franklin: A Sermon Preached at the Winnetka (Ill.) Congregational Church, 16 January 1927*.
54. *Parley's Book of Anecdotes* (1845), p. 127.
55. In *The Preacher's Assistant* for November 1890. For a clerical rebuttal, see Dr. Edward D. Neill, "The Ideal Versus the Real Benjamin Franklin," *Macalester College Contributions* (St. Paul, 1892), 2d series, pp. 97 ff.
56. J. E. Remsburg, *The Fathers of Our Republic* (1886), and M. M. Mangasarian, *The Religion of Washington, Jefferson, and Franklin* [1907?].
57. Q. in *Benjamin Franklin Gazette*, October 1927, p. 3.
58. *Archimedes and Franklin: A Lecture . . . Delivered Before the Massachusetts Charitable Mechanic Association* (Boston, 1853), p. 47.
59. *Memorial of the Inauguration of the Statue of Franklin*, p. 93.
60. *Illustrated Police News*, 25 January 1872.
61. Q. by Parton, II, 677–79. For a somewhat different comparison, weighted again in Washington's favor, see "Franklin and Washington," *New York World*, 17 January 1872.
62. *Ceremonies Attending the Unveiling of the Statue of Franklin, June 14, 1899*, p. 25.
63. See E. H. O'Neill, *A History of American Biography* (1935), p. 60, and "Bibliography."
64. See Julius F. Sachse, *Benjamin Franklin as a Freemason* (1906).
65. *Proceedings of the Printers' Banquet . . . on the Occasion of Franklin's Birthday, 17 Jan. 1850* (New York, 1850). Also John L. Jewett, *An Oration Delivered Before the N. Y. Typographical Society, on . . . the Birthday of Franklin, at the Printers' Festival, 17 Jan. 1849* (New York, 1849).
66. J. C. Oswald, *Benjamin Franklin in Oil and Bronze*, q. *B. F. Gazette*, Oct. 1928, p. 5.
67. For the Memorial, see *B. F. Gazette*, May 1928, pp. 5–6; for Mr. Huntington's impersonations, *ibid.*, Jan. 1929, p. 12.

THE EMBATTLED FARMERS

1. Raoul de Roussy de Sales, "What Makes an American," *Atlantic Monthly*, March 1939.
2. William H. Herndon, *Abraham Lincoln* (1st ed.), II, 340–42; and A. J. Beveridge, *Abraham Lincoln* (1928), I, 556–57.
3. Elbridge Colby, "An Army View of History Teaching in the Schools," *Current History*, Feb. 1928, p. 634.
4. For good discussion of this point, S. E. Morison and H. S. Commager, *The Growth of the American Republic* (1937), I, 87–88.
5. In *Collections of Connecticut Historical Society*, VII.
6. In *Mississippi Valley Historical Review*, XX.
7. *A Rebel of the Revolution* (Boston, 1847).

8. *The Historical Outlook,* Oct. 1922, pp. 250–55.
9. Bessie L. Pierce, *Public Opinion and the Teaching of History* (1926), p. 102.
10. *New York Times,* 19 March 1924.
11. *Chicago Herald & Examiner,* 3 July 1921.
12. See Howard K. Beale, *Are American Teachers Free?* (1936), p. 201.
13. *Ibid.,* pp. 192–93.
14. *Federated Press Bulletin,* 3 Nov. 1923, q. Beale, p. 301.
15. *New York Times,* 12 June and 28 July 1931.
16. *New York Times,* 12 March 1933.
17. *D. A. R. Manual for Citizenship,* 14th English ed. (revised 1936), pp. 12–13.
18. Bessie L. Pierce, *Civic Attitudes in American Textbooks* (1930), ch. II; and Beale, *op. cit.,* p. 187.
19. Emerson Taylor, *Paul Revere* (1930), p. 14.
20. See the account of Revere in *Dictionary of Amer. Biography;* a court-martial in 1782 eventually restored him to official favor.
21. Samuel Longfellow, *Life of H. W. Longfellow* (1886), II, 352.
22. See J. C. Fitzpatrick, *George Washington Himself* (1933), pp. 523–24.
23. T. Dwight, *The Conquest of Canaan* (Hartford, 1785), pp. 3–4.
24. Henry Phelps Johnston, *Nathan Hale: 1776* (1901), p. 36.
25. *Putnam's Magazine,* May 1856, p. 476; and a MS. essay by Edward Hale Brush, "Alice Adams: Nathan Hale's Sweetheart," in Rare Book Collection, Sterling Library, Yale University.
26. George Dudley Seymour, *Hale and Wyllys* (1933), pp. 1–3.
27. Q. by Lorado Taft, *History of American Sculpture* (1925), p. 339.
28. Fitzpatrick, *op. cit.,* p. 167.
29. W. Hunt, *American Anecdotes* (1830), I, 146.
30. *Biographical Sketches of Great and Good Men, Designed for the Instruction and Amusement of Young Persons* (1828), p. 30.
31. O. J. Victor, *Life and Times of Israel Putnam* (Beadle Library [1876]), p. 26.
32. Hunt, *op. cit.,* I, 123.
33. R. Frothingham, *History of the Siege of Boston* (1849), p. 140 n.
34. *The History of America Abridged for the Use of Children of All Denominations;* cf. A. S. W. Rosenbach, *Early American Children's Books* (1933), p. 81.
35. Constance Rourke, *American Humor* (1931), p. 116.
36. Pauline C. Bouvé, *American Heroes and Heroines* (1905), p. 89.
37. *The Green Mountain Boys* (Montpelier, 1839), II, 10.
38. Ethan Allen's *Narrative* (Philadelphia, 1779), pp. 33–34.
39. See Daniel P. Thompson, *The Shaker Lovers* (Burlington, Vt., 1849), under story called "Ethan Allen and the Lost Children"; and Hugh Moore, *Memoir of Col. Ethan Allen* (Plattsburg, N. Y., 1834), p. 245.
40. John Pell, *Ethan Allen* (1929), pp. 139–41.
41. For late impartial accounts of these transactions, see G. H. Doane, "Ethan Allen," *Dict. Amer. Biog.,* and Morison and Commager, *op. cit.,* I, 137. Stewart Holbrook's *Ethan Allen* (1940), a frankly admiring biography, takes the indulgent view that Allen's flirtations with the British were just good Yankee bargaining, to assure Vermont her statehood in the Union.
42. Mrs. St. Julien Ravenel, *Charleston: The Place and the People* (1929), p. 306.
43. Charles Jacobs Peterson, *The Oath of Marion: A Story of the Revolution* (1847), p. 39.
44. Ravenel, p. 376.

45. P. L. Ford and Emily E. Ford Skeel, *Mason Locke Weems: His Works and Ways* (1929), I, 101.
46. See Cecil B. Hartley, *The Life of Gen. Francis Marion* (Philadelphia, 1866).
47. J. T. Howard, "The Music of George Washington's Time," *History Washington Bicentennial Celebration*, II, 240.
48. Achille Murat, *America and the Americans* (1849), p. 157. *Cf.* J. Bennett Nolan, *Lafayette in America Day by Day* (1934), part IV.
49. *The Aristocratic Journey: Letters of Mrs. Basil Hall*, ed. Una Pope-Hennessy (1931), pp. 50–51.
50. "Paul Jones," in Burton E. Stevenson, *Poems of American History*, p. 224.
51. Alan Cunningham, *Paul Jones: A Romance* (3 vols., Philadelphia, 1827), I, 122.
52. *The Sea-King; Or, The Two Corvettes* (New York, 1873), pp. 18–19.
53. O. J. Victor, *Life and exploits of John Paul Jones* [New York, 1861], p. 29.
54. This life was first called, upon its American appearance, *The Interesting Life, Travels, Voyages, and Daring Engagements of That Celebrated and Justly Notorious Pirate Paul Jones* . . . (New York, 1807). It was issued later as *The Life of Paul Jones, Containing His Travels, Voyages, and Daring Engagements.* I quote here from the 30th ed., Philadelphia, 1831.
55. S. Putnam Waldo, *American Naval Heroes* (Hartford, 1823), p. 78. For another treatment of the sadism of Jones, see [Nathaniel Fanning], *The Life, Travels, Voyages . . . of Paul Jones* (New York, 1806), p. 5.
56. [Benjamin Walker], *Life of John Paul Jones* (Philadelphia, 1849), p. 396. Cf. A. S. Mackenzie, *Life of J. P. Jones* (Boston, 1841), II, 291–92: "No hero, indeed, ever sounded his own trumpet more unremittingly or with a louder blast."
57. See for example Charles J. Peterson, *The American Navy* (Philadelphia, 1859), p. 69.
58. Sarah Orne Jewett, *The Tory Lover* (1901), pp. 209, 214.
59. Mrs. Reginald De Koven, *A Fictitious Paul Jones Masquerading as the Real* (copyright 1906, *The New York Times*), p. 22.
60. *John Paul Jones Commemoration at Annapolis: April 24, 1906* (1907), p. 45.
61. Park Benjamin, "Is It Paul Jones's Body?" *New York Independent*, 20 July 1905; and C. H. Hart and E. Biddle, *Memoirs of . . . Houdon* (1911), pp. 125–154.

PRESIDENT WASHINGTON AND PARSON WEEMS

1. Some excellent remarks by the late Carl Russel Fish, "George Washington, the Man," are in *Transactions Illinois State Historical Society*, 1932, p. 24.
2. J. Franklin Jameson, *The American Revolution Considered as a Social Movement* (1926), p. 75.
3. John C. Fitzpatrick, *George Washington Himself* (1933), pp. 43, 112.
4. For these two quotations, see F. Hopkinson, *Miscellaneous Essays* (Philadelphia, 1792), II, 55–56, and I, 120.
5. William Carlos Williams, *In the American Grain* (1925), p. 142.
6. L. C. Hatch, *The Administration of the American Revolutionary Army* (1904), p. 122.
7. *Pennsylvania Magazine of History and Biography*, Vol. 56, p. 105.
8. Fitzpatrick, p. 330.
9. Q. by N. W. Stephenson and W. H. Dunn, *George Washington* (1940), II, 172–73.

10. Ezra Stiles, *The United States Elevated to Glory and Honor* (New Haven, 1783), pp. 42–43.

11. Jefferson to Walter Jones, 2 Jan. 1814.

12. James Parton, *Life of Thomas Jefferson* (1874), p. 369.

13. Q. by Fitzpatrick, p. 446.

14. *Ibid.*, p. 148.

15. *Writings of Washington* (Bicentennial ed.), Vol. 28, pp. 426–27 and 471.

16. Washington Papers, Library of Congress, under date of 14 Feb. 1784, for Mayor McWilliams's address and General Washington's rejoinder.

17. Rupert Hughes, *George Washington* (1926), I, 15.

18. Stephenson and Dunn, I, 201.

19. W. E. Woodward, *George Washington: The Image and the Man* (1926), p. 435.

20. *Writings of Washington,* ed. Worthington C. Ford, XI, 115 ff.

21. This is quoted from a sentimental description of Ferris's painting, in *History of the Bicentennial Celebration,* I, 237.

22. For an excellent résumé of the subject, John C. Fitzpatrick, *The George Washington Scandals* (Alexandria, Va., 1929).

23. *Writings of Washington* (Bicentennial ed.), Vol. 28, p. 83. This still unpublished volume is here cited by kind permission of the editor, the late Dr. Fitzpatrick. See also N. W. Stephenson, "The Romantics and George Washington," *Amer. Histor. Review,* Oct. 1933, pp. 274–283.

24. *Love Stories of Famous Virginians* (Richmond, 1925), p. 21.

25. See Fitzpatrick, *George Washington Himself,* p. 528, n. 4 to chap. LXI; also R. Hughes, *George Washington,* I, Appendix II, "The Spurious Prayers."

26. Related in W. Hunt's *American Anecdotes* (1830), I, 166–67, on the authority of Dr. David Hosack's *Memoir of DeWitt Clinton.*

27. Q. by P. L. Ford, *The True George Washington* (16th ed., 1896), p. 82.

28. Q. by J. C. Fitzpatrick, *George Washington and Religion* (Bicentennial Pamphlet No. 5), p. 6.

29. *New York Spectator,* 30 April 1839, interview with Captain Van Dyck.

30. I. N. P. Stokes, *The Iconography of Manhattan Island* (1915 *et seq.*), V, 1242–45.

31. *Writings,* ed. Ford, XIV, 143, under date 20 Jan. 1799.

32. Stephenson and Dunn, II, 269.

33. Edward Stanwood, *A History of the Presidency* (1906), p. 41.

34. *Writings,* ed. Ford, XIII, 76, 231.

35. Moncure D. Conway, *Life of Thomas Paine* (1892), II, 176–77.

36. Q. by Albert Jay Nock, *Jefferson* (1926), pp. 217–18.

37. Some 440 titles are given by Margaret B. Stilwell, *Washington Eulogies* (1916).

38. Carl Russel Fish, *op. cit.,* p. 40; to this essay I am indebted for suggestions in the following analysis.

39. *Poems by Noah Webster,* ed. Warfel (1936), p. 9.

40. For several profitable ideas on this topic I have consulted an unpublished Columbia M.A. thesis of 1920, Margaret Rowe's *George Washington: The Legend.*

41. These sentences are quoted from P. L. Ford and Emily E. Ford Skeel, *Mason Locke Weems: His Works and Ways* (1929), and Randolph G. Adams, "The Historical Illustrations in Weems's Washington," *Colophon,* part 8 (1931).

42. Joseph Rodman, in *The Critic*, Feb. 1904, cited by R. Hughes, *op. cit.*, I, 501; and compare Allan Nevins, *The Gateway to History* (1938), p. 121.

43. S. G. Fisher, "The Legendary and Myth-Making Process in Histories of the American Revolution," *Proc. Amer. Philos. Soc.*, Vol. 51 (1912); for an unconscious vindication of Fisher's conclusions, see Charles Altschul, *The American Revolution in Our School Text-books* (1917), a naïve but well-meant book by "a businessman," written apropos of America's entry into the World War.

44. Rhea M. Knittle, *Early Ohio Taverns* (priv. printed, 1937), pp. 29–30. Penn, Lafayette, Jefferson, Hamilton, and Wayne were also popular tavern names.

45. This mis-labeling occurred in the late eighteenth century, but specimens are still extant. One is owned by Dr. Max Farrand, San Marino, Calif. See also Albert Lee, *Portraits in Pottery* (1931), pp. 91–92.

46. N. Hudson Moore, *The Old China Book* (1903), pp. 64, 111.

47. Rhea M. Knittle, *Early American Glass* (1927), pp. 442–43.

48. Hewson L. Peeke, *Americana Ebrietatis; The Favorite Tipple of Our Fore-fathers* (priv. printed, 1917), chap. VI, "Relation of George Washington to the Liquor Traffic."

49. Jefferson's reply to Glass is found among the Jefferson MSS. in the Massachusetts Historical Society.

50. J. S. Bassett, *Middle Group of American Historians* (1917), pp. 103–110.

51. Albert Welles, *Pedigree and History of the Washington Family from Odin* (1879), and Anthony R. Wagner, "The Queen of England's American Ancestry and Cousinship to Washington and Lee," *Record of the N. Y. Genealog. and Biog. Soc.*, July 1939.

52. William Meade, *Old Churches, Ministers, and Families of Virginia* (1897), II, 242–255. This work was first published in 1857.

53. The episode, thinly veiled in anonymity, is described after an interview with Miss Greene by Edward Larocque Tinker, "Whitewashing," *The Bookman*, Feb. 1925. Information to the author from the late Dr. J. C. Fitzpatrick is also used.

54. *New York Times*, 7 Dec. 1921.

55. Hughes, *op. cit.*, I, 449–450.

56. *History of the Bicentennial Celebration*, II, 134.

57. Paul Wilstach, *Mount Vernon* (1916), pp. 250–53.

THOMAS JEFFERSON, THE GENTLE RADICAL

1. Jefferson's Autobiography, in *Works*, (ed. Ford), I, 2.

2. Information from Miss Maude H. Woodfin, University of Richmond, and from Professor T. P. Abernethy, University of Virginia. A scholarly study of Peter Jefferson, by Dr. Edgar Hickisch of Portsmouth, Va., is yet unpublished.

3. See Jefferson's Autobiography, *Works*, I, 29 and 38; Carl Becker, *The Declaration of Independence* (1922), p. 184; and John C. Fitzpatrick, *The Spirit of the Revolution* (1924), pp. 8 and 16.

4. It was published from the Jefferson Papers in the Library of Congress by Gilbert Chinard in 1929, in his *Thomas Jefferson, the Apostle of Americanism*, pp. 80–82. The distinction, of course, was implicit throughout Jefferson's thought.

5. Beveridge, *Life of John Marshall* (1916), I, 126–28.

6. As Chinard notes, p. 113. The quotation is from Jefferson to Duane, 1 Oct. 1812.

7. Jefferson to Short, 3 Jan. 1793, in *Memorial Edition, IX,* 9.

8. See Albert Jay Nock, *Jefferson* (1926), pp. 288–89.

9. Harriet Taylor Upton, *Our Early Presidents* (1890), pp. 165–66.

10. Thomas Harris to Jefferson, 26 March 1804, Jefferson Papers, Library of Congress.

11. "A Citizen of Washington County, Maryland" to Jefferson, 23 Feb. 1807.

12. Sarah N. Randolph, *The Domestic Life of Thomas Jefferson* (1871), p. 242.

13. Nock, pp. 260–61.

14. *Ibid.,* p. 266; cf. Henry Adams, *History of the United States* (1891–93), IV, chap. xii, "The Cost of Embargo."

15. F. Bremer, *America of the Fifties* (1924), pp. 124–25.

16. S. C. Carpenter, *Memoirs of the Hon. Thomas Jefferson,* printed for the purchasers, 1809, II, 93.

17. Dr. John Mason, *The Voice of Warning, to Christians, on the Ensuing Election of a President of the United States* (1800), p. 11.

18. G. A. Koch, *Republican Religion: The American Revolution and the Cult of Reason* (1933), p. 137. Dixon Ryan Fox, *The Decline of Aristocracy in the Politics of New York* (1919), chap. I, gives an excellent review of Jefferson the infidel as seen through Federalist eyes.

19. James Fenimore Cooper, *Gleanings in Europe: England* (1837), pp. 264–65.

20. Carl Sandburg, *Lincoln: The Prairie Years* (1926), II, 369.

21. Worthington C. Ford, *Thomas Jefferson Correspondence* (1916), p. 115.

22. Henry Lee to Jefferson, dated "Belvoir 8th Sep[r] 06," in the Jefferson Papers, Library of Congress, but apparently not listed in the *Catalogue of the Papers of Thomas Jefferson,* published by that Library.

23. Douglas S. Freeman, *R. E. Lee* (1935), I, 115.

24. T. P. Abernethy, *Western Lands and the American Revolution* (1937), p. 173 *et passim.*

25. Compare Chinard, pp. 312–13.

26. Fitzpatrick, *George Washington Himself,* p. 504; Beveridge, *John Marshall,* II, 375 and n. A late word on the subject, giving Jefferson the benefit of the doubt, is Manning J. Dauer, "The Two John Nicholases," *Amer. Histor. Review,* Jan. 1940, pp. 338 ff. No historian, I believe, has yet pointed out that among the Alexander Hamilton Papers in the Library of Congress is a letter from Washington's correspondent, John Nicholas, dated Richmond, 4 August 1803, offering Hamilton his services as a secret informer against "J" (plainly Jefferson): he adds that "being long intimately & personally acquainted with certain characters & their secret movements, I trust I can render my share of service."

27. J. Q. Adams, *Diary,* 11 Jan. 1831.

28. Jefferson to Dr. James Brown, 27 Oct. 1808.

29. Samuel Flagg Bemis, *Jay's Treaty* (1923), chap. V.

30. For the newspaper quotation, *The Norfolk* (Va.) *Herald,* 10 July 1826; for the comment, Randolph, *op. cit.,* p. 421 n.

31. *The New World* (New York), 25 Sept. 1841.

32. Newton Arvin, *Whitman* (1938), pp. 14–15.

33. Col. House's diary, 15 April 1914; q. by Dumas Malone, "Jefferson and the New Deal," *Scribner's Magazine,* June 1933.

34. Q. with disapproval in an editorial in *The New York World,* 6 Sept. 1928.

35. F. D. Roosevelt, *Public Papers and Addresses* (1938), V, 80.

36. C. M. Wiltse, *The Jeffersonian Tradition in American Democracy* (1935), pp. 261–67.

37. George Graham Vest, *Thomas Jefferson: An Address* (St. Louis, 1885), p. 24. For the Jesse incident, letter to the author from Mr. C. B. Rollins of Columbia, Mo., 24 April 1940; for the Bingham portrait, *Missouri Histor. Review*, Jan. 1938, pp. 196 ff.

38. Jefferson MSS., Mass. Histor. Soc., Jefferson to Robert Simpson of St. Louis, 14 Feb. 1824, saying characteristically: "It's [*sic*] object, agriculture, is certainly the first in human life and houshold [*sic*] manufacture is it's genuine companion & handmaid. I wish to them both all possible prosperity, and to the state in which the society is placed all those blessings which it's soil, climate, & government so richly promise it."

39. *Congressional Record,* 14 March 1939, in regard to the Interior Department Appropriation Bill for 1940, pp. 3839–3841. See also President Roosevelt's Executive Order of 21 Dec. 1935 respecting the Memorial. Other data in letter to the author from Mr. Daniel Cox Fahey, Jr., Executive Officer of the Memorial, 19 Jan. 1940.

WINNING OF THE FRONTIER: BOONE, CROCKETT, JOHNNY APPLESEED

1. Waldo Lincoln, *History of the Lincoln Family* (Worcester, 1923), p. 52.

2. Reproduced in Wm. S. Bryan, *History of the Boone-Bryan Family* (1913).

3. Clarence W. Alvord, "The Daniel Boone Myth," *Jour. Illinois Histor. Soc.,* April-July 1926, pp. 16–30.

4. J. Filson, *The Discovery, Settlement, and Present State of Kentucke* (Wilmington, 1784), pp. 51, 52, 58, 81. This purported autobiography of Boone was more widely circulated when Gilbert Imlay included it in his *Topographical Description of the Western Territory of North America* (1793, 1797).

5. John Bakeless, *Daniel Boone* (1939), p. 394.

6. Louise Phelps Kellogg, "The Fame of Daniel Boone," *Report of Boone Bicentennial Commission* (1936), p. 56.

7. *Ibid.,* p. 57.

8. Chester Harding, *My Egotistigraphy* (1866), pp. 35–36.

9. J. D. Bryan, *The Boone-Bryan History* (Kentucky Historical Society [1914]), p. 24.

10. *Literary Digest,* 9 Oct. 1937, p. 7.

11. J. K. Paulding, *Letters from the South* (1817), I, 199.

12. J. F. Cooper, *The Pioneers* (1831), p. 130.

13. *Ibid.,* p. 162.

14. Kellogg, *op. cit.,* p. 53.

15. Quoted *ibid.,* p. 50.

16. T. Flint, *Biographical Memoir of Daniel Boone, the First Settler of Kentucky* (1833), p. 263.

17. *Proceedings of the Meeting of the Kentucky State Historical Society on Boone Day 1912* (Frankfort), p. 9.

18. Edward J. White, *Daniel Boone: A Patriotic Drama in Five Acts* (1923), "Epilogue."

19. *In the American Grain* (1925), p. 130.

20. *Report of the Boone Bicentennial Commission* (1936). The Filson Club has also done much to keep alive the Boone legend. For its publications see the

Boone bibliographies compiled by Wm. Harvey Miner (1901) and Willard Rouse Jillson (1932).

21. *Literary Digest, loc. cit.*

22. Constance Rourke, *American Humor,* pp. 34–35.

23. J. K. Paulding, "The History of Uncle Sam and His Boys," *New York Mirror,* 19 Feb. 1831; Mark Twain, *Life on the Mississippi* (1899; first pub. 1874), pp. 32–33. Bird's *Nick of the Woods* presents a similar hero in Roaring Ralph Stackpole.

24. *Sketches and Eccentricities of Col. David Crockett, of West Tennessee* (1833), chap. XIII.

25. Constance Rourke, *Davy Crockett* (1934), and V. L. Parrington, "The Davy Crockett Myth," in *Main Currents in American Thought,* II, 172–79, are sources to which I am indebted.

26. *An Account of Col. Crockett's Tour to the North and Down East* (1835), p. 55.

27. *Lloyd's Ethiopian Song Book* (London, 1847), p. 25; John A. Lomax, *American Ballads* (1934), pp. 251–52.

28. W. H. Macleod, *The American Indian Frontier* (1928), p. 372.

29. Cited by J. L. Himrod, *Johnny Appleseed* (Chicago Historical Society, 1926).

30. [W. D. Haley], "Johnny Appleseed: A Pioneer Hero," *Harper's Magazine,* Vol. 43 (1871), pp. 830–836.

31. Himrod, p. 7.

32. See illustration in *Ohio Archæological and Historical Publications,* Vol. 9 (1901), p. 307, and compare with that given in Henry A. Pershing, *Johnny Appleseed and His Time* (Strasbourg, Va., 1930), Frontispiece.

33. W. D. Haley's article, pp. 835–36.

34. *Ohio Arch. and Histor. Publ.,* Vol. 9, p. 312 n.

35. Pershing, p. 354.

36. Q. by William A. Duff, *History of North Central Ohio* (Indianapolis, 1931), I, 68–69.

37. *Appleseed Johnny: A Poetic Drama of Pioneer Days* (St. Charles, Illinois, 1927).

38. Pershing, pp. 7–22.

39. *Ibid.,* p. 50.

40. *Ibid.,* p. 176.

41. *The Quest of John Chapman: The Story of a Forgotten Hero* (1904), Preface.

42. *The Adventures of Johnny Appleseed* (1930).

43. Duff, I, 64.

44. R. Price and F. E. Wheeler, "John Chapman's line of descent from Edward Chapman of Ipswich," *Ohio Arch. and Histor. Quarterly,* Jan., 1939; and R. Price, "The New England origins of 'Johnny Appleseed,'" *N. Eng. Quarterly,* Sept., 1939.

OLD HICKORY

1. James Parton, *Life of Andrew Jackson* (1860), III, 699.

2. Q. by Stuart P. Sherman, *Essays and Poems of Emerson* (1921), p. xxxii.

3. Edward Stanwood, *History of the Presidency,* I, 136 and 148.

4. Q. in *Washington Globe,* 24 Nov. 1832.

5. J. P. Kennedy, *Life of William Wirt* (1849), II, 331.

6. *New York Times Magazine,* 16 Aug. 1925, "Both Carolinas Claim Andrew Jackson."

7. Cf. John Trotwood Moore's article in *Memphis Commercial Appeal*, 8 April 1928, and other clippings on this subject in the Tennessee State Library, Nashville.

8. Parton, III, 554.

9. *A Brief and Impartial History of . . . Andrew Jackson. By a Free Man* (Boston, 1831), p. 7.

10. See Marquis James, *The Life of Andrew Jackson* (one-vol. ed., 1938), pp. 28–29 and 799; he casts some doubt upon the "last words" as reported by Thomas Butler, quoted in Augustus C. Buell's *History of Andrew Jackson* (1904), I, 56. The custodian of the Hermitage has for sale a leaflet called "Advice to Andrew Jackson by His Mother," following this more sentimental legend.

11. Parton, I, 104 and 107; James, p. 35.

12. Parton, I, 164; James, p. 94.

13. Charles Hammond, *A View of General Jackson's Domestic Relations* (1828).

14. T. P. Abernethy, *From Frontier to Plantation in Tennessee* (1932), pp. 262–276.

15. *A Brief and Impartial History,* p. 13.

16. *Correspondence of Andrew Jackson,* ed. J. S. Bassett (1926), I, 220.

17. Parton, I, 382.

18. Letter of 8 May 1814, *Correspondence,* II, 1.

19. Major A. L. Latour, *Historical Memoir of the War in the West* (1816), p. 199.

20. C. E. Gayarré, *History of Louisiana* (1866), IV, 625.

21. *Society in America* (1837), III, 166.

22. *Correspondence,* II, 213.

23. James, p. 266.

24. Jackson Papers, Library of Congress, A. Barratt to Jackson, 24 Feb. 1815.

25. Q. in James, p. 270.

26. Parton, II, 354.

27. To Dr. L. H. Coleman, 26 April 1824; see Parton, III, 35, and T. P. Abernethy, "Andrew Jackson and the Rise of Southwestern Democracy," *Amer. Histor. Review,* Oct. 1927, pp. 67–68.

28. *Folkways* (1906), p. 194.

29. Cf. James, p. 721.

30. *The Chronicles of Andrew* (Hamilton, Ohio, 1822), p. 103. A century later, John Trotwood Moore, ardent Jacksonian and Tennessee historian, wrote a poem glorifying Old Hickory's characteristic oath.

31. Q. from a contemporary newspaper in "Who Is the Real Jackson?" a manuscript essay by Mary French Caldwell, Tennessee State Library.

32. Parton, III, 51.

33. Washington *National Intelligencer,* 4 Aug. 1827.

34. A. Levasseur, *Lafayette in America* (1829), II, 24.

35. James, p. 449.

36. To W. B. Lewis, 31 March 1824.

37. *Correspondence,* III, 315.

38. John Finch, *Travels in the United States* (London, 1833), p. 141.

39. Emerson's *Journal,* 19 May 1828.

40. Charles Francis Adams, *Memoirs of J. Q. Adams* (1876), VI, 333.

41. *Writings of Daniel Webster* (National Edition), XVII, 371.

42. *An Address to the Citizens of Portage County, Ohio, by Disinterested Men* (1828).

43. Jackson to Andrew J. Donelson, 21 March 1822.

44. Jackson to Jefferson Club of Baltimore, 12 Sept. 1829 (MS., Library of Congress).
45. Cf. James, p. 404, for epithets of the previous campaign; in quotation here ellipses are omitted.
46. *Ibid.,* p. 469.
47. MSS., Library of Congress: Bledsoe to Jackson, 22 Sept. 1828; E. Patchell to Jackson, 30 Sept. 1828; R. Fenner to Jackson, 18 Dec. 1828; Capt. W. Alexander, 26 Dec. 1828; S. Hay to Jackson, 27 Dec. 1828.
48. *Private Corr. of Daniel Webster,* ed. F. Webster (1856), I, 473.
49. J. S. Bassett, *Life of Andrew Jackson* (1925), p. 422.
50. W. Peck to Jackson, 27 Feb. 1837 (MS., Library of Congress).
51. James, p. 639.
52. Josiah Quincy, *Figures of the Past* (1883), pp. 361-63.
53. *Ibid.,* p. 361.
54. It is doubtful whether this letter was genuine or a political jest; cf. James, p. 876, n. 57.
55. N. Arvin, *Whitman,* p. 15.
56. John Campbell of the Treasury, in a letter of 12 May 1833.
57. *Correspondence,* VI, 175.
58. Q. from *Harper's Magazine,* Jan. 1855, by James, p. 724.
59. *Correspondence,* V, 27.
60. Q. by James, pp. 779-780, from a clipping in the Tennessee State Library.
61. See Parton, III, 637; James, 741; Emerson's *Journal,* 30 Oct. 1841; *New York Evening Post,* 11 Sept. 1840.
62. *Works of Abraham Lincoln* (1905), II, 59-88, for this Congressional speech.
63. *New York Evening Post,* 3 Dec. 1836.
64. T. H. Benton, *Thirty Years' View* (1854), I, 735.
65. F. J. Grund, *Aristocracy in America* (1839), II, 241-43.
66. This sentiment, echoed in various public eulogies, is quoted from an unpublished letter in the Tennessee State Library, from the Rev. W. A. Scott, pastor of the Hermitage Church, to Mrs. Andrew Jackson, Jr., 30 July 1845.
67. See for example P. Merrick, *Eulogy on General Andrew Jackson* (Boston, 1845), p. 31.
68. Parton, III, 694-96 and 699.
69. House Document No. 430 of the 70th Congress, 2nd Session.
70. See Chicago *Daily Democratic Press,* 11 Dec. 1856, and *Public Papers and Addresses of Franklin D. Roosevelt,* II, 302.
71. Stanley F. Horn, *The Hermitage* (Richmond, 1938), pp. 86-87.
72. Theodore Roosevelt, "Andrew Jackson," *The Chautauquan,* Jan. 1891, p. 480.
73. Carl Sandburg, *Abraham Lincoln: The War Years* (1939), II, 240, and cf. 590-91.

LINCOLN: THE DEMOCRAT AS HERO

1. Albert J. Beveridge, *Abraham Lincoln* (1928), I, 16.
2. Phœbe Hanaford, *Abraham Lincoln: His Life and Public Services* (1865), p. 19.
3. Denton J. Snider, *Lincoln at Richmond* (1914), p. 17.
4. Q. by Roy P. Basler, *The Lincoln Legend* (1935), p. 132; to this excellent study I owe various suggestions in treating the Lincoln cult.
5. David Homer Bates, *Lincoln Stories* (1926), pp. 7-8.
6. Beveridge, I, 68.

7. *Works,* ed. Nicolay and Hay (1894), I, 142.
8. Beveridge, I, 534; and William H. Townsend, *Lincoln and Liquor* (1934), 16 *et passim.*
9. Townsend, 98 ff. Through a typographical blunder the date is incorrectly given as 1861.
10. Townsend, p. 79.
11. Paul Angle, *Herndon's Life of Lincoln* (1930), p. xli.
12. *The Kentucky Statesman,* q. by Sandburg, *Abraham Lincoln: The War Years,* I, 563; hereafter cited as Sandburg.
13. Sandburg, I, 653.
14. Weik MSS., q. by Beveridge, I, 300.
15. William E. Barton, *Life of Abraham Lincoln* (1925), I, 310 ff. and 506 ff.
16. On the authority of Professor J. B. Hubbell of Duke University, cited by Basler, p. 45 n.
17. Sandburg, II, 319.
18. *Ibid.,* II, 10.
19. Basler, p. 57.
20. Charles W. Ramsdell, "Lincoln and Fort Sumter," *Journal of Southern History,* Aug. 1937.
21. Lansing (Michigan) *State Republican,* 10 Feb. 1864.
22. Basler, p. 127.
23. Beveridge, I, 473.
24. J. G. Randall, *The Civil War and Reconstruction* (1937), pp. 478–480.
25. Nicolay and Hay ed., *Works,* II, 56–58; and Beveridge, I, 451 and II, 649.
26. Paul Angle, *The Foundations of Lincoln's Fame: An Address at Carleton College, Feb. 15, 1939,* p. 8; this pamphlet affords some very useful ideas upon its subject. See also J. G. Randall, "Lincoln's Task and Wilson's," *South Atlantic Quarterly,* Oct. 1930.
27. Charles W. Ramsdell, "Changing Interpretations of the Civil War," *Journal of Southern History,* Feb. 1937, p. 22.
28. Nicolay and Hay ed., *Works,* I, 57–64.
29. Paul Angle ed., *New Letters and Papers of Lincoln* (1930), pp. 356–59.
30. Henry C. Whitney, *Life on the Circuit with Lincoln* (1892), p. 47.
31. From transcript on exhibit in room where Lincoln died, 516 10th Street, Washington.
32. C. J. Furness ed., *Walt Whitman's Workshop* (1928), pp. 57–58.
33. Sandburg, III, 213.
34. Lloyd Lewis, *Myths after Lincoln* (1929), gives a detailed résumé of the Lincoln funeral oratory, and from contemporary newspapers supplies most of the facts here cited about the cortège from Washington to Springfield.
35. Helen Nicolay, *Personal Traits of Abraham Lincoln* (1913), pp. 379 ff.; Barton, II, 367.
36. Townsend, pp. 143–44.
37. Sandburg, II, 264.
38. H. K. Beale, *Are American Teachers Free?* (1936), p. 485.
39. *National Republic,* Feb. 1931, q. by Ralph H. Gabriel, *The Course of American Democratic Thought* (1940), p. 411.

LEE: THE ARISTOCRAT AS HERO

1. In treating the gentlemanly tradition I owe much to Ruth Kelso, *The Doctrine of the English Gentleman in the Sixteenth Century* (1929); Virgil B.

Heltzel, *Chesterfield and the Tradition of the Ideal Gentleman* (U. of Chicago dissertation, unpub., 1925); and Louis B. Wright, *The First Gentlemen of Virginia* (1940).

2. Douglas S. Freeman, *R. E. Lee* (1935), I, 159–60; this work of almost flawless scholarship, in seeking to correct Lee's error, makes another—an obvious typographical slip—by rendering the motto as "Non incantus futuri," instead of "incautus."

3. Henry Lee, *Memoirs of the War in the Southern Department of the United States,* ed. R. E. Lee (1869), p. 66.

4. The phrase is from Sir Thomas More's *Utopia,* tr. Robinson; q. by Heltzel, p. 257. And cf. Freeman, IV, 497.

5. Note E. Sprague Allen, "Chesterfield's objection to laughter," *Modern Language Notes,* Vol. 38, pp. 279–287; the tradition stems from Plato, Cicero, Barclay, Vivès, Hobbes, and others. For Lee, see Freeman, I, 451.

6. Douglas S. Freeman, *The South to Posterity* (1939), pp. 47–48. Information concerning the Hall of Fame, New York University, was given to me by the secretary, Mrs. N. Lyons.

7. Havelock Ellis, *From Rousseau to Proust* (1935), p. 253.

8. J. W. Jones, *Personal Reminiscences, Anecdotes, and Letters of Lee* (1874), p. 145.

9. *Journal of the Virginia Convention of 1861,* pp. 186–88.

10. Freeman, *Lee,* IV, 202 and I, 447.

11. For these impressions, see respectively A. L. Long, *Memoirs of Lee* (1886), pp. 66–67; C. Anderson, *Texas Before and on the Eve of the Rebellion* (1884), p. 24; Freeman, *Lee,* I, 450; A. S. L. Fremantle, *Three Months in the Southern States,* p. 253; Freeman, *The South to Posterity,* p. 157.

12. Emerson's *Journal,* 14 Dec. 1850.

13. See "Mrs. Lee's 'burial,'" leading editorial in the *Richmond* (Va.) *News Leader,* 24 May 1939.

14. Jones, *Personal Reminiscences,* p. 366.

15. Freeman, *Lee,* I, 25.

16. *Ibid.,* I, 272.

17. Cf. R. D. Meade, *Current History,* April 1929, pp. 55–60.

18. Freeman, *Lee,* I, 434.

19. John S. Mosby, *Memoirs,* ed. Russell (1917), p. 379, q. by Freeman, I, 439.

20. J. W. Jones, *Christ in the Camp, Or Religion in the Confederate Army* (1904), p. 100.

21. Q. by Freeman, *Lee,* II, 541–42.

22. *Ibid.,* II, 497–98; there are many versions of this story.

23. *Ibid.,* III, 287–88 and n. 5, 318, 321, 531.

24. R. E. Lee, Jr., *Recollections and Letters of General Lee* (1905), pp. 118–19.

25. John S. Wise, *The End of an Era* [1927], p. 435.

26. Cf. Freeman, *Lee,* IV, 142–43, n. 89.

27. Broadside published by James B. Rodgers, Philadelphia, 1865, from copy in Library of Congress.

28. Christiana Bond, *Memories of General R. E. Lee* (1926), pp. 32–34.

29. Jones, *Personal Reminiscences,* p. 174.

30. Freeman, *Lee,* IV, 317 n. 70, 260–61, and 358–59.

31. Bond, *op. cit.,* p. 18.

32. Q. by R. E. Lee, Jr., *op. cit.,* p. 405.

33. T. N. Page, *Robert E. Lee, the Southerner* (1908), p. 271.

34. The more realistic facts are given by Freeman's *Lee,* IV, 526.

GENERAL GRANT AND THE GILDED AGE

1. Timothy Dwight, *Travels in New England and New York* (New Haven, 1821), II, 460; the second quotation from Dwight is drawn from his *Discourse Occasioned by the Death of Jonathan Trumbull* (New Haven, 1809), p. 9. That from Mills will be found in *Cosmopolitan Magazine,* 1902, p. 292. Max Weber, R. H. Tawney, R. Niebuhr, and Clive Day have written ably on the capitalist implications of Puritanism. In applying this theory to American life one of the best discussions, in the main still unpublished, is A. Whitney Griswold's Yale dissertation of 1933, *The American Cult of Success.*
2. H. Bushnell, "How to Be a Christian in Trade," in *Sermons on Living Subjects* (1872). James Truslow Adams, "The North Begins to Hustle," chap. VII in *The Epic of America* (1931), illuminates the new philosophy of business. See also Miriam Beard, *A History of the Business Man* (1938), pp. 636 ff.
3. *The Nation,* 20 July 1871.
4. Samuel Insull, *Public Utilities in Modern Life* (1924), p. 137.
5. For a cross-section of McGuffey teaching see Harvey C. Minnich, *W. H. McGuffey and His Readers* (1937).
6. Charles A. and Mary R. Beard, *America in Midpassage* (1939), II, 734.
7. Howard Mumford Jones and Daniel Aaron, "Notes on the Napoleonic Legend in America," *Franco-American Review,* Summer 1937.
8. F. J. Grund, *The Americans* (1837), II, 9.
9. Robert S. and Helen M. Lynd, *Middletown in Transition* (1937), p. 423.
10. From Agnes K. Wagner's presentation copy of the song to Mrs. Frederick Dent Grant, Library of Congress, MSS. Division.
11. W. E. Woodward, *Meet General Grant* (1928), pp. 256–57.
12. William B. Hesseltine, *Ulysses S. Grant, Politician* (1935), p. 4 n. 4.
13. Ulysses S. Grant, *Personal Memoirs* (1885), I, 53.
14. Woodward, p. 262.
15. Allan Nevins, *Hamilton Fish* (1936), p. 609.
16. Q. Woodward, p. 185.
17. *Education of Henry Adams* (1918), p. 264.
18. Hesseltine, p. 120.
19. Lloyd Lewis, *Sherman—Fighting Prophet* (1932), p. 600.
20. Bishop Fallows, *Splendid Deeds of American Heroes* (1900), pp. 223–24.
21. Cf. Woodward, p. 402.
22. Nevins, *Hamilton Fish,* pp. 567–68.
23. James Schouler, *History of the United States* (1913), VII, 144–46.
24. Hesseltine, p. 303.
25. *New York Herald,* 25 Oct. 1870.
26. Cf. Nevins, p. 607 *et passim.*
27. Nevins, p. 641.
28. *Ibid.,* p. 804.
29. Horace Green, *General Grant's Last Stand* (1936), p. 297.
30. H. K. Beale, *Are American Teachers Free?* pp. 201, 301.

THE DIME NOVEL AND BUFFALO BILL

1. See James M. Harvey, "The Dime Novel in American Life," *Atlantic,* July 1907; *The Beadle Collection of Dime Novels* (New York Public Library,

1922); Edmund Pearson, *Dime Novels; Or, Following an Old Trail in Popular Literature* (1929); Merle Curti, "Dime Novels and the American Tradition," *Yale Review*, XXVI (1937), 761–68.

2. Richard J. Walsh, *The Making of Buffalo Bill* (1928), pp. 41, 81; this interesting and able, but little known, book was most helpful in the writing of this chapter.

3. Q. *Ibid.*, pp. 76–77.

4. John Levi Cutler, *Gilbert Patten and His Frank Merriwell Saga* (University of Maine, 1934).

5. This topic has been well handled by Emerson Hough, *The Story of the Cowboy* (1921), Douglas Branch, *The Cowboy and His Interpreters* (1926), and Philip Ashton Rollins, *The Cowboy* (revised ed., 1936).

6. Guy B. Johnson, *John Henry* (Chapel Hill, 1929); and Louis W. Chappell, *John Henry, a Folk-lore Study* (Jena, 1933).

7. For sentimental praise of Billy the Kid, see Walter Noble Burns, *The Saga of Billy the Kid* (1926), and Charles A. Siringo, *A Lone Star Cowboy* (Santa Fé, 1919).

8. W. M. Raine, *Famous Sheriffs and Western Outlaws* (1929), p. 159.

9. Cf. *Nebraska Historical Magazine*, April–June 1927, "Wild Bill-McCanles Tragedy."

10. Walsh's book, *The Making of Buffalo Bill*, based upon the Cody papers and written with the help of Milton Salsbury, Johnny Baker, and others who knew Cody best, is the chief source of the following statements.

11. *Ibid.*, p. 92.

12. *Ibid.*, p. 118.

13. James M. Cain, "The Man Merriwell," *Saturday Evening Post*, 11 June 1927.

14. Walsh, p. 289.

15. *Ibid.*, pp. 148–49.

16. As testified by Cody's protégé, Johnny Baker, in Walsh, p. 252.

17. *Ibid.*, p. 316. For data at the close of this chapter I am indebted to the secretary of the Cody Club, Cody, Wyoming.

COMMONER AND ROUGH RIDER

1. W. J. Bryan, *Memoirs* (1925), p. 86.

2. Paxton Hibben, *The Peerless Leader* (1929), p. 117.

3. Mark Sullivan, *Our Times* (1926), I, 126.

4. M. R. Werner, *Bryan* (1929), pp. 95–96.

5. *Ibid.*, p. 105.

6. An account of these presents will be found in W. J. Bryan, *The First Battle: A Story of the Campaign of 1896* (Chicago, n. d.), and in Werner, pp. 80 ff.

7. For a good résumé, Merle Curti, *Bryan and World Peace* (Smith College Studies in History, 1931), chap. I.

8. Hibben, p. 349.

9. Werner, p. 320.

10. Henry F. Pringle, *Theodore Roosevelt* (Blue Ribbon Books), p. 101.

11. *Ibid.*, pp. 4 and 490.

12. Edward S. Ellis, *From Ranch to White House* (1906), p. 17, and Pringle, p. 39.

13. Stuart P. Sherman, *Americans* (1922), p. 267.

14. Sullivan, *Our Times*, II, 226–29.

15. H. Hagedorn, *Roosevelt in the Bad Lands* (1930), p. 101.
16. Pringle, pp. 167–68.
17. See Fairfax Downey, *Richard Harding Davis and His Day* (1933).
18. H. C. Lodge, *Selections from the Correspondence of Theodore Roosevelt and Henry Cabot Lodge* (1925), I, 325–28.
19. An assortment of newspaper clippings on this subject will be found among the Roosevelt Papers in the Library of Congress.
20. Roosevelt to Von Sternberg, 19 July 1902.
21. *DeBow's Review*, September 1860.
22. *New York Tribune*, 19 Oct. 1898, q. by Pringle.
23. Roosevelt to Depew, 23 Jan. 1899.
24. Theodore Roosevelt, *Works* (1925), XI, 154–55.
25. Pringle, p. 35.
26. *Ibid.*, pp. 315–332.
27. *New York Times*, 3 Sept. 1906.
28. J. C. Sibley to J. D. Archbold, 7 March 1905, Clapp Committee, II, 1588.
29. Q. by Mark Sullivan, *op. cit.*, III, 71. *The Baltimore News*, 4 March 1905, contains an interesting analysis of Roosevelt's popularity as compared with that of Andrew Jackson, Clay, and Cleveland.
30. A. W. Dunn, *Gridiron Nights*, p. 154; cited Pringle, p. 368.
31. Joseph B. Bishop, *Theodore Roosevelt and His Times* (1920), II, 390.
32. *Ibid.*, II, 307–08.
33. *New York World*, 2 Jan. 1912.
34. Bishop, II, 427.
35. Sherman, *Americans*, p. 257.
36. Roosevelt, *Works*, XIX, 243–47.
37. Arthur H. Vandenburg, *The Greatest American: Alexander Hamilton* (1921), part I.

THE UNKNOWN SOLDIER

1. Q. from Ray Stannard Baker, *What Wilson Did at Paris*, by Sullivan, *Our Times*, V, 538–39.
2. Letter to the author from Miss Anne W. Trott, 16 Feb. 1940. In May 1940 the Wilson Birthplace was temporarily closed for the remainder of the year, to permit restoration and repairs.
3. Ray Stannard Baker, *Woodrow Wilson: Life and Letters* (1927), I, 35.
4. See Claude G. Bowers, "Woodrow Wilson: A Reappraisal," *Current History*, April 1931, p. 4.
5. Q. by Walter Millis, *Road to War* (1935), p. 430.
6. J. P. Tumulty, *Woodrow Wilson as I Know Him* (1921), p. 256.
7. Charles Seymour, *American Diplomacy During the World War* (1934), p. 399.
8. Cf. Lincoln Steffens, *Autobiography* (1931), II, 786–87.
9. These phrases are quoted from Harry F. Estill, *The Beginner's History of Our Country* (Dallas, 1919), p. 323.
10. From Halleck and Frantz, *Our Nation's Heritage*, p. 408; and W. B. Guitteau, *Our United States*, pp. 632–33.
11. Q. from George Creel, *Saturday Evening Post*, by Sullivan, *op. cit.*, V, 568. The last chapters of Edith Bolling Wilson's *My Memoir* (1939), offer the most detailed account of this phase in Wilson's life.
12. Charles A. and Mary R. Beard, *America in Midpassage* (1939), II, 925.

13. See B. H. Liddell Hart, "Pershing and His Critics," *Current History*, Nov. 1933; and Frederick B. Maurice, "Pershing and the A. E. F.," *Foreign Affairs*, July 1931.
14. Otto Eisenschiml, *Why Was Lincoln Murdered?* (1937), pp. 482–84.
15. *Literary Digest*, 7 Sept. 1918, pp. 58–64.
16. E. T. Tomlinson, *The Story of General Pershing* (1919), p. 20, and Howard McCracken, *Pershing: The Story of a Great Soldier* (1931), pp. 9–13)—the latter showing the increasing elaboration of myth, and even giving Pershing's birthdate (on p. 193) as 1855 instead of 1860.
17. Cf. Sandburg, *Lincoln: The War Years*, I, 494. The Confederate cried, "Come on, come on, you men! Do you want to live forever?" Carlyle's *The French Revolution*, II, 1, iv, quotes a similar remark from Frederick the Great.
18. According to a letter from Brigadier-General L. J. Wyatt to the London *Daily Telegraph*, 11 Nov. 1939.
19. *New York Times* editorial, 11 Nov. 1921.

GODS FROM THE MACHINE: EDISON, FORD, LINDBERGH

1. Q. by Gamaliel Bradford, *The Quick and the Dead* (1931), p. 108.
2. This and other realistic impressions of Edison are quoted in the section on that inventor in J. G. Crowther, *Famous American Men of Science* (1937).
3. Clara Burrus, *Life and Letters of John Burroughs* (1925), II, 196.
4. J. N. Leonard, *The Tragedy of Henry Ford* (1932), p. 15.
5. Information supplied to the author, on authority of the late Senator Dwight W. Morrow, by kindness of Professor Edwin F. Gay.
6. As reported in *The Literary Digest*, 1 Oct. 1927. Samples of the Lindbergh fan mail are quoted from the same source. An account of his gifts and trophies was published by the *Digest* on 18 May 1929.
7. See such popular accounts as the Lindbergh feature articles in *The New Yorker*, 20 Sept. 1930, by Morris Markey; in *The American Magazine*, April 1939, by Russell Owen; and in *Time*, 19 June 1939. A recent account, highly friendly to the aviator, is C. B. Allen's "The Facts about Lindbergh," *Saturday Evening Post*, 28 Dec. 1940.
8. For a sympathetic treatment of the incident, see Julian S. Mason (editor-in-chief of the *New York Evening Post*), "Lindbergh and the Press," *Saturday Evening Post*, 3 Aug. 1929.
9. Q. in *The Nation*, 8 Jan. 1936; cf. St. John Ervine, "Privacy and the Lindberghs," *Fortnightly*, Feb. 1936.
10. John S. Gregory, "What's Wrong with Lindbergh?" *Outlook*, 3 Dec. 1930.
11. Markey, *New Yorker*, 20 Sept. 1930.
12. *New York Times*, 31 Aug. 1929, p. 7:7.

CHAMPION OF THE NEW DEAL

1. *The Roosevelt Omnibus* (1934), p. 31.
2. *The Rocky Mountain Herald*, 10 Aug. 1940.
3. This campaign picture of Mr. Roosevelt, as presented in 1932, is deftly recalled by Charles A. and Mary R. Beard, *America in Midpassage*, I, 134–35.
4. *The Public Papers and Addresses of Franklin D. Roosevelt* (1938), IV, 96.
5. Mrs. James Roosevelt, *My Boy Franklin* (1933), p. 26.

6. *Ibid.*, p. 83.
7. Q. by Ernest K. Lindley, *Franklin D. Roosevelt: A Career in Progressive Democracy* (1931), p. 147.
8. Benjamin Thompson, Count Rumford, *Essays Political, Economic, and Philosophical* (Boston, 1798), I, 34.
9. Lindley, *op. cit.*, p. 21, citing the *New York Evening Post* and the *Herald Tribune*.
10. Raymond Moley, *After Seven Years* (1939), pp. 33–34.
11. Cf. Moley, p. 11, and Cyril Clemens, *Mark Twain and Mussolini* (Webster Groves, Mo., 1934), p. 51. W. G. Sumner's essay of 1883, *The Forgotten Man*, was the ultimate source of Mr. Roosevelt's phrase as first used in a radio address of 7 April 1932.
12. Robert S. Allen, "The Man Roosevelt," *American Mercury*, Jan. 1933.
13. Moley, p. 319 and n.
14. Q. in *Harper's Magazine*, Oct. 1939, p. 543.
15. Norman Hapgood, *Professional Patriots* (1927), p. 51.
16. Stephen T. Early, "Below the Belt," *Saturday Evening Post*, 10 June 1939.
17. *Ibid.*
18. Moley, p. 342.
19. *New York Times*, 6 Dec. 1936, IV, 9:1.
20. *Ibid.*, 24 Nov. 1937, 25:1.
21. Morris Markey, in *McCall's Magazine*, May 1934.
22. H. F. Pringle in *The New Yorker*, 16 June 1934.
23. Richard L. Neuberger, "They Love Roosevelt," *Forum*, Jan. 1939. Samples of the Roosevelt mail, from which extracts are here quoted, have been published in *Current History*, "Letters to the President," January and February 1938; other information is drawn from Ernest K. Lindley, "Roosevelt in Print," *Southern Review*, Autumn 1939. Although extensive direct quotation is discouraged until the end of the Roosevelt Administration, the kindness of Mr. Stephen T. Early allowed the present writer to make a cursory inspection of the files—of both fan and spite letters—and these results are here incorporated along with material previously published.
24. R. L. Neuberger, "Roosevelt Rides Again," *Current History*, Nov. 1937.
25. "Some Like Roosevelt," *Nation*, 2 July 1938.
26. *Fortune* Survey, July 1936; regarding the President's church attendance, see *Roosevelt Omnibus*, p. 68.
27. E. Ludwig, *Roosevelt: A Study in Fortune and Power* (1938), pp. 339–40.
28. *Ibid.*, p. 279.
29. *My Boy Franklin*, p. 88.
30. Q. by E. K. Lindley, *Roosevelt: A Career in Progressive Democracy*, p. 343.

INDEX